DEVON AND CORNWALL RECORD SOCIETY

New Series

Volume 65

DEVON PARISH TAXPAYERS 1500–1650

VOLUME 3

CHURCHSTOW TO DUNKESWELL

EDITED BY

TODD GRAY

DEVON AND CORNWALL RECORD SOCIETY

THE BOYDELL PRESS

First published 2023

A publication of the
Devon and Cornwall Record Society
published by The Boydell Press
an imprint of Boydell & Brewer Ltd
PO Box 9, Woodbridge, Suffolk IP12 3DF, UK
and of Boydell & Brewer Inc.
668 Mt Hope Avenue, Rochester, NY 14620–2731, USA
website: www.boydellandbrewer.com

ISBN   978 0 90185 310 3

Series information is printed at the back of this volume

A CIP catalogue record for this book is available
from the British Library

The publisher has no responsibility for the continued existence or accuracy
of URLs for external or third-party internet websites referred to in this book,
and does not guarantee that any content on such websites is,
or will remain, accurate or appropriate

This publication is printed on acid-free paper

Typeset by www.thewordservice.com

Printed and bound in Great Britain by
TJ Books Limited, Padstow, Cornwall

MIX
Paper from
responsible sources
FSC
www.fsc.org   FSC® C013056

CONTENTS

ILLUSTRATIONS

Plates

PREFACE

Since work for this volume began in 2014 a number of friends and colleagues have helped bring it to fruition. The state of some manuscripts, along with poor writing, has offered occasional challenges and I would like thank Elly Babbedge, Tony Gale, Dr Joanna Mattingly, Dr Oliver Padel and Jan Wood for their advice with niggles. Other forms of help have come from Dr Clive Burgess, Professor Tom Cain, Professor Sandra Cavallo, Sarah Charman, John Draisey, Gary Knaggs, Professor Maryanne Kowaleski, Elizabeth Lomas, Charlie Pritchard-Williams, Keith Stevens, Dr Jonathan Vage and Professor Jane Whittle. Tony Gale enthusiastically produced his text on Crediton and Professor Catherine Rider has, at every point, been a cheerful and supportive editor and who has, along with Dr Stephen Roberts, made many useful comments on the text. All remaining errors are, of course, my own. Each map was drawn by Tony Gale. The rates have been edited with the kind permission of the Colyton Chamber of Feoffees, Dartmouth Town Council, the Exeter Diocesan Secretary, Governors of Crediton Church and Plymouth Archive. All photographs have been taken by the editor. The cover illustration and Plate 2 (DHC, R9/1/Z/33) appears courtesy of Dartmouth Town Council and Plate 9 (DHC, 1660A/Add4/E1) courtesy of Credition Church Governors. Finally, a generous gift by Richard Moyse has helped the society fund publication.

Todd Gray
Taddyforde, Exeter

INTRODUCTION

This third volume of Devon's early taxation lists covers twenty-nine parishes and 112 taxation lists. Many of the documents are in a poor state of preservation through damp, tearing or have been damaged by rodents and Dean Prior, Dolton and Colyton have manuscripts which are too fragile for full examination. In contrast, the best-preserved collection is that of the borough of Dartmouth and this, as discussed on page xxxvii, was achieved partly through the work of the Devon & Cornwall Record Society nearly a century ago.

The lists have been drawn from archival collections in Barnstaple, Colyton, Exeter, Plymouth and Taunton. There are long sequences for Churston Ferrers, Coldridge, Crediton, Dartmouth and Dean Prior but many parishes have only one or two surviving rates. There are no surviving examples for the remaining twenty parishes in this alphabetical range (either for Clawton, Clyst Honiton, Clyst Hydon, Clyst St George, Clyst St Lawrence, Clyst St Mary, Cockington, Coffinswell, Colaton Raleigh, Combepyne, Countisbury, Creacombe, Cullompton, Culmstock, Dawlish, Denbury, Dowland, Down St Mary, Drewsteignton or Dunchideock).

As with the earlier volumes in this series, the parishes concerned are located across the county. Nearly all are rural in character but even the most urbanised, Crediton and Dartmouth, had extensive countryside. The lists comprise 1 churchyard rate, 2 hospital rates, 3 highway rates, 10 rates for military purposes including a Ship Money rate, 16 tithe accounts including 3 Easter Books, 29 church rates and 46 poor rates. There is one joint church and poor rate as well as four others for which no purpose was specified. The latter were undertaken by sidemen along with churchwardens or overseers of the poor and may also have been intended to maintain both the church building and the poor.

Rates, as discussed in Volume One, had distinct purposes: the church rate supported the maintenance of the building and those for bells, churchyards, clerks, highways, hospitals and the poor are equally self-explanatory. There were also rates which underpinned military activity. Eight parishes in this volume were assessed for their arms in the rate prompted by the general uncertainty following the defeat of the Armada in 1588.

The Easter Books, otherwise Paschal Books, recorded a portion of the 'offerings' and tithes due to clerics, lay people or institutions which were paid at Easter. This volume includes accounts for Clayhanger and Crediton, the former a rural parish and the latter a mix of both urban and countryside, while previous volumes have included similar ledgers for Awliscombe and Broadclyst.

'Offerings', an annual fee exacted on adult parishioners towards the maintenance of the parish priest, stood at two pence at Broadclyst and Crediton but Clayhanger had a wider range dependent upon gender, marital status, age and whether one was a head of household, servant or apprentice. Item 50 lists only the offerings paid at Crediton in 1574 while the Clayhanger accounts of c.1573 to 1582 (Items 13–22) recorded mixed tithes (those concerned with livestock, milk and eggs) and personal tithes (those relating to labour). A nominal fee was also paid for gardens as well as another for the tithe of hay. Praedial tithes (those concerned with grain) were collected separately.

Given that church attendance was mandatory, it is likely that payments were made in one central place, such as the parish church, but collectors may also have perambulated the parish and personally taken money.[1] The extent of many ledgers makes it likely that they were composed a reasonable time after the sums were paid. In most instances scribes would have access to previous accounts.

Few scribes have been identified. In some cases their writing and style of organisation can be identified amongst the lists. Some men, for instance, favoured particular symbols to note

[1] S. J. Wright, 'Easter Books and Parish Rate Books: a new source for the urban historian', *Urban History Yearbook* 12 (1985), pp. 30–5.

payment. Some included extraneous information in their tax lists and ledgers. One such notable example is Item 51 which includes details of the fees for nineteen christenings and five marriages at Crediton in December 1582 and January 1583. These were omitted from the parish register. He also listed twenty-three 'purifications', the ceremony in which women were churched after giving birth. Nearly every woman who gave birth had a churching ceremony between one and sixteen days later.

The portion of the population recorded in the lists varied not only from place to place but also according to the type of taxation. While all parishioners paid tithes, those who paid church and poor rates were mostly less than 20 per cent of the population.

Local parish administration and variations

A discussion in Volume One noted that the study of local taxation revealed the unsuspecting ways in which parish administration varied. These differences have largely escaped historians, at least those in Devon. Many parishes were run either by sidemen, questmen or even synodsmen, much like a parish council today, and they were known variously as the Four, Six, Seven or Eight Men. Their number differed from parish to parish and could change over time in one place. It is possible to confuse them with others similarly named such as the Twenty Men of Colyton who worked alongside the feoffees and were not in the same sense parish administrators.

National legislation on maintaining the poor and public highways increased the number of local officials, as parishes became the preferred administration unit in the late 1500s. Local people constructed different means to meet their ongoing and added responsibilities. For instance, in the late 1500s the parish of Milton Abbot had two collectors for the poor (who gathered the rates), eight bread wardens (of whom there were two in each quarter who sold bread, cheese, girts (coarsely ground oats), candles and meat), a high warden (who sold church property including parishioners' gifts of sheep and wool, and also collected fines and money for graves), two wardens of the common store (in the North or South Downs where they accounted for bread and ale made from the gathered oats), three receivers (who collected cash from all the wardens except the collectors of the poor) and one or two payers (who oversaw the costs for the maintenance of parish buildings, the military and policing).[2]

No other parish has yet been found that had that organisation. Dean Prior, for instance, appointed each year four new sidemen (the 'Four Men') from 1565 to 1622 (with the exception of 1584 to 1587 when there were eight), two wardens (otherwise churchwardens but sometimes known as the 'head wardens' or 'head wardens of the church') from 1554 to 1628, two 'supervisors of the ways' (waywardens who looked after public roads) from 1569 to 1616 and two, three or four 'collectors' (otherwise referred to as the 'overseers' of the poor) from 1569 to 1626.

Local government arrangements were made uniform through national legislation, particularly in 1835, 1878, 1888 and 1894, but in the period from 1500 to 1650 the local divergences were particularly marked. This can be seen in the establishment and use of sub-districts known as wards which existed in a handful of Devon localities including Dartmouth.

Another was Plymouth which comprised a large ecclesiastical parish but which had been divided into four wards by the late fifteenth century. Looe Street, Old Town, Venner and Vintry Wards each had two constables who were responsible for the collection of rates.[3]

Exeter had four wards which were named after the cardinal points and each had two aldermen who were assisted by two deputies. The aldermen were required to enquire:

[2]   Todd Gray (ed.), *Devon Parish Taxpayers, 1500–1650, Abbotskerswell to Beer & Seaton*, DCRS NS58 (2016), pp. 4–8.
[3]   R. N. Worth, *Calendar of the Plymouth Municipal Records* (Plymouth, 1893), pp. 26, 64, 73, 88, 118, 140.

'whether there be any nuisance or purprestures [the wrongful appropriation of land subject to the rights of others] in the city, as by setting of pales, walls, stalls, bulks, porches, windows, and such like, whereby any encroaching is used; or any timber, stones, dunghills or heaps of dirt, or any other thing be cast and laid in the streets to the letting or hindering of any way, or to the annoyance of any person. Also whether any do keep slaughtering within the city, or do keep and feed any hogs, ducks or any other filthy beast. Also whether the streets be kept clean and swept twice in the week at least. Also whether any house be ruinous and stand dangerously, and whether any chimney, oven or furnace, or backs or hearths for fire, do stand dangerously and in peril of fire, and the same not presented by the scavenger [a street cleaner]. Also whether there be crooks, ladders, and buckets in readiness to serve, if need should be, in peril of fire; and whether every man have in readiness a vessel of water at his door when any house is adventured with fire, and not advertised by the scavengers.'[4]

Each constable had to swear an oath that he would 'present all assaults, frays, bloodsheds, weapons drawn and all other things done against the King Majesty's peace'.[5] In the late sixteenth century John Hooker outlined the duties of watchmen and wardsmen who were appointed during times of war 'and troubles'. The former served at night and the latter during daylight hours.[6]

Exeter's wards were simultaneously known as quarters. An early fourteenth-century tax for the city walls was organised through the wards but sixteenth-century rates were arranged by parish, seventeen of which were located in part or in their entirety within the walls.[7] Exonians may not have identified themselves only as parishioners: it may be indicative that a petition of 1660 was written by residents of the South and West Quarters.[8] Ugborough also had North, South, East and West Quarters[9] while Plymstock had South, East, Oreston and Plymstock Churchtown divisions.[10] Cornwood, at least in its rate of 1628, had two 'sides', the east and the west.

Plymouth's constables may have had similar duties to their counterparts in Exeter and Dartmouth. The latter had wards from at least the fourteenth century.[11] It appointed two constables for each ward, through which the local militia was organised. The custom by 1579 was that two supervisors oversaw the twelve constables who were otherwise known as 'wardens of the peace'. The wards themselves were named after the first six days in the week.[12] The constables' other duties included overseeing butchers and innholders in the observation of Lenten restrictions.[13] Dartmouth's constables also monitored misdemeanours: in 1580, for example, those of Tuesday Ward presented one man for assault, those of Sunday Ward cited another for having an illegitimate child born in his house and those in Friday Ward accused Joan Green of illegally selling ale.[14]

4   Sidney & Beatrice Webb, *English Local Government from the revolution to: the municipal corporations act: the Manor and Borough* (London, 1908), pt 1, pp. 290–1, 334; Walter J. Harte, J. W. Schopp and H. Tapley-Soper (eds), *The Description of the Citie of Excester*, DCRS (1919), pt III, pp. 813, 838–40.

5   DHC, ECA, mayors' court books.

6   Harte et al., *The Description of the Citie of Excester*, p. 820.

7   J. H. Wylie & James Wylie (eds), *Report on the Records of the City of Exeter* (London, 1916), p. 402; Maryanne Kowaleski, 'Taxpayers in late Fourteenth Century Exeter: the 1577 Murage Roll', DCNQ XXXIV: VI (Autumn 1980), 217; Maryanne Kowaleski, *Local markets and Regional Trade in Medieval Exeter* (Cambridge, 1995), p. 372.

8   Wylie & Wylie, *Exeter*, p. 50.

9   PA, 1518A/PO1. They were also named after the cardinal points.

10   PA, 694/52/C2.

11   Hugh. R. Watkin, *Dartmouth, Volume One Preformation* (Exeter, 1935), p. 259.

12   DHC, DD61461, 4 June 1579 & 5 May 1580; Watkin, *Dartmouth*, p. 259.

13   DHC, DD62004-5, DD61970, DD62002-6, DD62008-9, DD62011.

14   DHC, DD61461.

The wards were also used for one-off purposes, such as raising money and materials to build the poorhouses in 1601,[15] and the corporation organised its manorial tenants by ward in the early 1600s. In 1625, in lieu of the danger from infectious disease and the attacks of North African pirates, the borough reaffirmed that all male inhabitants 'of what rank or quality soever they be' were required to either watch at night or ward during the day. The only exceptions were those who were ill and some officials. Councillors were also expected to regularly accompany the constables both during the day and at night.[16]

Parish taxation was organised by a handful of the community upon its wealthiest members for the benefit of all parishioners. Every known organiser was male and, given many could not sign their own names on the rates, it is questionable how many were literate.

No evidence has yet been found in this period of a woman having signed a Devon parish rate nor are there indications they had a direct role in taxation administration. Married women were generally not mentioned in tax lists except in regards to the payment of offerings in Crediton where all heads of households, whether male or female, were always listed. In general women headed less than 10 per cent of all households. However, in terms of receiving poor relief, the number of women was greater than that of men and this may have reflected a higher proportion of older women in the population who had fewer options in earning a living.

This raises the question as to whether women in Devon served as parish officers in any other capacity. It is known that women were actively involved in parish guilds in the period before the Reformation, particularly in the West Country,[17] and six women were named as churchwardens at St Petrock in Exeter in the early 1400s as well as another seven in Morebath and one in Meshaw in the early 1500s.[18] Some parishes chose their churchwardens on a rota system which was based on the occupancy of properties. Some men served who were not head of their households in places such as Dittisham.[19] At Dean Prior three women were named as churchwardens between 1554 and 1628. Margaret Phillip in 1599, Agnes Knowling in 1626 and Elizabeth Hore in 1628 were listed amongst the office holders of the parish. However, the church rate for 1599 was headed 'the account of John Phillip deputy for Peter Leate and Margaret Phillip, widow, churchwardens'. There was another unidentified woman who was a parish officer but her son John Collings also carried out her duties as an overseer of the poor.

Two other Devon church accounts have other further details. Kilmington's records show that thirteen of the 106 churchwardens between 1557 and 1595 were women. In one year, from 1559 to 1560, women occupied both posts. A male deputy replaced a female warden in 1557 as did another for male wardens in 1576 and 1578. Perhaps it should be expected that, like many other aspects, the inclusion of women in parish administration diverged from one place to another.[20] The parish accounts for Littleham in Exmouth are equally detailed and recorded that between 1563 and 1650 seven of the 174 churchwardens were women. It may be significant that two of the overseers of the poor were also women; they served in 1629 and 1630.[21] It could have been that women in some communities were largely marginalised from parish roles after the Reformation, if they had occupied them before, but that the tradition continued in others. However, the apparent absence of women involved in the administration of Devon's parish taxation suggests a parallel history.

[15] DHC, DD62278B.
[16] DHC, DD62202.
[17] Katherine L. French, 'Maiden's Lights and Wives' Stores: Women's Parish Guilds in Late Medieval England', *Sixteenth Century Journal* 29:2 (Summer 1998), 403–25.
[18] Katherine L. French, 'Women Churchwardens in Late Medieval England', in Clive Burgess & Eammon Duffy (eds), *The Parish in Late Medieval England*, Harlaxton Society NS XIV (2006), pp. 302–5.
[19] DHC, Chanter 857, folios 55–9.
[20] Robert Cornish, *Kilmington Church Wardens' Accounts* (Exeter, 1901); DHC, 3047A/PW1-2.
[21] J. M. Dixon, 'The Churchwarden's Accounts of the Parish of Luttleham-with-Exmouth, 1628–1760', *DCNQ* XXXII:1 (Spring 1971), 9; DHC, 2932A/PW7.

The exclusion of women in taxation documents extended to Crediton's scribe's notes of fees for weddings, christenings and purifications in 1582. He failed to record any woman's first name and noted the events in terms of men being grooms, fathers or husbands.

All known scribes were male. One document has two marginal notes which might impart insights into the perspective of the world as viewed from within the male oligarchy of the corporation of Dartmouth. A scribe wrote in 1613:

There are but six things we have need of in this life,
The grace of God, & a quiet life,
A contented mind and a honest wife,
A good report & a fund in store,
What need a man of any more?

Perhaps the absence of women emboldened a Dartmouth scribe to pen a few lines on the 'four natures in a woman':

A big woman is lazy,
A little woman is loud.
A fair woman is sluttish,
A black woman is proud.[22]

He may have used the latter term in its contemporary sense of describing an individual with dark hair. It is less likely that he was referring to a woman of African heritage and it is probably coincidental that 129 years earlier James Black, Devon's earliest recorded Black man, who was from 'Indea', had lived in Dartmouth. The port must have had African migrants similar to those living in Elizabethan Plymouth or Barnstaple.[23] Curiously, the scribe finished his poetry with 'and if she were as little as she is good, a peach red in June would make her a hood'.[24]

Only one of the thousands of men recorded in these tax lists wrote his memoirs. In it Robert Furse of Dean Prior recommended to his male descendants the best qualities for a wife as well as those to be avoided. Furse gave no guidance on potential husbands but did, however, advise his male descendants on how they should model their own behaviour.[25]

Some rates in this collection illustrate the influence of religion on local taxation. Combe Martin, Combe-in-Teignhead and Dolton each taxed their parishioners in quantities of grain. The barley and oats were likely to have been used for church ales which became obnoxious to convinced Protestants through the late sixteenth century. The rental by parishes of their brewing equipment is seen in Appendix 4. The sixteenth-century change from Roman Catholicism to Protestantism is also demonstrated by the use of a fourteenth-century wrapper for the Clayhanger tithe records. It may have been found in the parish chest and considered no longer to be sacred but regarded as useful only for recycling.

The format for rates differed from one parish to another because there was no template. This included the recording of numerals; some scribes used Roman, others Arabic numerals and a few used both. In 1549 a Crediton scribe also employed what was becoming an archaic system; he calculated using 'an arrangement of dots'. See page 92.

Some scribes neglected to note the purpose of particular rates. In listing contributors some scribes separated parishioners from those who held land but lived outside the parish. These men and women held agistments (also noted as 'justments' or 'jistments'), the practice whereby land was rented to others in order to graze livestock. The numbers of sheep, cattle and horses were not

[22]   DHC, DD61851.
[23]   Gray, *Devon's Last Slave-Owners*, pp. 26–7.
[24]   DHC, DD61851.
[25]   Anita Travers (ed.), *Robert Furse, a Devon family memoir of 1593*, DCRS, NS5 (2010), pp. 11–23.

noted but the landholder's name was generally recorded. Some individuals who held land in this fashion were noted as 'justment outholders', 'outholders' and 'holders' but the latter may have held property which was not in agricultural use.

Three urban areas

This volume includes rates for Colyton, Crediton and Dartmouth, three very different communities. Colyton, an inland market town in East Devon which had the lowest population, was largely unremarkable for a small market town. However, in the late twentieth century it became the focus of extraordinary attention of historians through the Cambridge Population Group's use of its remarkably complete parish register.[26] In contrast, Crediton, which, explained one local gentleman to Lord Burghley in 1579, 'we commonly call Kirton', was a larger and livelier town which benefitted from its proximity to Exeter where its woollen cloth was largely sold.[27] In contrast, Dartmouth's coastal position generated a wider interaction with the world. While Crediton and Colyton had travellers passing through much as other towns,[28] Dartmouth was constantly engaged with people from, or in, far flung parts of the world. Merchant vessels arrived and departed while plying their trades, fishermen were engaged in waters across the North Atlantic and in times of war the port was busy with privateers and prize ships. The common feature of these three places was that in the 1540s they were able to remove rivals and subsequently enjoyed generations of greater independence.

Colyton

Local administration in Colyton fundamentally altered with the execution in 1538 of Henry Courtenay, 1st Marquess of Exeter and 2nd Earl of Devon, a convicted traitor. Eight years after the Crown seized his property a group of local men purchased part of the manor and established themselves as the Feoffees of Colyton. Their most notable achievement was the establishment of the local grammar school but the feoffees' role in the community extended much further. They repaired bridges, the market house and water courses as well as maintained a fire brigade from 1641. The feoffees evolved to become 'a complete parochial corporation' of which 'all the social machinery of the town, short of the administration of the law, seemed to devolve'.[29]

The church was in the patronage of the Dean & Chapter of Exeter but repairs were undertaken partly through rates, by the feoffees and in 1606 through guaranteed loans (Appendix 1).[30] The geographical size of the parish was extensive and, like Crediton, it had tithings. A rent roll of the manor made in 1538 listed them as Colyton, Stowford, Woodland, Watchcombe and Yardbury[31] whereas Item 39 had a different organisation. In 1658 the parish was reorganised when Shute was divided from Colyton but shortly afterwards the older boundaries returned.[32]

---

[26] Pamela Sharpe, *Population and Society in an East Devon Parish* (Exeter, 2002), 8–11.
[27] TNA, SP63/68/78.
[28] It is paradoxical that it was probably because of Crediton's remoteness from the sea that Dartmouth's mayor sent Spanish prisoners there in 1598: TNA, SP16/266/1.
[29] Sharpe, *Population*, 16–17.
[30] V. J. Torr, 'Exeter Diocese in 1563', DCNQ XXX:II (April 1965), 47.
[31] James Gairdner (ed.), *Letters and Papers, Foreign and Domestic of the reign of Henry VIII* (London, 1886), Vol. 9, p. 307.
[32] C. E. Welch, 'The Division of Colyton and Shute in 1658', DCNQ XXVII:IV (Oct. 1959), 111–12.

Crediton (Tony Gale)

It may be just one of many unremarkable small Devon towns today, but in 1520 Crediton was one of the fifty largest towns in England; a place of some consequence.[33] In 1559, the population of the parish stood at 2,200.[34] The combined parishes of Sandford and Crediton – treated as one parish in the Tudor period – extended to 19,809 acres before the boundaries were re-drawn in the nineteenth century.[35] Situated at the junction of two major highways, the town was not only a hub for the agricultural community but was also an important centre for Devon's cloth industry. Early sources suggest that in mediaeval times it had held a monopoly on the sale of certain types of cloth; one commentator noted that it was 'the only Market in these Western parts, for the sale of Kersies, Wool, and Yarn' before the establishment of Exeter's weekly markets for those commodities during the sixteenth century.[36] Although those markets diminished Crediton's standing in the cloth industry, it continued to be a major manufacturing centre into the seventeenth century and beyond, with a notable speciality in spinning.[37] The records of tithes and other payments in this volume (Items 49–56) can be read alongside a rich collection of manorial and ecclesiastical documents to begin to understand these structures; what they represented; how they compare with other local towns; and how they changed during the sixteenth and early seventeenth centuries.

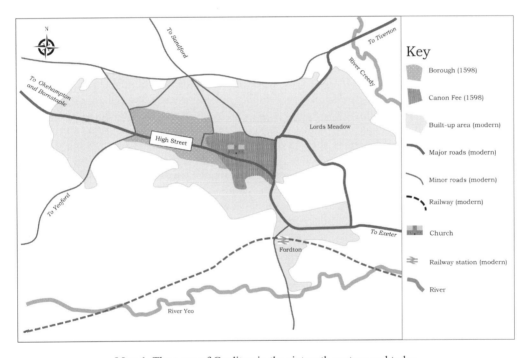

Map 1. The town of Crediton in the sixteenth century and today.

[33] Christopher Dyer, *Making a Living in the Middle Ages: The People of Britain 850–1520* (New Haven, 2002), p. 308.

[34] Beatrix Cresswell (ed.), *The Wardens' Accounts of the Governors of Crediton 1551–1599* (unpublished), p. 42.

[35] *White's Directory* (Sheffield, 1850), https://www.genuki.org.uk/big/eng/DEV/Crediton, accessed Feb. 2022.

[36] Richard Izacke, *Antiquities of the City of Exeter* (London, 1677), p. 119.

[37] Thomas Westcote, *A View of Devonshire in MDCXXX* (Exeter, 1845), p. 120.

Local governance: Crediton in context

A complicated ecclesiastical and manorial history created a confusing structure of institutions which managed community life in the town and the wider parish. This had a direct effect on the issuing of taxation. At the beginning of the sixteenth century there was an extensive manor, a seigneurial borough,[38] a 'canon fee', twelve prebends, an estate supporting a chapel and hospital, and five knights' fees. Before the Reformation these various institutions had formed two blocs. The bishop of Exeter held the manor and the borough. The church held the canon fee, which covered a large part of the town, and the twelve prebends – a substantial rural estate which funded the surprisingly large 'college' of local clergy in the town's collegiate church. Both the canon fee and the knights' fees each held their own manorial courts as sub-manors of the Manor of Crediton, but were for most purposes self-governing enclaves. The lordship of the manor changed hands several times during the course of the sixteenth century before Elizabeth I permanently vested it in private hands in 1595.[39] It was the secular role of the parish church which changed more dramatically. When the Crown dissolved collegiate churches in the 1540s, the inhabitants of Crediton purchased the strikingly large and imposing building and undertook to manage the church itself and the, 'Hereditaments and Goods of the Church of Crediton'. They were also to, 'create, erect, found, maintain, make and establish' a new grammar school. A corporation of twelve governors was established by royal charter to discharge these responsibilities.

As additional civic responsibilities passed to local communities under Elizabethan legislation, it was not the borough which took on those responsibilities for the town but the governors. They became, de facto, a 'closed vestry' – a prototype parish council whose members were selected for life. Whenever a vacancy arose, a new member was chosen by the remaining governors. Although their secular jurisdiction was initially limited to the canon fee – comprising something less than half of the urban area of Crediton – surviving records reveal that during this period they accrued responsibilities for matters such as the administration of the poor law, military musters and the maintenance of law and order on behalf of the whole of the parish, including all parts of the town.[40] The borough, meanwhile, remained in the ownership of the lord of the manor – an arrangement which persisted until the nineteenth century. Geographically, the borough formed a very small and tightly defined area, stretching for half a mile along the main street and for the most part just one burgage plot deep on either side of that street. The lord of the manor owned nearly all this property.[41] In the sixteenth century he also enjoyed – or assigned – the tolls and dues of Crediton's substantial market. It appears that although the borough was not set up to operate as a civic body, the trustees did make several payments to the poor and sick. The 1614 accounts for the market include in item, 'for the monthly payment to the poore owt of the said Borrough of Credyton .. at iijs iiijd p month'; another item 'for the repayringe of the Almes Houses'; a total of forty-one separate payments to inhabitants, 'in their sicknesse'; and ten payments for shrouds used at funerals. In total, the market authorities laid out just over £9 in payments to the poor and needy of the borough, representing about 11 per cent of the £80 total income – or about 70 per cent of the net profit of £13 9s 9d – from the market for that year.[42]

A schedule of 'Burrough Bonds' from the early seventeenth century reveals that they regularly loaned money at interest, 'out of the Issues and Profitts of the said Markett'.[43] A document of 1620 confirms how the market trustees were to use the profits of the market, together with the

---

[38] A seigneurial borough is controlled not by a corporate body of burgesses but by the lord of the manor.

[39] DHC, 2065M/SS5/21.

[40] Cresswell, *Wardens' Accounts*.

[41] Successive lords of the manor sold or otherwise disposed of many of these properties over the following centuries.

[42] DHC, 252B/APF75.

[43] TNA, C93/8/6.

interest on borough bonds, to the benefit of the townspeople. They were required to, 'dispose of and imploy such mony as shall be recovered and recoverable upon the… Bills Bondes and Accompts as aforesaid to the use and behoof of the poore and poore decayed tradesmen of the Town and Burrough of Crediton … according to an order and direction of a decree made by virtue of a Commission heretofore issuing out of the High Court of Chauncerie dated the Seaven and Twentieth Daye of Aprill 1620.'[44] Nonetheless, the chief responsibility of the borough trustees was to operate and sustain the market – which was how most of the income was used. Perhaps it is appropriate to regard the borough at that time as a charitable body with respect to profits from its activities, rather than as a civic entity collecting and distributing public funds specifically for charitable purposes.

How does this compare with other Devon towns during this period? The borough of Barnstaple, like that of Crediton, had mediaeval origins. As for Crediton, Barnstaple's founding charter no longer exists and the details are unknown. Unlike Crediton, Barnstaple's borough became incorporated by royal charter in the sixteenth century, with responsibilities for the government of the town through a mayor and a common council of 24 capital burgesses.[45] Like Crediton's twelve governors they were a closed body, electing their own successors. Tiverton, like Crediton, remained substantially under manorial control in the early part of this period, although unlike Crediton it never seems to have had a seigneurial borough. The population of the town grew dramatically during the course of the sixteenth century – from less than 2,000 in the 1520s to about 4,000 by 1615, when it became an incorporated borough.[46] Under its founding charter, the borough was to be run by a mayor, twelve capital burgesses and twelve assistant burgesses. They managed and regulated the market and maintained the roads and bridges. They had the authority to make their own byelaws and to hold their own courts. Unlike Crediton, where the borough covered only the small commercial centre of the town, the borough of Tiverton ran to 17,650 acres – the whole of the ecclesiastical parish. The local manor courts continued to function, but their residual roles were largely ceremonial.[47]

So by the early seventeenth century, both Barnstaple and Tiverton had incorporated boroughs with well-defined responsibilities for managing the civic lives of their respective communities, while in Crediton it was the church, through its twelve governors, which carried out most civic functions, largely eclipsing the manor and its seigneurial borough.

In some respects, Crediton evolved in ways which had more in common with the smaller East Devon towns of Colyton and Ottery St Mary. As noted earlier, the townspeople of Colyton had acquired local estates which were forfeited by the execution of the marquis of Exeter for treason and they assumed civic responsibilities for the town through a 'chamber' of twelve feoffees charged with, 'good, godly and commendable uses and purposes'. At Ottery St Mary, like Crediton, the local inhabitants purchased their collegiate church when it was dissolved in 1545. There was to be a corporation of four governors who were not only to govern the church but also – like their counterparts at Crediton – to establish and maintain, 'the kinges newe grammer scole of Seynt Marye Oterey'.[48] So the corporation at Ottery St Mary was set up along lines very similar to -that at Crediton: the feoffees of Colyton were charged with duties similar to those which the twelve governors at Crediton came to discharge later in the sixteenth century. These arrangements had more in common with rural communities – run by vestries – than with urban centres like Barnstaple and Tiverton, governed by their newly incorporated boroughs.

[44] TNA, C93/8/6.
[45] https://www.historyofparliamentonline.org/volume/1604-1629/constituencies/tiverton, accessed July 2021.
[46] Mike Sampson, *A History of Tiverton* (Tiverton, 2004), pp. 70, 89.
[47] Sampson, Tiverton, pp. 89–90.
[48] George Oliver, *Monasticon Diocesis Exoniensis* (Exeter, 1846), p. 262.

The manor of Crediton

At the beginning of the sixteenth century, the manor of Crediton formed part of the estates of the bishop of Exeter. In 1523, the bishop commissioned a *valor* – a valuation of his estates – which provides details of all its manorial tenants and their property holdings within the parishes of Crediton, Morchard Bishop and what are now Copplestone, Kennerleigh and Sandford. Many hamlets and farmsteads named in the *valor* can be identified to modern-day properties. Distinctive place names like Dunscombe, Hookway, Pydesleghe (Pidsley) and Yewford (Yeoford) form a useful starting point in understanding the geography of the manor – and parish – of Crediton as it stood in the sixteenth century. While the *valor* gives us a great deal of information about the tenants of the manorial properties, it does not include details of the occupiers – much of the land would have been sub-let.

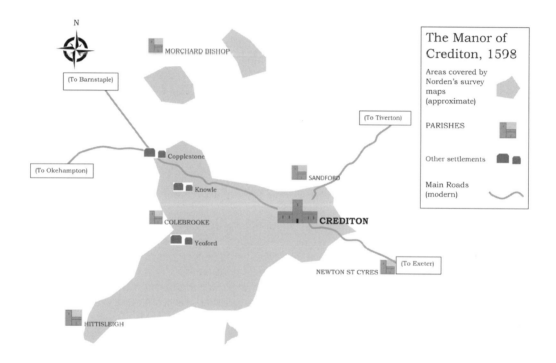

Map 2. The manor of Crediton in 1598.

The manor of Crediton changed hands several times during the sixteenth century, with numerous changes in the make-up of the estate. Bishop Turberville had leased some part of it to his 'kinsman' Nicholas Turberville before the lordship of the manor and the lease for the bulk of its lands passed to William Killigrew in 1570.[49] A contentiously worded document in the cathedral archives noted that 'Killigrewe had but eleven yeares to come in his Lease of the demeanes and Mannor of Crediton when he and his friends in court prevayled with her Queenes Mai'tie to make D Babbington B'p of Exeter'.[50] It was in 1595, during Babbington's incumbency, that Elizabeth secured the manor – now standing at about 6,000 acres – to the crown and almost immediately granted it to Killigrew on a permanent basis. This was just one of many manors lost to the bishopric following the Reformation; under Bishop Veysey (1519/51 and 1553/4), 'of two and

49   Oliver, *Monasticon*, p. 262.
50   Exeter Cathedral Archive, D&C861.

twenty Manors belonging to it [the bishopric], he scarcely left eight; and they none of the best'. Babbington's agreement signed away, 'that rich and noble Mannor of Crediton, a Bough as big near as the rest of the Tree'.[51]

Killigrew had already leased the manor for the previous twenty-five years, but from 1595 he held it under a grant in fee farm, an arrangement under which ownership passed to the grantee in return for an annual payment to the crown in perpetuity. It was at this point that he commissioned a survey with an unusually detailed set of maps and accompanying documentation. This was undertaken by the prominent cartographer and surveyor John Norden and provides a wealth of information which complements ecclesiastical and parochial records.[52]

Church and parish

Before the Reformation, much of the property in the parish of Crediton not held by the manor was in the hands of the local church rather than the bishop. In 1535, Henry VIII commissioned the *Valor Ecclesiasticus* – a valuation of the church lands across the whole country. This revealed that the temporal possessions of the local church at Crediton were valued at £17 18s per annum and the spiritual possessions at £238 11s 2½d per annum.[53]

Following the Reformation, Crediton's church ceased to be a collegiate establishment. The number of clergy was dramatically reduced, and the income available to the church was similarly slashed. The wardens' accounts for 1551 reveal that their total annual income was just £67 16s 9d.[54] The sum of £9 12s 10½d was payable to the crown for the 'Spiritualities of the late Prebend of Priestcombe'. The net income for the year was therefore less than £60: a massive reduction from the £238 assessment recorded sixteen years earlier. The prebends were no longer part of the church estate, and most of the tithes had been confiscated; the wardens' accounts reveal that the only tithe income in 1551 was £10 6s 8d received for privy tithes – levied on earnings or the value of labour.[55] Funding of the local church remained substantially unchanged during Mary's reign, but in 1560 Elizabeth I issued new letters patent which granted the governors an additional £100 a year in tithe income, coming from the prebends and the St Lawrence Lands. This might appear to be a nil-sum gift, as the grant was made in fee farm – with £100 a year payable to the crown. The arrangement took effect in 1563, when the governors managed to collect £100 15s 9½d in tithe income, only slightly more than they needed to pay the crown. However, it soon became clear that the tithes were worth more than this; by 1567 the governors were collecting over £120 a year from this source – and by 1582 it had risen to nearly £250 a year, while the annual payment to the crown remained at £100.

The accounts record payments each year in the 1580s and 1590s, 'for keeping the Easter Book of Crediton' (typically a payment of seven shillings) – and a separate Easter Book for Sandford (five shillings). In many parishes, the vicar's income was derived from the mandatory offerings collected from all communicants at Easter plus receipts from the small tithes.[56] Crediton took a different approach. The vicar was paid a stipend, while all tithe receipts and other collections – collectively referred to in the wardens' accounts as, 'spiritualities' – were paid into the church's general account. It would appear from the earlier of the two sets of sixteenth century Easter Book accounts included in this volume (1582) that the assessments included in the Easter returns were calculated on the same basis as those for the remainder of the year, as they total approximately 25 per cent of the full year's tithe income as revealed by the wardens' accounts for that year. For example, the Easter Book income from the tithing of Woolsgrove was £6 9s 8d: the total for the

[51] John Prince, *Worthies of Devon* (Exeter, 1701), p. 88.

[52] DHC, 1660/A add4/E1.

[53] Joseph Hunter (ed.), *Valor Ecclesiasticus* (London, 1834 edn), pp. 323–5.

[54] Cresswell, *Wardens' Accounts*, p. 1.

[55] Cresswell, *Wardens' Accounts*, p. 1.

[56] S. J. Wright, 'A Guide to Easter Books and related Parish Listings', *Local Population Studies* 43 (Autumn 1989), 18.

year from the same tithing was £25 18s 7d. The 1594 book (Item 52), however, explicitly records figures for the whole year.

However, the opening paragraph of each set of annual accounts states that they include, 'Receipts of Oblacions, Privy Tithes and Garden (i.e. Guardian) Money at Easter'. At Easter 1582, £22 6s 7d was received from oblations, £4 14s 4d from privy tithes and £2 3s ½d from garden money. It might appear that the records referred to in Crediton as Easter Books were in fact assessments of tithe liability for the whole year; and that while the 1582 accounts hark back to an earlier era when there was a separate calculation of income for the spring quarter, by 1594 they were treated as a record of all tithes payable during the year.

When it comes to the secular roles of the twelve governors, we find several references to payments entered in the wardens' accounts. In 1595, 7s 8d was paid, 'for the carriage of 12 men's armour to St Thomas Parish and to Alphington twice' and 3s 2d for, 'new sheafs for swords and daggers that were lost and mending of the rest' – clear evidence of their responsibilities for Crediton men at that year's militia muster. In the same year, the warden's own accountant claimed 2s 8d, 'for being Clerk to the Constables in writing of Hue and Cry precepts, Muster Book and all other their receipts and payments incident to their office as parcel of his fee of 5s a year for doing thereof'.[57] Regarding the governors' role in poor law administration, there are several entries each year from the Elizabethan era onwards, including the following from 1595. 'For a petticoat cloth for Wilmot Browning and for lining and making: 6s'; 'For curing the man that was hurted in the highway: 6s 8d'; 'Distributed to the poor in the East and West Towns against Easter: 41s'; 'Distributing money to the poor every week 5s: £8'.[58]

Tithings and prebends

For some years, the wardens' accounts also include details of individuals who had not paid their tithes. In 1597, the list of defaulters ran to sixty-eight names, including fifty-four who can be matched against the 1594 tithe list. Not only does the tithe list contain many more names; it also reveals further information not recorded elsewhere. For example, we learn that Margery Broadmead paid tithes for two adjoining holdings at Stockey Downs and Moore; that William Killigrew (Lord of the Manor) was paying tithes on, 'le Dye House' and for, 'a parcel of Dartes Downs' – and apparently nothing else; and not only that William Marten had taken over a tenement, 'which was Mr Wyvell's' but also that Marten was a merchant, 'of Exeter'. In an era when ready money was in short supply, the church authorities sometimes resorted to seizing goods in lieu of unpaid tithes. In 1540, the dean of Crediton seized a quantity of broom – presumably stock-in-trade? – from John Howe and John Walshe in lieu of overdue payments.[59]

Perhaps the most useful additional information afforded by these tithe lists is the light they shed on the evolving pattern of tithings within the parish of Crediton and the changing status of Sandford.

---

[57] Cresswell, *Wardens' Accounts*, p. 362.
[58] Cresswell, *Wardens' Accounts*, p. 363.
[59] TNA, C1/1011/50-52.

Table 1. Schedule of Tithings as included in the returns from 1549 to 1644 (NB All spellings have been standardised).

1549	1574	1582	1594	1619	1630	1636	1644
A Collection	Easter Book	Easter Book	Tithe Account	Church Rate	Tithe Account	Tithe Account	Tithe Account
East Town	East Town	Town Tithing	Town	Canon Fee	Canon Fee	Canon Fee	Canon Fee
Borough	West Town	Prebend	Poole	Borough	Borough	Borough	Borough
Kirton Tithing	Town Tithing	Priestcombe	Priestcombe	Town Tithing	Town Tithing	Town Tithing	Town Tithing
Rudge		Rudge	Rudge	Rudge	Rudge	Rudge	Rudge
		Stowford	Stowford	Knoll (Knowle)	Knoll	Knoll	Knoll
				Uton	Uton	Uton	Uton
Yewford		Crosse	Crosse	Yewford	Yewford	Yewford	Yewford
Woodland		Woodland	Woodland	Woodland	Woodland	Woodland	Woodland
		Aller	Aller				
		Carswell	Carswell				
		Henstill	Henstill				
		Woolsgrove	Woolsgrove				
				Sandford	Sandford	Sandford	Sandford
		Rents	Parish Rents		Parish Rents	Parish Rents	Parish Rents
			Exminster			Parke Ground	Parke Ground

Table 1 lists the breakdown of each return to facilitate comparisons. It must be noted that these and other contemporary records habitually use the terms 'prebends' and 'tithings' loosely, confusingly and interchangeably. Strictly speaking, Crediton had no 'prebends' – lands providing income for individual churchmen known as 'prebendaries' – following the dissolution of the collegiate church in 1546/7; but the names of the former prebends continued to be applied to several tithings throughout the following century. These are tithings – subdivisions of the parish for the purpose of collecting tithes – and would have had no role as prebends. In some instances the relationship between the name of each tithing and the land within it is unclear. Reichel's work on the hundreds of Devon goes some way towards clarifying the geography of the tithings as listed from 1619 onwards (Items 53–6), while leaving some unexplained gaps and ambiguities.[60]

For reasons described above, the urbanised area of Crediton is generally split between the East Town (or Canon Fee) and the West Town (or Borough). The return for 1594 anomalously includes a single entry for 'Town'. It appears that the surviving return for that year is incomplete; comparisons with returns for other years suggest that 'Town' relates to the Town Tithing (see notes relating to 'Town Tithing' and 'Poole', below). All the returns except for 1594 include the Town Tithing which was referred to in 1549 (Item 49) as 'Kerton Tithing' – Kirton being an alternative name for Crediton. Reichel commented that the Town Tithing included the estates of Newcombes, Downes, Little Fulford and Bradley – encompassing a swathe of the parish lying immediately north and east of the town.[61] See also the entry for Poole, below.

The Twelve Prebends

The 1594 return (Item 52) is the only one to refer to Poole by that name but the substantial overlap with the list of entries under 'Prebend' in the 1582 return suggests that the two were one and the same. Poole appears to have encompassed the Great Meadow (otherwise known as Lords Meadow) and a number of mills, including 'the Four Mills' at Fordton and Mr Dunscombe's 'New Mill' at what became Downes. From 1619 onwards, some or all of these properties – including 'the fower mills' and 'the great meadow' – are listed as part of the Town Tithing (see above).

Priestcombe gave its name to one of the tithings listed in 1582 and 1594 (Items 51 & 52). After the tithings were reorganised (between 1594 and 1619) it became part of the tithing of Knowle.

Rudge lent its name to one of the tithings listed in in 1549 and again from 1594 onwards. Reichel commented that it included Dunscombe, Fordton, Carsford and Trowbridge.[62] It was referred to in some accounts as, 'Rudge Episcopi' to avoid confusion with the farm of Rudge in Sandford. Reichel himself contributed to that confusion by a reference to the latter elsewhere in his Hundreds of Devon.[63]

Stowford gave its name to one of the tithings listed in in 1582 and 1594. After the tithings were reorganised it became part of the tithing of Knowle. From 1619 onwards the tithing of 'Knoll' (Knowle) subsumed the former prebends of Priestcombe and Stowford. Reichel noted that it included Spencecombe and Ford (south-east of Yeoford).[64]

Uton was one of the eighteen tithings of Crediton in the 1340s, but had lost that status by the beginning of the sixteenth century.[65] It appeared as one of the tithings from 1619 onwards. Reichel noted that it included Uton Arundel, Yew and Venny Tedburn as well as the settlement of Uton.

[60] Reichel, 'The manor and hundred of Crediton', *DAT* LIV (1922), 165–8. The estates and settlements are listed using the names that would have been familiar to Reichel's contemporaries.
[61] Reichel, 'The manor', 154.
[62] Reichel, 'The manor', 154.
[63] Reichel, 'The manor', 166.
[64] Reichel, 'The manor', 154.
[65] Reichel, 'The manor', 153.

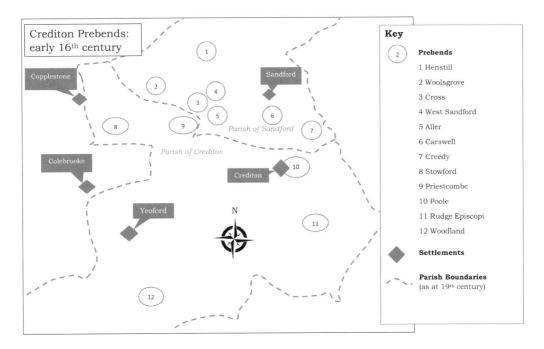

Map 3. The prebends of Crediton, early sixteenth century.

Yewford is listed as a tithing in 1549. That name did not appear in the returns for 1574 (which appears to relate only to the town of Crediton and its immediate surrounds), 1582 or 1594(Items 50–2). In those returns, the tithing of Crosse appears to subsume the holdings of Yewford. The name of Yewford appears once again from 1619 onwards. Reichel noted that it included Hollacombe, Keymelford and Posbury as well as Yewford (i.e. Yeoford) itself.[66]

Although Woodland was another prebend there does not appear to have been a prebendal farm associated with it. Reichel suggested that Woodland 'is really in the parish of Colebrook' but the whole range of returns from 1549 to 1644 clearly identify it as one of the tithings of the parish of Crediton.[67]

Aller was also one of the tithings in 1582 and again in 1594. From 1619 onwards it is subsumed into 'Sandford'. Carswell, a prebend, appeared as one of the tithings in 1582 and again in 1594. From 1619 onwards it was subsumed into 'Sandford'. Creedy, a prebend, did not appear in any of these returns as a 'tithing'. It lay within what became the parish of Sandford. Crosse, another prebend, gave its name to one of the tithings listed in in 1582 and 1594. The prebendal farm of Crosse lay within what became the parish of Sandford, but many of the other properties in the tithing lay within Crediton. After the tithings were reorganised, those properties became part of the tithing of Yewford (i.e. Yeoford).

Henstill also appeared as one of the tithings in 1582 and again in 1594. The prebendal farm of Henstill lay within what became the parish of Sandford, but many of the properties within the tithing lay within Crediton. After the tithings were reorganised, those properties became part of the tithings of either Yewford or Uton (the exact boundaries of each are not known). West Sandford, another prebend, does not appear in any of these returns as a 'tithing'. It lay within what became the parish of Sandford.

---

[66] Reichel, 'The manor', 154.
[67] Reichel, 'The manor', 154.

Woolsgrove was a tithing in 1582 and again in 1594 but from 1619 onwards it was subsumed into 'Sandford'. When the corporation of twelve governors of Crediton church was established in 1547/8, it was specified that three should be from Sandford, 'a village and hamlet within the said parish'. The wardens' accounts for 1559 referred to Sandford as 'a next [i.e. annexed] unto Crediton and a daughter to the same even now at this daye'.[68] Where Norden's survey of 1598 lists the local parishes, it cited Sandford as being 'a chapple to Crediton'.[69] But Sandford's status was ambiguous. The lay subsidy returns for 1544 and 1581 list the inhabitants of Sandford as if it was a separate parish: but there was no 'Sandford' list in the lay subsidy returns for 1524 or the muster roll for 1569. Stoate, who edited those returns, commented that the Sandford return for the muster roll 'appears to be missing'.[70] It seems rather that it is the lay subsidies of 1544 and 1581 which are anomalous, as Sandford was not a parish in its own right. Crediton and Sandford were two substantial and distinct settlements within the same parish, one with the parish church, the other with a chapel of ease. The antiquarian William Pole noted in the early 1600s 'Sandford hath his church, but is of the parish of Crediton'.[71] Reverend George Oliver, writing in 1846, commented that Sandford had long been a chapel of ease within the parish of Crediton, which by his time was, 'reputed a distinct parish for all secular purposes'.[72]

The manor of Crediton as granted to Sir Thomas Darcy when it was first wrested from the bishops of Exeter in the 1540s included all twelve prebends; but the grant to Killigrew in the 1590s did not include any land in what became the parish of Sandford. Rudge Episcopi, Priestcombe, Woodland, Yewford, Uton and Knowle all lay within the Manor of Crediton (as did Poole): the former prebends of Aller, Carswell, Creedy, Cross, Henstill, West Sandford and Woolsgrove all lay beyond the boundaries of the manor. It might be that for a period in the sixteenth century it was deemed appropriate and convenient to use the names of former prebends for the tithings, but in the seventeenth century it seemed more appropriate to group together the cohesive collection of prebends which lay outside the manor of Crediton under the name of Sandford; and to name the tithings within the manor after the principal settlements in each.

Parish rents appear as a separate item in several of these returns. It will be noted that they are rents, not tithe payments. The individual rents included in these lists change over time. Most of the parish church's real estate lay within the Canon Fee or the Town Tithing, so individual 'rents' sometimes appear under one or other of those schedules.

The former Great Park had been disparked by 1571.[73] At the time of Norden's survey of 1598 there were no less than twenty-two tenants holding closes within the area he still referred to as 'The Great Park'.[74] It is not clear why the 'Park Ground' was only listed separately in the returns from 1619 onwards – or indeed how it had been treated for tithing purposes before that date.

Exminster is and was a separate parish, lying some twelve miles south-east of Crediton. The twelve governors became responsible for its parochial affairs under the terms of Edward VI's Charter of 1547 and the accretion of local government responsibilities later in the sixteenth century.[75] Contemporary records relating to Exminster typically record it separately from Crediton, but for some unspecified reason it was named and listed in the 1594 tithe returns as one of the 'prebends'.

Crediton's complex and shifting parochial and manorial arrangements have long been a source of confusion, but by studying these tithe returns, church rates and Easter Books alongside other

[68]   Cresswell, *Wardens' Accounts*, p. 42.
[69]   DHC, 1660/A add4/E1/p. 6.
[70]   T. L. Stoate & A. J. Howard (eds), *The Muster Roll of Devon for 1569* (Paignton, 2004), p. iii.
[71]   William Pole, *Collections towards a Description of the County of Devon* (London, 1791), p. 226.
[72]   Oliver, *Monasticon*, p. 79.
[73]   Lincolns Inn Library and Archive, Maynard M.45, fol. 16r.
[74]   DHC, 1660A/add 4/E1, p. 26.
[75]   Samuel Lysons, *Magna Brittania being a concise topographical account of the several counties of Great Britain; Volume the Sixth containing Devonshire* (London, 1822), p. 148.

manorial and ecclesiastical records we can get a better understanding of how they evolved over the century following the Reformation. A comparison with other small towns in Devon highlights the surprising diversity of institutions which developed during that time. It is possible to track the evolution of the various tithings within the parish – and the changing relationship between Sandford and Crediton – by a close examination of these eight sets of returns, stretching across almost one hundred years.

Dartmouth

In terms of the history of parish taxation, Dartmouth is perhaps unique in Devon for its parishioners not having to pay church rates. A scribe acknowledged this in 1613 when he wrote the glebe terrier for St Saviour:

> 'there was never any rate made to the knowledge of the said churchwarden for the reparation of the said chapel but the same is and hath always been repaired at the charge of the corporation of the said town and by their common stock'.[76]

The history of the town's finances, and the manner in which it taxed local people, can be found in the corporation's archive, one of the most extensive such collections in Devon. Its landscape was a particular reason for its prosperity and thus the healthy state of the borough's finances.

Map 4. Dartmouth, 1500 to 1650.

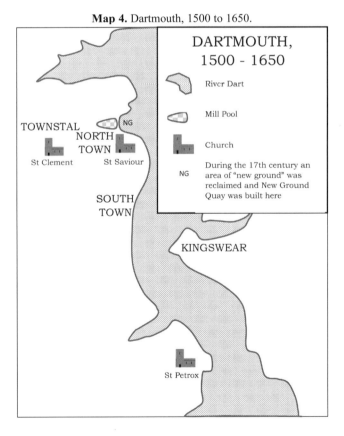

---

76   DHC, Diocese of Exeter, Principal Registry, Glebe Terriers, Dartmouth, 1613.

Dartmouth is situated on the west bank of the Dart directly across from the village and parish of Kingswear. The town lies between two promontories with a tidal inlet which lay in between. Across this was built The Fosse, a causeway on which stood two grist mills with a salt-water pool on the inner side. In this period they were known as 'the salt mills'.[77] The northern promontory, which rises to 354 feet in height, was named Townstal and its ridge of land falling to the river, Hardness. Most of the town of Dartmouth lay to the south and the southern promontory was known as Clifton. During this period there was extensive development along the river, in building houses and quays on the mud. A variety of rival interests had civil and ecclesiastical jurisdiction in the port but in the early sixteenth century the corporation, led by the small mercantile elect who comprised the council, increasingly became independent.

Dartmouth's topography at the mouth of the river contributed to a complicated pattern of legal jurisdictions. It derived a commercial advantage from being a deep-water port with easy access to Devon's main foreign trading ports. In 1522 the Earl of Surrey advised Henry VIII:

'In my life I saw never a goodlier haven... at the entry of the haven there is a blockhouse made of stone and of the same side another old castle, on the other side there is another other old castle and besides that another other blockhouse, and a chain ready to be laid over the haven and all things ready for the same. The town is not two arrows' shot from thence. And the ships may lie two miles further within the haven, under John Gilbert's house, and at the least five fathoms at a low water. The chain that is at Portsmouth may be laid within the other chain, so that we here think it shall not be possible for any ships to come within the haven, the most danger we see is that if the enemies would come with a great pinnace and land at a place called Torbay, which is but two miles from the place where the ships shall ride, they might with casting fire into them do some hurt or else some fellow in the night might steal near them and throw wildfire into them. The remedies whereof after our opinions is this: that your grace should write unto the bishop of Exeter, and to all the best gentlemen of Devonshire showing unto them that your grace is informed that they be now making a blockhouse a little beside Brixham within Torbay, and if they would make another at Churston, within the said Torbay, your grace would help them with ordnance and powder.'[78]

In 1599 an Italian summarised Dartmouth as:

'a large port [with capacity] for 600 vessels, and at low tide five yards of water; at the entrance [is] a bastion of earth with six or eight pieces of artillery; [and] further in a castle with 24 pieces and 50 men; and more inside and then another earth bastion with six pieces or iron all in good order. The place is not very large but not walled, the mountains serving for walls. The people are warlike, and constantly at sea with vessels to attack the Spaniards and other enemies. On the other side [of the river] there is a very beautiful village with good people. In the port are generally 30 vessels of merchandise or war'.[79]

Throughout this period the Crown arranged that the borough would maintain the port's defence: an annuity was paid out of the port's customs to the corporation.[80] Dartmouth trained its militia independently of the rest of Devon.[81] Dartmouth's unusually high number of wards may be connected to the borough's military responsibilities.

The vulnerability to landings continued into the seventeenth century. In 1626 the mayor warned national government that Torbay and Blackpool Sands in Stoke Fleming were ideal landing places

---

[77] DHC, DD61441.

[78] J. S. Brewer (ed.), *Letters and Papers, Foreign and Domestic, of the Reign of Henry VIII* (London, 1867), Vol. 3, p. 997.

[79] TNA, SP12/270/139. I am grateful to Sandra Cavallo for her translation of the Italian text.

[80] Watkin, *Dartmouth*, p. 156; Russell, *Dartmouth*, pp. 53–6.

[81] DHC, DD61858.

for enemies who could 'take the hills which are above us and beat us out of the town'.[82] Visitors repeatedly noticed the deep river channel and the steep hills. In the 1690s Reverend John Prince, the author of *The Worthies of Devon*, described it as:

'A large populous town, situate on the south side of a very steep hill, which runneth from east to west a considerable length of near a mile, whereby the houses as you pass on the water seem pensil and to hang along in rows, like gallipots in an apothecary's shop, for so high and steep is it, that you go from the lower to the higher part thereof by stairs and from the bottom to top requires no less, in some places many more, than an hundred'.[83]

A century later another visitor centred on the buildings and the people who lived in them. Daniel Carless Webb wrote Dartmouth:

'has a peculiar appearance, the houses seeming to be placed one on the top of another… I am sorry to observe that the inhabitants were as much in want of cleanliness as their neighbours.'[84]

Another traveller later made equally disparaging remarks about local people when he observed it was:

'a seaport, built upon the side of a rock, the scent of which greets the traveller with pitch, tar and dried fish. Nature seems to have kept her original rudeness here, for they are all very rough, and if they possess any improvement from art, it is the art of swearing, in which few could beat them. The women being the most vulgar, they go a fishing, row passengers over in the boats, with their petticoats tied between their legs like trousers, and a short pipe in their mouths. They therefore being no very desirable objects it was no great wonder the captain was not tempted to break his [marital] oath'.[85]

Throughout this period Dartmouth was nationally prominent in times of war, particularly during the long Elizabethan conflict with Spain, which involved the seizure of merchant vessels. The most famous incident took place in 1592 when the *Madre de Dios* was brought into the port. This Portuguese carrack had been captured off the Azores and Robert Cecil, later Secretary of State, rushed from London to secure the Crown's portion of the East Indian cargo. He famously commented:

'I am passed by Exeter where I did take this course, whomsoever I met by the way, within seven miles that either had anything in cloak, bag or malle which did but smell of the prizes, either at Dartmouth or Plymouth (for I assure your lordship I could well smell them almost), such hath been the spoils of amber & musk amongst them. I did (though he had little about here) returned him with me to the town of Exeter where I stayed any which could convey news to Dartmouth and Plymouth at the gates of the town. I compelled them also to tell me where any trunks or malls were, and I by this inquisition finding the people stubborn till I had committed two innkeepers to prison, which example would have won the Queen £20,000 a week past… My lord, there was never such spoil.'[86]

---

[82]   TNA, SP16/32/120.

[83]   John Prince, *The Worthies of Devon* (Plymouth, 1810 edn), p. 477.

[84]   Daniel Carless Webb, *Observations and remarks during four excursions made to various parts of Great Britain* (London, c.1811).

[85]   *A Trip to Bath and a tour through the west* (London, c.1790), p. 35.

[86]   M. Oppenheim, *The Maritime History of Devon* (Exeter, 1968), pp. 49–50; John Appleby, 'Devon privateering from early times to 1688', in Michael Duffy et al. (eds), *The New Maritime History of Devon* (Exeter, 1992), p. 94; TNA, SP12/243/26, 19 Sept. 1592.

The cargo included porcelain dishes, ivory, 'Turkey carpets', rubies, silk and spices.[87] Cecil seized at Exeter:

> 'A great pot of musk, 26 pieces of calico lawn, 1 piece of calico, 8 bundles of twisted satin, 2 pieces of white silk, 59 pieces of white cipres, carnation taffeta a remnant, checked taffeta a remnant, a white quilted kirtle, three spoons of mother of pearl, a bag of pearl wherein is two or three pieces of gold string work with rubies and crystal, a bag of seed pearl and a quilt for a bed and a canopy.'

The value was estimated at half a million pounds but a considerable portion was stolen or embezzled.[88]

In 1625, twenty years after the declaration of peace between England and Spain, the country was again at war and for five years prize ships were once again brought into Dartmouth. The war also brought French and Spanish privateers which attacked English vessels including those of Dartmouth. From the early 1600s the port also suffered from the depravations of corsairs from North Africa.

In this period Dartmouth's commerce was dominated by cloth which was transported from Totnes down the river and by overseas fishing. Dartmouth was involved in a network of fisheries which extended from the inshore fisheries, particularly that for pilchards along the south coast, to others in the English Channel, the North Sea, Ireland, Iceland, New England and Newfoundland. The latter was the preferred fishery and in 1619 no less than twenty-four Dartmouth ships returned directly from Newfoundland. The *Nicholas, Falcon, Christopher, Comfort, Grace, Gabriel, Sweepstake, Content, Edward Bonaventure, Anne, Holligrove, Rose, Handmaid, Revenge, Swiftsure, William, Mayflower, Primrose, Gift, Prosperous, Unity, Hopewell, Valentine* and *Mary* were joined by the *Blessing* of Kingswear, *Eleanor* of Salcombe, *Samuel* of Dittisham, *Jonas* of Kingswear and the *Minion* of Dittisham. Other ships sailed first to Portuguese, Spanish or French ports where they sold cured fish and subsequently returned home to Dartmouth.[89] By the early 1600s the port had become the greatest centre for shipping and seafarers in South Devon.[90]

In 1619 ships also arrived from the Channel Islands, Scotland, Ireland and even the Amazon. The port's records are riddled with references to men from distant places. They included seven Dutch men who died shortly after arriving in 1610 from the East Indies[91] and in 1619 the mayor provided assistance to men from Germany, Ireland, France and the Low Countries as well as others from across Great Britain; amongst them were several dozen shipwrecked men.[92] Individual events were responsible for sizeable numbers of aliens in the port: in 1637 over one hundred shipwrecked French mariners needed financial help for their maintenance and for their return home.[93] There were also some foreign women in the port such as Marie Parie, from France, who had an illegitimate child with local mariner John Pre, and who in 1625 was pregnant with his second but Pre, he explained, could not marry her until his wife died.[94] Visitors occasionally included illustrious people such as the Persian Ambassador in 1626 and explorers such as Henry Hudson.[95]

---

[87] R. A. Roberts (ed.), *Calendar of the Manuscripts of the Most Hon. the Marquis of Salisbury, Preserved at Hatfield House, Hertfordshire* (London, 1892), p. 231.

[88] TNA, SP12/243/27; Russell, *Dartmouth*, pp. 75–8.

[89] DHC, DD61979.

[90] Todd Gray (ed.), *Early-Stuart Mariners and Shipping*, DCRS NS33 (1990), xvi–xxii.

[91] DHC, Dartmouth St Saviour, PR1, 11–18 May 1610.

[92] DHC, DD61978 & DD61793.

[93] TNA, SP16/363/115.

[94] DHC, DD62149.

[95] DHC, DD62213.

Plate 1. Lithograph showing the west end of St Saviour's Church from the Fosse, Dartmouth, 1845.

The mayor cited this 'intercourse of strangers' as one of the chief characteristics of the town when in 1604 he asked James I to renew the charter.[96] The corporation was expected to interrogate suspicious men who had come from abroad such as Nicholas Flute, a local man, who voyaged in the *Samaritan* of Dartmouth to visit Rome in 1594[97] and the travels of Christopher Hubbard caused the mayor to write to Cecil four years later. Hubbard had been born in Padstow, was taken prisoner by the Spanish and served in the galleys off Mexico and Cuba before returning to Spain.[98] In 1619 the son of a Londoner was imprisoned when he arrived from Spain: John Davis was 'a professed and dangerous Roman Catholic… apt to infect his Majesty's subjects with the dangerous positions of popery and disloyalty'.[99] Other men were questioned for Continental news particularly regarding foreign military movements.

When Dartmouth officials examined foreign visitors they drew upon their mercantile skills in being conversant in other European languages or were able to enlist other local men. In this the character of Dartmouth was most likely dissimilar to Colyton or Crediton. Men arrived in the port and their behaviour at sea required investigation. For instance, it transpired in 1613 that Captain 'Cutting Dick' had recruited crewmembers in a wine tavern in Brixham before going on to take some sixty French, Flemish, Scottish and English vessels in the Channel. John Tooley, John Pomeroy and John Humphrey were some of the Brixham men who subsequently faced charges of piracy.[100] That year another vessel, crewed mainly by local men, also came into Dartmouth. They were also suspected of piracy and their examinations revealed inconsistencies which suggest the mayor had been right to question them. The company of thirteen included Nicholas Shere of Plymouth, Nicholas Norracott of Dartmouth, Thomas Martin of Salcombe, Andrew Duloe, a Frenchman, Simon Croote of Totnes, John Allen of Frome in Somerset, Arthur Halse of Plymstock, James Chamberlain of Plymouth, Pascoe Westcoat of Stonehouse, Anthony Orenge of Stonehouse, Nathaniel Babb and William Carey of either Stonehouse or Truro. They had set sail in a small vessel of some six tons from Salcombe in April 1613 and three days later entered Dartmouth aboard the *Cod Fish*, a Flemish ship en route to Bristol with a cargo of hemp, madder and flax. Although most of the men agreed that they had originally intended to fish for rays in the Isles of Scilly and sell them in Brittany, they admitted that they had neglected to bring any nets, lines or hooks with them. Chamberlain claimed to have been onboard merely to sail to France where he had wanted to sell six pounds of tobacco and Arthur Halse's stated purpose was to travel in order to learn the French language.

However, when the mayor examined two sailors from Zeeland they revealed they had been robbed and held below deck for three days (with the only exception being allowed to come on deck 'to ease themselves') before finally being set free in Dartmouth. None of the English 'fishermen' could explain why they had stopped the Flemish vessel and boarded her 'having ciphers over their faces', and with drawn swords, nor could they satisfactorily clarify why they seized the ship and took the cargo.[101]

The course of religious change in Dartmouth was much like that in other Devon market towns. One early indication of popular sentiment took place on 28 October 1537 when Emelima Petyfen cried out in the port 'the devil take the king and his lady both'.[102] She was referring to Henry VIII but was unlikely to have known that the king's third wife, Jane Seymour, had died four days

---

[96] M. S. Guiseppi (ed.), *Calendar of the manuscripts of the most Hon. the Marquis of Salisbury* (London, 1933), XVI, p. 128. In 1631 another mayor also observed Dartmouth was 'much resorted unto by strangers': TNA, SP16/186/27.

[97] Roberts, *Calendar*, IV, p. 598.

[98] TNA, SP12/266/1.

[99] TNA, SP14/107/70 & 74 & SP14/108/60.

[100] DHC, DD61843.

[101] DHC, DD61829.

[102] Russell, *Dartmouth*, p. 92; James Gairdner & R. H. Brodie (eds), *Letters and Papers, Foreign and Domestic, Henry VIII* (London, 1896), Vol. 15, item 34; John P. D. Cooper, *Propaganda and the Tudor State; Political Culture in the Westcountry* (Oxford, 2003), p. 95.

earlier. Dartmouth's records noted the course of the Reformation with the disposal of holy relics to the employment of puritan preachers.[103] By the early 1600s there was a substantial puritan element which would have pleased the 'Pilgrims' aboard the *Mayflower* when they visited in 1620. In 1642, at the outbreak of the Civil War, the town supported parliament and that autumn the mayor was appointed the port's military governor by Westminster. Dartmouth fell to the Royalists in October 1643 and it was not until January 1646 that Parliament recaptured it.[104]

It could be indicative of the town's support for Parliament that it took part in the colonisation of Ireland. The events of the Irish Rebellion in 1641, one of the issues which led to civil war the following year, would have been well known in Dartmouth. In March 1642 parliament passed the Adventurers' Act, in which Irish land was sold to private individuals, and Dartmouth Corporation arranged for sixty-three men and women to contribute some £2,397 for more than 3,291 acres.[105] This was part of the wider transfer of Catholic land ownership from 1641 to 1688 when the Protestant share increased from 41 to 78 per cent of all Ireland.[106]

Plate 2. Detail from a map of Dartmouth, early 1600s, depicting the
Church of St Saviour, the Fosse and the Salt Mills.

[103] Watkin, *Dartmouth*, pp. 322, 325, 313.

[104] Russell, *Dartmouth*, pp. 109–19; Eugene A. Andriette, *Devon and Exeter in the Civil War* (Newton Abbot, 1971), pp. 159–60; Mark Stoyle, *Loyalty & Locality* (Exeter, 1995), pp. 45–8, 197–200.

[105] Russell, *Dartmouth*, p. 109; David Brown, *Empire and Enterprise* (Manchester, 2020), 73–4; DHC, DD62700a-b. In 1642 the corporation sanctioned a fourth payment of £2,668 7s 6d: DHC, DD62712. The land was calculated in terms of English acreage.

[106] Russell, *Dartmouth*, p. 109; Karl S. Bottigeimer, 'English Money and Irish Land: the Adventurers in the Cromwellian Settlement of Ireland', *Journal of British Studies* 1 (Nov. 1967), 12–27.

Jurisdictions

Dartmouth had a tangled character of legal and fiscal jurisdictions which has left a rich archival legacy relating to character of local taxation. In 1341 the Crown granted a charter to the borough of Clifton-Dartmouth-Hardness and the geographical bounds were extended in 1463 with the annexation of Southtown 'that they may keep watch at a certain place called Gallion's Bower to guard against our enemies'. The corporation had the right to elect a mayor who by 1500 was assisted by two bailiffs, twelve burgesses and a town clerk. As early as 1590 the councillors referred to themselves as 'the brethren'[107] but like other places, local politics in Dartmouth were not always brotherly. In 1625 'confusion and disorder' in the council prompted new procedures for the election of the mayor. It was claimed that in the past 'sundry factions and sects' had been 'nourished and maintained within the borough'. The corporation experienced 'certain factious spirits who being never contented with any order in government but with such as suiteth with their humours'. It was agreed that the mayor and his twelve 'masters' (otherwise councillors) would nominate two 'free burgesses' (otherwise freeman) to stand for election as mayor. Thirty-seven freemen, along with the bailiffs and some other men, would then vote for the two candidates along with those to be elected for other offices.[108]

Between 1500 and 1650 the borough vied for control of various different types of jurisdictions with five manorial lords, the Duchy of Cornwall, Torre Abbey, the Admiralty and the Diocese of Exeter. There were risks of confrontation as happened with the visit of an Admiralty official in 1558. When John Reynolds arrived he felt that the borough had infringed the Admiralty's rights and was angered when the mayor contradicted him regarding what he asserted were traditional liberties. Tempers flared, Reynolds called the mayor a knave and was arrested. While being taken to gaol Reynolds plucked the mayor's cap from his head and declared 'thou shall not wear a cap and I to go bare-head'.[109] The dispute between the corporation and the Admiralty continued for years.[110]

The De Bryan family held the lordship of the manor of Clifton-Dartmouth-Hardness until about 1400 when it appears to have lapsed or at least ownership became murky. A descendant of the family made an unsuccessful claim nearly two hundred years later[111] and in 1620 the corporation purchased the manorial rights.[112]

Townstal, Southtown, Clifton and Norton Dawney were Dartmouth's four other manors. In 1545 Nicholas Adams of Dartmouth acquired the manor of Townstal from Torre Abbey.[113] The Seale family later owned the manor of Southtown.[114] The manor of Clifton was held by the Carew family and subsequently by the Southcote family from about 1589 to 1670.[115] The manor of Norton Dawney, which lies on the borough's northern edge in the parish of Townstal, was by 1346 held by the Courtenay family and afterwards, from 1539, by the Crown. The corporation held Town Park in the manor.[116]

---

[107] Edward Windeatt, 'The borough of Clifton-Dartmouth-Hardness and its mayors and mayoralties', *DAT* 43 (1911), 124; Watkin, *Dartmouth*, p. 155; DHC, DD61461, p. 92.

[108] DHC, DD62208.

[109] DHC, DD61415.

[110] DHC, DD61420.

[111] DHC, 4088/Box 1/58.

[112] Russell, *Dartmouth*, pp. 31–2.

[113] Joyce Youings, *Devon Monastic Lands*, DCRS NS1 (1955), pp. 68–70; Russell, *Dartmouth*, pp. 28–9.

[114] DHC, 4088/Box 1/58, 902M/M/1 & 3353M/M/1; Suffolk Archives (Bury St Edmunds), 449/1/ E3/15.51/1.5–8, 1.10–13, 1.15, 1.17–18, 1.20–24 & 449/1/E3/15.51/1.2–4; *White's Directory* (Sheffield, 1850), p. 486.

[115] Maxwell Adams, 'The castle, manor-house and church of Clifton, near Dartmouth', *DAT* 32 (1900), 503–4; Suffolk Archives (Bury St Edmunds), 449/1/E3/15.51/1.5–8, 1.10–13, 1.15, 1.17–18, 1.20–24 & 449/1/E3/15.51/1.2–4.

[116] Watkins, *Dartmouth*, p. 274; Russell, *Dartmouth*, pp. 29–30; DHC, CR/532; TNA, SC6/HENVII/1096 & 1098; TNA, SC6/HENVIII/523-33; DHC, DD61838.

The rights of the river, port and waters of Dartmouth have been owned by the Duchy of Cornwall since the 1330s following a visit by Edward I in 1285. A water bailiff appointed by the Duke of Cornwall, or by the crown when holding the Duchy collected Port dues, but the borough leased the office from 1511 through to 1860. The rights had to be periodically renegotiated. During these years the corporation had the maritime jurisdiction of the Dart and the coastline westward to Salcombe and eastward into Torbay.[117]

The corporation held regular water bailiff courts, from 1584 there was one in the spring and another in the autumn,[118] in which men were prosecuted for maritime misdemeanours. From 1500 to 1650 men were prosecuted for throwing ballast out of their ships, allowing rubble to be cast from the quarries sited along the river, using fishing nets without permission and creating public nuisances in creating docks (or pits) in the mud along the shore. The borough licensed the use of fishing seines: in 1577 twelve nets brought in £3 14s 4d, the equivalent of more than £760 today. Of considerable practical use was the borough's ability to control petty customs.[119]

By 1500 Dartmouth had been sending members to parliament for just over two hundred years. In the first half of the sixteenth century one of the two was normally a resident of the port and during the early years of Elizabeth's reign the Earl of Bedford, lord lieutenant of Devon, dominated the elections. His death in 1589 left a vacuum in the following decades and the selection of candidates became closely controlled by the mayor and his council: six representatives (John Upton, Thomas Holland, Thomas Gourney, William Nyell, Roger Mathew, William Plumleigh) served in the seven parliaments of 1604–10, 1614, 1621, 1624, 1625, 1626 and 1628–9. They were all local men and, with the exception of Upton, were merchants who had served the borough as mayors, receivers or town clerks. Nyell had represented the borough at the assizes in Exeter and had kept the water bailiwick court.[120] In 1626 sixty men voted for three candidates who vied for the two places. One had forty-nine 'voices' while the others had forty and twenty-seven (Appendix 3).[121]

The town had three parishes which extended some two miles across the landscape. In about 1198 Torre Abbey built St Clement's Church at the crest of the hill at Townstal. The abbey remained its patron until 1539 and the abbot, Simon Rede, became the vicar a few months before the Dissolution. He remained at Townstal until his death sixteen years later. When in 1545 the manor was acquired by Nicholas Adams of Dartmouth the rectorial rights were retained by the Crown. Forty-one years later they were acquired by Thomas Plumleighe, Robert Smythe, John Smythe and John Follett the younger, four Dartmouth merchants, in part for an annual fee of £6 13s 4d to the Crown. The four feoffees also agreed to pay £13 6s 8d for the Townstal vicar's pension and £5 to the St Saviour chaplain for his stipend. The initial part of a further fee was to be given between one and four in the afternoon on 1 November 1587 at Chaucer's Tomb in Westminster Abbey. The borough retained the rights for 250.[122] The corporation had sub-leased with the stipulation that the licensee would pay the crown's fee, the rector's pension and repair the chancel.[123]

---

[117] Russell, *Dartmouth*, pp. 7, 56–7; DHC, DD61895 & DD61899.

[118] DHC, DD61461, 14 May 1584.

[119] DHC, DD61429, DD61877, DD62096 & DD61454.

[120] P. W. Hasler, 'Dartmouth' in Hasler (ed.), *The History of Parliament: the House of Commons, 1558–1603* (London, 1981), I, p. 145; George Yerby & Paul Hunneyball, 'Dartmouth' in Andrew Thrush & John P. Ferris (eds), *The History of Parliament: the House of Commons, 1604–1629* (Woodbridge, 2010), II, pp. 93–4; DHC, DD61903.

[121] DHC, 3889M/Box 7.

[122] Youings, *Devon Monastic Lands*, pp. 68–70, 130; Russell, *Dartmouth*, pp. 28–9, 93; DHC, R9/1-0/Z/2. The rights were in the possession of Robert Petre and had been held by Edmund Downyinge and Peter Aishton from a grant of 1581.

[123] DHC, DD61461, 1 March 1591.

A chapel, which was to become St Saviour's Church, was built below St Clement's Church in the town but ecclesiastical rivalries delayed its consecration until 1344. Townstal remained the mother church and the borough agreed in 1395 to pay the salary of the cleric at St Saviour.[124] As noted above, from 1587 the borough became the patron of both Townstal and St Saviour.[125]

The third church, that dedicated to St Petrox, is situated adjacent to the castle at the mouth of the Dart and a mile from the town. It is the oldest of the three churches. The church was recorded in 1192 and rebuilt between 1636 and 1641. Until 1822 the patron of St Petrox was the rector of nearby Stoke Fleming.[126]

For the organisation of poor rates the parishes were referred to as Townstal (St Clement), Southtown (St Petrox) and Northtown (St Saviour).[127] Rate-paying could be problematical. In 1610 ninety-seven parishioners of St Saviour refused to pay their poor rates and the mayor instructed the churchwardens and overseers of the poor to distrain the recalcitrants' goods (Appendix 2). An average of 160 individuals, or 16 per cent of the general population of about 2,577 people, contributed to the Dartmouth poor rates edited in this volume; of these men and women there were on average 130 ratepayers in St Petrox, 187 in St Saviour and 132 in Townstal. They were 17, 14 and 26 per cent of their respective populations.

By 1393 two churchwardens administered funds for St Saviour and a century later there were another two wardens who looked after property bequeathed for obits for the chantry chapel in the church. The principal wardens raised the church's maintenance costs and the salaries of the priests and other clerics through donations, Sunday collections particularly one at Michaelmas, the rental of church property, the selling of pardons, houseling money (an Easter fee), seat rentals, the sale of candles and fees for burials and the ringing of bells. The highest sum came from property rentals. One means of raising income may have been peculiar to Dartmouth: ship's masters occasionally paid to moor their ships against the wall of the churchyard.

After the Reformation the number of wardens was reduced by half. Their descriptions evolved: in 1542 they were either the 'warden of the stores of the high altar and St Mary' or the 'warden of the chantry'. The following year they were termed the 'receiver of the monies of the high store and the blessed Virgin Mary and of certain lands appertaining to the said town' or the 'receiver of certain lands there'. A year later their names were simplified: they were the 'receivers of certain lands and tenements appertaining to the town aforesaid'. The complication for the wardens, and thus the corporation, was that properties given to support 'superstitious uses', that is outlawed Roman Catholic practices, were required to be handed over to the Crown but the borough retained or recovered possession of all those properties which had been previously administered by the churchwardens. Following the Reformation the wardens continued to raise money through charges for seats, fees for burials and rentals of property.[128] Individuals also gave property for charitable purposes.[129] In 1586 the rights to the tithes were purchased[130] and it was from this source that the wages of the clerics were paid. In the early 1600s the combined salaries for the clergy of the two churches of St Clement and St Saviour was £26 13s 4d. An additional fee was paid for recording baptisms, marriages and burials.[131]

The arrangement for paying clerical salaries was repeatedly questioned. In 1613 the crown's auditor noted that the rectorial tithes were being charged and cited the agreement made in 1395

---

[124] DHC, DD61837.

[125] Watkins, *Dartmouth*, pp. 278–80; Russell, *Dartmouth*, pp. 28–30, 38–9.

[126] Adams, 'The castle', pp. 510–14.

[127] Russell, *Dartmouth*, pp. 28–30, 38–9.

[128] Watkins, *Dartmouth*, pp. 294–301, 304; Russell, *Dartmouth*, p. 94.

[129] *The report of the commissioners concerning charities containing that part which relates to the county of Devon* (Exeter, 1826), I, p. 27.

[130] DHC, R9/1-0/Z/2.

[131] DHC, DD61670, DD61675 & DD61809. By 1610 the salary was raised to £40 per year: DD661783.

between the borough and Torre Abbey clarifying its responsibility. James Altham determined that there were seventy-three years of back payments, totalling £365 (the equivalent of some £50,000 today), since the Reformation. The case was settled two years later.[132]

The corporation paid the Crown an annual fee of £14 13s 4d for the rights to tithes and although there were complications with the collection, particularly during the Civil War, in 1647 they brought in £145 6s. The assessments were based on land holdings but in 1637 eight men also paid a sum for their boats.[133]

Church rates were not issued in Dartmouth. The three churches were partly maintained by feoffees, the trustees who looked after property generally for charitable purposes. They were in place at Townstal in 1560 and utilised income from land holdings to repair the nave of St Clement's Church whereas the corporation maintained the chancel. Feoffees were also established in St Petrox from at least the fifteenth century and were concerned with the water supply. St Saviour's feoffees were operating since at least 1576.[134] In 1599 the town's feoffees outlined their income was intended to maintain the church of St Saviour, the poor and local defences.[135]

Dartmouth residents paid other rates which were not collected on every Devonian; this included the half penny paid by shipowners on the tonnage of ships which helped pay for the lighthouse built in Cornwall in the early 1620s.[136] Merchants were regularly required to pay towards other causes such as the naval fleet for North Africa in 1619[137] and in about 1570 contributions, probably voluntary and possibly loans, were made by over one hundred men and women to build the new quay.[138]

Each of Dartmouth's three parishes had two collectors for the poor rate but the number of overseers of the poor varied between two and four men. The rates themselves were signed by men acting in various capacities; some poor rates were even signed by waywardens.

Dartmouth's documents

The Dartmouth documents in this volume are part of the corporation's main collection, which number more than 8,000 items. They were first investigated, and partially listed, by the Historical Manuscripts Commission which published a report in 1875.[139] The HMC had been established six years earlier to identify records and papers held outside the Public Record Office in Chancery Lane, London. From 1879 to 1880 Stuart A. Moore of the Public Record Office calendared the archive in Dartmouth. His bound calendar is housed with the collection at the Devon Heritage Centre. Moore had, in the mid-1860s, completed the same task in relation to Exeter's records; he had 'turned chaos into cosmos'. Moore subsequently worked on the papers of the Dean & Chapter and six years after that task finished he began work in Dartmouth.

In 1879 the mayor admitted that Moore's 'inspection was due to the hostility of the late vicar but out of evil often came good'. The cleric had disputed the council's liability for repairs at St Saviour's Church.[140] Moore pointed out in 1880 that there was a good survival rate of documents but that there was a glaring lack of ancient correspondence. The papers were placed in two presses and Moore expressed the hope that after any consultation the documents would be replaced in sequential order.[141]

---

[132] DHC, DD61837, DD61798, DD61809, DD61815-6, DD61853-7, DD61859-60, DD61867-8.
[133] DHC, DD62672 & DD62671. For the payments in arrears see DD62670, DD62742, DD62727, DD62676.
[134] DHC, 1163/F/T/1; *The charities in the county of Devon* (London, 1839), I, pp. 35–40; DHC, DD61444.
[135] DHC, DD61626,
[136] TNA, SP14/152/110.
[137] DHC, DD61940 edited in Gray, *Early-Stuart Mariners*, pp. 103–5.
[138] DHC, DD61434.
[139] *Fifth Report of the Royal Commission on Historical Manuscripts, Part 1* (London, 1876), pp. 597–606.
[140] *Exeter & Plymouth Gazette*, 1 Aug. 1873; *Exeter Flying Post*, 12 Feb. 1868, 12 Nov. 1879; *Western Times*, 13 Oct. 1868.
[141] DHC, Stuart A. Moore, A calendar of the archives of the borough of Dartmouth, Introduction.

The former gaol was converted to serve as a muniments office in 1898 but subsequently the papers were said to have descended into an 'indescribable condition'. By 1910 there was disquiet amongst council officers on the manuscripts' condition; it was alleged that papers had an inch and a half of mildew. The next year Mr R. A. Roberts of the Public Record Office visited Dartmouth to advise on the care of the archive. Some papers were placed in a safe in the guildhall parlour[142] and there was discussion about cleaning; a fine rubber or pieces of bread were suggested as the most effective means to remove the 'beastly' dust and dirt.[143]

The council subsequently sent its collection to Exeter Library which had appropriate storage. Librarian H. Tapley Soper, who was also Honorary Secretary of the Devon & Cornwall Record Society, was then gathering documents from across the county. These became the core of a collection which would evolve into the Devon Record Office (now Devon Heritage Centre). Soper listed some documents because of a possibility they may have been returned to Dartmouth.[144] However, the papers remained in Exeter with the exception of six years of the Second World War when they, along with nearly all of the other records in the library, were removed for their safety.

A fourth individual also listed the collection. Hugh R. Watkin, president of the Devonshire Association in 1918 and council member of the Devon & Cornwall Record Society from 1915 to 1937, began work in September 1925 and it was then noted 'the work is expected to occupy a considerable time'. The documents 'had been got ready' by two women, Miss Northmore and Miss Sybil Davies. Ten years later the Devonshire Association published his analysis of the pre-Reformation records but his second and third volumes were uncompleted at the time of his death in 1937. Watkin stated 'where possible every parchment and paper has been transcribed and the contents embodied in a précis'.[145] His work included recovering a collection of some sixty early deeds which were recorded in 1875 but had been loaned to a private gentleman in 1913.[146] After Watkin's death, and by 1950, each précis was typed at Exeter City Library and bound into eighteen volumes. They serve as the only catalogue.[147]

The collection has been organised in at least three separate periods. At some point each document was stamped 'Corporation of Dartmouth' often in purple ink. In the 1870s Moore stamped each cover page with a four-digit numeral taken from his catalogue. These are in black ink. Subsequently a second series of markings were made in red ink. These were presumably applied by Soper, Northmore, Davies or a combination of the three in Exeter Library. In the top left corner of the same page the year of the document was written and in some instances this was followed by a pair of Arabic and Roman numerals to note the day and month on which the document began. Below this a second or third individual wrote, also in red ink, a five-digit reference number mostly preceded by 'DD' (which stood for Deeds & Documents). An unknown person or persons also wrote the year of each document in pencil and these were later nearly entirely erased. A few documents have a short descriptive note which had been written in red ink. Most documents also have an original description, made in black ink at the time by the scribe, which includes the year. These were sometimes written in Latin.

Ancillary documents occasionally provide significant details which reveal the background to the tax lists. These have normally been utilised, when identified, for the notes preceding each document. A church court case of 1561 for two parishes in this volume, Crediton and Sandford,

[142] *Dartmouth & South Hams Chronicle*, 12 Aug. 1910, 3 March 1911 & 28 April 1911; Watkin, *Dartmouth*, iii; *Western Morning News*, 7 Feb. 1925.

[143] *Dartmouth & South Hams Chronicle*, 6 Oct. 1911.

[144] *Dartmouth & South Hams Chronicle*, 7 July 1911; *Express & Echo*, 5 June 1939; *Western Times*, 7 July 1939; DHC, bound volume of Soper's Dartmouth précis for DD6501-3.

[145] *Exeter & Plymouth Gazette*, 18 Sept. 1925; *Western Morning News*, 16 Sept. 1925; Watkin, *Dartmouth; Western Times*, 19 Nov. 1937.

[146] *Western Morning News*, 12 March 1927.

[147] *Western Morning News*, 18 Nov. 1937; *The Cornishman*, 2 Nov. 1950.

details local variations which were otherwise not recorded. That year parishioners disputed the custom of paying their tithe of hay. They argued that grass was first made into a pook from which 10 per cent was extracted for the cleric or his representative and immediately removed from the meadow ground. Eight men testified as to the legally binding traditions within their own prebends. In doing so they revealed an awareness of the history of their local tax obligations to Crediton Church which went back to the 1530s when a previous chancellor had unsuccessfully attempted to change the custom.[148] Their evidence also disclosed how local frameworks could differ not merely across parishes but within them.

---

[148] DHC, Chanter 855A/100-105.

EDITORIAL CONVENTIONS

The spelling of first names has generally been modernised except in ambiguous cases or when they were written in abbreviated forms. Place names appear as in the originals and modern spellings have been given in square brackets generally in the first instance. These have been derived from the English Place Name Society's two volumes on Devon, ordnance survey maps and mid-nineteenth-century tithe apportionments. Some lists included field names such as 'Blackman's Combe', noted in Item 54, which later became known as Blackmoor Combe and was recorded as early as 1333.[1] Population estimates for 1642 have been derived from the formula in which the number of male parishioners who signed the Protestation Oath is multiplied by 1.66 and then doubled.[2]

Parish church rates in the diocesan collection were, at some point, possibly in the early seventeenth century, organised with a number system. These figures have been retained in the rates' editing. The use of bold for lettering has also been kept and Latin words have usually been translated and placed in italics. Summaries have been provided for some lengthy Latin texts. The physical construction of the edited manuscripts is described differently from volumes One and Two in this series. It became apparent that record offices house nearly all of the surviving examples of locally made thread and string. These were used in stitching paper to construct booklets. The editing of Claude Passavant's eighteenth-century Exeter cloth book[3] made me aware of the otherwise rare survival of this material although their modern equivalents do not seem to match what may be better termed 'stread' or 'thring'.

Some scribes used crosses or tally marks to note the payment of contributions. These have been retained. Other scribes noted reasons for non-payment including 'left', 'gone', 'away', 'runaway', 'too much', 'not able', 'poor', 'drowned' and 'dead'. These have also been retained. All words which were crossed through have been identified as such in the text.

Abbreviations

DAT	*Devonshire Association Transactions*
DCNQ	*Devon & Cornwall Notes & Queries*
DCRS	Devon & Cornwall Record Society
DHC	Devon Heritage Centre
KK	Kresen Kernow
NDRO	North Devon Record Office
PA	Plymouth Archives
TNA	The National Archives

---

[1] J. E. B. Gover, A. Mawer & F. M. Stenton, *The Place-Names of Devon* (Cambridge, 1932), p. 413.
[2] Nigel Goose & Andrew Hinde, 'Estimating local population sizes at fixed points in time', *Local Population Studies* 77 (1977), 83.
[3] Todd Gray (ed.), *The Exeter Cloth Dispatch Book*, 1763–1765, DCRS NS63 (2012).

THE LISTS

CHURCHSTOW

Two rates survive for this South Hams parish located less than two miles north-west of Kingsbridge. A note from three men, who were presumably the churchwardens, was written on 20 June 1613 and recorded that 'for the repairing of our church and the rate for the poor this we can signify & nothing else: first our rate for repairing is uncertain but there is gathered yearly to the value of £9 or £10 agreed as a composition between the parishioners according to every man's singular living. Rents belonging to the church 20s 6d. Rate for the poor Item our rate amounteth yearly to £5 and upward, some years more saving some years decreasing. Item there is given in fee for ever 20s by Mr John Petre'.[1] Three years after the rate the vicar, Nicholas Costerd, faced a defamation case in which he was called a rogue, rascal, woodcock, ass, knave, sinner and 'shutman' [spendthrift].[2] In 1616 fifty individuals, approximately 23 per cent of the population, contributed to the church rates in contrast to only seven men who were assessed for military equipment twenty-four years earlier.

1. Churchstow, Military Rate, c.1592

DHC, 3799M/3/O/4/50, no page numbers

Note: This rate is recorded in a volume with pages approximately 7¾ inches in width and 12 inches in length. About a decade before, in 1581, eleven parishioners paid the subsidy and their surnames were Birdwood, Brown, Gilbert, Head, Knowling, Lapthorne, Leigh, Lidstone, Nichel, Putt, Tirrey and White. Five names also appear in the military rate.[3] The armour for the survey comprised almain rivets, bandoleers, corslets, head pieces, jacks and morions while for weapons there were bills, bows, calivers, daggers, halberds, muskets, pikes, sallets, shear hooks, splints and swords.

Churstowe

John Liston	a musket performed	John Browne	a musket performed
	a Corslr performed	William Putt	a Callr performed
Richard Tyrrie	a Corslet performed	Robert Knowling	a musket performed
James Tyrrie	a musket performed	John Hingston	a bill

2. Churchstow, Church Rate, 1616

DHC, Devon Glebe Terriers

Note: This rate was written on a piece of vellum which measures approximately 7 inches in width and 18 inches in length. The numerals are Roman with the exception of the year. At the bottom and the reverse side of the document is a terrier. An agreement made in 1414 stipulated the mandatory attendance of Kingsbridge's parishioners at their mother church of Churchstow on the Feast Day of the Assumption. They paid a penny if married and a half penny if single.[4] Many of the surnames in the military rate appear in this church rate. There was no listing in this rate for Thomas Gillard who in 1613 signed a lease with an annual rental of two shillings for a house with a herbgarden

[1] DHC, Diocese of Exeter, Principal Registry, Churchstow Church Rates.
[2] Todd Gray, *Strumpets & Ninnycocks* (Exeter, 2016), p. 127.
[3] T. L. Stoate (ed.), *Devon Taxes, 1581–1660* (Bristol, 1988), p. 48.
[4] DHC, 215M/ZP2.

near the Bakehouse at Fenn in the parish.[5] Six years later some of these individuals were listed as being the most substantial arable farmers in the parish (Arthur Harris, John Rider, Richard Tyrry, William Putt, Edward Finch, John Heed, John Tolman, Pascoe Ward and Nicholas Knowling). Andrew Bardens and Matthew Castleman were also recorded in that list but may not have been resident in the parish.[6]

Churstowe 24 of September 1616 168 A terrier is endorsed.

The Ratte for the Maintenance of the Church

Nicholas Gilbert Esquire	13s 4d	Stephen Nycholls	5s
Arthur Harris gent.	20s	John Harris	10s
Robert Gilbert gentleman	[worn]s	John Luccraste *wid.*	11d
John Rider gent.	13s 4d	John Chrispen	6d
John Lidston	20s	John Tyrry	11d
William Head	13s 4d	William Horswell	6d
John Heed	3s 8d	Simon Loxe	4d
William Putt	11s	William Putt senior	2s 8d
Robert Knowlinge	6s 8d	John Lapp	3d
William head John Lidston & Andrew		Mr Richard Baker	21d
Cornishe	16s 8d	John Howse	8d
Philip Foxworthy	6s 1d	Pascoe Lapp Junior	20d
Edward Fynch	3s 11d	Alexander Woulcoytt	15d
Julian Leigh	2s 8d	Pascoe Warde	3s
John Tolman	3s 4d	James Weamouth	3d
James Tyrry	3s	Margaret Yabb	4d
Richard Tyrry	3s	John Hingston	6s 8d
Simon Coytt	20d	Nicholas Knowlinge	20d
Thomas Putt	20d	Thomas Lidston	8d
Bridget Elliott	20d	Richard Collinge	10d
John Lidson Thomas Lidson and Katherin		Hugh Leigh	8d
Hingston *wid.*	3s 4d	William Horswell	3d
Elizabeth Bunckerd *wid.*	20d	George Lapp	3d
Thomas Bunckerd	20d	George Pinwell	12d

Sum total [blank]
Witnessed by me Richard Costerd, vicar 1616

---

5   DHC, 2779 M/6/2.
6   Todd Gray (ed.), *Harvest Failure in Cornwall and Devon* (Camborne, 1992), p. 13.

CHURSTON FERRERS

A long series of rates survives for this parish located between Torbay and the river Dart, lying some four miles south of Paignton. Galmpton and Greenway are noted throughout and the former is sometimes listed as a distinct part of the parish. At this time the Yarde family lived at Churston Court while the Gilberts were at Greenway. Two volumes of Poor Rates are in the parish collection and cover the years from 1599 to 1607 and 1628 to 1661. The first manuscript has had minor water damage and tearing to its final pages. The latter volume has more substantial damage. Only a portion of the rates have been edited: those not in this volume includes those for 1600, 1601, 1603, 1604, 1605 and 1606. There are also two Church Rates; one is located in the diocesan records while the second is part of the parish collection. In total ten rates have been edited for this volume. It appears as though a number of scribes were employed to write the rates. Some 8 per cent of the population contributed to the poor and church rates. The tithe apportionment of 1844 has been used to supply alternative spellings to archaic spellings of places in these rates.[1]

3. Churston Ferrers, Poor Rate, 1599

DHC, 1235A-2/PO1

Note: This rate is part of a damaged volume made up of sheets of paper stitched together to provide unnumbered pages which are approximately 6 inches in width and 15½ in length. The numerals are Roman with the exception of the year. The subsidy of 1581 indicates the Yard family was then the greatest landowner.[2] Of much less consequence was Nicholas Lewes, a mariner who was rated in 1595 for two shillings through his annual property rental of 21 shillings. His details were recorded in a lease for the Westerhouse, a tenement which had a rent of 15s 4d. This included 'all buildings, stables & bakehouses', one orchard or 'apple garden', a herbgarden, a parcel of land called the hemphay which comprised one acre, a second close of land called the South Down which comprised three acres, a third close of land called the Foordon which was one acre, a fourth close of land called the rewe which comprised three acres and finally four closes of land called the leases which were twelve acres in extent. He also signed the lease of a cellar (a storehouse) at Churston Quay which had an annual rental of 5s 8d and a capon.[3]

The rate for 1600, which is in the same manuscript, recorded nearly every parishioner in the same order although some had different contributions. That year the churchwardens were William Cornishe and William Harry while the overseers of the poor were John Skirdon, Nicholas Lewes, Walter Chenicke and Andrew King. The total sum raised was £11 17s 8d. Amongst the poor who were given financial assistance were Gillian Speare, Joan Sheway, Joan Ulcombe, Elizabeth Gardner, Robert Payne, Wilmot Mayne and Anne Cranburie's child.

1599
Wardones for the pore in Churston and Galmpton in the yer above written are Thes Peter Vitterye & Richard Speark

[1]   DHC, Churston Ferrers, tithe apportionment.
[2]   Stoate, *Devon Taxes*, p. 64.
[3]   TNA, SP13/256/5. The lease was made with George Yarde of Bowden and the other leasees were Lewis' wife Agnes and son John.

The collection

First my lady gilberte	16s	Richard Philpe	2s 6d
Mystres An Yeard	13s 4d	Richard Cardy	2s 4d
Mr John Upton for Lowere enwilles [Endville]	4s	Walter Kelly	12d
Toby Symons	4s 4d	John Lamesed	20d
John Skirdon of galmpton	8s	Richard Harry	2s
John Blaccoler	2s	Robert Wheatton	2s
Peter Hassard	9s	John Roper	2s 6d
John Harry	5s	Richard Clark	4s
Thomas Blaccoler	3s 4d	Harry Roe	2s 4d
Joan Clowter	16d	Andrew Kinge	2s 8d
Thomas Chube	2s	John Boinge elder	2s 8d
Joan Blaccoler widdow	16d	Nicholas Gardner	12d
William Harry	6s	Nicholas Lewes	2s
Walter Chinck	2s	John Torrin	7s
John Chedder	8s	William Ulcu'	8d
Lewis Shere	7s	John Squier	16d
William Gillard	2s 6d	William Beard	16d
William Showringe	2s 4d	William Weymoth	16d
William Addames	12d	Thomas Bolter	2s
John Skirdon of Churston	2s 8d	William Farwell	[torn]
Robert Chard	16d	Edward Cardy	12d
William Churchyete	12d	Thomas Blaccole	8d
William Langdon	9s	lambes ground	6d
Edward Cock	16d		

[new page]

1599 Collection

William Cardy	8d	Andrew Kinge for John Edwards garden	8d
John Clowter	12d	Thomas Blaccaler for John Edwards ground	7d
William Cornishe	2s	Thomas Food for John Edwards ground	8d
Nicholas Morrishe	6d	William Harry for John Edwards ground	6d
Thomas Lykey	8d	John Blaccoler for John Edwards ground	6d
Peter Vittery	2s	John Skirdon for John Edwards ground	6d
Nicholas Lee & Alice Hine	16d	Nicholas Preter for Thomas Chambes ground	9d
Michael Philpe	12d	Andrew Kinge & John Cole for mistres	
Phillip Jane	12d	holcomes ground	8d
Gregory Cade	8d	Lewis shere for enwilles	16d
Peter Chinick	2s 6d	Nicholas Lewes for Joan Fords ground	16d
Mr Lucmore	4d	John preter for jistment ground	4d
William minnifee justments	2s	William Langdon for Mark Clarks ground	4d
Thomas Blaccoler Justments	2s	Mr Langdon for panks mead	4d
Henry Cordnell	2s	William minifee for Mark Clarks ground	
John Lyley	6s 8d	[torn]	
Harry Roe for justments which he holdeth of		John Chedder for Ulcumes Kittingames	[torn]
Mr Edwards in galmpeton	4s 4d	Sum is	[torn]
Peter Hassard for John Edwards gardenes	20d	Whereof sobers	18s 6d
John Chedder for yearnbery [Yarnberry]	8d	to the next Collectors	[torn]

4. Churston Ferrers, Poor Rate, 1602

DHC, 1235A-2/PO1

Note: See Item 3. The payments to the poor included sums given to Wilmot Mayne, Gillian Speare, Richard Blackston, Elizabeth Gardner, Elizabeth Robert and Isabel Robert for 'fetching of water for Isabel Gardener', 'Lowries' child', Robert Payne, Isabel Gardener, Margaret Knight, William Carter, Peter Hassard 'for Isabel Philipe's bastard', Richard Clowte and Richard Squier. Rates for 1603 and 1604 were headed by Sir Henry Thine and mostly followed the order of the 1602 rate. That for 1605 was headed by Sir John Gilbert who replaced Thine. The list of the remaining parishioners was mostly similar to those of 1602 to 1604.

Churston Ferrers: The rate made for the relyefe for the pore for the yere 1602 by vertue of warrant from the worshipfull Sir Thomas Ridgeway knight & Richard Sparrye esquire Twoo of her Majests Justices of the peace by the Churchwardens John Boinge & Richard Ponnde, & us the overseers William Cornishe, Humphrey Shere John Blaccoler & Thomas Blaccolere The 18th of April According to the Statute in that behalfe made & pvided.

Maister George Yard esquiere	4s	William Cornishe	16d
Mistress Anne Yard	13s 4d	William Showringe	20d
Mr William Langdone	9s 8d	Mark Clark	8d
Joan Harries	12d	John Repere	2s 4d
John Torrine	6s 8d	Phillip Keyton	4d
Lewis Shere	6s 8d	Nicholas Morishe	4d
Edward Cocke	20d	Peter Vitterye	2s 4d
Gregory Cade	6d	Mr Henry Thine esquire	26s
William Churchyete	12d	~~Jone~~ John Clowter	12d
Robert Chard	10d	Joan Clowtere	14d
William Farwell	12d	Peter Hassard	8s 8d
John Boyne eldere	2s 4d	Harry Roe	22d
John Boyne youngere	8d	Andrew Kinge	2s 8d
John Skirdon	2s 4d	John Skirdon	6s 8d
Nicholas Lewes	20d	William Harrys	5s 8d
John Lamsed	18d	Thoma Leykey	4d
Walter Kelly	12d	Thomas May	6d
John Squiere	12d	Thomas Chubbe	2s
Alice Gillard	12d	Thomas Blaccolere	2s 8d
William Ulcombe	4d	[new page] John Harrye	4s
William Adames	10d	Peter Chenick	3s
Richard Cardye	2s	Walter Chenick	22d
Edward Cardy	4d	Harry Cordnele	20d
William Bearde	12d	John Blaccolere	20d
Nicholas Gardnere	10d	John Cheddere	7s 8d
Richard Clark	3s 4d	Richard Powne	8d

Justmente holders

Mr George Yard for Skirdons Enwiles	2s
more for gillards grounde	10d
Mr Langdon for Mark Clarks ground called foven	4d
Mr Landgon for gillards grounde	8d
William minifee & David Farwell for Toby Symons ground	4s 4d
Mr Richard Hucmore for ground that he holdeth him selefe in alsone [Alstone]	4d

William minifee for ground that he holdeth of Mr Hucmore	2s
William minifee for Joan Fords ground	4d
Lewis Shere for Isaac Roberts grounde	4d
Nicholas Lewes for Michael Philps & kittinganes ground	4d
John Preter for Alice gillards grounde	6d
Richord Clark for Mr Hucmors ground called alsone downe	12d
Richard Clarke for hiles meade	4d
William Showringe for Michael philpes ground	16d
John Eme for the widdowe hines	2s
Phillip Jane	4d
Harry Woddle for Joan Fords grownde	16d
John Philpe for millond [Mill Land] park	4d
Mr Arthur Upton for lowere enwiles	4s
Mr Arthur Upton for wheattones bargine	11d
Mr pollarde [continued]	

[new page]

Mr Pollard for the three weeks	13s
John Cheddere for milland	4d
John Cheddere for kittinganes ground	4d
John Chedder for yarnbury	12d
for John Cheddere for paulks grounde	4d
John Chedder for Chubes meade	8d
Harry Roe for blynwill [Blindwell] & warbury pke	10d
Harry Roe for viders garden	3d
Harry Roe for bromfille & ford lake	8d
Harry Roe for John Codners ground	20d
Walter Chericke for rods & Mr Hucmors grounde	10d
John Cole for mistres Holcomebes ground	4d
William Harry for prickshill	2d
John Blaccoler for shilston & hayle	8d
Peter Ellete for butts	2d
Thomas Ford for for [sic] Crownell	4d
Richard Speark for Tuves & breakridge [Brakridge]	6d
Thomas Leykey for John Edwards grounde	8d
Richard Norway for Tuvaheard & Thorne	8d
John Skirdon for Pudsdon & yedsone	4d
John Skirdon for badwill	4d
John Skirdon for Turve	4d
John Skirdon poorehows pke & bere garden	18d
John Skirdon for Langston	4d
John Skirdon for Castell hay [Castle hayes]	3d
John Edwards ground Called bittombe	8d
Hi[gh]er Langston [Langstone]	4d
John Squiere for margeret lystones ground & the leases	8d

Sum total	£10 07 1d
R[eceive]d at our firste entry of the old collectours in *the year* 1602	17s
Sum total of our R[eceipt]s is	£11 4s 1d

5. Churston Ferrers, Poor Rate, 1607

DHC, 1235A-2/PO1

Note: See Item 3. This rate followed the form of the rate written in the previous year which listed contributors in an initial list followed by a section headed Churston Ferrers and a third entitled 'justment holders in Churston'. The latter has more differences. It recorded 'Mr George Yard for Enwills 2s, for Tobie Symones mead 8d, for Gillardes ground 10d, Mr William Langdonn for a Close he houldeth of Mark Clark 6d, William Furnish for one Close he houldeth of Mark Clark 6d, Mr Langdon for Churchet's 2 Closes 6d, Mr Langdon for two Closes of Mr Huckmore 12d, Thomas Blackeller of Paintonn for kettingane's ground 2d, Thomas Blackler of Painnton for the 3 Corner Close 2d, Samuel Chinock of Paintonn for kettingane's ground 2d, Davy Farwell for Toby Symond's ground 3s 4d, William Minifer for Joan Foarde's ground 4d, William Minifer for Mr Huckmore's ground 2s, John Squire for bond's meade 6d, Nicholas Lewis for Michael Philp's ground 10d, Phillip Jean for one Close of Philp's ground 4d, Phillip Hassard for Forde's ground 16d, Nicholas Neck for Millande 12d, Mr Arthur Uptonn Esquire for Enwills 4s, Mr Hugh Pollard Esquire for Weekses 13s, Thomas Edwards for Milland 4d, Thomas Edwards for Yearnburie 12d, Thomas Edwards for Bittombe 8d, Thomas Edwards for Mark Clark's ground 6d, Thomas Edwards for Luckcraft 16d, Mr Huckmore for 2 Closes in hand 6d, Wiliam Furnish for Mr Gyfford's ground 8d, William Furnish for Mr Edward's ground 6d, William Furnish for Michael Harris ground 6d, John Skerfonn for Mr Edward's Land 5s, Thomas Hunt for Rider's garden 4d, Henry Rowe for Codnerel's ground 2s 4d, Walter Chinnock for Mr Huckmore ground 3d, Walter Chinnock for Mr Eawe's ground 2d, Mr Laingdonn for Walter Kellis 2 Closes and Land at Bascum 8d, William Harrie the yonger for Mr Eawe's and Mr Gyfforde's ground 8d, Thomas Blackler for shelstonn 4d, Thomas Blackler for Ulcombe's ground 2d, Richard Hassard for kellis ground 2d, John Squire for Listone's ground 8d, Nicholas Jeane 4d, Nicholas Lewis for Giffard's ground 2s 4d, Nicholas Lewis for Philp's ground 6d, Richard Sperk for Brekredge 4d, John Squire for Mark Clark's backsides 3d, Mr Laingdonn for Padsonn 4d, Henry Rowe for Yeadsomm 1d, Richard Pownd for Higher Langstonn 4d, Richard Pownd for Prick's Hill 4d, William Cornish for Ulcombe's ground 2d, Richard Norowaie for Pauck's prick hill 2d, Mr Laingdonn for Keybone Tobie 8d, Humphrey Sshere for Keygone 2 Closes 6d, Edward Cocke for Keybone 4d, John Eaue for Cowparck 8d, William Showringe for prierie garden 2d, William Minifer for clowters ground 2d, Mr Laingdonn for Alice Cad's Croste ground 4d, Christopher Clark for Alice Charde's 2 Closes 5d, John Skerdonn for Alice Charde's Close 4d, Richard Hassard for Alice Charde's Close 4d and Richard Rop for Garnzey Close 4d'. Amongst the poor who were helped in 1607 were Julian Speare, Wilmot Maine, Margaret Knight, Elizabeth Gardner and Agnes Philpe.

Churston ferris the booke for the pore ther for the yeare of our lord god 1607 Thomas Edwards Humphrey sheare wardens wm adams wm Churchward Andrew King Richard pound overseers.

Sir John Gilbert knyght	20s	Thomas Blackler	2s
Joan Clouter	10d	John Harrye	3s 4d
John Clouter	9d	Peter Chenocke	2s 4d
Ede hassard	4s 4d	Walter Chenocke	18d
Henry Rowe	2s	Michael harry	18d
Andrew king	2s	John blackler	16d
John skerdon	5s	Thomas Edwards	5s
Christopher Newland	4s 6d	Richard pound	8d
Thomas leekey	4d	Joan waymouth	8d
Thomas Chub	2s	Wm Furnis	6d

Churston Ferris

Sir Henry Thynne	6s 8d	Walter Kelley	4d
Mr George Yarde	4s	Mr yard for Ametts bargaine	8d
Mrs Ann Yard Wid	10s	John squire	12d
Wm langdon	7s	Alice gillard	4d
John Feris	3s	Wm Adams	[torn]
Lewis sheare	5s	Richard Cardye	[torn]
Edward Cocke	12d	Edward Cardy	[torn]
Alice Chard	8d	Wm bearde	[torn]
Annis harris	4d	Nicholas gardn	[torn]
John Bowing elder	12d	Thomas blackler	[torn]
John Bowing yonger	8d	Christopher Clark	[torn]
John skerdon	20d	Wm Cornish	[torn]
Nicholas lewes	18d	Wm Shorringe	[torn]
John lamsitt	12d		

[new page]

John Rop	20d	Wm Cardy	8d
Philip Ketor	8d	John hasard for Robins land	2s
Nicholas Morishe	6d	John hutchins the younger	4d
John eyme	2s	Wm Churchward	4d
peter vittry	2s 4d		

Justment holders

Mr george yard for enwill	2s	John squire for listons ground	8d
more for toby symons meado	8d	Nicholas lewes for Michael philps ground	10d
more for Wm gillards ground	10d	Nicholas Lewes for gillards ground	2s 4d
wm langdon for mark clarkes ground	6d	Nicholas Jane & Michael Philp for the ground	
more for bowings ground	8d	at ther lands 10d	
more for churchwards ground	6d	Richard hassard for Fords ground	16d
more for 2 closes Mr hucmores ground	12d	Richard hassard for kellyes ground	2d
more for pidstone	4d	Richard hassard for Alice chards ground	4d
more for chards 2 closes	4d	Nicholas neck for melland	10d
more for keeboones ground	12d	Arthur Upton esquire for enwells	4s
Thomas blackler for mark clarks ground	6d	Sir Hugh pollard for 3 weekeses	13d
Thomas blackler for kellyes ground	6d	Joan Palke widow	4d
Thomas blackler for shilstone	4d	Thomas Edwards for melland	4d
Tho. blackler of peinton [Paignton] for 2 of		[torn] Yarnbury	12d
kittinghams grounds 4d		[torn]	8d
walter chennock for kittinghamss ground	2d	[torn]	6d
walter chennock for Mr hucmores ground	4d	[torn] his land	6d
david farwell for toby symons ground	3s 4d	[torn] Fords ground	8d
wm minnifye for Joan Fords ground	4d	[torn] Edwards ground	6d
wm minnifye for Mr huckmores ground	2s	[torn] es lane	[torn]
John squire for bands meade	6d	[torn] gardin	[torn]
John squire for mark clarks backside	4d		

[new page]

Henry Rowe for Codners ground	2s 3d	Richard Pennd for higher longston	3d
Wm harris the yonger for Mr geffords ground	8d	more for prickeshill	3d
Richard Sperke for Breakridge	[torn]	wm Cornish for Wolcombs ground	2d
Henry Rowe for yadston	2d	Richard Norwaie for prickshill	2d

John Lamsitt for kittinghams	2d	Christopher clark for Robt sheares ground	2d
wm shouringe for priory garden	2d	Walter chenocke for Mr giffords ground	1d
wm shouring for Chards ground	3d	John Keton	4d
John skerdon for alice chards ground	4d	John Arundell for kneboones ground	4d
John Rop for gardners ground	4d	*Sum*	£9 2s 11d

6. Churston Ferrers, Church Rate, 1612

DHC, 1235A-2/PW1

Note: This rate was written on a piece of vellum which measures 14 inches in width and nearly 21 inches in length. The numerals are Roman with the exception of the year. This Church Rate is more detailed regarding tenements than the earlier Poor Rates.

A Copy of A Rate or Taxacion for Reparacion of the Chappell or Church of Churston Ferrers made the Sixth day of January in the yeare of our Lord God One Thousand Six hundred and Eleven [sic] by Rawleigh Gilbert & George Yarde Esquyre Together with the Consent of the greater & better sorte of the Inhabitants there whose names are there Underwrytten.

Edward Yarde Esq. for the Barton of Churston And Burlinke Close thereunto added	13s 8d
Henry Browse for the Tnement wherein Nicholas Jane did dwell	1s 8d
Susan Chant for the Tenement where in shee dwelleth	0 6d
Humphrey Sheere gentleman for Janes Tenement	1s 8d
Henry Yarde gentleman for the Tenement wherein Giles Furneaux did dwell	2s 0
John Harris for the Tenement wherein John Roper did dwell	2s 2d
George Yarde gentleman for the Tenement wherein Harry Leeky did dwell	2s 2d
Eleanor Barter for the Tenement wherein she dwelleth	0 10d
Christian Furneaux for Perrotts ground	0 10d
John Moore for the Tenement wherein he dwelleth	1s 10d
Andrew Beard for the Tenement which was Michael Cranberyes	0 8d
Roger Furlong gentleman for the Tenement wch was Richard Candyes	1s 0
Henry Scobble for the Tenement where he dwelleth	0 10d
Daniel Wadland for the Tenement wherein he dwelleth	0 8d
William Lange for the Tenement wherein John Harris did dwell	2s 2d
John Lambshead for the Tenement wherein he dwelleth	0 10d
Thomas Lauerence for the Tenement wherein he dwelleth	0 10d
John Bovey for the Tenement wherein John Lewes did dwell	1s 10d
William Skyrdon for the tenement wherein he dwelleth	1s 8d
John Moore for the tenement wch was William Churchwards	0 8d
Peter Dyer for his Cote and for Lystons Close	0 8d
John Evens for the Tenement wherein he dwelleth	1s 2d
William Harris for the Tenement wherein he dwelleth	1s 8d
William Downe for the Cote wherein Edward Tyllard dwelleth	0 6d
William Berry for the Tenement wherein he dwelleth	1s 6d
John Little for the Tenement wherein Keeboone Toby dwelt	1s 6d
Anstice Wheeler for the Tenement wherein Mr William Langdon dwelt	6s 8d
Peter Harrys for the Tenement wherein he dwelleth	0 6d
John Weymouth for the Cote wherein he dwelleth	0 2d
Mrs Ebbot Yarde for the Tenement wherein she dwelleth	5s 0
Edmund Wakeham for the Tenement wherein John Fennes did dwell	2s 4d
Mr George Yarde for Pinstone pcell of the Tenement next abovesayd	0 4d

Robert Evens for the Tenement wherein he dwelleth	0 6d
Mrs Elizabeth Yarde for the Tenement wherein Joan Harris did dwell	1s 3d
The same for Robyns land	1s 4d
The same for higher Ewills	1s 0
The same for Symons grownd	0 8d
Mrs Anne Yarde for the Tenement wherein William Cornish did dwell	4s 0
The same for the Tenement wherein George Yarde Esquire did dwell	3s 0
The same for the two closes & for Ropetackle	0 8d
Dunes Clarke for the Tenement wherein shee dwelleth	1s 4d
John Pitts for the Cote wherein he dwelleth	0 4d
Gilbert Hody for the Tenement wch was Mr Humphrey Sheers	0 8d
Amy Dyer for the Tenement wherein Richard Pretor did dwell	0 10d
Emlyn Laurerence for the Tenement wherein she dwelleth	0 6d
Richard Downe for the Cote wherein he dwelleth	0 4d
William Avery for the Cote wherein he dwelleth	0 4d
John Nicholls for the Cote wherein he dwelleth	0 4d
The two George Yards for Lower Euwills and a Meadowe	2s 4d
William Browse for Mylland	0 6d
John Full for his Cote	0 4d
Edward Coxworthy for the Tenement wherein he dwelleth	1s 8d
Roger Garde for his Cote	0 2d
Henry Knight for his Cote	0 2d
Richard Clarke for the Tenement wherein he dwelleth	2s 0
Alice Berry for her Close at Poundfold	0 2d
[column total]	[£]4 4[s] 4[d]
Thomas Boone Esquire for the Barton of Greenway	20s 0d
Sir Peter Lear Barronet for the three Weekles	6 8
William Clarke for his Bargayne and Commons	2 1½
William Wilcocks for his Tenement	0 6 ½
Roger Templeman for his Tenement	1s 4d
Joan Clarke for her Tenement	0 10d
Mrs Elizabeth Yarde for her Tenement & Commons & for Chapple land	2s 1d
Henry Furneaux for Thomas Edwards for his Tenement for Blackallers and his home Bargayne	6s 4d
Richard Crowt & Sarah Burton for Kings Tenement	3s 2d
John Harris for Honypincke	0 2d
John & Timothy Skirdon for theyr Bargayne & Commons	5s 0
Robert Phillipps for Newlands two Tenements	6s 8d
Phillip Hooper for his Cote	0 6d
Thomas Cruse for Chubbs bargayne and Commons	2s 4d
Rawleigh Blackhaller for his bargayne & Commons	3s 8d
The same for Moors Cote	1s 0
The same for Heale & a Land at Bremell Grove	0 4d
Richard Skirdon for Winckles Bargayne	2s 0
The same for Bearehouse & Commons	1s 8d
John Pretor & James Necke for Ellis Mathews Tenement	2s 0
Richard Clyffe & William Harris for Pearse his Tenement	1s 4d
Richard Harris for his Tenement & Commons	5s 0
William Blackaller for his Bargayne & Commons	3s 8d
Richard Clarke for Ryders bargayne & Commons	2s 2d
The same for Pudson Hayes and lyttle Pudson	3s 3d
Joan Burton for her bargayne & Commons & Chapple lands	1s 8d

Honor Mellowes for her Tenement	2s 4d
Katheryne Blackaller for her Tenement ['& Commons' inserted]	2s
Samuel Cauley for his Cote	0 8d
Pentecost Chynnocke	0 10d
Elizabeth Lewes	5s 0
[column total]	4 16 5
Sum total	£9 0s 9d

This is a true Coppy of the established Rate abovesayd assented unto and agreed upon to be Contynued by the Gentlemen & other the Inhabitants of Churston Ferrers aforesayd, whose names are underwrytten.

7. **Churston Ferrers**, Church Rate, 1613

DHC, Diocese of Exeter, Principal Registry, Churston Ferrers Church Rates, 1613

Note: The rate, a fair copy, was written on a sheet of paper which has been folded in half to make four pages which measure 6 inches in width and 15½ inches in length. It is endorsed '1613 Churston'. The numerals are Roman with the exception of the year and the document sequence numbers. There is minor water damage.

Chursten (42

John Preter Church Wardon For Churston In the yere of our Lord God
In the yere of our Lord God [sic] 1613

A Ratte For to gether the Church monye

Mistris Anne yards Barton	13s 4d	William Churchward	8d
Mr George yard esquier	3s	John squier	4d
Mr Arthur Uptone esquier for Euwills	2s 4d	Nicholas Lewes	14d
Mr William Langdon	6s 8d	Henry Rowe	20d
Nicholas Jane	20d	Richard Hassard	20d
Joan Kittingehame	6d	Tookers howse	6d
Peter Vittery	2s	John Ferres	18d
Humphrey Shere	20d	Keybonn Toby	18d
John Glanfelle	10d	Edward Cocke	6d
Edward Coocke	6d	George Waymouth	2d
Humphrey Shere	8d	Gartred Boulter	5s
John Harry	2s 2d	John Ferres	2s 8d
Thomas Leykey	2s 2d	David Emabrouck	6d
William Cornishe	20d	Joan Harres	20d
Thomas Blakler	22d	Cartters bargaine	3s
Thomsin gardner	8d	Elizabeth Cardy	16d
Johne Nicolls	4d	Toby Semons Bargine	3s 4d
Elizabeth Cardye	12d	William Minifey	4d
William Adames	10d	Robins Lande	16d
William Ulcome	8d	John Skirdons enwilles	12d
Alice gellard	2s 2d	['Nicholas Necke for' in margin] Milland	
John Lamsed	10d	parke	6d
Walter Kellye	10d	Listons Closse	4d
Nicholas Lewes	22d	showrings Closse	4d
John Skirdon	20d	skirdons Closse	4d

| Tamsin Ewines | 2d | John squier | 4d |
| Ane Bowine | 4d | Amyes Bonde | 2d |

8. Churston Ferrers, Poor Rate, 1629

DHC, 1235A-2/PO2

Note: The rate was written in a volume of poor rates which date from 1628 to 1661. There is substantial damage in tearing to the outside edges of many pages. The paper pages, which are not numbered, are approximately 8¼ inches in width and 12 inches in length. The numerals are Roman with the exception of the year. The first resident named, Lady Alice Dormer, was the widow of both Sir William Dormer and Sir John Gilbert of Compton. The poor rate for the previous year was undertaken by John Skerdon and Michael Harrie, churchwardens, and Mr Thomas Edwardes, Nicholas Lewes, Walter Chinnocke and John Bickeforde, overseers of the poor. The order of names is similar on both rates.

Churston Ferres

The booke of the recetes for the poore for this yeare of our Lord god 1629
Christopher Newland and Thomas Blackler wardens
Humphrey Shear John Vettry Micheall Harry Over Seers for the poore

Churston

The Lady Alice Dormer for the tith of		Humphrey Sheare	4s 8d
Churston & gampton	20s	Richard Hassard	1s 6d
George Yard Esquier	22s	Christopher Clowke	3s 4d
John Upton Esquier for Wheatons bargens	1s 4d	John bickford & his mother	1s 6d
William Langdon	6s	Samuel Knowling	1s 6d
John Ferres & his tennets	3s	William Volcombe	8d
Mary Berrey	1s	John Skerdon	8d
Henry Dugdall	6s	Nicholas Harres	6d
Peter Dyer	8d	Roger Norrocot	4d
Margaret Skerden	1s	William Chollwill	1s
Nicholas Lewes	3s 6d	Johen Vettrey	1s 4d
Walter Lamshead	8d	John Clarke	1s 6d
James Petter	8d	John Amery	6d
Edward Cardy	1s	John Lewes	6d
Thomas Leesue	1s 8d	Thomas Bllackler	6d
John More	2s 8d	Simon Tucker	1s
John Nickell	1s	Emanuell Lavers	6d
William Cornish	10d	Richard Langdon for the lower mielles	1s
John Parry	5s	[column] *sum*	£4 19s 6d

Gampton

My Laday Alice Dormer for the Barton of		Thomas Leckey	[torn]
grenawaye	[torn]	John Butland & his tenetes	[torn]
Eleanor Clowter	[torn]	William Tulley & his tenets	[torn]
John Toucker & his tenetes	6[torn]	William Hollowaye	[torn]
Leonard Templeman	8[torn]	Richard Harrye	[torn]
Richard Sparke & his tenetes	2s [torn]	Peter Chennick	[torn]
Andrew King & his tenetes	[torn]	Michael Harry	[torn]
Richard skerdon & his tenetes	[torn]	Walter Chennick	[torn]
Christopher Newland &	[torn]	John Blackler	[torn]

Thomas Edwardes	[torn]	John Morris	6d
Robert skerdon & his tenets	[torn]	Margaret Blackler & her tennets	3s
Odes Cullen	[torn]	Odes Hyne	6d
Thomas Carter	[torn]		
Cicily Powen	6d	John Pretor	1s 4d

Justment holders			
Mr John Travers vicker	2s	John Harryes for heale	4d
John Mor for neckes milland	[torn]	Alice Perret & her tenetes	4d
Samuel Knowling for Yables ground	[torn]	Sum [illegible]	4d
William Chader for yables ground	[torn]		

The holl som is [torn] over recetes & is [torn] 7s 8d

9. Churston Ferrers, Poor Rate, 1633

DHC, 1235A-2/PO2

Note: See Item 8. Amongst the poor who received financial assistance in 1633 were Joan Squier, Judith Jey, Elizabeth Sheere, Walter Ferres, Richard Burly, Peter Ellot, Grace Skinner, Alice Parrott, Tamsin Heyward, Joan Ashe and Richard Burley. Three years later some were still receiving help: in 1636 the parish gave money to Claire Liston, Judith Jey, Elizabeth Shere, Walter Ferres, Joan Squier, Peter Elliott, Nicholl Jane and Edward Fox amongst others.

The list of contributors from Galmpton is more complete in the 1634 rate that that of 1633; they included Nicholas Shipheard, a gentleman, Mr John Travers, Thomas Leekey, Eleanor Clowter, Richard Skirdon and his tenants, John Butland, Nicholas Lewes, Richard Harris, Richoard Harris, Peter Chinnick, Michael Harris, Elizabeth Chinnick, John Blackaller, Mr Thomas Edwards, Robert Skirdon, Oades Cullin, Thomas Cater, Cicily Pound, Thomas Blackaller, Margaret Blackaller, William Tullie, John Necke, Michael Harris, William Downe, Thomas Blackaller, Oades Hine, John Clarke and John Clowter.

The booke for the poore of Churston ferres for the [torn] yere of our Lord god 1633 Nicholas Lewes and Richard Harry Churchwardens Robert Skerden and John More overseers and Collectors for the pore of the pishe aforenamed 1633.

Churston			
Rayleigh Gilbert Esq	5s	Mr Gils Yard for his house and ground to the	
William Langdon for the ground that he		same	5s
holdeth of mr gilbert	5s	Mr George Yard for his house and ground to	
Thomas Leykey for the ground that he holdeth		the same	2s
of mr gilbert	2s 6d	John Upton Esquire for wheatons bargaine	1s 4d
Peter Chenicke for the ground that he holdeth		William Langdon	6s
of mr gilbert	2s	John ferres and his tennats	3s
Edward Michelmore for the ground that he		Marie Berrie	[blank]
holdeth of mr gilbert	2s 8d	William Skerdon	1s
Christopher Clarke for the ground that he		James Pits	8d
holdeth of mr gilbert	2s 8d	Elizabeth Lamsed	6d
William Downe for the mill	1s 2d	John Lewes	4s
George Yard Esquire for the bartan	1s 6d	Peter Dire	1s 6d
for the lower Elwels	1s 6d	Edward Cardie	8d
for the Cae parks	1s	Thomas Leykey	1s 8d
for Henry Dugdals Livinge	3s	John More	1s 8d

for Churchwards bargaine	0 8d	Nicholas Harvie	[illegible]
Agnes Nicle	1s [torn]	Roger Norracott	[torn]
John Perret	1s [torn]	John Vittrie	[torn]
John Harrie	1s [torn]	John Clarke	[torn]
Richard Harrie	2s [torn]	John Averie	[torn]
Humphrey Sherrs	4s 8d	Mr Nicholas Sheapheard	[torn]
Joan Hassard	1s 6d	Simon Qucker	[torn]
Nicholas Lewes	1s [illegible]	Richard Langdon	[torn]
Christopher Clarke	2s [illegible]	John Bickford and his mother	[torn]
Samuel Knowling	[illegible]	Richard Harrie	[torn]
Alice Woolcombe	[torn]	Gillards ground	[torn]
Barberry Skerdon	[illegible]	Henry Leykey	[torn]
Emanuell Lauerence	[illegible]	John West	[torn]

Galmton

Eleanor Clowter	[torn]	Richard Skerdons & his tennats [torn]	
Mr Tucking and his tennants	[torn]	Nicholas Lewes	[illegible]
Richard Sparkes & his tennats [torn]		John Morrish	[illegiblc]
Henry Kinge & his tennats	[torn]	John Butland & his	[illegible]
Thomas Blackler	[torn]		

[new page] [illegible]

his tennats	2s 6d	[torn, illegible] for milland	1s 4d
[torn, illegible]	3s	[torn, illegible]	12d
[torn, illegible] Chenocke	2s 6d	[torn, illegible] heale	4d
[torn, illegible]ell Harrie	1s 6d	[torn, illegible] for yarnberrie	1s 4d
[torn] Elizabeth Chenocke	1s 4d	[torn, illegible] for [illegible] ground	1s 2d
[torn] John Blackler	1s 4d	[torn, illegible]	8d
[torn] Thomas Edwards	5s	[torn, illegible] Chenocke for [torn, illegible]	
[torn]obert Skerdon	2s 4d	ground	3d
[torn, illegible]	1s 2d	[torn, illegible]	3d
[torn]homas Cater	1s	[torn, illegible]	4d
[torn] Cicily Pound	0 6d	[torn, illegible] Clarke	8d
Thomas Leykey	4s	[torn, illegible]kings and [torn, illegible]	
Margaret Blackler	3s	tennats	1s
Odes Hyne	0 6d	[torn, illegible] galmton	4d
[torn]er Chenocke for [torn]	0 8d	[torn, illegible] Clowter	4d
[torn, illegible]don	4d	[torn, illegible]	£3 12s 2d
John Trevil	2d	[torn, illegible]	

10. Churston Ferrers, Poor Rate, 1639

DHC, 1235A-2/PO2

Note: See Item 8. An additional rate was issued in 1639 for a quarter of the annual assessment.

The booke for the poore of the pishe of Churst[torn] this yere of our Lord god 1639 Richard Harris and Peter Blac[torn] Churchwardens Nicholas Lewes John Gardner & John Harris Overseers & Collectors for the poore this yere first above writen
Receipts
Churston
Received at our Cominge in of the old Collectors the some of   38s 8d

Edward Yard Esquire for the barten	18s	Mr Humphrey Sheeres	7s 6d
John Upton for Wheatons bargaine	1s 6d	Edward Coxwarthie	2s 2d
Mr Giles yard	7s 6d	Nicho Lewes	1s 4d
Mr George yard	3s	Christopher Clarke	5s
more for Harris livinge	2s 2d	John Cardye	6d
Mr Henry yard	5s	John Chadder	1s
the two George Yards the younger for the		John Hendlie	1s
Lower Eawells & the meaddow	2s 6d	Emanuell Lauerence	8d
Mr William Langdon	9s 6d	Nicholas Harris	8d
Edmund Wakeham	3s 6d	Roger Narrocott	2s 6d
Mary Berrye	1s	John Vittrie	2s 6d
William Skerdon & his holders	2s	John Clarke	2s 2d
James Pits	0 8d	Simon Tucker	1s 6d
Elizabeth Lamshead	10d	Richard Langdon for the lower mill	2s
John Lewes	5s	John Averrye or his Tents	6d
Peter Dier	2s 2d	Nicholas Put	4d
Tho: Leeykey	2s 2d	John Harris	3s 4d
John moore	2s 6d	John West	1s
more for Churchwards Livinge	1s	William menyfey	6d
John Gardner	1s 6d	Lewis Gold or his Tents	2s
John Perrat & James Barter	2s 7d	Richard Sparpoynt or his ten[an]ts	8d
Richard Harris	3s 8d	William Jolliffe	8d

Galmpton

Rayleigh Gilbert Esquire for the sheaffe	[torn]	Gads Cullinge	[torn]
Nicholas Sharpham Esquire	[torn]	Tho: Oates	[torn]
Mr John Travers	[torn]	Cicily Powne	[torn]
Thomas Leykey	[torn]	Margaret Chenocke for Kings Langdons	[torn]
Eleanor Clowter	[torn]	Christo Clearke for Kings Brome pke	[torn]
Richard Skerdon	[torn]	William Dininge for Kings Luccrafte	[torn]
John Butland or his holders	[torn]	Oads Cullinge for Kings meadow	[torn]
Nicholas Lewes	[torn]	Tho: Blackler thelder for Kings Langstone	
Richard Harrye	[torn]	[torn]	
Margaret Chanocke	[torn]	Tho: blacker the younger	[torn]
John Tuckerman or John P[errott] or Mr		William Tallie	[torn]
Tawlie for the tenement in Gamton	[torn]	Jo: Necke for melland	[torn]
The holders of the t[enement] late in the		Jo: Clowter the younger	[torn]
possession	[torn]	Jo: Harrye for huny parke	[torn]
Joan Harrye	[torn]	Jo: Bickford	[torn]
Peter Harrye Junior	[torn]	William Furnex Junior	[torn]
John Borton	[torn]	Humphrey sheree	[torn]
Tho Blacklen the	[torn]	Tho: Bennett	[torn]
Mr Edwards	[torn]	Richard Harrye	[torn]
William Furnex thelder	[torn]	Jo: Clarke	[torn]
Robert Skerden	[torn]		

[new page]

Justment Holders
Mr Rawleigh Gilbert or Mr William Langdon for the ground hee holdeth of Greenaway Barton 10s
Mr Rawleigh Gilbert or Thomas Blackaller to Beere for the ground hee holdeth of Greenaway
Barton   2s 4d

Mr Gilbert or Christopher Clearke for the ground hee holdeth of Greenaway Barton	3s 3d
Mr Gilbert or Edward Michelmore for the ground hee holdeth of Greenaway Barton	4s
John Lewes for the ground hee holdeth of Greenaway Barton	3s 10d
Thomas Blackaller to Beere for the ground he holdeth of Greenaway Barton	4s
Christopher Clearke for the ground he holdeth of Greenaway Barton	1s 9d
William Furneaux senior for the ground he holdeth of Greenaway Barton	2s 2d
John Toope for the ground he holdeth of Greenaway Barton	2s 10d
John Beeton for the ground he holdeth of Greenaway Barton	1s 2d
Mr Gilbert or William Dunning for Cow pke	1s 9d
John Clarke for the ground hee holdeth of Greenaway Barton	1s 3d
Mr Gilbert or William Downe for the ground hee holdeth of Greenaway Barton	5s
John Hoskins & his holders	2s 6d
John Clearke for John Weymouths ground	3d
Thomas Blackaller for Templemans Living	2s
Mr Edwards for Sparkes ground	9d
Emanuell Lauerence for Sparkes ground	9d
William Lake for Sparkes ground	1s 4d
George Clowter for kings ground	4d
William Pearce & his Holders	1s 6d
John Harry for yadson & Prixell	6d
John Morrish	6d
John Harris	6d
Sum	~~£14 6s 3d~~ £16 4s 11d

11. Churston Ferrers, Poor Rate, 1645

DHC, 1235A-2/PO2

Note: See Item 8. In 1643 financial assistance was given to George Weymouth, John Liston, Walter Ferris, Joan Ash, Joan Hoop, Joan Clowter, John Weekes, Julian Abraham, Otho Cullyn and 'Lancelot'. In 1644 the same parishioners, except for Ash and Cullyn, once again received help along with Richard Knight, Agnes Mitchell, James Hanes, Elizabeth Martyn and Philip Ferris.

Churston Ferrers: 1645:
A Rate made for the Releife of the Pore of our pish by George Yard gentleman and Thomas Bennett Churchwardens William Furneax Richard Skirdon John Moore Michael Cranbery Overseers of the Poore

Receipts

Rec att our Coming in from the old Collectors		The 2 George Yards Junior for the lower	
	£2 4s 4d	Enwills & Meadowe	2s 6d
Edward Yard Esquire	18s	Mr William Langdon	10s 6d
Arthur Upton Esquire for Wheatons tenement		Mr Humphry sheeres	7s 6d
	1s 6d	John Lewes	4s 6d
Mrs Ann Yard *widow*	7s 6d	more for the tenement in Galmpton	6s
Mr George Yard	3s	Richard Clarke & his mother	5s
more for Harris his Living	2s 2d	Richard Harris	3s 8d
Mrs Ebbot Yard *widow*	5s	Edmund Wakeham & his holders	4s
more for the tenement in Galmpton or his		John Harris	3s
holders	2s 6d	John Moore	2s 6d
		more for Churchwards Living	1s

Peter Dyer	2s 2d	James Pitts for his holders	6d
Giles Furneax	2s 6d	John Chadder	8d
more for Perretts tenement	2s	Thomas Bennett for holding of Elizabeth	
Thomas Leekey	2s 2d	Yards living	[blank]
James Barter	8d	Roger Norrowcot	8d
William skirdon or his holders	1s 8d	William Jollife	8d
Edward Covery	2s 2d	John Bickeford	8d
Thomas Pooling	2s	Peter Harry	8d
John Clarke	2s 2d	John Averie	6d
John Gardner	1s 6d	Nicholas Putt	4d
Mary Berry	1s 4d	William Minefee	6d
Emanuell Laverence	1s	Richard Downe	4[torn]
Barbery Penley or her holders	1s 4d	Jon Moore	6d
Simon Tucker	1s 8d	Jon Lamshead	4d
Michael Cranbery	1s 4d	John Downe	4d
Elizabeth Lamshead	10d	Jon Lauerence	4d
Nicholas Harris	10d		

Galmpton

Mrs Joan Gilbert for the Sheefe	18[torn]	Henry Cordall	1s [torn]
Nicholas Shepherd Esquire	10[torn]	Jon Mellows & Richard Harris	1s [torn]
Mr Jn Traverse vicer	[torn]	Otho Cullyn	1s [torn]
Nicholas Lewes	[torn]	Nicholas Necke for Millond	1s [torn]
William Furueax	[torn]	Thomas Cater	1s [torn]
Richard Skirdon Senior	[torn]	Richorde Harris *widow*	1s [torn]
Richard Harris	[torn]	Jn Harris for heale	[torn]
Richard Skirdon Junior	[torn]	more for Hunnipinke	[torn]
Thomas Blackeller Junior	[torn]	John Clarke	1s [torn]
Mr Henry Stroude for his tenement in		Peter Chinnicke	1s [torn]
Galmpton	[torn]	Leonard Newland	[torn]
Jon Perret for litle pudson	[torn]	John Blackeller	[torn]
Margaret Butland or her Tents	3s [torn]	Henry Scobble	[torn]
Mr Christopher Beere or his Tents for his Tenemt		Wm Pearse	1s 6d
in Galmpt that was Margaret Chinnickes	4s [torn]	Wm Downe	[torn]
John Borton	6s [torn]	Wm Wilcox	[torn]
Wm Tilley or his holders	3s [torn]	Jon Skirdon	[torn]
Eleanor Clowter	2s [torn]	John Marish	[torn]
Thomas Blackeller Senior	2s [torn]	Edward Gregory	[torn]

[new page]

[torn – Just]ments Mrs Joan Gilbert for the Barton of Grinaway	18s 9d	Avice Woodely for the ground shee holdeth of Greenawy Barton	4s
Mr William Langdon for the ground hee holdeth of Grinaway Barton	10s	Jon Hoskins or his holders	2s 6d
Thomas Blackler for the ground hee holdeth of Greenaway Barton	2s 3d	Jon Avery for Wemouth ground	4d
Richard Clarke for the ground hee holdeth of Greenaway Barton	3s 3d	Thomas Blackeller senior for Templemans living	2s
		Jon Clarke for Spareponts ground	3d
		Richard Harris for Spareponts ground	2d
		The whole som of receipts	£16 4s 11d

12. Churston Ferrers, Poor Rate, 1650

DHC, 1235A-2/PO2

Note: See Item 8. The numerals are Roman with the exception of the year and the totals of the money received from the previous collectors and the year's rate. Amongst the parishioners who received financial assistance in 1649 were Agnes Michell, Frances Stone, Margaret Waymouth, Claire Liston, Richard Tapper, Joseph Salter, Richard Knight and John Weekes.

Churston Ferrers 1650
A Rate made for the relife of the poore of our pishe by Humphrey Sheares and John Milloes Church Wardens Richard Clarke William Berry John Bourten John Blackaller overseers for this yeare past for the poore

Rec of the old Collectors at our coming in the som of £0 15s 1d

Edward Yard Esquire	13s 6d	Edward Coxwerthy	2s 6d
Arthur Upton Esquire	1s 2d	Tristrim Irish	4d
George Yard	2s 3d	John Clarke	1s 8d
more for Harris living	1s 8d	John Gardnor	1s 2d
more for one tenement in gampton	1s 11d	Mary Berrey	1s 2d
Mrs Ann Yard	5s 8d	Alice Lauerance	6d
Mr Ebbot Yard	3s 11d	Emanuell Lauerance an Thomas Lauerance	
the two George Yard for medow and the			1s 1d
loweremoels	1s 11d	Simon Tucker	1s 4d
Mr William Langdon	6s 9d	Michael Crambry	1s [torn]
Mr Humphrey Sheares	4s 6d	Elizabeth Lambshed [torn]	
John Lewes for his home tenement	1s 6d	Nicholas Harris	1s 2d
more for Rowes tenement	1s	James Pikes	4d
more for his tenement in gampton	4s 6d	Elizabeth Yard	1s 2d
Susanna Lewes	1s	Roger Narrocte [torn]	
Richard Clarke and his mother	3s 9d	William Jollife [torn]	
Richard Harris	2s 9d	Henry Hyne [torn]	
Edmund Wakham	3s	Peter Harris [torn]	
John Harris	2s 4d	John Avery [torn]	
Willimouth Moore	1s 11d	Nicholas Putt [torn]	
more for Churhward	9d	William Minnene [torn]	
Peter Dyer	1s 8d	Richard Downe [torn]	
Giles Furneaux	1s 11d	John Moore [torn]	
more for pettets tenement	1s 6d	John Lambshed [torn]	
Henry Leakey for his mother	1s 6d	Henry Scobbell [torn]	
James Barter	6d	John Lawerance [torn]	
William Skerdon	1s 3d		

Gampton

Nicholas Sheperd Esquire	9s [torn]	William Furneax	3s [torn]
Mrs Jane Gilbert for Shefe	18[torn]	John Harris for his wife tenement	2s [torn]
Nicholas Lewes	6s [torn]	more for heale [torn]	

[new page]

more for hony pinke	3d	Thomas Blackaller Junior	3s 5d
Richard Skerdon Senior	4s 6d	Richard Clarke for perrets pudsen	2d

Margaret Butland	2s 3d	John Clarke	11d
William Bradell	3s	Peter Chinnocke	11d
John Bourten	4s 6d	John Blackaller	4d
Dunes Talley	2s 3d	Thomas Powling	1s 2d
Eleanor Clowter	1s 11d	William Downe	5d
John Milles	1s 8d	John Skerdon Senior	4d
Thomas Blackaller senior	1s 11d	John Morris	3d
Grace Collen Mary Coullen & Elizabeth		Edward Gregory	3d
Coullen for the house orchard and meddowe	7d	Richard Harris	3s 6d
Tobias Coullen for prickshill	2d	Richard Skerdon	2s 8d
Nicholas Necke for milland	1s	John Skerdon Junior	4d
Thomas Cater	1s	Henry Strowde or his holders	3s 5d

Justment holders

Mrs Joan Gilbert for the barten	18s	Anes Woodley for the ground hee holdeth of	
Mr William Langdon for the ground hee		greneway barten	3s
holdeth of Greneway barten	7s 6d	John Hoskengs	2s 11d
Thomas Blackaller for the pound hee holdeth		John Waymouth	4d
of greneway barten	1s 9d	Thomas Blackaller for Tempellman Living	1s 6d
Richard Clarke for the ground hee holdeth of		Richard Spearepoints or his holders	4d
greneway barten	2s 6d	The whole some of our receipts	£11 6s 0d

Plate 3. Carving of a labourer on a bench end in St Peter's Church, Clayhanger, c.1600.

CLAYHANGER

A series of Easter Books survives for this parish which is located on the county border with Somerset, ten miles north-east of Tiverton and five miles east of Bampton. A comparison between the individuals listed in these accounts and with the subsidy list of 1581 shows a nearly exact match[1] but with additional individuals paying their tithes. In the early 1600s Tristram Risdon noted the parish 'bordereth upon the bounds of Somersetshire, where at the conquest, William Mohun was seized of three rods and three farthings of land, by the conqueror's gift'.[2] Robert Chollacombe was appointed vicar in August 1582.[3] It appears that one scribe was responsible for writing the ten accounts.

13–22. CLAYHANGER, Easter Books, c.1573–82

PA, 3338/1

Note: In 1535 the *Valor Ecclesiasticus* recorded the rector received for the tithes of grain £6 6s 8d, for lambs 48s, for calves 8s, for wool 23s and for Easter Offerings 43s 11d ½.[4] This amounted to £12 9s 7½d whereas in the 1570s his successor received more than £3 in mixed and personal tithes. Predial tithes, such as that for grain, appear to have been excluded. The Elizabethan vicar made two personal notes in his Easter Books. He wrote of one parishioner's account 'I must have a tithing calf' and of another he noted he had received the tithe. It can be deduced from the Easter Books that the rates were two pence for the ownership of a cow, a penny for all ewes and a penny for a garden. However, the system was more complex. A terrier of 1634 recorded that the milk of every heiffer at her first calving was assessed at ¾ pence, the milk of every cow in the summer was 2d, and the milk of every cow during the winter was only a penny. The milk of ten ewes required the payment of a penny but if there were nine ewes or less than no tithe was paid. Perhaps the most complicated arrangement concerned the tithe of lambs. The terrier recorded 'they pay the tenth lamb in this manner: of twenty five, or of a greater or less number, they first take up two of the best lambs for themselves and the third best for the parson, and then do take up seven more of the next best for themselves to make up ten (sending home the parson's lamb to the parsonage) and so again, until the number remanining be under ten, which is to be added to such number of lambs which is at Saint Mark's Day [25 April], they pay the tenth calf when he falleth and is to be kept by them until he be of the age of seven weeks (if the parson so please) at which time, upon notice given, the parson is to send for him. They pay the tenth pig, when he falleth, at one farrowing, or at several by addition, keep him the like time, they take up two of the best & upon notice given, the parson the third best. The like custom for geese, as for pigs, saving that they are to be taken up at Lammas [1 August] and the odds of lambs, calves, pigs, geese, yearly, until they come to the tenth, are to be numbered'. A penny was paid for every colt at its birth. There was also a tenth due of all 'corn, grain, apples, pears, hops, honey and wax in kind sent for the parson'. Wool also generated a payment of a tenth which was paid in kind and sent to the parsonage or the chancel of the church. The wool tithe was termed a 'stent', a tax assessment calculated on a property. It was noted for 1634 this was 6d for West Nutcombe and 6d for East

[1] Stoate, *Devon Taxes*, p. 80.
[2] Tristram Risdon, *The Chorographical Description or Survey of the County of Devon* (London, 1811 edn), p. 65.
[3] www.theclergydatabase.org.uk, accessed 2 June 2015.
[4] J. Caley & J. Hunter (eds), *Valor Ecclesiasticus* (London, 1814 edn), II, p. 331.

Nutcombe (both payments by John Nutcombe), 3d for Dunginston Mill Tenement (William Stone) and for his mill 15d, 3d for Hookhay (Richard Frogspitt), 3d for Perry (Joan Frogspitt, widow), 2d for Berry (Anstice Burdge), 2d for West Friars, 2½d for Bushays, 3d for Manley (Nicholas Hartnoll, clerk) and 2d for Downe as well as 2d for East Friars also for Hartnoll, 9½d for Honleigh (Robert Norman), 3d for Woodland (Christopher Stone), 6d for Hillcombe (John Talbitt), 3d for Vellayne (Thomas Stone) and 3d for him for Willhayes, 3½d for Woodcocks (Joseph Yawe), 3½d for Willball (John Head), 3d for Hobhouse and Little Ham (Richard Stone), 5d for Upcott and 4d for Marshall (Honor Stone, widow), 6d for part of Northheale (Christopher Stone) and 5d for another part of it (Roger Southell). Robert Adams was assessed at 2d for part of Northeale and for Southmore. 6d was due for part of Southel (Roger Southel) and James Corner paid 2d for another part. 3d was paid by Dorothy Sully, widow, for Brockham while Nicholas Nutcombe paid 8d for Hele Wood, Jane Wipple paid 3d for Woodhayes, John Hill paid 3d for Bond House and Henry Farthing paid 3d for Crosses. Other inhabitants who were assessed were Nicholas Tucker paid 6d for Hearne also called Hooreplace, James Corner paid 4d for South Bulcombe and William Burdge paid 2d for North Bulcombe and another 2d for Crooks Berry. Finally, Robert Potter paid 5d for West Clayhanger and 4d for East Clayhanger. Juillet Meadow was assessed at 3d. Many of the place names were noted in the church rate of 1603. The terrier also outlined the complex scale for the offerings of communicants: these were 3½d for a married couple or 2d for unmarried men or women who were the head of their household. Children and apprentices also paid. They contributed ½d for their first year and ¾d for subsequent years. Male servants were assessed at 4d while female servants paid 3d.[5]

The volume contains complete accounts for the years 1574 to 1582 and a partial rate at the beginning of the volume. This was probably that of 1573. An X precedes each entry which (presumably) indicated payment. There were about 65 household entries for each year with an additional thirty or so other individuals noted as children, sons, daughters, sisters, servants, maids or 'folks'. This could indicate the parish had a population of about 100 people.

The inside page noted 'This is a private book of the Vicar of some Parish for the receiptes of the vicarial tithes in the reign of Queen Elizabeth from 1574 to 1582, but for what Parish, or in what County does not appear, and is therefore uninteresting. The cover is evidently taken from the leaves of a Book (after the Reformation considered useless) containing part of the services according to the Roman Catholic Church, Athenaeum, 29th April 1834. Presented by Lt Coll. Smith'. The Plymouth Athenaeum presented the document to the Plymouth & West Devon Record Office in 2007. The binding, which is illuminated, is noted as 'part of a church service breviary, containing Mattins and Lauds, with musical notation for the Epiphany and feast days, circa 1300'.[6] It comprises ten pages. The document has been given two numbering sequences: one for the illuminated manuscript and the second for the Easter Book. The accounts were written on pieces of paper which have been bound and stitched together to make up 58 pages each of which measures approximately 8½ inches in width and 12 inches in length. A slip of paper has also been included in the binding. Thomasine Crosse, one of the parishioners listed in the Easter Books, was prosecuted in the church court in 1585 for not properly tithing her grain.[7]

13. Account, c.1573

+ Harry Osmonnde for privy tythes & offerings 7d
+ Thomas Osmonnde for 3 kye 6d for a gardyne 1d for his greest myll 14d for haye 3d & for

5   DHC, Diocese of Exeter, Principal Registry, Glebe Terriers, Clayhanger.
6   J. Brooking Rowe, 'Fifth Report of the Committee on Devonshire Records', *DAT* 25 (1893), 221, 244;
J. Brooking Rowe, 'Sixth Report of the Committee on Devonshire Records', *DAT* 26 (1894), 98.
7   DHC, Chanter 862, fols 99, 100, 117.

the newe meade for his offerings 3d ½ for 2 meadous 3d [total] 2s 6d ½ behind ½ & for the new meade a tythynge clafe

+ Elizabeth Farthinge for 3 kye & heaffer 7d ½ for haye 2d for a gardyn 1d for her yowes 1d for offerings 2d ½ for hes daughter & her servannt 3d [total] 17d

+ Andrew Norman for his offerings 3d ½ for a gardyne 1d ½ behind ½

+ Geoffrey stone for prvy tythes & offerings 5d ½

+ Thomas Stone for prvytythes & offerings 6d

+ John Stone at Woodlande for privy tythes & offerings 5d

+ James St burge for pvytythes & offerings 4d

+ John Stone at heale for one kowe & a heaffer 3d ½ for yowes 1d for his offerings 3d ½

+ Harry Stone for prvy tythes & offerings 6d

+ John Thorne for his offerings 4d for a gardyne 1d

+ Hugh Skynner for prvy tythes & offerings 4d

+ Thomas Stone for 5 kye 10d for haye 6d for a gardyne 1d for yowes 1d for a colte 1d for offerings 3d ½ [total] 22d ½

+ John Mortimore for a gardyne 1d for his offerings 3d ½ for 2 children 3d [total] 7d ½

+ Nicholas Lonynge for his offerings 3d ½ for 2 children 3d [total] 6d ½

+ James Estcote for a wynter cowe 2d for his offerings 3d ½ [total] 5d ½

+ John Genyngs for one Cowe 2d for other 2 kye 3d for a gardyne 1d for yowes 1d for his offerings 3d ½ for haye behind for haye

+ Hugh Osmonde for prvy tythes & offerings 8d

+ Michael Parkhowse for 2 yeares

+ Joan Potter [blank]

+ Elizabeth potter [blank]

+ Richard Potter [blank]

+ John Parkhowse for 2 yewes a heaffer 1d for his offerings 3d ½

+ Thomas Harte

[page 1b] + Elizabeth Stone for 2 yeres

Justment for lye woode for 3 yeres

+ Edmund Crosse for Justment of frogpits meade 2d

+ John Coram for his offerings 3d ½ behind ½

+ Ede Apole for prvy tythes & offerings 4d

+ Joan capren for prvy tythes & offerings 4d

+ Margaret Capron for prvy tythes & offerings 4d

+ Thamassyn Thorne [blank]

+ John Hill the elder for his offerings 2d

+ Ede Holman for privy tythes & offerings 4d

+ John Tawbot of chipstable for healewoode meade [illegible]s 8d

+ John Cranklond at Redingeton [Raddington] [blank]

+ Robert Fleade [blank]

+ John Burge at Sowthell [South Hele] for 2 kye 4d for a gardyne 1d for haye 1d for his offerings 3d ½ for his Daughter 1d ½

John Burge his sonne for privy tythes & offerings [blank]

+ John Hill at bampton for twylete meade 2d

+ Richarde Martimore for privy tythes & offerings 5d

23 *September in the year of our Lord* 1601
Memorandum that this boocke was showed unto us whose names are here under written by William Coleman at the tyme of the taking of this Deposition concerning the same
[signed] Humphrey Winter Humphrey Were Thomas Osmond

14. Account, 1574

[page 2]

In the yere of oure lorde 1574 ['16 Elizabeth' in another hand]
+ Geoffrey Potter for vyve kye & two heaffers 13d for haye at home 7d for a gardyne 1d for yowes 1d for two coults 2d for offerings 3d ½ for haye at Clehanger 4d for a gardyn there 1d for thre of his folks 4d ½ [total] 3s
+ Geoffrey ~~pott~~ Stone for fowre kye 8d for haye 12d for a gardyne 1d for yowes 1d for his offerings 3d ½ 1d ½ for Richardes offerings 1d ½ besides 1d ½ for a theynge callffe 5s 8d
+ John Crose for fyve kyve 10d for hay 7d for a gardyne 1d for yowes 1d for his offerings 3d ½ for his children 4d ½   Some 2s 3d
+ John Nutcombe for 8 kye & a heaffer 17d ½ for hay 12d for a gardyne 1d for yowes 3d for a colte 1d for his offerings 3d ½ for his sone 1d ½ [total] 3s 4d
+ John Hill *otherwise* Pery for his two kye & two heaffers 7d for hay 3d for a gardine 1d for yowes 1d ½ for his offerings 3d ½ for his children 3d ½ [total] 19d ½

the first Cow a theyng callffe
+ Richard Applye for 2 kye 4d for haye in the miode 4d for haye behinde the howse 1d for a gardyne 1d for yowes 1d for his offerings 3d ½ [total] 14d ½
+ Robert Burge for 3 kye & a heaffer 7d ½ for hay 6d for a gardyne 1d for yowes 1d for his offerings 3d ½ for his sone Christopher 1d ½ [total] 20d ½ owed ½

[page 2b]

+ a tethinge calfe 5s
+ Roger Burge for 4 kye & a wynter kowe 9d for haye 6d ½ for a gardyne 1d for yowes 2d for his offerings 3d ½ for a colt 1d for his children 6d for Roger 2d ½ [total] 2s 8d

a tethinge calfe 4s
+ Thomas Stone for 5 kye 10d for haye 6d for a gardine 1d for yowes 1d for a colt 1d for his offerings 3d ½ [total] 22d ½

+ Andrew Stone for 4 kye 8d for hay 9d for a gardyne 1d for yowes 2d for his offerings 3d ½ for his 2 Daughers 3d [total] 2s 2d ½ owe[illegible] ½
+Harry Tooker for 3 kye 6d a heaffer 1d ½ a wynter kowe 1d for hay 4d for newe meade 3d for a gardyne 1d for yowes 1d for his offerings 3d for 2 children 3d for Richard 1d ½ [total] behind ½
+ John Burge at bulcombe for a kowe & a heaffer 3d ½ for meade 4d for his offerings 3d ½ [total] 11d
+ Ellen Burge for 3 kye 6d for a gardyne 1d for yewes 1d for offerings 2d for her 2 daughters 3d [total] 13d
+ Elizabeth Stone for 3 yeres 5d
+ Roger Capren for offerings & a gardyne 4d ½
+ Dorothy stone for offerings 1d ½
+ Ede Pole for privye tithes & offerings 5d

[page 3]

+ Thomas Giafford for 3 kye 5d for haye 4d for a gardyne 1d for yowes 1d for his offerings 4d ½ for his daughter 1d ½ for a colt 1d [total] 18d ½
+ John Sowthell for his offerings 3d ½
+ Robert Stone at heale for privy tythes & offerings 7d
+ Margaret Packhowse for one kowe 2d for haye 3d for a gardyne 1d for her offerings 2d for her daugher 1d ½ for a calfe 4d Some 13d ½
+ John Stone for Justment 10d for offerings 3d ½ [total] 13d ½

+ Geoffrey Stone for privye tythes & offerings 5d ½

+ John Stone at heale for a kowe & a heaffer 3d ½ for yowes 1d for his offerings 3d ½ [total] 8d

+ Stephen Croker for privy tythes & offerings 5d

+ Robert Croker for his privy tythes & offerings 7d

+ Joan Southell for 4 keye & 2 heaffers 11d for hay 6d for a gardeyne 1d for yowes 1d for her offerings 3d [total] 21d

+ Agnes Mortimore for her offerings 2d for a gardyne 1d for her Daughter 1d ½

+ William Poole for 3 kye 6d for hay 3d for a gardyne 1d for yowes 1d² ½ for his offerings 3d ½ [total] 14d ½

[page 3b]

+ Thomas Stone for privytythes & offerings 7d

+ John Stone at Woodlond for 2 kye & heaffers 5d ½ for haye 2d for a gardyne 1d for yowes 1d for his offerings 3d ½ [total] 13d

+ Thamassyne Baldwyne for offerings 2d

+ John Parkhowse for the yere of oure lord 1572 for 2 kye 4d for his offerings 3d ½ for yowes ½d payd for 4 yeres 20d

+ Joan Newe for her offerings 2d for a gardyne 1d for her Daughter 1d ½ behind

+ Harry Osmonde for privye tythes & offerings 7d

+ John Genyngs for a wynger kowe 1d for a gardyne 1d for yowes 1d for his offerings 3d ½ behinde for haye for 2 yeres

+ John Thorne for a gardyne 1d for offerings 3d ½ for his Daughter 1d ½

+ Elizabeth Farthinge for 3 kyne 6d for haye 2d for a gardyne 1d for yowes 1d for her offerings 2d for her daughter 1d ½ [total] 13d ½ behind ½

+ John Frogpite for 4 kye & a wynter kowe 9d for haye 6d for a gardyne 1d for yowes for a colte 2d for yowes 2d for his offerings 3d ½ for seaven fyve childre 7d ½ [total] 2s 6d

[page 4]

+ Harry Stone at Woodlon [Woodlands] for privy tythes & offerings [total] 6d

+ George Herrishe for privi tythes & offerings 5d

+ Thomas Osmonnd for 3 kowe 6d for a gardine 1d for his grist mill 14d for haye 3d for his offerings 3d ½ for his Daughter 1d ½ [total] 2s 5d

+ Hugh Osmond for privy tythes & offerings 8d

for tythinge of calfe 4d

+ James Estcote for a cowe 2d for his offerings 3d ½

+ Harry ffrowg frogpit for his privy tithes & offerings [blank]

+ John William Stone the yonger at Woodlon [blank]

+ James Burge at hilcombe 4d

+ Nicholas Lonynge for offerings 3d ½ for 2 children 3d for last yere ½

+ Sander Crocker for privy tythes & offerings 3d

+ Michael Parkhowse for 2 yeres his offrings 3d ½

+ Joan Potter [blank]

+ Elizabeth Potter [blank]

+ Thomas harte [blank]

Justments for bye woode

+ Edmund Crosse for frogpits meade 2d

[page 4b]

for heafer 1d ½ for a gardin 1d   ½ behinde

+ John Coram for last yere behind ½ for his offerings 3d ½

+ Joan Capren for privy tythes & offerings 5d

+ Margaret Capren for privy tythes & offerings 5d
+ Thursten the servannt of John nutcombe for privy tythes & offerings
+ John Tawbot for Justment of healwood meade 2s 8d
+ Robert Floade for Justment
+ John Burge at Sowthell [South Hele] for kye 1 2d for a gardne 1d for hay 1d for offerings 3d ½ for his Daughter 1d ½
+ John Hill at hampton for knylet meade
+ Harry to pay for Justment 23d
+ Mary Geafforde for privy tythes & offerings 4d
+ Robert Hyll of Clepstabell [Chipstable] for Justment 8d
+ Hugh hosegood for his privityes 6d
+ ~~hary Frogpyt 4d~~

15. Account, 1575

[page 5]

In the yeare of the lord 1575 (1575)

+ First Geoffrey stone fower kyne 8d for hey 12d for one gardin 1d for yewes 1d for his offerings 3d ½ [total] 2s 3d ½
+ Robert Stone gefferyes sonne for his privye tythes & offerings & for his mannes 1d ½ [total] 8d
+ Thomas Stone the elder four kyne & a heafer 9d ½ for hey 6d a gardin 1d yewes 1d offerings 3d ½ [total] 21d
+ John Sowthele for five kine 10d for hey 6d yewes a 1d for a gardin 1d for his mothers offings 2d for his offrings 2d ½
+ Geoffrey Stone for his privye tythes & offrings 9d
+ Ede Axole for her privie tythes & offrings 5d
+ Andrew Stone three kyne & a heafer 7d ½ for hey 9d for a garden 1d for yewes 2d for his ofrings 2d ½ for his two doughters 3d [total] 2s 2d

+ John Hill *otherwise* pirrey for three kyne & a heafer 7d ½ for hey 3d for a gardin 1d for yewes 1d ½ for his offrings 3d ½ for his towe sonnes & his doughters 3d ½ ½ behind
+ John Crose for fower kyne 8d for hey 7d for a gardin 1d for yewes 1d for his offerings 3d ½ for his Children 4d ½ [total] 2s 1d

a tythinge Calfe
+ John frogpitt for ~~fower~~ three kyne ~~& a winter kowe 7d~~ 9d for hey 6d for a gardin 1d for two Colts 2d for yewes 2d for his offrings 3d ½ for fower Children 6d [total] 2s 2d ~~½ ½ behind~~ ffor florence his sonne 1d ½ 2

[page 5b]

a tythinge Calfe
+ Geoffrey Potter for six kyne 12d for hay at home 7d for a gardin 1d for yewes 1d for offrings 3d ½ for haye at Clehanger 4d for a gardin 1d for three of his folks 4d ½ [total] 2s 10d

+ Robert Burge for fower kyne 8d for hay 6d for a gardin 1d for yewes 1d for his offrings 3d ½ for his sonne Christpfer 1d ½ [total] 21d
+ James Burge for his prime tythes & offrings 6d
+ Joan Newe for her gardin 1d for her doughters offrings & hers 5d
+ Roger Burge for fouor kyne & a winter kow 9d for haye 6d ½ for a gardin 1d for yewes 2d for his offrings 3d for a Colte 1d for his Children 6d [total] 2s 5d

+ Harry Toker ~~fower kyne~~ fower kyne & a winter kowe 9d for haye ~~fo~~ 4d for a newe meadowe 2d for a gardn 1d for yewes 1d for his offrings 3d ½ for 2 Children 3d [total] 23d ½

[page 6]

for one tything Calfe 13 grotts [4s 4d]

+ John Burge at Bulcombe for 1 cowe & a heaffer 3d ½ for a meadowe 4d for his offrings 3d ½ ~~11d~~ for yewes 1d [total] 12d

+ Ellen Burge for one cowe & a winter Cowe 3d for a gardin 1d for yewes 1d for offrings 2d for one doughter 1d ½ [total] 8d ½

+ Richard Applye for 1 Cow & a winter Cowe & a heaffer 4d ½ for haye 4d for a gardin 1d for yewes 1d for his offrings 3d ½ [total] 14d

+ ~~G~~ Joan Capron for her privie tythes & offrings 5d

+ Christian the servante of John Nutcobe & offrings 5d

+ Margaret Capron the servannte of John Nutcombe 5d

+ Elizabeth farthinge for 3 kyne & a heaffer 7d ½ for haye 2d for a gardin 1d for yewes 1d for her offrings 2d for her doughters 1d ½ [total] 13d ½

+ John Nutcombe for fower kyne & three winter kyne 11d for haye 12d for 2 gardins for yewes 2d for his offrings 3d ½ for his sonne 1d ½ for houslye meadowe laste yeare & this yeare ~~16 16d~~ ~~10d~~ 5d [total] 3s 1d

+ John Stone the younger sonne of Thomas for Justment 4d & more for Justment 8d for his offrings 3d ½ ~~½ to muche~~ [total] 15d ½

+ William Stone sonne of John 2 yeares for his privie tythes & offrings ~~9d~~ 12d

[page 6b]

+ John Burge at Sowthele for 1 Cowe 2d for haye 1d for one gardin 1d for his offrings 3d ½ for his doughters 1d ½ [total] 9d

+ Michael Parkehouse for offrings 3d ½

+ Margaret parkehouse for her offrings 2d & for her 2 Doughters 3d ~~for our gardin 1d for one Cowe 2d~~ [total] 8d

+ Richard Tocker for his offrings ~~3d ½~~ 4d

+ Thomas Osmunde for 3 kyne 6d for his grist mill 14d for haye 3d for a gardin 1d for his offrings 3d ½ for his doughter 1d ½ [total] 2s 5d

+ Hugh Osmunde for his privie tythes & offrings 8d

+ Geoffrey Stone for privie tythes & offrings 6d

+ Roger Capron for ~~privie tythes~~ & offrings ~~3d ½~~ 3d ½ for one Cowe 2d for a gardin 1d [total] 6d ½ – ½ behinde

+ Thomas Stone for his privie tythes & ofrings & for his servannte John frogpitt 8d

+ John Stone at Woodlande for 2 kyne & ~~one~~ 2 winter ~~Cowe~~ kyne 4d for haye 2d for a gardin 1d for yewes 1d for his offrings 3d ½ [total] 11d ½

Robert Stone sonne of Geffrye

+ Humphrey Stone for his offrings 3d ½

[page 7]

+ George Harrishe for privie tytes & offrings 6d

+ John Stone at heale for 1 Cowe 2d for one heaffer 1d ½ for ~~a gardin 1d~~ for yewes 1d for offrings 3d ½ [total] 8d

+ Stephen Trocke for privie tythes & offrings 6d

+ John Stone at Woodlonde for privie tythes & offrings 6d

+ John Potter for privie tythes & offrings 3d ½

the laste heaffer for one tythinge Calfe 5s

+ Thomas Geafferde for 3 kyne 6d for one winter Cowe 1d for haye 4d for a gardin 1d for his offrings 3d ½ for yewes 1d for his Childrens offrings 3d [total] 19d ½

+ John Hurford for his privie tythes & offrings 6d

+ Harry Stone for his privie tythes & offrings 6d

for tythinge Calfe 4d

+ James Adams for one Cowe 2d for his offerings 3d ½ [total] 5d ½

+ John Thorne for a gardin 1d for his offrings 3d ½ for his Doughter 1d ½ [total] 6d

+ Elizabeth Stone Doughter of John for her offrings 2d

+ John parkehowse for one Cowe 2d for haye 1d ½ for his offrings 3d ½ for yewes ½ 1d 8d [sic] for Justment 8d [total] 15d

+ Agnes Mortimere for a gardin 1d for her offrings 2d for her Doughter 1d ½ [total] 4d ½

+ Thomasin Bowdwyne for her offrings 2d

+ John Coram for one Cowe 2d for his gardin 1d for offrings 3d ½

+ John Hill at Bampton for twylet meadowe [blank]

+ Edmund Crosse Frogpitts meadowe [blank]

+ John Talbot for healewood meade [blank]

[page 7b] + Robert Fleade for Frogpitts ~~meade~~ Closes [blank]

+ Harry Hill at Bampton for Justment 23d

Robert Hill of Chipchable [blank]

+ John Tanckins for his privie tythes & offrings [blank]

+ Margaret Pester for privie tythes & offrings [blank]

+ Sannder Trocke for privie tythes & offrings 4d

[blank] Sampforde for lye woode [blank]

+ John Genings for haye for 2 yeares 5d for a gardin 1d for his offrings 3d ½ for a Colte 1d [total] 10d ½ ½

+ John Perrett for henlye Justment 6s 8d

+ William Poole for 3 kyne 6d for havye 3d ~~for ye~~ for gardin 1d for his offrings 3d ½ & for a nother kowe 2d [total] 15d ½

+ Thomas Hill *otherwise* Chubworthye for one lambe 2s 4d

16. Account, 1576

[page 8]

In the yere of our Lorde god *in the year* 1576

X *First* Geoffrey stone for 2 key and A heyfer 5d ½ for a winter Cow 1d for hey 14d for a garden 1d for yewes 1d for his offerings 3d ½ [total] ~~22s~~ 2s 2d

the first Cowes caulfe was the tithinge Caulfe 5s & 8d

X John Hill for 3 kye 6d for a Winter Cow 1d for hey 3d for a garden 1d for yewes 1d ½ for offerings 3d ½ for his Children 4d ½ [total] ½ behind 20d ½

X John Crosse for 4 kye 8d for 2 heyfors 3d for hey 7d for a garden 1d for yewes 1d for his offerings 3d ½ for 2 Children 3d [total] 2s 2d ½

the first Cow A tethinge Caulfe

X John Notcombe for 6 kye and a heyfer 13d ½ for hey 12d for 2 gardins 2d for yewes 2d for a colt 1d for his offerings 3d ½ for houly meadow 3d [total] 3s 1d

the firste cow a tethinge caulfe

X Harry Toker for 3 kye & three heffors 10d ½ for hey 3d for new meadow 2d for a garden 1d for yewes 1d for his offerings 3d ½ for 2 Children 3d ~~for a colt a 1d~~ [total] 2s 2d

[page 8b]

X Richarde Appye for 2 kye and a Winter cowe 5d for hey 4d for yewes 1d for a Garden 1d for his offerings 3d ½ [total] 14d ½
X Grace Kinge for her prevetis and her offerings 4d
X Andrew Stone for 4 kye 8d for hey 9d for a gardyne 1d for yewes 2d for his offerings 3d ½ for his twoe daughters 3d for his sone ½
X for Christian his Daughter 4d [total] 2s 7d

the ~~seven~~ thirde cowes caulfe is the tethinge Caulfe
X Robert burdge for 3 kye and a heffer 7d ½ for hey 6d for a Garden 1d for yewes 1d for his offerings 3d ½ for twoe Children 1d [total] 20d

X John froggpitt for 5 kye 9d ½ for hey 6[d] for a a [sic] garden 1d for yewes 2d for a colt 1d for his offerings 3d ½ for 5 Children 7d ½ [total] 2s 9d
for Thomas Hyll at Skilgate for Justment 2s 9d
Edward Edmondes for Justment [blank]

X Thomas stone the Elder for 4 kye 8d for hey 6d for yewes 1d for a Garden 1d for on colt 1d for his offerings 3d ½ [total] 20d ½

[page 9]

X Geoffrey Potter for sixe kye 12d for hey at home 7d for a garden 1d for yewes 1d for offerings 3d ½ for hey at Clehenger 4d for a garden 1d for a colt 1d for ~~three~~ two of his Children 3d ½ total] 2s 9d ½
and for his Daughter Joan 1d ½
X Nicholas Loringe the younger for his prevites and offering [blank]
X James Adams for his offerings 3d ½ for a Cowe heffer 2d
X John burdge for two kyne and a heffer 5d ½ for hey 4d for A colt 1d for his offerings 3d ½ [total] 14d
X Elizabeth stone for her offerings 1d
X Roger Caprone for 2 kye 4d for his offerings 3d ½ for a garden 1d [total inserted] 8d ½ for Susan his servant for her prevetis and offerings
X Christian Chilcotte for her prevites and offerings [blank]
X Margaret Capron for her prevetis & offerings [blank]
X Geoffrey stone for his privye tethes and offerings 6d for Justment of pkhouse Close 6d
X John Coram for a Cow 2d for his offerings 3d ½ for garden 1d for a caulf that he sold 5d ½
[page 9b]

X Ellen burdge for ~~twoe kye~~ a Cow and heffer 3d ½ for a garden 1d for yewes 1d for her offerings 2d for her daughter 1d ½ [total] 9d
X Roger burdge for 4 kye and a heiffer a winter Cow 9d for hey 6d for a garden 1d for yewes 2d for a colt a pe 1d for his offerings 3d ½ for five of his Children 7d ½ And for Annes burdge her offerings 2d for hey at parkhouse 1d ½ [total] 2s 8d ½
X John stone the sone of Thomas stone for his offerings 3d ½ for a Cow 2d [total] 5d ½
X Robert Camary for his prevites a offerings 6d

The thirde Cow is the tethinge Calfe
X John Soughtheale for fourthe kye and a Winter Cow 9d for hey 6d for yewes 1d for a garden 1d for his mothers offerings 2d for his offerings 3d ½ for Humphrey Clarke his svannt ½ [total] 23d
X John Parckhouse for a kow and a winter Cow 3d for yewes 1d for his offerings 3d ½

X Robert stone for his privie tethes & offerings and for Richard Toss his svannte his offerings 7d 7d

[page 10]

X Margaret Packhouse for a cow and a Caulfe 8d for her offerings 2d for a garden 1d [total] 11d

X Stephen Trocke for his previe tethes and offerings 7d

X John stone for twoe heffers 3d for yewes d for his offerings 3d ½

X George Harris for his prevetethes & offeringes 7d

X Edmund Capron for his prevetethes & offerings 4d

X John Potter for his offerings 3d ½

X James burdge for his privie tethes & offerings 7d

X William stone for his privie tythes & offerings 7d

X John brdge at sougtheale for a Winter Cow and heffer 2d ½ for a gardan 1d for hey 1d for his offerings 3d ½ for his daughter 1d ½

X Thomas stone ys sonne Thomas the elder for his for his [sic] preve tythes and offerings

[page 10b]

X Thomasin Thorne Widdowe for her offerings 2d

X Joan Newe for her offerings 2d for a garden 1d for her daughter 1d ½

X Humphrey Stone for his offerings 3d ½ for hym

X Richard Toker for his offerings 3d ½ for hym

X William Pole for three kye and a Winter cow 7d for hey 3d for a garden 1d for his offerings 3d ½ [total] 14d

X Geoffrey stone for his privie tythes 6d

X Christopher burdge for his prevettethes & offerings 4d

X John Gennyns for a cow & a heffer 3d ½ for hey 2d ½ for his offerings 3d ½ for a garden 1d ½ behind   [total] 10d ½

The firste cow was the tethinge Caulfe

X Elizabeth farthinge Widow for 3 ky 11d for hey 2d for a garden 1d for a colt 1d for her offerings 3d for yewes ½ for her daughter 1d ½ [total] 13d

X George Wyne for his prevetethes and offerings 6d

[page 11]

X John Thorne for his offerings 3d ½ for his daughters 1d for a garden 1d [total] 6d

X Annes Mortimer for her offerings 2d for a garden 1d for her daughter 1d ½

X Harry stone for privie tethers & offerings 7d

X John stone the elder for 2 keye and a Winter cow 5d for hey 2d for a garden 1d for yewes 1d for his offerings 3d ½ [total] 12d ½   ½ behynd

John stone the sone of John stone the elder at woodland for his previtethes & offerings [blank]

X Thomas Gefferde for three key 6d for three heffers 4d ½ for hey 4d for a garden 1d for yewes 1d for his offerings 3d ½ for three Children 4d ½ [total] 2s ½   ½ behind

X Hugh Osmonde for his previtythes and offerings 7d

X Thomas Harte for his offerings 3d ½   ½ for his boye

[page 11b]

X Sander troke for his privie tythes and offerings

X John talbote of Chipstable for Justment 7d

X Thomas Osmonde for three ky 6d for hey 3d for a garden 1d for his offerings 3d ½ for a griste 19d

X Ursula Bult for her previtythes and offerings 5d

X Nicholas Loring the elder for his offerings 5d 3d ½

X Joan Gefforde for her privitythes and offerings [blank]
X John and Elizabeth Potter for there offerings 3d [total] 3d
X Hary hill at Bampton fo twoe yeres Justment
X Joan Loringe for her prive tethes & offerings 1d ½
Robert hill at Chipstable
X Edmund Hawkyns st for his privetythes & his offeryngs 5d
John Tauckings for his prive tythes and offerings
X Susan Hill for her prive tethes & offerings 2d
~~Magarit Jackhouse for her~~
X John Peret at Chipstable
X John Capron at Ashbritle for Justment 2d
[blank] forde at Skilgate for Justment [blank]
Michael Parckhouse for his offerings 3d ½

17. Account, 1577

[page 12]

In the year of our Lord 1577

X Richard Applye for twoe kyne 4d and for twoe heiffers 3d for Hey 4d and a gardine 1d for yewes 1d for his offerings 3d ½ for his servannte 1d ½ for a colt 1d [total] 19d
X Geoffrey Stone for three kyne 6d for hey 12d for a garden 1d for yewes 1d for his offerings 3d ½ [total] 23d ½
X Roger Burdge tythinge Calfe 6s for foure kyne a Winter cow 9d for hey 6d ½ for a garden 1d for yewes 1d for his offeringes 3d ½ for twoe Children 3d [total] 22d
X Robert Burdge for three kyne and heifer 7d ½ for hey 6d for a garden 1d for yewes 1d for his offringes 3d ½ for two Children 3d

X for a tethinge caulfe 5s 8d
X John Notcombe for sixe kyne and a heiffer 13d ½ for hey 12d for twoe gardens 2d for yewes 2d for his offerings 3d ½ for houlye meade 3d [total] 3s
X John Crosse for foure kyne a heiffer 9d ½ for a winterr Cowe 1d for yewes 1d for a garden 1d for hey 7d for his offeringes 3d ½ for twoe children 3d [total] 2s 2d
X John Perye *otherwise* Hill for three kyne and a heiffer 7d ½ for hey 3d for a garden 1d for yewes 2d for his offerings 3d ½ for three of his Children 4d ½ [total] 22d

[page 12b]

X Thomas Stone for three kyne a twoe haffers 9d for hey 6d for a garden 1d for yewes 1d for his offerings 3d ½ ~~I have ½ to much~~
                                                            X for a tethinge calfe 5s 4d
X Andrew Stone for foure kyne 8d for hey 9d for yewes 2d for a garden 1d for his offerings 3d ½ for three Children 4d ½ [total] 2s 4d
X and for his daughter Christian 4d
X John Gennings for hey 2d ½ for his offerings 3d ½ for a Winter Cowe 1d for a garden 1d [total] 8d
X John Stone at woodlond the elder for twone kyne and a Winter 5d for hey 2d for a garden 1d for his offering 3d ½ [total] 11d ½
Peter Shcorlande at Ebwerthye [blank]
X John Parckhouse for twoe kyne 4d for hey 3d ½ for yewes ½ for his offeringes 3d ½ ~~11d~~ 11d ½
X Christian Chilcott for her prevites and offerings 5d
X Margaret Capron for her prevites and offerings 5d

X Henry Tocker for five kyne and a heyffer 11d ½ for hey for the great meade 4d for the newe mead 2d for yewes 1d for a garden 1d for his offerings 3d ½ and for his sonn John 1d ½ [total] 2s ½

X for his servant Joan Dowdnye 5d

X John Stone at heale for one cowe and a Winter cowe 3d for yewes 1d for hey 2d for his offerings 3d ½

[page 13]

X John Sowtheale for foure kyne and a Winter Cowe 8d ½ for hey 6d for yewes 1d for a garden 1d for her [sic] offeringes 2d for his offerings 3d ½ and for his Boye 1d ½ [total] 23d

X Joan Chamerlen for her prevyteythes and offerings 5d ½

X Robert Bowkere for his previteythes and offerings 8d

X Elizabeth Farrthinge widow for three kyne 6d for hey 2d for a garden 1d for her offerings 2d for her daughter Annes 1d ½ [total] 12d ½

I must have a tething calfe

X Ellen Burdge for three kyne 6d for a garden 1d for yewes 1d for her offerings 2d for her daughter Joan 1d ½ and for hey 1d [total] 12d ½

X James Burdge for his previteythes and offeringes 7d

X James Adams for twoe Heyffers and a Cowe 5d For his offerings 3d ½ [total] 8d ½ and for twoe caulfes

X William Stone at Woodlond for his previtethes and offerings 7d

X John Burdge at berye for his offeringes 3d ½

X William Pole for Three kyne 6d for hey 3d for a garden 1d for his offeringes 3d ½ [total] 14d

I had a tethinge calf

X Geoffrey Potter for sixe kyne and a winter kowe and a heiffer 14d ½ for haye at home 7d for a garden 1d for yewes 1d for his offeringes 3d ½ for hey at clehenger 4d for a garden 1d for twoe of his children 3d [total] 2s 12d

X Roger Capron for [illegible crossed through] twoe kyne 4d for a garden 1d for his offerings 3d ½ [total] 8d ½. ½ behynde

X John Corame for one Cowe 2d and winter cow 1d for a garden 1d for hey ½ and for his offeringes 3d ½ [total] 8d

[page 13b]

X John Frogpitt for three kyne and a winter Cow 7d for hey 6d for a garden a 1d for yewes 2d for his offeringes 3d ½ for som of his children 6d ½ [total] 2s 1d

X Emund Crosse for Justment 22d

X Joan new[,] widow for her offerings and for her daughter 3d ½ and for a garden 1d   4d

X John Stone the sonne of Thomas Stone for one cowe 2d for his offerings 3d ½ [total] 5d ½

X Thomas Geyfferde for ~~Sixe kye &~~ five kyne and a winter cow 10d for hey 4d for a garden 1d for yewes 1d for a colt 1d for his offeringes 3d ½ for three of his daughters 4d ½ [total] 2s 2d

X Nicholas Lovinge thelder for his offeringes 3d ½ and for his daughter Joan 2d [total] 5d ½

X and for his sone Nicholas [blank]

X John Burge at Holcombe for twoe kyne and a heiffer 5d ½ for heye ~~2d~~ 2d for yewes ½ for a garden 1d for his offeringes 3d ½ [total] 12d ½

X Humphrey Stone at heale for his offeringes 3d ½

X Hugh Osmonde for his prevites and offeringes 7d

X Geoffrey Stone for his offeringes 3d ½

X Edmund Capron for his prevites and offeringes 5d

X For Elizabeth and Joan Poter for her offerings 3d

X Elizabeth stone at woodland widow for her offerings 2d

X Annes Exale for her offerings and prevites 5d

X Geoffrey stone the Sone of Thomas stone for his privtie and offeringes 6d

[page 14]

X Christopher Burdge for his ~~prevites and~~ offerings 1d ½

X Margaret Parckhouse for a cowe and a caulfe 8d for a garden 1d for her offeringes 2d [total] 11d

X John Sayer at sowtheale for twoe kyne 4d for hey 1d garden 1d for his offeringes 3d ½ and for his daughter Alice 1d ½

X Thomasine Boaden widow for her offerings 2d

X Stephen Trocke for his prevites & offeringes 7d

X Richard Towsse for his ~~prevites~~ and offerings 1d ½

X Annes Martymere for her offeringes 2d for a garden 1d and for her daughter Elizabeth 1d ½

X John Hurford for his prevites and offeringes 9d

X Richard Tocker for his offeringes 3d ½

X Henry Stone for his prevites and offeringes 6d

X John Thorne for a garden 1d for his offerings 3d ½ and for his daughter Elizabeth 1d ½ [total] 6d

X Michael Pkchouse for his offeringes for twoe yeres 6d

X John Potter for his offeringes 3d ½, and for Justment 16d

X John Whit for his offeringes 4d ½

X George Wyne for his previteythes and offerings 6d

XX Thomas Stone for his prevites and offeringes for twoe yeres 12d

Martin Samford for Jistment of Lye woode [blank]

[page 14b]

X Mary ~~eyer~~ Bocher the Servante of Thomas Osmonde for her prevytes and offeringes 5d

William Applie for his prevites and offerings

X Thomas Harte for his offeringes 3d ½

X John Stone a[t] Woodland for twoe yeres his privites and offeringes [total] 12d

X Thomas Osmond for hey 3d for a garden 1d for a cow 2d for his offerings 3d ½ for ~~agayn~~ griste mill 14d [total] 2s 3d

X John Hill for Twilet meadow 2d

Henry Hill for Justment of the lower dustone 23d

End   1567 8 [1578]
paye Richard Hill *of* Bampton

18. Account, 1578

[page 15]

In the year of our Lord 1578

X Geoffrey Potter for five kye and a heyffer 11d ½ and a winter Cow 1d for hey at home 7d for a Garden 1d for yewes 1d for his offerings 3d ½ for his twoe Children 3d for hey at Cleyenger 4d for a garden 1d [total] 2s 8d

X Robert Burdge for twoe kye and a heyfer 5d ½ and a winter Cow 1d for hey 6d for a garden 1d for yewes 1d for his offerings 3d ½ for andrew and Thomasin his Children 3d [total] 21d

X John Pery for foure kye 8d for a winter cowe a peny for hey 3d for a garden 1d for yewes 2d for his offerings 3d ½ for two of his Children 3d [total] 21d ½

X John Burdge for twoe ky and a heiffer 5d ½ for hey 3d for a Colt a 1d for a garden a 1d for yews 1d for his offerings 3d ½ and for Justment [total] 2s 6d

X William Poole for foure kye 8d for a meadow 3d for a garden 1d for his offerings 3d ½ and for his sonne ½ [total] 16d

X Thomas Stone for foure kye 8d for hey 6d for a garden for yewes 1d for his offerings 3d ½ for a colte 1d [total] 19d

X Richard Applye for thre kye 6d for hey 4d yewes 1d garden 1d for his offerings 3d ½ for a colt 1d [total] 16d ½

X Andrew stone for foure kye 8d for hey 9d for yewes 2d for a garden 1d for his offerings 3d ½ for his three daughtors 4d and for his mancs offerings and privitethes 3d

[page 15b]

X John Stone for his offerings 3d ½ for a cowe 2d [total] 5d ½

X John hurforde for his privitethes and offerings 10d

X John Notcombe for seven kye and a heifer 15d ½ for hey 12d for twoe gardens 2d for yewes 2d for a colt 1d for his offerings 2d ob for houely meadow 3d [total] 3s 3d

X John Nottcombe the yonger for his offrings 3d ½   ½ behinde

X Henry Manninge for the mill 10s and for his offering & for thomas his man 3d

X Thomas Martimere for his offerings 4d

Heughe Osmonde for two

Hugh Osmond for his prevites and offerings 10d

X Michael pkhouse for his offerings 3d ½

X John Southeale for foure kye 8d for hey 6d for yewes 1d for a garden 1d for his mothers offerings 2d for his owne offerings 3d ½ for his servint 1d ½ [total] 24d for John Chamberlyn 6d

X Roger Capron for twoe kyne 4d for a garden 1d for his offerings 3d ½ [total] 8d ½

X Thomas Geyfforde for foure kye and a winter cowe 9d for hey 4d for a garden 1d for yewes 1d for a garden 1d for his offerings 3d ½ for three of his daughters 4d ½ [total] 22d

X Thomas Osmound for twoe ky and a heifer 5d ½ for hey 3d for a garden 1d for his offerings 3d ½ [total] 13d

X Geoffrey stone for his privetithes and offerings 6d

[page 16]

X Geoffrey stone for his privites and offerings 6d

X James Burdge for his privites and offerings 7d

Elizabeth farthinge &

X Elizabeth farthinge widowe for twoe kye and a heyfer 5d ½ for hey 2d for a garden 1d for her offerings 2d for her Daughter Annes offerings 1d ½ [total] 12d

X Thomasin Thorne for her offerings 2d

X John Burdge one cowe and a heifer 3d ½ for his offerings 3d ½

X Roger Burdge for four ['5' inserted] ky 8d and a heiffer 11d ½ for hey 6d ½ for a garden 1d for yewes 2d for his offerings 3d ½ for foure Children 6d for a Colt 1d ½ behinde

X John Frogpitt for his privites and offerings 2d

X Thomasin Frogpitt widowe for foure kye and a heyffer 9d ½ for heye 6d for yewes 2d for a garden 1d for her offeringes 2d for a colt 1d for three of her children 4d ½ [total] 2s 2d

X Henry Frogpitt for privities and offerings 4d

X and for mary pratt her offerings 2d

X Humphrey stone for his offerings 3d ½

X William Stone for his privites and offerings 6d

X Robert anery for his privityes and offerings [blank]

X Joan newe widowe for her offerings 2d and for her daughter 1d ½ and for a garden 1d

X Nicholas Loringe for his offeringes 3d ½ and for his daughter ½

X John stone at woodlonde for his previties offerings 4d

[page 16b]

X Christopher burrdge for his privities and offerings 5d

X John Bawden *otherwise* thorne for a garden 1d for his offerings 3d ½ for his daughter 1d ½

X John Burdge for a cowe 2d for a garden 1[d] for his offerings 2d ½ for hey 1d ½ ~~behind~~
X John Stone at Woodlonde for twoe ky and a Wynter cowe5d for hey 2d for a garden 1d for his offerings 3d ½ [total] 11d ½
X John stone at heale for twoe [kine] and heiffor 5d ½ for yewes 1d for his offerings 3d ½
X Annes Martymer for her offerings 2d and her daughter 1d ½ for a garden 1d
X Henry stone for his priviteths and offerings 6d
X John Coram for a cowe 2d for a garden 1d for hey ½ for his offerings 3d ½
X Stephen Trocke for his privities and offerings 7d
X Richard Tosse for his privities and offerings 4d
X Christian Chilcott for her privities and offerings 6d
X Margaret Capron for her privities & oferings 5d
X John Loringe for her privitys and offerings 4d
X Elizabeth stone widow for her offerings 2d

[page 17]

X James Adams for two kye 4d for his offerings 3d ½ ~~and for~~ the towe calfes [blank]
X Edmund capron for his priviteis and offerings 5d
X William pridham for his privites and offerings 4d
X Joan Dandry for her privityes and offerings 5d
X Geoffrey Stone for three kye 6d for hey 12d for a garden 1d for yewes 1d for his offerings 3d ½ [total] 23d ½
X Thomasin Crosse for five kye 10d for hey 7d for a garden 1d for her offerings 2d for her three children 2d ½   2s ½
X John Potter for his offerings 3d ½
X John Pkchouse for twoe kye 4d for yewes 1d for his offerings 3d ½ for hey 1d ½   9 ½ behind John Genings [blank]
X Thomas Harte for offerings 3d ½
X John Hill for Twylot meadow
Henry Hill for Justment for twoe for lower dunstone
+ Margaret pkhouse for a cow and calf 8d for a garden 1d for her offerings 2d & for her daughter 1d ½ [total] 2s

[page 17b]

X Joan and Elizabeth Potter
Martin Samforde for lye woode
John Perot for houly meadow
X Harry Tocker for twoe kye and a heyfer 5[d] ½ for hey 6d for yewes 1d for a garden 1d for a Colt 1d for for [sic] John & his mothers offerings 3d [total] 16d ½
X Richard Tocker for one kowe for his offerings 3d ½ for his servant margery pearce 4d

19. Account, 1579

[page 18]

In the year of our Lord 1579

X Geoffrey Stone for three kye 6d for hey 12d for a garden 1d for yewes 1d for his offerings 3d ½ [total] 23d ½
X John Perrye *otherwise* Hill for five kye 10d for hey 3d for a garden 1d for yewes 2d for his offerings 3d ½ for twoe of his Children 3d [total] 22d ½

the forthe cowe is the tethinge caulfe

X Thomas Stone for five kye 10d for hey6d for a garden 1d for yewes 1d for his offeringes 2d and
for a colte.   Re. for the calfe 5s 8d [total] 20d
                                           the seconde cowes calf is the tethinge caulfe

X John Burdge at Bolcombe for twoe kye 4d for twoe heiffers 3d for hey 4d for a garden 1d for
yewes 1d for his offeringes 3d ½ for his boy ½ ~~2s 9d 17d~~ for Justment of a meadowe 16d
                                           The third cows caulfe is the tethinge caulfe 5d

X Roger Burdge for three kye and a winter Cowe 7d for hey 6d ½ for a garden 1d for yewes 2d
for his offeringes 3d of for three of his Children 4d ½ for twoe colts 2d [total] 2s 2d

[page 18b]

X Andrew Stone for foure kye 8d for hey 9d for a garden 1d for yewes 2d for his offeringes 3d ½
for three of his Children 4d ½ [total] 2s 4d
                                           the second kowe is the tethinge caulfe

X John Notcombe for seven kye a heiffer 15d ½ for hey 12d for twoe gardens 2d for yewes 2d
for his offeringes 3d ½ [total] 2s 11d
                                           the firste cows calfe is the tethinge caulfe

X John Stone at woodlonde for twoe kye and a winter Cowe 5d for hey 2d for a garden for yewes
2d for his offeringes 3d ½ [total] 12d ½
                                           the thirde cowes caulfe is the tethinge caulfe

X Alice Burdge Widowe for ~~three foure~~ three kye ~~and a heifer~~ & a heiffer ~~9d~~ 8d for hey 6d for
a garden 1d for yewes 1d for your offeringes 3d ½ for the offeringes of the twoe maydens 2d
[total] 21d ½

X Christopher Burdge for privites & offerings 6d

X John Coram for a cowe and a heifer 3d ½ for hey ½ for a garden 1d for his offeringes 3d ½
[total] 8d ½ ½ behind

X Joan Sheiphearde for privities and offerings 5d

[page 19]

X Richard Appley for three key and a heiffer 7d ½ for hey 4d for a garden 1d for yewes 1d for a
Colte 1d for his offeringes 3d ½ [total] 18d

X John Southcate for foure key 8d ofr hey 6d for a garden 1d for yewes 1d for his offeringes 3d
½ and for his servante Humphrey Clerke 1d ½ [total] 21d

X Edmund Capron for his priviteithes and offerings 5d

X Thomas Geiffarde for five key and a winter Cowe 11d for hey 4d for a garden 1d for his
offeringes 3d ½ and for twoe of youre daughters 3d [total] 22d ½

X Thomasine Crose widowe for foure kye 8d for three heiffers 4d ½ for hey 2d for a garden a 1d
for yewes 1d for her offeringes 2d and for twoe of her Children 3d [total] 21d ½
                                           Justment for healwodde meadow

X William Poole for thre kie and a heiffer 7d ½ for hey 3d for a garden 1d for yewes ½ for his
offeringes 3d ½ and for his Children 2d [total] 16d ½ also received pitt money 7d ~~½ behinde~~
                   x I have received of Thomas Osmonde for twoe tethinge Caulfes 13s 4d

X Thomas Osmonde for three key 6d for hey 3d for a garden 1d for offeringes 3d ½ [total] 13d ½

X Agnes Amerye for privityes and offeringes 5d

[page 19b]

X Margaret Parckhouse for a cowe beinge winter mylche 1d for a garden 1d for her offeringes 2d
for her daughter 1d ½ behinde

X John Parckhouse for twoe kye 4d for hey 1d ½ for yewes 1d for his offerings 3d ½ [total] 10d
½ behind

X John Stone for a cowe 2d for his offeringes 3d ½ [total] 5d ½ ~~½ to pay~~

X Michael Parckhouse for ~~privteithes and~~ offeringes [total] 3d ½

X Geoffrey Stone for prviteithes and offeringes 6d

X Humphrey Stone for offeringes 3d ½ ½ to muche
X Elizabeth Stone for her offeringes 2d
X Grace Wodrousse servant of thomas Stone theld the elder for privitethes and offeringes 5d

Justment

X Richard Tocker for three kye 6d for a garden 1d for yewes 1d for his offeringes 3d ½ and for his brother John 1d ½
X James Adames for twoe kye 4d for his offeringes 3d ½ ½ to muche 6d ½
X Christian Chilcote servant of John Notcombe for priveteithes and offeringes 5d

[page 20]

X Margaret Capron for priviteithes & offeringes 5d
X John Chamberlin for priveteithes and offeringes 5d
X Dunstan Skilmer for offerings 3d ½
X John Notcombe the yonger for offerings 3d ½
X Joan Newe & her daughter 3d for a garden 1d
X John Burdge for one Cowe 2d for hey 1d for a garden 1d for his offeringes 3d ½ ½ to muche
X Stephen Troke for privtethes & offeringes 7d
X Thomasine Throne for her offeringes 2d
X William Stone for priviteithes and offeringes 6d
X Richard Froggpitt for offeringes 3d ½
X Thomasine Frogpitt widowe for a kowe 2d for three heiffers 4d ½ & for twoe winter keye 2d for hey 6d for yewes 2d for twoe colts 2d for a garden 1d for her offeringes 2d and for her sone Michael 1d ½ [total] 23d
X Richard Cousse for priviteithes and offeringes 6d
X Robert Canworthie for privitethes & offeringes 7d

[page 20b]

X John Frogpitt for priviteithes and offeringes 5d
X Elizabeth Farthinge widowe for twoe kye 4d for twoe heiffers 3d for hey 2d for yewes 1d for a garden 1d and for her offeringes 2d & for daughter Agnes 1d ½ [total] 14d ½ ½ behinde
X James Burdge for priviteithes & offeringes 7d
& for his brother 1d ½
X Joan Geiffard for priviteithes & offeringes 5d
X John Thorne for a garden 1d for his offeringes 3d ½ and for his daughter 1d ½
X Agnes Stockcombe for her offerings 2d for a garden 1d & for her daughter Elizabeth 1d ½
X John Stone for priveteithes and offeringes 6d
X Thomas Courte for a garden 1d & for his offeringes 2d ½
the first cowes calfe is the tethinge caulfe
X John Stone for three kye 6d for yewes 1d for a garden 1d & for his offeringes 3d ½
X Henry Stone for privites & offeringes 6d
X John Potter for twoe heiffers 3d for youre offeringes 3d ½

[page 21]

X Lucy Tosse for her offeringes & her boyes offeringes 3d ½
X John Burdge for twoe kye and heiffer 5d ½ and for his offeringes 3d ½
X William Pridey for priviteithes & offeringes 5d
X Geoffrey Potter for six key and a heiffer 13d ½ for hey at whome 7d & for hey at Clehenger 4d for a garden 1d for yewes 1d for his offeringes 3d ½ for twoe of his Children 3d [total] 2s 10d & a garden at Clehenger 1d
X Michael Roe for Justment 2s 4d
X Joan & Elizabeth Potter for offeringes 3d

Martin Sanforde for Justment [blank]
Harry Hill Justmente [blank]
X John Hill for Twillet Meadow 2d
John Talbote for Houlie Bargain Justment
X Henry Manninge for Thomas Osmonds Mill 6s 3d
X Thomas Harte for offerings 3d ½
X Joan Dowdney for priviteightes & offeringes
X Alice Longe for priviteithes & offeringes 4d

[page 21b]

John Genninges [blank]
Robert Harte of Aishebrytle for a cowe & towe heiffers 5d
John Bowbere for Justment [blank]
X Nicholas Lovering the elder for offeringes 3d ½ and for his daughters 3d ½ behinde

20. Account, 1580

[page 22]

In the year of our Lord 1580

X John Hill *otherwise* Pery for foure kye 8d a heiffer 1d ½ a winter kowe 1d for hey 3d for a garden a 1d for yewes 2d for his offerings 3d ½ and for three of his children 4d ½ [total] 2s ½ Justments 4d
the kowes caulfe is the tethinge calfe
X Geoffrey Stone for three ky 6d for hey 12d for a garden 1d for yewes 1d for his offerings 3d ½ [total] 23d ½
X Edmund Capron servante unto John Nutcomb thelder for previteith and offeringes 6d
for a tething calfe
X John Nutcombe the elder for five kye and a heiffer 11d ½ for hey 6d for a garden 1d for yewes 1 [sic] 2d for his offerings 3d ½ [total] 2s
X John Stone at Woodlande thelder for twoe kye & and [sic] a winter kow 5d for hey 2d for yewes 1d for a garden 1d for his offerings 3d ½ [total] 12d ½. ½ behinde
X John Southeale for three kye 6d & a heiffer 1d ½ for hey 6d for a garden 1d for yewes 1d and for his offerings 3d ½ and for his servante Humphrey Clarcke 1d ½ [total] 20d ½. ½ to muche
X Richard Appley for three kye 6d for hey 4d for a garden 1d for yewes 1d for his offerings 3d ½ [total] 15d ½
X Thomas Stone for foure ky and a heiffer 9d ½ for hey 6d for a garden 1d for yewes 1d for his offerings 3d ½ [total] 19d ½
X Alice Saier widowe for twoe ky and a heiffer and a winter kowe 1d 5d ½ for hey 6d for a garden 1d for a garden 1d for her offerings 2d and for her twoe daughters 4d & for her sone Christopher 1d ½ [total] 19d ½

[page 22b]

X Andrew Stone for three kye & a winter kowe 7d for hey 9d for a garden 1d for yewes 1d for his offerings 3d ½ and for thre of his children 4d ½ [total] 2s 3d
X Richard Tocker for [a] kowe 2d for a heiffer & a winter kowe 2d ½ for hey 2d for a garden 1d for yewes 1d for his offerings 3d ½ for a colte 1d & for his brother John 1d [total] 14d ½
William Roe for Justment [blank]
X John Corame for a Cowe 2d & for a heiffer 1d ½ for hey ½ for a garden 1d for his offerings 3d ½ [total] 9d
and for Justmente [blank]

X John Stone for a kowe 2d & for his offeringes 3d ½ and for Justmente 3d. ½ behinde

X Geoffrey Stone for preivtethes and offeringes 6d

X Roger Burdge for twoe kye and a heifer 5d ½ for hey 6d ½ for yewes 2d for a garden 1d for his offerings 2d for three of his children 3d ½ Justment for lye woode 4s [total] 21d ½

X John Nutcombe the younger for three kye 6d for a winter kowe 1d for yewes 1d for hey 6d for a garden 1d for a Colte 1d for his offerings 2d ½ . ½ behinde. [total] 19d ½.

X John Burdge the younger for a kow 2d for a heiffer 1d ½ & a winter Cowe 1d & for his offeringes 3d ½ [total] 8d

X and for the medo that brimpe hereth.

X John Burdge for three kye and a winter kowe 7d for hey 4d for yewes 1d for a garden 1d for his offeringes 3d ½ [total] 16d ½. & for Justment of Richard Tockers meade.

[page 23]

X Robert Camworthie for previteithes & offeringes 7d

X John Baker for priveteithes and offeringes 7d

X James Adams for a kowe 2d & twoe winter ~~kye~~ kow 1d and for offeringes [total] 6d

                                   the second kowes is the tething calfe.

X John Crosse for five kye 10d for twoe old heiffers 2d for hey 7d for yewes 1d for a garden 1d for ~~ye~~ her offerings 2d & for twoe of her Children 3d [total] 2s 3d

X William Poole for three kye 6d for hey 3d for a garden 1d for his offeringes 3d ½ for his sone William 1d ½ [total] 15d

and for Justment for hele wod mede for twoe yews 5s

X Thomas Osmonde for three kye 6d for hey 3d for a garden 1d and for his offeringes 3d ½ [total] 13d ½

X Thomasin Frogpitt for ~~eight~~ sixe kye 12d for twoe winter kye 2d for hey 6d for a garden 1d for yewes 2d and for her offerings 2d and for her twoe sones 3d & for her servant 2d ½ [total] 2s 4d

X Henry Osmonde for his offeringes 3d ½

X Richard Frogpitt for his offeringes 3d ½

X John Chamberlin for privteithes and offeringes [blank]

X Alice Boyce for privteithes and offeringes [blank]

X Humphrey Stone for his offeringes 3d ½

X Stephen Trocke for privteithes & offeringes 7d

X James Burdge for privteithes and offeringes 7d

& for his brothers offeringes 1d ½

[page 23b]

X William Stone for privteithes and offeringes 6d

X Richard Towse for privteithes and offeringes 6d

X Elizabeth Farthinge for foure kye 8d for hey 2d for a garden 1d for yewes 1d for her offeringes 2d and for her daughter Agnes 1d ½ [total] 16d

X William Preddise for privteithes and offeringes 7d

X Henry Thorn for previteithes and offeringes 7d

X Henry Frogpitt for privteithes and offeringes [blank]

X Thomas Stalenge *otherwise* Colman for his offeringes and for his daughters offeringes 1d ½ [total] 5d ½

X Agnes Stocombe for her offeringes 2d for a garden 1d and for her daughter Elizabeth 1d ½ [total] 4d ½

X Joan Newe for her offeringes 2d for a garden 1d & for her daughter Anstice 1d ½ [total] 4d ½

                                   & for a tethinge Caulfe

X John Burdge for a winter kowe 1d for heie 1d for a garden 1d for his offerings 2d [total] 5d & for a tethinge calves 4s

X John Stone at heale for his offeringe 3d ½ & and [sic] for his sones offeringes ~~1d~~ ½ 4d
& for mortalond 12d

X John Burdge for previteithes and offerings 4d

X Thomas Courte for his offerings 3d ½ for a garden 1d

[page 24]

X John Thorne for his offeringes 3d ½ for a garden 1d and for his daughter Elizabeth 1d ½ [total]
6d

X Lucy Morr for privteithes and offeringes 5d

X Margaret Parckhowse for ~~privteithes~~ her offerings 2d for a kowe 2d & for the calfe 6d for a
garden 1d & for her daughter Joan 1d ½ [total] 12 ½. ½

X Agnes Capron servant of John Notcombe thelder for privteithes and offerings [total] 3d

X Thomas Geiffarde for fhree kye 6d for winter kowe 1d & for a heiffer 1d ½ for hey 4d for a
garden 1d for his offeringes 3d ½ & for twoe of his daughters 3d [total] 20d

X Joan Dadreye for privteithes and offeringes 5d

John Hurfor for privteithes and offeringes 10d

X John Peter for a kowe 2d for a winter kowe 1d and for his offeringes 3d ½ [total] 6d ½

X Dionis Tymwell for privtethes and offerings 4d

X Nicholas Lorring thelder for his offeringes 3d ½ and for his twoe daughters 3d [total] 7d

X Geoffrey Potter for five kye 10d for a heiffer 1d ½ for a winter kowe 1d for hey at home 7d for
hey a Clehenger 4d for yewes 1d for twoe colts 2d for a garden 1d for a garden at Clehenger 1d
for his offeringes 3d ½ & for twoe of his children 3d [total] 3s. ½ behinde.

John ~~Stone at woodland for a barren~~

X Joan and Elizabeth Potter for offeringes 3d

[page 24b]

 X Joan Geiffard for privteithes and offeringes 4d

Martin Sanford for Justment [blank]

Harry Hill [blank]

John Hill for Tmllit Meadowe Justment 2d

John Talbot Justment for Houlie Bargaine [blank]

Thomas Harte for offeringes 3d ½

John Genings [blank]

Robert Hart for [blank]

X Henry Stone for previteithes and offerings 6d

X William Stone for privteithes and offerings 6d

X John Stone for privteithes and offerings [blank]

Michael Parckhouse for his offeringes 3d ½

21. Account, 1581

[page 25]

In the year of our Lord 1581

X Geoffrey Stone for three kye 6d for hey 12d for a Colt 1d for a garden 1d for yewes 1d and for
his offeringes 3d ½ [total] 2s 2d and for his daughter Lucy 1d ½

X John Perye *otherwise* Hill for twooe kye 4d for twoe ~~kye~~ wynter kye 2d, and for a heaffer 1d
½ for hey 3d for a garden 1d for yewes 2d for his offeringes 3d ½ and for three of his children
4d ½ [total] 21d ½

X John Coram for a kowe 2d for hey ½ for a garden 1d and for his offeringes 3d ½ [total] 7d
and for Justment

                                              this yere the last calfe was the tithing calfe
X Richarde Tucker *otherwise* Hearne for twoe kye 4d for a heaffer 1d ½ for yewes [1d] for a
garden 1d and for his offeringes 3d ½ [total] 11d
John Stone for his offeringes 3d ½ for a garden 1d and for Justm[en]t 23d & for his sone 1d ½
[total] 2s 5d
                                                              for a tethinge Calfe
X Andrew Stone for fowre kye 8d for hey 9d for a garden 1d for yewes 1d for his offeringes 3d
½ and for three of his cheldren 4d ½ [total] 2s 2d
X John Nutcombe for five ky and a heaffer 11d ½ for hey 6d for yewes 2d for a garden 1d for his
offeringes 3d ½ [total] 2s ½ behend
X John Southeale for three kye and a winter kowe 7d for heyfer 1d ½ for hey 6d for yewes 1d
for a garden 1d for his offeringes 3d ½ and for his svante Humphrey Clarcke 1d ½ [total] 22d ½

[page 25b]

In the year of our Lord 1581.
X Alice Burdge for twoe kye 4d for a heaffer 1d ½ for a wynter kowe 1d for hey 6d for yewes 1d
for garden for her offeringes 1d and for three children 3d ½ [total] 20d
X John Stone for fowre kye and a heiffer 9d ½ for hey 6d for yewes 1d for a garden 1d for his
Fathers offerings twoe pence, and for his owne offeringes 3d ½ [total] 23d
Joan Goefferde daughter of Thomas Geifforde thelder
X Joan Brice for previteithes and offerings 5d
X Lucy More for previtethes and offerings 4d
X Roger Burdge for three ky 6d for hey 6d ½ for yewes 2d for a garden 1d for his offeringes 2d
for twoe of his Children 3d [total] 20d ½
& for Justment for lye woode 3s 4d not paide
X John Burdge the yonger at bery for twoe ky and a wynter kow 5d for his offerings 3d ½ [total]
8d ½
X John Burdge att Bulcombe for three ky and a heaffor 7d ½ for hey 4d for a garden 1d for yewes
1d for his offeringes 3d ½ Justmente for Krimpe and for his servant William Grannt 1d ½
                                              the tithinge Caulfe is the first caulfe
John Nutcombe the yonger foure kye 8d for a Wynter kowe 1d for hey 7d for yewes 1d for a
garden 1d for his offeringes 3d ½ [total] [illegible sum crossed through] 20d ½

[page 26]

X Richard Appley for three kye 6d for hey 4d for yewes 1d [torn] garden 1d for his offrings 3d ½
and for Justment for Rch[torn] Tuckers meadowe
and for Justmente ~~of~~ for ground wch he holdeth of John Toheal[torn]
X Richard Towse for previteithes and offerings 8d and for William Touse
X John Touse for prevytithes & offerings 5d
X John Packhouse for twoe yeres for hey 3d for twoe kye & a heaffer 5d ½ for offrings 7d & for
his boy 2d ½ [total] 12d ½
X Stephen Tooke for privetethes & offerings 7d
X Thomas Stallinge for offerings 5d ½
X Alice Boyce for priveteithes & offrings 5d
X Henry Smythe for previtethes and offrings 3d
X Alice Geafforde for privetethes & offerings 4d
X Agnes Pearse for privetethes & offerings 5d
X Joan New & Anstice her Daughter 3d ½
X James Adames for a kowe 2d for a heiffer 1d ½ for his offerings 3d ½ [total] 6d ½
X Michael Pkhouse for offerings & for twoe yeres 7d
X Robert Noryshe for privetethes & offerings 5d
X William Predis for privetethes & offerings 5d

Thomas Cock for a garden 1d for his offerings 3d ½

[page 26b]

X William Poole for three ky 6d for hey 3d for yewes for a garden 1d for his offerings 3d ½ & for his boy 1d ½ [total] 15d ½ ½ behind

X Thomas Osmonde for three kye 6d for hey 2d for a garden 1d for a Chriske [grist] Mill 14d for his offerings 3d ½ [total] 2s 4d ½

X Henry Osmonde for offerings 3d ½

X William Colman for his offerings 3d ½ for a garden 1d and for his brother and his servant 3d

X Edmund Way for priviteithes & offerings 4d

X John Potter for twoe ky 4d & for his offerings 3d ½ [total] 7d

X John Packhouse for privetethes & offerings 4d

X John Burdge for privethes & offerings 7d & for his brother 1d ½

X Thomasine Frogpitt widowe for five kye 10d for a wynter kowe 1d for hey 6d for yewes 2d for a garden 1d for her offerings 2d & for her sonne Michael 1d ½ [total] 23d ½ & for Stoke her servant 2d ½

X Richard Frogpitt for his offerings 3d ½

X William Stone for privitethes & offrings 6d

X Henry Frogpitt for offerings 1d ½

X John Burdge at Come for offerings 2d for hey 1d for a garden 1d [total] 4d

X John Thorne for his offerings 3d ½ for a garden 1d 3d ½

X John Bunker for privtethes & offerings 6d

X John Stone the Bucher for privetethes & offerings 6d

[page 27]

X Henry Bowden for privetethes & offerings 6d

X Henry Stone for privetethes & offerings 6d

                              & for a tithinge caulfe beinge the second cowe

X Elizabeth Farthinge for three ky 6d for heifor 1d ½ for hey 2d for a garden 1d for yewes 1d for her offrings 2d & for her daughter 1d ½ [total] 15d

X Agnes Stoccomb for her offerings 2d for a garden 1d and for her daughter Eilizabethe 1d ½ [total] 4d ½

X Joan Bryce for privetethes & offerings 4d

X Thomasine Bowden for offrings 2d

X Thomas Geiffarde for six kye 12d three kye 6d for twoe Winter kye 2d for a heiffer 1d ½ for hey 4d for a garden 1d for yewes 1d for his offerings 3d ½ and for twooe of his Childrene 3d [total] 22d

X Thomasine Crosse for five kye 10d for a heiffer 1d ½ for a winter kowe 1d for yewes 1d for a garden 1d for her offerings 2d & for twoe of her Children 3d 19d ½ ½ behinge & for hey shee is behinde 3 yeres.

                              the therd cowes calfe is the tetheinge calf

X Geoffrey Potter for foure kye 8d for twoe winter ky 2d for a heiffer 1d ½ for hey 7d at home & for hey at Clehenger 3d for a garden 1d for his offerings 3d ½ for twoe of his children 3d for his servante Peter Stocker 1d ½ & for a garden 1d [total] 2s 10d

X Thomas Harte for twoe yeres all his duties 9d

X John Gennings for that he was behind for three yeres for his wyves offerings 4d ½ for a kow 2d for a heaffer 1d ½ for two ky 4d for a kow & a heffer 3d ½ for hey 6d for a garden 3d [total] 2s ½

X Margerit Parckhouse for a kow 2d & for the caulfe 6d & her offerings 2d & for a garden 1d [total] 11d

[page 27b]

John Hill for Twylett meadow 2d

Henry Hill for [blank]
John Talbote [blank]
Robert Harte [blank]
X John & Elizabeth Potter [blank]
X Michael Roe for wole 2s
John Dewdney for priviteithes & offerings 4d
Nicholas Loringe for his offerings & 3d ½ & for twoe of his chilldrene 3d [total] 6d ½   ½ behinde
X John Perret for Justmente 16d & Robt Tynwell
Nicholas Perret for Justmente 16d

22. Account, 1582

[page 28]

In the year of our Lord 1582

+ Geoffrey Stone for one cowe 2d a heatter 1d ½ a wenter cowe 1d for yewes 1d for a gardinge
1d for meadewes 12d for his offering 3d ½ for his dausters offerings & here sones 3d [total] 2s 1d
+ John Hill *otherwise* Peri for 3 kine 6d for 3 heaffers 4d ½ for yewes 2d for a gardinge 1d for
meadewes 3d for his offeringes 3d ½ for two of his chelder 3d [total] 23d

                    Justment for healwood meadewe 2s 6d
                    the second cowes calfe is was the tathinge
+ John Nutcomb for 6 kine 12d for a heaffer 1d ½ for yewes 2d for a gardinge 1d for meadewes
6d for his offering 3d ½ for Michael harts offerings 1d ½ [total] 2s 4d
+ Richard tocker for 2 kine 4d for twoe heaffers 3d for yewes 1d for agardinge 1d for meadewe
3d for his offerings 3d ½ for Welmots offerings 1d ½. [total] 18d
+ Roger Burdge for 2 kine 4d a heaffer 1d ½ for yewes 2d for gardinge 1d for meadewes 6d ½
for his offerings 2d for a colte 1d for two of his sones offerings 3d [total] 21d
+ Andrew Stone for 3 kine 6d for a heafer 1d ½ for yewes 1d for garding 1d for his meadewes 9d
for his offerings 3d ½ for 3 of his cheldere 4d ½ [total] 2s 2d ½
+ John Stone for 2 kine 4d for 2 heafers 3d for yewes 1d for agardinge 1d meadewes 6d for his
offerings 3d ½ 18d ½ ½ not payed

                    John Stones tything Calfe sold for 5s yt is descharged for his due
                    the second cowes calfe was the tithing
+ Alice burdge for 4 kine 8d for yewes 1d agardinge 1d meadewes 6d for here offerings 2d for 3
of here cheldes 4d ½ [total] 22d ½. ½ not payd

                    the second cows calfe was the tithinge
+ John burdge at bulcombe for 2 kine 4d 2 heaffers 3d yewes 1d agardinge 1d Meadewes 4d for
his offerings 3d ½ for mathewes offerings ½ Justment for Crempe 12d [total] 2s 5d
+ for the tythinge Calfe 6s 4d
+ John Nutcomb the younger for 2 kine 4d 2 heafferes 3d yewes 1d agardinge 1d a wenter cowe
for haye 6d for his offering 3d ½ [total] 19d ½
+ Agnes Osmonde for one cowe 2d a wenter cowe 1d agardinge 1d meadewe 3d for here offerings
2d for a grest myle 14d [total] 23d

                    the seconde calfe the next yere is the tithinge
+ Henry Osmonde for his offerings 3d ½ for the tithinge of one calfe 7d
+ John burdge at berry for 3 kine 6d for his offerings 3d ½ [total] 9d ½

                                                    ½ not payd

[page 28b]

+ Richard applie for 3 kine 6d yewes 1d agardinge 1d for his offerings 3d ½ for his mayd
offeringes ellinge hill ½ [total] 16d

Justment for Richard Tackers meade 2s 8d
Justment for John Stones ground 2s 8d
this yere the 4 Cowes Calfe was the tithinge Calfe
+ Thomas gefford for 4 kine 8d for 3 wenter kye 3d a garding 1d for his offerings 3d ½ for meadewes 4d a colte 1d for one of his dahters offerings 1d ½ [total] 22d
+ William Poole for 2 kine 4d for a wenter cowe 1d a garding 1d for meadewes 3d for yewes 1d a colte 1d for his offerings 3d ½ [total] 14d ½
+ Richard froggpit for 2 kine 4d a heaffer 1d ½ yewes 1d for his offeringes 3d ½ [total] 10d
the last cowse calfe this yere is the tithinge Calfe
+ Thomasine froggpit for 4 kine 8d a heaffer 1d ½ yewes 1d agardinge 1d for meadewes 6d for here offerings 1d for one of here Sonnes & here servants stocke 3d [total] 22d ½
the seconde Cowes cafle was the tithinge Calf
+ Thomasine Crosse for 5 kine 10d a heaffer 1d ½ a wenter cowe 1d yewes 1d gardinge 2d a colte 1d meadewes 4d ½ here offerings 2d here sonnes offerings 1d ½ [total] 2s ½
+ Elizabeth southinge for 4 kine 8d for yewes 1d agardinge 1d for meadewes 2d a heaffer 1d ½ for here offerings 1d for here Daufters offerings 1d ½ [total] 18d
+ John pkhowse for 2 kine 4d for meadewe 1d ½ for his offerings 3d ½ for 2 of his chelder offerings 2d [total] 11d
+ Geoffrey potter for 5 kine 10d a heaffer 1d ½ for yewes 1d for gardings 2d for his meadewes at home 7d for his meadewes at Clehanger 4d for his offerings 3d ½ for Joan his dausters offerings 1d ½ [total] 2s 6d ½. ½ not payed
this yere a tithinge Calfe sold for 5s
+ John Corram for one Cowe 2d for agardinge 1d for meade ½ for his offerings 3d ½ [total] 7d
Justment for John to heales Downe 10d
+ Margaret pkhowse for one cowe 2d for a gardinge 1d for here offerings 2d for here mayds offering ½ for one calfe 6d [total] 11d ½
+ Thomas Cocke for agardinge 1d for his oferings 3d ½ [total] 4d
+ John potter for a cowe 2d for a Wenter Cowe 1d for his offerings 3d ½ [total] 6d ½. ½ not payed.
[page 29]
+ John thorne for agardinge 1d for his offerings 3d ½. ½ not payed
+ James Adames for a cowe 2d for his offerings 3d ½ [total] 5d ½
+ Agnes Slocombe for a gardinge 1d for her offering 2d for here dauters offerings 1d ½ [total] 4d ½
+ Joan Newe for here offerings 2d for here dauters offerings 1d ½
+ Thomas Stone for his offerings 2d
+ Michael pkhowse for his offerings 3d ½
+ James burdge for his privitethes and offerings 8d
+ Richard Uphame for his privtethes & offerings 8d
+ Robert Nories for his privetethes & oferings 7d
+ Stephen Trocke for his privitethes & offerings 8d
+ John Tawse for his privitethes & offerings 7d
+ Andrew burdge for his privitethes & offerings 6d
+ William Stone for his privitethes & offerings 6d
+ Henry Stone for his privitethes & offerings 6d
+ Edmund Waye for his privitethes & offerings & for the offerings of his Sister 8d
+ John backer for his privitethes & offerings 6d
+ John Perrye servant of Andrew Stone for his privitethes & offerings 6d
+ Nicholas Stone for his privitethes & offerings [torn]
+ William grant for his pritethes & offerings [torn]

[page 29b]

+Thomasinge Lynell for here privitethes & offerings 5d

+ Alice Boayes for here privitethis & offerings 4d

+ Agnes Capren for here privitethes & offerings 4d

+ Lucy more for here privitethes & offerings 5d

+ Alice gefford for here privitethes & offerings 4d

+ Joan pkhowse for here privitethes & offerings 4d

+ Joan pkhowse for here privitethes & offerings 3d

+ Alice Dallye for towe of here Chelder offerings 1d

Henry froggpit for his offerings 1d ½

+ Cherstone burdge for his privitethes & offerings 3d

X Marian bowden for here privitethes & offerings 4d

+ John burdge at Colme for his offerings 2d

+ Thomas hart for his privitethes & offerings 3d ½ not payed

          the therd cowse calfe is the tathinge calfe

John Sowthell for 3 kine 6d a heaffer 1d ½ for yewes 1d for a gardinge 1d for haye 6d for his offerings 3d ½ & for his boayes offerings 1d ½ [total] 20d ½

Nicholas Loringe for his offerings 3d ½ for too of his dauters offerings 3d [total] 6d ½   ½ not payed

John genninges for his wifes offerings 1d ½ for a gardinge [torn 1d] for too kine 4d for a heiffer 1d ½ for meadowes 2d ½

[torn]ddow for his privitethes & offerings 6d

[page 30, a slip of paper]

the names

John Hill *otherwise*	Thomasine
pery hathe 4	Joan & Roger
Andrew hill	Nicholas loring
Ellen hill	Agnes lorringe
John hill	Andrew stone
Agnes hill	hath three
Robert burdge	Alice
hathe 4 5	William & Thomas
John burdge	Thomas
Andrew burdge	Stone Serse

Receaved the Sume of 32s 2d before eyster daye
[?total] 59s 6d ½

23. CLAYHANGER, Church Rate, 1603

DHC, Diocese of Exeter, Principal Registry, Clayhanger Church Rates, 1603

Note: This rate, a fair copy, has been written on a sheet of paper which has been folded to make up four pages each of which measures approximately 6 inches in width and 16 inches in length. The numerals are Roman with the exception of the final tally and the year. There is a copy of this rate in this collection and it has the signatures of Thomas Stone, sideman, and Richard Stone, churchwarden.

Clehanger prshe 31

A Rate toward the repacon of the pishe Church of Clehanger made and confirmed wth the consent & agreement of Mr Emanuel Maxhey Clerke pson there John Potter, John Nutcombe, John

Parkehowse, John Burdge of Berry, John Burdge of Bullcombe, John Toker, John Stone, William Comer, John Sowthell, John Hill, John Perrot, Agnes Burdge widowe, Florence Frogpitt wydowe, John Moore, Christopher Cornishe & others of the sayd pishe.

Confirmed

First John Nutcombe for west Nutcombe	17d
John Burdge of Berry [Bury] for West friers and Bulhayes	17d
William Comer for South Bullcombe [Bulcombe]	11d
Michael Frogpitt for Hoockehaye [Hookhays]	9d ½
Florence Frogpitt for Perrye	9d ½
John Perrett for Dunnyngeston [Donningstone] Mill	14d
Dunsham *otherwise* Dunstone	19d
Toolett meade	1d ½
The widowe Chrimpe for her Close	1d
Andrew Stone for Upcott & Chappell rewe	21d
John Potter for Marly Downe & East Fryers [Friars]	2s
John Stone for Lane & East F Willhayes 12d	
Thomas Stone for Woodelande [Woodlands]	7d
John Parkehowse for woode Coocks [Woodcocks] & wildballe [Wild Ball]	12d
Alice Gifforde widowe for the Tenement of Hobbhowse	10d
William & Christopher Stone for one pte of the Tenement of Northheale [North Hele]	8d
Robert Potter for West & East Clehanger	14d
Thomas Hudford *otherwise* Burston for wade Wadehayes	9d
John & Joan Hill for Band howse [Bond House]	13d
John Tucker for Hearne place or Hore place	13d
Henry Farthinge for Crosse	11d
Thomas Court for Morterlande	2d
All the Tenements of Polletesleigh [?Pollards Lee] Downe & leigh woode Rynes Chrust & Little	
Leigh the Tenements of George Sandforde	23d
John Nutcombe for East Nutcombe	18d
Agnes Burdge for Hillcombe [Helecombe]	7d
John Sowthwell for Southeale [South Hele]	17d
John Norman for Homleigh	16d
Joan Stone the wife of Mathewe Byndon for one pte of Northeale Tenement	6d
Christopher Cornishe for Brockecombe [Brockham]	4d
John Burdge for Bullcombe & Cranchberrye	18d
John Toase for one pte of Southe heale	1d
turn	

[page 2]

John Moore for one pte of Northeale	3d
James Addames for one pte of Northheale Tenement	2d
Bowden Coram	1d
New Close Hie	1d
Heale Wood the Tenement of John Nuttcombe	14d
Sum total	32s 2d ½

This Rate was appved & Confirmed by Evanns Morrice Docter of the Lawe *fourth of November in the year of our Lord* 1603.

CLAYHIDON

Four rates survive for this parish, near the Somerset border, which is located eleven miles north of Honiton. The parish had a population in 1642 of approximately 518 persons of whom some 14 per cent had paid the church rate.

24. CLAYHIDON, Church Rate, c.1613

DHC, Diocese of Exeter, Principal Registry, Clayhidon Church Rates, c.1613

Note: This rate, a fair copy with the signature added later, was written on a piece of vellum which measures approximately 4½ inches in width and 18¾ inches in length. It is endorsed 'Cleyhidon Rate'.

3. Cleyhidon **A copie of the Rate** made for the repation of the Churche by the Parson & Churchwardens with the Consent of the prshioners after the rate of 1d in the pounde and to be encreased as occasion shall serve.

£63	Culmepine [Culm Pyne] Farme nowe in the tenure of John Chase	5s 3d	£13	Nicholas Marke	13d
£14	John Genninges	14d	£8	Alexander Pyke	8d
£12	Tristram Courte	12d	£10	George Somerhaies	11d
£8	John Everye	8d	£17	Alice Rudge *wid.*	
£6	Simon Tozer	6d		[illegible crossed through]	17d
£4	Alex & Robert Colsworthy	4d	£8	William Searle	8d
£12	Helen Lee	12d	£5	Edward Barefoote	5d
£11	Mark Crosse	11d	£5	Stephen Morris	5d
£27	Henry Charde	2s 3d	£5	Pococke & Trickhey	5d
£8	Robert Franke	8d	£3	William Batten	3d
£3	Thomas Pyke & Mary Pyke *wid*	3d	40s	Richard Pearse	2d
£12	Joan Pyke & Ric. Crosse	12d	20s	Roger Franke	1d
£18	Joan Bellwaye *wid.*	18d	40s	John Hurforde	2d
£4	John Browne	4d	£9 10s	John Troke	9d ½
£12	Thomas Cordent	12d	£9	Henry Heardman	9d
30s	Ric Hooper & Anne Harris	1d ½	£9	John Cooke	9d
£32	Joan Godderd *wid*	2s 8d	£10	Alex L[illegible]trewe	10d
£18	Richard Crosse	18d	£0	Ellorye Morris *wid.*	6d
£0	John Clappe	6d	£0	Edward Powlett Esquier & John Newcombe Clercke	5s
£5	Nicholas Blackmore	5d	£4	Richard Collins & Nic. Callowe	4d
£12	Thomas Somerhaies	12d	£3	Jerom Hunte	3d
£12	Stephen Wiett	12d	£3	John Harris	3d
20s	John Helton	1d	£1	Elizeus Peirce	7d
£5	Richard Conibeare	5d	£12	John Tawton & Hugh Gatchell	12d
£12	John Austin	12d	£5	~~Margerye~~ Joan Nicolls *wid.*	5d
£15	John Quanse	15d	£8	Henry Allforde	8d
£3	Alexander Pester & John Poole	3d	£7	William Burrowe	7d
£10	Andrew Tucker	10d	£6	John Berrye	6d
£12	Mark & Ric. Bradbere	12d	£6	Margaret Tucker *wid*	6d
£18	Nicholas Bradforde	18d	£9	Anthony Maye	9d

£20	Tristram Tucker	20d	20s	John Pringe	1d
£14	Martin Crocker	14d	*Sum*		[blank]
40	Richard Pringe	2d			

[signed] William Lee Rector *there*

25. CLAYHIDON, Church Rate, 1615

DHC, Diocese of Exeter, Principal Registry, Clayhidon Church Rates, 1613

Note: This rate, a fair copy, was written on a sheet of paper which makes up four pages each of which measure approximately 4 inches in width and 12 inches in length. There is some slight water and rodent damage. The rate was endorsed in a later hand 'Cleyhidon Rate'. The numerals are Roman with the exception of the year.

Cleyhiden   **A** true Copie of the rate made for the repation of the Churche 2 *April in the year* 1615 by William Lee Clerke, John Page and Nicholas Nicholls Churchwardens George Summerhaies & John Tawker Sidemen, Tristram Tucker Harry Charde John Geninges Senior Tristram Corrte John Quante Nicholas Bradford John Austin, Martin Crocker and John Treke at 1d the pounde.

John Colles Esquier & his ten[an]ts	4s 7d	Nic. Bradforde	15d
John Chase & his tents	3s 4d	Mark Bradbere & his sonne	8d ½
John Geninges Senior	11d	A. Tucker & Page	6d ½
Tristram Courte	9d	John Hurforde	1d ½
Mary & Wm Toser	5d	Ric Pearse	1d ½
Mrs Everye	6d	Wm Batten	2d ½
Mrs Lee	10d	Tristram Tucker	17d
Michael Crosse	8d	Henry Pococke	7d
Henry & Wm Charde	20d	John Morris	6d
Alex: Colsworthy	4d	John Leyman	13d ½
Robert Franke	6d	Justinian Sawnders	5d ½
John Charde	6d	for Brownes land	5d
Richard Crosse & others	8d	Trickhey & Pococke	4d
Joan Kellwaye & others	18d	Ellis Peirce	7d
John Browne	4d	Nic. Collins	2d ½
John Cordent & his mother	10d	Wm Awton	3d
John Clappe & his mother	7d	Anthony Maye	7d ½
Joan Godderde	2s 1d	Mary Tucker widowe	5d
Nic. Blackmore	3d ½	John Berrye	[torn]
Tho: Somerhaies	15d	William Burrowe	[torn]
Eliz: Bennett	3d	Henry Alforde	6[torn]
Joan Wiett for her Mills	5d	John Tawton	4[torn]
Tho: Crosse & J Austin	11d	Ellis Maye	4d ½
John Sommerhaies	5d	Martin Crocker	9d
A Pyke & Tooker	6d	John Troke	8d ½
John Quante	18d ½	Hugh Gatchell	6d
A: Paster & John Poole	2d	Jerom Hunte	4d
Robert Leyman	20d	John Harris	3d
Richard Crosse	17d	Anth. Roswell & A. Harris	1d ½
[page 2] Nicholas Marke	12d	John Hilton	1d

George Mitchell	1d	John Troke & Peirce	1d ½
Ric. Peter	½	Nic. Callowe	1d
Joan Wiett for Pringe	½	*Sum*	45s 10d

In Agreement with the original
W Lee Rector *of* Clehidon

26. CLAYHIDON, Church Rate, 1615

DHC, Diocese of Exeter, Principal Registry, Clayhidon Church Rates, 1615

Note: This rate, a fair copy with the confirmation, signatures and signs added later, was written on a sheet of paper which measures approximately 8 inches in width and 12 inches in length. There is water damage. The numerals are Roman. It is endorsed 'Exeter 3 Sept 1616' and in a later hand '1613 Clayhidon Rate'.

Cleyhidon   A true copie of the confirmed rate after 1d of the pounde. 123
Clayhidon

£55	Edward Paulett	4s 7d	30s	Richard Pearse		1d ½
£40	John Chase	3s 4d	50s	William Batten		2d ½
£11	John Gennings senior	11d	£17	Tristram Tucker		17d
£9	Tristram Courte	9d	£7	Widdowe Hardman		7d
£5	Simon & Wm Toser	5d	£6	Widdowe Morrishe		6d
£6	John Every	6d	£10	John Leyman		10d
£10	Mrs Lee	10d	£5 10s	George Searle		5d ½
£8	Michael Crosse	8d	£5 10s	Edward Barffoote *and* Saunders		5d ½
£20	Henry & Wm Chard	20d	£5	Stephen Morrish		5d
£4	Alex: & Robert Colesery	4d	£3 10s	Alex: Lantroe		3d ½
£6	Robert Francke	6d	£4	George Trickey *and* Pococke		4d
£6	Thomas Pike *with* 52s	6d	£7	Ellis Pearse		7d
£8	Joan Pyke *and* Richard Crosse	8d	50s	Nic Callowe for Collines		2d ½
£18	Joan ~~Pyke and~~ Kellway Joan Wyatt	18d	£3	Robert Browne		3d
£4	John Browne	4d	£7 10s	Anthony Maye		7d ½
£10	John Corden & his mother	10d	£5	Margaret Tucker		5d
£7	John Clappe & his mother	7d	£4	John Berry		4d
£25	Joan Goddard	2s 1d	£5	William Burrowe		5d
£3 10s	Nicholas Blackmore	3d ½	£6	Henry Allforde		6d
£10	Tho: Somerhayes	10d	£4	John Taunton		4d
£3	Joan Conibeare	3d	£4	Jo: Nicholes		4d
£6	Jo: Anstey *and* Tho: Crosse	£11	£9	Martin Crocker		9d
£10	George Somerhayes	10d	£8 10s	John Trose		9s ½
£6	Alex: Pyke *with* Tucker	6d	£6	Hugh Gatchell		6d
£13	John Quante	13d	£4	Jerom Hunte		4d
£2	Alex: Pester *and* John Poole	2d	£3	John Harris		3d
£20	Alice Rudge	20d	20s	Ric Hoop & Ann Harris		1d
£17	Richard Crosse	17d	20s	John Hilton		1d
£12	Nicholas Marke	12d	20s	Alex: Michell		1d
£15	Nicholas Broadford	15d	10s	Richard Peeter		½
£6 10s	Andrew Tucker & Page	6d ½	10s	John Pringe		½
£8 10s	Mark Broadbere & Richard	8d ½	£5	Joan Wiett for her milles		5d
30s	John Hurford	1d ½		*Sum*		45s 6d

This rate was confirmed at the Consisterie of *Exeter* the 11th of December *in the year* 1615 as appeareth under seale
[signed] W. Lee Marten Crocker [sign of] Simon Kelwaye
[signed] Tristram Tucker [sign of] Richard Smythe

27. CLAYHIDON, Church Rate, 1615

DHC, Diocese of Exeter, Principal Registry, Clayhidon Church Rates, 1615

Note: This rate, a fair copy, was written on a sheet of paper which measures approximately 12 inches in width and 15½ inches in length. There is discolouring at the bottom and along the right hand side of the document. The numerals are Roman with the exception of the year. Church court records show Michael Crosse, who was not listed on this rate, had grown cabbages, carrots, turnips, parsnips, onions 'and such like herbs' in 1622. The records also detail an Elizabethan harvest dinner as having taken place in the parish in which men played cards for horse shoe nails.[1]

Clehidon ['1615' in later hand]
A Rate made for the reparation of the Church at 1d of the pounde the second day of Aprill *in the year of our Lord* 1615 by William Lee clark John Page & Nicholas Nicholls church wardens George Somerhaies & John Tawton Sydemen Tristram Tucker Henry Charde John Gennyngs senior Tristram Court John Quant Nicholas Broadford John Austen Martin Crocker and John Troke *as that follows*

£55	Edward Pawlett Esquire for Middleton		£13	John Quante	13d
		4s 7d	£2	Alexander Pester & John Poole	2d
£40	John Chase gent	3s 4d	£20	Alice Rudge Weddow for the	
£11	John Gennyngs senior	11d		home Livinge, the Land at Densehaies	
£9	Tristram Courte	9d		[Denceshayes] & the land wth Richard Pearse	
£5	Simon & William Toser	5d		and Hasslebeare feildes	20d
£6	John Everye gent.	6d	£17	Richard Crosse	17d
£10	Mrs Lee	10d	£12	Nicholas Marke	12d
£8	Mark Crosse	8d	£15	Nicholas Broadforde	15d
£20	Henry Charde and William	20d	£8 10s	Mark & Richard Broadbeere	8d ½
£4	Alexander Colesery & Robert	4d	£6 10s	Andrew Tucker and Page	6d ½
£6	Robert Francke	6d	30s	John Hurford	1d ½
£6	Thomas Pyke [a]nd Alys	6d	30s	Richard Pearse	1d ½
£8	Joan Pyke & Richard Crosse	8d	50s	William Batten	2d ½
£18	Joan Kelway and Joan Wyatt	18d	[illegible]	Tristram Tucker	16d
£4	John Browne	4d	[illegible]	Henry H[illegible]	7d
£10	John Cordinge & his mother	10d	£6	Ellery Morrish *wid.*	6d
£7	John Clapp & Ellen Clapp *wid.*	7d	£10	John Leman	10d
£25	Joan Godderd *wid.*	2s 1d	£5 10s	George Searle	5d ½
£3 10s	Nicholas Blackmore	3d ½	£5 10s	Edward Barffoote & Saunders	5d ½
£10	Thomas Somerhayes	10d	£5	Stephen Morrishe	5d
£3	Joan Conibeare	3d	£3 10s	Alexander Lantrowe for lychard	3d ½
£5	Joan Wyatt for the Mill	5d	£4	George Trickey & Pococke	4d
£11	Sir Francis Popham & Jo: Austen	11d	£7	Ellis Pearse	7d
£10	George Somerhaies	10d	50s	Nicholas Callowe	2d ½
£6	Alexander Pyke & Andrew Tucker	6d	£3	Robert Browne	3d

---

[1]   DHC, CC5/310 & Chanter 856/90.

£7 10s	Anthony Maye	7d ½	£6	Hugh Gatchell	6d
£5	Margaret Tucker	5d	£4	Jerome Hunt	4d
£4	John Berrye	4d	£3	John Harris	3d
£5	William Burrowe	5d	20s	Richard Hooper & Ann Harris	1d
£6	Henry Alforde	6d	20s	John Hilton	1d
£4	John Tawton	4d	20s	Alexander Michell	1d
£4	Joan Nicholes	4d	10s	Richard Peter	½
£9	Martin Crocker	9d	10s	John Prynge	½
£5	John Troke for Fraunsis	5d	*Sum total*		[blank]
£3 10s	And for his lande being pcell of denshaies	3d ½			

John Chasse William Lee Rector *of* Clehidon
Tristram Tucker John Page Churchwarden
Henry Charde
Sideman Tristram Court   Sideman George Somerhaies
Sideman John Troke   Nicholas Bradford Sidemen

CLOVELLY

One rate survives for this North Devon coastal parish located eleven miles west of Bideford and five miles from the Cornish border. Clovelly Court was the residence of the Cary family who built the pier in the 1580s, the decade in which herring returned to the North Devon shore. Presumably the profits of that fishery are reflected in the assessments. The village is the most distinctive in Devon with its houses straddling the single street which leads from the harbour to the top of the cliff. In this it was similar to two other Devon's ports. Place names reflect this: Brixham has 'Cowtown' (Upper Brixham) and 'Fishtown' (Lower Brixham), Dartmouth has had 'Above Town' since at least the sixteenth century[1] and Clovelly has 'Upalong' and 'Downalong'. Clovelly, unlike its counterparts, did not have as substantial expansion as Dartmouth or Brixham and in consequence is more similar in size to its state from 1500 to 1650: the population stood at about 252 people in 1642 whereas there were 443 resident in 2011. Seventy-seven individuals contributed to the rate in 1613.

28. CLOVELLY, Eight Men Rate, 1613

DHC, Diocese of Exeter, Principal Registry, Clovelly Church Rates, 1613

Note: This rate, a working copy, was written on a sheet of paper which has been folded in half to make up four pages each of which measure approximately 8 inches in width and 12 inches in length. It was endorsed 'Clovelly Rate' and made by the Eight Men although only seven signed the document. The numerals are Roman with the exception of the year and document sequence number. The rate may have been intended to maintain the church but its purpose was not specified on the document.

Clovellye **103**

A rate made by the Eight men of the prshe of Clovelly the 17th Daye of Januarie *in the year of our Lord* 1612 [1613]

Mr Francis Cary	5s 4d	John Verechild	2s
Mr Harry Cary	5s 4d	John Tricke	2s
Robert Shapleigh	2s 8d	Peter Blackdon	8d
Peter Hill	2s 8d	Michael Proosse	8d
Peter Proosse	2s 4d	Joan Snowe	2s
Thomas Wheler	1s 4d	Michael Shapleigh	2s
Joan Wheler	8d	Harry Coole	2s
William Hoop	1s 4d	John Rud	2s
Elizabeth Shorte	3d	Isaac Buckenham	2s
Peter Nicholl	2s 8d	Francis Bonntie	2s
John Southcot	2s 8d & 2s	William Reede	2s
Lefte unp[ai]d of the Laste rate		William Lange	2s
Thomas Grudgworthie	2d	Giles Beapell	2d
Edw: Garratt	4d	+ Margeret Shapleighe		2s 10d
William Wollacott	2s	Walter Heard	4s 2d

---

[1] DHC, Chanter 864/10-11; Abovetown can also be found as a place name in Cornwall including in Padstow, Blisland and Morval: KK, PB/1/26, BRA2606/45, & WM/11.

John Warring	2s	John Clevden	2d
John Heard	1s 4d	William Reede	2d
Martin Shorte	1s 4d	Daniel Fryer	2d
Richard Old	1s 4d	John Madge	1d
Peter Quance	1s 4d	Peter Sannder	2d
John Moyse	18d	James Heard	1d
Gabriel King	1s 4d	John pnacott	1d
William Heard	1s 4d	Lawrence warring	1d
William Skinner	2s 8d	George warring	1d
[page 3] Hugh hunt	1s 4d	Robert pker	3d
P: for making all accounts	8d	Barnaby pker	2d
Peter acland	1s 4d	Paule Sannder	1d
William Burgeiss	2s 2d	Joan [blank]	1d
Humphrey Sampson	2s	Michael Reynold	1d
Anthony Curteis	8d	Will Cleark	1d
Richard Proosse	2s	John Julyans	1d
Lawrence Can	1s 4d	William Horrowd	1d
Robert Wysse	2s	Francis mylls	1d
John Tooker	1s 4d	John Hoop	1d
Thomas Wysse	8d	Andrew pollerd	1d
George Rudmoore	1s 4d	Andrew Smyth	1d
Harry Pode	1s 4d	John Basse	1d
Thomas Sterry	1s 4d	Robert Hunt	1d
Rober[t] Bountie	1d	Roger Whyte	1d
Daniel Sannder	2d	*Sum*	£4 13s

[page 2] 1612. The names of the Eight [sic] men:
The signe [of] John Bonntie thelder [signature] Richard Proosse [sign] Peter Proosse [sign]
Thomas Wheeler [sign] Robert Shaplighe [signature] William Wollard [sign] John Moyse

The *sum* of bothe Rates £8 4s

COLDRIDGE

Six rates survive for this parish located ten miles north-west from Crediton. It was renowned for its park, described in 1630 as having once been 'garnished with goodly woods and timber'. In 1567 it was alleged that it was under one of the oak trees in Coldridge Park that for several successive Sundays Sir Thomas Stukley 'had to do' with Wilmot Berry, named then as 'a whore'.[1] The population of the parish was some 360 persons in 1642. Approximately 14 per cent of the parish contributed to the church rates and marginally more in Ship Money.

29. COLDRIDGE, Church Rate, early 1600s

DHC, Diocese of Exeter, Principal Registry, Coldridge Church Rates

Note: The rate, a fair copy, was written on a sheet of paper which measures approximately 8 inches in width and 12 inches in length. All the figures are Roman except for the number 101. There is some water and possibly fire damage.

Colrudg parish **101**

A rate for the reparacon of the Church

Mr Slee for the barten	21d	Thomas Dracke	5d
Mr Wm Moulford	18d	Mr Wm Holcomb for Batfields tenement	
George Radford gent.	23d	& predhams	7d
Richard Densham	21d	Richard Flacchr	4d
Richard Evans	21d	Wm Wilcocks	4d
Augustine Slee	2s 6d	Nicholas Shabrooke	4d
Nicholas Dier	20d	John Flaccher thounger	3d
Philip Luxton	18d	Thomas Pridham	2d
Henry Reed	13d	Isatt Darke	2d
Thomas Slee	12d	Roger Peckes	2d
Thomas Holcomb gent	11d	John Kelly	2d
Christopher Kingdome	11d	Richard Rogers	2d
Joan Mors	11d	Wm Lillicrapp	2d
Wm Warren	10d	Lawrence Haine	2d
Thomas Sticke	9d	Thomas Pearse	2d
Mrs Katherine Wood	8d	Wm Hurler	2d
Henry Spaxton	8d	Christopher Sommer	2d
John Buckingham	8d	Richard Band	2d
Walter Gibbings	7d	Edward Harvie	2d
John Underhill	7d	Richard Radford	1d ½
John Picke	6d	John Avery	1d
John Flacchr thelder	6d	Thomas Varley	1d
Simon Underhill	6d	Nicholas Reed	1d
Jonas Harvie	5d	John Dracke	3d
Christopher Kelland	5d		

---

[1] Risdon, *Chorographical*, p. 294; DHC, Chanter 856/74-5.

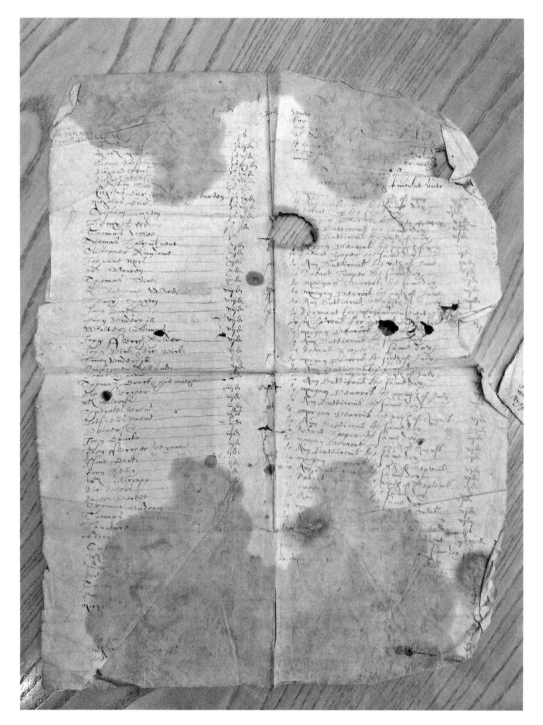

Plate 4. Coldridge church rate, 1613.

30. COLDRIDGE, Church Rate, 1613

DHC, 272A/PO6

Note: This rate was written on a piece of paper which measures nearly 12 inches in width and 15 inches in length. Part of the document is illegible due to fire and having been covered in part with rat urine. The remainder of the document, which lists disbursements, has not been transcribed because of this illegibility. The numerals are Roman.

Colrudge parish

[illegible]
the rate of the parishioners residents

Mr [illegible]	1s	Jonas Harvie	5d
Mr Slee	1s 3d	Thomas Drack & his mother	5d
Mr Wm Moulford	1s 6d	Ric Flecher	4d
George Radford gent.	1s 11d	Wm Wilcocks	4d
Richard Evans	1s 9d	Spabrookes tenement	4d
Richard Densham	1s 8d	Botfields tenement	4d ½
Augustine Slee	2s 6d	Pethersh'd	3d
Nicholas Dier & others for the barten	1s 11d	John Dracke	3d
Nicholas Dier	1s 8d	John Fletcher the younger	3d
Christian Luxton	1s 6d	Isault Darke	2d
Henry Reed	13d	John Kelly	2d
Thomas Slee	12d	Wm Lillicrapp	2d
Thomas Holcomb gent	11d	Ric Rogers	2d
Christopher Kingdome	11d	Roger Pecket	2d
Joan Mors	11d	Thomas Pridham	2d
Wm Warren	10d	Thomas P[illegible]	
Thomas Sticke	9d	Lawrence Haine	2d
Mrs Katherine Wood	8d	Edward [illegible]	
Henry Spaxton	8d	Christopher [illegible]	
John Buckingham	8d	Wm [illegible]	
John Underhill	7d	[illegible]	
Walter Gibbings	7d	Ric R[illegible]	
John Flecher thelder	6d	Thomas [illegible]	
John Picke & Ric: Picke	6d	John [illegible]	
Simon Underhill	6d	Nicholas [illegible]	
Cristopher Kelland	5d	[illegible]	

31. COLDRIDGE, Poor Rate, 1619

DHC, 272A/PO8

Note: The rate, a fair copy, was written on a sheet of paper which measures approximately 16 inches in width and 12 inches in length. The numerals are Roman except for those of the year.

The accompte of William Darte and Henry Dier collectors for the poore in the yeere of our Lord god 1619

Our Rts

First R[eceived]d of Mr John Woode Esquire
4s

Mr Nicholas Greedie	8s
Mr William Molforde	9s
Mr George Radforde	11s 6d
Mytres Slee for the sheafe	7s 6d
Richard Evans	10s 6d
Nicholas Dier	10s
Augustine Slee	18s 6d
Christian Denshame	13s
Henry Reede	6s 6d
Alice Slee wydowe	6s
Thomas Holcombe	5s 6d
Christopher Kingedon	5s 6d
Peter Northcott	5s
Thomas Sticke	4s 6d
Phillip Pile	4s
William Buckenhame	4s
John Underhill	3s 6d
John Denshame	3s 6d
Walter Gibbons	3s 6d
Richard Pricke	3s
Jonas Hervye	3s
Simond Underhill	3s
John Lee	3s

Christopher Killande	2s 6d
Jane Drake & Tho: Drake	2s 6d
William Darcke	2s 6d
Roger Peckett	2s 6d
John Drake	3s
John Babbacombe	2s
William Willcockes	2s
Richard Flatcher	1s 6d
John Flatcher	6d
John Kellye	11d
William Lillicrapp	12d
Richard Vogers	12d

[second column] Rts

Thomas Pridhame	12d
Thomas Pearse	12d
Robert Westorne	12d
Thomas Varley	12d
Christopher Somer	12d
William Hurler	12d
Edward Harvye	9d
Widow Lande	9d
John Averye	6d
Nicholas Reede	6d
Anthony Norrishe	4d

The barten of Colerudge

Mr Roger Slee for the barten moore	1s 4d
Nicholas Dier	4s 9d
Henry Dier	3s 9d
John Ryse	9d

The some of all our Rts is £9 17s 10d

The Eight Daye of Maye *in the year of our Lord* 1620
Our Expenses towards the releife of the poore and ther other charges

First paide towardes the releife of Morgan Peacocke & his wyfe	£1 8s 3d
Item paide for his howse rente	10s
Item payde to Henry Reed beinge collector the yeare befor us wch he hade layd out	1s 6d
Item payde for the releife of the wydow Leymondes Children	£1 9s 1d
Item payde for her howse rente	3s 4d
Item payde towardes the releife of the widowe Garnses Children	£1 11s 10d
Item payde for her howse rent	4s 6d
Item payde to Margeret hoop for keepinge of Mary Reed 16 weekes 10d the weeke	13s 4d
Item payde to Agnes battinge for keepinge of the forsayde Mary Reede 37 weekes 9d the weeke	£1 7s 9d
Item payd for her coate cloathe & the making of it	4s 5d
Item payde towarde the reliefe of anne butticombe	13s 9d
Item payde for one payre of shoes for her	1s 6d
Item payde for her howse rent	8s 10d

Item payde for one payre of shoes for Margery Sutter   1s 9d
Item payd for one yearde & halfe of canvas   1s 4d
for yearde & quarter of chrease   1s 2d
Item payd towardes her releife   3d
Item payde towardes the releife of gilling Pricke   2s 1d
Item payde to Mr Nicholas Gredey for John Grimslades howse rente for three quarters   9s
Item payde to Roger Cookerye for one quarter   4s
Item payd to Walter Gillinge for makine of a peare Indentures for ann butticombs Daughter 1s
The some of our expenses is   £9 8s 8d
so ther is Dewe to us from the pisheners   10d

Collectors for the next yeare Peter Northcoote & Robert Picket

32. COLDRIDGE, Church Rate, 1621

DHC, 272A/PW6

Note: This rate was written on a piece of vellum some 11 inches in width and 28 inches in length. It recorded parishioners in thirty-eight named places in the parish. In 1708 this rate was reproduced alongside a new one.[2]

Coleridge A Rate Made for the Reperacion of the Church of Coleridge and other ornaments and necessaries belonging to the same, Made by George Radford Gent. Thomas Callard Gent. Richard Evans, Nicholas Dyer, John Densham, Christopher Kingdon, Peter Northcott, Thomas Stycke and John Drake yeoman, Parishioners and Inhabitants within the said pish, And Henry Reed & John Underhill Churchwardens and Inhabitants there, together wth the consent of the Major and better part of the rest of the pishioners of the said parrish. Confirmed and approved by lawfull Authoritie. In the yeere of our Lord God One thowsand six hundred Twentie and One as followeth, *Vizt*

Barton of Coleridge	Roger Sleigh gent. for the Barton	22d
Milson [Millsome]	John Wood Esquire for Milson marshes	8d
	William Molford gent. for his Tenement in Milson	18d
	Richaurd Bond wid, for part of Milson	1d ½
Hawkeridg [Hawkridge]	George Radforde gent. for east Hawkeridge & West Hawkeridge	17d
Wiseland	The same George for Wiseland	6d
Frogbery [Frogbury]	Roger Slee gent. for frogberye	5d
Parcke [Park]	Thomas Callard gent. for his Tenement in the parcke	14d
Burch haies [Birch Hayes]	Richard Evans for his Tenement in Burch haies	21d
Gilscott	Nicholas Dyer for Gilscott Tenement	9d
Chilverton	The same Nicholas for Heigher Chilverton	11d
	Thomas Cookerowe for Lower Chilverton	7d
	Agnes Shebbrooke and Roger Shebbrooke for parte of Lower Chilverton	1d
	Thomas Westerne for parcel of the same	1d
Oke [Oak]	The Tenement of Oke	14d
Eastlee [East Leigh]	Christopher Kingdon for his Tenement in Eastlee	11d
	William Buckingham for his Tenement in Eastlee	8d
	Thomas Drake for his Tenement in Eastlee and Milparck	5d

2   DHC, 272A/PW6.

	Isott Darke widow for her Tenement in Eastlee	2d
Westlee [West Leigh]	Peter Northcott for his Tenement in West Lee	10d
	Roger Slee & Walter Slee for a Tenement in West Lee	10d
	Nicholas Greedy for his Tenement in West Lee	4d
Southmore [South Moor]	Henry Reed for the Tenement in South More	13d
Frost	Thomas Slee for his Tenement of Lower Frost	9d
	Walter Gybbins for his Tenement of Heigher Frost	8d
	Walter Gybbins for his Tenement of Heigher Frost	14d
Westacott	Paul Wheatton for Westacott Tenement	12d
Holmes [Holm]	Thomas Sticke for his Tenement called Holmes	9d
Colehouse [Cholhouse]	John Underhill for his Tenement called Colehouse	7d
	George Pyle for his Tenement called Fursdon	8d
Parcke of Coleridge	John Densham for his Tenment once part of Coleridge parck & for his other Tenement	21d
	John Drake thelder for his Tenement part of the parcke	1d ½
	Roger Cookerow for his Tenement part of the Parcke	2d
	The same Roger for his Tenement at the North parcke gate	3d
	Thomas Varley for his Tenement pte of the parck	3d
	Richard Fletcher for his Tenement part of the parck	2d
	Robert Westerne for his tenement part of the parcke	2d
	Edward Harvey for his tenement part of the parcke	1d ½
	Thomas Reymond for his tenement parte of the parcke	½
Meryfeild	John Drake thelder for his Tenement in Meryfield	2d
Pedersham	The same John Drake for his Tenement of Pedersham	3d
Northparke	Thomas Drake for Northparck Tenement	2d
Venn	Jonas Harvey for his Tenement in Ven	6d
Springsland	Richard Peike for his Tenement in Springsland	6d
Banckland [Bankland]	John Flatcher for his tenement called Banckland	6d
Totterton [Titterton]	Simon Underhill for his Agistment called Totterton	6d
	Richard Rogers for his Agistment in Tottorton	2d
Walsham	Isott Drake widow for Walsham Meadowe	3d
Parcke Milles	John Babbacomb for the Parck Mills	4d
Rawleigh	William Wylcocks for his Tenement in Rawleigh	4d
Milallers	Thomas Prydham for Millallers Tenement	2d ½
East Cross	John Kelley for his Tenement called Eastcrosse	2d
Woodbridg	William Hurler for his Tenement at Woodbridge	2d
Smythhouse	Thomas Varley senior for his Tenement in Smythhouse	1d
Westminster	John Avery for his Tenement in Westminster	1d
Gylhouse	Thomas Varley Junior for the Tenement in Gylhouse	1d
Little Silver	Joan Reed widow for her tenement in Littlesilver	1d
Towbridge	Nathaniel Slee for his Tenement at Towbridge	1d
Skinnerland	Christopher Somer for the Agistlment of Skimmerland	2d
Leedownes	William Lyllycrapp for Lee Downes	2d
Frogberry	Thomas Pearse for a Tenement part of Frogbery	2d
Hawkridge	Christopher Kellande for part of Hawkridge	5d
Parcke	John Flatcher for pte of the Parcke	1d
Totterton	Richard Edgcomb for his Tenement in Tottorton	1d ½
	John Rice for parcel of the Barton	1d

Sum total   31s 6d

By the import of these present [writings] *we **Barnaby Goche**, doctor of laws, the delegate of the reverend father in Christ [etc.] of the Archbishop of Canterbury, primate of all England, appointed to exercise jurisdiction within the diocese of Exeter while the episcopal seat there is empty* [William Cotton died on 26 August 1621 and was succeeded by Valentine Carey who was consecrated on 18 November]: *We make it **known** to all that a Rate or Taxation having been heard, viewed and examined by us or our substitute concerning all the inhabitants and others holding an estate (fundus), lands, or tenements within the parish of Coleridge, to support the fabric and repair of the church of the aforesaid Coleridge, and* [to support] *other necessary burdens of the said church occurring...*

***Because** we have found and established that the same said Rate or Taxation has been correctly made and ordained by and with the agreement of the greater and better part of the said parishioners, and proclaimed in the parish church there on three Sundays or feast days at the time* [of divine service] *and approved by us,*

***Therefore** we by these present* [writings] *ratify, approve and confirm, as much as lies in us and as the laws of this kingdom of England allow, the same present above-written Rate or Taxation, to be observed at all times in the future, by the said parishioners and all and singular others holding an estate, lands or tenements within the said parish.*

***In witness** of which we have had attached to these presents the seal which we use in this role; given 25th October in the year of our Lord 1621.* [signed] *Robert* Michell, *the deputed registrar.*

33. COLDRIDGE, Poor Rate, 1632

DHC, 272A/PO10

Note: This rate, a fair copy, was written on a sheet of paper which measures approximately 11 inches in width and nearly 16 inches in length. There has been considerable damage caused by tearing and the chewing of vermin. The income has Roman numerals but the expenditure has Arabic.

Colrudge   The Accompt of Christopher Gummer and John Babbacomb Church Wardens and John Buderhill and William Darte Overseers theire for the poore for the yeare 1632 and published in the pishe Church the 23 of Aprill 1633

Receipts   Rec. of the last collectors £1 10s 8d 6d

John Wood *Esquire*	4s	Mary Slee *widow*	4s 6d
John Cooke cler.	6s	John Underhill	4s 3d
Roger Slee gentleman	16s 2d	Phillip Pile	4s
William Moulford gentleman	9s	Will. Buckingham	4s
Thomas Radford gentleman	11s 6d	Walter Gibbings	3s 6d
Rich: Evans	6s	Thomas Cookerey	6s 6d
Henry Reede	10s 4d ½	John Dart	3s
Tho: Parker	7s	Jonas Harvie	3s
Mary Sticke *widow*	7s	Robert Cookerey	3s
Richard Sticke	7s	Ric Peeke	3s
Elizabeth Northcott	6s 6d	Ric Rogers	3s
Paul Wheaton	6s	Will Dart	2s 6d
John Kingdon	5s 6d	Tho Farley	1s 6d
Ric: Reed	5s 6d	Tho: Drake	1s
Ric. Drake	5s 9d	Christ Somer	1s
Roger Slee	5s	John Lillicrapp	1s
Henry Dyer	4s 7d ½	Ric Rogers	1s

Tho Pridham	1s	Rob Pugsley	9d
Tho Pearse	1s	Rog Shabrooke	6s [sic]
Ric Drake	1s 6d	John Averie	6d
Edward Harvie	1s	Joan Reed *widow*	6d
Mary Hame *widow*	1s	Christian barley *widow*	6d
John Dart	1s	Ric Shabrooke	[blank]
Thomas Westerne	10d	John Helliar	[blank]
John Drake	1s	Ric Dart	[blank]
Catherine Rice *widow*	9d		

Received from Bundleigh for Elizabeth Glasse 4s
the whole summ of our receits is £11 7s 6d

Disbursements

pd to Anna Butticomb 55 Weekes 15d the Weeke	£3 8s 9d
pd to Agnes Batten 55 Weekes tenn pence the weeke	£2 5s 10d
pd to Margaret Pridham 55 weekes 6d the weeke	£1 7s 6d
pd to Anna Tucker 25 weekes 3d the weeke, 12 weekes 5d [torn] the weeke 18 weekes 6d [torn] the weeke	£1 3d
[torn] to Alice Wescotl 13 weekes 8d the weeke	8s 8d
pd to John Greeneslade 22 weekes 12 the weeke	£1 2s
pd more to John Greenslade	6d
pd to Lews Harden [torn] for this year	7s 10d
pd to Barnard Somer for a house for Elizabeth Glasse	5s [torn]
pd for two yeards and halfe of canvasse for the saide Elizabeth	2s 4d
pd for a payre of shoes for the said Elizabeth	22d
pd for a payre of shoes for Margaret Pridham	2s
pd for two yeards and three quarters of linen cloth and thread for the sayd Margaret	2s 7d
pd for a payre of cardes for Agnes Batten	1s
pd for a payre of Shoes for the sayde Agnes	2s 4d
pd for 16 seames of Wood for the poore this yeare	10s 8d
pd for tending of Elizabeth Glasse	6d
pd more to Anna Butticomb	7d
pd more to Agnes Batten	8d
pd to Nicholas Shabrooke for a house for Alice Wescotl	1s
pd to Wilmot Batten for tending of Agnes Batten	6d
pd for a precept for Ric Evans	4d
pd for a precept Richard Grady and John Drake for keeping this booke and making the accompt	2s

The whole some of our disbursements [torn] Soe theire remaneth due unto [torn] pishoners.

34. COLDRIDGE, Ship Money Rate, 1639

Somerset Heritage Centre, DD\SAS\C/795/HV/36

Note: This rate was written on a sheet of paper which measures approximately 6 inches in width and 15 inches in length. The numerals are Arabic. It is endorsed with a series of figures. This national tax was raised in 1628 by Charles I by prerogative without the approval of Parliament and assisted him in meeting government expenditure through the 1630s. Its unpopularity led to its repeal with the Ship Money Act of 1640.[3] It raised more in Coldridge than the church and poor

---

[3]   Oppenheim, *Maritime*, pp. 62–3.

rates. Some 15 per cent of the population was assessed for this rate.

Coleridge pishe: northtawton hundred 1639

A Rate made by Richard Peeke Roger Slee & John Parker for the raising of £5 5s 5d for his maities service for shipping wthin the pishe aforsaid

Christopher Wood Esquire £0 4s 9d	£5 2s 5d	Mistres Grace Monlford		0 15 6
John newcomb for Castle medowe	0 2 2			
[marginal note 'Ecclesiasticall'] John Cooke Clarke for his ecclesiaticall mean				2 0
Roger Slee gent on the acconpts	1 1 11	Thomas Westerne		0 1 3
Phillip Elston gent or the occupants	0 19 10	Robert Dyer		0 1 10
Thomas Parker	1 5 1	John Lillicrap		0 2 0
Henry Reed	0 11 2	Richard Creemer		0 1 10
Richard Sticke	0 12 1	Christopher Sommer	0 1 10 ['3 2 7' in	
Thomas Sticke	0 12 1	margin]		
Richard Drake	0 14 4	Thomas Pridham		0 1 0
John Parker	0 7 11	Thomas Rice		0 2 0
Robert Cookerye	0 7 11	Edward Harvie		0 1 0
Joanne Cookerye or the occupants	0 3 5	Robert Puggeslye or the occupants		0 1 3
John Kingdon	0 9 6	Thomazine Shobrooke		0 1 7
Richard Reede	0 9 6	Roger Shobrooke		0 0 10
for pte of the Barton	0 1 3	Anthony Clatworthye		0 1 4
Henry Babbacomb	0 11 2	Archelans Searell		0 1 4
Roger Slee	0 8 8	Augustin Reymond		0 1 0
William Warren 0 8 8 ['5 8 11' in margin]		Nathaniel Slee		0 0 6
Robert Waye	0 7 9	Phillip Pile for pte of the barton		0 3 5
William Buckingham	0 5 11	William Darte for pte of the barton		0 1 9
Walter Gibbings	0 5 2	William Darte for pet of the glebe land		2 –
John Reed	0 7 8	Thomas Balkwell for pte of the glebe land 2 –		
Jonas Harvie	0 6 2	William Waye		0 4 0
Richard Peeke	0 5 2	William Sannders		0 1 0
Thomas Pearse	0 3 5	Zachery Sannders		0 0 10
William Darke	0 4 4	William Darte		0 2 0
Barnard Sommer	0 3 6	John Saffin gent		0 1 0
John Darte	0 2 2	*Total*	15 5 3 ['1 11 6' in margin]	
John Drake	0 2 7			

[signed] Henry Reed head constable
Roger Slee, Richard Peeke, John Parker Raters
The 28th day of Januarye. I require you the Pettye Constables of this pishe to collecte the summes of money herein mentoned & to paye it to the head constables at or before the 16th daye of Februarye nexte.
Nich. Martyn vic.

COLEBROOKE

Two rates survive for this parish located five miles west of Crediton. In this parish church ales continued through to 1637 at least. That of 1621 brought in £5 3s 4d. In 1623 14s were received 'for malt and money collected out of the parish to the parish use' while the rate brought in £2 9s 5d. The following year two rates raised £6 11s 4d.[1]

35. COLEBROOKE, Church Rate, 1623

DHC, 4203Z/PW1

Note: These rates were recorded in the churchwardens' account book and appear following expenditure. For other years there is no list of contributors but merely a recorded total sum. The bound volume has paper pages which measure approximately 7 inches in width and 11 inches in length. The accounts for some subsequent years have shorter lists of parishioners who have not paid towards the rate. This includes the years 1627, 1630, 1634, 1640, 1644, 1645, 1646 and 1649. In 1623 the total sum of £2 9s 5d was collected by the rate.[2] The numerals are Roman. The population stood at some 668 persons and less than 4 per cent contributed to the rate. Parishioners who were not contributors included John Pary the younger who in 1623 was excommunicated for 'incontinentcy' with Joan Trend.[3] This rate was collected by Thomas Reeve and Matthew Froste, churchwardens, and amongst their expenditure were repairs for the tower, windows and the church bells.

[page 20]

The names of those have allowances uppon the Church Rate as followeth

Robt Yong gent	4s 1d	John Ballamy att Pemston	4d
Mr Eaton	8d	John Temblett	2d
Mr Mills	2s 6d		

The names of those that are to pay uppon the Church Rate as followeth

John Pey gent	4s	Jo: Necomb	2d
and for Strangs tenemt	2d	[illegible crossed through]	
William Pyddsley	3s	Robert Skemmer	4d
Robt Hooke	12d	Gregory Bolte	2d
John Hooke	18d	Phillip Thomas	2d
Thomas Hill	8d	William Forlong	4d
John Trowe	3d	Stoddens tenemt	2d
Christopher Bolte	14d	Katherine Hormott	2d
John Baker	20d	Walter Reeve	2d
William Reed Mary Down	12d	Andrew Eastbrooke	2d
Sampson Bolte	10d	Richard Knight	2d
[in margin 'Sampson Bolt for Will Reede']		Mr Steer for that that was Jo: Bolts tent	2d

---

[1] DHC, 4203Z/PW1, accounts for 1621, 1623, 1624.
[2] DHC, 4203Z/PW1, pp. 33, 40, 42, 58, 65, 6, 72, 73–4.
[3] DHC, CC134/61.

36. COLEBROOKE, Church Rate, 1625

DHC, 4203Z/PW1

Note: This list appears in the same account book as that of 1623. The numerals are Roman. At the bottom of the page is a list of individuals who received money from Ellize Westaway. These were John Hoper for 1s, Wm Smyth (8d), Alice Daymond (4d), Christian Collings (4d), Nicholas Labdon (4d), Alice Jewell (4d), Joan Bryce (4d), Andrew White (4d), Pascoe Swadle (6d), John Wonston (4d), Elizabeth Locke (4d), Henry Gribble's wife (4d), William Eastabroke (4d), Ellize Hoper (4d), Joan Bryce (2d), Amy Trevant (4d) and Alice Daymond (4d). In 1625 two church rates were paid by the parishioners. The expenditure included mending the church forms.

[page 26] The names of those that are to pay to these 2 Rates

Robert Younge gent	11s 9d	['Sampson' in margin] Henry Hoper	1s
['Allowed' in margin] Christopher Eaton	1s 8d	['Boalt' in margin] John Ballamey thelder	6d
['alowed' in margin] Roger Myles	6s	['J: Bellamy' in margin] Walter Reeve	5d
John Ballamey the yonger	1s 4d	Richard Knight	5d
John Hooke	9d	Mr Steer	5d
Robert Frost	5d	John Trowe	5d
Christopher Boult	1s 4d	Gregory Boult	2d
Sampson Boulte	2s 1d		

Rec. by the Wardens of money dew from Ellize Westway to the pish of Colbroke for 2 yeeres – 6s

Plate 5. Monument to Pole family, Colyton, 1605.

COLYTON

A number of rates survive for this market town located six miles south-west of Axminster and three miles north of Seaton. The Dean and Chapter of Exeter were the patrons of the parish church. The fall of the Courtenay family with the execution on 9 December 1538 of Henry Marquess of Exeter brought substantial local independence to Colyton; in 1547 the Crown sold the manor to twenty residents of the town (see p.000). Colyton has the most explicit quote regarding taxation in this period. In 1637 Richard Drake, a gentleman, complained that he was slandered when Joan Sincock said 'Joan Dodge is thine whore and if that my cunt had been as good as Joan Dodge's I had not paid so much to the rate'.[1]

37. COLYTON, Church Rate, 1579

DHC, 1585F/14/8a

Note: This rate has been written on two pieces of paper which were folded and stitched with brown thread to make up pages measuring 8 inches in width and 12 inches in length. Half of one of the pieces of paper has not survived. The document includes expenses notably for communion bread and wine, the recording of christenings, marriages and burials, and twelve pence 'paid to the bellfounder in earnest'.

The accompe made by William bocknolle of puddelbrydge and Robert Dolbere of cadden Wardens in the yeare of our Lord god 1579 as followethe
Recepts

Collyton

Roger Hoopper	4d	Peter bagwyll	4d
Thomas byrd	1d	George Maye	4d
John carpenter	3d	John mander	1d
Thomas Fryer	1d	John Woode	1d
Thomas tycken	4d	John yonge	6d
Joan hayman	1d	Thomas spyller	1d
John tyeppe	4d	John crosse	1d
Robert Wylls	1d	Thomas sampson	3d
James Carswyll	5d	Thomas markell	3d
William Rackeye	1d	John tyckel	1d
John Knowels	1d	Thomas newberye	3d
Walter Vye	1d	John spyller	1d
Christopher collens	2d	Francis Reede	8d
Robert catte	1d	Alexander sande	1d
Francis pennye	1d	Bartholomew spracke	2d
Andrew tyrlyng	8d	William torner	1d
John Leslond	2d	Raffe hardy	2d
Syblye Maye	1d	John hardye	3d
Thomas hayman	1d	Thomas bagwyll	4d
Robert Hamlyn	4d	John cowper	1d

---

[1] Gray, *Strumpets*, p. 46; DHC, CC25/125.

Walter bawden	4d	John greene	1d
John haine	3d	Robert byrd	4d
John byrd	6d	Walter morris	2d
Walter Rawlyn	4d	William byrd	1d
Richard byrd	1d	John whyber	1d
sum 10s 5d			

[page 2]

Watchcombe
Woodland

		Mr Westover	6d
Walter Weston	4d	John byrd	4d
Peter Whetcombe	4d	John Freer	4d
John Newton of Willen	4d	John Howcke	2d
Simon Repyngton	4d	John Bennett	4d
John Newton tryten	2d	John Wydslade	2d
Rooter Holle	4d	John Gye	2d
John Horsland	4d	Sum 2s	8d
Robert Weston	8d	Thomas Whyttye	2d
John Rowe	2d	John stocker	5d
Edward Drake	4d		

Mynchensome

Agnes Leasley 2d		John Dennett	4d
John newton & Joan stocker widow	6d	Sum	4s 4d
agnes newton wid.	4d	Peter Batstone	1d
sum 3s 16d		John mychell elder	4d

Whytwyll [Whitwell] & holesayne

John mychell younger	8d	Peter bagwyll & Edmund Lowde	10d
Walter chepe	4d	Henry quynten	9d
Edith quynten	8d	Alan markell	4d
Raffe butter	4d	Francis carswyll	8d
Mr John strobrydg	6d	Sum	2s 4d
Robert Redwoode	4d	John sande	1d
Mr George strobrydg	6d		
Thomas markell	2d	Robert Dolbere	2d

Farwood

Thomas Sampson	4d	William Hocknolle	4d
Richard Collmado	6d	Sum	5s 9d
Robert toker	2d	John Reede	4d
Thomas Marrode	4d	William Wydslade	4d
Joan Whotonne	2d	Sum	22d

[page 3]

Stopford the towne borrowe [borough]

John Whyke	2d	John bevyes	2d
Robert tanner	1d	Roger Kyng	1d
Allan Markell	2d	Walter bawden	2d
John bevis	1d	Walter Waklyn	1d
Richard Atkyns	2d	Robert Dolbere	2d
William yeate	1d	Richard tredewe	1d

John Walkelyn	4d	John Whyker	1d
John perrye	1d	Simon Repyngton	4d
Richard tyepe	4d	Sum	19d
Ellen torner	1d	William tanner	6d
John Whyker	1d	Richard Newton	4d
John Bartlett	1d	Richard Lugge	1d
Mr Hoopper	4d	Sum	3s 6d

~~sume of the holle offerings of whytson boke 32s 5d~~

the borrow of Collyforde
Receaved of Richard Calmadye gent for the burials

John parson	1d	Joan Daisell	1d
of his son in the church of Colyton	6s 8d	John Wytte	4d
Thomas harris	1d	John Whyker	1d
John marwoode	4d	Walter Marwoode	2d
John Rooke	1d	Raffe harris	1d
John m[obscured]		Francis bagwell	4d
George tanner	1d	John Hoeke	2d
John Read	2d	John makye	6d
Mary seward	1d	John habell	1d
John Clarke	6d	sum	2s 7d

38. COLYTON, Church Rate, 1618

Colyton Feoffees Archive, Colyton Town Hall, Great Book, page 9

Note: This book, which has not been paginated, measures some 17 inches in length and 11¾ inches in width. It is part of a small collection of manuscripts which have not been lodged by the feoffees in the Devon Heritage Centre. This page is headed 'The account of John Tirlinge & Edward Michell then Churchwardens'. Included in the receipts is income from seat rentals, knells and graves. A list of payments follows including for communion bread and wine.

Receipts
Receaved of the Rate made for the repairing of the Churche:

Of Mr Jo[h]n Sampson senior	6s	Of Francis Lockyer	6d
Or Mr Jo[h]n Ham	6s 8d	Of John Sprake	4d
Of Mr Joseph Longe	2s 8d	Of William Stocker	4d
Of Nicholas Salter	2s	Of John Watcomb	4d
Of George Saunder	8d	Of John Fludd senior	4d
Of John Ticken at Elme	10d	Of William Fludd	4d
Of the widdow Rawlyn	1s	Of William Drewe	4d
Of Jo[h]n Newton *of* Gollacre	2s 2d	Of Roger Deyman	4d
Of Hugh Harding	10d	Of the widdow Sprake	4d
Of Henry Newton	10d	Of John Kent	4d
Of John Bird	1s	Of Erasmus Bondfielde	4d
Of William Bird senior	8d	Of John Frenche	4d
Of Hugh Buckland	6d	Of Joanne Skair	4d
Of John Spiller	6d	Of Peter Turner	8d
Of James Daniell	4d	Of Mr Burnard	8s 8d
Of George Weekes	4d	Of Mr Jo[h]n Marwood	7s 10d

| Of Tristram Bowdige | 8s | Of Jo[h]n Hooke | 4s |
| Of Tristram Pearce | 10d | Of Ebdon for Kingsdon west | 8d |

39. COLYTON, Poor Rate, 1639

DHC, 1585F/14/9c

Note: This rate is incorporated within a churchwarden account in which there are three copies dated (A) 9 June, (B) 1 September and (C) 26 June. Rate C has been edited below. Rate A has additional entries for those who occupied lands and tenements which belonged to Walter Yonge and other men and women.

Each rate covered the period up to Easter 1640 although a later hand noted of Rate A 'this rate is to be continued but until the 26th of January 1639 [1640]'. There are occasional differences in the spelling of surnames and in the weekly assessments. Some pages have substantial damage from tearing. Names are followed by tally marks to indicate that the rate had been paid. These differ between the three rates as it appears the rates covered different time periods. Rate C is relatively undamaged.

The churchwarden account includes several lists of the recipients of the tax. One page is headed 'the names of the poor & Impotent that are to have weekly reliefe out of the rate aforesaid'. It lists individuals along with tally rates to show receipt of the named weekly sum they were given. They included 'Moor's Dumb Child, Peter Row and his wyfe, Old Bull and his wyfe, Walter Corkyn, Widdow Farbye, Henry Norrington, Blynd Holwell, Edith Hoor, Widow Pease, Veryard's Dumb Child, Ann Whitmore, Widdow Cluttery, John Carpenter, Edward Norrington's lame child, Widdow Cranly, Widdow Court, Widdow Seller senior, Widow Plumly, Hercules Carswell, Jonathan Markell for nursing, Thomasin Rutter, Frances Basley, Widdow Trall, Widdow Stile, William Manlyes Wyfe, Widdow godwood, William Marshel's Children, Robert Tarner's Grandchild, Robert Bastone, William Ralph, Ellis Tickens, Peter Noller, Richard Joanes & his wife, Elizabeth Kellander, Widdow Bartlet and Alice Addems'.

A Weekly rate made for the releife of the poore by James Bussell and Ellis Coxe Churchwardens, Philip Michell, Allan Abbot, John Teape & Francis Lockier, Overseers of the poor, to indure from the Sixe and Twentye day of June 1639 untill Easter 1640 Aswell Upon the Inhabitants of the said pish as on the lande and occupiers thereof.

Colyton Tythinge

The Lady Jane Poole IIIII x	3s	Barnard Dossell senior IIIII x	4d
William Poole Esq. IIIII x	8d	Roger Marwood IIIII x	2d
Mr Tho: Collyns vicar IIIII x	8d	John Farthinge gent. IIIII x	1½d
John Tyrlinge IIIII x	1s	Peter Ticken IIIII x	5d
Walter Macy IIIII x	1s	John Whicker IIIII x	3d
Edward Bagwell IIIII x	1s	Thomas Drake IIIII x	3d
John Hopth Doct. IIIII x	4d	John Cox IIIII x	2d
Katherine Weeks wid. IIIII x	7d	Robert Hamlyn sen. IIIII x	2d
Tho: Holmes IIIII x	7d	Peter Turner IIIII x	2d
Edmund Turner IIIII x	6d	William Stocker senior IIIII x	2d
Evan Stocker IIIII x	4d	Ellis Coxe IIIII x	2d
Simon Bird IIIII x	5d	Syth Haymond IIIII x	2d
William Tanner IIIII	6d	Elizabeth Stone widow IIIIII x	2d
Simon Vye IIIII x	5d	John Knott IIIII x	2d
Robert Burges IIIII x	4d	Robert Luson IIIII x	2d
Henry Parsons IIIII x	5d	Robert Steevens IIIII x	2d

Peter Bagwell IIIII x	1d
Ellis Holcombe IIIII x	2d
Alan Abbot IIIII x	2d
John Clarke IIIII x	1d
Robert Dolbeir IIIII x	1d
John Turner IIIII x	1d
Andrew Ham IIIII x	1d
Barnard Dwyth IIIII x	1d
[page 2] Peter Palfrey IIIII x	½d
Joan Standinough widow IIIII x	½d
John Freeke IIIII x	½d
John Parker IIIII x	½d
Edmund Clarke IIIII x	½d
Richard Dier IIIII x	½d
Mary Sampson widow IIIII x	½d
Philip Searle IIIII x	½d
John Halston IIIII x	½d
Henry Tanner senior IIIII x	½d
Francis Penny IIIII x	½d
Robert Porter IIIII x	½d
William Orum IIIII x	½d
Francis Lockier IIIII x	½d
Elizabeth Stone widow IIIII x	½d
John Nutton IIIII x	½d
Widow Penny IIIII x	½d
The occuipers of that was the widow	
Northerns IIIII x	½d
Nathaniel Sweett IIIII x	½d

Robert Hamlyn Junior IIIII x	½d
William Stocker Junior IIIII x	½d
Nicholas Wislake IIIII x	½d
Henry Tanner junior IIIII x	½d
Walter Vye IIIII x	½d
Eleanor Holwell widow IIIII x	½d
Ralph Bagwell IIIII x	½d
John Holman IIIII x	½d
John Cleeve IIIII x	½d
William Band IIIII x	½d
Mary Bird widow IIIII x	½d
The Lady Drake for haggr plots IIIII x	½d
Mr William Ham IIIII x	6d
John Wislake IIIII x	8d
William Raynolds gent IIIII x	1s 3d
Mrs Katherine Sampson IIIII x	1s
Nicholas Moxham Junior IIIII x	1s ½d
Theires of Mr Edward Clarkes land IIIII x	4s
John Knights tenement IIIII x	1s ½d
The widow Duckes tenement IIIII x	1s ½d
Francis Carswells tenement IIIII x	1s
Hugh Bucklands tenement IIIII x	1s
Thoccupiers of Elminge stubs IIIII x	1s
Thoccupiers of the lands and tenements of	
Walter Young esq.	
That which Edmund Clarke hath IIIII x	3s
That which Evan Stocker hath IIIII x	2s
That which john Francklyn hath IIIII x	1s ½d

[page 3]

Farwood

Mrs Margaret Haydon widow IIIII x	1s 9d
Mrs Bridget Marwood widow IIIII x	1s 7d
Clement Bowdage IIIII x	1s 1d
Mr Upton for Hornshaynes IIIII x	10d

Thomas Bowdage IIIII x	11d
John Reed Senior IIIII x	5d
William Bucknole IIIII x	4d
Philip Collyns IIIII x	1d

Woodland

Edward Searle IIIII x	9d
Thoccupiers of Bornehayne IIIII x	1s 4d
Thoccupiers of Happerhaine IIIII x	8d
John Hooks ground Called Radeis IIIII x	4d
Mrs Hooks ground IIIII x	4d
Thoccupiers of Colchayne IIIII x	4d
Robert Farrant gent. IIIII x	4d
Mrs Katherine Weston widow IIIII x	4d
Edward Drake IIIII x	4d
William Whicker IIIII x	4d
Thoccupiers of Mr Richard Rose for that was	
whickers IIIII x	1d
Thoccupiers of that was hardies IIIII x	2d

Thoccupiers of Mr Waldrons Borcombe IIIII x	
	4d
Thoccupiers of Mr Burroughs ground IIIII x	
	3d
Thoccupiers of Frances Clarkes Radish IIIII x	
	1d
Thoccupiers of Kingsdowne IIIII x	1d
Robert Turner for balsame felds IIIII x	3d
John Weslade IIIII x	2d
Thomas Collyer IIIII x	1d
John Reed Junior IIIII x	2d
Philip Wilcoxe IIIII x	1d
John Maston *otherwise* Lake IIIII x	1d

Michinholme

John Burnard gent. IIII x	1s 4d	[page 4]William Tucker IIII x	2d
John Holwell & his Mother IIII x	1s 3d	John Rutter IIII x	2d
John Carswell gent. IIII x	6d	Thoccupiers of Goodges ground IIII x	2d
Edward Michell II	6d	Richard godwood IIII x	1d
Thoccupiers of Thomas Marwoods ground		Thoccupiers of the lands & tenements of the	
IIII x	6d	late wiy Drake Esq.	
Philip Michell IIII x	4d	Yarbury IIII x	1s 3d
Rockey Dolbeire IIII x	2d	Luggshaine IIII x	8d
Gideon Hall IIII x	4d	Colesmiths & the grounds IIII x	6d
William Michell IIII x	3d	Gollacars tenement IIII x	3d

Watchcombe

John Crosse gent. IIII x	8d	Widow Chancellour IIII x	3d
John Newton IIII x	5d	Nicholas Sander IIII x	3d
William Stocker IIII x	6d	Silas Stocker IIII x	3d
Sparkehayne ground IIII x	9d	Paryn ground IIII x	2d
Tho: Seaward IIII x	4d	Richard Newton IIII x	2d
Robert Cox IIII x	4d	John Seller IIII x	2d
Hugh Newton IIII x	4d	Chapleland IIII x	1d
Parkehaine tenement IIII x	4d	William Marwood IIII x	1d
John Buckland IIII x	3d	John Quentors ground IIII x	1d
Alice Buckland widow IIII x	3d	Henry Chancellour IIII x	1d
Robert Basley IIII x	3d	Henry Michell IIII x	1d

Stoford Whitwell Collyford & Gatcombe

Thomas Blackaller gent. IIII x	7d	William Newton IIII x	3d
John Butter IIII x	6d	Ralph Teape Junior IIII x	2d
Carswells land per 36 per 36 9 ½	7d	Robert Tucker IIII x	2d
James Bussell IIII x	5d	Robert Moxhams tenement IIII x	2d
Theodore Marwood IIII x	4d	Robert Martyne IIII x	1½d
[page 5] Mr Philip Drakes land IIII x	4d	Thomas Kerby IIII x	2d
Boorsdowne IIII x	[torn]	Preslies ground IIII x	1½d
Sommer lease IIII x	[torn]	Francis Francklyn IIII x	2d
Robert loudr IIII x	4d	New Close IIII x	2d
Ralph Teape senior IIII x	4d	Thomas Francklen IIII x	1d
Mr Richard Mallackes land IIII x	6d	Walter Franches tenement IIII x	1d
Mr Simon Potters tenement IIII x	5d	Widow Luggr IIII x	1d
Mr Whits Gatcombe IIII x	4d	John Whicker IIII x	1d
John Perry IIII x	4d	Walter Teapes tenement IIII x	1½d
Mrs Bartlett IIII x	6d	Swaynes tenement IIII x	1d
Nicholas Moxham senior tenement	3d	Charles Follett IIII x	1d
Mr Wilsman's land	4d	Seraphim Phillips IIII x	1d
Mr Edmund Waldrons or thoccupiers of bovie		Mr Rendalls tenement	1d
downe & Collyford meadow x x	3d	Peter Francklyn	1d
Richard manings tenement IIII x	3d	John Teape IIII x	2d

[signatures] John Pole Walter Yonge

COMBE MARTIN

Two rates survive for this North Devon coastal parish located eleven miles north of Barnstaple. In 1630 Thomas Westcote noted in his *A View of Devonshire* 'this borough deriveth its name of the situation, being a low and deep valley, surrounded with very high hills on every side (toward the sea excepted)... A little river (that hath as great a name as the second river of England) Humber [sic], cleaveth it throughout, making, at the town's end, a poor haven, which yieldeth a like commodity'. He also wrote 'the town is not rich: yet are the people industrious and painful: their greatest trade and profit is the making of shoemakers' thread, by spinning whereof they maintain themselves, funishing therewith the most part of the shire. The soil is not naturally fruitful; but manured and improved with sand, lime and such like, is made much richer and yields increase to their satisfaction'.[1] Tristram Risdon added it 'lieth low as the name implieth and near the sea having a cove for boats to land; a place noted for yielding the best hemp in all this country, and that in great abundance; but in former times famous for mining of tin, and (that which is better merchandise) silver, hath been found since our remembrance'.[2] Both rates were confirmed by Matthew Sutcliffe, the chief judge of the court as Diocesan Chancellor from 1582.[3] These appear to be copies but were recorded in different formats. The parish had a population of about 800 persons of which less than 10 per cent contributed to the church rate.

From at least 1565 through to at least 1631 the parish had four sidemen who were annually 'chosen by the assent of the whole parish'. Their duties included receiving money for church seats.[4] The parish clerk in the late sixteenth century was, according to the testimony of one parishioner, given a penny by parishioners four times a year and he had variable quantities of bread at Christmas, a piece of bacon and eggs at Easter, wool at Midsummer and grain at the harvest. Robert Gyll also claimed in addition a workman gave half a day's labour during the harvest. The custom was subsequently replaced by a monetary tax.[5]

40. COMBE MARTIN, Church Rate, 1583

DHC, Diocese of Exeter, Principal Registry, Combe Martin Church Rates, 1583

Note: This rate, a fair copy, was written on a sheet of paper which measures approximately 8 inches in width and 13½ inches in length. The numerals are Arabic. In 1583 a dispute regarding this rate reached the church court. Richard Lerewell, John Chalecombe, John Robert and Nicholas Nutt, who had all lived in the parish throughout their lives, testified before William Miricke and Peter Medford, the parsons of Berrynarbor and Combe Martin. Lerewell, aged forty, Chalecombe, aged 83, Robert, aged 77 and Nutt, aged 33, thought the rate was fair except for five shillings in the the valuation for the ground of William Handcock, John Herding and John Pecke for Vellacote.[6]

[1]   Thomas Westcote, *A View of Devonshire in MDCXXX* (Exeter, 1845), pp. 252–3.
[2]   Risdon, *Chorographical*, pp. 347–8.
[3]   Frances B. Troup, 'Biographical notes on Doctor Matthew Sutcliffe, Dean of Exeter, 1588–1629', *DAT* XXIII (1891), 173; Jonathan Andrew Vage, 'The diocese of Exeter, 1519–1641: a study of church government in the age of Reformation', PhD thesis, Cambridge, 1991, p. 278.
[4]   DHC, Chanter 854d.
[5]   DHC, CC85.
[6]   DHC, CC84 & CC85.

Combmartyn pishe 13

The Copie of the Rate for the repation of the Church made and Confermed by the Reverend Matthew Sutclyffe Doctor of th~~~~ lawe &c: the 18th day of July *in the year of our Lord* 1583

Oates

West Challacomb [Challacombe]	bushels	5
East Challacomb [Challacombe]	bush.	3 and half & half peck
Gurton [Girt]	bush.	3 & a peck
Vellacote [Vellacott]	bushe.	2 & a halfe
Holson [Holdstone] Holland & the meadow at townsend	bush.	5 & a halfe
Higher verefyld	bush.	3
Lower verefylde	bushe.	3
Colsworthy [Coulsworthy]	bushe.	5
Trackcomb [Truckham]	bushe.	3 and a peck
Blackwell	b.	2
Nutcomb [Nutcombe]	bushe.	3
Colscott [Coulscott]	bush.	4
Loughwood	bush.	1 & one peck
Lower Bussacott [Buzzacott] & Fludyeat	bush.	2 & a halfe
Higher Bussacott	bushe.	2
Beare	bushe.	2 & a half
Greater Netherton	bushe.	1 & one peck
The two greistmyls		
Easter dear pke and wydecomb		
moore meade 2 ham[illegible] & conypke	bushe.	7 & one peck
Wossomland [Wilsomland]	bushe.	1 1 peck and half
Wester dear pke [Wester Park]	bush.	2
Eastacott }		
Berryes }	bush.	4
Libland }		
Byckham		half a peck
Lyttle Neytherton [Netherton]		one peck
Higher Knole		half a peck
Lower Knole		half a peck
Toote [Touts]		one pottle
Three Closes of Land in the teanure of John Thorne in nytherton [Netherton]		one pottle
A Close sometyme Balle the Mellers		one quart and halfe

Item Agreethe with the Originage under the seale of Mr Doctor Sutclyffe

41. Combe Martin, Church Rate, 1583

DHC, Diocese of Exeter, Principal Registry, Combe Martin Church Rates, 1583

Note: This rate, a fair copy, was written on a sheet of paper which measures approximately 10 inches in width and 15 inches in length. The numerals are Roman with the exception of the year. The right hand side has been destroyed. Tristram Risdon noted in the early 1600s that the first family noted on the rate, Prouse, which did not pay the highest amount, came to the parish through marriage with the last member of the Orchard family of Orchard.[7] The Challacombe family at Nutcombe had been resident in Combe Martin since at least the fifteenth century.[8] The subsidy rate of 1581 only listed ten parishioners each of whom were assessed for their goods and not for land. Each is on the church rate: these are John Beare, John Challacombe, Thomas Eastaway, William Hancock, Richard Lerawill, John Ley, John Norman, Nicholas Nutt, John Peake and John Roberts.[9] The heading, in Latin, confirmed the rate was approved by Mathew Sutcliffe in July, 1583.

	[value]	[grain amount]
Combmartyn		
Mr Prouse	£27 10s	[torn]
Thomas Eastwaie	£18 18s 9d	Three [torn]
Mr William Hancocke for Gurte	£17 17s 6d	three b[torn]
Mr William Hancoke for Vellacotte	£13 15s	two bushels & [torn]
William Heardinge for Holson hollande & the meadow at towens ends	£30 5s	five bushels and a [torn]
John Norman at Verivill	£16 10s	three bushels
William Blackemore	£16 10s	th[torn] bushels
Richard Lerywill for Culsworthie	£27 10s	five b[torn]
William Tucker for Truccombe	£17 17s 6d	[torn]
David Smyth for Blakewill	£11	Tw[torn]
John Chollacombe of Nutcomb	£16 10s	Three [torn]
Nicholas Nutt of Colscotte	£22	ffower[torn]
William Hartnoll for longste woode	£7	one bush[torn]
John Heardinge for Bussacott & the Meadow att fludyeate £13 15s		two bush[torn]
& the Meadow att Fludyeate	£13 15s	two bush[torn]
John Beare in Bussacott	£11	Two bushels [torn]
John Peake to Beare	£13 15s	two bush[torn] &
Adrian Reede at Netherton	£6 17s 6d	one bushels one pecke [torn]
Mr William Hancocke for two griste Mills	£20}	
Mr Willliam Hancocke for the east deare pke & widecom	£13 15s} £40 10s	Seaven bushels & [torn]
Mr William Hancocke for two Hammes Moore meade & the Connie pke	£6 15s }	one bushel peck
John Hancocke for woosomelande	£7 11s 3d	one bushel [torn]
Nicholas Berrie Esquire for the west Deare pke	£11	Two bushels [torn]
John Roberts for Eastacott	£10	} [torn]
John Roberts for Lieblande	40s	} [torn] Fower bush[torn]
Richard Roberts for the Berries	£22	} [torn]
Alexander Laurie for Bickham	16s	halfe a pec[torn]
The old Mother Ley for Netherton	27s 6d half a [torn]	
John Ley of Shutte for the Knowell	16s	half a pecke [torn]
John Baylie for the Knowell	16s	half a peck [torn]
Mr John Chollacombe for the Toote	8s	One pecke [torn]
Catherine Thorne for three Closes	8s	One pecke [torn]
John Bale the Miller for one peece of grounde	6s 8d	One quarte & [torn]

These hereafter named are agreed to this Rate

7   Risdon, *Chorographical*, p. 348.
8   DHC, 1262M/T/163.
9   Stoate, *Devon Taxes*, p. 14.

Richard Leriwill By me John Chollacombe John Roberts Nicholas Nutte
[Confirmation in Latin of the rate with the seal of the church court]

COMBE RALEIGH

One rate survives for this East Devon parish located less than two miles north of Honiton. Between 1518 and 1529 John Adams was involved in a court case which involved lands, rents and services in Combe Raleigh and Awliscombe which were intended to support the chantry. He served as the chantry priest for Our Blessed Lady and St Erasmus the Martyr which had been established in 1498 by John and Alice Bonevyle on the north side of the church.[1] At the time this church rate was made there was a dispute over the rector,[2] which was less colourful than that involving a subsequent vicar, Samuel Knott, who was accused of trying to put his hands up a parishioner's skirt.[3] Knott may have been the parish's vicar who had the most unusual character. It was said that he wore 'an old, torn, furred cap which was a very uncomely sight and made him look both ugly and ridiculous, thereby causing very much laughter in the congregation, it being a thing fitter to be worn by a player upon the stage than by a minister in the church'.[4] In 1714 John Walker wrote he lived 'a sort of retired and melancholy life, was looked upon by the generality of the common people as a conjurer. He pretended likewise to, and practiced physic. I have been informed that he was in truth an excellent scholar; but was certainly altogether unfit for any ecclesiastical cure'.[5] The British Library holds a number of rare twelfth- to fifteenth-century medical and theological manuscripts which had belonged to Knott.[6]

42. COMBE RALEIGH, Church Rate, 1596

DHC, Diocese of Exeter, Principal Registry, Combe Raleigh Church Rates, 1596

Note: The rate, a fair copy to which the signatures and signs were added in a darker ink, was written on a sheet of paper which measures approximately 6 inches in width and 14½ inches in length. The sheet has been torn along the top edge. The numerals are Roman with the exception of the year and the total sum. At the base are the rental fees for three seats.

[torn] *in the year of our Lord* 1596. 127
[torn] the day aforesaid [torn] agreed uppon by the parishioners [torn]gh aforesaid for the reparacon of theire Church there: copied and taken out of the Roll wherunto the late Lord Bishopps seale was ~~the~~ sette 8th *February in the year of our Lord* 1596 as followeth.

First the Right Worshipful Mr Serjeant Drewe for the Barton	7s 4d	Michael Sampford for Stonehaies [Stonehayes]	2s 8d
John Mantell gentleman for Ellishaies [Elishayes]	3s 3d	John Foxwell for Aller haies	2s 2d
		John Levermore for Lower Crooke [Crook]	1s 2d
John Mantell gentleman for Walles	2s 2d	Alice Foxwell for higher Crooke [Crook]	2s 2d
William Palfrey gentleman for Combe haies	2s	Richard Carpenter	22d

1   TNA, C 1/462/29, C 1/381/4 & REQ 2/8/324.
2   TNA, C 3/252/59.
3   DHC, CC178.
4   www.comberaleigh.org, accessed 3 June 2015.
5   John Walker, *An Attempt towards recovering an account of the numbers and sufferings of the clergy* (?London, 1714), II, p. 287.
6   British Library, Harley Mss 1913, 1917, 2257, 2270, 2274, 2347, 2399, 2729, 3334, 3371, 3372, 3383, 3388, 3407, 3542, 3594, 3665, 3719, 3768 and 3770.

Edward Ford for Wyndyeat [Windgate]	16d	John Mantell gentleman for the Channtery	
James Hardinge for Reddishaies [Raddishayes]	2s 1d	[Chantry]	3d
Thomas Husey	16d	Thomas Chowne	3d
John Roddon	15d	Edward Salter	3d
Hercules Willes	14d	Ellize Bussell	2d
Lawrence Vicarie for Woodhaine [Woodhayne]	17d	Phillip Lucas	1d
		Friswill Dowan	1d
Susanna Woodrowe for Jugglers land	8d	Hercules Barton for the Church house	1d ½
Robert Benett	8d	William Mynifee for Agnes Hame	2d
George Ford for Aller	10d	Richard Norcotte	1d
Augustine Lane for Lake	10d	Robert Searle	1d
John Way for Wyndyeat [Windgate]	13d	George Awton	2d
Ambrose Stephen	6d	Walter Peirce for the Parkes & Redstones	
John Shapton for Scottishaies [Scotchhayes]	10d	Close	8d
John Foxwell thelder	8d	James Hardinge for his gleabe land	4d
William Carter	7d	Alexander Searle for his gleabe land	3d
William Forwood	6d	Michael Sampford for his gleabe acre	½
William Middleton	6d		
Arundell & Rolles Esquires for Cheesway		Mark Foxwell for his seate	1d
[Cheeseway]	4s 4d	George Foxwell for his seate	1d
James Burnard for Zarte	6d	John Hardinge for his seates	1d
Robert Rowdon for the Mill	6d	*Sum total*	£1 11s 9d

The mrke of John foxwell   The marke of Argenton Middleton sideman
The mrke of Alexander Foorde Church Wardens

COMBE-IN-TEIGNHEAD

One rate survives for this parish located on the southern shore of the Teign estuary three miles from Teignmouth. In the early 1600s Tristram Risdon described 'the two Teign Heads' of 'which with high cliffs look to seawards; from which towering hills trickleth such moisture as makes the valleys for fertility inferior to few places in the county'.[1] Some 28 per cent of the population contributed to the church rate which collected pecks and bushels of grain.

43. COMBE-IN-TEIGNHEAD, Church Rate, 1600

DHC, Diocese of Exeter, Principal Registry, Combe-in-Teignhead Church Rates, 1600

Note: The rate, a fair copy, was written on one piece of vellum which measures 13 inches in width and 23 inches in length. The numerals are Roman.

Combyntinhed   The Rate of the pishe of Combyntinhed for the reparation of theare Church [obscured] as it hath ben used of old ensuing, as followeth: Coppyed out *in the year of our Lord* 1600

	Wheate	Barlye	Otes
Mr William Hockmore	one pecke	Two bushells	Two bushells
Mr John Carewe			one bushell
Joan Longn [sic]	one pecke	one pecke	one bushelle
William Kellond		Two pecks	
William Long		Two pecks	
Gregory Gardner		Two pecks	
Henry Longe		halfe pecks	on bushell
Mark Bickford		Two pecks	
William Long		one peck	one bushill
Charity Long		Two pecks	
John Godbed	one pecke		one bushell
Thomas Melberye			Three peecks
Margaret Raddone	one peecke		one bushill
Francis and margaret Radon			Two peck & halfe
Alice Poocke		half pecke	halfe bushille
James Melbery and Roger Thorne		half pecke	halfe bushill
Gregory Clampitte			a bushille
Thomas Haylere			half a bushille
Andrew Marten			one bushille
John Babb & Barbarye	two peecke		
Richard Haywood	one pecke	one peecke	one bushille
Simon Bickford	one pecke		
Peter Clampit		one pecke	one bushille
Alice Bickford and		one peecke	one bushille

---

[1] Risdon, *Chorographical*, p. 141.

for her Cotte		one pecke	
Gregory Worthey for his barten grownd Cote & myll			one bushille
Richard Haywoode	one pecke	one pecke	one bushille
Mr John Seyward	one pecke	one pecke	one bushille
William Whatawaie		Two peckes	
William Stoneman		Two peckes	
[illegible]	[torn] pecke	one pecke	one bushille
[illegible]			
[illegible]			7d
[illegible]			3d
Roger Long	one pecke	one peck & halfe	one bushill
John Melbery		halfe a pecke	halfe a bushill
John Browne		halfe a pecke	halfe a bushill
Henry & Richard Codner		one pecke	one bushille
Gregory Webber	12d		
Nicholas Thorne			one bushille
Mary Fletcher		one pecke	one bushille
Thomas Braddon		one pecke	one bushille
Peter Braddon		one pecke	one bushille
Richard Drewe			one bushille
Anthony Gotbed		one pecke	one bushelle
Oliver Tamlyne		one pecke	one bushille
ffreyswide Gunhame	one pecke	one pecke	one bushille
Margaret Cleere	one pecke		
Geoffery Long	one pecke		one bushille
Thomas Gothem			one bushille
Joan Cade		one pecke	one bushille
Christopher Bickford & Robert Stevens	one pecke	one pecke	one bushille
Barnabas Randoll	one pecke	one pecke	one bushille
Gregory Froode		one pecke	one bushille
William Taylore		one pecke	one bushille
William Frayer		one pecke	one bushille
John Gord & Wilmot Bakor	one pecke	one pecke	one bushille
Henry Blackler for the meadowe at aller			6d
Gilbert Rondille			6d
[illegible] Bickford for her [illegible]an land			8d

[second column]

Joan Phipps	2d	Nicholas Flatcher	4d
Anthony Taplye	2d	Edward Bickford	2d
Thomas Dayvd	2d	Edward Cleeve	2d
John Dayvd	[blank]	William Drewe	2d
Alice Voysaye & Alice Chudley	4d	Thomas Hubber	2d
Thomas Wills	2d	Edward Langlye	2d
John Foyle	2d	John Chade	2d
John Poule	4d	George Parker	2d
John Grabrille	2d	Roger Codner	4d
Catherine Alward	2d	John Braddon	2d
Thomas Lambord	2d	Roger Long	2d
Geoffrey Byckford	4d	Geoffrey Babb	2d

Edward Cleere	2d	Margaret Cleeve	2d
John Cawsaye	2d	Richard Bowden	2d
Henry Codner	2d	Mary Eastabrooke	2d
Christopher Tap[torn]	2d	Thomas Braddon	2d
[illegible] Fletcher	2d	Andrew Wallyes	2d
[illegible]	2d	Gregory Webber for grublond	3d
[illegible]	2d	Roger Long for Come marsh	10d
William Balle	2d	Anthony Longe for wooltocome	4d
Thomas Frayer	2d	Nicholas Codner for dwale	4d
James Frayer	2d	Robert Culling	2d

Witnessed by me Thomas *preacher of this place*
[signed by] Andrew martyn church warden
signe of William wataway side man
sign of Olliver Tamline

COOKBURY

Two rates survive for this parish located four miles north-east of Holsworthy. In about 1500 John Gay, churchwarden, was in dispute with his parishioners regarding 'Wrenne Park' which is not noted on this rate.[1] Some 15 per cent of the population contributed to the rates.

44. COOKBURY, Church Rate, 1613

DHC, Diocese of Exeter, Principal Registry, Cookbury Church Rates, 1613

Note: This rate, a fair copy, was written on a sheet of paper which measures 8 inches in width and 11 inches in length. It is endorsed '1613 Cookbury Rate'. There is a copy within at the Devon Heritage Centre which also includes parish boundaries. This rate has been torn along the upper right hand corner. The numerals are Roman with the exception of the year and the document sequence number.

Cookburie in Devon (26

A Coppie of the Rate formerlie had and made fo[torn] reparacon of the church aforesaid exhibited v[torn] Right reverent Father in god the L. Bishopp of E[torn] in his visitacon holden at Okehampton the 28th of May *in the year of our Lord* 1613

First Sir Henry Rolls knight	7s	Abraham Salterne	16d
Ellis Standon gent.	4s	John Reech	16d
Clement Huddle	4s	John Knapman	16d
William Hutchings	2s 8d	Tristerham Bremacomb	16d
Benjamin Jewell	16d	Phillip Crellake	16d
Richard Martyn	16d	John Tom thelder	20d
John Metherill	16d	Richard James Clarcke	2s 4d
Gregory Jefferie	16d	Thomas Knapman	16d
John Gaie for his tenement in Cookberie		Nicholas Simcocke	2s
towne	12d	John Gaye for his tenement at Upcott	16d
Richard Glawen *otherwise* Glandfild	12d	John Lange	20d
Nicholas Priddam	6d	Walter Bremacomb	12d
John Knight	2s 8d	Digory Peard	8d
Humphrey Jefferie of Vaggellfild [Vaglefield]	4s	Widdow Dier & Oliver Axworthie	4d
Robert Browne	16d	Roger Glawens tenement	8d

The Church Meddow given by the Ancestors of the worshipful John Arscott Esquier for ever to the reparacon of a certaine Eile in our Church.

Justment holders

Robert Morckham for walland	3s	Humphrey Jefferie for Justment pks	
Benjamin Jewell for Cundaies pke	8d	[Agistment Parks]	6d
		William Hutchings for Ashmans hill	4d
		Sum total 57s 8d	

---

[1] TNA, C 1/138/39.

[signs of] Nyatt Cragoe Churchwarden *John* Metherill Sideman
thus witnessed Richard Oxenham *clerk*

45. COOKBURY, Church Rate, early 1600s

DHC, Diocese of Exeter, Principal Registry, Cookbury Church Rates, early 1600s

Note: The rate, a fair copy, was written on a sheet of paper which measures approximately 6 inches in width and 14¾ inches in length. The numerals are Roman.

Cookbury

A Copy of the Church Rate as it is yearle gathered.

Richard Rolle gen[tleman]	7s	Joan James	16d
Ellis Standon	4s	Susan Swanson	20d
Clement Huddle	4s	Jo: Lange	20d
Humphrey Jeffry	4s	Walter Brenacombe	12d
Jo: Knight for Weeke [Wick]	2s 8d	Jo: Knight for Cookbury towne	2s 8d
Joan Brondene	16d	Benjamin Jewell	16d
Gideon Venton	16d	Gregory Jeffry	16d
Phillip Crellake	16d	Nyatt Crago	16d
Katherine Burnard	16d	Jo: Prydham	6d
Honor Brenacombe	16d	Elizabeth Peard *wid.*	8d
John Knapman	16d	Richard Glowen	12d
Wm Syncocke	2s	Jo: Gay	12d
Jo Gay sen.	16d	Roger Glowen	8d
Jo: James	2s 4d	Metherells Tenement	16d

Justments

Phillippe Morkombe *wid*	3s	Condyes	8d
Humphrey Jeffry	6d	Oliver Axworthy	2d
Ashmant hill	4d	Ellen Dyar	2d

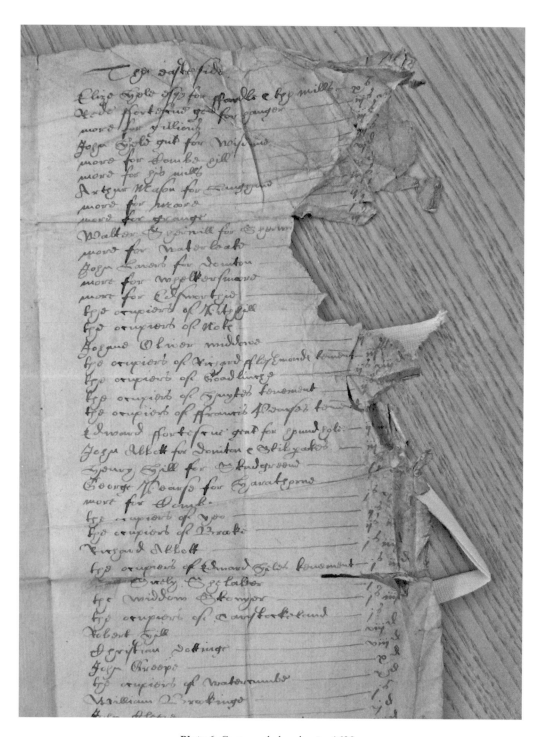

Plate 6. Cornwood church rate, 1628.

CORNWOOD

One rate survives for this parish located ten miles north-east of Plymouth. In 1630 Thomas Westcote noted in his *A View of Devonshire* that Slade, the first property noted on the church rate, was 'inhabited by a worshipful race of long continuance of the Coles'.[1] Henry Smith, 'a man of worth and learning', was appointed vicar the year following this rate and during the Civil War was forcibly removed from his post. He escaped from his persecutors by fleeing out of a garret window.[2] The contributors to the church rate were nearly 10 per cent of the parish population from whom a considerable number of legal suits reached the London Courts. This included a mid-sixteenth-century dispute between the vicar, who was also treasurer of Exeter Cathedral, and Walter Hele regarding the rental of houses in the parish.[3] Before this four parishioners had argued over alleged assaults and forcible entry[4] and about this time the Countess of Devon had her oxen seized which were grazing on Penmore Common.[5]

46. CORNWOOD, Church Rate, 1628

DHC, Diocese of Exeter, Principal Registry, Cornwood Church Rates, 1628

Note: This rate, a fair copy, was written on a sheet of paper which has been folded to make four pages, each of which measures approximately 6 inches in width and 15½ inches in length. There has been considerable damage to the right hand side. The numerals are Roman. It is endorsed 'Cornewood pishe. A rate for the maintenance of the Church 1628', and in a later hand 'Cornwood Rate 1628'.

Cornewoode pishe the West side [torn]

A rate for the maintenance of the Ch[torn]

The ocupiers of Slade & the mills	[torn]	more for pkeland	2s
Richard Bellman gentleman for Dallamoore		more for Fosters tenement	1s 4d
[Delamore]	2s 4d	Adam Williams gentleman for Stert	3s
more for Rooke [Rook]	2s 8d	more for his tenement in Cornetowne	
more for hellamoore	2s 6d	[Corntown]	1s 4d
more for Church pke	6d	more for Churchtowne	1s 4d
more for Crosse Meddowe & the gaule	8d	William Pearse for Rake [Rook]	2s 4d
John Hele gentleman for Hele & North hele		more for Hangers tenement	8d
	3s 8d	more for Tokermans tenement	8d
more for Denells [Dendles]	1s	more for Hingstons tenement	8d
more for Rode pitts	1s	Mary Rice widdow for Southhele	3s
The ocupiers of Mr Sprats tenement	4s 8d	The ocupiers of Mr Wakhams tenement	1s 4d
William Cholwitche gentleman for		Richard Foster	2s 4d
Cholwichetowne [Cholwichtown] and		Geoffrey Edwardes	2s 8d
lower Bromewich [Broomage]	6s	Soloman Andrew for Gadabrooke	
more for higher Bromewich	2s	[Goodabrook]	1s 4d

1   Westcote, *View of Devonshire*, p. 384.
2   Walker, *An Attempt*, II, p. 355.
3   TNA, C 1/1381/68.
4   TNA, STAC 2/29/164.
5   TNA, REQ 2/5/334.

more for Pitmans pkes	6d	more for his howse at Crose	2d
the ocupiers of Hane	1s 4d	Richard Worth	8d
the ocupiers of Highehowse	1s 4d	Walter Saugwill	6d
the widdowe Higgons	1s 4d	Edmund Symons	6d
Walter Sherwill of Northwood	1s 4d	Arthur Tonson	6d
John Stephen	1s 4d	more for Gabb hill	4d
John Browne for his tenement	6d	Eleanor Skerte	2d
more for Austine Beeres tenement	1s	William Foster	6d
John Mason	1s	Mark Tayler	2d
Thomas Greepe	1s	Thomas Thorne	2d
Phillip Pearse	6d	William Hanaford	2d
Thomas Turpine	1s 4d	Margaret Foster widdowe	2d
John Bamlett	8d	Henry Abbott	2d
George Woolcombe	8d	Eleanor Burch	2d
John Browne Junior	8d	James Beere for his howse at heathfield	2d
Elizabeth Skert	8d	John Symons	2d
John Tucker	8d	William Browne	2d
Henry Kent Harris tenement	6d	John Bowden	2d
more for Ferne land	6d		

[page 2]

[torn]n Blackler	2d	Thomas Hanaford	6d
[torn]e occupiers of Berryes tenenet	2d	John Barret	6d
the ocupiers of Poyles howse	2d	James Hanaford	6d
Robert Woolcombe	2d	Michael Harris	6d
William Burche	2d	Digory Baskervile	6d
John Gibb	6d	Richard Higgons	6d
Thomas Browne	6d		

[page 3]

The easte side

Elize Hele esquire for Fardle [Fardel] & the mills	10s	the ocupiers of Francis Pearses tenement	2s
Rede Fortescue gentleman for hanger	3s 7d	Edward Fortescue gentleman for hound hole	2s 4d
more for gillions	3s	John Abbott for Doniton & Stib parkes	3s 6d
John Hele gentleman for Wisdom	3s	Henry Hill for Stadgreene	1s
more for Combe hill	6d	George Pearse for Harathorne	1s 8d
more for his mills	6d	more for Combe	1s 6d
Arthur Mason for Langhame [Langham]	3s	the ocupiers of yeo	2s
more for moore	2s	the ocupiers of Brooke	2s 6d
more for grange	1s	Richard Abbott	1s 4d
Walter Sherwill for Sherw[torn]		the ocupiers of Edward Heles tenement	1s 3d
more for Waterleake	[torn]	Sicely Shelalier	1s [torn]
John Lavers for Doniton [Dinnaton]	[torn]	the widdow Skowyer	1s 4d
more for Whelkersmoore [Wilkeysmoor]	[torn]	the ocupiers of Tavystockeland	1s
more for Edsworthie [Yadsworthy]	[torn]	Robert Hill	8d
the ocupiers of Pitchhill [Pit Hill]	[torn]	Christian Dottinge	8d
the ocupiers of Nots	[torn]	John Greepe	10d
Joan Oliver widdowe	3s [torn]	the ocupiers of Watercumbe [Watercombe]	10d
the ocupiers of Richard Fleshmonds tenement	3s	William Brookinge	1s
the ocupiers of Goadlinche	2s 8d	John Cleeve	6d
the ocupiers of Huytes tenement	2s 8d	Christopher Welche	4d

John Skidston	4d	John Denborde	4d
Richard Wilkey	6d	William Collinge	4d
the ocupiers of Stone	2s 4d	John Davy	2d
John Holmes	6d	John Wyett	2d
Nicholas Abbott of Doniton	4d	Christopher Badford	2d
Thomas Langford & William Abbott	6d	of John Mayes wife	3d
Nicholas Abbott of Fursgoycot	4d		

Plate 7. Monument to Lady Elizabeth Harris, 1633.

CORNWORTHY

One rate survives for this parish located on the west bank of the river Dart and four miles upriver from Dartmouth. In about 1558 parishioners disputed their tithes with John Peter.[1] It was also at that time that Edward Harris was at variance with William Giles regarding a share in a ship bought of Thomas Stuckley.[2] The parishioners also went to court regarding their church house which had been given by the ancestors of Sir Peirs Edgcombe.[3] The Harris family were listed first in both this rate and in the subsidy of 1581.[4]

47. CORNWORTHY, Military Rate, c.1592

DHC, 3799M/3/O/4/50, pages 32–3

Note: This rate is recorded in a volume with pages approximately 7¾ inches in width and 12 inches in length.The numerals are Roman. The armour for the survey included almain rivets, bandoleers, corslets, head pieces, jacks and morions while for weapons there were bills, bows, calivers, daggers, halberds, muskets, pikes, sallets, shear hooks, splints and swords. Twenty-eight men and one woman were assessed for this rate.

Cornworthie

The Lady Harris a Corsl ps a musket ps
Robert Tookerman a musket ps
John Richards a Call ps sword & dagger
Edward Luke a musket ps a bill
John Efford a muskett a Corsl ps a bill
Thomas Efford a Callr ps a bill
Robert Soryer a bow sheaf arr sword a bill
Robert Parrat a paire of almainer 2 swords 2 daggers a Callr ps a musket ps a Corslett
Christopher Sharpham a Callr ps
John Parratt a musket ps
James Tuckerman a musket a ps a Corsl ps
John Holdiche a Callr ps a Corsl ps a Carare
John Crease a musket ps
[page 33] John Curtise & William Parrat a muskett ps a Corsl ps
John Coake a bill a dagger
Richard Pomeroye gentleman a musket ps
John White a bill a paire of splints
Christopher Madford a bill a sallett
Edward Penny a musket ps
John Yelland a sword dagger a bill a sallet she[a]f arr[ows] a Callr ps
Henry Fortescue gentleman a musket ps
Stephen Waymoth a musket ps
Stephen Holdiche a musket ps

---

[1]   TNA, C 3/42/76 & C 3/38/90.
[2]   TNA, C 1/1440/10-12.
[3]   TNA, C 2/Eliz/C6/28.
[4]   Stoate, *Devon Taxes*, p. 55.

Anstice Hooper a halbert
John Pearse a Callr ps
Peter Waymoth a musket & bandalere
Samuel Waymoth sword & dagger
English Farewood a hedpece

The psihe armour Pikes 2, Corsli ps 1, almanr 4, blacke armes 1, musket ps 1

CORYTON

Two militia rates survive for this West Devon parish located twelve miles south-west of Okehampton and seven miles north of Tavistock. In 1630 Thomas Westcote wrote in *A View of Devonshire* that this parish was 'a place of no great note'. He also noted that the Coryton family had moved to Cornwall.[1]

48. CORYTON, Militia Rates, 1643

DHC, 189M-1/F8/3

Note: This rate was written on a sheet of paper which measures nearly 12 inches in width and 7¾ inches in length. The numerals are Roman. The heading refers to the Grand Subsidy of May 1643 which was concerned with Ireland. About 3 per cent of the population contributed to the rates.

Coriton pish

The money wch Thomas Steert, Walter Hollock & William Nicole gathered of the Gransipsidie rate wthin the pish of Coriton having neither rate nor Warrant but gathered it for the militia wth out any authoryty

Francis Buller Esqr.	£0 15s	Anne Beale widdow	0 13s 0
William Williams clerk	£1 0	Richard Doidg	0 11s 0
Thomas Steert	0 16s 6d	John Harry	0 6s 6d
Walter Hollock	0 16s 0	John Doidg	0 6s 0
William Williams	0 18s 0	Pancras Courteis	0 3s 0
William Nicole	0 16s 0	Pascoe hearne widdow	0 5s 0
Thomas Bickell	0 18s 0	Jasper Vinton	0 1s 6d
Digory Hore	0 13s 0	William Pophom	0 1s 6d
['Justment holders' in margin]			
William With for the mills	0 10s 0	William Reccord for his kill	0 3s 0
William Williams of Sourton	0 4s 6d	Arthur Collen	0 1s 0
Hugh Fortescu esqr.	0 1s 6d	Thomasine Gloine	0 3s

Some is nine Pounds & fowerteen shillings Besides two horses Thomas Steert put forth out of the pish when the militia was going for Stratton.

Martiall rates wch Thomas Steert Walter Holles William Nicole gathered for the militia

William Williams Clerk	18s 2d	Pascoe Hearn	4s 8d
Thomas Steert	8s 2d	John Harris	4s 0
Walter Hollock	11s 8d	Ann Beale widdow	7s 6d
William Nicole	9s 8d	Arthur Collin	0 10d
William Williams	9s 8d		
Thomas Bickell	8s 2d		
Digory Hore	8s 2d		
Richard Doidg	6s 2d		
John Doidg	3s 6d		

---

[1] Westcote, *View of Devonshire*, p. 355.

['Justment holders' in margin]
William With   8s 8d   Hugh Fortescu esqr.   1s 2d

Some is Five pounds six shillings & two pence
Besides one rate more wch Thomas Steert gathered since for Carryage of his owne hay to
Ockehampton to the Militia Army when the weare for Stratton he gathered this rate since
Whitsontide.

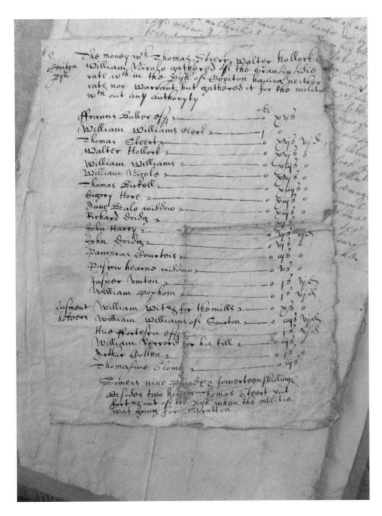

Plate 8. Coryton militia rate, 1643.

CREDITON

Detailed Elizabethan and early Stuart taxation records survive for this market town located eight miles north-west of Exeter. Crediton's history relating to financial administration has been examined more fully in pages xvii to xxxix.

In 1549 the scribe used Kirton, the alternative name for Crediton, as had John Leland seven years earlier when he noted 'there is a pretty [prosperous] market in Kirton. The town useth clothing and most thereby liveth'.[1] A century later Tristram Risdon wrote it was 'the principal town upon this river [the Creedy]; an ancient borough, seated in the heart of the shire, partaking of the best, both for air and soil, of a red mould, and such as for the most part is accounted fertile land. Famous was this place in the time of the Saxons for an episcopal see here erected, in which sundry bishops successivley sat, until the reign of Edward, that holy king and confessor',[2] In 1644 a Royalist commented that Crediton was called 'in the common manner' Kirton and that it was 'a great lowsy town, a corporate town governed by a bailiff'.[3]

Sandford was a chapelry of Crediton and its parishioners were included in the latter's tax lists. In some they were separated from those who lived in the parish of Crediton. In 1559 it was claimed that 'there containeth in Kirton parish the number of 16 hundred people & besides six hundred in Sandford which is annexed unto Crediton and a daughter to the same even now at this day'.[4] The records include a long series of warden accounts, which specify the income streams available to the corporation, which cover the years 1550 through to the 1770s.[5] The scribe from 1551 to 1583 was Hugh Deane, clerk to the twelve governors.[6]

49. CREDITON, Church Rate, 1549

DHC, 1660A/0/A/4

Note: This rate was written, on sheets of paper which were folded to make twelve pages 4 inches in width and 12 inches in length, during the year of the Prayer Book Rebellion in which Crediton played a key part. The rebels gathered in the town and a skirmish took place in which several barns were set on fire in the king's cause. It was later claimed that 'The Barns of Crediton' became a rallying cry 'flaming the beacon of insurrection'. No comment was made regarding damage to the church either at the time or in the heading to this rate.[7] However, the the wardens' accounts for 1551 noted that the church governors paid John Courtenay and Edward Ford forty shillings 'for our bell clappers and Sandford bell clappers of them bought upon a gift from the king to Arthur Champernon Knight and John Chichester Esquire this yere'.[8] In 1550 Thomas and John Harrys were granted additional time to pay their debts to the crown because 'they were spoiled in the

[1] Lucy Toulmin-Smith (ed.), *The Itinerary of John Leland* (London, 1907), p. 239.
[2] Risdon, *Chorographical*, pp. 97–8.
[3] C. E. Long (ed.), *Diary of the Marches of the Royal Army* (Cambridge, 1997 edn), p. 40.
[4] DHC, 1660A/12.
[5] DHC, 1660A/8-56.
[6] Beatrix F. Cresswell, 'Hugh Deane, clerk to the governors of the corporation, 1551–1583', *DAT* LIV (1922), 199–204.
[7] Frances Rose-Troup, *The Western Rebellion of 1549* (London, 1913), pp. 140–9; Prebendary Smith, 'The early history of Christianity', *DAT* XIV (1882), 198.
[8] Cresswell, *Wardens' Accounts*, p. 5. I am grateful to Tony Gale for this reference.

last commotion by the rebels'.[9] Thomas Harrys was recorded in this rate without a contribution. It is not known if Crediton lost any documents but Plymouth's town papers were burned during the rebellion and one individual in Hatherleigh, twenty miles from Crediton, lost a lease because of the 'late rebellion'.[10] The rate covered the town and three tithings but not those of Sandford.

The writing is unusual in several respects. There are two styles of secretary hand: the last three pages were possibly written by a second scribe or a different implement was used. There were also two forms of accounting. On the first page the scribe tabulated the sums in Roman numerals (xviiis iid) as he did on the third page (xliiis xd *ob*). He also employed the system which in 1910 Charles Trice Martin, then Assistant Keeper at the Public Record Office, referred to as 'an arrangement of dots'. This separated numerals into four columns; these were pounds, shillings, pence and farthings. On the principal line, and the line below, each dot counted as a unit. Dots above the line on the left hand side in the pence column counted for six units. Dots above the line on the left hand side in the pound and shillings columns counted for ten while those on the right hand side counted for five units.[11] The Crediton scribe also calculated his totals in Roman numerals and differences between these sums may be a reflection of the nature of the account as a working document.

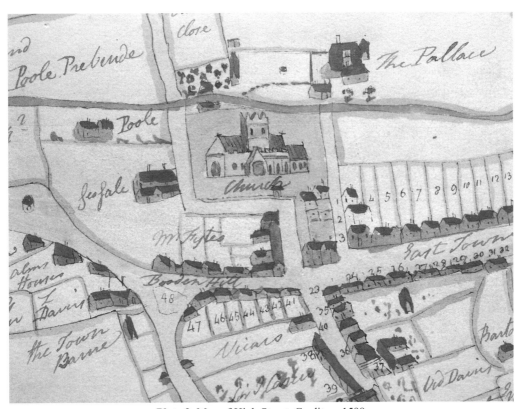

Plate 9. Map of High Street, Crediton, 1598.

[9]   DHC, PC2/4/240.
[10] Rose-Troup, *Western Rebellion*, p. 130; TNA, C1/1726/1-4.
[11] Charles Trice Martin, *The Record Interpreter* (London, 1910), xii–xiii.

The E[a]st Towne of Kerton

Mony Gevyn towardye the rep[at]acons of the Churche *in the third year of our Lord* Edward *Sixth*

John Rawe	2d	William Chase	4d
Harry Kensall	2d	Margaret Robyns	1d
Geoffrey Merfyld	2d	Sulpie Newcomb	12d
William Chagford	1d	Ric' Chnlder	4d
Robt Bodlegh	4d	John Wotton in Pe tethinge	2d
Richard Middelton	8d	Robt Cryce	6d
John Marshall	1d	John Chudlaye	4d
John Richard	1d	John Honywyll	2d
John Moggrege	8d	Elizabeth Winter	2d
Edward Smyth	12d	Robt Clarke	4d
William Lee	4d	Willm Pawnsford	4d
Thomas Chamber	8d	Amy Crosse	8d
John Cornyshe	4d	Ric L'nne	4d
William Laye	12d	William Shilston Junior	4d
John [worn]	12d	John Quashe	12d
Ric' Gibb	2d	Gilbert Slader	12d
John Norden	2d	[total]	18s 2d
James Nevyll	4d		

[page 2]

Willm ~~Calsyll~~ Cawle	~~1d~~ ½	+ Ric Bawdon	1d
John Whytrawe	1d	Joan Becher	[blank]
Elizabeth Symons	1d	John Raynold	2d
John Dirler	1d	John Prudham	[blank]
	. .|	+ Michael Browing	1d
	. . .| . . . . [18s 4d]	+ Robert Peritt	2d
no. Tybitt Molle	[blank]	James Verrytt	[blank]
Thomas Brownyng	2d	+ Richard Whytrawe	1d
Thomas Farewell	[blank]	+ William Barber	1d
John Crier	[blank]	+ Simon Shapcote	2d
John Fylipp	[blank]	+ John Byrche	1d
Humphrey Spurwaye	[blank]	John Clarke	[blank]
Nicholas Bokingham	12d	Mathe Snell	[blank]
Patrick Kyng	[blank]	+ Alyc Wynter	4d
John Gurnard	[blank]	[dots crossed through] + John Webber A	
+ John Shore	4d	bolhand	4d
+ John Caron	2d		. . .|. [4s 1d]
Tamsin Edbury	[blank]	+ Elizabeth Rewe	2d
Derek Trose	8d	Thomas Clogg	[blank]
~~Nicholes Kere~~		John Miller	[blank]
John Sawnder	[blank]	no Willm Moxhaye at Credi.	[blank]

[page 3]

The Tething of Kerton

John Bond	3s 4d	William Pawnsford	4d
Roger Burshe	2d	Matho Edbury	20d
John Gullocke of Chedingbroke [Chiddenbrook]		William Mayne	3s 4d
	4d	William Shute	[blank]
Thomas Bichill	[blank]	Christopher Clarke	2d

Robert Cawe	6d	John Butler	2d
Alyc Carrs	2d	Phillip Alkocke	12d
Robert Browning	4d	Christopher his wiffe	8d
John Pawnsford	4d	James Drwe	1d
Robt Middelton	4d	John Adams	2d
William Middelton	2d	Peter Lengdon	12d
John Cloyn	2d	John Lang	[blank]
John Waye	12d	John Kensall	[blank]
Gilbert Shylston	8d	William Lobdon	8d
Robert Brodmad	4d	[dots crossed through] John Ford	12d
Nicholas Bremrigge	20d	Bawdon bugbroke	4d
William Lake	12d	Margery Bremrigge	4d
Robt Wolwaye	12d	. .|. .|. .	[£2 2s 4d]
Rich Rawe	12d	|. . *total* 44s	[illegible]
Gilbert Browning	1d		

[page 4]

The Tething of Wodland

Mathe[w] Gullocke	12d	Alson Crosse	12d
John Gullocke Junior	1d	Harey 2 maydys	2d
Bennet Burnell	4d	no. Harry Gullocke	[blank]
Rose Burnell	2d	no. John Venycombe	[blank]
Richard Collehole	4d	Marian Trend	4d
John Burgyn	[blank]	Joan Temlett	2d
Harry Truman	20d	John Wrayford	12d
John Gullocke of Winstawe [Winstout]	4d	Too of his maydes	2d
Thomas Frawnce	12d	William Skynner	4d
Robert Lengdon	2d	[blank] Skynner his son	[blank]
John Lengdon	2d	no. William Halse	[blank]
William Bayle	8d	no. William Bradlee Senior	4d
John Bayle	2d	Lucy Estabroke by Mal.	6d 4d
John Delve	3d	Thomas Flud	4d
Ric' Venycomb	4d	James Bayle	3d
Edmund Venycomb	4d	Joan Sowthcote	2d
John Sowthecote	1d	Catherine Canne	1d
William Collehole	1d	John Frawnes	4d
Annys Collehole	1d	Thomas Truman	4d
John Prudham Senior	4d	Rc Prudham	1d
John Prudham Junior	2d		

John Prudham John Gullocke and Racherd Collehole Collecters Recayved   13s 6d' 14s 7d

[page 5]

The Tething of Uford

John Pytwod	20d	Robt Venycomb	8d
John Venycomb	12d	Thomas Reve	4d
William Lee	12d	John Strang	[blank]
Roger Burrayge	[blank]	John Burrage	4d
Robt Strange	8d	Phillip Burrage	2d
Hugh Whyte	4d	Robt Lyngdon	4d
Walter Strang	8d	Phillip Gullocke	16d
John Exmbere	2d	John Gulloc	2d
John Lee of holcomb [Hollacombe]	6d	Walter Waylshe	4d

Sible Lengdon	6d	John Truman	12d
Harry Lengdon	4d	Robt Gullocke	2d
Robt Waryn	12d	Robt Comyng	12d
no Joan Waye widdo	2d	John Borage	4d
Nicholas Temlett	2d	Richard Waryn	4d
Thomas Temlett	2d	John Exmbere	4d
John Drayton	4d	no. Richarde Jurdyn Widdo	[blank]
Cicily Gornard	8d	Robt Hoke	12d
Thomas Lee	2d	. .	
Richerd Nucomb	4d	. . .	[18s]
John Flud	4d		

[page 6]

Uford

John Lee of Gunston [Gunstone] 20d		William Pytwod	2d
Walter Waye	16d	Ric Dayman	2d
John Hoke	[blank]	Margaret Waylshe	1d
John Dicleg	8d	Mawte Wele	2d
Peter Strang	2d	Roger Reve	1d
John Burgyn	[blank]	William Reve	8d
John Diclegge Junior	2d	Richard Frawnce	4d
Robt Waring Junior	2d	John Gullocke Junior	1d
William Wering	12d	John Quycke	1d
John Reve	4d	Walter Lee	4d
Catherine Bowden	1d	Roger Laye	2d
Eleanor Flud	2d	. |	
Peter Warryn	2d	. . . | . .	[8s 2d]

Thomas Reve William Lee & Robt Hoker Collectere
payde of this tething   25s 9d

[page 7]

The burro of Kerton

Richard Maunder	2d	James Braye	2d
William Cornyshe	4d	Margyt Holmes	2d
William Bakyr	1d	John Leyngdon	8d
Robt Ragge	[blank]	Robt Basse	2d
Rose Bullyn	1d	Robt skynner	1d
John Marod	2d	Simon Rogyr	4d
Garot Aslyn	2d	Robt Chyse	2d
John Skyre	2d	Phillip Conebye	16d
Nicholas Moxhaye	12d	Phillip Elyott	6d
William Shilston	3d	John Gore	[blank]
Nicholas Roger	4d	John horwyll	4d
Humphrey slee	4d	William Keman	2d
John Mannder	4d	John Chobbe	[blank]
Gilbert sladyr	[blank]	Davye Cheryton	6d
George sladyr	2d	William Downe	[blank]
George Champon	4d	John Settyll	4d
John Gurrode Spycer	2d	Rycharde Hyll	[blank]
William hurston	[blank]	Robt downe	1d
John Venycomb	22d	. . .| . .	[14s 2d]
William Leche	8d		

[page 8]

John Gye the Eldar	1d	Rycharde doderyge	12d
Peter Smale	[blank]	Thomas harrys	[blank]
John Pawnsforde	4d	John Waylshe	[blank]
Thomas perse	2d	Thomas Hunt	12d
John Ven	4d	Walter parre	2d
Ryc Braye	4d	John Bonde	[blank]
John Petron	[blank]	Phillip squyre	4d
John Rawe	4d	William squyre	2d
Edmund Smale	2d	William prescon	2d
John Gye the yonnger	1d	John Luxton	1d ½
William Payne	3d	Thomas Morrys	12d
Thomas Perse	[blank]	Ryc sowthecotte	2d
Ryc Balhachyt	2d	John Julett	2d
William Balhachyt	2d	Alice Barle	2d
Walter Northecot	16d	John Bond	2d
John Dyer	2d	John Charde	2d
Humphrey Gerde	2d	Edward Allyn	2d
Joan Prestle	[blank]	John Pope	12d
William honywyll	4d		
John Clawe	[blank]	.| .|	
Robt Coocke	2d	. . .|. .|. . [10s 11½d]	
John Ellys	2d	. . |. .|	
Thomas Basse	[blank]	.	
John Wellcote	4d		

[page 9]

John Shute	4d	Walter Moore	2d
Roger Darte	1d	John Whyterow	½
John Baron	4d	John Samyn	2d
John Brodmede	1d	Isabel Laueryns	1d
John Tokefylde	2d	William Treveryn	1d
John Whytte	4d	Thomas Gullocke	2d
Davye Pemeton	1d	Thomas Delfe	1d
Gelys Tokar	2d	Thomas Bushe	2d
John Dere young man	4d	John Roche	4d
John Goslynge	2d	John Herrys younge man	2d
Rycharde Can	2d	John Shaver	2d
Ryc Broke	2d	Walter Baren	1d
Walter dene	2d	Thomas Garett	[blank]
John pope younger	2d		
Harry palmar	4d	. . .|. .|	
Thomas Ryde	1d	. |. .| . [4s 4½d] [total] 29s 6d	
Nicholas Moryfelde	[blank]		

[page 10]

The Tething of Rudge

Robert Trobrydge	6s 8d	Ryc Weste	[blank]
John Bodelaye	10s	Pedrycke Foyle	8s
John Dunscombe	16d	John Whyte	4d
Elyis Lee	2s	John West Senior	4d

Alys West Junior	[blank]	John Gescon	[blank]
Thomas Rawe	[blank]	William Gescon	[blank]
John Bodelye At Rudge	12d	John Gryne	8d
Thomas Sannder	[blank]	John Benet	2d
Ryc Lee	8d	Thomas Basse	12d
John Averye	8d	Ryc Lake	[blank]
Joan Baker wydoo	[blank]	John Strange	2d
James Geston Senior	12d	John Payne	[blank]
James Geston Junior	[blank]		
Joan Northecotte Wyddo	[blank]	. . .|. .|	
John Northecote	[blank]	. |. .|. .	[total] 19s 6d

50. CREDITON, Easter Book, 1574

DHC, 1660A/O/A/193

Note: The account has been written on twelve pieces of paper which have been golded and stitched with white thread in order to provide a booklet of twenty-four pages which are 4 inches in width and 12 inches in length. The numerals are Roman. In 1550 a lease of twenty-one years had been assigned from John Harrys, Crediton clothier, to Griffin Ameredethe, for the tithes of the prebend of Pruscombe of grain, wool, lambs and 'all spiritualities'.[12] Seven years later the Archbishop of Canterbury granted John Nicholles, clerk rector of Crediton, the tithes of grain, wool, lambs, other tithes, oblations, 'profits and ecclesiastical and spiritual emoluments' from Crediton and Sandford. They were then worth £122 7s 10½d.[13] In this Easter Book the scribe used horizontal lines to separate parishioners. These have been retained as underscoring. His intention may have been to show separate households; the 1,271 individuals noted in the urban parts of the parish were living in some 162 households in West Town, 163 in East Town and twenty-two in Town Tithing. There may have been as many as 347 households. Unlike the Easter Book for Clayhanger, this account was restricted to collecting offerings of two pence from each adult.

---

[12]   DHC, 1660A, two unnumbered deeds (listed on page 6 of collection catalogue in searchroom).

[13]   DHC, 1660A/9. The grant was made on 12 Nov. 1557. In 1563 John Chichester was given rights to the prebends of Aller and (Kerswill) Westsampford: DHC, DD1629.

Plate 10. Mediaeval roof boss, Holy Trinity Church, Crediton.

A bocke off East[er] Duties for the east & Weast town & town tethinge 1574

The Weast Towne

2d John Cowke
2d and his wyffe
2d Christopher Clowltte
~~Jone~~ Clowlltte
John Comb Widower
Richerd ellis & his wyff
ellys basse & his wyffe
2d Wydow Cornyshe
X ~~sybly cornyshe~~
2d John cornyshe
and his wyffe

[page 2]

2d annes Deman widowe
2d Katherine Whyttrowe widowe
2d Andrew trencher
2d and his Wyffe
2d Walter Deane
2d and his Wyffe
2d thomas myller
2d and his Wyffe
2d Elizabeth myller

2d george hamatte
2d and his wyffe
2d gilbert ballom 2d
2d geoffrey myryfild
2d and his Wyffe
2d Joan meryfild
2d thomas maryne 3d
2d thomas playe 2d
2d Jane a mayd
2d William renolde
[total]   2s 6d   8d

2d Edmund Venycomb & his Wyfe
2d nicholas davye
2d and his Wyffe
2d nicholas hore
2d and his wyffe
2d Edward hore
2d Richard hore
2d John marwode
2d and his Wyffe

1d Richard Marrowde
2d John Roche
2d and his Wyff
2d John Waye

[page 3]

2d John Dullinge
2d and his Wyffe
2d thomas ford
+ Edmund Kensall
2d thomas Kensall
2d Thomas Roger
2d ~~simon Rapientt~~
['edward pery' inserted]
2d and his Wyff
2d edward perry 3d
2d anthony buller
2d michael bykely
2d John perry
2d mary Pope
2d thomas more

[page 4]

2d Alice Bradmed Widowe
2d Walttin Bradmed
2d John myller bangeles
2d Phillip smytth
2d and his Wyff
2d Rose morrys
2d Annes Butte 4d
2d Elizabeth swete
2d Walter shylston
2d thomas shore
mary his doghter

[page 5]

2d sybly omfre widowe
2d Rose Bullinge Widowe
2d nicholas slee
2d Richard Marwode
2d simon brocke
2d and his Wyffe
2d Katherine trend 2d
2d Alice more widowe
2d John bykly a pore man
2d nycoll Lydford 2d
+ John lydford
2d Alice mylford
2d thomas champeyn
2d and his wyff
2d John Dyklege
2d bykly 1d

2d edward Dunster
2d harry Venycomb
2d Richard Roche

[totals] 3s 14d

2d John Skear
2d and his Wyffe
2d William Skear
2d edward skear
2d mary annery 2d
2d William morys
2d and his Wyffe
~~Myghell marttin~~
2d John farwell 5d
2d Richard mogridge 5d
2d a servannt of his more
2d Joan softon
2d Joan Jones 2d

[totals] 4s 2d   [total] 17d

2d Richard Leye
2d and his Wyffe
2d Hugh haywode
2d Kirste Rogers widow
2d Elizabeth Roger
2d John Roger
2d and his Wyffe
2d Alice Roger
2d Robert Led
2d Eleanor Garland

[totals] 3s 4d   [total] 10d

2d William hurston
2d and his Wyffe
2d John Robins
2d William John pinson first
2d and his Wyffe
2d thomas berry 3d
4d William smyth & his Wyffe
John veyncomb
2d and his Wyffe
2d John venycomb
2d Margaret ~~Joan~~
2d Owins Wyffe   1s 9d
2d Joan Owins
2d Gilbartt
[totals]   4s 8d   [total] 8d

[page 6]

2d nicholas Leche
2d and his Wyffe
2d Mably leche
2d Alice boltt
2d John leche
2d thomas huntt
2d and his Wyffe
2d John huntt
2d a mayd svanntt
2d John Isake
1d Mary his doghter
2d thomas fowler
2d and his Wyffe
2d thomas duke
2d stephen skelhorne

+ Jone
2d dukes Wyffe shalbe
2d annes watt
2d Joan Luxton widowe
2d elizabeth luxton
a mayd more
2d John panchard
2d and his Wyffe
2d Alice panchard
2d Alice fare 2d
2d florens his mayd 1d
2d John legg
2d and his Wyffe

[totals] 4s 3d   [total] 3d

[page 7]

2d Randell
2d and his Wyffe
2d Marion small 2d
+ sybly [illegible crossed through]
2d Robert delve 4d
2d John berry
2d and his Wyffe
nicholas berry
2d george berry
2d Jane berry 2d
Robert horwill
Nicholas Rede
2d 2d nicholas delve
2d and his Wyffe
2d Richard Sweete
nicholas myller
and his Wyffe

2d John Walshe
2d and his Wyffe
2d Christopher Row 2d
2d Richard Walshe 2d
2d Joan Basse Widowe
2d John Petherton
2d and his wyffe
2d Joan his mayde 2d
2d Joan Down widowe
2d Mary Down
Joan Down
2d Simon Roger
2d and his Wyffe
2d Gawain cowch
2d and his Wyffe

[totals] 3s 4d   [total] 13d

[page 8]

2d Margaret Webbe Widowe
2d Alice skinner
2d Widowe Chese
2d anne chese
2d William Pogier
2d and his Wyffe
2d Robert browne
2d Phillip Cony'by
2d and his Wyffe
2d Robert more 4d
2d frysyld tukfild
2d Pascoe Rapientt 4d
2d John Thorne
2d William Collins

2d and his Wyffe
2d Alice Delve
2d Richard more 4d
2d Peter Webber
2d thomas plushen
for his Wyffe
2d John Venner
2d nicholas meryfild
2d and his Wyffe
2d Walter meryfild
2d Margaret meryfild
2d Richard Wyghte

[totals] 4s 2d 12d

[page 9]

2d Richard more
2d and his Wyffe
2d Richard more
2d Joan More
2d Michael Haus
2d and his Wyffe
2d Watt' Ellyott
2d and his Wyffe
2d Robert brownscomb
2d and his Wyffe
2d George cokshed
2d and his Wyffe
2d Eleanor cockshed

2d John Whytte 4d
2d John farsdon 2d
2d John taylore 1d
2d William dodrydge
2d and his Wyffe
2d William Dodrygde
2d John Warringe
2d and his Wyffe
2d Alice Warringe
2d Elizabeth Lorng Widowe
Watt avery and his Wyffe

[totals] 3s 10d 7d

[page 10]

2d nicholas myller
2d and his wyffe
2d the Wydowe smale
2d mary small
2d and his Wyffe emlyn
margett Cheryton
1d Robert cheryton and his Wyff
2d thomas gillocks
2d for his daughter
2d John Prowes
2d and his Wyffe
2d John Holway
2d and his Wyffe
2d clementt frenchen

2d and his Wyffe
2d adam scott
2d and his Wyffe
2d mary broke Widowe
2d Phillip broke
2d Phillip brayd
2d and his wyffe
2d John Upcott
2d Joan his mayd
2d Kateren Davy Widowe
2d Richard ford
2d and his Wyffe

[total] 4s 1d

[page 11]

2d marian collins Widowe
2d Joan Wodhear Widowe
2d Joan Hyll Wydowe
1d John Wodhore
1d James Penyton
2d and his Wyffe
2d Harry Huntt
2d and his Wyffe
2d Joan Huntt
2d Stephen bowdyn
2d and his Wyffe
2d William
1d John

2d Alice bushe Widowe
2d Jeyse bushe
2d William Averye
2d ane his wyffe
2d Widowe hogge
2d a mayd more
2d a mayd
2d Richard Deman
2d and his Wyffe
2d William Evenns
2d and his Wyffe

[total] 3s 8d

[page 12]

2d Widowe taller
2d mathy Borrayge
2d and his Wyff
Katherine Lorrayge Walter Borrayge
2d John Strange

2d and his Wyffe
2d Humphrey morrys
2d Margaret penyton
2d Alice his mayd
Robert Reve

2d John Mayne
2d and his Wyffe
2d Robert bowden
2d and his Wyffe
Elizabeth howper Widow
Joan Dear
2d John Veane

[page 13]

2d John Kine
2d and his Wyffe
2d Alice kine
2d Phillip Peetr
2d and his Wyffe
2d Joan cornyshe
2d Robert cornyshe
2d John Stabacke
2d and his wyffe
2d John Rewe
2d and his Wyffe
2d Richard yard
2d and his Wyffe
a boye

[page 14]

2d John chub widower
2d Joan Bond
2d Peternell Bond
2d Eleanor Glas
John haydon
2d and his Wyffe
2d Robert bentt
2d and his Wyffe
Joan Peryam
2d Joan beard widowe
Watt averye and his wyffe
2d John Strannge
2d and his Wyffe

[page 15]

2d a old woman srvanntte
2d Richard att will
2d John Demens
2d John dear
2d and his Wyffe
2d Joan Dear
2d Widowe gird
2d John gird
2d and his Wyffe
Thomas Plushen and his Wyffe
2d Ellen [illegible]
2d Widow Borrayhe

2d and his Wyffe
Jelyan Venner
2d Richard Venner
2d and his Wyffe
2d Margaret Venner
2d thomas veane [total] 2d

[total] 3s

Christopher Bushe
2d Joan Reade Widowe
2d John David Wotton
2d and his wyffe
2d Richard smalridge
2d and his Wyffe
Elizabeth drake
Margaret ottway
and her daughter
2d Jarvis Lindon
2d and his Wyffe
2d Phillip gried
2d Dorothy berry

[totals] 3s 8d [total] 8d

2d William balhachett Wid
a mayd
2d Alice Shear Widow
2d Watt Shear
2d Anne Shear
2d Mrs nortthcott Widowe
2d Phillip nortthcott
2d Elizabeth Rowe 4d
katheren hington
2d Hugh [illegible]
2d Elizabeth moxham

[total] 3s

2d mary Burrayhe
2d John horwill
2d and his Wyffe
mark berry
2d Phillip delve
2d John horwill
2d nicholas demmet
2d george leigh
2d annes dune 2d
2d Alice horwill
2d Margaret down
2d Kingwell William

2d gilbert steven
2d and his wyffe
2d mariutt more
2d John Tooker
2d Robert Reve

[page 16]

2d Watt gyffry
2d and his Wyffe
2d thomas cowke
2d and his Wyffe
2d Argent honywell 4d
2d John ford 1d
2d John ellis
2d and his Wyffe
[illegible crossed through]
2d a boye
2d thomas basse
2d and his Wyff
2d ellis weast
2d Joan his mayd
2d thomas Lyr.
2d and his wyffe
2d John Squyer

[page 17]

2d Richard come
2d and his Wyffe
1d Margaret smyth
2d ebett strange Widowe
2d Joan Velacott
2d anthony Poyntt
2d and his Wyffe
2d John Grantt
2d and his Wyff
2d a boye
2d Joan smartt
emen bowdyn John Huntt younger
2d Richard [illegible]
2d John sherlond
2d and his wyff
2d Joan koman 1d
2d Richard orchard

[page 18]

2d Elizabeth leigh widowe
2d Margaret leigh
2d Joan Leache
2d William Sqwyer
2d & his Wyffe
2d William Sqwyer
2d Kirsten haydon 4d

John Reve
2d nicholas bery
2d Richard Waltam

           [totals] 4s 3d   [total] 10d

2d and his Wyffe
2d mark stone
2d and his Wyffe
2d Edward allin
Jane stone
2d William Webber 2d
2d John Page 2d
2d William gaybell
2d Thomas beman
2d John Walsh
2d and his Wyffe
2d Richard Walshe
2d and his Wyffe
2d Anne hole widowe
2d elizabeth amery 3d

                     [total] 12d

2d Harry palmer
2d and his wyffe
2d Margaret palmer
2d John palmer
2d Margaret ponsworthy
Peter palmer
2d margaret ellis
2d thomas steven 1d
2d Alice anne of marg hollis
2d John byrd
2d avis davye
2d thomas noryshe
2d giles delve
2d and his Wyffe
2d a mayd 2d
2d Richard ellis 2d [total] 6d

         [totals] 3s 8d   [total] 1s 12d

2d Anne Pryston Widow
2d William Pryston
2d and his Wyffe
2d John Wotton
2d and his Wyffe
2d Robert Wotton
2d Sabyan his mayd

2d simon his man 2d
2d Robert skinner 2d
2d widow lindon 2d
2d gilbert slader 2d
2d george slader
2d and his slader [sic]
2d tomsin hole
2d alice moyse Wydowe

[page 19]

2d John French
2d and his Wyffe
2d nicholas holmes
2d John Lee
2d burnard Young
2d elzabeth Choane widow
2d thomas george his man 4d
2d Richard Sowthcott
2d and his Wyffe
2d John barttlett
2d John Cowch
2d and his Wyffe
2d John Squyer
2d and his Wyffe

[page 20]

2d Katern Chard Wydowe
2d Watt Chard
2d and his Wyffe
2d Richard sattingwod 3d
a boye
2d Joan Clarke
2d Joan Weaste 2d
1d Margaret Hoke
2d Edward Allen
2d and his wyffe
2d ellis alline
2d John allin
2d Alice allin
2d grace allin
2d John Pope the elder
2d and his Wyffe
2d John Pope
2d and his Wyffe

[page 21]

2d John Leche
2d and his Wyffe
2d Joan Leche
barnard Leche
2d Watt Keman 3d
2d John Rowe 2d

frances branche
2d Robert [illegible]
2d and his Wyffe
george his sevannte
William bykly
2d Richard buryan

[totals] 4s 1d   [total] 12d

2d annes Densam Widowe
Jone Clark
Panll and his Wyffe
2d Thomas Hukby
2d and his Wyffe
2d Thomas bryge
2d and his Wyffe
Widowe Kinge
2d Ane Taylour
2d Joan grybell
anne grybell
1d ½ clemeantt

[total] 3s 7d ½

2d John Chard
2d george pryste
2d thomas smytth
2d Robert tenther
2d Andrew Row
Bridget R[illegible]
haydon
2d Elizabeth his mayd
2d John stevens
2d and his Wyffe
gilbartt mader
2d John leche
2d Tristram way 1d
2d Richard Vyell
2d and his Wyffe
2d Joan Waye
2d John Simons

[total] 4s 10d 5d

2d a mayd more
2d John Richard sewell
2d Elizabeth brocke
2d and his daughter
2d thomas kensall
2d and his Wyffe

2d Margaret kensall
2d william tuckett
2d and his Wyffe
2d John gyll
2d and his wyffe
2d Richard Roche

[page 22]

The east towne
2d ellis Rowe
2d and his Wyffe
2d elizabeth ellis
2d John Rowe
2d simon brodmed
2d and his ~~brodmed~~ wyffe
2d gilbert brodmed
2d bennett brodmed
2d besse brodmed
2d william temlett
2d gilbert shylston ½
2d and his Wyffe

[page 23]

2d John Marks
2d and his Wyffe
2d John Marks
2d and his Wyffe
2d florens
1d Richard Moreman
2d John Edwards
2d and his Wyffe
2d kriste edwards
2d william myddeldon
2d Richard myddeldon
2d william myddeldon
2d Richard myddeldon
2d William tolly
2d Richard
2d Robert myddeldon ½

[page 24]

2d John Krocker
2d Margaret gallen
2d Rawdon
2d bushe
2d John Whytrowe 2d
2d John collins
2d and his [blank]
2d william colle
2d and his wyffe
2d ~~ede~~ colle
~~Rose colle~~

2d Nicholas Ryche 1d
2d thomas neld
2d and his Wyffe
2d ysett Rede

[totals] 3s 6d 6d
end

2d John shylston
1d Margaret shylston
1d tamsin bremridge
2d Robin bond
2d and his Wyffe
~~Richard~~ his mayd
2d John lydford
2d Joan bond
2d John bond 1d
2d a man more

[total] 3s 2d [total] 3d ½

2d and his Wyffe
2d Phillip buckingham
2d & his Wyffe
~~Richard~~ edwards
2d cicily ponford Widowe
2d Gilbert ponford
2d elizabeth ponford
2 kirsten ponford
2d annes ponford
2d william ponford
2d Richard bond ½
2d & his wyff
2d Robert butte 4d
2d kirste edwards 4d

[totals] 4s 7d 4d 2 [illegible] 9d ½

2d annes chese widowe
2d Edmund bond ½
2d and his Wyffe
2d gilbert bond
2d Joan bremridge
2d William bond
2d Robert Peynton
2d nicholas bond
~~John more~~
2d a servannte
2d Gilbert myddeldon

2d and his Wyffee
2d bartholomew beard
2d John Comb ½

[page 25]

2d John chuble
2d and his Wyffe
2d Mary
2d Richard Weast
2d and his Wyffe
2d Mary Weast
2d thomas Bittell
2d & his Wyff
2d bennett tubfild
2d and his Wyffe
1d Margaret weast
2d Edmund byryton
2d and his Wyffe

[page 26]

2d margery snell
2d and his Wyffe
2d mary snell
~~Richard~~ snell
2d Robert snell
2d John Kensall
2d and his Wyffe
~~Robartt~~ Kensall
2d gilbert Kensall
2d John Kensall

[page 27]

2d John Lyvton bacheler 2d
2d John clarke
2d and his Wyffe
2d William tonnge 4d
classe his mayd
~~Joan Ware~~
2d John chese
2d Robert myddeldon
2d and his Wyffe
2d John quoyshe
2d tomsin Wyks 2d
2d nicholas his boye
2d Joan Wakman Widowe
~~Joan shutt~~ Widowe

[page 28]

2d Richard Stevens
2d Lawrence Davy 5d
2d William Crybell 6d
2d John byrd

2d and his Wyffe

[total] 3s 10d 3d

2d Richard Lenne
2d William baron
2d and his Wyff
2d William Rowe
1d May baron
2d thomas spenser
2d and his Wyffe
~~Nicholas~~ berttlett
2d elsabetth
~~thomas~~ Venner
~~baron his man~~
2d boye

[total] 3s 6d

2d Kirste Kensall
2d Joan Kensall
2d Nicholas Bradmed
2d and his Wyffe
~~John bradmed~~
2d Joan his mayd
2d Richard Venner
2d and his Wyff
1d a boye

[total] 3s 6d 3d

2d Joan ley Widowe
2d thomas Rowe
2d and his Wyffe
2d ede plommer
~~Kirsten~~ Rowe
2d John Rowe
2d and his Wyffe
2d Margaret Rowe
2d Margaret Rede 4d
2d Alice Roger 4d
2d Rowllinge 4d
~~myller~~

[total] 3s 6d 20d

2d ede colle 4d
2d nycoll lindon 4d
2d Robert bab
2d and his wyff

2d franncis lyddon
2d and his Wyffe
2d tomsin strange
2d Richard dabaway
2d William Watts
2d and his Wyffe
2d John Watts
2d Kirsten Watts
2d Margaret Watts
2d ede watts

[page 29]

2d Robert m'bels
2d and his Wyffe
2d Margaret Varder
2d John his servanntt
2d William Rowe
2d Robert bodly
2d bartholmew myddeldon
2d and his Wyffe
2d ede his mayd
2d William
2d Wilmett 2d
2d John bodly
2d Elizabeth prydym
2d Eleanor bodly
2d petrnyll molle widowe

[page 30]

2d garrett osen
2d and his Wyffe
2d John gey
2d and his Wyffe
2d Robert baker
2d and his Wyffe
2d Jane baker
2d James baker
2d Roger Perrs
2d Nicholas mameduke
2d thomas bodly

[page 31]

2d James Parrett
2d and his Wyffe
Martin Trodylfild
and his Wyffe
2d William Spenser 4d
2d hugh Deman 5d
William Deman
2d Margaret Raddin 4d
George Rowe
Thomas Turbevile

2d alexander cadworthy 3d
2d John Worthy
and his Wyff
2d wilmett cokeram
2d Richard body
2d Elizabeth clarke 2d
2d John Wortth
2d george bowdych

[total] 3s 4d 12d 2s

2d John
2d Joan molle
2d edward commings
2d and his Wyffe
2d esett mayor widowe
Joan Lokear
2d John busell
2d and his Wyffe
2d William frye
2d and his Wyffe
kirsten Waye
Joan Waye
Paull frye

[totals] 4s 2d

2d and his Wyffe
2d William Whyttger
2d and his Wyffe
2d John Webber the younger
2d and his Wyffe
2d Eleanor 4d
2d annes Rowe 4d
2d gilbert mader
2d Pascoe satyrrly 4d

[total] 3s 4d 12d

Anne fayire
[illegible crossed through] bronescomb
2d Elizabeth strange 2d
2d Widowe Deyll
2d and her doughter
2d Mr John Davy
2d and his Wyff
2d Kirstofer snell
2d Kirsten Davy
2d Joan blase

2d Robert Davye
2d Wilmot veyncomb 4d
2d waltt bord 5d ½
~~elsabetth~~ lindon

[page 32]

2d John Nortthcott
2d and his Wyffe
2d Edward steven 8d
2d John salter
2d Matheys his mayd 4d
2d John ballom
2d Richard dark 2d
2d Dimmes his mayd 4d
2d Joan Bremiscombe 2d
2d nicholas tok' 6d
2d Kirstyon jollett widow
[illegible crossed through] Jollett
2d Elizabeth Jollett
2d Thomas Jollett
2d John Danyell 4d
2d Richard [illegible] 4d

[page 33]

2d Joan norawaye
2d Widow moo'
2d Edmund Whytt
2d and his Wyffe
2d John Bykly
2d and his Wyffe
2d William Lucas 4d
2d John Saltern
2d and his Wyffe
2d John adams
2d and his Wyffe
2d thomas bushe
2d and his Wyffe
2d Gilbert Ware
2d and his Wyffe
2d Thomas bennett

[page 34]

2d John gurnard
2d and his Wyffe
2d John Wylles
2d and his Wyffe
2d Joan Wylls
2d grace Wylls
2d Anne
2d John corbyn
2d and his Wyffe
2d John Varder

2d jane mychell 2d
2d Joan ware 3d
2d thomas barry

[totals] 3s 2d 2s 6d

2d Thomas mychell
2d and his Wyffe
2d a mayd
1d Resons Wyffe
2d thomas Chambr
2d and his Wyff
2d Margaret Chambr
2d Elizabeth Winter
2d george wyncott
2d and his Wyffe
2d Richard holmes 2d
~~bartibmew~~ berd
2d thomas back
2d James his man

[total] 4s 6d

2d and his Wyffe
2d Margaret Wotton Widowe
2d William tok
2d and his Wyffe
2d Thomas Crowther
~~2d~~ Alice Webber ~~1d~~
~~tamsen~~ Wryght
2d Margaret balcom 1d
2d William Down
2d Thomas toker
2d simon avery
2d Robert gunstande 6d
2d thomas Russel
2d [illegible] 1d

[total] 4s 8d

2d Harry Brocke
2d John Brocke
2d Richard Winsor 2d
2d gilbert pope
2d and his Wyffe
2d thomas Delve
2d giles lendon
Robert lee
2d nicholas buckingham
2d and his Wyffe

2d Margaret buckingham
2d Joan Buckingham
2d Richard buckingham

[page 35]

2d Richard bray
2d and his Wyff
2d Katherine a mayd
2d Richard Sarnder
2d and his Wyff
2d alice
2d John Wolwaye
2d and his Wyffe
2d Robert tok
nicholas Whytte
and his Wyffe
2d Joan Baron Widowe
2d John shore
2d and his Wyffe
2d thomas Loveringe
2d and his Wyffe

[page 36]

2d Richard Herman
2d and his Wyff
2d David Treyes
2d and his Wyff
2d Jone
John browninge
and his Wyffe
2d Richard Mayberry
2d and his wyfe
2d nicholas mychell
2d and his Wyffe
2d Joan Clemett
2d his mother
1d a mayd more
2d Richard Pope
2d and his Wyffe
2d thomas palme

[page 37]

2d James wyre
2d and his Wyff
2d gilbert wyre 2d
2d John Egbeare
2d and his Wyff
2d mother garnsey Widow
2d Phillip garnsey
2d and his Wyff
2d William Steyner
2d Richard hill

2d simon buckingham
2d kristofer Waye

[total] 4s 2d

Robert Browninge
2d george Rodd
2d anne his Wyff
2d thomas browninge
2d Richard burgess
2d and his Wyff
Ellen Balachott
2d Richard pope
2d and his Wyffe
2d John Goltin 2d
2d Elizabeth browninge
2d her doughter
2d annes
2d mother brown

[total] 4s 4d 2d

2d Joan Lokear 2d
2d tomsin payn 4d
2d thomas howper
2d and his Wyffe
2d Matthew gold
2d and his Wyffe
2d thomas tompson
2d Arthur godsland
2d John ford
2d William Randell
ede sawnder widowe
2d Joan sander Widowe
2d stephin Brocke
2d and his Wyff
2d her doughtr

[total] 4s 9d 6d

2d and his Wyffe
2d Joan Tok 2d
2d Alice gallin
2d William Furler
2d and his Wyff
2d Ellen balachatt
aves bak
2d tomsin seller
2d hugh dene
2d and his Wyffe

2d Joan Deane 4d

~~a mayde more~~

[page 38]

2d ellis basse

2d ane his Wyff

2d Reynold penyton

2d and his Wyff

annes his doughter

2d William Robartt

2d & his Wyff

2d Phillip Wade

2d and his Wyffe

2d Richawd his ~~wyff~~ 3d

2d John Reynsyn 2d

2d John Borengge 2d

2d Edward Cleale

2d & his Wyffe

[page 39]

2d thomas delve

2d and his Wyff

2d & his doughtr

2d William Jak'

2d and his Wyffe

2d John Marsford

2d and his Wyffe

2d Jane lindon Widowe

2d John lindon 4d

2d Richard seldyn

2d and his Wyffe

[page 40]

2d thomas ware

2d and his Wyff

2d Humphrey Jule

2d and his Wyff

2d Richard Hansford

2d & his Wyffe

2d Joan bryce

~~Phillip basse and his Wyff~~

2d gilbert Jak'

2d & his Wyffe

2d thomas R[illegible]

2d Hugh babb

2d and his Wyff

2d Christopher myddeldon

[page 41]

2d 2d John Webber the elder

2d 2d and his Wyffe

2d 2d annes Webber

[total] 2s 10d 6d

2d & his mayd

2d Robert venycomb ½

2d John Davy

Eleanor lange Widowe

2d Margaret fryshe

2d Richard bowdin

2d and his Wyffe

2d Jane bowdin

2d Mr harcourtt scolemaster

2d Robert clarke

2d and his Wyffe

2d Joan herd Widowe

[totals] 4s 7s ½

2d bridget seldon

2d Richard seldon

2d annes seldon

~~nyell~~

2d Joan slocomb

2d Edmund deryke

2d and his Wyffe

2d Joan the Wyff to Ratt

2d John Ponford

2d and his Wyff

[total] 3s 2d 2d 4d

2d and his Wyff

2d William

2d Peter

2d thomas holland

2d and his Wyff

2d Joan Plimsher

~~Joan Plimshen~~

2d William garrett

2d and his Wyff

2d Alice Whytrowe

2d thomas [illegible] 2d

2d Joan Garratt

[totals] 4s 2d

2d Joan Varder 2d

2d annes Ponsfard

2d Richard Snell

2d and his Wyff
2d simon shapcott
2d and his Wyffe
2d thomas sander
2d anne his Wyff
2d William Gibs
2d John honnywell
2d and his Wyffe
2d Mary honywell
2d Joan honnywell
2d John Adam
2d John bond

[page 42]

2d Anne
2d & her doughter

[page 43]

The town tething
2d Elizabeth baker Widowe
2d William Lake
2d and his wife
2d tomsin more
2d William more
2d Wilmot Ride
2d Margaret Scutt
1d Elizabeth brocke
2d John Wolwoth
2d and his Wyff
2d Joan stander garett 2d
2d John Ellis
2d Anne Rugge
2d William Wall

[page 44]

2d Robert Endtt ½
2d and his wyffe att be
2d Joan basse 2d
2d John seryll
2d and his Wyff
gilbartt lendon
2d Margaret lendon
2d thomas lane
2d John toker
2d Widowe stapill
2d John Jordeyn
1d thomas Goodwyn
2d John Edbery
2d and his Wyffe
2d William edbey
Joan edbery
1d John edbery

2d John Honnywell 4d

2d thomas Sawnder
2d and his Wyff
1d Joan
2d John Halle
2d and his Wyffe
2d Peter gidly
2d and a mayde of his
2d anne heliar
Joan barell

[totals] 4s 3d 6d

[total] 4d

2d and his Wyff
2d Cristen Wall
2d Robert Wall
2d thomas bray 4d
2d Garshay 1d
1d Joan Wall
2d Richawde a mayd 2d
William payn
and his wyff
2d John truman
2d and his Wyff
2d Joan truman
2d William Honywell

[total] 4s 4d 9d

2d and his wyff
2d William Edbery
Joan Edbery
1d John Edbery
[illegible crossed through]
2d Joan his mayd
2d Giles Pope
2d and his Wyffe
2d Joan pope
2d lucy pope
2d Widowe grillocke
2d gilbert shylston
1d and his Wyff
2d katherine Kine
2d Joan smythe
2d John smyth 2d

[totals] 4s 2d 5d ½

[page 45]

2d Gilbert bykly	2d Andrew flaye
2d and his Wyff	2d James gibs
2d Elizabeth tob	2d Robert [illegible]
2d thomas swettlond	2d and his Wyff
2d John gibs	2d Richard pinsan
2d and his Wyffe	2d and his wyff
2d William Nott 3d	

John Callow

[totals]	2s 3d

oblacions	£8 14s 10d ½
oblacons more	£6 9s 7d ½
totall	£15 4s 6d
privy tytthes	56s 1d ¾
garden mony	27s 1d ½
total	£19 17s 11d

51. CREDITON, Easter Book, 1582

DHC, 1660A/O/A/193

Note: The account has been written on thirteen pieces of paper of about 4 inches in width and 12 inches in length which have been folded and stitched with white thread in order to provide a booklet of twenty-six pages. The numerals are Roman with an occasional Arabic one included. At the end of the book are notes of arrearages, payments, christenings, purifications and weddings for a few months from 1582 to 1583. In 1577 the tithes for lands formerly part of the Deer Park were leased from the governors to Robert Denys, of Bicton, and his family.[14] In this Easter Book the scribe recorded the names of 329 individuals in nine prebends (Aller, Henstill, Kerswill, Priestcombe, Rudge, Stowford, Town, Woodland and Woolsgrove), the geographical areas of the parish which supported canons before the Reformation. A manuscript regarding prebends, possibly relating to this document, was destroyed in a Crediton fire in 1915.[15] Like Item 52, this book appears to be a collection of tithes which have been commuted to a fixed annual payment. This was similar to arrangements elsewhere, such as in Coventry, Leicester, Winchester and other urban areas, where tithes were commuted to rents.[16]

Prebendal Rental Book in the 25th year of the reign of Queen Elizabeth

Wolsgrove [Woolsgrove] prebend		+ Mat. Elston	12d
Mr Coplestone [blank]		Joan Northcott	2s 3d
Mr Alford	4s 6d	+ Egidig Weast	20d
+ Mortymer *of* Ranscomb [Ranscombe]	12s 6d	+ Lane *of* Wolsgrove	2s 6d
+ Walter Bound	3s 8d	+ George Northcott	3s 4d
+ Jo. Wall *otherwise* Bey	3s 6d	Ed: Morishe	7s 3d
+ Jo. Delve senior	2s	+ Henry Hore	3s 6d
	2s	+ William Jacobb	20d
William Heard	4s 9d	Robert Reed	10d

14 DHC, 1660A/190.
15 *E&E*, 24 Feb. 1939. Some papers were seen by Ethel Lega Weekes: DHC, DD1772-4.
16 Wright, 'Easter Books', 33.

John Boroughe	3s 4d	Gilbert Wall	16d
more for Armely	6d	+ Robert Gover	21d
Ro: bowrington & Armely	9d	+ Thomas Delve p ar	3d

[page 2]

Wolsgrove prebend

+ William Elston	4s 10d	+ Kene *of* Ken[ner]ly	4s 7d
+ Simon gover	12s	Couche *of* sand	4s 7d
+ Gilbert Predam	6s 8d	Pet' Rock	18d
+ William Claishe	2s 6d	Hugh Mortymer	3s 4d
+ Reed *of* Aishe	12d	+ Mat. fooost	12d
+ Ro: Bound	20d	Ro fooost	4s 6d
+ Pope *of* Elston	3s 6d	+ Jo. wilcotts	2s
more for Armely	1d ¾	Tho. Gribbell	5d
+ Robert Towker	4s 3d	+ Clearke *of* downe	21d
+ William Shoubook	4s	Thomas Reed	2s
John Gellard	6d	phus pond	1d

[page 3]

Henstell [Henstill]

Mr Marshall	3s 9d	William Reve	2s 9d
+ Henry Kingwell	6s 3d	+ Gilbert Bradmed	2s
+ Tho: Tuckfild	5s	+ Andrew Strangg	2s 3d
+ Joan Pitwood	5s	+ Richard Cobley	4s 6d
+ Joan Lee *of* Gunston *widow*	5s	+ Bennot Weale	6s 6d
+ William Ley	3s 9d	+ Shilston of hid	2s 6d
John Whites bargayne	3s 4d	+ John Borage	2s 3d
+ John Howke	4s	John Chard *for* stokey	10d
John Dreaton	13d ½	+ Jo: Roberts	4d
Anthony Rowe	4s ¼d	Walter Gullock	13d
Kyne *of* Hollacomb	3s 6d	+ Bennet Dicklegg	5d
+ Jonaa' Dyker *widow*	6s ¼d	William Comb	5d
+ Rafe Towker	3s 6d		

and this prebend is increased upon the widow Lee of Gunston this yeare   12d

[page 4]

Carswell [Kerswill]

Howke mede	3d	Ric Howkeway	21d
George Trobridge gentleman	5s	+ Peter Reed	4s
+ William Trewman	13s 4d	+ Jo. Dunscomb	3s
+ John Tuckfild	7s 6d	+ Walter Connybye	13d
+ Nicholas thomas	5s 5d	Davy *of* Ted	3s 4d
+ Nicholas Atwill	3s 4d	+ Jo. Woodley	3s 6d
+ Henry Kingwell	4s 9d	Lendon *of* posbery [Posbury]	12d
+ James Temlett	3s 3d	+ John Skutt	2s 9d
+ Jo. Whitrowe	4s	Ro. Gullokk	5d
+ Jo. Ballaman	2s 6d	+ Tho: Strongg	3d
+ James Banton	4s		

[page 5]

Rudge

Mr John Trobridge	12s 1d	+ Ric Hoole	2s
more for Towker	18d	Bennot *of* old rudge	4s ½
+ Mr Gilbert Davie	10s	Petherick	7d
+ Mr William Bodleighe	15s	Tho. Lake	7d
+ Mr Dunscomb	17s 11d ½	Jo. Foot	7d
Mr Wevill	3s 4d	Ric Potter	5d
+ Robert Davye	5s	+ William Jeston	9d
+ James Jeston	8s 6d	Ric Clatworthey	15d
+ Jo. Burgyn	5s 3d	+ Widow Lane	15d
+ Ric Serell	2s 6d	Elezeus Jeston	5d
+ Jo. Helior	3s	Jo. Bennot *of* New	
+ Widow Basse	3s	Edbury *of* Rud	4d
Jo. Newale	6d	John Delve	3d
+ Geoffrey Kyngwell	9d	John Foot *for* kettell	7d ½
+ Jo. Gryne	4d		

[page 6]

Aller

Joan Atwill *widow*	16s8d	Roger Badkock	5s 6d
+ Robert Lane	17d	+ Pope *of* East Pid[sley]	7s 6d
+ Reed of storge	2s	+ Pope *of* Weast Pid	3s 6d
+ Ric Hoole'	18d	+ John Eliot	2s 6d
+ Robert Melhuish	3s 4d	+ Widow Howkway	2s 3d
+ Ric Potter	3s 4d	+ Jo. Trencher	2s 3d
+ Ro. Philpp	2s 9d	Ro fooost	3s 10d
+ William Mortymer	3s 9d	+ Tho Please	9s 2d
+ William Lake	9s 2d	+ Shilston de hid	10d
+ Moxsay Thac	18d	+ Tho. Basse	4d
+ Jo. Haydon	5s 3d	+ Wearyn *of* pit	7d ½
+ Land *of* Sto.	2s 6d	+ Jo. Rollond	12d
+ Ro. Wreaford	4s 3d	Collyns *of* comb	3d
+ Gilbert Bokley	18d	Love mede	2d
+ Ellis Davy *widow*	5d	Edbury *of* Weastwood [Westwood]	4s 3d
Jo. Leache	6d	Gilbert Trobridge	3d
+ Jo. ford	5s		

[page 7]

Crosse [Cross]

Anthony Copleston gentleman	2s 9d	+ Bennet Weale	16d ½
+ Widow Steere	2s 9d	+ Bennot Dicklegg	4s 11d
+ Hollacomb *of* crose	9s 2d	+ Trewman *of* eweford	4s 7d
+ John Tuckfeld	3s 6d	Jo. Dreaton	3s 4d
+ Robert Werryn	3s 4d	+ Widow Osborne	10d
Peter Werryn	2s 6d	+ Andrew Lee	20d
+ William Werryn	2s 6d	+ Gullokk *of* ewe	4s 6d
+ Widow Reve	2s 6d	Gullokk *of* vost	4d
+ Borage *of* Eweford [Yeoford]	2s 6d	+ Jo. Flud	3s 4d
Philip Chapplyn	2s 6d	+ John Comyns	4s
+ Tho. Lee	5s	+ William Venicomb	4s

+ Gilbert Venicomb 4s   Bennot Way 6d
memorandum encreased uppon the widow osborne paid 8d

[page 8]

Priscomb [Priestcombe]

Mr Jo. Northcott	11s 8d	+ Jo. Robertts	3s
+ Mr Tho Moxsay	2s 6d	+ Gullokk *of* instowe	3s 4d
George Trobridge gentleman	20d	+ Towker of Uton	12d
Jo. Hollcomb	7s 6d	Widow Bennott	16d
Tho: Edbury	5s	Gullokk *of* Uton	4d
+ Jo. Mortymer	7s 6d	+ Widow bornell	2s
+ Tho. Gullolk	5s 10d	+ gilbert bornell	15d
+ Lane *of* hill	3s 4d	+ bennot Colehole	2s
+ Nichas Atwyll	15s	+ Werryn *of* pit	22d ½
+ Tho Callowe	2s 6d	+ Jo. Jocks	10d

memorandum increased uppon Ben. Colehold for the year 12d
[total] 10s ¼

[page 9]

Stowford

Mr Coplestone *of* colbroke [Colebrooke]		+ Jo Lobdon	7s 6d
+ Mr Humphrey Copleston	11s 8d	+ Jo. Delve senior	2s
+ Robert Lee	13s 4d	Ric kinston	3s 6d
+ William Elston	8s 9d	+ Jo Fooost	5s
+ Pope *of* Elston	4s 6d	+ Matthew fooost	7s
Ro Foost *for* elston	5s	+ Gater of wolsgrove	2s 6d
Giles Hoop	3s	+ Gater of Sandford	21d
+ Jo. Gover	2s	+ Jo. Wilcokks	2s 6d
+ William banton	7s 6d	+ George Claish	2s
+ Ro. Towker	3s	John Elston *for* Nov	8d
Jo. Lightfoot	10d	Austin Hoop	9d
+ Simon brock *for* White	5s	Ric Peake	1d
Widow Clase	6s 8d	Gilbert fooost	1d
+ Michus Thomas	3s 3d		

memorandum this prebend is increased uppon [illegible] boock *for the year* 4s for Whit Tithes of knoll 31s 1d

[page 10]

Woodland

John Fursse	9s	+ Tho. Frances	4s
+ Henry Trewman	5s 10d	+ Edmund Venicomb	4s 0d
+ Jo. bradley	3s 9d	+ John Lendon	2s
+ John Swanson	6s 8d	Gullokk de vost	18d
Widow Wreaford	5s	+ Gullokk *of* instowe	3s 4d
Jo. Wollacott	9s 2d	+ Bennot Colehole	2s
Joan Skynner	3s 4d	+ Widow Miller	4s
+ Eliz Torner	5s	+ John Land	4s
Walter Delve	5s	+ Thomas Delve	4s
+ Michus Mannd'	4s	+ Lendon *of* Colbrok	12d
Skynner *of* Colbrok	4s	Richard Arnold	10d
+ Predam of Rock	7s	Bawdwyn Towker	2d

memorandum this prebend is increased more uppon Colehole *for the year* 6d

~~49s 9d~~ 36s 11d

[page 11]

Towne prebend

Mr Periyam	7s 6d	+ Michus Bokenam	21d
+ Sir Robert Denys	13s 4d	Jo. Ballam for potters close	2d
+ Mr Gale	2s 9d	+ Jo. Rowe	15d
Mr Jo. Trobridge	17d	Tho. Rowe	6d
+ Mr Troblevile	9s 8d	Bennot Tuckfild	3s 6d
Mr Jo. Northcott	2s 9d ½	+ William Wall	12d
+ Mr Gilbert Davy	4s 1d	+ Jo. Wolwey	6d
Mr Lawrens Davy	4s 7d	+ Widow Cornyshe	12d
Mr Philipp Nothcott	3s 4d	Widow Pleace	4s 6d
+ Mr John Davy	2s 4d	+Widow Denssam	4d
George Trobridge gentleman	5s	Widow Gird	1d ½
+ Eliz Davy *widow*	11d	*Philip* Baker	19d
John Woorthe	15d	Robert Middleton *otherwise* Peni	5d
+ Walter Harres	7s 6d		

[page 12]

Towne prebend

Mr Edward Denys	10s 6d	Jo. Leache senior	4d
Mr Anthony Copleston	2s	Jo. Leache Junior	5d
+ Mr John Davy	12d	+ William Squyre	10d
+ *Philip* Smythe	8s 2d	Jo. Rondell	3d
Mrs Northcott	4s 6d	+ Simon brock *for* marrod	3d
Jo. Stephens	20d	Jo. pope	2d
+ Walter Chard	5s 6d	Jo. borington	5s
more for his orchard	1d	+ Tho. Swetelond	3s
Strangg *of* Capella	2s	Tho. Nild	3d
Jo. Pynsson *otherwise* Edbu.	5d	Jo. Venncomb *or* pker	3d
Jo. Horwell	9d ½	Ric Wealshe	8d
+ Jo. Tuckfild	16d	Mortymer *or* Jo. leache	3d
Ric. Ven	3d	Jo. Pemerton	1d ½
Jo. Kellond	3d	Miller *of* sandford	½
Gilbert Stephins	2d ½		

[page 13]

Towne prebend

Jo. Ware	16s 4d ½	Tho. Ware	19d ¼
+ Ric. Lane 3	s	+ Spensser	3s 3d
+ Gil. Shilston	2s 6d	Jo. Cutler	2d
+ Jo. Clearke	2s	Philip bray	2s
+ Philip bokenam	2s 6d	+ Gilbert Lendon	12d
	6s 6d	+ Robert Quicke	12d
+ Gilbert bradmed	6s 6d	+ Jervis Lendon	6d
+ Gilbert Ponsford	3s 3d	+ Nicholas slee	7d
Robert bennot p ohol	9d	+ Trewman *of* Ewe [?Yeoford]	2d
Edmund bond	20d		

Rentts

+ Mr Turbervile	6s 8d	+ Philip Smythe	15d

+ William Smythe	5s	John wills	2s
+ Jo. ballam	21d	Robert Clearke	12d
Reynolls	2s 3d	Pitts howsse	
+ Goddefray	3s	+ Ponsford als Deane	2s

[page 14]

prea bends

Mr Trobridge	53s 11d	Tho. Rowe *for* mol	2s 6d
+ Mr Turbervile *for* prats	5s 4d	Ro. Bennott	12d
John Howe	5s 10d	+ bennot Dicklegg	10d
+ John Rowe *for* mol	6s 3d	Philip Baker	6d

for Molt

21 January 1582

Rec for Christ quarter 1582 for bred for the poore by the hands of Edward Sweetland 13s [total] 13s

[page 21]

Christenyngs from the 13th day of Decembre 1582

+ Jo. Borane child christened the 25 of December

+ Ro. Petener the 27 of Decem. 1582

+ Gil[bert] Brodmede child the 29 of Decem.

+ Jo. Strang the last of Decem. 1582

+ Hugh Demans Child the 10th of January

+ Jo. Gibbes child the 13 of Jan. 1582 [sic]

+ Hen. Kingwells child Christyd the 14 of Jann.

+ Colyholes child Christened at Cheriton the 15 of January

+ Flods child Christened the 21 of Ja. 1582

+ Garnsers child christened the 29 of Ja.

+ Hawkyns child christ. the 30 of Ja. 1582

+ Eliot a stranger of opsam Christened the 3 of Febru.

+ Thomas Furlers child Christ the 4 of Febru.

+ Mark Stones child Christ. the 4 of february

+ Thomas Gullock child Christ the 5 of February

+ Vens child Christ. the 6 of February 1582

Dreatons child Christened the 9 of February

Dunster Glasses child Christ. the 10th of february

Jordens child Christened the 10th of February

[page 23]

Rec[eipts] for purificatons sithe the 13 day of Decembre 1582 unto the 12 of the same Monethe 1582 as followethe &c

b. *for the wife of John* Vencomb 13 December 1582	6d
w. *for the wife of George* Trobridge gentleman 14 December	6d
So. *for the wife of Philip* Frances 16 December 1582	6d
b. *for the wife of Egidge* Delve 23 December 1582	6d
w. *for the wife of Thomas* Busshe the 23 December 1582	6d
for the wife of bond *of* old rudge 1582	6d
So. *for the wife of Thomas* Borage the 3 January 1582 [sic]	6d
b. *for the wife of* Thomas Couche 22 December 1582	6d
for the wife of Gilbert Brodmede 12 January 1582	6d
w *for the wife of* Pettner 12 January 1582	6d
for the wife of Colyhole the 16 of January 1582	6d
S. *for the daughter of* Strang of morelak 20 Ja. 1582	6d
b. *for the wife of Hugh* Deman 26 Ja. 1582	6d
S. *for the wife* Henry Kyngwell 27 of Ja. of 1582	6d
w. *for the wife of John* Gybb the 27 of Ja. 1582	6d
S. *for the wife of* Fend the 3 of February 1582	6d

w. *for the wife of* Eliot a stranger of opsam the 9 of Febuary

for the wife of hawkyns the 10 of February 1582	6d
for the wife of Garnsey 11 February 1582	6d
b. *for the wife of Mark* Ston the 17 of February 1582	6d
b. *for the wife of* Furler the 17 of February 1582	6d
b. *for the wife of* Ven the 17 of February 1582	6d
S. *for the wife of* Gullokk *of* Lee 17 of Febru. 1582	6d

[page 23]

Rec[eipts] for Weddings sithe the 13 day of Decembre 1582 unto the 12 of the same month 1583 as follows

w. Rec. for Thomas Delve wedd. the 17 of Ja.	16d
b. Rec. for Robert Davy gentleman the 21 of Ja. 1582	16d
b. Thomas Sherelond wed the 21 of Ja.	16d
b. Gilbert Stephins wed the 24 of Ja.	16d
w. Jo. Jeston wed the 27 of Ja. 1582	16d

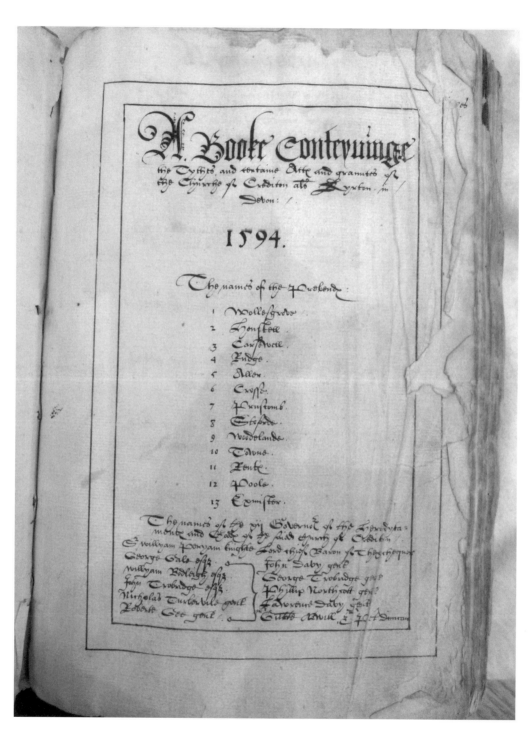

Plate 11. Crediton Easter Book, 1594.

52. CREDITON, Easter Book, 1594

DHC, 1660A/O/A/13

Note: This bound volume has several hundred unnumbered paper pages which are approximately 4 inches in width and 12 inches in length. Some initial pages were given folio numbers and incorporate the Easter Book which includes blank pages headed with the names of the prebends. The organisation of this account differs in its prebends with that written in 1582. It was during 1594 that the bishop surrendered the manor and borough of Crediton to the Crown.[17] The tithes had been commuted into a fixed annual payment and the wardens' accounts recorded significant non-payments.[18]

A Booke Conteyninge the Tythes and certain Acts and grauntes of the Churche of Crediton *otherwise* Kyrton in Devon.

1594
The names of the Prebends: 1 Wollesgrove, 2 Henstell, 3 Carsewell, 4 Rudge, 5 Aller, 6 Crosse, 7 Pruscomb, 8 Stoforde, 9 Woodelande, 10 Towne, 11 Rents, 12 Poole, 13 Exmi[n]ster

The names of the 12 Governors of the Heredytaments and Goods of the saidd Church of Crediton. Sir William Peryam Knighte Lord Chief Baron of Thexchequer

George Gale Esquire   John Davy gentleman
William Bodleigh Esquire   George Trobridge gentleman
John Trobridge Esquire   Phillip Northcott gentleman
Nicholas Turbervile gentleman   Lawrence Davy gentleman
Robert Gee gentleman   Mr Gilbert Atwill & Peter Duncan

[new page]

Wollesgrove fo.1
Note, that the grauntes made to the Parishioners of their Tithes doe endure and contynew no longer, but whilest the taker of theym is livinge, and is the Lords Teanante, unles it be by some speciall graunte made to the contrary.

John Coplestone esquyre for the Tithes of his pte in Aishmoore [Ashmoor] *for the year*	**6s 8d**
John Borrington for the tithes of his pte in Aishmoore *for the year*	**6s 8d**
John Pope for the tithes of the Tenemente called Barrough [Borough] *for the year*	18s 8d
John Mortymer of Remyscomb [Ramscombe] *for the year* 50s	
Agnes Bond and William her sonne *for the year*	16s
John Walle *otherwise* Bea *for the year*	~~14s~~ 10s
Phillip Ponde payeth for som pte of Aishmoore wch was John Walles *otherwise* Bea	~~10s~~ 4s
John Delve thelder *for the year*	**8s**
William Hearde and John his sonne *for the year*	**19s**

[new page]

Wollesgrove

Matthew Elsonne for his Tenement called		sett againe to his wife for the same price	
Davyes Lande *for the year*	4s	**Alice** weste wyddow *for the year*	6s
John Adams *otherwise* Forde *for the year*	9s	**John** Lane of Wollesgrove *for the year*	10s
dead **Thomas** Rood *for the year*	8s	**George** Northcott *for the year*	13s 4d

---

[17]   DHC, sB/CRE7/1551/CRE, Beatrix Cresswell, *Fifty Tudor Years*, p. 141.
[18]   Cresswell, *Wardens' Accounts*, pp. 355–6. I am grateful to Tony Gale for this reference.

Roger Selby of *Exeter for the year*   32s   **Roger** Jacob *for the year*   6s 8d
Simon Legg and his mother *for the year*   16s

[new page]

Wollesgrove fo.2
John Prowse *for the year*   3s 4d   **Simon** Gover *for the year*   43s 4d
John Borrough *for the year*   18s   **Joan** Pryddam wydd *for the year*   28s
Robert Treip *for the year*   30s   **Robert** Wilcocks *for the year*   10s
Margery Elsen wydd *for the year*   10s   [blank] Reede of Aysh *for the year*   4s
John Elsen *for the year*   10s

[new page]

Wollesgrove
Robert Bonde *of* Morchard *Bishop for the year*   **William** Keene *of* Kennarleigh [Kennerleigh]
          6s 8d   18s 4d
John Pope of Elsen [Elston]   14s   **John** Rowlande *for the year*   20s
Amy Tucker wyddow   17s 8d   **Peter** Rocke *for the year*   6s
William Shobbrocke *for the year*   18s   **Hugh** Mortymer *for the year*   13s 4d
John Gellard *of* Downe St Mary   2s

[new page]

Wollesgrove fo. 3
Matthew Froste *for the year*   4s   **Thomas** Gribbell *for the year*   20d
Robert Froste *for the year*   18s   **Peter** Pope *for the year*   9s
John Wilcocks *for the year*   8s   **Phillip** Ponde *for the year*   4d
Sum total for the tolls of the prebend of wollesgrove *for the year*   £27 17s 8d

[new page]

Henstil fo.5
William Lee in Gunston *for the year*   15s   **Thomazine** Pitwood for the moytie of her
Emblyn Kingwill wydd *for the year*   14s   Customary Tenemente   10s
Henry Kingwill *for the year*   7s   **Giles** Spicer for thone moitie of his
Thomas Tuckfeild *for the year*   20s   Customary Tenemente   10s
Margery Brodmeade wydd for stuckey   **Christopher** Lee **for the year**   20s
downes [Stockeydown] 3s 4d and for Moore   **William** Lee in Hollocomb [Hollocombe] **13s**
16s **19s 4d**   **4d**

[new page]

Henstill
Joan Ley Widd *for the year*   15s   **John** Davye of Sandford gentleman *for the*
John Reve *for the year*   11s   *year*   26s 8d
John Hooke *for the year*   16s   **Anthony** Raw *for the year*   18s 8d
John Keene *of* Hollocombe   14s   **John** Dreyton *for the year*   4s 6d
John Borreige *for the year*   9s   **Ralfe** Tucker   14s

[new page]

Hanstall fo.6
Andrew Strange *for the year*   9s   **Thomas** Lane att Hill   16d
Richerde Cobleigh *for the year*   18s   **Walter** Gullocke *for the year*   4s 4d
Christopher Lee weale *for the year*   26s   **Robert** Dicklegg *for the year*   2s
Gilbert Shilston of Chuddenbroke   **William** Coombe *for the year*   20d
[Chiddenbrook]   10s
Sum total of the prebend of Henstell for the year   £16 9s 10d

[new page]
Carswell fo. 8
George Trobridge gentleman *for the year* **36s
8d**
William Trewman *for the year*   **53s 4d**
John Tuckfeild *for the year*   **30s**
John Tuckfeild aforesayd *for the year*   **2s 4d**

Margaret Atwill wydd *for the year*   **14s 4d**
John Scutt *for the year*   **12s**
Walter Conneby *for the year*   **4s 4d**
Henry Kingwill *for the year*   **9s**
James Bruton *for the year*   **16s**

[new page]
Carswell
James Tremblett *for the year*   **10s**
James Tremblett aforesaid *for the year* **13s**
John Whitrawe *for the year*   **16s**
Augustine Bearde *for the year*   **8s**
Peter Reede *for the year*   **16s**

John Bronnscomb att Pytt [Pitt]   **12s**
Walter Woodleigh *for the year*   **14s**
John Hooke *for the year*   **4s 4d**
John Fea *for the year*   **2s**

[new page]
Carswell fo. 9
Robert Ware *for the year*   **8s**
Thomas Strange *for the year*   **2d**
Sum total of that prebend of Carswell for the year

[blank] **Davye** *now* Lendon *of* Tedborne
[Tedburn St Mary]   **13s 4d**
                                            £14 14s 8d

[new page]
Rudge
John Trobridge esquyre *for the year*   **48s 4d**
of the same for Carsforde *for the year*   **12s**
*of the same for the tenement recently in the
tenure of* Tucker   **6s**
of the same for the tenement formerly Greene
for the year   **16d**
William Bodleigh esquire *for the year*   **50s**
George Trobridge gentleman *for the year* **30s**
Thomas Dunscomb gentleman *for the year*
                                           29s 4d

besyds his mylls
Walter Dunscomb *for the year*   **26s 8d**
Phillip Buckingham for his Tenement
at Howkeway [Hookway] and for halfe
Brodepke   **15s**
John Davy gentleman *for the year*   **20s**
William Marten of *Exeter* merchante for the
Tenement which was Mr Wyvells   **10s**
Agnes Jurston wyddow   **24s**
Richard Newman merchant *for the year*   **20s**

[new page]
Rudge fo. 11
dead John Burgaine *for the year*   **21s**
of the same for half Brodepke *for the year* **6s
8d**
sett againe to Allyce his late wife for the same
price
Richerde Searell *for the year*   **10s**
Robert Kemyll *for the year*   **3s**
Richerd Bawdonne *for the year*   **8s**

William Slade *otherwise* Gregory *for the year*
                                             20d
Robert Pewtner *for the year*   **2s 4d**
Thomas West *for the year*   **2s 4d**
John Foote *for the year*   **2s 6d**
of the same John for the year   **2s 4d**
Richerd Potter *for the year*   **20d**
William Jurston *for the year*   **3s**

[new page]
Rudge
Richerd Clatwourthy *for the year*   **5s**
[blank] Lane *for the year*   **5s**
Ellize Jurstone *for the year*   **20d**
Sum total of that prebend of Rudge for the year

John Bennet *of* Newgate *for the year*   **16d**
John Delve *for the year*   **12d**
[blank] **Edbery** *of* Rudge *for the year* **16d**
                                           £18 12s 6d

[new page]

Aller fo. 13

Gilbert Atwill gentleman *for the year* £3 6s 8d

Thomas Lane att Hill *for the year*   **5s 8d**

Thomas Lane of Storedge [Sturridge] *for the year*   **13s 4d**

Gilbert Borredge *for the year*   6s

John Melhuish *for the year*   14s

Richerd Reed of Storidge *for the year*   10s

Robert Froste *for the year*   15s 4d

Thomas Handon and Mylden *for the year* **12s**

Wm Mortymer *for the year*   **15s**

[new page]

Aller

Wm Lake of Bradly [Bradleigh] *for the year*   **36s 8d**

Hugh Sampford *for the year*   **6s**

John Haydon *for the year*   **21s**

Wydd Lane of storedge & Tho. hei somme **10s**

Robert Wreyforde *for the year*   **17s**

John Clarke *for the year*   **20d**

Gilbt Bukle *otherwise* Thressher *for the year*   **6s**

John Leache theldei *for the year*   **2s**

[new page]

Aller fo. 14

John F[smudged] Forde *for the year*   **20s**

voyd **Roger** Preston *otherwise* Budbrooke *for the year*   **22s**

sett againe to Mr Robert Davye for the same price

John Pope *of* Pydgeleigh *for the year*   **30s**

Wydd Ellett *for the year* ~~15s~~   **12s**

dead **Wydd** Hookeway *otherwise* Charells *for the year*   **9s**

sett againe to Wm Charles for the same price

John Lee *of* Aller *for the year*   **36s 8d**

John Trencher *for the year*   **9s**

Gilbert Trobridge gentleman *for the year* **16d**

Gilbert Trobridge gentleman *for the year* **12d**

[new page]

Aller

Wydd Pope *of* Pydgeleigh [Pidsley]   **15s**

Gilbt Shilston *of* Chuddenbroke   **3s 4d**

John Warryn att pitt *for the year*   **2s 6d**

Nicholas Rowland *for the year*   **4s**

Sum total of the whole Prebend paid for this year

Collens *of* Comellanncy [Combelancey] *recently* labdon   **12d**

Wydd Lovemeade *for the year*   **89**

Mark Townesend *for the year*   **17s**

£22 2s 10d

[new page]

Crosse fo. 16

voyd **Anthony** Copleston gentleman **for the year**   ~~22s~~

17 Dec 1595 sett againe to Giles Kingwell for   24s

Thomas Warryn *for the year*   **13s 4d**

Thomazine Holcomb *widow for the year* **40s**

John Tuckfeild *for the year*   **14s**

Peter Warryn *for the year*   **10s**

William Warryn *for the year*   **10s**

Martin Warryn *for the year*   **10s**

Ursula Borredge widow *for the year*   **11s**

Phillip Chaplinge *for the year*   **10s**

[new page]

Crosse

John Lee *for the year*   **22s**

John Hooke *for the year*   **5s 6d**

Wydd Baily *for the year*   **13s 4d**

Robt Dycklegg *for the year*   **7s**

Wydd Trewman   **14s**

John Dreyton   **13s 4d**

Walter Trewman   **5s**

Giles Delve   **3s 4d**

Andrew Lee   **6s 8d**

John Gullick *of* Uforde   **18s**

[new page]

Crosse fol. 17

Thomas Underhill *formerly* Gullock *of* Vosse **2s**		**William** Vynnecomb	**16s**
John Flodd *for the year*	**13s 4d**	**Giles** Vynnecomb	**16s**
Robt Commyns *for the year*	**17s**	**Wydd** Way and John Way *for the year*	**3s**

Sum total of whole of the prebend of Crosse for the year   **£15 15s 10d**

[new page] ~~Crosse~~

Pruscomb

John Northcott gentleman *for the year*	46s 8d	**Thomas** Gullock of Winstock [Winstout]	13s 4d
George Trobridge gentleman *for the year*	6s 8d	**John** Tucker of Uton	4s
Wm Holcomb gentleman *for the year*	26s 8d	**Wydd** Bennett	5s 4d
Thomas Edbery *for the year*	20s	**Gullocke** of Uton *for the year*	16d
John Mortymer *for the year*	40s	**John** Weste	8s
Thomas Gullock att Lee	23s 4d	**Bennett** Callihall	8s
Thomas Lane att hill	13s 4d	**John** Warren of Pitt	7s 6d
Wydd Atwill	£3	**Wm** Jakes *for the year*	3s 4d
Wydd Callow *for the year*	10s	**Gilbert** Burnell	5s
John Clarke	12s		

Sum total of that prebend of Pruscombe for the year   £15 14s 6d

[new page]

Stowforde

John Coplestone esquire for som pte of his pke	3s 4d	**Robert** Froste	20s
Humphrey Copleston gentleman *for the year*	46s 8d	**Giles** Hooper *for the year*	12s
		Willm Bruton *for the year*	30s
Robt Lee of Spenserscoomb	53s 4d	**Amy** Tucker wydd *for the year*	12s 4d
Wydd Elsen & John her sonne	35s	**Thomas** Lightfoote *for the year*	3s 4d
John Pope of Elsen [Elston]	18s	**John** White *for the year* 1	6s

[new page]

Stowforde

Robert Clase *for the year*	26s 8d	**John** Froste *for the year*	20s
Wm Thomas *for the year*	13s	**Matthew** Frost *for the year*	28s
John Labdonne *for the year*	30s	**John** Gater of Sandford	7s
John Delve senior *for the year*	8s	**John** Gater of Woolesgrove	10s
John Davy gentleman	14s	**John** Wilcocks	8s

[new page]

Stowforde fo: 19

George Clase *for the year*	8s	**Richerd** Peake *for the year*	4d
John Elsen *for the year*	2s 8d	**Gilbert** Froste *for the year*	4d
Austin Hoop *for the year*	3s	**John** Gover *for the year*	8s

Sum total of that prebend of Stowford for the year   £21 17s

[new page]

Woodelande fo: 20

John Furse gentleman *for the year*	36s	**William** Swanson *for the year*	26s 8d
decrese upon Mr Furse	6s	**Richerd** Lillicrop *for the year*	20s
Henry Trewman *for the year*	23s 4d	**Joan** Wolcott *widow for the year*	36s 8d
John Bradly *for the year*	15s	**Henry** Skynner *for the year*	13s 4d

Wydd Turner *for the year*   20s   **Wydd** Delve *for the year*   **20s 8d**

[new page]

Woodeland

Nicholas Maunder *for the year*	16s	**John** Pryddam	10s
Christopher Skynner *for the year*	16s	Robert Gullocke *of* Rocke	[blank]
Maude Pryddam at Rocke [Rock] ~~28s~~	29s	**John** Lendon	8s
Phillip Frannces *for the year*	16s	**Wm** Turner *formerly* Gullock	6s

[new page]

Woodelande   fo: 21

Thomas Gullocke *of* Wynstocke	13s 4d	sett againe to Robert Lane for the same price	
Bennett Collihale	8s	**Thomas** Delve *for the year*	16s
dead **Thomas** Phillip	16s	[blank] Lendon of Colbrocke [Colebrooke]	**4s**
sett againe to John Phillip for the same price.		**Christopher** Adames *for the year*	3s 4d
dead **John** Lane	16s	**Baldwin** Tucker *for the year*	8d

Sum total of that prebend of Woodland for the year £19 9s 4d

[new page]

Towne   fo: 22

Sir Wm Peryam knighte L: chief Baron	30s	**Nicholas** Turbervile gentleman *for the year*	
Sir Thomas Denys knighte *for the year*	53s 4d		**38s 8d**
George Gale esquyre *for the year*	13s	**John** Northcott gentleman *for the year*	7s 6d
John Trobridge esquyre *for the year*	5s 8d	**Anthony** Copleston gentleman *for the year*	20s

[total] £8 8s 2d

[new page]

Towne

Robert Davye gentleman *for the year*	32s 4d	**George** Trobridge gentleman *for the year*	5s
Lawrence Davye gentleman *for the year*	18s 4d	*of the same* George Trobridge for the year	**13s 4d**
John Moxsay *for* Northams *now Philip*		**Elizabeth** Davye Wyddow for the year	10s
Northcott gentleman *for the year*	8s 4d	John Wourth for the year	5s

[total] £4 13s 6d   *of the same* John Wourth *for the year* **14d**

[new page]

Towne   fo: 23

of the same John Wourth *for the year*	4s	**Jervice** Lendon *for the year*	4s 6d
of the same John Wourth *for the year*	4s	*of the same* Jervacio *for the year*	2s
The Sonnes of Walter Harrys *for the year*	26s 8d	**Thomas** Bodleigh *for the year*	8d
		of the same Thoma *for the year*	10d
Ellize Bodleigh *for the year*	2s 6d	**Bennet** Tuckfeild *for the year*	14s
of the same Elize Bodleigh *for the year*	6s 6d		

[total] £3 5s 08d

[new page]

Towne

Thomas Raw *for the year*	8s	**Edward** Denys esquire *for the year*	42s
John Wall *for the year*	4s	**Phillip** Smyth gentleman *for the year*	24s
John Lee *for the year*	18s	Thomas Lightfoote *for the year*	2s
John Davye gentleman *for the year*	7s 8d	**Phillip** Northcott gentleman *for the year* 16s ~~2s~~	
Wydd Nevye *for the year*	2s	**of the same** Phillip *for* Lame Johns Close	**20d**

[total] 6 5 4

[new page]

Towne fo: 24

Walter Shilston *for the year*	**4s 2d**	**Walter** Charde *for the year*	**22s 4d**
of the same Waltero formerly Budbrooke	**16d**	**John** Strange *for the year*	**8s**
Mr Wm Kelligrew for *le* dye howse	**12d**	**John** Horwill *for the year*	**10d**
of the same William for a parcell of Darts		**Richerde** wonnston *for the year*	**20d**
Downes *recently* Gilbert Brodmeade *for the*		**John** Tuckfeild *for the year*	**5s 4d**
year	**10s**	*of the same John for the year*	**20d**
		[total] 2 16 4	

[new page]

Towne

John Gearde *for the year*	**6d**	**Nicholas** Crodenne	**3s 4d**
Richerde Venne *for the year*	**12d**	**Simon** Rocke	**12d**
Thomas Rendell *for the year*	**12d**	**George** Preston	**8d**
John Lech sonne of Nicholas Leache	**20d**	**John** Borrington **20s**	

[new page]

Towne   fo: 25

Humphrey Prydeaux gentleman *for the year*	**12s**	**Lawrence** Mortymer *for the year*	**12d**
Wydd Neilde *for the year*	**12d**	**John** Miller *for the year*	**2d**
John Vynnecomb *for the year*	**12d**	**John** Ware *for the year*	**£3 5s 6d**
William Trewman *for the year*	**3s 4d**	*of the same John for the year*	**6s 4d**
of the same William for the year	**8d**	[total] £4 11s	

[new page]

Towne

Richerd Lane *for the year*	**9s**	of ground pcell of Darts Downes *for the year*	
Gilbert Shilston *for the year*	**10s**		**4s 16s 8d**
John Lech sonne of Simon Leach	**16d**	**Gilbert** Pannsford *for the year*	**13s 4d**
John Clarcke *for the year*	**8s**	**Gilbert** Bonde *for the year*	**7s**
Philip Buckingham *for the year*	**10s**	**Thomas** Spenser *for the year*	**13s**
Margery Brodmead for her customary		**Phillip** Bray *for the year*	**8s**
tenement *for the year* 12s 8d and for 7 acres		[total] 4 16s	

[new page]

Towne   fo: 26

Robt Quyck *for the year*	**4s**	**Roger** Tucker *for the year*	**8d**
John Davye gentleman & Trewman for the		**Gilbert** Lendon *for the year*	**4s**
ground formerly Wydd Slees	**2s 4d**	**Thomas** Furlor *for the year*	**6d**
Wydd Densam *for the year*	**16d**	**John** Tucker *for the year*	**20d**
John Robyns *for the year*	**6d**	**Gilbert** Stevyn *for the year*	**10d**
Wm Eastbroke *for the year*	**8d**	[total]	**16s 6d**

Sum total of the whole of the prebend of Towne for the year £37 1s 8d

[new page]

Parish Rents   fo: 27

Nicholas Turbervile gentleman *for the year*		**Robt** Clarcke *for the year*	**4s**
	26s 8d	**Joan** Deane wydd *for the year*	**8s**
Phillip Smyth gentleman *for the year*	**5s**	**Wydd** Brocke *for the year*	**8s**
Thomas Smyth *for the year*	**20s**	**Wydd** Pope *for the year*	**6s**
Wm Smyth for the year	**9s**	*Sum of the parish rents for the year* £4 6s 8d	

[new page]

prebend of poole [Pool]   fo: 28

Prebend of Poole *for the year*   £10 15s 8d
wheareof Mr John Trobridge doth pay
~~quarterly halfe y~~ every halfe yeare 36s and Mr
Newman doth pay every halfe yeare £3 11s 10d
John How for his Barton yearely   **26s 8d**
Mr William Kelligrew for the 4 mills yearely   **25s**
Robt Bennett for his mills yearely   **4s**

Wydd Baily for her mills yearely   **3s 4d**
Thomas Raw for his mills yearely   **10s**
Thomas Dunscomb for his mills yearely   **4s**
Mr Turbervile for the great meadow yearely
                                          21s 4d
Phillip Wade for the 10th of the faires y'rly 2s
                               Sum total £15 12s

[new page]

Exmyster   fo: 29

The Farmers of the Tithes for the year £104 3s 4d

Mr Southcott *for the year*   40s
Mr Edmund Parker *for the year*   £5 10s
Mr Henry Tottell *for the year*   £4

Mr John Davy of *Exeter for the year* 3   0s
Mr Style *for the year*   13s 4d
Thomas Crockhey *for rent for the year*   40s
                           Sum total £119 16s 8d

[new page]

fo. 30

Tithes payde for piggs
John Robyns *for the year*   4d
Robert Bolt *for the year*   4d
John Snell *for the year*   6d
John Welsh *for the year*   8d
Robert Webber for the year   16d
John Adames for the year   8d

Mr Lawrence Davy *for the year*   4d
Richerd Hill *for the year*   6d
John Salter *for the year*   6d
Henry Brocke *for the year*   6d
John Berry *for the year*   8d
John Miller *for the year*   4d
Humphrey Jellett *for the year*   4d
                           Sum total 7s

53. CREDITON including SANDFORD, Church Rate, 1619

DHC, Diocese of Exeter, Principal Registry, Crediton Church Rates, 1619

Note: This rate, a fair copy, was written on sheets of paper which measure approximately 6 inches in width and 12 inches in length and which have been stitched together to form a book of twenty-four pages. The numerals are mostly but not exclusively in Roman. Residents of Crediton and Sandford were assessed separately for this rate along with those who held agistments. The use of the names for the tithings and prebends continued to change according to the scribe's preferred organisation. It may have been the churchwarden of the same name, William Lee, who was later presented for talking during divine service with William Vynycombe.[19]

A Noote of Rates made the 4th day of November *in the year of our Lord* 1619 by William Lee and John Pridham Churchwardens and Christopher Weale sideman of Crediton, upon the Inhabitants of Crediton and hamblett of Sandforde for the repairing of the Church of Crediton aforesaid

Borowghe Receits

Mr Phillip Smyth   1s 8d   Gilbert Lendon   8d
Mrs Buckingham   2s 4d   Simon Leach tanner   1s 4d
Walter shilston   1s   Robert Tucker   8d

---

[19]   DHC, CC170 (no item number).

Gervase Lendon	8d	Thomas Hollande	8d
Nicholas Slee	1s	John Leach weaver	8d
Roger Bolte	8d	John Challacombe	1s
widowe Preston	4d	Phillip Smyth cordwainer	4d
Hugh Parker	6d	William Leach	4d
Lawrence Darte	8d	Clement Pidsleigh	4d
John Saunders	1s 4d	Walter Kensall	8d
Peter Palmer	8d	William stronge	8d
~~Leonard~~ Widow Leach	2s	Thomas Rowcley	8d
Henry Lake	1s	John Osborne	4d
Gawen Reeve	1s 4d	John Perrie	4d

Sum total [damaged] 10d

[page 2]

Nicholas Osborne	[torn]	John Furler	6d
Simon Lee	4d	James Sannders	4d
Arthur Rowden	4d	John Snell	4d
Humphrey Waldron	4d	the Occupiers of Mr Yonngs howses in the	
Robert Hooper	4d	Borowghe	4d
The occupiers of John Please his tenement	4d	Aaron Smyth	4d
Edward Perrie	4d		

Justments

~~Leonard~~ Widow Leach for Mr Turners tenement	4d
John Jellett for a tenement *once upon a time* Mr Northcots	8d
~~Leonard~~ Widow Leach for Robert Quicks grounde	4d
Mrs Buckingham for the widow Bodleighes ground	2d

Sum 5s 8d

Cannon Fee

Mr Thomas Gale	2s 8d	George Bodleigh	1s 4d
Mr George Gale	1s 4d	Widowe Lane	8d
Mr George Wilton	1s 4d	The occupiers of Henry Bourtons howse 4d	
Mrs Turbervile	3s 4d	Henry Marles	8d
John Brocke	1s 4d	Mrs Woode	1s 4d
Thomas Edberrie	8d	Stephen Neabels	4d
Bartholomew Tucker	4d	Hercules Stockman	4d
Richard Bourton	4d	Robert Welshe	2d
Henry Rowe	2d	John Stevins	4d
Matthew Ware	8d	Henry Northdram	8d
John Cleeve	4d		*Sum* 18s 8d

[page 3]

Towne tithinge

Sir Robert Bassett knight	2s 8d	Richarde Phillip	4s
Mr Bevill Prideaux	1s 4d	Robert shilston	1s
Mr Roger Trobridge	2s 8d	The occupiers of Mr yonngs tenement	1s 4d
Mr William Yeollande	3s	['Meadland' in margin] The occupiers of Mr	
Mr Daniel Hamblyn	3s 8d	Davies tenement	1s
Mrs Cooke	8d	Phillip Lake	1s 8d
Widow ware	4s	Robert Brownscombe	4d
Henry Harris	2s 8d	Joan Whiterow widowe	10d

John Buckingham	8d	walter Levitt	8d
Mark Townsend	1s 4d	Robert Harris	8d
Thomas Sannders	8d	Richarde Bickle	4d
John Lendon for shilstons tenement	4d	marie ware widowe	8d
Widowe Spenser	1s	William Rogers	4d
Thomas Trewman	4d	John Lendon for his owne abilitie	4d
William Honiwill	1s	John Pope	8d
John Adams	4d	The Occupiers of lower Forton [Fordton] and	
John Rowe	1s	of Elworthies Childrens Mylls	1s 4d
Phillip Buckingham	1s 4d	*Sum £2 4s 10d*	

[page 4]

Towne tithing justments

William Helmore and Phillip Bourton for Mr Prowse his tenemente	2s
Mark Townsend and Roger Bolte for Chittenbrooke	4d
Thomas sannders for Andrew Horsewills tenement	4d
John Pridham for his Justment	8d
Mr Champneis tenement	8d
Richard Bourton for Mr Northcots gronnde	8d
Phillip Bourton for Mr Northcots gronnde	4d
John sannders and ~~Leonard~~ widow Leach for Mr Tickels ground in the pke	1s 4d
The Occupiers of Mr maynes tenement	8d
John sannders ~~Leonard~~ widow Leach and f Robert Harris for Mr Trobridges gronnde in the pke	8d
Widow Potter	2d
Mr Christopher stronge and Simon Row for pte of will pke	4d
Sum 8s 2d	

[page 5]

Rudeg [Rudge] tithing

John Trobridge Esquire	4s	Walter Lane	1s 4d
Thomas Bodleigh Esquire	6s	Henry Weivill	8d
George Trobridge senior gent.	3s 4d	Henry Lendon	4d
George Trobridge Junior Esquire	4s	George Woolridge	4d
The Occupiers of Mr George Dunscombs		Gilbert Jeston	4d
Barton	3s 4d	Richarde Burnell	4d
Mr Walter Dunscombe	1s 4d	Walter Tapper	2d
Simon Lane	1s 4d	John Pitts	2d
Robert Keymell	4d	['Justment' in margin] Simon Lane for pte of	
William Tarr & James Jeston	4d	Aishmoore	2d
Widow Buckingham	1s 8d	*Sum 29s 6d*	

[page 6]

Ewton [Uton] tithing

John Northcot Esquire		Walter Woodleigh	4d
William Holcombe gent.	3s 4d	John Woodleigh	4d
John Tuckfeild gent.	4s 8d	John Edberie	1s 4d
Walter Conibie	2s	William Jakes	4d
['for Radfords tenement' in margin] William		Widow Bennett	4d
Gullocks	8d	Widowe Tucker	4d
Benjamin Bremblecombe	1s 4d	James Lendon	4d
Nicholas Britten	1s 8d	John Callowe	1s
Robert Ware	1s	Bennet Kingwill	8d

John Conibie	1s	William Lake	6d
Phillip Temblet	4d	The Occupiers of Mr Bermans tenement	2s 8d
Bennet Allyn	4d	Mr Yonnge for Tedborne	2s 4d
['Justments' in margin] Phillip Temblet for Mr		Bennet Brodmead	4s
Tuckfeilds tenement	8d	Mark Townsend for pte of moore	8d
Gilbert shilston Junior	4d	John Hooke for posberie	4d
Elize Trewman for pte of Ewe [Yeo] Barton	10d		*Sum* 39s 2d
Bennet Kingwill for pte of the same Barton	2d		

[page 7]

Knoll [Knowle] tithinge

Thomas Please	2s 8d	Matthew Hooper	8d
Phillip Elston	2s 4d	Giles White	1s
Robert Lee	3s 4d	John Morrishe	4d
Giles Britten	1s 8d	Barnarde Smale	4d
Richarde Frost	1s 4d	Robert Phillip weaver	4d
Robert Clase	1s 4d	['Justments' in margin] Amias Coplestone	
Widowe Lobdon	2s	Esquire for pte of his pke	4d
Gilbert Frost and his mother	1s 6d	Nicholas Pope for the Barton of Knoll	2s 8d
widow Frost at Knoll	1s	Thomas Please for Chapple Downe	4d
Edward Dulyn	1s	Thomas Please for a tenement in tymes past	
Mr Yeollande for goldwill [Goldwell]	2s	Lightfootes	2d
William Thomas	1s		*Sum* 27s 4d

[page 8]

Woodland tithinge

George Wolcott	1s 8d	Robert skinner	8d
Widowe Lilicrope	1s	George Trewman	1s
Widowe Pridham	4d	Thomas Collihall	1s
William Gullocke	1s 4d	Widowe Bradleighe	8d
Robert Hooke	1s 4d	Phillip Frannces	10d
Thomas Temblet	10d	William Hooke	8d
Matthew Caseleigh	1s	John Burnell	8d
John Pridham	1s 4d	Widow Burnell	4d
Henry Keymell	8d	John Gullocke	4d
George Gullocke	1s 4d		

['Justments' in margin]			
The Occupiers of Mr Furse his Barton	1s 8d	Bawden Sannders	2d
John Lee of Colbrooke	8d	Edward Aishe for Bowden ground	2d
			Sum 19s 8d

[page 9]

Ewforde [Yeoford] tithinge

Robert Gullocke	1s 4d	Widowe Morrishe	1s
Edward Martyn	1s	Giles Vinecombe	1s 4d
Gilbert Trewman	2s	Christopher Lee	1s
Thomas Warren	1s	['hollacombe' in margin] William Vinecombe	
John Dreaton	1s		1s 8d
['Kemelford' in margin] William Vinecombe		Robert Hooke	1s
	1s 4d	Widowe Floodd	1s
Widowe Burridge	8d	Lawrence Chollishe	8d

Christopher Weale	1s	Widowe Lee	1s 4d
Robert Bayleighe	1s 8d	John Weeks	1s
Giles Kingwill	1s 4d	Nathaniel Lee	8d
William Lee	1s 4d	Thomas Temblet	4d
Thomas Ley	8d	Robert Brownscombe	8d
Bennet Temblet	8d	Walter Trewman	4d
Peter Trewman	1s	['Justments' in margin] Mr Christopher	
Robert Warren	8d	Stronge for Jewes [Jew's] Hollacombe	4s
John Reeve	8d	Bennet Temblet for two Justments	2d
Robert Dicklegge	8d	John Weeks and Gilbert Shilston Junior for	
Robert Burridge	8d	Fursedowne	4d
Andrew Stronge	8d	*Sum* 35s 10d	
		Sum total of Crediton £12 13s 8d	

[page 10]

A Rate made upon the Inhabitants of Sandford for the repayringe of the church of Crediton, 1619.

Sir Edward Chechister knight	3s	Matthew Pope	1s 2d
Thomas Dowriche Esquire	2s	Simon Pridham	8d
John Davie Esquire	2s 4d	Thomas Mortimer & his Brother	6d
Emmanuell Davie gent	2s 8d	Robert Mildon	8d
The occupiers of Mr Gyes tenemente	1s	Gilbert Mortimer	8d
George White gent.	1s 4d	Thomas Cobleigh	8d
James Aishe gent	1s 4d	Thomas Haydon	2s 6d
Robert Tripe gent	1s	Richarde Lane	6d
['for a tenemente at Sandford towne' in		Richarde Bawden	4d
margin] Mr John Davie	1s	John Clase	4d
Robert Burrington gent.	2s	Widowe Bande	8d
Richarde Clarke	1s 6d	John Reede of Henstill	4d
Henry Harris	1s	Robert Smale	2d
Robert Phillip	2s 4d	John Northcot	6d
John Holcombe	1s 6d	Widowe Paidge	1s 2d
John Howe	1s 4d	William Myller Senior	2d
John Mortimer of Remscombe [Ranscombe]		Roger Jacob	4d
	1s 6d	Thomas Northcot	6d
John Tucker	1s	William Miller Junior	2d
Thomas Lane at hill	1s 2d	*Sum* £2 1s	

[page 11]

William Brembridge	6d	John Adams	2d
Arthur Whiterow	4d	William Densham	4d
Christopher Pope	6d	Robert Wrayforde	8d
Samuel Coxe	6d	Hugh Heis	4d
John Reede	8d	Robert Borowgh for henstill	6d
Richarde Borowghe	4d	William Mortimer of Coombe	4d
Richarde Coxe	6d	Peter Rocke	2d
David Beere	2d	Agnes Gater	4d
Simon Legge	4d	Widow Lane of storidge	6d
John Mortimer of Levibrooke	1d	Robert Lane	9d
Roger Pitts	2d	John Forde	8d
John Hall	8d	John Rowlande	1s 6d
Richarde Delve	6d	John Phillip	10d
James Vicarie	1s 8d	Gilbert Burrington	6d

Thomas Coake	4d	Thomazine Delve widow	2d
Robert Gardner	2d	Robert Taylor	1d
John Beare	4d	Ellize Breedie	2d
John Lane of Burridge	4d	John Hill	2d
Robert Waye	2d	William Burrington	2d
John Adams Junior	2d		*Sum* 16s 9d

[page 12]

Justments

Nicholas keene	6d	John Mortimer for Creedie	4d
Widowe Weareman	6d	the Occupiers of the tenement of Beere [Bere]	
['for Borow' in margin] William Pope &		mils	4d
Richard wearmen	8d	the Occupiers of ~~Beere~~ deedie mills	2d
George Prior & Robert sannders	6d	John Holcombe for Wolsegrove	2d
Widow maunder & Thomas Bradford	2d	Robert Lane for pte of Aishmoore	2d
Robert Gribble	1d	John Hall for a Justment	4d
Henry Pope	3d	Peter Snow for Furse pke	2d
Robert Bande	2d	Peter Rocke for Aishe	2d
John Mortimer for swelthill	4d	Roger Selbie	8d
John Gillerd	1d		Sum 6s 5d
John Lane for henstill	4d	*Sum total of* Sandforde £3 4s 2d	
Peter Lobdon for heards tenemente	4d		

[sign of] John Pridham
[signed] William Lee Christopher Weale

54. CREDITON including SANDFORD, Tithe Account, 1630

DHC, 1660A/O/A/261

Note: There are tithe accounts for the years 1630, 1631, 1633, 1635, 1639 twenty-four pages which are approximately 6 inches in width and 16 inches in length. This is a working copy with some tally marks recorded to show payment. Amongst the place names noted were Lame John's Close. The numerals are Arabic. The organisation of the account was similar to that of the rate of 1619.

1630

A Booke whereby to collect the money to be due and payable for the Tythes of Crediton and Sandford in the yeere aforesaid

Quarterly

Towne Tything

Thomas Tucfeld gent	£01 00s 00d
Thomas Poyntingdon gent for Westwood late Mr Yollands	00 10 01 ½
Silvanus Evans for (*once upon a time*) Mr Yollands houses and grounde in the Borrowgh	00 01 01 ½
Roger Trobridge for Uton and Yew mills	00 03 00
Wm Elworthie for the one moytie of the Fower mills	00 05 00
Wm Holcombe gent for the other moyty of the said Fower mills	00 05 00
~~John Trend for~~ The occupiers of lower Forton	00 06 00
[illegible & ~~Pontingdon gent~~ Mr Wilston for late Mr Newcombes houses & backsides	00 01 01 ½
of him for late Cornishes ground	00 02 07 ½
of him for stonie crosse & other ground	00 03 09

of him for Goldwill	00 13 01 ½
of him for Northams and Downes	00 07 06
Mr Hamlyn for the great meadow	01 03 03
of him for his Copy hold Tenement	00 05 00
of him for George Hill grounde	00 01 09
wid: Buckingham for her copie holde tenement	00 08 01 ½
John ware for pte of the same tenement	00 05 00
~~Widow~~ John Buckingham for her grounde in the commonmarshlane	00 01 10 ½
John Buckingham for howkway ground	00 07 06
Mr Richard Phillip for wares downes	01 10 00
of him for Pallace ground	00 05 00
Mr Robert young for his Tenement	00 11 03
~~of him~~ Peter Keene for southwoods house & ground	00 00 09
Thomas Channon for late Mr Phillip Nothcots house & grounde	00 01 03

[new page]

Mr John Davie of meadland for his house and Tenement	£00 04s 00d
of him for pte of the Common marshes	00 06 03
of him for pte of Coplestons marshes	00 02 03
Phillip Lake of Bradleigh	00 11 03
John Buckingham for his Tenement	00 03 09
Robert Brownscombe of Bradleigh	00 01 10 ½
John Trend *once upon a time* Townsend [added 'abated 6d quarterly *for the year* 2s']	00 07 06
Simon Burridge *once upon a time* Saunders	00 02 03
Thomas Sannders for his ground and house att Bowden Hill	00 00 04 ½
Mr Richard Coles for late horses ground	00 02 03
Gilbert Shilston for Chiddenbrooke	00 02 03
of him for his owne Tenement	00 03 09
John Lendon for his ground in Towne	00 01 01 ½
of him for Sarehills	00 03 09
John Adams for his house & garden	00 00 01 ½
Mr John Row for his Tenement and for his houses in the Churchyarde	00 06 03
Philip Buckingham for his Copy hold tenement	00 05 00
Walter Levitt for his Tenement	00 05 00
John Pope of Westwood for his Tenement and for Fulfords houses and ground	00 03 09
Marie Edberie for Fulfords meadow	00 00 09
Joseph Slee for Selwood meadowes	00 02 07 ½
Mr Carow for the Newmills & ground	00 03 00
Widow Potter for her meadow	00 00 09
John Phillip for his ground in Towne	00 00 09
Mr Samuel mayne clerke for his Tenement	00 02 06
warren and Fursdon for pte of Common marshes	00 01 10 ½
George Gale gent for his Tenement	00 04 06
of him for Creedy Bridge marsh	00 01 06
of him for Crayl hayes	00 00 09
Emanuell Davie gent for his tenement	00 03 09
of him for lame John's Close	00 01 00

[new page]

Leases

Sir Robert Killigrew Knight for the pke	£00 13s 04d
The occupiers of late Mr Wm Prowses Tenement	00 09 0

Mr George Trobridge for Beere	00 03 04
Henry Harris for winsor	00 07 06
John Furse gent for his Copy hold tenement	00 00 09
Mrs Buckingham	00 07 06
Walter Shilston	00 00 10
Richard Shilston	00 07 06
Phillip Buckingham for Darts Downes	00 03 04
Elizabeth Spenser	00 04 00
Bennett Allen	00 03 04
Richard Bickell	00 02 00

Parish Rents

Mr John Row	00 01 08	Wm Elston	00 05 00
Mrs Turbevile	00 06 08	The Occupiers of the Church hous	00 08 04
Mrs Buckingham	00 01 07	Thomas Smith	00 01 00

Cannon Fee

Mrs Elizabeth Gale widow	00 07 06	of him for the Common marshes	00 03 00
Mrs Turbervile widow	01 06 0 3	Henry Harris for pte of the Widow Bodleighs	
~~Richard~~ Phillip Borton	00 00 06	ground	00 03 09
Mr Reeve for late George Bodleighs ground		of him for the fair Parke ~~and other ground~~	
	00 06 09	[added '& 2 marshes *once upon a time* Mr	
Robert Lane	00 03 00	Davie of meadland']	00 03 00
Mr George Wilton by lease	00 03 06		

[new page]

Burrow

Mrs Buckingham for dickers ham and delbridge	£00 03s 09d	Andrew Quicke John Pope of westwood and Walter Kensall	00 03 00
of her for Buckinghams Close	00 00 09	[added 'Widow Reeve for the pke house & garden 2d quarterly']	
John Trend for Simon Leaches house and grounde	00 01 10 ½	Gawyne Reeve	00 01 00
George Gale gent for Chiddenbrooke ground		[added 'set the occupyers Richard Reeve £1 10d ½ and {illegible} Reeve 4d quarterly']	
	00 02 03	William Leach	00 00 03
Eleanor Tucker widow	00 00 01 ½	Thomas Chanon	00 00 04
Roger Bolte	00 00 09	Walter Kensall	00 00 09
Samuel Parker	00 00 01 ½	Widow Osborne for house & ground	00 01 06
Lawrence Darte	00 00 01	William Collins	00 00 01
John Saunders	00 00 04 ½	John Furler	00 00 03
John Vinecomb	00 00 03	John Jellett	00 03 09
Henry Lake	00 00 01 ½	Widow Gearde	00 00 03
John Pope for wearesfoote	00 01 01 ½	Widow Bolte	00 00 09
of him for three other closes	00 01 06	Edward Dicker	00 00 01
of him for Turners grounde	00 02 09	Phillip Tule	00 00 03
of him for Chiddenbrooke	00 01 08	John Forde	00 00 04
of him for Mrs Gales pte of Chddenbrooke		John Lane of Sandford for pte of the Common	
	00 01 08	marshes	00 06 00
of him for the ground under the Parke	00 01 09	William Strong	00 00 01
of him for a close at Bowden Hill	00 00 04 ½	Phillip Stevins	00 00 01
of him for Augustyne Randells ground		~~Robte~~ Phillip wrayford	00 00 03
	00 00 04 ½		
John Lyde for his house	00 00 03		

[added 'set the ocuppiers'] Mr Wm Holcomb
for Mr Chards garden   00 00 05
Thomas Robts of Stockly pomeroy   00 00 03

Nicholas Slee by lease   00 02 03
Simon Leach Chandler   00 00 01
James Sannders   00 00 03

[new page]

Woodland

George Woolcott   £00 11s 03d
Wilmot Lillicropp widow | 00 07 06
william Gullocke | 00 07 06
Thomas Temblett   00 05 07 ½
Widow Caseleigh   00 11 03
John Pridham of Rocke   00 09 04 ½
of him for his Tenement in Towne 00 05 07 ½
of him for the widow Pridham's tenement
                                  00 02 09 ¼
of him for the widow Clashes tenement
                                  00 00 04 ½
William Hooke   00 03 09
Robert Skinner   00 03 09
George Trewman | 00 07 06
Thomas Collihole   00 06 00

Phillip Frannces | 00 06 00
Robert Westington   00 03 09
John Burnell   00 02 03
John Gullocke | 00 02 09 ¼
John Lendon of Colbrock || 00 01 01 ½
John Skinner | 00 05 07 ½
Thomas Furse gent   00 11 03
William Aish   00 01 00
John Furse gent for Bradly   00 05 07
Peter Tucker   00 00 03
Robert Hooke for Gunston | 00 07 06
of him for Surtacomb | 00 07 06
Henry Delve by lease   00 05 02
George Gullocke | 00 09 04 ½

[new page]

Knoll

Thomas Please for Lightfoote   £00 02s 03d
William Thomas for Eastland | 00 03 00
Robert Lee of Spenscoomb [Spence Combe]
                                     01 10 00
Widow Frost of Elston | 00 07 06
Amy Frost widow   00 09 04 ½
Widow Duling | 00 07 06
Richard Burredge | 00 05 07 ½
William Thomas | 00 05 07 ½
Giles White   00 07 06

John Morrish [added 'for the moity of
Daviesland']   00 01 10 ½
Widow Lobdon | 00 13 01 ½
Robert Clase | 00 09 04 ½
Barnard Smale   00 01 10 ½
Matthew Frost | 00 00 04 ½
Phillip Elston | 00 11 11
widow Britten | 00 10 00
William Yeo | 00 05 07 ½
Mr John Venner   00 15 00

[new page]

Uforde

Widow Gullocke | £00 07s 06d
Zachary Martyn   00 06 00
Gilbert Trewman   00 08 07 ½
Widow Dreyton | 00 06 00
John Pring Weeks   00 01 06
William Vinecombe of Kemelford [Keymelford]
                             | 00 07 06
John Burredge   00 04 10 ½
John Lee of Gunston | 00 08 03
Robert How of Hollocomb | 00 08 03
Widow Fludd | 00 06 00
Lawrence Chollice   00 04 10 ½
Christopher Weale   00 09 04 ½
Robert Bayleigh   00 09 00
Giles Kingwill   00 09 04 ½

John Burrington for Hollcomb | 00 05 07 ½
of him for Chapple Downe | 00 02 03
John Dunscomb late Thomas Ley   00 04 06
Bennett Temblett | 00 03 04 ½
of him ['Nicholas Lee' inserted] for
Northdownes   00 01 06
Peter Trewman & John Pidsleigh   00 06 00
Robert Warren | 00 04 06
Robert Dicklegg   00 03 09
Andrew Lee & his mother | 00 08 06
John Weeks for his Tenement   00 04 10 ½
Walter Trewman & his sonne John | 00 02 03
Robert Burredge   00 03 09
Mr Christopher Strang   01 02 06
Widdow Mortimer of Gunnston | 00 00 09

Thomas Warren by lease | 00 03 04	Giles Vinecomb by lease [added 'sett the
~~William Strang~~ ['now John Mildon' added]	ocupyers 7s 6d but we wish yt only 6s p[er]
00 03 09	quarter because of her povertie'] 00 04 00
Nathaniel Lee by lease 00 03 06	William Lee by lease | 00 03 09
Widow Morrish by lease [added 'she is Dead	John Reeve by lease 00 02 09
set Jo. Pitwood 7s 6d *by* quarterly'] 00 05 00	Robert Brownscombe by lease 00 03 00
Thomas Temblett att Pitt [added 'set Jo Temlet	
3s quarterly'] 00 02 06	

[new page]

Rudge

George Trobridge Esquire £01 06s 03d	Henry Lendon | 00 01 01 ½
George Trobridge Junior gent for Upcott 00 07 06	Gilbert Jurston 00 01 01 ½
of him for Westacott ~~by lease~~ 00 10 00	Richard Burnell 00 00 09 ½
William Payne 00 07 06	John Foote 00 01 01 ½
Mr Wm Golde for Dunscomb 01 06 03	Walter Lee 00 01 01 ½
of him for pte of Copstons marshes 00 03 09	William Slade 00 00 09
Mr Doctor Westcomb 00 10 06	William Trobridge gent 00 01 06
Richard Prowze gent for Forton and serells	John Newcomb of Trobridge Downe 00 00 11 ½
01 01 00	Robert Mortimer 00 00 09
Mr Waldron for lower Dunscomb 01 02 06	Nicholas West 00 01 01 ½
Catherine Lane widow 00 06 04 ½	Widow Dunscomb 00 11 03
of her for Hooke meadow 00 02 07 ½	John Pitts 00 00 04
Paul Bery *once upon a time* Kemill | 00 01 01 ½	Walter Tapper 00 01 01 ½
Edward Jeffrey 00 00 04 ½	Henry Searell 00 00 02 ½
Walter Lane for his Tenement 00 08 03	John Bennett 00 00 01 ½
of him for Kerswills 00 03 09	Roger Tucker 00 00 02 ½
of him for pte of wyvills Tenement 00 00 09	Lewis Marrell 00 00 02 ½
Henry Wyvell 00 03 04 ½	Richard Tapper 00 00 02 ½
Widow Woolridge 00 01 01 ½	

[new page]

Uton

Wor[shipfu]ll John Northcott Esquire for Uton by lease	£00 11s 08d
of him for a Tenement in Towne by lease	00 01 10½
of him for Goose Allers	00 01 10½
of him for pte of Harves lease	00 12 09
[added 'Mr Walter Tuckfild for Uton and pt the Cleaves 4s 6d quarterly']	
John Tuckfeld gent for Uton by lease	00 05 00
[added 'Mr Roger Tuckfild for the Cleeves & Edburies 9s quarterly']	
of him for another Tenement by lease	00 03 06
[added 'Mr Walter & Roger Tuckfild for [illegible] 4s 3d quarterly']	
of him for pte of Hoopers Tenement	00 02 06
[added 'sett Mr Ro Tuckfield']	
of him for pte of Mr Yonngs Tenement	00 00 06
John Woodleigh	00 04 06
Margery Radford by lease	00 03 06
Thomas Holland *once upon a time* Tucker	00 02 09¼
Thomas Holcomb gent |	00 18 03
Bennett Kingwell |	00 05 03
Nicholas Pope *once upon a time* John Conesbye	00 05 00
of him for pte of Mr Youngs Tenement	00 02 06

George Conesbie late his Fathers	00 02 06
Benjamin Bremelcomb for his Tenement	00 06 00
of him for Posbery	00 02 03
Widow Britten for her tenement	00 03 09
of her for Posberie	00 03 09
| Robert Britten for pte of Mr Yonngs tenement	00 03 06
ffor late Robert Wares Tenement	00 04 06
John Edbury and his sonne	00 07 06
[added 'Mr Roger Tuckfil & Mr Walter Tucfield']	
John Tucfeld gent for pte of Edburis tenement	00 03 00
Silvanus Evans for pte of Edburies tenement	00 00 09
[added 'Wm' illegible]	
Widow Jakes	00 01 06
Widow Bennett	00 02 09¼
Nicholas Lee late Hookes tenement	00 01 06
John Callow	00 06 00
of him for late Lendons Tenement	00 02 03
Widow Handcock	00 01 00
Widow Hawkins	00 00 09
Walter Young Esquire for pte of Tedborne	00 09 04½
Widow Symons	00 00 04½
Richard Phillip for moore	00 08 03
John Frannces for moore lake	00 00 09
William Tarr for pte of hoops tenement	00 00 04½
Robert Harris for pte of hoops	00 00 04½
John Lee for pte of Hoopers	00 00 04½
Robert Quash for pte of Hoopers	00 00 03
Mr Champnowne for yew	00 17 06
William Lake for pte of yew	00 03 00
Bennett Kingwell for pte of yew	00 01 01½
Nathaniel Reeve for pte of yew	00 02 03
Thomas Edbury for pte of yew	00 01 06
Thomas Bussell for pte of yew	00 00 04½
John Clarke for pte of yew	00 04½
Walter Reeve for pte of yew 00 01 00	
Ellize Trewman ['Giles Kingwill' added] for pte of yew	00 00 03
Walter Deyman for pte of yew	00 01 03
Wm moore for pte of yew	00 00 04½
Thomas Holland for pte of symons tenement	00 00 01½
James Jurston for pte of hoopers tenement	00 00 04½
Mr John Tucfeld for Walter Hoop and Peter Hooper's tenement	00 00 04½

[new page]

Sandford

Emanuel Davy gentleman for Ruxford	£02 00s 00d
of him for Fenne	00 07 06
of him for Gaters Tenement	00 03 09
of him for Govers Tenement	00 03 04
of him for his owne Tenement by lease	00 06 08
of him for Dowrich walls	00 02 03
of him for late John Davies Tenement	00 09 00

Wor[shipfu]ll John Davie Esquire for his home Tenement	01 00 00
of him for long barne	01 09 00
of him for late Howes Tenement	01 00 00
Wor[shipfu]ll John Nortchott Esquire for late Lanes tenement	00 09 00
George White gentleman by lease	00 05 10
John Helmer for pte of Mr Whites tenement	00 05 00
Mrs Grace Davie and Mr Bellew	00 14 03
Mr Bellew for that Phillip Lake held	00 02 00
Mr Robert Burrington	01 00 00
Walter Young Esquire late Aishes tenement	01 00 00
Lewis Dowrich gentleman *once upon a time* Mr Treepe	00 10 00
James Vicary	00 05 03
Robert Lane Junior for pte of Jo: Davies tenement	00 05 03
Widow Clarke for Creedy	00 19 06
of her for her Cottaige	00 02 07 ½
Margery Phillip widow	00 02 03
Henry Harris for Sutton	00 11 03
John Holcomb for Crosse	01 02 06
of him for late Wests tenment by lease	00 01 09
John Mortimer of Remscomb	01 02 06
of him for Creedy	00 05 07 ½
for him for swetshill	00 02 07 ½
John Tucker of wollesgrove	00 15 04 ½
Robert Lane Junior for Baunton hayes	00 05 07 ½
of him for Cleyland	00 00 04 ½
widow Pope for Pidgley	00 11 03
Simon Pridham	00 08 07 ½
John Pridham of Rocke *once upon a time* mortimer	00 05 07 ½
widow mildon	00 08 07 ½
widow mortimer	00 08 06
Thomas Cobly	00 06 09
Thomas Haydon	00 11 03
of him for his lower Tenement	00 08 03
of him for pte of Coomblanncy	00 07 06
more of him for pte of Coomblanncy	00 08 03

[new page]

John Clase [added 'we think the lease not good so he must pay this']	£00 05s 07d ½
Jo: Jacob *otherwise* Stevyn	00 03 00
William Charells *otherwise* miller	00 04 06
Arthur Whitraw	00 03 09
+ William Pope	00 06 09
+ of the same William *once upon a time* warman	00 06 00
Samuel Cox	00 05 03
John Reed of Storidge & of him for Aller Downe	00 07 01 ½
Roger Bond	00 07 06
Widow Burrow	00 03 09
Richard Cox	00 06 09
David Beere	00 01 06
Widow Legg	00 04 06

John Mortimer of Lethybrooke	00 01 06
Thomas Reed of Priston [added 'John Hale']	00 01 06
Roger Lobdon	00 01 02
Richard Delve for his tenement	00 03 09
of him for Fursland	00 01 06
John Vicary	00 12 06
John Adams	00 03 04 ½
Charles Adams & Richard Adams	00 03 04 ½
John Lane for Yolland	00 03 09
- of him & lee for blackmanscombe [Blackmoore Combe]	00 03 03
- John Cockerham for Burredge	00 04 10 ½
Roger Lane of Storidge	00 05 03
Robert Lane senior for Aishmoore	00 03 04 ½
of him for Brendons and for Culv' Cleeves	00 04 10
Mr Cotton *once upon a time* Frosts ['Walter Harvie' added]	00 01 01 ½
John Ellett *once upon a time* Densham	00 03 09
Thomas Wrayford	[added 'now John Jellett']	00 09 00
John Bere	00 03 09
John Ford *otherwise* his widow	00 09 09
John Hall for wollesgrove	00 04 06

[new page]

John Phillip of Creedy	00 01 06
Thomas Coake	00 04 06
Gilbert Burrington	00 00 09
Widow Keene	00 05 07 ½
Robert Sannders *once upon a time* Pryor	00 04 06
John Haunce	00 06 09
John Lane	00 04 01 ½
Peter Lobdon	00 03 04 ½
Widow Potter	00 02 00
it should be 2s *for the year* more but it is given to the widow because of her poverty	
Richard Please for deedy mill	00 02 00
Peter Rocke	00 01 06
& of him for Aish	00 01 06
Robert Teylder	00 01 01 ½
John Adams of Fen lake	00 01 00
Widow Mannder	00 00 09
Widow Bradford	00 01 06
Phillip Way	00 01 06
Richard Atwill	00 00 06
Henry Pope	00 02 03
Robert Bond of morchard	00 01 01 ½
[added 'by Aishmoore'] John Geallard of Downe St Mary	00 01 01 ½
Robert Gribble	00 01 01 ½
Phillip Elston *once upon a time* Frosts	00 02 03
Edward Delve	00 02 07 ½
Widow Delve	00 01 10 ½
Robert Collens	00 00 06
Richard Phillip	00 00 09
John Butcher	00 00 04 ½

Elizabeth Paige widow   00 05 07 ½
William Tucker *once upon a time* Pound   00 00 04 ½
John Paige   00 05 07 ½
John Rowland of sammaton *by* lease   00 05 00

[new page]

John Reed by lease	£00 02s 00d	John Phillip ~~of Creedy~~	00 04 00
Gilbert Northcott	00 05 09	John Hall	00 04 00
Robert Burrow by Lease	00 05 00	Robert Lane senior [added 'qr to see his lease']	00 04 00
Gilbert mayer of Aish	00 01 10 ½		
+ John Rowland *once upon a time* Rowe *by* lease	00 04 08	Gilbert Burrington [added 'senior']	00 02 03
		William Bremridge |	00 05 00
Thomas Northcott by lease |	00 03 04	The occupiers of Dowrich Barton	01 01 00
~~Widow Bawdon~~ ['Robert Small' added] |	00 02 00	John Lane for Halscom meadow and wall downe	00 03 00
Richard Lane	00 03 04	The Occupiers of the Burrowgh Land	00 05 00
Widow Warman	00 04 06	The Occupiers of Rookwood and the Copps	00 01 04
Thomas Please senior by lease	00 11 03		
Peter Snow	00 03 09		

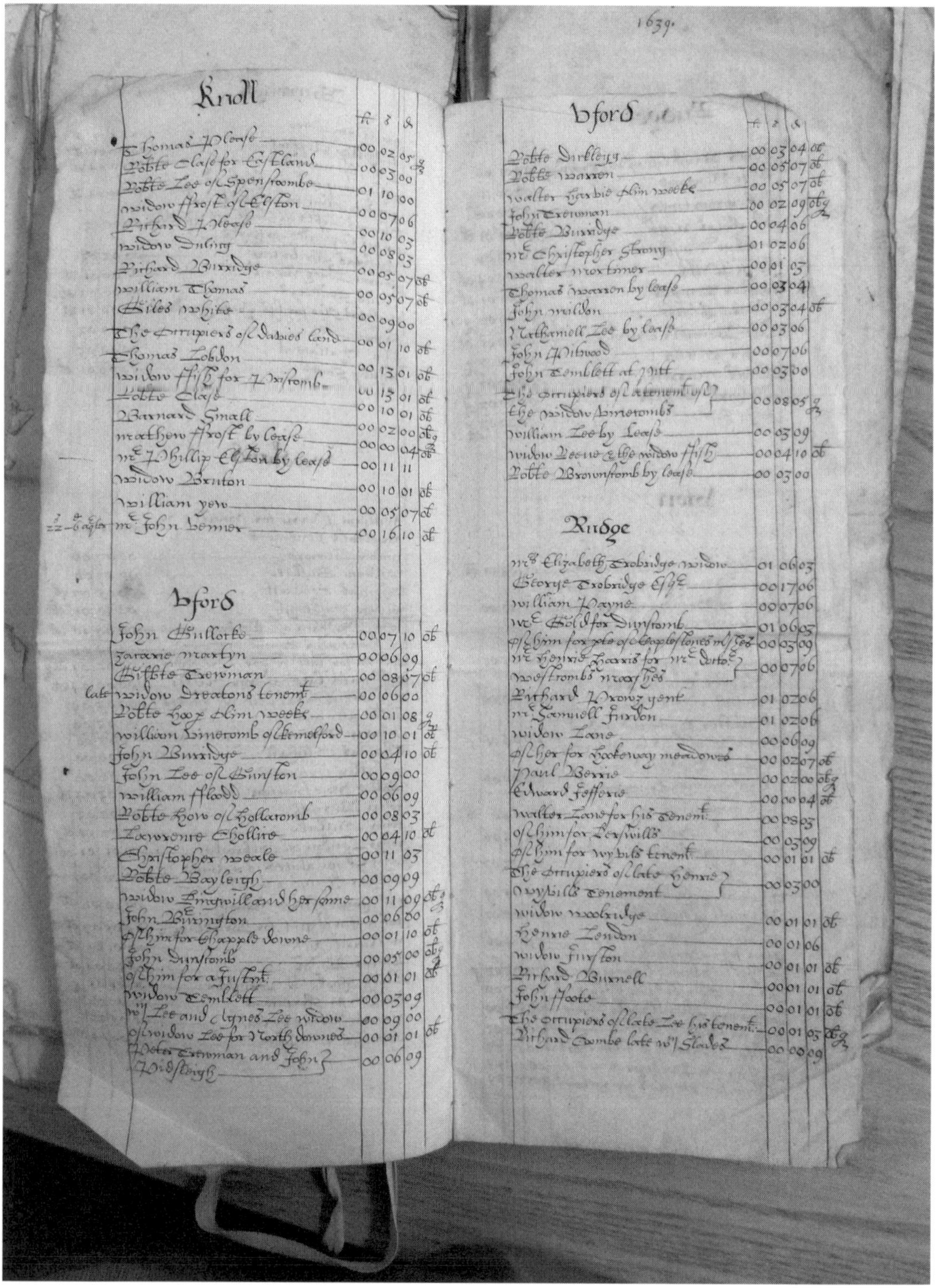

1639.

Knoll

	li	s	d	
Thomas Pearse	00	02	05	q
Robte Clase for Estland	00	03	00	
Robte Lee of Spencecombe	01	10	00	
widow ffrost of Elston	00	07	06	
Richard Pearse	00	10	03	
widow Duling	00	08	03	
Richard Burridge	00	05	07	ob
William Thomas	00	05	07	ob
Giles White	00	09	00	
The occupiers of Davies land	00	01	10	ob
Thomas Lobdon	00	13	01	ob
widow ffish for Pitscomb	00	13	01	ob
Robte Clase	00	10	01	ob
Barnard Small	00	02	00	ob q
Mathew ffrost by lease	00	00	04	ob q
Mr Phillip Elston by lease	00	11	11	
widow Brinton	00	10	01	ob
William Yew	00	05	07	ob
Mr John Bemer	00	16	10	ob

Uford

	li	s	d	
John Bullocke	00	07	10	ob
Zacharie Martyn	00	06	09	
Gilbte Crewman	00	08	07	ob
widow Dreatons tenemt	00	06	00	
Robte Hore for Ilim weeke	00	01	08	q
William Vincombe of Kemelsford	00	10	01	ob
John Burridge	00	04	10	ob
John Lee of Bunston	00	09	00	
William ffloode	00	06	09	
Robte How of Hollacomb	00	08	03	
Lawrence Chollice	00	04	10	ob
Christopher Weale	00	11	03	
Robte Bayleigh	00	09	09	
widow Bingwill and her sonne	00	11	09	ob q
Mr John Burington	00	06	00	
of him for Chapple downe	00	01	10	ob
John Dunscomb	00	05	00	ob q
of him for a tenemt	00	01	01	ob
widow Tomblett	00	03	09	
Wm Lee and Agnes Lee widow	00	09	00	
of widow Lee for North downes	00	01	01	ob
Peter Crewman and John Widslegh	00	06	09	

Uford

	li	s	d	
Robte Dirkleys	00	03	04	ob
Robte Warren	00	05	07	ob
Walter Harbis for Ilim weeke	00	05	07	ob
John Crewman	00	02	09	ob q
Robte Burridge	00	04	06	
Mr Christopher Strong	01	02	06	
Walter Mortimer	00	01	05	
Thomas Warren by lease	00	03	04	
John Wildon	00	03	04	ob
Nathaniell Lee by lease	00	03	06	
John Pitwood	00	07	06	
John Tomblett at Pitt	00	03	00	
The occupiers of a tenement of the widow Vincombe	00	08	05	q
William Lee by lease	00	03	09	
widow Reene & the widow ffish	00	04	10	ob
Robte Brownscomb by lease	00	03	00	

Rudge

	li	s	d	
Mrs Elizabeth Trobridge widow	01	06	03	
George Trobridge Esqr	00	17	06	
William Payne	00	07	06	
Mr Gold for Dunscomb	01	06	03	
of him for pte of Copplestone mills	00	03	09	
Mr Henrie Harris for Mr Dertos Westcombs Marshes	00	07	06	
Richard Prouz gent	01	02	06	
Mr Samuell Furlon	01	02	06	
widow Lane	00	06	09	
of her for Hockway meadowe	00	02	07	ob
Paul Berrie	00	02	00	ob q
Edward Jefferie	00	00	04	ob
Walter Lane for his tenemt	00	08	03	
of him for Corswills	00	03	09	
of him for Wykills tenemt	00	01	01	ob
The occupiers of late Henrie Wykills tenement	00	03	00	
widow Woolridge	00	01	01	ob
Henrie London	00	01	06	
widow Furston	00	01	01	ob
Richard Burnell	00	01	01	ob
John ffoote	00	01	01	ob
The occupiers of late Lee his tenemt	00	01	03	ob q
Richard Combe late Wm Slades	00	00	09	

Plate 12. Crediton tithe account, 1636.

55. CREDITON including SANDFORD, Tithe Account, 1636

DHC, 1660A/O/A/261

Note: See Item 54. This account was written in a volume of five pieces of paper stitched together to make up thirty pages which are approximately 6 inches in width and 16 inches in length. It is endorsed 'Rate & tithe 1636' along with some calculations.

1636

A Booke to Collect the Tithes of Crediton and Sandford.

Towne tithing

Worll Thomas Tuckfeild Esquire	£00 18s 09d
Mr Thomas Pointingdon for Westwoode late Mr Yollands	00 08 01
Silvanus Evans for *formerly* Mr Yollands house and ground in the Burrowgh	00 01 01 ½
Mr Roger Trobridge for Uton	00 02 06
Wm Elworthie for one moytie of the Fower mills	00 05 00
Mr Wm Holcomb for thother moytie of the Fower mills	00 05 00
The occupiers of Lower Forton	00 04 06
Mr John Newbomd for late Cornishes ground for storie Crosse and other ground and for Northams and the Downes	00 13 1 ½
Mr Hamblyn for the great meadow	01 05 00
Of him for his Copiehold Tenemt	00 05 00
Of him for George Hill ground	00 01 09
John Ware	00 12 04 ½
Phillip Buckingham for ground in the Common Marsh Lane	00 01 08 ¼
Thomazine Buckingham widow for hookeway ground	00 08 05 ¼
Of her for her home Tenemt	00 03 00
Nicholas Ware for wares downes	01 10 00
Mr Richard Phillip for Pallace ground	00 05 00
Of him for moore Tenemt	00 11 03
Of him for another pte of the Common marshes	00 07 06
Mr Robert Young for his Tenemt	00 10 00
Peter Keene for late Southwoods house and ground	00 00 06 ¾
Thomas Channon for late Mr Phillip Northcots	00 01 06
Mr John Davie of Meadland for his Tenement	00 04 06
Of him for pte of Common marsh	00 06 04 ½
Of him for late Coplestones marsh	00 02 07 ½
Phillip Lake of Bradleigh	00 12 04 ½
Robert Brownscomb	00 02 04 ½

[new page] towne tithing

Mr George young *formerly* Townsends	£00 09s 09d
Simon Burridge *formerly* Sannders	00 02 03
Robert Welsh *formerly* Sannders	00 00 03 ¾
Mr Richard Coles late horses	00 02 07 ½
Gilbert Shilston for Chiddenbrooke	00 02 07 ½
Robert Hoop late Gilbert Shilston senior Deceased	00 03 09
Worll John Northcot Esquire for Beere	00 10 00
John Lendon for his ground in Towne	00 01 02
of him for Sarehills	00 03 09
John Adamas for his house and garden	00 00 02
Mr John Rowe for his Tenemt and his house in the Churchyard	00 06 03
Phillip Buckingham for his tenemt	00 05 00
Walter Levitt for his Tenemt	00 05 00
John Pope at Westwood for his Tenemt & Fulfords house & ground	00 03 09
Thomas Lodbon for late Fulfords meadow	00 00 09

Joseph Slee for Selwood meadowes   00 03 00
Mr Carrow for the new mils ground   00 03 00
for a meadow late the wid: Potters   00 00 09
John Phillip for his ground in Towne 00 00 10 ¾
late Mrs John Gales tenemt   00 05 07 ½
Of her for Creedie Bridge marsh   00 01 06
Mrs Anne Mayne widow   00 02 06
Robtes of Stockleigh   00 01 00
Emmanuell Davie Esquire for his Tenement
                                    00 03 11 ¼
Of him for lame John's Close   00 00 10 ½
Mr Henry Harris for Winsore   00 07 06

Parke ground
Partrack Newcomb   00 05 00 ¾
Mr Whitehorne late Mr Honiwils   00 07 06
Mrs Tickels ground   00 06 00
Robert Harris   00 07 06
Mr Phillip Buckingham   00 07 06
Of him for late Trewmans ground   00 03 11 ¼
[new page] Peter Palmes ground   00 02 03
Robert Harris for now Peter Palmers 00 01 01 ½
Robert Harris for Challacombes ground
                                    00 01 01 ½
Roger Bolte for late Elizabeth Gratleighs
ground   00 01 01 ½

Parrish Rents
Mr John Rowe   00 03 04
Mrs Turbervile   00 06 08
Humphrey Pits for a Barne at Bowdon Hill
                                    00 05 00

Cannonffee
Mrs Elizabeth Gale widow   00 05 07 ½
Mrs Turbervile widow   01 06 03
Mr Knaplocke for late George Bodleighs
ground   00 06 06
Phillip Borton   00 00 10
Mrs Wilton   00 03 06
Of her for Common marshes   00 03 00
Of her for her house and ground   00 01 01 ½
[new page]

Burrowgh
Mr Phillip Buckingham for Dickers Hames and
Delbridge   00 03 09
Of him for Buckinghams Close   00 00 09
Mr George Young for *formerly* Simon Leach
his house and ground   00 02 03
Late Mrs Joan Gale for pte of Chiddenbrooke
                                    00 02 03

Mrs Honor Furse for Copiehold   00 02 07
Mr Phillip Buckingham for late his mothers
Tenemt   00 07 06
Of him for Darts Downes   00 04 01 ½
Mr William Shilston   00 01 06
Richard Shilston   00 01 06
Elizabeth Spenser widow   00 05 07 ½
Bennett Allyn   00 02 03
John Pope at Westwood   00 02 03
Richard Bickle   00 03 09
John Babb formerly Mrs Prowze   00 08 03

Silvanus Evans late Walter Popes 00 01 08 ¼
Of him for late Bands ground   00 02 03
Henry Spenser for late Osbornes   00 01 01 ½
William Still for Anstice Bickels ground
                                   00 01 01 ½
Widow Tucker   00 02 00 ¾
John Heard late Reeves   00 02 03
Mr Henry Harris for late Leaches ground
                                    00 02 03
Sebastian Penicot late Mr Henry Harris 00 00 10
Thomas Edberie late Peries   00 01 01 ½
John Pope at Westwoode for late Snells 00 02 03

William Elston   00 05 00
Mr Forward for the Church house   00 08 04
Thomas Smith   00 01 00

Robert Lane   00 03 00
Mr Henry Harris for the Widow Bodleighs
ground   00 03 04 ½
Of him for the Faire pks and the marshes
formerly Mr Davies of Meadland   00 03 00
John Backe *formerly* John Lanes 00 00 04 ½
Mr Gye for *formerly* Worthes   00 00 04 ½

Eleanor Tucker widow   00 00 01 ½
Roger Bolte   00 00 09
Widow Parker   00 00 04 ½
Phillip Darte and the Occupiers of mils his
house   00 00 01 ½
Samuel Sannders   00 00 04 ½
John Vinecomb   00 00 04 ½

Widow Lake	00 00 03	Mrs Reynell *formerly* Reeves	00 00 06
John Pope for Weares Foote	00 01 01 ½	John Dunscomb *formerly* Reeves	00 00 05 ½
Of him for 3 other Closes	00 01 06	6d a piece *for the year* John Leach Robert	
Of him for Turners ground	00 02 09	Hoop and Lewis Bremblecomb	00 00 04 ½
Of him for Chiddenbrooke	00 01 08	Thomas Channon for a Close	00 00 06
Of him for pte of Mrs Gales tenemt at		Walter Kensall for ground	00 00 11 ¼
Chiddenbrooke	00 01 08	Widow Osborne for house & ground	00 01 06
Of him for a Close at Bowden hill	00 00 04 ½	John Furler	00 00 03
Of him for late Augustyne Randels	00 00 06 ¾	William Osborne	00 00 01 ½
John Pope at Westwood for ground under the		John Jellett	00 04 01 ½
pke	00 01 06	Gervase Geard	00 00 04 ½
John Lyde for his house	00 00 03	Widow Bolte	00 00 10 ½
John Taylor formerly Quicks	00 03 04 ½	Edward Dicker	00 00 01 ½
Widow Reeve for the pke house and garden		Widow Tule	00 00 04 ½
and for the other house and garden	00 00 07	*formerly* John Fords tenemt	00 00 04 ½

[new page]

Burrough

William Rowe	00 00 01 ½	Simon Leach weaver	00 00 01 ½
Phillip Stephins	00 00 01 ½	James Sannders	00 00 04 ½
Phillip Wrayford	00 00 04 ½	Nicholas Slee for his house & garden	
The Occupiers of a house and garden formerly			00 00 01 ½
Mr Chards	00 00 04 ½	Simon Lee	00 00 03
Thomas Roberts of Stockleigh for his house		John Challacomb	00 00 03
and Orchards	00 00 03	Phillip Smith	00 00 01 ½
Nicholas Slee by lease	00 02 03		

Woodland

William Perrie for Walter Woolcots tenement		Robert Westington	00 03 04 ½
	00 11 03	John Burnell	00 02 03
Widow Lilicrope	00 07 06	John Gullocke	00 02 09 ¾
William Gullocke	00 07 06	John Lendon of Colbrooke	00 01 01 ½
Thomas Temblett	00 05 07 ½	John Skinner abated 1s *for the year* if there be	
Widow Caseleigh	00 10 01 ½	cause so to doe	00 06 00
John Pridham of Rocke	00 09 10 ½	Mrs Honor Furse widow	00 10 01 ½
Of him for his Tenemt in Towne	00 04 06	John Furse gentleman for Bradleigh	00 05 07 ½
Of him for late Widow Pridhams	00 02 09 ¾	William Aish	00 01 01 ½
Of him for late Widow Clashes	00 00 04 ½	Peter Bishop	00 00 04 ½
The Occupiers of late Wm Hookes	00 03 09	Robert Hooke for Gunston	00 08 05 ¼
Robert Skinner	00 03 09	Of him for Shortacomb [Shortacombe]	00 07 06
George Trewman & his sonne	00 07 06	Henry Delve by lease	00 05 02
Thomas Collihall	00 06 00	George Gullocke	00 09 04 ½
Phillip Frannces	00 06 00		

[new page]

Knoll

Thomas Please	£00 02s 05d ¼	Richard Burridge	00 05 07 ½
Robert Clase for Eastland	00 03 00	William Thomas	00 05 07 ½
Robert Lee of Spenscoombe	01 10 00	Giles White	00 09 00
Widow Frost of Elston	00 07 06	The Occupiers of Davies land	00 01 10 ½
Richard Please	00 10 03	Thomas Lobdon	00 13 01 ½
Widow Duling	00 08 03	Widow Fish for Priscomb	00 13 01 ½

Robert Clase	00 10 01 ½	Widow Bruton	00 10 01 ½
Barnard Small	00 02 00 ¾	William Yew	00 05 07 ½
Matthew Frost by lease	00 00 04 ½	4s 6d a quarter Mr John Venner	00 16 10 ½
Mr Phillip Elston by lease	00 11 11		

Uford

John Gullocke	00 07 10 ½	Christopher Weale	00 11 03
Zacarie Martyn	00 06 09	Robert Bayleigh	00 09 09
Gilbert Trewman	00 08 07 ½	Widow Kingwill and her sonne	00 11 09 ¾
late Widow Dreatons tenemt	00 06 00	John Burrington	00 06 00
Robert Hoope *formerly* Weeks	00 01 08 ¼	Of him for Chapple Downe	00 01 10 ½
William Vinecomb of Kemelford	00 10 01 ½	John Dunscomb	00 05 00 ¾
John Burridge	00 04 10 ½	Of him for Justmt	00 01 01 ½
John Lee of Gunston	00 09 00	Widow Temblett	00 03 09
William Floodd	00 06 09	Wm Lee and Agnes Lee Widow	00 09 00
Robert How of Hollacomb	00 08 03	Of widow Lee for North Downes	00 01 01 ½
Lawrence Chollice	00 04 10 ½	Peter Trewman and John Pidsleigh	00 06 09

[new page]

Uford

Robert Dicklegg	£00 03s 04d ½	John Temblett at Pitt	00 03 00
Robert Warren	00 05 07 ½	The Occupiers of a tenemt of the widow	
Walter Harvie *formerly* Weeks	00 05 07 ½	Vinecombs	00 08 05 ¼
Thomas Warren by lease	00 03 04	William Lee by Lease	00 03 09
John mildon	00 03 04 ½	Widow Reeve & the widow Fish	00 04 10 ½
Nathaniel Lee by lease	00 03 06	Robert Brownscomb by lease	00 03 00
John Pitwood	00 07 06		

Rudge

Mrs Elizabeth Trobridge widow	01 06 03	Walter Lane for his Tenemt	00 08 03
George Trobridge Esquire	00 17 06	Of him for Kerswills	00 03 09
William Payne	00 07 06	Of him for Wyils tenemt	00 01 01 ½
Mr Gold for Dunscomb	01 06 03	The occupiers of late Henry Wyvills	
Of him for pte of Coplestones marshes	00 03 09	Tenement	00 03 00
Mr Henry Harris for Mr Doctor Westcombs		Widow Woolridge	00 01 01 ½
marshes	00 07 06	Henry Lendon	00 01 06
Richard Prowz gent	01 02 06	Widow Jurston	00 01 01 ½
Mr Samuel Jurdon	01 02 06	Richard Burnell	00 01 01 ½
Widow Lane	00 06 09	John Foote	00 01 01 ½
Of her for Hookeway meadowes	0 02 07 ½	The occupiers of late Lee his tenemt	00 01 03
Paul Berrie	00 02 00 ¾	¾	
Edward Jefferie	00 00 04 ½	Richard Coombe late Wm Slades	00 00 09

[new page]

Rudge

Roger Band late Mr Wm Trobridge	£00 01s 06d	Henry Searle	00 00 02 ¼
John Newcomb	00 00 11 ¼	late Bennets tenemt	00 00 01 ½
Robert Mortimer	00 00 06	Roger Tucker	00 00 02 ¼
Nicholas West	00 01 01 ½	Lewis Marrell	00 00 02 ¼
Widow Dunscombe	00 10 06	Richard Tapper	00 00 02 ¼
John Pitts	00 00 04 ½	John Silke	00 00 02 ¼
Walter Tapper	00 01 01 ½		

Uton

Worll John Northcot Esquire for Uton	01 08 01 ½
Lewis Northcot gent for his house in Towne for Goose Allers and for pte of Harvies lease	01 10 00
Mr Walter Tuckfeild for Uton except the Cleeves	00 05 03
Mr Roger Tuckfeild for the Cleeves and Tedborne	00 10 00
Mr Walter Tuckfeild and Mr Roger Tuckfeild for Posberie	00 04 06
Mr Roger Tuckfeild for pte of Mr Younngs Tenement	00 00 06
John Woodleigh	00 04 01 ½
Edmund Browne	00 03 06
The occupiers of a Tenemt *formerly* John Tuckers	00 02 03
Thomas Holcomb gent	00 18 09
Bennett Kingwill	00 05 03
Mr Robert Davies tenemt formerly John Conisbies	00 04 06
Of him for pte of Mr youngs tenemt	00 03 02 ¼
George Conisbies late his Fathers	00 03 00
Benjamin Bremblecombe	00 06 00
Of him for Posberie	00 02 03
Robert Bruton late his mothers	00 03 09
Of him for Posberie	00 03 09
Of him for pte of Mr youngs tenemt	00 03 09

[new page]

Uton

William Gullocke formerly Mildons	£00 04s 06d
John Elberrie and his sonne	00 07 06
Mr Roger Tuckfeild for pte of John Edberies Tenement	00 03 00
William Commins	00 01 06
Silvanus Evans for pte of John Elberies tenemt	00 00 11 ¼
Widow Bennet *otherwise* Reynels	00 02 09 ¾
Nicholas Lee late Hookes tenemt	00 02 03
John Callow	00 07 06
Henry Harris Junior *formerly* Callowes	00 02 09 ¾
Widow Handcocke	00 01 00
Widow Hawkins *otherwise* Fey	00 00 09
Worll Walter Young Esquire for pte of Tedborne	00 09 04 ½
John Frannces for moore lake	00 01 01 ½
Wm Tarr for pte of Hoops tenemt	00 00 04 ½
Robert Harris for pte of Hoops tenemt	00 00 05
John Lee for pte of Hoops tenemt	00 00 04 ½
Mr Heale for Yew Barton	00 17 06
Wm Lake or Robert Brownscomb for pte of Yew	00 01 01 ½
Bennett Kingwill for pte of Yew	00 01 01 ½
Humphrey West for pet of the same tenement	00 00 04 ½
Robert Warren late Hodge	00 00 04 ½
Nathaniel ~~Lee~~ Reeve for pte of yew	00 02 03
John Pope of Westwood for pte of Ewe	00 01 06
Thomas Bussell for pte of Ewe	00 00 04 ½
Of him for pte of Lockes ground	00 00 10 ½
Widow Clarke for pte of yew	00 00 09 ¼
Walter Reeve for pte of yew	00 01 00
Late Giles Kingwill for pte of yew	00 00 03
Walter Deamond for pte of yew	00 01 03
William Moore for pte of yew	00 00 04 ½
Thomas Holland late Symons	00 00 09
James Jurstons for pte of Hooops	00 00 04 ½
Mr Roger Tuckfeild for pte of Walter & Peter Hoops tenemt	00 00 04 ½
Richard Fraunces for pte of Wm Lakes	00 00 10 ¾
The Occupiers of Ice meadow	00 00 09
for pte of yew late Gilbert Brodmeads	00 00 11 ¼
Simon Lee for marshes of yew Barton	00 04 06
Late Robert Quash his tenemt	00 00 04 ½

[new page]

Sandford

Emmanuel Davie Esquire for Ruxford	£02 06s 10d ½
of him for Fenne	00 09 04 ½
of him for Gaters Tenemt	00 03 09
Of him for his owne tenemt by lease	00 06 08
Of him for Gov's tenement	00 03 09

Of him for Dowrich mills	00 01 10 ½		Of her for her Cottage	00 02 05 ¼
of him for late John Davies tenemt	00 08 09		Margery Phillip widow	00 02 03
¾			Mr Henry Harris for Sutton	00 12 00
Worll John Davie Esquire for his home tenemt			John Holcomb for Crosse	01 02 06
	01 00 07 ½		Of him for Wests tenemt by lease	00 01 09
Of him for Long Barne	01 10 00		John Mortimer of Remscomb	01 02 06
Of him for late Howes Tenemt	00 18 09		Of him for Creedie	00 05 07 ½
9s 6d a quarter abated 3d a quarter Mr			Of him for Swelts hill	00 02 07 ½
Wrayford late Lane's Tenemt	00 09 09		John Tucker for Woolsgrove	00 15 00
George White gent by lease	00 05 10		Robert Lane Junior for Bampton Heys	00 06 00
John Helmore for pte of Mr Whites Tenement			Of him for Clealand	00 00 04 ½
	00 05 00		widow Pope for Pidsleigh	00 11 03
Mrs Grace Davie widow and Mr Bellew			Simon Pridham	00 08 07 ½
	00 14 03		John Pridham of Rock *formerly* mortimer	
Mr Bellew for htat Lake held	00 02 00			00 05 03
Robert Burrington Esquire	01 00 00		widow mildon	00 08 07 ½
Mr Aishes Tenement	01 04 09		widow mortimer	00 08 07 ½
Lewis Dowrich gent	00 09 00		Thomas Cobleigh	00 07 06
William Vicarie	00 06 00		Thomas Haydon	00 11 03
Robert Lane Junior for pte of Mr John Davies			of him for his Tenement	00 08 03
Tenemt	00 05 05 ¼		Of him for Coombelansie	00 15 09
Widow Clarke for Creedie	00 19 06		John Clase	00 05 07 ½

[new page]

John Jacob *otherwise* Stevins	£00 03s 04d ½		Roger Lane of Storidge	00 05 07 ½
William Charles *otherwise* Miller	00 04 10 ½		Robert Lane senior fo Aishmoore	00 03 04 ½
Arthur Whitrow	00 03 09		Of him for Brendons and Culver Cleaves	
William Pope	00 06 09			00 05 00 ¾
Of him for *formerly* warman	00 06 00		Walter Harvie *formerly* Frosts	00 01 01 ½
John Vicarie *formerly* Coxes tenemt	00 03 11 ¼		John Elliott *formerly* Denshams	00 04 06
John How for pte of the same tenemt			John Jellett *formerly* Wrayfords	00 09 00
	00 01 08 ¼		John Beere	00 03 09
John Reed of storidge & Aller downes	00 08 03		Widow Forde	00 09 09
Roger Band	00 07 06		John Hall for Woolsgrove	00 05 00
widow Burrowgh	00 03 09		Robert Phillip of Creedie	00 01 06
widow Cox	00 07 01 ½		Thomas Coake	00 05 00 ¾
David Beere	00 01 06		William Burrington	00 00 11 ¼
widow Legg	00 04 06		Robert Lanes Junior *formerly* Keenes	
John mortimer of Lethebrooke	00 01 06			00 04 10 ½
John Hall *formerly* Reed	00 02 00		Robert Sannders *formerly* Priors	00 04 10 ½
Roger Lobdon	00 01 03		John Hannce	00 06 09
Richard Delve for his Tenemt of Burrowgh			Richard Delve late Lanes	00 04 01 ½
	00 03 09		Peter Lobdon	00 03 04 ½
Of him for Fursland	00 01 06		Christopher Potter for mills	00 03 04 ½
John Vicarie for his home tenemt	00 11 10 ¼		[highlighted] Richard Please for Deedie mils	
John Adams of henstill	00 03 04 ½			00 02 00
Richard Adams & Charles Adams	00 03 04 ½		George Rocke	00 02 00
John Lane for yolland	00 04 01 ½		Of him for Aish	00 02 00
Wm Lee for Blackman's Coombe [Blackmoor			Robt Taylor	00 01 03 ¾
Coombe]	00 03 05 ¼		John Adams of Felllake	00 01 06
John Cockerham for Burridge	00 05 03		Andrew Budd	00 00 09

widow Bradford	00 01 06	John Reed *formerly* Atwills	00 00 09
Phillip Way	00 01 06		

[new page]

Henry Pope	£00 02s 03d	Peter Snow	00 04 06
William Thomas formerly Lanes	00 01 01 ½	John Phillip senior	00 04 00
Mrs Berrie formerly Geallards	00 01 01 ½	John Hall senior	00 04 00
Wm Thomas late Gribbles	00 01 01 ½	Robert Lane senior	00 04 00
- Mr Elston formerly Frosts	00 02 09 ¾	widow Burrington	00 02 03
Edward Delve	00 02 07 ½	william Brembridge	00 05 00
widow Delve	00 01 10 ½	The occupiers of Dowrich Barton	00 17 00
Robert Collens	00 00 06 ¾	John Lane for Halscombe meadow and wall	
Richard Phillip	00 00 09	Downe	00 03 00
John Butcher	00 00 04 ½	Lewis Dowrich gent for pte of Dowrich	00 02 03
John Paige	00 07 06	Peter Smarte for Burrow land	00 02 09
quere Roger Lane for pte of Paiges tenemet		John Lane for Burrow land	00 02 00
	00 00 06	Thomas Spiser for Burrow land	00 00 09
Thomas Cobleigh for pt of pages	00 01 08	Charles Admas for Rooke wood and the	
Roger Lane for pt of pages tenemt	00 01 02	Copps	00 02 03
John Adams	00 01 02	William Vicarie *formerly* Robert Priors	
['Wm' inserted] ~~Widow~~ Tucker *formerly* Pond			00 00 06 ¾
	00 00 04 ½	Peter Snow for Furse pks	00 01 10 ½
Gilbert Pridham for sanniton	00 09 00	- Mr Phillip Elston for Aish please	00 05 00
John Reed by lease	00 02 00	John Yeo	00 02 ¼
John Mildon late Gilbert Northcot	00 06 09	rated 18d *for the year* widow Breedie	
Robert Burrowgh by lease	00 05 00		00 00 04 ½
Thomas White *formerly* mayers	00 02 03	William Ballamey	00 00 02 ¼
widow Rowland *formerly* Rowe	00 04 08	John Colborne	00 00 02 ¼
Thomas Northcot by Lease	00 03 04	William Gover	00 00 04 ½
Robert Lane Junior late Smales	00 04 01 ½	John Bartlets	00 04 ½
widow Lane	00 06 09	Thomas Pitts	00 00 02 ¼
John warman	00 05 07 ½	Hugh Quicke	00 02 ¼
Thomas Please senior by lease	00 11 03	4d *for the year* John Lane for Gorfords tenemt	
of him for a tenemt in West Sandford	00 00 09	which was pte of hill tenemt	00 00 01

56. CREDITON including SANDFORD, Tithe Account, 1644

DHC, 1660A/O/A/261

Note: See Item 54. The account was written in a volume of five pieces of paper stitched together to make up thirty pages which are approximately 6 inches in width and 16 inches in length.

1644
A Booke where by to Collect the money to be Dew and payable for the Tithes of Crediton and Sandford in the yeere aforesaid
quarterlie **Towne Tithing**

John Tuckfeild Esquire	£00 18s 09d
Thomas Ponntingdon gent for westwood late mr yollands	00 08 01
Silvanus Evans for *once upon a time* mr yollands house and ground in the Burrowgh	00 01 01 ½
Mr Roger Trobridge for Uton	00 02 06
William Elworthie for one moytie of the Flower mills	00 05 00

Thomas Holcomb gent for thother moytie of the Fower mills	00 05 00
George young gent for Lower Forton	00 04 06
Mr John Newcomb for late Cornishes ground for stone Crosse and other ground, and for Northams	
& the downes	00 13 10 ½
Mr Hamblyn for the great meadow	01 05 00
of him for the great m his Copie hold	00 05 00
Widow Ware at Townes end for her tenement	00 12 04 ½
John Jeston for ground in the Common Marsh Lane	00 01 08 ¼
Thomazine Buckingham widow for her home Tenement	00 03 00
John Buckingham for a tenement at Hookeway	00 08 05 ¼
George Young gent for wares downes	01 10 00
Mr Richard Phillip for Pallace ground	00 05 00
of him for moore Tenement	00 11 03
Mr John Averie for Common marshes late Mr Richard Phillips	00 07[s] ½
of him for ground late Mr Davies of meadland	00 06 04 ½
of him for ground late Mrs Wiltons	00 03 00
Mr Thomas Young for late his Fathers Tenement	00 10 00
Peter Keene for late Richard Southwoods house and ground	00 00 06 ¼
Thomas Channon for late Mr Phillip Northcots	00 01 06
Peter Keene for ground at George Hill	00 01 09

[new page]

Mr John Davie of meadland for his Tenement	00 04 06
William Payne of Newton St Cires for Coplestones marshes	00 02 07 ½
Phillip Lake for Bradleigh	00 12 04 ½
Robert Brownscomb of Bradleigh	00 02 04 ½
Mr George Young for *once upon a time* Mark Townsend	00 09 09
Thomas Bridgman for late Simon Burridges tenement	00 02 03
Gilbert Trewman late welsh	00 00 03 ¼
Mr Richard Coles for pte of Chiddenbrooke	00 02 07 ½
Gilbert Shilston for pte of Chiddenbrooke	00 02 07 ½
Robert Hoop for late Gilbert Shilstons Tenement	00 03 09
Right Worshipful John Northcot Barronat for Beere Tenement	00 10 00
John Lendon for his ground in the Burrowgh	00 01 02
of him for Sarehills	00 03 09
John Adams for house and garden	00 00 02
Mr John Row for his Tenement and houses in the Churchyard	00 06 03
Phillip Buckingham	00 02 06
Robert Buckingham	00 02 06
widow Levitt for her Tenement	00 05 00
widow Pope at Westwood for a Tenement & for late Fulfords house and orchard	00 03 09
Thomas Lobidn for late Fulford meadow at westwood	00 00 09
Simon Lee for Selwood meadows	00 03 00
Thomas Berrie for Mr Carrowes Mills	00 03 00
James Quick for late widow Potters meadow	00 00 09
Silvanus Evans for late John Phillips ground in Towne	00 00 10 ¼
Clement Pidsleigh for Mr huddies ground	00 05 07 ½
of him for Credie [Creedy] Bridge marsh	00 01 06
Mrs Anne Mayne for her tenement	00 02 06
John Robts of Stockleigh	00 01 00
Robert Davie gent for late his Fathers Tenement	00 03 11 ¼

of him for lame Johns Close   00 00 10 ½
Mr Henry Harris for winsore   00 07 06
[new page] Mrs Honor Furse for her copiehold   00 02 07
Mr Phillip Buckingham for late his mothers Tenement   00 07 06
of him for darts downes   00 04 01 ½
Mr William Shilston   00 01 06
Widow Shilston   00 07 06
Widow Spenser   00 05 07 ½
Bennett Allyn   00 02 03
Widow Pope at Westwood   00 02 03
Richard Bickle   00 03 09
John Babb for late Mrs Prowses ground   00 08 03

Parke ground

Patrack Newcomb   00 05 00 ¼   of him for late Bounds ground in the pke
Mr Whithorne for late Wm Honywill 00 07 06   00 02 03
Mrs Tickle for pkeground   00 06 00   Henry Spenser for pke ground   00 01 01 ½
Robert Harris   00 07 06   Wm Still for Anstice Bickels Parke ground
Mr Phillip Buckingham   00 07 06   00 01 01 ½
Of him for late Trewmans   00 03 11 ¼ widow Tucker   00 02 00 ¼
Robert Herris for late Peter Palmers ground   John Heard for late Richard Reeves ground
                                       00 02 03   00 02 03
John Backe for late Palmers ground 00 01 01 ½   John Back for late Leaches ground   00 02 03
Robert Harris for John Challacombs ground   John Back for late Mr Harris ground 00 00 10
                                       00 01 01 ½   John Lane for late Edward Perries ground in
Silvanus Evans for late Elizabeth Gratleighs   the pke   00 01 01 ½
ground   00 01 01 ½   James Pope for late Snells ground in the pke
of him for late Walter Popes ground ~~ground~~   00 02 03
                                       00 01 08 ¼

[new page]

Parish Rents

Mr John Rowe   00 03 04   Wm Elston or Nicholas Melhuish   00 05 00
George Turbervile gent   00 06 08   Mrs Forward for the Church house 00 08 04
for a Barne at Bowdon hill   00 05 00   Wm Strong for late Smiths house   00 01 00

Canon Fee

Mrs Elizabeth Gale widow   00 05 07 ½ Mr Henry Harris for the ground late widow
Giles Vinecomb for Penton   01 05 00   Bodleighs   00 03 04 ½
Mr Knaplocke for wynsore   00 06 06   Of him for the Faire pks and the marshes late
Phillip Borton or Wm Rogers   ⸱00 00 10   Mr Davies of meadland   00 03 00
Mrs Wilton widow   00 03 06   John Backe for late John Lanes of Sandford
of her for Common marshes now Mr Avery   00 00 04 ½
                                       00 00 00   Mr Peter Gye for late Robert worthes house
of her for her house and ground   00 01 01 ½ and orchard   00 00 04 ½
Robert Lane   00 03 00

[new page]

Burrough

Sir John Northcot Barranat for dickers hams and delbridge   £00 03s 09d
Mrs Buckingham for Buckinghams Close   00 00 09

Mr George Young *for once upon a time* Simon Leachers ground	00 02 03
widow Leach for pte of Chittenbrooke	00 02 03
Eleanor Tucker widow	00 00 01 ½
Roger Bolte	00 00 09
Widow Parker	00 00 04 ½
Phillip Darte & Robert Harris	00 00 01 ½
Samuel Sannders	00 00 04 ½
Widow Vinecomb	00 00 04 ½
Robert Bolte mercer for late the widow Lakes house	00 00 03
Wm Costyn for weares Foote	00 01 01 ½
Silvanus Evans for 3 Closes	00 01 06
Wm Brocking for Turners ground	00 02 09
Richard Haydon for Chiddenbrake	00 01 08
of him for Mr Gales Chiddenbrocke	00 01 08
Wm Bray for a Close at Bowdon hill	00 00 04 ½
Christopher Pope for Whitfilds house and ground *once upon a time* Randels	00 00 06 ¾
Wm Heale for ground under the pke at westwood	00 01 06
William Brooking for Lides house	00 00 03
John Taillor for late Quicks ground	00 03 04 ½
of him for late the widow Reeves pke house and garden and of John Corbyn for another house and garden late widow Reeves also	00 00 07
Mrs Reynols for *once upon a time* Reeves	00 00 06
John Dunscomb for *once upon a time* Reeves	00 00 05 ½
John Leach Robert Hoop and Lewis Bremblecomb	00 00 04 ½
Thomas Channon for a Close	00 00 06
Walter Kensall for ground	00 00 11 ¼
Widow Clase for a house and ground at Forches	00 01 06
Richard Shapland for late Furlers house and ground	00 00 03

[new page]

Burrowgh

William Holmes late Osbornes £00 00s 01d ½		Thomas Robts of Stockleigh for a house and orchard	00 00 03
John Jellett	00 04 01 ½	Simon Lee for Chapple Downe	00 03 03
Richard Balkewell	00 00 04 ½	Simon Leach weaver	00 00 01 ½
Widow Bolte	00 00 10 ½	James Sannders	00 00 04 ½
Edward Dicker	00 00 01 ½	Simon Lee for his house & garden	00 00 01 ½
Simon Lee late Tule	00 00 04 ½	more Simon Lee	00 00 03
Peter Keene late Fords	00 00 04 ½	John Challacomb	00 00 03
Wm Row *otherwise* widow Treherne	00 00 01 ½	Thomas Bickle for his house	00 00 01 ½
Widow Stevins	00 00 01 ½	William Leach	00 00 03
Phillip Wrayford	00 00 04 ½		
John Masie for a house and a garden *once upon a time* Mr Chards	00 00 04 ½		

[new page]

Woodland tithing

John Furse gent for Bradleigh £00 05s 07d ½		Robert Brownscomb Junior late Temblets	00 05 07 ½
John Furse Junior gent	00 10 01 ½	Widow Caseleigh	00 10 01 ½
Walter Woolcott	00 11 03	John Pridham of Rocke	00 09 10 ½
Widow Lilicrope	00 07 06	of him for his Tenement in Towne	00 04 06
William Gullocke	00 07 06	of him for late widow Pridhams	00 02 09 ¾
George Gullocke	00 09 04 ½		

of him for late widow Clashes 00 00 04 ½
John Frances for late Wm Hookers tenement
00 03 09
Robert Skinner 00 03 09
George Truman 00 07 06
Thomas Collyhall 00 06 00
Robert Westington 00 03 04 ½
John Burnell 00 02 03
John Gullocke of Rocke 00 02 09 ¾
John Lendon of Colbrooke 00 01 01 ½
John Skinner of Colbrooke abated 1s *for the*
year if there be cause 00 06 00
Wm Aish for Bowdon ground 00 01 01 ½

[new page]

knoll tithing
Mr John Venner for Knoll [Knowle] Barton
£00 19s 08d ¼
Mr Phillip Elston *by* lease 00 11 11
Widow Lee of Spenscoomb 01 10 00
John Please for knoll 00 10 03
John Please for Lightfootes 00 02 05 ¼
Roger Skinner for Eastland 00 03 00
widow Forst of Elston 00 07 06
widow Duling 00 08 03
Richard Burrage 00 05 07 ½
widow Thomas 00 05 07 ½

[new page]

Uford tithing
John Gullock Junior £00 07s 10d ½
Zachary Martyn 00 06 09
Roger moore for late Trewmans 00 08 05 ¼
Peter Trewman Butcher for pte of the same
00 03 09
Widow Pring *once upon a time* Dreatons
00 06 00
John Hoop for *once upon a time* weeks 00 02 06
William Vinecomb of Kemelford [Keymelford]
00 10 01 ½
John Burrage 00 04 10 ½
John Lee of Gunston 00 09 00
William Flood 00 06 09
Robert How of hollacomb 00 08 03
Lawrence Chollish 00 04 10 ½
Christopher Weale 00 11 03
Robert Bayleigh 00 09 09
widow Kingwill and her sonne 00 11 09 ¾
Mr John Burrington 00 06 00
of him for Chapple Downe 00 01 10 ½
John Dunscomb 00 05 00 ¾
of him for a Justment 00 01 01 ½

John Hooke for Shortacomb 00 05 00
Late George Hill for *once upon a time* Frosts
Tenement 00 02 06
Henry Delve *by* lease 00 05 02
John Frances and william Frances for their
Tenement 00 06 00
Peter Bishop 00 00 04 ½
7 14 6
7 14 6
7 14 5
7 14 6
total 30 18

widow white 00 09 00
~~Richard Appledon~~ William Hockwell for
Davies Land 00 01 10 ½
Thomas Lobdon 00 13 01 ½
John Hill for late Fishes tenement 00 13 01 ½
Robert Clase and the widow Clase 00 10 01 ½
widow Britten 00 10 01 ½
william yeo 00 05 07 ½
Barnard Smale 00 02 00 ¾
Matthew Frost *by* lease 00 00 04 ½

John Hoop senior for late Templetts 00 03 09
Wm Lee and Agnes Lee widow 00 09 00
of the widow Lee for North Downes 00 01 01 ½
Peter Trewman & widow Pidsleigh 00 06 09
Widow Dicklegg 00 03 04 ½
Robert warren senior 00 05 07 ½
George Butler *once upon a time* weeks
00 05 07 ½
John Trewman 00 02 09 ¾
Mr Bodleigh and Mr John Burrington for
Jewes hollacomb 01 02 06
Walter Mortymer 00 01 03
Thomas warren by lease 00 03 04
John Mildon 00 03 04 ½
Widow Lee in hollacomb 00 05 07 ½
Widow Pitwood 00 07 06
John Templet of Pitt 00 03 00
The occupiers of a tenement of the widow
Vinecombs at kemelford 00 08 05 ¼
William Lee senior *by* lease 00 03 09
Widow Reeve and widow Fish 00 04 10 ½
Robert Brownscombe *by* lease 00 03 00

Robert Hooke for Gunston   00 08 05 ¼   Robert Burridge   00 04 06
[new page]

Rudge tithing

Mrs Elizabeth Trobridge widow   £01 06s 03d
George Trobridge Esquire   00 17 06
William Payne   00 07 06
Mr Gold for Dunscomb Barton   01 06 03
of him for pte of Coplestones Marshes 00 03 09
Richard Prowz gent   01 02 06
Mr Henry Harris for Mr Doctor Westcomb
Marshes   00 07 06
John Pits Junior for lower Dunscomb 01 02 06
widow Lane of Rudge   00 06 09
of her for hookeway meadow   00 02 07 ½
George Trobridge Esquire for *once upon a*
time keymels   00 02 00 ¾
Edward Jefferie   00 00 04 ½
Walter Lane for his Tenement   00 08 03
of him for kerswils   00 03 09
of him for pte of weyvils tenement 00 01 01 ½
John Mychell for *once upon a time* weyvils
                                  00 03 00
Robert Bond for late woolridges tenement
                                  00 01 01 ½
widow Lendon   00 01 06
[new page]

Henry Jurston for late widow Jurstons
Tenement   00 01 01 ½
John Egbeare for late Burnels tenement
                                  00 01 01 ½
widow Foote   00 01 01 ½
The occupiers of late Lees tenement lying in
Hookeway   00 01 03 ¾
George Gosse late Slades   00 00 09
Roger Bond   00 01 06
John Newcomb   00 00 11 ¼
James Jurston for late Cleeves   00 00 06
Nicholas West   00 01 01 ½
widow Dunscomb   00 10 06
John Pits senior   00 00 04 ½
Walter Tapper   00 01 01 ½
Henry Searle   00 00 02 ¼
widow Newall   00 00 01 ½
widow Tucker   00 00 02 ¼
Lewis marle   00 00 02 ¼
Richard Tapper   00 00 02 ¼
John Silke   00 00 02 ¼

Uton tithing

Sir John Northcot Barronat for his Barton at
Uton   £01 08s 01d ½
of him for late Mr Holcombs ground 00 04 06
Lewis Northcot gent for his house in Towne
for Goose Allers and for pte of Harvies lease
                                  01 10 00
Thomas Holcomb gent   00 12 03
Mr Roger Tuckfeild for the Cleeves and
Tedborne   00 10 00
of him for Posberie   00 04 06
John Tuckfeild Esquire for Uton   00 05 03
Mr Roger Tuckfeild for pte of Mr Walter
Youngs Tenement   00 00 06
Wor[sipfu]ll Walter Young Esquire for his pte
of Tedborne   00 09 04 ½
The heires of John Woodleigh   00 04 01 ½
Edmund Browne   00 03 06
of him for late Mr Holcombe   00 01 06
John Tucker for his tenement   00 02 03
Bennet Kingwill   00 05 03
Mr Robert Davie for his Tenemt *once upon a*
time Conisbies   00 04 06

of him for pte of Mr Youngs Tenement
                                  00 03 02 ¼
Christopher Pope for George Conisbies
Tenement   00 03 00
Benjamin Bremblecomb   00 06 00
of him for Posberie   00 02 03
Robert Bruton for late his mothers 00 03 09
Of him for Posberie   00 03 09
Of him for pte of Mr Youngs Tenement 00 03 09
William Gullocke for *once upon a time* John
Mildons Tenement   00 04 06
John Edberie and his sonne Thomas 00 07 06
Mr Roger Tuckfeild for pte of John Edberies
Tenement   00 03 00
William Commins   00 01 06
Silvanus Evans for pte of John Edberies
Tenement   00 00 11 ¼
Mr John Holcomb for late the widow Bennets
Tenement   00 02 09 ¾
Nicholas Lee for late Hookes tenement 00 02 03
John Callow Junior   00 07 06
Henry Harris Junior for late Callowes 00 02 09 ¾
Thomas Handcocke   00 01 00

widow hawkins *otherwise* Fey   00 00 09   John Frances for moorelake   00 01 01 ½

[new page]

Uton tithing

Widow yeo for pte of hoops Tenement
            £00 00s 04d ½
Robert Harris for pte of hoops Tenement
            00 00 05
John Lee for pte of Hoops Tenement 00 00 04
½
Mr Heale for pte of Yew Barton   00 17 06
Wm Lake and Robert Brownscomb for
another pte of yew Barton   00 01 01 ½
Bennet Kingwill for pte of yew Barton
            00 01 01 ½
Humphrey West for pte of the same Barton
            00 00 04 ½
Robert Warren for late Hodges tenement
            00 00 04 ½
Peter Growdon for late Nathaniel Reeves
tenement   00 02 03
Widow Pope at Westwood for pte of yew
Barton   00 01 06
Nathaniel Reeve for late Thomas Bussells
Tenement   00 00 04 ½

Nathaniel Reeve for late William Lakes
ground   00 00 10 ½
Widow Clarke for pte of yew   00 00 09 ¼
Walter Reeve for pte of yew   00 01 00
John Kingwill for pte of yew   00 00 03
Walter Deamond for pte of yew   00 01 03
William Moore for pte of yew   00 00 04 ½
Widow Holland for late Symons   00 00 09
James Jurston for pte of hoops tenement
            00 00 04 ½
Mr Roger Tuckfeild for pte of Hoopers
Tenement   00 00 04 ½
Richard Frances for late William Lakes
Tenement   00 00 10 ¾
The occupiers of Jce meadwo   00 00 09
Gilbert Brodmead for pte of yew Barton
            00 00 11 ½
Mr Heale for marshes of yew Barton late
Simon Lees   00 04 06
Late Frances Conant for *once upon a time*
Quashes tenement   00 00 04 ½

[new page]

Sandford

Right Wor[shipfu]ll Sir John Davie Barranat
for his home Tenement   £01 00s 07d ½
of him for Long Barne   01 10 00
of him for late Howes Tenement   00 18 09
Worll Walter Young Esquire   01 04 09
John Davie Junior Esquire for Ruxford
            02 06 10 ½
of him for Fenne   00 09 04 ½
for him for Gaters Tenement   00 03 09
of him for his owne Tenement   01 02 06
of him for Gov's Tenement   00 03 09
of him for Dowrich mills   00 01 01 ½
of him for late John Davies Tenement
            00 08 09 ½
Robert Burrington Esquire   01 02 06
Mrs Wrayford for late Lanes tenement 00 09 06
George White gent   00 05 10
Lewis Dowrich gent   00 09 00
William Helmore   00 05 00
Mrs Grace Davie widow & Mr Bellew 00 14 03
Mr Bellow for that once Lake held   00 02 00
William Vicarie   00 06 00

Richard Lane for late Mr John Davies
Tenement   00 05 05 ¼
Late the widow Clarke for Credie   00 19 06
and for late widow Clarks Cottage 00 02 05 ¼
Robert Phillip late Widow Phillip   00 02 03
Mr Henry Harris for Sutton   00 12 00
Roger Snow late John Holcomb for Crosse
            01 02 06
Widow Holcomb for Wests Tenement 00 01 09
Robert Mortymer and Thomas Mortymer
            01 02 06
late widow Mortymer for Credie   00 05 07 ½
Robert Mortymer for swelthill   00 02 07 ½
John Tucker for woolgrove   00 15 00
Richard Lane for Banton heys   00 06 00
of him for Clealand   00 00 04 ½
widow Pope for Pidsleigh   00 11 03
Roger Pridham   00 08 07 ½
John Pridham of Rocke for late Mortymers
tenement   00 05 03
Thomas Cobleigh   00 07 06
Roger Mortymer   00 08 07 ½
widow mildon   00 08 07 ½

[new page]

Sandford

The occupiers of late Mr Hanres tenement
£00 06s 09d

Richard Delve late Lane	00 04 01 ½
Peter Lobdon	00 03 04 ½
Christopher Potter for mills	00 03 04 ½
The occupiers of Deedie mills	00 02 00
George Rocke	00 02 00
of him for Aish	00 02 00
late Robert Taylors	00 01 03 ¾
John Adams for Fellocke	00 01 06
Andrew Budd	00 00 09
John Belworthie late Bradford	00 01 06
William Helmore late wayes	00 01 06
John Adams *once upon a time* Atwils	00 00 09
Henry Pope	00 02 03
late widow Thomas	00 01 01 ½
Mr Berrie *once upon a time* Gillerds	00 01 01 ½
Late Gribbels now Thomas	00 01 01 ½
Mr Phillip Elstons late Frosts	00 02 09 ¾
Edward Delve	00 02 07 ½
widow Holcomb for late widow Delves	00 01 10 ½
Robert Collins Cordwainer	00 00 06 ¾
Richard Phillip	00 00 09
late John Butcher	00 00 04 ½

widow Page	00 07 06
Thomas Cobleigh for pte of Pages Tenement	00 01 08
Roger Lane for another pte of the same Pages Tenement	00 01 02
William Tucker *once upon a time* Pond	00 00 04 ½
John Adams	00 01 02
Gilbert Pridham for swannaton	00 09 00
John Reed *by* lease	00 02 00
John Mildon late Northcots	00 06 09
Robert Burrowgh *by* lease	00 05 00
Thomas White late mayers	00 02 03
Widow Rowland *once upon a time* Row	00 04 08
John Browne	00 06 09
Richard Lane late Smales	00 04 01 ½
of him for late Widow Lanes	00 06 09
John Wearman	00 05 07 ½
Mrs Please for Aller	01 02 06
of her for a tenement in west Sandford	00 00 09
Peter Snow	00 04 06
John Phillip	00 08 03
John Hall senior	00 04 00

[new page]

Sandford

Thomas Haydon	£00 11s 03d
of him for another Tenement	00 08 03
of him for Coomblansie	00 15 09
John Reed for pte of Clases Tenement	00 01 10 ½
Widow Clase for pte of her Tenement	00 04 00
John Jacob *otherwise* Stevins	00 03 04 ½
William Charles *otherwise* Miller	00 04 10 ½
Arthur Whitrow	00 03 09
Widow Pope of henstill	00 06 09
of her for late wearmans	00 06 00
John Vicarie for late Coxes Tenement	00 03 11 ¼
late widow how for pte of the same tenement	00 01 08 ¼
John Reed for Storidge and Aller Downe	00 08 03
Roger Bond	00 07 06 00 [sic]
widow Burrowgh	00 03 09
widow Cox	00 7 01 ½
late David Beeres Tenement	00 01 06
George Gay for late Legs tenement	00 04 06

widow mortymer of Levibrooke	00 01 06
John Hall *once upon a time* Reed	00 02 00
Roger Lobdon	00 01 03
Richard Delve for his Tenement Mr Burrowghe	00 03 06
Of him for Fursland	00 01 06
John Vicarie for his home Tenement	00 11 10 ¼
John Adams of henstill	00 03 04 ½
Charles Adams and Richard Adams	00 03 04 ½
John Lane for yolland	00 04 01 ½
widow Lee for Blackmans Coombe	00 03 05 ¼
John Cockerham for Burridge	00 05 03
Roger Lane of Storidge	00 05 07 ½
Robert Lane for Aishmoore	00 03 04 ½
of him for Brindons and Culver Cleeves	00 05 00 ¾
Richard Appledon for Walter Harvies Tenement	00 01 01 ½
John Elliot *once upon a time* Densham	00 04 06
John Jellett *once upon a time* Wrayford	00 09 00
Widow Beere	00 03 09

Thomas Ford	00 09 09	William Burrington	00 00 11 ¼
John Hall for Wolsgrove	00 05 00	Richard Lane for late Keenes	00 04 10 ½
Robert Phillip for Credie	00 01 06	Widow Sannders late Pryers	00 04 10 ½
Thomas Coake *otherwise* Wilcox	00 05 00 ¾		

[new page]

Sandford

Robert Lane senior	£00 04s 00d	William Vicarie for late Pryors	00 00 06
widow Burrington	00 02 03	Peter Snow for Furspks	00 01 10 ½
william Brembridge	00 05 00	Mr Elston for Aish *by* lease	00 05 00
The occupiers of Dowrich Barton	00 17 00	John Yeo	00 00 02 ¼
John Lane for Halscomb meadow and wall downe	00 03 00	widow Breedie	00 00 04 ½
		William Ballamey	00 00 02 ¼
Lewis Dowrich gent for pte of Dowrich Barton	00 02 03	John Colborne	00 00 02 ¼
		widow Page late Wm Gov's	00 00 04 ½
Peter Smarte for Burrowgh land	00 02 06	John Bartlets	00 00 04 ½
John Lane for Burrowgh land	00 02 00	Thomas Pitts	00 00 02 ¼
William Vicarie for Burrowgh land	00 00 09	Hugh Quicke	00 00 02 ¼
Charles Adams for Rookewood and the Cops	00 02 03		

John Lane for Gorfords tenement *once upon a time* pte of hill tenement 00 00 01

CRUWYS MORCHARD

One rate survives for this parish located six miles west of Tiverton. The Cruwys family was listed as the principal residents in this rate and as the largest landowners in the subsidy of 1581.[1]

57. CRUWYS MORCHARD, Church Rate, 1604

DHC, Diocese of Exeter, Principal Registry, Cruwys Morchard Church Rates, 1604

Note: The rate, a fair copy, has been written on a sheet of paper which has been folded to make four pages each of which is approximately 8 inches in width and 10¾ inches in length. The numerals are Roman with the exception of the document sequence number. John Cruse was recorded as the wealthiest parishioner in the 1524 subsidy list.[2]

[illegible] of morchaid **36**

[illegible] a rate made concluded and agreed uppon the thirtith day of November in *the year* 1604 for the mainetenannce of the Church of Morchard Cruise in the Countie of Devon and for all manners matters and Chardges concernynge the church there by Hugh Croock beinge church-warden in the behalfe of Mary Mander at more and George her sonne and Thomas Melhuishe Thomas Wright George Bodley and John Chamberlen sidemen for the time beinge there and divers other inhabitance of Morchard Cruise, aforesaid all wch have hereunto sett there hands

First Humphrey Cruise Esquir for his Barton	4s 4d
Mary Maunder & George her sonne for more	2s 6d
John Melhuise for Agerye	2s 2d
Thomas Shapcott for Norracott [Northcote]	2s 2d
Grace Melhuise for Woode and for a parte volscom [Vulscombe]	2d [total] 2s 2d
Robert Jerden for one moitie in hockway [Hookway]	12d
John Fugars for other pte in hockway	12d
Walter Thomas for nether Edbury [Yeadbury]	21d
Thomas Wright for litell heath and cotten heath	21d
Joan Jervice for east hill & west hill	19d
William Shilston for east hil lane	19d
Thomas Melhuise for Parke	19d
George Bodlye for wicke [Week] dipford & yolland	19d
John Losomor for Gogland	19d
Humphrey Westorne for east Rockcomb [Ruckham]	19d
John Drake for littaland thornehease and the moiti in east waie and Stuckridge [Stickridge] Downe	20d
John Chamberlene for Downe	12d
Alexander Mander for scoultis thorne	12d
William Westorne for west lane	10d

1 Stoate, *Devon Taxes*, p. 35.
2 T. L. Stoate (ed.), *Devon Lay Subsidy Rolls 1524–7* (Bristol, 1979), p. 86.

[page 2]

Joan Shapcot for morchard mill	11d
Richard Drake for west waye	10d
Thomas Gallen for Beare	10d
James Holmeade for Forde	10d
Thomas Fursdon for edburiye [Edbury] mill	10d
Robert Losamore for higher edburie	10d
Walter Thomas for west wringland [Wringsland]	10d
Wilmot Broocke for Chaple [Chapple]	9d
Hugh Croocke for Foorse [Furze]	9d
Alice Quicke for three ptes in kelle	7d ½ ¼
Margaret Norrich for one pte in kelle	2d ¼
Matthew Melhuise for fill knape	9d
George Manly for the more part in Lugsland	9d
Robert Jetsame for Comeland [Coombeland]	9d
Robert Willes for West Cotton	9d
Christopher fenner for middeth waye	9d
Niccolas Hill in North Lusland [Lugsland]	8d
Robert Wills for east cotten	8d
Thomas Manly for middill cotton & a moitie in east waye	7d
Alice Melhuise for Broockes heane	6d
Humphrey Drake for Grobeare	5d
Anne Bidgoode for Ford	5d
Robert Thomas Hugh Thomas for nether west Rockecome	5d
John Beddill for higther West Roccombe	5d
John Mogford for come	4d
John ashelford for south Lustand	4d
Julian Donstome for a pt in Lugstand	4d
William Lane for higher Stuckridge	4d

[page 3]

Richard Drak for nether Stuckridge	4d
Mathu Cocke for west North Ruckcombe	4d
John Skinner for a part in Littiland [Lythe-Land]	2d ½
Davi[d] Goune for a part in Littaland	2d
Joan Hill for a part in Volscom [Vulscombe]& Littiland	2d
Joan Shapcot for a part in Lugsland	2d
Anne Woode for a part in Lugsland	2d
Bartholomew Beri for a pte in hockwaie [Hookway]	2d
Humphrey Melhuise for Ufferland	2d
Nicholas Woode for a part in Scoltis thorne	1d
Catherine Geston for a part in Lugland	1d
George Manley for a part in Volskomes	1d
Lawrence Wilcocke for the winde mill and our Ladi Parcke	1d
Joan Short for a part in east waies	1d
John Polsworthe for f [sic] a part a [sic] Tenement by Stuckridge Downe	1d
Richard Herrell for Clowe [Claw]	1d
Roger Hanksland for a part in Volscombe	½
Peter Sander for Stuckride Downe	½
Joan Tacke for Tithingland	½

Also it is further Concluded agreed and confirmed by all the persons aforesaid that the four said sidemen for the time beinge three or tow of them at the lest shall go wth the warding for the time beinge to gather the forsaid rate and the same collected to remaine in their hands and after ward to be delivered to the warden as occasion shall require to use The same and the sonday next uppon Easter day yearelie they all To geve in their accompts to the pishoners of Morchard aforesaid of their receipts and paiment and the said [ac]counts to be writen then and theare in a Boke to be made and kept.

[page 4]

for that purpose and the rate aforsaid to be collected as often or occassioon shall requir Provided alwaies and it is further Concluded and agred by all the pishoners aforsaid That If anie person or persons do refuse or neglect the payment of his [illegible] rate by the space of Twentie Daies after laufull demande made or ~~knowing~~ warning given in the Church of Cruise Morchard [illegible] or her sonne of his or her housholde That then pces to be payd for that ptie for the having of said rate and that he or she have the Chardge of the said the p[ro]ces and suit over and besides his or her Rate for such neglience or Will fullness in not payment.

[sign of] Humphrey Cruise
Hugh Croock Thomas Melhuise Thomas Wright George Bodlye John Chamberlen Walter Thomas Thomas Manly George Manly Matthew Melhuise Humphrey Drake Humphrey Westorne Christover fenner William Shilston Robert Losmore Robert Jetsame Alexander Shapcot John Fugars John Skinner Robert Thomas Hugh Thomas Matthu Coock James Holmead John Mogford John Beddill Thomas Galling William Smale Robert Jerden

DARTINGTON

A small number of rates survive for this parish located two miles north of Totnes. The tower is the only vestige left of the ancient parish church at Dartington Hall, the home of the Champerknowne family throughout the period of these rates. The rate of 1593 outlines the parish including Northford, an elusive manor.[1] Twenty-six men and women were assessed for the military rate whereas the church rate a year later involved nearly four times more parishioners.

58. DARTINGTON, Military Rate, c.1592

DHC, 3799M/3/O/4/50, no page numbers

Note: This rate is recorded in a volume with pages approximately 7¾ inches in width and 12 inches in length.

Dartington

Arthur Champnowne Esq	[blank]
Henry Farwell	a musket ps
Roger Marten	a musket ps a Calbr ps
William Burte	a Calbr ps a musket ps
Andrew Searell	a Corslet ps
John Tucker junior	a musket ps, an almaine a halbert
Richard Tucker	a musket ps a Call. ps
Edward Skynner	a musket ps
Margaret Willyams, Richard Willyams & William Pottle	a Corslet ps
Peter Ewen	a Corslet ps
Nicholas Searell	an almayne a bill a musket ps
George Arscott & Sibley Preston widow	a Corslet ps
Thomas Harder	a Calbr ps
John Hawkyn	a muskett ps
John Tucker	a muskett ps
Robert Stidson	a Corslet ps
Nicholas Bidlake & Mary Marten	a Corslet ps
Nicholas Howse	a Corslett
Christopher Willyam	a pike sword dagger & moeryon
Edward Edward	a musket ps
Geoffrey Myller	a Calbr ps
William Bidlake	a halbert
The parish armour	corsletts ps 2, muskets ps 3

59. DARTINGTON, Church Rate, 1593

DHC, Glebe Terriers

Note: The terrier, written on four pieces of vellum of varying sizes stitched together, is worn in

---

[1] Julian Wright, 'Finding Northford: Dartington's Lost Manor', *DAT* 147 (2015), 253–72.

various places with missing letters. A second item, edited below, may relate to an accompanying terrier for 1613.

Dartington

A rate [illegible] Thomas Beard Nicholas Searle and John Tucker Sydemen by Authorytie to them Committed With the consent and agrement of the reste of the parishoners there the 12th of Februarye *in the year of our Lord one thousand five hundred and ninety three.*

Byllerswill [Billerswill]

Thomas Maddocke	halfe a bushell of Otes	Mr Sargent Glanfield	twoo Bushells of Otes
Edmund Moyse	a Bushell of Otes		halfe Bushell of Wheate
ffenton [Venton]			

Brocking [Brook]

Edward Williams	halfe a Bushell of Otes	William Pottell	halfe a Bushell of Otes
Jane Williams widdowe	halfe a Bushell of Otes	Edmund Abraham	half a Bushell of Otes

Cobbetonn [Cobberton]

John Tucker	three peckes of Otes half a pecke of wheate
Leonard Williams	a Bushell of Otes and a pecke of Wheate
Nicholas Adams	a peck of Bareley

Petowe [Petoe]

William Burte	three pecke of Otes

Allerton

Lawrence Issell	a bushell of Otes and a pecke of wheate
Thomas Beard	three peckes of Otes and halfe a pecke of wheate
Nicholas Searell	a Bushell of Otes and a pecke of wheate

Westcombe

Thomas Martyne	a Bushell of Otes and a pecke of wheate
Mrs Saverye	a Bushell of Otes and half a pecke of wheate
Nicholas Bidlacke	three peckes of Otes
James Farwell	three peckes of Otes and halfe a pecke of wheate

Coxelacke [Coxlake]

Richard Driston	three pecke of Otes and halfe a pecke of wheate

Belley [Belleigh]

Joan Myllar	halfe a bushell of Otes and halfe a peck of wheate
Joan Michell	halfe a Bushell of Otes and half a pecke of wheate
Mary Martyn	half a Bushell of Otes and half a pecke of wheate
Alice Ford	half a Bushell of Otes

Byllynhey [Billany]

John Lavers	three peck of Otes

Weeke [Week]

James Searell	a Bushell of Otes

Edward Searell   half a Bushell of Otes & a pecke of Wheate
[Page 2]

Dartington   102

Oldinge
Mrs Joan Kerswill   a Bushell of Otes   Walter Windeat   half a bushell of Otes

Yeanard [Yarner]
John Hawking   half a Bushell of Otes   Peter Come
Margery Williams   halfe a Bushell of Otes   three pecke of Otes and half a peck of wheate
Allen hendlye   half a Bushell of Otes

ffoorde
Edward Shinner   halfe a Bushell of Otes   Dewnes Beard   three pecke of Otes
Thomas Shinner   halfe a Bushell of Otes

Staple
David Mannning   half a bushell of Otes   Mr Geoffrey Babb [faded] the [faded]
John Tucker   half a bushell of Otes   a pecke of wheate
Alice Martyn   a peck of Barley   John Tucker for the barton   a pecke of otes
Nicholas Huxham   Robert Shorton   a peck of Otes
          [faded] and a pecke of wheate   Thomas Hawkyng   a pecke of Otes
John Chattell for Barton meadow   Allan Sarell half   a pecke of Otes
          [faded] half a pecke of Otes   Dewnes Beard for the Barton a pecke of Otes
William Goale for his ground   Edward Shinner for Bromehaye
          half a Bushell of Otes   a pecke of Otes
John Lavers for his Barton   Elizabeth Williams for Wests and
          half of a pecke of wheate   half a pecke of wheate
Edward Abraham for [faded] pecke of wheate   Leonard Williams for Cobbeton
Thomas Martyn for   half a pecke of wheate
          [faded] half a pecke of wheat   John Luscombe for whiteley   a pecke of Otes
Mr Geoffrey Babb for the   [faded and torn]

Northford
Mr Richard Sparrowe esquire for three peeces of ground   halfe a Bushell of Bareley
Robert Bullye for three peeces of ground and   a pecke of wheate
Mr John Voysey for one Close of   a half a pecke of Otes
Mrs Saverye for three Closes half   a bushell of barley
Peter Pytford one Close and a Medowe   a pecke of Bareley
Edward Goule for twoo Closes   a pecke of Bareley
John Nele for two Closes & a Meadowe   a pecke of wheate
Edward Beare for one Close   half a peck of Bareley
Mr Richard Hackwill for one Close   a pecke of Bareley
Walter Weaver for one Close   a pecke of bareley
Robert Bullie for the Conygers   halfe a bushell of barley
Mr Geoffrey Babbe for two Closes   a pecke of wheate
Robert Bullie one close in Copperland   a pecke of bareley
John Glanfield one Close   half a pecke of Bareley
Richard Dotting one Close   half a peck of Bareley
Nicholas Rider and the rest for Copperland   half a bushell of wheate
Henry Hacker for twoo Closes   a pecke of Barlye

Mr Thomas Every one Close	a pecke of Bareley
Mr Richard Every for three Closes	halfe a bushell of bareley
Mr Christopher Savery for fower Closes	three pecke of bareley
John Twiggs for two Closes	a pecke of Barley
Alexander English for fower Closes	half a bushell of...
Phillip Sheere for two Closes	a pecke of wheate
Agnes Hatton for two Closses that...	a pecke of wheate
Hext Abell for two Closes	halfe a Bushell of wheate
[blank] Comminge for one Close	a pecke of Barley
Mr John Wisse for three Closes	halfe a bushell of barley
Mr Nicholas Newman for two Closes	a pecke of wheate
Mr Richard Baggins for a meadow	a pecke of bareley
Mr Edward Blackaler one Close	a pecke of barley
Mr Gabriel Lenicott for three Closes	halfe a Bushell of Bareley
Mr John Neyle for the ground at paddeven [Puddavine]	a pecke of otes
John Seaver for his tenement	three pecke of Otes
Mr Walter Dotting for poddeven myll	a pecke of wheate
[Item 2] Joan Carswill for two Closes and one grove	half a bushell of wheate
William Come one Close & a meadow	a pecke of bareley
Mr Richard Hackwill for one Close	halfe a pecke of bareley
Mr Lucke Serrett for two Closes and one grove	halfe a bushell of Barely
William Brocking one Close	a pecke of bareley
Mr Richard Buggins three Closes and one grove	half a bushell of bareley
Mr Walter Dotting one close	a pecke of bareley
John Norrys for two meadowes	a pecke of bareley
Nicholas Norman for two Closes	a pecke of wheate
David Mannyng for two Closes	a pecke of wheate
Thomas Martyne for his ground at forches	halfe a bushell of Otes
David Manning	a pecke of Otes
John Tucker	a pecke of Otes
William Averye for the land he holdeth of Agnes Haston	a bushell of Bareley
William Averye for two Closes in the styrtes	a pecke of barelye
William Averye for one Close and a Meddowe	a pecke of Bareley

60. DARTINGTON, Churchwardens and Overseers of the Poor Rate, 1642

DHC, 347A-99/PX1

Note: This rate was written on a single sheet of paper of 14½ inches in width and 11½ inches in length which has been folded to provide four pages. The purpose of the rate is unspecified and may have been to maintain both the church and the poor.

The rate and Taxasione of Everie Inhabitant possessor and Occupier of land within the pish of Dartington made by Williame Searle theelder Churchwarden Robbart Stidston and Henry Searle Overseers of the poore Appointed there unto by his Maits Justices of the peace Whose names are heare under written *in the year of our Lord* 1642

First the worshipful Arthur Champnowne Esqr.	£2 3s 4d	Mrs Marie or the holders of harders living	00 02 00
Mr Arthur Rowse gentellman or the holders	1 00 00	Edward Williames	00 01 00
		Henry Harder or the holders	00 01 3

Gawen Shinner	00 01 4
Henry Farlye	00 00 6
Christopher Williames	00 02 6
Henry Searle	00 03 4
Nicholas Lucke	00 03 0
Margaret Shinner wido	00 05 0
John Tucker of Cobbaton [Cobberton]	00 06 1
Edmund Williames	00 04 0
Robert Smardon or the holders	00 02 8
Nicholas Addames	00 00 10
Joan Jssell wido	00 04 8
Thomas Bearde	00 04 4
William Searle of Allorton [Allerton]	00 11 0

William Addomes	00 10 4
John Gill or the holders	00 05 4
Roger Marten or the holders	00 03 0
John Bidlake	00 04 0
Alice Varwell widdo	00 04 4
John Bidlake for Mr Sandries ~~living~~ ground	00 03 10
William Searle for pt of the same	00 00 6
George Distine for pt of the same	00 00 4
Thomas Beard for pt of the same	00 00 4
John Preston Senior	00 03 4
John Preston Junior	00 01 00
William Crossing	00 02 0

[page 2]

['0' in margin]	
John White or the holders ~~for parsonage~~	2s 0d
Mr Robert Savery esquire or the holders	7 8
John Luscombe or the holders	4 2
Thomas Luscombe	1 0
James Emett senior	0 8
John Kinge or the holders	0 6
['0' in margin] Henry Pearce	1 0
Giles Bidlake	1 0
John Tayler	0 6
Even Martin	1 3
['John' added later in margin] John Coale	0 4
Peter Windeate	0 6
Nicholas Belson	0 4
John Maxsie	0 4
Lawrence Beard	0 4
Christopher Edwards	0 6
John Weecher	1 6
Christopher Bidlake	0 8
John Hawkings Junior	1 0

Christopher Williams Junior	0 4
William Busshell	1 0
Thomas Booking	0 8
William Searle Junior	0 4
James Emett ~~Junior~~	0 4
Richard Reede	0 6
Phileman Filpe of the holders	0 4
Nicholas Emott for michels Close	0 6
['0' in margin] Elizabeth Westawey widowe	1 0
Andrew Choake for the holders	0 8
Edward Beard	0 4
Allan Edwards	0 6
Thomas Hearle	0 6
Nicholas Halle	0 4
['0' in margin] Thomas Sheepane	0 4
['0' in margin] William Ford	0 6
['0' in margin] Martin Lavers	1 0
William Evens	0 4
[added] William Evens	0 4

[page 3]

Norfoote Rate

Mr Richard Voysie	5s 0d
Mr Walter Donise	0 9
Stephen Kellond	0 8
Mr Docter Whachabb	2 0
Mr Garratt	5 0
Mr William Bogans	1 8
the same for a close that William Farwell hath	0 6
Thomas Panchin	1 4
The same for a close that waes Caselies	0 6
the same for a Close that was Mr Bogans of Dartmouth	0 6
William Farwell	1 2

Mr James Roods	0 10
Mr John Wise for 4 peeces or the holders	2 0
Mr Richard Wise for 2 peeces or the holders	1 0
Mr John Pitts for a Close above the Coome	0 8
John Weeger for Austins land	2 0
The widowe pinson or the holders	2 0
Geoffrey Barber	0 6
John Drewe or the holders	0 8
Mrs Macye or the holders	8 4
Dewenes weaver or the holders	1 4
Mr Thomas Beare	2 0
Richard Parker	0 3
Whater Reefe or the holders	2 0

Christopher Farwell	0 3
Joan Tucker widowe	1 2
Francis Bickford	2 6
Mr Thomas Prestwood	0 6
Mrs Kinncott or the holders	2 4
John Attwill	1 2
Mr Richard Harvey	1 4

Robert Parker	0 4
Richard Hannaford for 2 peeces of land of Mr Blacklers wch William Farwell had	1 2
['0' in margin] James Rowe or the holders for medowe Smalebridge	0 6

The *sum* of our Receytes £16 2s 8d

DARTMOUTH

One of the main ports in Devon, the borough was named Clifton-Dartmouth-Hardness and was divided into the three parishes of St Petrox (in which lie Clifton and Southtown), St Saviour (in which lies Northtown) and Townstal (of which the church was dedicated to St Clement and in which Hardness and Norton lie). For the purposes relating to policing and the militia the port was divided into six wards which were named after each day of the week except for Saturday. The port's records are extensive and it has not been possible to include poor rates for St Saviour's parish for 1604, 1608, 1609 and 1610.[1] The population of the port was about 2,577 in 1642. Some 16 per cent of the borough contributed to the poor rates. An average of 130 St Petrox parishioners paid their poor rates, some 17 per cent of the parish population of about 760. In comparison an average of 187 people, or 14 per cent, of the estimated 1,305 parishioners of St Saviour were ratepayers. The parish of Townstal had a population estimated at 512 and 26 per cent of them, or an average of 132, paid the poor rates.

61. DARTMOUTH (St Petrox), Poor Rate, 1604

DHC, DD61699

Note: This rate was written on seven sheets of paper which measure 8 inches in width by 12 inches in length. These have been folded and stitched together with white thread to form a booklet of 28 pages. The rate is preceded by notes of two payments over twenty-six weeks each to several individuals.

A booke of ratemente for the poore people of the parish of St Pethericks in the sowthe towne dartmowthe for the yeare of our Lord god 1604 begininge the 25th of march to be Collected bye William Plumly and John Newman Collectors for the yere

[illegible crossed through]

June 8th

James Saverye	|||||||||||||||||||||||||	10d
Geoffrey Leagar	|||||||||||||||||||||||||	08
mother Lettys	|||||||||||||||||||||||||	04
To efford	|||||||||||||||||||||||||	04
To agnes flecher	|||||||||||||||||||||||||	04

More I gave to mother Lettys & unte efford for one weeke over & above be cawse the were sycke
01s 00d.

Allso I dyd Receave of Robert Downes to Use of the poore twentye shyllyngs & thre pence more I have reseaved of the wyddowe towpe as a gyft gevn to the paryshe by hyr deseased husband thre shyllynges & fower pence so the holle is   23s 07d

and I have payd over to the poore twente thre shyllynges and syx pence so hyr [obscured] to the parryshe one pennye [signed] William plomleyghe

I J||||ohn Newman have pd for a quarters Rents Eferds hose latt medsomer 1s 8d
I John Newman have pd tell the laste of September wch is 16 wekes is in all 40s

---

[1]   DHC, DD61698, DD61788 & DD61789.

Plate 13. Brass of John Roope, early 1600s.

[total] 2 1 8
1 11 4   Itt[em] I have Rec of quarting 9 3
1 12 4   The resteth to me 1 12 5
1 17 6   Delivered to Mr Newman the sum of 12s 5d
1 16 8
6 17 10d

[page 2]

James Saverye																						10d	To efford																				04
Geoffrey Legar																						08	To Agnes flacher																				04
mother Lettys																						04			

Begynynge agayne to paye ~~the~~ to the sayd poore the 8th of october.
I Wm plumleyghe here payde for mychelmas Rent to speed for effordes howse 1s 8d
Memorennd that I John Numan Doe acknowlgde to be faullye satysfyed of wm plumleyghe for
all the monye wyche I payd to the poor of the parryshe. [signed] Jn Newman
I wm plomleyghe have payde to speed for Chrystmas quartters Rent for effordes howse 1s 8d
I wm plumleyghe have payd to speed for ower ladyes quartters Rent for effords howse 1s 8d

[page 3]

A.

	Nicholas Adams						4s 0d	Gregory Arther						0 4
John Anthonye						1 8	Richard Androwes						0 8
Edmund Averye						2 0	Henry Asheberye 0 8		

B.

John BrinJohn [sic]						2 0	Phillip Boorne				0 4
+ John Blackaller						2 0	John Beare						0 8
Robert Bicklye						1 4	Lambert Bastwill		0 8
John Barnes						0 8	John Bartlet						0 4
John Bennet						1 0	John Bayleye						0 8
Nicholas baple						0 4	['Dennys bucklond 0 4' in later hand]		

C

Robert Constable		0 5	Humphrey Crosse					0 8
William Constable						0 8	thomas Carter		0 8
Thomas Cane						0 8	Robert Careye		0 8
William Collin				0 4	stephen Chappell		0 8

D.

George Duringe						2 0	walter Demante						0 8
		Robert Downe						1 0	Henry Daye						1 0
thomas Downinge						1 0	[total]		31s
george Davis						0 4			31s 4d
John Davy 1 0					

[page 4]

E. F.

Nicholas Eastcotte						1s 0d	James fosten						0 8
John Furnes						0 [0]	Robert Fust						1 0
Robert fursman						0 0 [sic]	William Freend						0 4
				Robert fletcher						0 8	~~John fyllypes~~	#	~~0 8~~

G.

Name		Amount	Name		Amount
Arthur goodridge	||||	0 8	Hugh gefforde	|||||	0 8
|| Walter gunne	||||	0 8	William ginkins		0 4
Richard greesacke	|||||	0 4			

H. J.

Name		Amount	Name		Amount
John Hawkins	||||	4 0	Richard Harris	|||	1 0
James Haward	||||	1 8	tryamor harvy		0 4
| George Hambleton	||||	1 4	william homes	||||	0 4
|||| Richard Hocken	||||	0 8	Nicholas Jeffrye	||||	0 8
~~Thomas Hixan~~		~~0 8~~			

K. L.

Name		Amount	Name		Amount
Robert Knighte	||||	1 0	John Lynes	||||	1 0
John Knowles	||||	0 8	William Lerefant	||||	1 0
Elizabeth Lewes	||||	4 0	['Edmund Lapthorne	||||	
Elizabeth Leye	||||	4 0			0 4' in later hand]
John Lewes	||||	1 0	[total]		32s [obscured]d
John Lukum	||||	1 4			

[page 5]

Name		Amount	Name		Amount
Robert M.			Peter Miller		0 4
| ~~Thomas~~ midwinter	||||	2s 0d	John Martin		0 4
William Morris	||||	3 0			

N.

Name		Amount	Name		Amount
Mr William Norris or Wynchyster		1 8	John Newman	||||	1 4
Richarde Newall	||||	2 0			

P.

Name		Amount	Name		Amount
| John Plomleighe	||||	6 0	William Pethibridge	||	0 6
Robert Phillpot	||||	2 0	William Prowse	||	1 0
William plomlye	||||	1 4	| John prince	||||	0 8
John Phillippes	||||	0 8			

R.

Name		Amount	Name		Amount
Nicholas Rowpe	||||	8 0	John Rocker		0 4
| John Rowswell	||||	3 0	[total]		37s 6d
John Runnsevall	||||	1 0			1 16 0
William Roper		1 0			3 13 0
Robert Rule		0 8		37 6d	6 17 2
Edmund Raymonde		0 8			

[page 6]

S.

Name		Amount	Name		Amount
Mr Gilbert Staplehill	||||	4s 0d	James Savvrye	||||	0 6
|| Thomas Spurwaye	||||	4 0	Robert sparke senior	||||	0 4
James Searle	||||	1 4	Robert sparke Junior	||||	1 0
John Searle	||||	1 4	|| John sparke Junior	||||	1 0
|| William Sayer	||||	0 8	thomas Smithe	||||	1 0
george sparke	||||	1 0	John Strange	||||	0 6

T.

| Richarde trosse		2 0	stephen tayller ||	1 0
William tollocke ||||		1 0	george tizarde	0 8
phillip taplye ||||		1 0		

W.

| Mr Richarde wakeham ||||		6 0	|||| Christopher willson ||||	1 0
nicholas waterton ||||		2 0	thomas wardroppe ||||	1 0
William White ||||		1 4	Anthony white ||||	0 4
thomas weekes ||||		1 0	William Wakeham ||||	0 4
|| thomas watson ||||		1 0		

[page 6]

Resevyd of Robert Downe the 9ᵗʰ of apryll for the pore twentye shillynges and three pene

first payd weeklye to the pore	2 06
more for Effordes howse for the yeare	6 08
more Deleveryd to efford and to mother Lettys when the were sycke	1 00
more collectyd the som of	£6 7s 02d
the holle that I have Reasevyd is seaven pownd seaven shyllynges and fyve pence	7 7 5
And I have payd owt the sum of seven pownd and towe pence	7 0 2
so thyr restythe Due to the Parryshe from me seven shyllynges and thre pence	0 7 3

[signed] William Plomleyghe

More that cannot be collectyd of this acownt 9s 9d.

['31s	
32	[0]d
37	6
36	8
137	2 Recepts
20	3 [Robert] downe
	6d
157s	5' on opposite sheet]

[page 7]

William plumly Receyned from Robert Downe the 9ᵗʰ of Aprill for the poore twenty shillings and three pence and doth begin his first paymente to the poore upon Sonday next after Easter beinge the 15ᵗʰ of Aprill & so to contynew till thannuciacon of mary the blessed virgin next ensewing and to paye weekely to every pticuler poore body as herafter followeth

to paules childe wth geffry leager	8d
to Worthlyes child wth James savery	10d
to Lettis weekelye	4d
to Agnes fletcher weekly	4d
to efford weekelye	4d
more effords rent yerlye	6s 8d
The whole some weekely to be payde is 2s 8d wch makes in the yeere	£6 10s 0d
~~It there is dew from the wydow tenpe by her husbands bequest~~	~~3s 4d~~
Item there is dew from the parishoners by this booke of ratement as by the book appeerethe the some of	£6 17s 10d all beinge collected.

And the yeerely payment is	£6 16s 8d
More Resevyd of Elexsander cossullyn	2d

62. DARTMOUTH (St Petrox), Poor Rate, 1609

DHC, DD61776

Note: This rate was written on six pieces of paper which measure some 7½ inches in width and 12 inches in length, which have been folded and stitched with white thread to make up a booklet of twenty-four pages. Payments to the poor are recorded at the end of the rate including financial support in May and June for Agnes Fletcher, Margaret Skynner, Joan Grant and Elizabeth Archer. These payments are preceded by a short account of expenditure on Widow Grant, 'Rodger's Bastard' and for Eleanor Reeve's shroud and burial.

A booke of ratement wherin is conteyned how much each parishoner within the parish of St petherick in the Sowthtowne Dartemowth is to paye to the reliefe of the poore of the same parish from the 25th daye of march 1609 untill the 25th daye of march 1610. Nicholas Deane and John Bowdon Collectors and Robert Midwinter and William Plumleighe overseers for the said year.

A.

Edmund Averie	||||	1s 0d	Richard Androes	||||	1 8
John Athonie *otherwise* gunnell	||||	1 4	Richard Archer	||||	1 0

B.

John Blackaller	||||	2 0	Henry Butland	||||	0 4
Alice Barnes Widow	||||	0 4	John Bartelet Junior	||||	0 4
John Bennet	||||	1 4	John Bowdon	||||	0 8
John Barrette	||||	1 0	John Bryn	||||	0 4
Henry Bacun	||||	1 0	John Bingly	||	0 4
Nicholas Baple	||||	0 4	[in later hand] Arthur Browne		0 4
Phillippe Boorne	||||	0 4	[in later hand] Nicholas Bennett		0 4
John Baillie	||||	0 8			

C

John Chapell	||||	2 0	Robert Carey	||||	0 8
Alexander Cosens	||||	1 8	Stephen Chapin	||||	0 8
William Constable	||||	1 0	Widow Clynnick	||||	0 4
gon Nicholas Constable		0 4	George Combe	||||	1 0
Thomas Cane	||||	0 4	[in later hand] Jn Creese		0 8
Humphrey Crosman		0 4			

D

George Duringe	||||	2 0	Robert Downe	||||	0 4
George Davis	||||	1 0	John Duyn *otherwise* Cornish	||||	1 0
Walter Deament	||||	1 4	[total]		1 11 8
Nicholas Deane	||||	1 8			1 11 8
Henry Daye	||||	1 0			

[page 2]

E

Nicholas Estcote	||||	0s 8d	[in later hand] Wm Jerman	||||	2 0
John Efforde	||||	0 4			

ff

Edmund Follet	||||	1 0	John Furnes	||||	0 8
Robert Fost	||||	1 0	Robert Furseman	||||	0 4

Name		Amount	Name		Amount
James Foskew	||||	0 8	Run A way Robert Fisher	||||	0 8
William Freend	||||	0 4	gon ~~Joan Flute wyddowe~~		~~0 4~~

G

Name		Amount	Name		Amount
|||| Robert Giles	||||	[0] 8	John Gulborne	||||	1 0
Arthur Goodridge	||||	0 8	Andrew Gribble	||||	1 0
Richard Gressack	||||	0 4	[in later hand] Robert grindall	||||	2 0
Hugh Gefford	||||	0 8			

[H]

Name		Amount	Name		Amount
drownd Edward Hynde			1 0	William Homes	||||	0 4
James Hawarde	||||	2 0	John Ham	||||	0 6
George Hambleton	||||	1 0	John hamon	||||	0 4
Richard Harris	||||	0 4	Julian hoggett wyddowe	||||	0 4
Tryamor Harvye	|||	0 4			

J. K. L.

Name		Amount	Name		Amount
Nicholas Jefferye	||||	0 6	John Lukum	||||	1 4
Phillippe Joslyn	||||	0 4	Edmund Lapthorne	||||	1 0
John Knowles	||||	0 8	Robert Lome	||||	1 0
John Jefferie	||||	0 8	Nicholas Leach		0 4
|||| Elizabeth Ley Widow	||||	4 0	[total]		1 12 4
John Lewes	||||	1 0	[numbers crossed through]		1 12 4

[page 3]

J. K. L.

Name		Amount	Name		Amount
John Leye	||||	0s 8d	Wm Jago	||||	1 0
Wm Lappam	||||	0 4			

M. N.

Name		Amount	Name		Amount
Robert Midwinter	||||	2 0	John Newman	||||	2 0
William Morris	||||	2 0	Margaret Nowall Widow	||	0 8
Thomas Newman	||||	4 0	Robert Modie	||||	0 6

P

Name		Amount	Name		Amount
John Plumleigh gent.	||||	6 8	William Pethibridge	||||	0 4
Robert Philpotte	||||	3 0	*John* Prince *clerk*	||||	1 0
William Plumleigh	||||	3 4	Walter Pecke	||||	2 0
John Phillippes	||||	1 0			

R

Name		Amount	Name		Amount
Nicholas Rowpe	||||	10 0	John Rocker Senior	||||	0 4
John Rowswell	||||	2 8	Robert Rogers	||||	0 4
John Rounsenall	||||	1 0	Joyce Roper Widow	||||	1 0
Edmund Reymond	||||	1 0	Richard reynelles	||||	0 6

S.

Name		Amount	Name		Amount
|||| Gilbert Staplehill	||||	4 4	William Sayer	||||	0 8
|||| Thomas Spurway	||||	4 8	James Saverie	||||	0 4
Edward Stevens	||||	3 0	Robert Sparke Senior	||||	0 4
James Searle	||||	1 8	Robert Sparke Junior	||||	1 4
John Searle	||||	1 4	[total]		3 6 04
John Sumers	||||	1 4			

[page 4]

S.

John Sparke	||||	1s 0d	Giles Sillie	||||	0 8
Thomas Smithe	||||	1 0	Reuben Skynner	|||	0 4
Widow Strange	||||	0 4	Robert Sallett	||||	0 4
John Sheere	||||	0 4			

T.

~~Ma~~ Richard Trosse	||||	3 4	Thomas Terrye	||||	1 0
William Tollocke	||||	1 4	Christopher Taplie	||||	0 4
Phillip Taplye	||||	0 4	[in margin 'dead'] Thomas Vine		0 4

W.

Margery Wakeham Wido	||||	4 0	Richard Waterton	||||	1 0
Andrew Wakeham	||||	2 0	William Wakeham	||||	0 6
Nicholas waterton	||||	2 0	John Weeks	||||	0 4
John Winchester	||||	3 4	John Waymouthe	||||	0 8
William White	||||	1 0	Edmund White *clerk*	||||	1 4
Thomas Weekes	||||	1 0	John Wellshe	||||	0 4
Thomas Watson	||||		[total]		1 9 8
Widow Willson	||||	1 0			

ordinary paymentes Weekely to be paide for this presente yere 1609.

To Joan Rogers bastard	12d	To Joan grannte	4d
To Agnes Fletcher for Caverly	8d	To Elizabeth Archer	4d
To Agnes Fletcher for her self	4d		

Mother Grant died 7 daies before Crismas.

And I praysent we pd to be good in the [illegible] his hand and

[page 5]

[signed] Nicholas waterton Edward stevens Churchewardens
Gilbert Staplehill, *Sign of* Robert Geilles Robert mydwinter William Plumleighe Overseers
[signed] Thomas Payge mayor John Follet

The wholl Raats of the book A monts unto the som of £7 18s 8d
Rec of the old Raters 0 7 9
[total] 8 6 5
Resting unpaid the som of 0 4 6
[new total] 8 1 2

[page 6]

Delivered over to the overseeres the 3th of maye 1609 3s 5d
Rec by William Plumleighe to Nyc Deanes and Jn boddlye the 3th of maye 1609 3s 5d
~~Rec by me Nyc Dean of Wm plomlye the 3th of may 3s 5d. Rec by me Nyc Dean of Andrew Walkham the som of 4 4d~~
~~I Nyc Dean have pd out more then this 7s 9d that I have Receaved the som of 16s 7d as p this book appears beffor the 26th of June of the wch som I have Receaved as Followth~~
~~Mr Gilbert Staplehill 4s 4d Mr Thomas Spurway 4s 8d Mr Robert Gyles 4 8d Mrs Elizabeth Lea 4 0~~
~~17 8~~
~~So I am debtter to this Accompt 1s 1d~~

I sett in my plac be the Conselll of the pish Samuwell weeks
by me Nyc Dean

63. DARTMOUTH (St Petrox), Poor Rate, 1611

DHC, DD61811

Note: This rate was written on five sheets of paper, approximately 8 inches in width and 12 inches in length, which have been folded and stitched to provide a booklet of ten pages.

1611

A boke of ratement wherin is Conteined how much each parishoner within the parish of St Pethericks in the sowthtowne Dartemowth is to paye towards the reliefe of the poore people of the same parish ~~fo~~ from the 25th day of march 1611 untill the 25th daye of march 1612. Robert Grindall & Richard Archer Collecters, Nicholas Roope Robert Giles John Winchester & William Plumleighe overseers of the poore for the said yeer 1611

[page 2]

A.

Edmund Averie	‖‖	0s 8d	William Ashford	‖‖		0 8
John Anthony *otherwise* guynell	‖	1 4	‖ Lewis Amerideth gentleman	‖‖‖		2 0
Richard Archer		1 0				

B.

John Blackaller	‖‖‖	2 00	Henry Butland	‖‖‖	0 4
Alice Bacon Widow	‖‖‖	0 4	John Bartlett Junior		0 4
John Bennet	‖‖‖	1 4	John Bowden	‖‖‖	0 8
‖ John Barret	‖‖‖	1 0	‖ Arthur Browne	‖‖‖	1 0
Henry Babon	‖‖‖	1 0	Nicholas Bennet	‖‖‖	0 4
poore ~~Widow Baple~~		~~0 4~~	Nicholas Babbe		1 0
Philip Boorne	‖‖‖	0 4	William Bowdon	‖‖‖	0 8
John Bayly	‖‖‖	0 8			

C.

John Chapell	‖‖‖	1 4	Robert Carey	‖‖‖	0 8
Alexander Cosen	‖‖‖	1 8	Stephen Chapen	‖‖‖	0 8
poor William Constable		~~1 0~~	George Comb	‖‖‖	0 4
Thomas Kane	‖‖‖	0 4	[total]		23s 0d Rcd 21s

[page 3]

D. E.

gon ~~George During~~		~~1 4~~	~~Robert Downe~~		0 0
George Davye		1 0	gon John Dinnis *otherwise* Cornish		1 0
Nicholas Deane	‖‖‖	1 8	John Davys	‖‖‖	0 4
Walter Deament		1 4	Nicholas Eastcote	‖‖‖	0 8
Henry Daye	‖‖‖	1 0			

ff

Edmund Follet	‖‖‖	1 4	Robert Fursman	‖‖‖	0 4
Robert Fust	‖‖‖	1 0	William Freende	‖‖‖	0 4
John Furnes	‖	0 8	Anthony Fletcher	‖‖‖	0 4
James Foskew	‖‖‖	0 8	gon John Filp		0 4

G

Robert Giles	||||	4 8	John Golborne	||||	1 0
Arthur goodridge	||||	0 8	Andrew gribble		1 0
Richard Gressack		0 4	Robert grindall	||||	2 8
Hugh gefford	||||	0 4			

H

James Haward	||||	2 0	William Homes	||||	0 4
George Hambleton	||||	1 0	[total]		28s 0d
Joan Hareson	||||	0 4	Rc		d 23s
Tryamor Harvye	||||	0 4			

[page 4]

H.

John Ham	||||	0 4	Julian Hogget	||||	0 4
John Hamond	||||	0 4			

J. K. L.

Nicholas Jeffrie	||||	0 6	John Lukem	||||	1 4
gon Philip Joslin	||	0 4	Edmund Laptherne	||||	1 0
John Jeffrie	||||	0 8	Robert Lamb	||||	1 0
William Jago	||||	1 0	William Luken	||	0 4
gon 1s William Jarman	||||	1 0	John Leye	||||	0 8
John Knowles	||||	0 8	William Lapham	||||	0 4
Elizabeth Ley Widow	||||	4 0	Robert Knighte	||||	1 0
John Lewes	||||	1 0			

M. N.

|| Robert Midwinter	||||	2 0	Margaret Newall	||||	0 4
Widow Morris	||||	1 0	William Neale	||||	1 0
Robert Moodyn	||||	0 6	Robert Norber		0 4
Thomas Newman	||||	2 0	Ric Norber		
gon ~~John Newman~~	|||	~~1 0~~			

P.

John Plumleighe gentleman	||||	6 8	*John* Prince *clerk*	||||	1 0
William Plumleigh	||||	3 4	[total]		40s 4d
Robert Philpot	||||	3 0	Rcd		28s 10d
Walter Pecke	||||	2 0			

[page 5]

P.

John Phillippes	||||	1 0	William Pethibridge	||||	0 4

R.

Nicholas Roupe	||||	8 0	|| Richard Reinolds	||||	0 4
John Rowswell	||||	2 8	Gilbert Roope		1 4
John Rowsevall	||||	2 8	Nicholas Roope the yonge		2 0
Emline Reymont		1 0			
poore ~~John Ricket senior~~		~~0 4~~			
Robert Rogers	||	0 4			
Richard Robins	||||	0 4			

S.

Gilbert Staplehill	||||	4 0	James Savery	||	0 4
Thomas Spurwaie	||||	4 8	John Spark	||||	1 0
James Searle	||||	1 0	Thomas Smythe	||||	1 0
John Searle	||||	1 4	gon John Sheere	||||	0 4
William Sayer	||||	0 8	Reuben skynner	||||	0 4
Mary Sumers	||||	1 4	Robert Sallet	||||	0 4
Robert Sparke senior	||||	0 4	Walter Shut	||||	0 4
Robert Spark Junior	||||	1 4			

T.

Richard Trosse	||||	4 0	Philip Taplyn	||||	0 4
William Tollock	||||	1 4	[total]	40s 6d Rcd 39s 6d	

[page 6]

T.

Thomas Terrie	||||	1 0	Richard Tooker	||||	0 4
Christopher Taply	||||	0 4			

W.

Andrew Wakeham	||||	4 0	Poore John Walshe	||||	0 4
John Winchester	||||	3 4	*Edmund* White *clerk*	|||	1 0
Richard Waterton	||||	1 0	Robert Windet	||||	0 4
Nicholas Waterton	||||	2 0	[total]	19s 8d	
William White	||||	1 0	Rcd	1 1 0	
Thomas Weeks	||||	1 0		1 3 0	
Thomas Watson	||||	1 0		1 18 10	
|| Widow Wilson	||||	1 0		1 19 6	
William Wakeham	||||	0 8		0 18 5d	
John Waymowth	||	1 0		7 0 9d	
~~John Weeks 0 4~~					

ordinarie payments weekely to be paid this presente yeer 1611

To Agnes fletcher for Caverley	0s 8d	To the Widow Archer	0 6
To Agnes fletcher for her selfe	0 4	To Joan Downes Child	1 0
To Joan Rogers Bastard	1 0		

[page 7]

the sine of William Wakeham

[signed by] And: Wakeham   churchwardens
The singe of Robert Gilles [signed by] William Plumlighe overseers for the por
[signed by] Nic Roupe   John Wynchester

[page 8]

the 15th of December I payd by the order of the sidmen unto the widoe Bartlet £00 7s 00
the 27th of this p John follet did take Joan Rogers bastard and from the 25th of march to this daye
A bove writen I have payd for the keeping of it 1s p weeke which Amounts to 39s
~~payd unto John foliet for Joan Rogers bastard~~
witnesseth that I Robert Grindlle have receaved in stocke nyntiene shillinges and three pense
[signed] Robt Grindle

[page 9]

Rcd when we took our office	£0 19s 3d
Rcd by the booke of rates as by the pticulers appeereth	7 0 9
The whole receipts	28 0 0

[page 10]

pd for the keepinge of the boy wyth Agnes fletcher for 59 weeks at 8d the weeke and to Agnes fletcher for her selfe so many weeks at 4d the weeke £2 17s 0d

to the widow Archer for 57 weeks at 6d the week	1 8 6
for Joan Downes child for 3 weeks at 1s the week	0 8 0
for Joan Rogers bastard for 39 weeks at 1s the week	1 19 0
dlld to the wydow bartlet in her sickness by order from the pisheners	0 1 0
pd to the churchwardens fos so much they layd unto for clothes for the poor Children	0 19 9
to Emlyn Hart for 3 weeks kepinge another child of Joan Downes	0 2 6

Rest due to the parish and is delivered with this account to the churchwardens the third day of May 1602 1612 to ballanc this account   0 4 3

The whole is   8 0 0

the signe of Robert Marten maior   [signed] Jn Smyth

64. DARTMOUTH (St Petrox), Poor Rate, 1613

DHC, DD61844

Note: This rate was written on seven sheets of paper, approximately 8 inches in width and 12 inches in length, which have been folded and stitched to provide a booklet of fourteen pages.
1613 A Booke of ratement Wherin is Conteined how much each parishoner within the parish of Saint Pethericks in the Sowthtowne Dartmowth is to paye towards the reliefe of the poore people of the same parish From the 25th daye of march 1613, untill the 25th daye of march 1614. John Dottin and Edmund Lapthrne Collectors. Thomas Newman, John Lewes and Alexander Cosen overseers for the poore for the said yeer 1613.

Robert Philpot & Thomas Wecks Churchwardens

[page 2]

Mr Lewis Amerideth	||||	2s 0d	Richard Archer	||||	1 4
Mr Edward Amerideth	||||	2 0	William Ashford	||||	0 8
John Anthony *otherwise* guynell	||||	1 4	Walter Androes	||||	0 6
Edmund Averye		0 4	Henry Ashley	|	0 8

B.

John Blackaller	||||	2 0	Philip Boorne	||||	0 4
John Bennet	||||	1 4	John Bailie	||||	0 4
John Barrat	||||	1 0	Henry Butland	||||	0 4
Henry Baker	||||	1 0	John Bartlet Junior	||||	0 4
Arthur Browne	||||	1 0	Nicholas Bennet	||||	0 4
John Bowden	||||	0 8	Lodowick Blackler	||	0 4
William Bowdon	||||	0 8	Edward Brand	||||	1 4
Alice Barnes widow	||||	0 4	Mr Edward Beare	||	2 0

C

John Chapell	||||	1 4	- William Constable	|	0 8
Alexander Cosen	||||	2 0	1s Thomas Cane	||||	1 0

Robert Carey	||||	0 8	Henry Chillie	||||	0 4
Stephen Chapin	||||	1 0	Christopher Cade	||	0 8
George Comb		0 4			

D. E.

Nicholas Deane	||||	2 0	John Dotterell	||||	0 8
Henry Daye	||||	1 0	John Davis	||||	0 8
John Dotten	||||	1 4	[totals]	11s 6d	1 11 6

[page 3]

D. E.

Grace Duringe	||||	0s 4d	+ John Efford		0 0
Nicholas Eastcote	||	1 0	Andrew Gribble	||||	1 0

F.

+Anthony Follet	||||	2 0	Robert Fursman	||||	0 4
Robert Foss	||||	1 0	William Freend	||||	0 4
John Furnes	||||	0 8	Anthony Fletcher	||||	0 8
James Foskyn	|||	0 8	Jn fursman & his mother	||||	1 0

G. [H]

Robert Giles	||||	4 8	George Hambleton	||||	1 0
Widow Grindall		2 0	Triamor Harvye	||	0 4
John Golborne	||||	1 4	William Humes	||||	0 4
Arthur Goodridge	||||	0 6	John Ham	||||	0 4
Hugh Gefford	||||	0 8	John Hamons	||||	0 4
Richard Greasacke	||||	0 4	Julian Hogget	||||	0 4
William Gourney	||||	2 0	Robert Haward	||||	0 4
Gilbert Hellier	||||	0 8	Richard Hawkins	||||	0 4
James Haward	||||	2 0			

J. K. L.

John Jefferie	||||	1 0	Elizabeth Ley Widow	||||	4 0
Nicholas Jefferie	||||	0 6	John Lewes	||||	1 0
William Jago		1 0	John Lukom	||||	1 0
20d Robert Knighte	||||	1 8	Edmund Lapthorne	||||	1 0
John Knowles	||||	0 8	[total]		£1 17s 0d

[page 4]

L.

Robert Lambe	||||	1s 0d	~~John Lidstone~~		
John Leye	||||	1 4	Phillip Josline	||||	0 4d
William Lopham	||||	0 4			

M. N.

Katherine Morris	||||	1 0	William Nealle	||||	1 0
Robert Moodie	||	1 0	Richard Norber	||||	0 8
Thomas Newman	||||	2 8	Robert Norber	||||	0 4
Widow Newall	||||	0 4			

P.

Jn Plumleighe gentleman	||||	6 8	Robert Philpot	||||	3 4
William Plumleighe	||||	3 4	Walter Pecke	||||	2 0

John Prince *clerk*	||||	1 0	John Phillips	||||	1 0
John Pascoe	||||	1 4	William Pethibridge	||||	0 4

R.

Nicholas Roope thelder	||||	8 0	Richard Robins	||||	0 4
Nicholas Roope Junior	||||	2 0	Richard Reynolds	|	0 4
John Rowswell	||||	1 0	David Rogers	||||	0 4
Michael Roade	||||	1 0	Arthur Rous gentleman	||||	2 0
John Rounsevall	||||	0 8	Richard Rendall 2 q[uarte]r	||	2 0
- Robert Rogers		0 4	[total]		£2 5s 0d

[page 5]

S.

Mrs Staplehill Widow	||||	2s 0d	Thomas Smith	||||	0 8
Thomas Spurwaie	||||	4 8	James Saverie	||||	0 4
Aldred Staplehill	||||	2 8	16d Nicholas Skinner	||||	1 4
John Searle	||||	1 4	John Sheere	||||	0 8
James Searle	||||	1 0	- John Savorie		0 4
- William Sayer		0 8	Reuben Skynner	||||	0 4
Robert Sparke senior	||||	0 4	Walter Shut	||||	0 8
Robert Sparke Junior	||||	1 0	John Stone	||	0 8
John Sparke	||||	1 5	Nicholas Straw 3 q[uarte]r	|||	2 8

T

Richard Trosse	||||	3 4	William White	||||	1 0
William Tollocke	||||	1 0	Thomas Weeks	||||	1 0
Philip Taply	||||	0 8	Thomas Watson	||||	1 0
Thomas Terrie	||||	0 8	Widow Wakham	||||	0 4
Christopher Taply	||||	0 8	John Waymowth	||||	1 0
- Richard Tooker		0 4	John Walch	||||	0 4
Robert Teage	||	10	- John Watson	||||	0 4
Nico Towse	||	1 0	*Edmund* White *clerk*	||||	1 0
Andrew Wakeham	||||	4 8	William Waymouthe	|||	0 8
John Winchester	||||	4 8	Richard Waymowth		0 4
Nicholas Waterton	||||	1 4	- [total]		£2 5s 4d
Richard Waterton	||||	1 0			

[page 6]

In the year of our Lord 1613

Robert Philpot Thomas Weeks   Churchwardens
Thomas Newman John Lewes Alexander Cosen   overseers of the pore°
John Dotten Edmund Laptherne   Collecters for the pore
Robert Philpot Thomas Weekes his marke
[signed] Tho: Newman John Lewes Alexander Cosen Walter Francis maior RM
[page 7]

1613

oirdinaries payments weekelie to bee paid to the poore this yeer from the first of May 1613

To Agnes Fletcher widow	0s 4d	To Caverlies child	0 8
To the Widow Archer	0 6	To Barbara Sallet	0 4
To Joan bartlet Widow	0 6		

[page 8]

John Dotin and Edmund Lapthorne Collecters for the poore for this yeer begin theire first payment to the poore the second daye of maye 1613 and they Rcd then from the Collectors of the last yeere the *sum* of   £1 11s 6d

more for English grace to buy her hose & shoes delieevered by the curate which was collected for her in the church   0 3 4½

[page 9]

M[emorandu]m the account for this yere was passed in this yere in this sorte
The receipts this yer amounnte to   £10 00s 02d ½
The paiments amount to the some of   08 02 03
So there remaineth in stock to balance this accompt wch is delivered to Nicholas Strawe Collector for the yere to come and is   £01 17s 02d

65. **Dartmouth** (St Petrox), Poor Rate, 1619

DHC, DD61974

Note: This rate was written on six pieces of paper, 7¾ inches in width and 12 inches in length, which have been stitched together with white thread to make a book of twelve pages. In addition to the marks given for each individual's quarterly payments some names have a slash mark.

A Booke of rates wherin is conteined what each parishoner within the parish of St pethericks in the Sowthtowne Darmowth is to paye towards the reliefe of the poore people of the same parish, from the 25th day of March 1619 untill the 25th daye of march 1620. Thomas Harte and Thomas Lewes beeing then Collectors *that is*

[page 1]

A.

William Ashford	||||	00 08d	Thomas Adrescull	||||	00 04
Mary Archer Widow	||||	00 08	~~William Allen~~		00 00
Henry Ashley	||||	00 08	Walter Androwes	||||	00 06

B.

John Blackaller	||||	02 00	Henry Bacon	||||	00 04
Edward Brawne	||||	01 08	/ Phillip Borne	||||	00 04
/ John Bennet	||||	01 04	John Baylye	||||	00 04
Arthur Browne	||||	02 00	Nicholas Bennet	||||	00 04
John Boden	||||	01 00	/ Stephen Bowdon	||||	00 04
William Bodon	||||	00 08	James Bond	||||	01 00

C. D.

Alexander Cosen	||	02 00	gon Margery Deane Wido	||	01 00
gon ~~John Chapell~~		00 00	gon Henry Daye	|||	01 04
Stephen Chapin	||||	01 00	John David	||||	00 08
Henry Chillye	||||	00 04	gon Anthony Deament	||	01 00
/ Christopher Cade	||||	00 06	George Devonshier *otherwise* Andrues	||||	00 04
Richard Crocker	||||	00 08	~~George Deering~~		00 00
Thomas Cowle	||||	00 04	[total]		£1 4s 8d
/ John Cornish	||||	00 04			

[page 2]

E. F.

Anthony Follet	||||	02s 08d	Robert Fursman	||||	00 04
['2s 8d' in margin] Edmund Follet	||||	02 08	/ Nicholas Eastcote	||||	01 00
James Foskew	||||	00 08	William Evans	||||	00 04
/ Anthony Fletcher	||||	01 00	gon ~~Gilbert Follet~~		~~00 8~~
gon John Furnes	||||	00 04			

G. H.

Robert Giles	||||	05 00	Mary haward widow	||||	00 08
William Gurney	||||	02 04	Gilbert Hellier	||||	00 08
John Golborne	||||	01 00	George Hambleton	||||	01 04
Andrew Gribble	||||	00 08	William Humes	||||	00 04
Arthur Goodridge	||||	00 04	John Ham	||||	00 08
Widow Gressacke	||||	00 04	Johh Hamonds	||||	00 04
Timothy Geate	||||	00 04	Henry Haward	||||	01 00
William Hogget	||||	01 00	/ Christopher Harper	||||	00 08
Thomas Harte	||||	01 04	gon Thomas Hodge	|	00 8
John Harvye	||||	01 04	~~Davye Hooper~~		~~00 08d~~

J. K. L.

John Jefferie	||||	01 04	Andrew Langdon	||||	02 00
Nicholas Jefferie	||||	00 06	Joan Lewes Widow	||||	00 04
Philip Joslin	||||	00 04	Edmund Lapthorne	||||	01 04
William Kent	||||	02 08	Robert Lamb	||||	01 00
John Kingman	||||	00 08	[total]		£1 18s 6d

[page 3]

J. K. L.

Richard Lomer	||||	00 04	Thomas Lewes	||||	00 08
Robert Lenagen	||||	01 00	/ Thomas Kane	||||	01 0

M. N.

Catherine Morris	||||	01 00	Nicholas Norton	||||	01 00
Widow Malber	||||	00 04	/ Richard Norbor	||||	00 08
Nathaniel Martin	||||	01 00	Robert Norbor	||||	00 04
['pd' in margin] Edward Moore	||||	00 08	William Noy	||||	00 08
John Newman	||||	02 00	~~Thomas~~ William Martyn	||||	00 04
Thomas Newcomen	||||	01 00	John Nickelles	||||	00 04
John Norbor	||||	00 08	Thomas Mosse	||||	00 04

P. Q.

John Plumleigh gent	||||	06 08	/ Henry Peeke	||||	01 00
William Plumleighe	||||	05 00	Richard Piper	||||	01 00
Robert Philpot	||||	03 04	|||| Nicholas Pimple for silver park		01 00
Walter Parke	||||	02 00	and for the meadow		00 00
John Prince *clerk*	||||	01 00	Henry Quash	||||	00 04
William Petheridge	||||	01 04			

R. S.

Mr Nicholas Roupe thelder	||||	08 00	Thomas Spurwaye	||||	05 00
Nicholas Roupe the yonger	||||	04 00	William Spurway	||||	02 00

[total] £2 13s 8d

[page 4]

R. S.

Aldred Staplehill	||||	02 08	John Strell	||||	00 08
Gilbert Staplehill	||||	02 08	John Stone	||||	00 08
Nicholas Straw	||||	02 08	Nicholas Snelling	||||	00 08
Richard Randall	||||	02 00	~~James Savury~~		00 00
John Rounsevall	||||	01 04	Reuben Skynner	||||	00 04
~~David Rogers~~		~~00 0~~	/ Walter Shut	||||	00 04
Walter Rounsevall	||||	00 04	vincent Skynner	||||	00 08
James Searle	||||	02 00	John Sparke senior	||||	01 04
Nicholas Skynner	||||	02 00	Thomas Smyth	||||	00 08
William Symons	||||	01 04	/ William Speering	||||	00 04
Robert Sparke	||||	01 04	Joan Sayer	||||	00 04
Joan Searle widow	||||	01 00	Andrew Sam'oys	||||	01 04
John Spark Junior	||||	00 08	John Sayer	||||	00 04
John Sparke Tailor	||||	00 08	David Rogers	||||	0 4

T.

Thomas Terry	||||	01 04	John Tozer	||||	00 04
Philip Taplye	||||	00 08	Matthew Tucker	||||	01 04
Christopher Taplye	||||	00 08	Thomas Tucker	||||	00 04
Alice Tollock Widow	||||	00 08	Richard Terrye	||||	00 08

[page 5]

W.

John Winchester	||||	05 00	Robert Winder	||||	00 04
Andrew Wakeham	||||	04 08	Joan Wakeham Widow	||||	00 04
Edmund White *clerk*	||||	01 04	/ John Walsh	||||	00 08
Widow Watson	||||	01 00	/ Nicholas Babbe	||||	00 04
John Watson	||||	01 00	Richard Waterton	||||	02 00
Widow Wardrope	||||	01 00	William White	||||	01 00
John Waymowthe	||||	01 00	[total]		20 4
Henry Woolcot	||||	00 08			

[on opposite sheet ' £1 0s 4d

1 13 4

2 13 8

1 18 6

1 4 8

8 10 2']

in the first leaf £1 4s 8d

in the second leaf 1 18 6

in the third leaf 2 13 8

in the fourth ~~lyne~~ leaf 1 13 4

in the fifth leaf <u>1 0 4</u>

the whole rcd is £8 10 6

more as apperth <u>2 19 5</u>

11 9 11

[page 6]

1619

Walter Park Nicholas Skynner Churchwardens
Robert Philipt Gilbert Staplehill William Pethibridge Overseers for the poore
Thomas Harte Thomas Lewes Collectors for the poore

Weekely payments
6d   To Catherine Waterman 6d
            To the Widow Archer 4d
            To Barbara Bennet 4d
            To William freend 4d
            To Marion Jago Widow 4d
            To Thomas Ruswell 4d

The whole weekely payments is twoe shillings & twoe pence 22d 2s 2d
[signed] John Smyth maior Tho: Payge

[page 7]

pd the 19 of July 1619 for so much geven to Joan Rocket the wyfe of Walter tocker with c[on]sent	£0 1s 0d
pd to Mr freend the 11th of august with consent of the pishoners	0 1 0
more on 2 other severall tymes	0 2 0
deld to John efford in his sicknes	0 1 0
pd to Mary frankling the 14 of desember	0 1 0
pd to William freend the 20 of desember	0 1 0
ped to Richard Efford in his sicknes the 9 of January	0 2 0
ped to William freend 16 of January	0 1 0
ped to Richard Effording [sic] his sickines the 23 of January	0 2 0
ped to William frind 23 of Janiary 1619	0 1 0
the 13 of march d[elivere]d to Efford the tayller 4s and the last day of march 2s all is	0 6 0
d[elivere]d to Jn salters wyfe as 2 tymes being sick	0 2 0
pd for the rent of the howse of Jn weeks for one yeer	0 10 0
for a shrowd cloth for efford the tayller	0 3 6
for apparrell for Joan Vyn	1 3 0

[page 8]

Collected the 14th of march 1619

of Christopher harper	0s 8d	of William Spearing	0 4
of henry Peek	1 0	of Christopher Cade	[0] 3
of Anthony fletcher	1 0	of Richard norber	0 8
ot Thomas kaine	1 0	of Jn bennet	0 8
of William Ashford	0 8	of Richard terry	0 8
of Anthony f²			
of John Walsh	0 8	the whoe *sum* is	8s 2d
of Walter Shut	0 4	of Stephen Bowden	0 4
of phillip borne	0 1	of Thomas Adresce	0 4
of Jn Cornish	0 2	of Nicholas bab	0 8

[page 9]

Rcd out of the poore menes box the 4th of Aprill 1619   £0 5s 8d

more of Joan Lewes widow for so much dew by the last will of her husband John Lewes
deceased   0 10 0
more Red of the Collectoers of the last year   1 3 9
more Rcd of Gilbert Staplehill for thuse of £5 of the poores   0 10 0
Rcd of Mr Aldred Staplehill for thuse of fyv pounds   0 1 0
[total] the some of   2 19 5
begun with Jn efford a groat awecke the 21th day of September 1619 pd for a shurte for the old
efford the tayleor £0 3s 6d I begun wth John Efford six [illegible] a weeke.

[page 10]

The names of those that have not paid to the poor 1618 Anthony follet & Arthur brown Collectors
for that yeer

Thomas Cane	||||	1s 0d	Walter tucker gon		0 4
Thomas Cowle		0 4	Thomas Tucker		0 4
gon. William Hames		2 0	Nicholas Bak	||||	0 4
Richard Hawkins		0 6	James Savag		0 4
trihamor harvy dead		0 3	Walter Androes		0 3
Wm Lapham gon		0 4	Stephen Bondon		0 4
Robert Norbor poore	|	0 4	Henry Butland gon		0 4
Vincent skynner		0 8			

[miscellaneous figures]

66. DARTMOUTH (St Petrox), Hospital Rate, 1627

DHC, DD62283

Note: This rate was written on a single sheet of paper, approximately 16 inches in width by 12
inches in length which has been folded to provide four pages which are each approximately 4
inches in width and 12 inches in length. It is endorsed 'Anthony Folletts booke'. The corporation
asked the crown to be able to purchase the *Madre de Dios* in 1594 as a means towards building a
hospital.[2] In 1604 a Parliamentary Act was passed enabling officials of cities, boroughs, corporate
towns and priveleged places to 'assess all and every inhabitant and all houses of habitation,
lands, tenements and hereditaments' at 'such reasonable taxes and payments as they shall think
fit' towards the relief and ordering of persons afflicted with the plague.[3] It was this rate which
was enforced in 1627. Plague and other infectious diseases were prevalent across Devon between
1626 and 1628 including, notably, Plymouth and Exeter. On 20th June 1626 Dartmouth's mayor
wrote that 'it has pleased the Almighty to visit our town with the plague, the fear whereof hath so
possessed the inhabitants that almost all men of ability in body and purse have left their houses
to make their residence in other places though there be not yet above ten houses infected to our
knowledge so that the ablest men having withdrawn themselves and many others being at sea and
in his Majesty's service, the town is left to be a prey for the enemy, and a great number of poor
people remaining in the town cannot be relieved by reason of the absence of the men of ability, nor
well be governed for that divers of my brethren, one of the bailiffs and most part of the constables
have withdrawn themselves together with the rest'. A month later he wrote again that he had
instructed Dartmouth's residents to return 'but the greatest part of them seem so little to regard
your lordships' command in that behalf that they come not home though there be no cause why
they should withdraw themselves there having been but fifteen houses infected, all which being

2   TNA, Lansdowne Mss 115, fol. 233.
3   Edwin Cannan, The History of Local Rates in England (Westminster, 1912), pp. 46–7.

separated into pesthouses remote from the town. The town is now in perfect health'.[4] In January 1626 there had already been an outbreak of illness amongst conscripted soldiers.[5]

A rate for the poore people in the hospetale made by Andrew Voysey maior & William Plumligh Justice for the south towne Dartemouth this 21th of May 1627.

Name	Tally	Amount	Name	Tally	Amount
Mr William Plumligh	||||	.s 9d	Anthony Follett	||||	0 6
Mr John Plumligh	||||	1 0	Edmund Follett	||||	0 6
Mr Thomas Spurwaie	||||	. 9	Thomas Smyth	||||	0 3
Mr Thomas Abraham	||||	. 6	John Penney	||||	0 3
Mr John Croockherne	||||	. 4	John Newman	||||	0 6
Mr William Gurney	||||	. 6	John Norber	||||	0 3
Mr Edmund Whytaker	||||	. 4	Thomas Newcomyn	||||	0 3
Aldred Staplehill	||	. 4	Wydow Braund	||||	0 3
Gilbert Staplehill	||||	0 6	Wydow Bacon	||||	0 3
William Spurway	||||	0 4	Henry Peeke	||||	0 3
Robert Phylpott	||||	0 6	Hugh Peryn		0 6
Andrew Wackham	|||	0 6	Nicholas Norton	||||	0 3
Walter Pecke	||||	0 4	Stephen Chappen	||||	0 3
Christopher Searle	||||	0 6	Thomas Drew	||||	0 3
Richard Randell	||||	0 3	John Forde	||||	0 3
Thomas Hart	||||	0 3	John Rounsevall	||||	0 4
James Band	||||	0 3	Nicholas Skynner	||||	0 6
Henry Penney	||||	0 3	John Sparke thelder paid		4d 0 6
Alexander Cousens	||||	0 4	Robert Sparke	||||	0 3
William Symons	||||	0 3	John Watson	||||	0 6
Andrew Samwayes	||||	0 4	Nicholas Smellyn	||||	03
James Searell	||||	0 4			

[page 2]

Name	Tally	Amount	Name	Tally	Amount
Gilbert Roope	||||	0 3	John Geffery		
John Stowell		0 3	James Knyght	||||	0 2
Matthew Tucker	||||	0 3	Thomas Lewes	||||	0 3
Christopher Toney	||||	0 3	Nicholas Luce	||||	0 2
Vincent Winchester	||||	0 4	Robert Lome	||||	0 3
Lawrence Wheeler	||||	0 3	Edward More	||||	0 3
Daniel Travell	||||	0 6	Nicholas Morrish	||||	0 3
Jereme Salter	|	0 6	William Morrish	||||	0 2
John Lomer	||||	0 3	Leonard May	||||	0 3
John Terrey	||||	0 3	Nathaniel Marten	||||	0 3
William Aklynes	||||	0 3	Walter Dymond	||||	0 6
William Hocket	||||	0 3	John Fabyn	||||	0 3

This is a Rate to be gathred wekeley
[signed] Andrew Voysey maior   William Plumligh
The hoolle is 22s 70d

4   DHC, DQS, OB 1/6, p. 113; TNA, SP16/526/135 & SP16/71/7.
5   TNA, SP16/18/18.

67. DARTMOUTH (St Petrox), Hospital Rate, 1627

DHC, DD62284

Note: This rate was written on two pieces of paper to make a booklet of eight pages which are nearly 4 inches in width and 12 inches in length. The cover has a series of sums totalling 28s 7d and is endorsed 'This Booke is to be Coleckted by Alexsander Carye'. Less than three months later the mayor and burgesses petitioned the Privy Council that John Plumleigh had refused to serve his term as mayor as had John Budley, John Shapleigh and John Richards other civic roles.[6] Amongst those on this rate were men identified separately this year as shipowners including Andrew Voysey (*Blessing*, *Flower*), Gilbert Staplehill (*An Advisor*) and William Plumley (*Burnt Cow*).[7]

A rate for the maintenance of the poor people in the pesthouses to be paidd wekelie made bie Andrew Voysie Maior and William Plumligh Justices etc the 18th of June 1627

weekly

Mr William Plumeigh	||||	1s 6d	Alexander Coosens	||||	0 8
Mr Tho Spurway	||||	1 4	William Symons	||||	0 6
Mr John Plumleigh	||||	2 6	Andrew Sammes	||||	0 8
Mr Tho: Abraham	||||	1 0	James Searle	||||	0 8
Mr William Gourney	||||	1 0	Anthony Follett	||||	1 0
John Crewkerne	||||	0 6	Thomas Smith	||||	0 3
Mr Thomas Woodward		0 8	John Penny	||||	0 3
Edmund White	||||	0 8	John Newman	||||	1 0
Aldred Staplehill		0 8	John Norber	||||	0 6
Gilbert Staplehill		0 6	Thomas Newcomin	||||	0 6
William Spurway	||||	0 [torn]	Widow Brawer	||||	0 3
Robert Fillpott	||||	[torn]	Widow Bruartt	||||	0 4
Andrew Wakeham	||||	1 0	Widow Bacon	||||	0 4
Walter Peck	||||	0 8	Henry Peke	||||	0 4
Christopher Searle	||||	0 [torn]	Mr Hugh Perrin	||||	0 8
Richard Randall		0 4	Mr Nicholas Norten		0 6
Thomas Hart	||||	0 6	Stephen Shapen	||||	0 4
James Band	||||	0 6	[total]		25s 9d
Henry Pennie	||||	0 6			

[page 2]

before I receaved this booke Mr Maior receved of Mr Wm Wakham 6s 0d Mr John Spurway 5 4
Mr Abraham 4 0 Mr Crukerne 2 3
Rec seventeen shilleings & fowr penc [signed] Andrew Voysey
August 24th 1627: Receved mor in pt of this booke six pownds therteie shillings & fower penc
Andrew Voysey
8 01 00

10 04 not pd
7 10 08

[page 3]

Thomas Drewe	||||	0s 4d	Edmund Follet	||||	0 3
John Foord	||||	0 4	William Pethebredg	||||	0 3

---

6   TNA, PC2/36/128.
7   TNA, SP16/80/194.

John Rounsevall	IIII	0 6	James Knight	IIII	0 2
Nicholas Skinner	IIII	1 9	Thomas Lewis	IIII	0 4
John Spark thelder	IIII	0 6	Nicholas Luce	IIII	0 3
Robert Spark	IIII	0 4	Robert Lover	IIII	0 3
John Wattson	IIII	1 0	L Nicholas Morris	IIII	0 3
Nicholas Snelling	IIII	0 4	L William Morris	IIII	0 2
Gilbert Roop		0 3	Leonard May	IIII	0 4
John Stowell	IIII	0 3	Nathaniel Martinn	IIII	0 4
Matthew Tucker	IIII	0 4	Walter Dymont	IIII	0 8
Christopher Toney	IIII	0 4	John Fabian	IIII	0 6
Vincent Winchester		0 6	John Sanders	IIII	0 4
Lawrence Wheeler	IIII	0 6	Nicholas Cole	IIII	0 4
Daniel Travell	IIII	1 0	William Rewe	IIII	0 4
Jerome Salter	IIII	0 8	John Jeffrey	IIII	0 3
John Lomer	IIII	0 4	[total]		2 00 03
John Terric	IIII	0 4			14 6d
William Alkins	IIII	0 4			1 5 9
William Hocket	IIII	0 4	[total]		2 0 3

[signed]   Andrew Voysey Maior   Will Plumleigh

68. **DARTMOUTH** (St Petrox), Poor Rate, 1649

DHC, DD62748

Note: This rate was written on five pieces of paper, which measure some 6 inches in width and 16 in length, which have been folded and stitched together to form a booklet. The rate was signed by two collectors, two overseers of the poor, two churchwardens and two waywardens.

A Booke of Rates for the poore of the parish of St Patricke Aprill the 19th *in the year of our Lord* 1649

Mrs Barbara Woodwards houses	£00 08s 00d	Mrs Phillpotts houses	00 02 00
Mrs Holletts house	00 01 04	Mrs Shapleigh & Charles Plumleigh	
William Lees house	00 01 08	for Mr Kingmans house	00 02 00
Francis Barnards house	00 02 00	Mr Pascoe Jagoe his house	00 01 00
Mr Trynnick's houses	00 03 00	Mr Tristram Lane for the house	
Stokefleminge Tenements	00 01 04	Mrs Randall Lives in	00 01 04
Mr Anthony Folletts houses	00 08 00	Willmott Sammoys widow	00 01 06
Mr Thomas Newcomens house	00 01 04	Mr Lawrence Wheeler	00 01 00
Mrs Whites houses	00 01 04	Mr Thomas Halswill	00 05 00
Halce Phillips Tenement	00 00 08	Richard Halswill	00 01 08
Mr Thomas Leighs houses	00 02 00	John Stone	00 01 06

[page 2]

A

Mr Gregory Alford Re	IIII	00 01 00	Elizabeth Axforde	IIII	00 01 00
William Alkins	IIII	00 03 00	George Andrewes		00 00 08
Thomas Attwill		.. .. ..	[total]		07s 00
Thomas Adames	IIII	00 02 00			

B

Mr John Buttler	IIII	00 04 00	Widdow Brand	IIII	00 02 00

	William Bragg	||||	00 01 00		Phillip Bawden	||||	00 01 04
	Stephen Booden	||||	00 00 08		~~Richard Beaden~~		.. .. ..
	~~Widdow Bagwell~~		~~00 00 08~~		Robert Browne		.. .. ..
	John Bracey	||||	00 01 00		Richard Bond	||||	00 00 08
	John Bagwell Walfleete		.. .. ..		Thomas Bawdon	||||	00 00 04
	Robert Byffyn	||||	00 01 00		[total]		13s 4d
	John Bush	||||	00 01 04				

C

3s	Nicholas Cawley	||||	00 03 06		Daniel Clase	||||	00 01 00
~~Alexander Cossens~~			.. .. ..		Richard Cole	||||	00 01 00
	John Churchwill	||||	00 00 08		~~Widdow Churchward~~		.. .. ..
	Widdow Constable		.. .. ..		Mr Courtney	||||	00 02 06
	Robert Clapp	||||	00 04 00		John Cockewell	||||	00 00 08
Rec. 6d	William Cutt junior	||||	00 01 06		[total]		15s 6d
	William Cooke	||||	00 01 08				

[page 3]

D

	Margaret Downeinge	||||	00 01 04	[total]	2s 00d
	Henry Dight	||||	00 00 08		

E

Thomas Elliott Rec. 18d	||||	00 02 00	William Ellmore	||||	00 00 08
John Elliott	||||	00 02 00	[total]		6s 8d
Ephraim Eastcott	||||	00 02 00			

F

Mr	Anthony Follett	||||	00 06 00		John Fosse	||||	00 00 08
	Alice Foxworthy widdow	||||	00 02 04		Edward Fosterd	||||	00 01 08
Anthony Fletcher ~~rec. 3s~~		||||	00 03 04		[total]		14s 00d

G

Mrs	Grace Gourney	||||	00 10 00		~~Nicholas Gill~~		~~4d~~
	Arthur Goodridge	||||	00 01 08	Mr	~~John Godolphin~~	||||	~~00 01 00~~
~~Andrew Gribble~~			~~00 00 08~~		~~Gosse~~		~~00 01 00~~
Nicholas Geffry		||||	00 00 08		[total]		13s 4d

H

Thomas Horsman		00 01 06			~~William Hockett'~~		.. .. ..
	John Horwill	||||	00 01 00		Oliver Hawke	||||	00 02 08
Mrs	~~Margerett Hill widdow~~				John Huntt ~~rec. 6d~~		00 01 00
Mr	William Hammett	||||	00 06 06		Jonathan Hodge	||||	00 01 00
	George Huntt	||||	00 01 00		Robert Horswill	||||	00 00 08
	Roger Hync	||||	00 02 00		[total]		15s 10d

[page 4]

H

	Richard Huxham	||||	00 02	20s 6d ~~Thomas Halswill 00 05 00~~	
	~~Richard Hooper~~			[total]	4s 8d 15 10 20s 6d
	Sargeant Higgesson	||||	00 01 00		
	Richard Halswill	||||	00 01 08		

J

	Widdow Jeffery	||||	00 01 00	Thomas Joyslynn	||||	00 01 00
	John Jeffers widdo.	||||	00 01 00	[total]		3 00d

K

Mr	Edward Kingman	||||	00 02 00	~~John Knowlinge~~		~~00 01 00~~
	James Knight	||||	00 01 04	John Kinge	||||	00 01 08
	Joan Kelly widow	||||	00 01 00	[total]		5s 4d

L

Thomas Lewes	||||	00 04 00	Rowland Lovell	||||	00 00 08
John Lomer ~~rec. 4d~~	||||	00 02 04	William Luscombe	||||	00 01 00
Samuel Langmeade ~~rec. 1s~~	||||	00 03 00	William Luckeys ~~rec. 1s~~	||||	00 01 04
Nicholas Luist	.. .. ..		Anthony Lane	||||	00 01 00
Robert Lome ~~rec. 8d~~	||||	00 01 06	Richard Leigh 6d	||||	 6
Richard Lomer ~~rec. 8d 16d~~	||||	00 01 08	Thomas Lee	||||	00 01 08
Richard Laffatus	||||	00 02 00	[total]		1 0 8

M

William Martyn *otherwise* Parkes	||||	00 01 08	Robert Millman	||||	00 00 04
James Martyn	||||	00 01 00	John Martyn	||||	00 00 04
William Mathewes	||||	00 00 08	~~Edward Marten~~		~~00 01 00~~
Rice Maurice	||||	00 00 08			~~6s 8d~~
Richard Manninge	||||	00 01 04	[total]		7s 00d
Edward Muchamore	||||	00 01 00			

[page 5]

N

Mrs	Newman Widdow	||||	00 03 00	Mr	John Norrish ~~rec. 8d~~	||||	00 03 04
	Anastace Norton Wid.	||||	00 01 04	[total]		8s 8d
	Matthew Nickles	||||	00 01 00			

O

[blank]

P

Mr	John Plumleigh	||||	00 12 00	John Pepperell	||||	00 00 04
Mrs	~~Phillpott widdow~~	.. .. ..	William Prideaux	||||	00 01 04
	Henry Pike	||||	00 02 08	Richard Parker	||||	00 05 00
	Henry Penny	||||	00 01 04	~~Peter Preston~~			00 00 02
	William Powell ~~Rec. 1s~~	||||	00 01 04	John Penny	||	00 00 06
	Roger Pepperell ~~Rec. 8d~~	||||	00 01 08	John Possott ~~Rec. 6d~~	|||	00 01 06
	~~Thomas Pooleinge~~	.. .. ..	John Poole		.. .. ..
	William Parnell ~~Rec. 8d 6d~~	||||	00 02 00	Mrs	~~Katherin Plumleigh~~		~~00 04 08~~
	~~Lewes Pooleinge~~		[total]		1 9 8d
	John Prestor	||||	00 00 06			

R

	Nicholas Roope Esquire	||||	00 16 00	Christopher Row		00 02 00
	~~Mrs Randall wid.~~		~~00 02 00~~	Mr	George Roope [illegible crossed
	Nicholas Risdon	||||	00 02 00	through]		||||	00 04 08
	John Rich	||||	00 03 00	~~Henry Ryder~~		.. .. ..

	Nicholas Redwood	||||	00 04 08	John Randell basket maker ||||00 01 . 4
	~~Henry Roberts~~		~~00 01 00~~	[total]	1 11 8d

[page 6]

S

Mr	Thomas Spurwaie Senior	||||00 06 08		Edward Straw	||||	00 03 00
Mr	~~Aldred Staplehill~~	.. .. ..		Thomas Smyth	||||	00 02 08
Mr	Gilbert Staplehill ~~Rec. 8s~~-||||	00 10 00		Thomas Spurwaie junior	||||00 03 08
Mr	William Spurwaie	||||	00 06 08	Thomas Sparke	||||	00 00 08
	Widdow Skinner |||| ~~Rec. 18d~~ 00 06 08			~~Richard Skinner~~	.. .. ..
	Widdow Sammoys	||||	00 01 00	John Sherrome	||||	00 00 08
	Nicholas Snellinge	||||	00 01 06	~~Andrew Salleys~~	.. .. ..
	John Sayre	||||	00 01 00	Andrew Samwoys ~~Rec. 4d~~	||||	.. .. ..
	John Starr	||||	00 00 08	Peter Styrgis	||||	00 00 08
	George Sommers	||||	00 01 04	Thomas Shepherd Rec. 8d	||||00 00 08
	Nicholas Sparke	||||	00 03 04	Mr	Samuel Stone	||||	00 03 10
	George Sparke	||||	00 02 00	Christopher Searle	||||	00 02 00
	John Sparke	||||	00 03 00	John Stone	||||	00 02 04
	John Sadler	||||	00 01 00	[total]	3 0 06

T

~~Rec 6d   Rec 6d   Rec 8d   Rec 6d~~

Christopher Toney	||||	00 03 04	Thomas Trounsonn	||||	00 01 00
Samuel Tylt	||||	00 00 08	[total]	7s
William Taylor	||||	00 02 08		

V

Francis Vryne	||	00 04 00	[total]	2s 8d

W

Mrs	White widdow	||||	00 01 04	John Wakeley Rec 8d|||	00 01 00
	Thomas Wallys	||||	00 01 04	Thomas Williams	||||	00 01 00
	John Weekes	||||	00 01 00	~~Thomas White~~	.. .. ..
	Crispin Wadland	||||	00 00 08	~~Thomas Wilkens~~	00 01 00
	Edward Wrethford Rec 1s	||||00 02 00	[total]	10 4d

[page 7]

A noate of the weekely payments to the poore of St Patricke this present yeare *in the year* 1649.

William Holmes		00 00 03	Frizett Deereinge	00 00 06
Andrew Gribble senior	XX	00 00 06	Elizabeth Hooper	.. .. ..
Widdow Hammett		00 00 06	Rebecca Robins	.. .. ..
Edward More		00 01 06	Elizabeth Coytt	00 00 03
Avis Teage wid.		.. .. ..	~~Widdow Roe~~ Widdow Collings	00 00 02
Widdow Crocker	XX	00 01 00	~~Pascoe Stone~~	00 00 06
Barbara Salleys		00 00 04	Widdow Weekes	00 00 06
~~Widdow Nichole~~		.. .. ..	Katherine Coombe	00 00 04

Robert Clapp   Nicholas Calley   Mr George Roope   Tho: Leuvise overseers
John Sparke   William Taylor   Churchwardens
Edward fosterd   Christopher Searle   Collectors

John Penny   John Churchwill   Way Wardens
Jo: Staplehill Mayor   William Barnes

69. DARTMOUTH (St Petrox), Poor Rate Account, 1649

DHC, DD62749

Note: This summary account was written on a single sheet of paper which measures 7¾ inches in length and 12 inches in width.

Year past for the poore of St Patricke May 11ᵗʰ 1650
13 18 10   A note of monyes Rec. on the poore Booke for the parish of
[-] <u>11 3 9</u>   St Patrix for the yeare 1649
2 15 1

By letter A as appeareth	00 07 00	By Letter L is	01 00 08
By Letter B is	00 13 04	By Letter M is	00 07 00
By Letter C is	00 15 06	By Letter N is	00 08 08
By Letter D is	00 02 00	By Letter P is	01 09 08
By Letter E is	00 06 08	By Letter R is	01 11 08
By Letter F is	00 14 00	By Letter S is	03 00 06
By Letter G is	00 13 04	By Letter T is	00 07 08
By Letter H is	01 00 06	By Letter V is	00 02 00
By Letter I is	00 03 00	By Letter W is	00 10 04
By Letter K is	00 05 04	[total]	13 18 10

p Contra Creditor to monye paid to the poor of St Patrix 1649

To Will: holmes in full	00 12 02	To Anstice weekes	00 07 02
To Edward Modre	03 12 00	To Alice weekes	00 10 06
To Andrew Grible the tyme he lived	00 06 00	To Katherine Coombe	00 08 08
To widow Crocker	01 04 02	To Joan Cowle	00 01 06
To widow hammet	01 04 00	To Dorothy snelling	00 01 00
To widow hallos	00 16 00	to Mary in the Almes houses	00 00 06
To widow Dearing	01 04 00	~~for making the poore book~~	00 0 0
To widow Coyte	00 12 03	for making the warrant	00 01 00
To John Stone	00 02 10	[total]	11 03 09

Due for Ballance pd in to the new overseers the 11ᵗʰ day of may 1650 the
some of   02 15 01
 [total]   13 18 10
[signed] Robert Clapp Edward Foster

70. Dartmouth (St Saviour), Poor Rate, 1601

DHC, DD61641

Note: This rate was written on five pieces of paper, of about 12 inches in width and 16 in length, which have been folded and stitched with white thread to make a booklet of twenty pages. Two pins provide bindings at the top and base of the booklet. Some of the names are grouped in unusual alphabetical clusters.

Dartmouth   The rate for the poor of North Towne Dartmouth received at Easter 1601 for one yere followinge.

Henry Heyward Maior	13s 4d	William Flute	10s 8d
Nicholas Heyman	13s 4d	Bennett Flute	10s 8d
John Follett	10s 8d	John Newbye	10s 8d
Thomas Holland	13s 4d	Walter Francis	10s 8d
Robert Martin	13s 4d		

A:

Thomas Abraham	4s		

B.

Edward Breckland	1s 4d	Henry Bowne	1s 4d
John Baker	1s 4d	John Baylye	0 8d
Christopher Blackaller	1s 4d	Lawrence Brocke	0 8d
Andrew Bickelye	1s 4d		

C.

William Cade	4s	William Cutt	1s 4d
Richard Crusce	4s	John Collins	1s 4d
Thomas Crockwell	2s	William Coxe	1s 4d
John Cutte	1s 4d	Edward Coake	4s
Henry Collins	2s	Walter Cheswill	0 8d
William Cannell	1s 4d	John Chanterell	1s

D.

George Duringe	4s	John Dotterell	2s 8d
John Dreyton	1s 4d		

E.

Hugh Edwardes	2s	John Ellett	1s 4d

[page 2]

F.

Thomas Fortescue gentleman	10s	Nicholas Flute thelder	2s
x Walter Francis	8s	Nicholas Flute the yonger	1s 4d

G.

Thomas Gourneye	6s	Richard Grappelle	2s
Zachary Goold	6s	John Garnesey *otherwise* Aprey	1s 4d

H.

[blank] Hallett widow	2s	William Hankes	5s 4d
John Holligrove	4s	Henricke Clarsen	2s
Robert Hullett	1s 4d	Robert Harwood	0 8d
Thomas Hodge	1s 4d		

I.

William Irishe	2s 8d	Pascoe Jagoe	1s 4d
John Gefferye	4s		

K.

John Kidlye *otherwise* Pointer	4s	John Keymor	1s 4d
William Kempe	2s 8d	John Kinge	2s 8d
John Kellye	2s 8d	Richard Kennawaye	1s

L.

x Elizabeth Langdon widow	2s	John Londewell	2s
Thomas Luke	2s	Tristram Lane	1s 4d
John Laye	4s	x Ralphe Liston	0 8d

M.

Walter Miller	4s	William Mayne	1s 4d
Henry Maine	2s 8d	Ellis Maye	1s 4d
x Thomas Martin	1s 4d	Richard Manfild	0 8d

N.

John Newman thelder	5s 4d	Thomas Norracott	1s 4d
William Nyell	4s	Martin Norman	1s 4d
William Nuland	1s 4d	Widow Norman	1s
Nicholas Norracott	2s	Robert Nicholls	0 4d

[page 3]

O.

| John Olliver thelder | 1s 4d | John Olliver the yonger | 1s 4d |

P.

Edmund Pinkell	2s	Nicholas Pleyar	0 8d
Thomas Paige	4s	Vincent Paine	1s
H John Paige	4s	John Plumleigh thelder	2s
John Paschow	2s	Robert Paschow	1s 4d
widow Perrin	1s 4d	Bartholomew Pitcher	0 8d

R.

| John Randall gent. | 6s 8d | William Richardes | 1s |

S.

Agnes Smith widow	8s	Matthew Sheere	0 8d
John Smith	5s 4d	Walter Simons	1s
James Searle	2s 8d	Lawrence Swanson	4s
Robert Stabb	1s 4d	[blank] Sayer	2s
Nicholas Squyre	2s	Thomas Smith	1s 4d
John Stearte	0 8d		

T.

| Lancelott Teape | 2s 8d | James Trenills | 1s 4d |

W.

Arthur Wotton gentleman	5s 4d	John Whyte	1s 4d
John Winchester	4s	Widow Whyteinge	1s 4d
Penticost Walter	2s	Christopher Woode	1s 4d
Andrew Weekes	2s	[page 4] Thomas Whyte	1s
Edward Winchester	2s	Giles Walle	0 8d
Christopher Wallis	2s 8d		

Sum total £17 16s

[signed] Nicholas Hayman Junior John Follet Gylbart Staplehyll Thomas Holland Thomas Ridgeway Edward Seymour

[page 5]

Dartmouth. An accompt of the monyes collected for the poore *in the year* 1601.

Paid to 10 poore impotent people weekelye *namely*

To Alice Blunt	4d	To Joan Nowell	12d
To Ciprian Sudden	6d	To Cicily Borage	2d
to Willmot Berrye	6d	To Jackett Seymour & to Joan Hodge	10d
To Jn Skynner	6d	To Jn. Cornew	4d
To Ursula Garman	4d	*Sum*	4s 6d

These weekely payments by the yeere amount to the some of £11 14s

Item paid for the house rente of certaine poore people, and toward the maintenance and duracon of poore Orphan children by the yere the some of £3 12s

Item paid for shroudes for 3 poore people buryed this yere 0 11s 4d

Item toward the releif of other poore people by occasion of sicknes 0 12s 0

Item we crave allowance of monyes not to be had, from such as are dead, and depted the Towne sithence the rate made, the severall somes whereof & the pties names are as followeth *namely*

Jn. Randall gentleman	11s 8d	Jn. Baylye	0 8d
Elizabeth Langdon wid.	2s	Ralph Liston	0 8d
Henry Collins	2s	Richard Manfill	0 8d
Wm Cammell	1s 4d	The somme of this allowance is	18s 4d
Thomas Martin	1s 4d	The total *sum* is	£17 7s 8d
Jn. Chanterell	1s		rest 13s 4d
Edmund Puckell	2s		

[signed] Nicholas Hayman Junior   Robert Holland   John Follet   Gylbart Staplehill   Thomas Ridgeway   Richard Spurway

71. **Dartmouth** (St Saviour), Poor Rate, 1603

DHC, DD61664

Note: This rate was written on four pieces of paper, which measure 8 inches in width and 12 inches in length, which have been folded and stitched with brown thread to make up a booklet of sixteen pages.

1603

The rat for the pore of the northtowne Dartmouth recd at our Ladie daie 1603 for one yere followinge to be Collected by Lawrence Cranston & Trastram Lane

|||| Mr Walter Francis	8s	|||| Mr Henry Heyward	10s
|||| Mr Nicholas Heymond	12s	|||| Mr William Flut	8s
|||| Mr John Follet	5s	|||| Mr Bennet flut	8s
|||| Mr Thomas Holland	10s	|||| Mr John Newby	8s
|||| Mr Robert Martin	10s		

A

|||| Thomas Abraham	3s 4d

B

|||| Edward Bere	1s	|||| Thomas Balle	1s 4d
|||| Edward Breckard	1s 4d	|||| Christopher Blacler	8d

				Andrew Bricleye	1s 4d					Lawrence Brocke	8d
				Henry Bowne	1s 4d	John Borne	8d
				William Beyly	1s		

[page 2]

C

				William Cad	3s					Wililam Cutt	1s 4d
				Richard Crust	3s 4d					William Coxsall	1s 4d
				Thomas Crokwill	1s 4d					Edward Coke	3s 4d

D

| |||| John Dreytton | 1s | |||| Roger Drew | 8d |
| |||| John Doldred | 2s 8d | |||| William Daved | 8d |

E

| |||| Henry Edwards | 2s | |||| John Edes | 8d |
| |||| John Ellet | 2s 4d | | |

ff

| |||| Nicholas flut thelder | 1s | |||| Robert Follet | 8d |
| |||| nicholas flut theyonger | 1s | |||| William French | 1s |

G

				Thomas gurney	6s					Jo. garnesey *otherwise* Apre	1s
				Zachary goold	5s					John Geffery	4s
				Widdo grapolle	2s					Peter Goodridge	1s

[page 3]

H

				Julian hallet widow	2s	Mr Hendrick	2s
|||| John Holligrove	4s	|||| Roger Harwood	8d
William Hawker	5s					Robert Hooper	8d
|||| Robert Hallet	1s	|||| Alexander Hellier	8d
				Thomas Hoge	1s 4d		

J

| |||| Wm Irishe | 2s | |||| Pascoe Jagoe | 1s |

K

				John Keley *otherwise* poynter 3 4						Richard Kennaway	8d
				Wm Kempe	2s					John Knight	1s
				John Kelly	2s 8d					Jos. Knowller	1s 4d
				John Kenne	1s					John Kingman	1s 4d

L

				John Leye	3s 4d					Trustram Lane	1s 4d
				Thomas Linke	2s					Richard Luke	1s
				John Londewed	1s 4d	Richard Lane	[0]

[page 4]

M

|||| Walter Myller 3s 4d |||| William Mayne 1s 4d
|||| Henry Maine 2s |||| Ellis Mayne 1s

N

|||| John Newman thelder 4s |||| Martin Normand 1s 4d
|||| Wm Nyell 3s 4d |||| Widdo Nancarrow 8d
|||| Wm Newland 1s |||| Robert Nicholls 8d
|||| Nicholas Norracott 1s 4d |||| Thomas Nevell 1s 4d
|||| Thomas Norracott 8d

O

|||| John Ollyver thelder 8d

P

|||| Thomas Payge 4s |||| Bartholomew Prynn 8d
|||| John Paige 3s |||| Walter Phillpe 8d
|||| John Paschow 1s 4d |||| John Pratten 8d
|||| Vincent Pane 1s Walter Pecke 8d
|||| Jon Plumley thelder 1s 4d

[page 5]

R

|||| Wm Richardes 8d |||| Henry Robens 8d

S

|||| Mrs Agnes Smyth 5s 4d |||| Nicholas Sqyer 1s 4d
|||| John Smyth 5s 4d |||| Lawrence Samson 4s
|||| Robert Stabb 1s |||| Edward Stevens 1s 4d

T

John Toser 1s 4d |||| Stephen Taller 1s
|||| Lancelot Teape 2s |||| Evan Tyrrey 1s 4d
|||| James Tremylts 1s

W

Arthur Wotten gentleman 4s |||| Christopher Wade 1s
|||| John Winchester 3s 4d |||| Thomas Whitte 8d
|||| Andrew Weye 2s |||| Henry Wheeler 10s
|||| Edward Winchester 1s 4d |||| Christopher Wellworth 2s
|||| Christopher Wallis 2s |||| Wm Wonchester 1s
|||| John Whitte 1s John Wallter 1s
|||| Margaret Whitting 1s 4d

the *sum total* £13 17s 4d
[signatures of] E. Ameridith Nicholas Gillbert
[page 13]

1603

Pascoe Jago delievered me in money the 5th day of Maie of this Collection £2 6s 10d.
plus gathered of the Arerages in all

hereof I paid John Risdon to have some Aprentise 1 6 8
paid Trustram Lane 1 – 2

The names of the pore that are to have Relife wicley as follo

Christian Siddon	6d	Sysley Brydge	2d
Wilmot Berry	4d	Mary Frye	6d
John Skinner	6d	John Cormewe	4d
Item to German	4d	sum	4s 8d
Joan Nowell	12d		

72. DARTMOUTH (St Saviour), Poor Rate, 1605

DHC, DD61726

Note: This rate was written on three pieces of paper which measure 12 inches in width and nearly 16 inches in length, which have been folded and stitched with white string to provide a booklet of twelve pages.

St Saviors in Dartmouth

A rate for the poore of the same pishe for one yere next insueing, made by the churchwardens and overseers of the same mediated and appointed by his Majesty's Justices of the peace according to the forme of the statute in that behalf made, the 18th daie of April 1605: to be Colllected quarterlie.

Quarterlie pamments

|||| Mr Thomas Gourney maior ~~10s~~	2s 6d	|||| Mr Robert Martin	2s 6d
|||| Mr Jn Nubye ~~10s~~	2s 6d	|||| Mr Henry Heyward	2s 6d
|||| Mr Nicholas Hayman	3s 1d	|||| Mr Walter Francis	2s 6d
|||| Mr Jn Follett	2s	|||| Mr William Flute	2s
|||| Mr Thomas Holland	3s 6d	|||| Mr Bennett Flute	2s

A

	Thomas Abraham	1s 0 in the sowth	Thomas Adams a paynter	0 1d
|||| Henry Ashlie	0 2d		

B

|||| Edward Beere	0 10d	|| Gregory Band for Mr Plumley [illegible]	1s
|||| Edward Breckard	0 4d	2s was accepted	
|||| Thomas Balle	0 9d	|||| Lawrence Brocke	0 1d
|||| Christopher Blackler	0 2d	|||| John Barber	0 2d
|||| Andrew Bicklie	0 6d	|||| Geoffrey Bande	0 1d
|||| Henry Boone	0 8d	|||| John Bowden	0 2d
|||| William Baite	0 6d	||| Alexander Barter	0 1d

C

|||| William Cade	0 10d	|||| Edward Coke	1s 0
|||| Richard Croste	1s 0	|||| Jn Cutte	0 2d
in the Sowthe Thomas Crockwell	0 4d	|||| William Chambers	0 8d
|||| William Cutt	0 4d	£1 11s 11d Rd in this sched £6 4s 4d for the	
|||| William Coxsaid	0 6d	hole yeare	

[page 2]

|||| William Courte	9s 2d	|||| William Cammell	0 1d
|||| Henry Churchard	0 2d		

D

| |||| John Dotterell | 0 3d | |||| William Daniell | 0 2d |
| |||| the widow Drewe | 0 2d | |||| Jn Dalle | 0 2d |

E

| | Hugh Edwardes | 0 4d | |||| Jn Edes | 0 2d |
| |||| Jn Ellett | 0 11d | | |

ff

				Lewis Fortescue	1s					William Fursman	0 3d
	Nicholas Flute thelder	0 3d					Bartholomew Frye	0 2d
				Nic: Flute the yonger	0 6d	Osmond Follett	0 1d
				Robert Follet	0 4d		

G

				Zachary Goold	1 6d					Phillip Godfrey the yonger	0 1d
				Jn. Jefferie	1s					Ric. Goslin	0 1d
				Jn Garnesey *otherwise* Leprey	0 4d					James Goodridge	0 2d
				Peter Goodridge	0 3d					Moses Gilford	0 2d

H

				Widow Hallett	0 2d					Roger Harwood	0 2d
				William Hawkes	1s					Alexander Hollier	0 3d
				Jn Holligrove	1s	Ellis Harradon	0 2d
				Thomas Hodge	0 10d					Jn. Heywood	0 1d
				Robert Hallett	0 3d		22s 02d

Some of moneys receieved on this shde for the holle yeare is   £1 18s 1d

[page 3]

J

| |||| William Irishe | 8d | |||| Pascoe Jagoe | 8d |

K

				Jn. Kidlie *otherwise* Pointer	1s					Jn Knight	0 4d
				William Kempe	0s 8d					Joseph Knolles	0 6d
				Jn Kellye	0 8d					Jn Kingman	0 4d
				Jn Keymor	0 2d	Benjamin Knowlles	0 1d
				Ric: Kenwaye	0 3d					Edward Kingman	0 2d

L

Phillip Loveringe gentleman	0 4d					Ric: Luke	0 2d
|||| Anstice Leye	0 6d	|||| Ric: Lumlye	0 4d
|||| Thomas Luke *otherwise* Sander	0 4d	|||| Henry Longe	0 10d
|||| Jn Lundwell	0 4d	|||| Jn Lome	0 2d
				Tristram Lane	0 4d		

M

				Walter Miller	1s					Ellis Maye	0 4d
				Jn Morris *otherwise* Tozer	0 8d					William Maine	0 4d
				Henry Maine	0 6d			Thomas Mackrell	0 3d

N

| |||| Wm Niell | 1s | |||| Jn Newman thelder for his house | 0 10d |

|||| Wm Nuland	0 3d	|||| Thomas Newell	0 4d
|| Thomas Norracott	0 2d	|||| Robert Nicholls	0 3d
|||| Martin Norman	0 4d	|||| Nic. Norber	0 1d
|||| Widow Nancarrow	0 1d	[total]	15s 02d

Receved on this shete as apperethe   £2 12s 4d

[page 4]

O

|||| Jn Olliver thelder   0 2d

P

|||| Thomas Paige	1s 6d	|||| Vincent Paine	0 3d
|||| John Plumleigh Junior	1s 6d	|||| Walter Pecke	0 3d
|||| John Plumleigh Senior	0 8d	|||| Thomas Pennye	0 1d
|||| Jn Paige	0 10d	|||| Thomas Pillaton	0 3d
|||| Jn Pascoe	0 4d	|||| William Putt	0 6d

R

|||| Jn Roope gentleman for the malt mill	1s	|||| Arthur Richards	0 2d
|||| William Richardes	1 2d	|||| John Risdon	0 1d
|||| Henry Robins *otherwise* Johns	0 3d	|||| Ric: Renolls	0 2d

S

|||| Mrs Agnes Smith	1s	|||| Adrian Staplehill	0 4d
|||| Jn Smith	1s 6d	||| Gawen Starkey	0 1d
|||| Robert Stabb	0 3d	|||| Lewis Strublin	0 1d
|||| Lawrence Swainson	1s	Jn Stoyle hath a child of Stones	[blank]
|||| Nicholas Squyre	0 4d	|| Jane Somes widow	0 4d
['In the Sowth' in the margin] || Edward Stevens	0 4d	Ric. Sanders the plomber	1 1d

T

	Lancelot Teape	0 2d Irland	|||| George Tapper	0 2d
|||| Even Terye	0 6d	|||| Robert Lemington *otherwise* Teage	0 1d
|||| James Tremills	0 3d	Matthew Tooker	0 2d
|||| Peter Terrye	0 2d	[total]	15s 9d
|||| Nic. Townesend	0 1d	Some of this sched. Received	£2 16s 5d

[page 5]

W

|||| Henry Wheeler	2s 6d	|||| Margaret Whyteing	0 4d
|||| Arthur Wotten gentleman	0 6d	|||| Chr. Wood	0 4d
|||| Andrew Weekes	0 6d	- Chr. Wellworth	0 8d
|||| Edward Winchester	0 6d	|||| Ric. Wallis	0 1d
|||| Chr. Wallis	0 6d	|||| William Widger	0 3d

Y

| William Yongge   0 4d   [total]   6s 6d

delivered by the Overseers of the yere past unto Overseers under named & is £4 3s 10d
|||| due to the poore by the gift of Customer Peter at Christide 1604 & is 20s
|||| more wch will be due for the yere to come at Christmas 1605 20s

due to the poore from Mr Ingram by the will of Mrs B[torn] £5
[signed] John Follet Thomas Holland Thomas Payge John Kydsey Thomas Gourney Mayor
John Newbye
the signe of Robert Martyn

Received on this sched.	£7 0s 9d
Received in folio the first	6 4 9
Received in folio the second	1 18 1
Received in folio the fowrthe	2 12 4
Received in folio the fyfthe	2 16 5
Some of the monyes Rec by this bowke of Ratts amownpts the some of	£14 12s 4d

[enclosure]

A note of those that have not payd

Mr Heawode 2 quarters	5s	Benjamin Knolles 4 quarters	4d
Henry Ashe 2 quarters	4d	Phillip Loveringe 4 quarters	1s 4d
Thomas Adams 4 quarters all per a.	4d	Ellis Maye 1 quarter	4d
Andrew Byckle 4 quarters	2s	Thomas Mackrell 2 quarters	6d
Gregory Bande 4 quarters	4s	Thomas Naracott 4 quarters	8d
John Barber 4 quarters	8d	Martin Norman 2 quarters	8d
John Bowden 1 quarter	2d	Widow Nan Carrow 4 quarters	4d
William Court 4 quarters	8d	Thomas Nevell 3 quarters	1s
Henry Churchwode 4 quarters	8d	Nicholas Narbor 4 quarters	4d
William Cannyll 4 quarters	4d	Arther Richards 1 quarter	2s
John Dottrell 2 quarters	6d	Gawen Starkey 1 quarter	1s
the Widow Drew 4 quarters	8d	Evon Tyrrey 1 quarter	6d
Jn Dalle 4 quarters	8d	Peter Terrye 2 quarters	4d
Osmond Follett 4 quarters	4d	Matthew Tooker 4 quarters	8d
Ellis Harradon 4 quarters	8d	Arthur Wotton 2 quarters	1s
Jn Knyght 3 quarters	1s	Ric: Wallis 4 quarters	4d
Joseph Knowlles 3 quarters	1s 6d	William Widger 1 quarter	3d

Memorandum for your arrerage of last year for the poore
~~to rember Mrs Dyers bequeathd the poor~~
to remember Mr barters will to the poor.
0 7 2
0 15 0
1 2 2

[page 7]
1 15 05d   1 15 05
0 11 02
0 15 00
0 15 01
0 06 06
[total] 4 03 2

Chardges

p *year* the Book is by collecon	£16 12 08d
Rec. of Customer Peters Gift the yere past	01 19 06
Rec. allso of the yere past	04 03 10
	[total] 22 16 08

Dischardges

Weekelie paiements at 3s 4d	£09 00s 00d	H. Edwards	01 0
pd for a child & for the poor Lepar	05 16 00	Nic: Flute senior	00 9
pd for other uses as wthin appereth	00 15 04	O. Follett	00 4
pd in mony in all at the writing of	06 04 10	Ellis Harradon	00 8
hereof is	00 01 00	B Knowlles	00 4
pd in charges for a warrant	[total] 21 17 2	P Lewis	01 4
annercast & is	01 02 2	T. Mackrell	00 6
ancegh of such as are given		T. Norracott	00 4
namely Tho: Abram	03s 0d	E. Stevens	00 8
Tho: Parker	00 4	R. Sanders	00 4
Greg. Band	02 0	L. Teage	00 6
A Barter	00 1	M. Toker	00 8
T. Crockwell	01 4	w. Hawkes & William 06 8 young 4s 00	
W. Cannell	00 4		

[page 8]

A Count of monyes Receved by William Howckes and Christopher Wellworthe collecttores appointed by his majestes Justice for the yeare 1605 begynninge the 18th daye of Aprill
First Receved of thomas Ball Collector for the yeare 1604 the somme of £4 3s 10d
Receved by the gifte of Custemer Peter dew at Cristyde 1604 £1
Receved more by the sayd gifte of Customer Peter Dew at Cristyde 1605 £20. The quitance 6s paid by Edward Coke 00 19 6
['£14 12s 4d' in margin] Recved of the use of the poore as by the Booke of Rattes Dothe appere is 14 12 4
Some of the holle Recepts 20 18 8
[signed] William Hawckr

Memorandum A Count of moneys pd Owt by us the Collecores as apereth payd by us unto the poore of the parishe of st Saviours in Dartmoothe accordinge Unto the Rate made by the Church Wardens and overseers appointed by his majestys Justice at 3 of 4d the wicke begynyng the 18th daye of aprill Unto this present daye being the 2th of Maye is 54 Wicks whiche some were unto the some of £9.
Memorandum payd unto alice Barenes for monyes Restying Dew to hir before our coming is 5s.
Memorandum Payd unto hir sythe thence for One holle yeare at 13s the quarter £2 12s.
Memorandum payd Edward Cocke as by his acqutance maye appere for Walter Husbandes being in the Mawdling at Tottnis 2 19 0
Memorandum payd unto William Whitt for One holle yeare for the keping of sartayn poore chilldren 10s.
September the 4th given to a poore man by Mr Maiores command 4d
Occtobour the 9th pd mr maior for monyes he Distrybuted 2s
January the 18th pd by mr maiors command unto sartyn frenchmen that had Lost ther shipp 3s.
1606 Maye the 8th payd unto mr maior to Levell this account the some of 5 4 4
[total] 20 15 8
[signed] William Hawck
Receaved by his accompt from Wm Hawkes the some of £5 4s 4d wch was dd to Mr Follett Overseer for the yere past to be kept by him till the accompt for that yere to be pfected.

73. **DARTMOUTH** (St Saviour), Poor Rate, 1609

DHC, DD61759A

Note: This rate was written on three pieces of paper 12 inches in width and 15½ inches in length which have been folded and stitched together with white thread to make up a booklet.

for the poore: 1609

The Second Rate from Mich[aelmas] till our Lady Day.

[page 2]

Dartmouth A Rate for the poore of the pishe of St Saviors reced at Michall 1609 and is for one half yeere from thence untill the 25th of Marche next quarterlie.

Mr Thomas Holland maior	3s 4d	Mr Thomas Gourney	3s 4d
Mr Thomas Paige	3s 4d	Mr Bennett Flute	3s
Mr John Follett	3s	Mr William Flute	3s
Mr Robert Martin	3s 4d	Mr John Smith	3s
Mr Walter Frauncis	3s 4d	Mr William Niell	2s
Mr John Newebye	3s 4d	[total]	1 14 0

Thomas Abraham	15d	Andrew Brickley	4d
Henry Aishlie	3d	Henry Bounde	12d
Thomas Adames	1d	William Baite	8d
Christopher Adames	1d	Lawrence Brocke	3d
John Austin	1d	Geoffrey Bande	2d
[total figure '0 1 9' in margin] John Aishlye		Alexander Barter	2d
2d		William Booden	2d
Peter Bastard	2d	Simon Browne	2d
John Branson	1d	Phillip Boyes	2d
William Bogan	20d	~~Willm~~ Thomas Bodman	1d
Edward Beare	15d	Roger Browne	1d
Thomas Ball	15d	William Bradford	1d
Edward Breckard	6d	[blank] Baits sonne in law	2d
Christopher Blackler	3d		

[page 3]

William Cade	15d	Nicholas Coyte	3d
Edward Cooke	15d	John Coleserye	2d
John Collins	1d	William Cole	1d
Amy Collins widdowe	3d	[blank] Coome a Taylor	~~2d~~
William Cutt	6d	Esdras Cole	3d
William Coxall	8d	Francis Cooke	3d
John Cutt	3d	[total]	0 5 3
Henry Churchward	[blank]		

John Dottrell	3d	~~John Drake~~	~~1d~~
Christopher Drewe	4d	John Davye	2d
William Dannell	1d	John Ellett	12d
Widdowe Dale	[blank]	[total]	0 2 0
John Dottin	2d		

Lewis Fortescue	15d	Mr Edmund Fortescue for half a house	5d
Nicholas Flute 10d	15d	John Follett senior	2d
Robert Follett	10d	William Foster	2d
Jn Fursman & his mother	3d	Christopher Ford	
Bartholomew Frye	3d	Matthew Fisher	3d
Osmond Follett	1d		

John Jefferye [sic]	16d	Phillip Godfreye	1d
John Garneseye	11d	Richard Goslin	1d
Peter Goodridge	2d	[total]	0 7 7

[page 4]

James Goodridge	3d	William Grose	1d
Moses Gilforde	6d	Thomas Goffe	2d
Robert Grindell	12d	[total]	0 2 0

Henry Heyward	8d	Roger Harwood	2d
Mary Hawkes widdowe	8d	Ellis Harradon	2d
Widdowe Hullett	1d	John Heawood	1d
John Holligrove	15d	Thomas Harte	4d
Thomas Hodge	15d	Nicholas Hand	2d
William Hooper	1d	[total] 0 5 5	
Robert Hullett	6d		

Pascoe Jagoe	12d	Walter Jackman	2d
William Irishe	8d	Timothy Jette	1d
William Jackman	2d	Robert Jefferye	2d
Thomas Jackman	2d	[total]	0 2 5

John Kidlie *otherwise* Pointer	12d	Edward Kingman	3d
William Kempe *otherwise* Wenman	12d	Robert Knight	6d
Widdowe Kellye	8d	Stephen Knowlinge	4d
Widdowe Kennawaye	1d	Thomas Knowlles	6d
John Knight 7d	6d	Gilbert Kidlie	2d
Alice Knowles	6d	Richard Kingdome	1d
John Kingman	4d	[total]	0 6 2
Benjamin Knowlles	3d		

[page 5]

John Loweye	2d	John Luxe occupier of the salt mills	20d
Phillip Loveringe gent.	[blank]	Trustram Langedon	6d
Widdowe Luke *otherwise* Sanders	2d	William Lerefaite	2d
Widdowe Lowdwell	4d	Peter Luscombe	6d
Tristram Lane	8d	John Lome	2d
Richard Luke	2d	Ledowick [blank] a Taylor	2d
Richard Lumleighe	13d	John Lower	2d
Henry Longe	10d	[total]	0 6 8

Walter Miller	16d	William Maine	6d
Thomas Martin	2d	Leonrad Maye	2d
John Morris *otherwise* Toser	4d	Roger Mathewe	13d
Henry Maine	1d	[total '0 4 1' in margin] John Maye	3d
Elllis Maye	6d	William Manne	1d
John Neweman senior	10d	Thomas Nevell	3d
William Neweland	6d	Robert Nicholles	8d
Martin Norman	3d	Phillip Norton	2d
Widdowe Nancarrowe	1d	[total]	0 2 9
John Olliver senior	2d	Henry Oldinge	3d
Thomas Oxford	6d	[total]	0 0 11

[page 6]

Alexander Pomrey 3d		John Pascowe cooper	3d
John Plumleighe senior	12d	William Plumleighe Junior	2d
John Paige	14d	Widdowe Paine	1d
John Pascowe	4d	Nicholas Pinbelle	2d
Vincent Paine	4d	John Paddon	2d
Thomas Penney	2d	Thomas Parsons	2d
Thomas Pillaton	3d	[total]	0 4 6
Widdowe Richardes	1d	Richard Randall	4d
Henry Robins	6d	Walter Rownsivall	2d
Arthur Richardes	3d	Robert Rule	2d
John Risdon	4d	John Rowe	2d
Nicholas Reddwoodd	3d	[total]	0 2 3
Mrs Agnes Smith	8d	Robert Stabb	4d
Nicholas Strawb	12d	William Shercombe	3d
Lawrence Swainson	10d	John Sayer	4d
Widdowe Squire	6d	Richard Speede	1d
John Streate	3s 4d	John Stone	3d
Alexander Staplehill	6d	John Stoyle	4d
Aldred Staplehill	12d	[total] 0 9 6	
Gawen Starckeye	2d		
Widdowe Terrye	3d	Robert Teage *otherwise* Lenington	3d
James Tremlles	1d	Mathew Tooker	4d
Peter T	[blank]	Nicholas Townsende	3d
George Tapper	3d		

[page 7]

Mr Walter Willesman	6d	Christopher Wood	6d
Arthur Wotton	6d	Christopher Wellworth	15d
Andrew Weekes senior	6d	Widdowe Wallis	1d
Edward Winchester	8d	Thomas Weste	12d
Margaret Whitinge widdowe	4d	Andrew Weekese Junior	2d

Peter Willes	1d	Chr: Wallis his widowe	2d
Gilles Walle	2d	Jerome Wilcocks	2d
William Whiteheare	2d	[total]	0 6 4
Richard Waye	1d		

This Booke amounteth to by the Quarter £05 14s 00d
& is for the half yere 11 08 00
The Account of the Overseers for the poore in the yere begone the 4th of Aprill *in the year* 1609 and ended in ~~the year~~ the last of March 1610
They are chardged wth two severall books of Rates made in the said yere the one of the said books for the first half yere amounteing to the some of £08 13s 06d.
The second Reate for the last half yere from Mich. to our Lady Day amounteing to the some of 11 08 00
wth money delivered them in stock and is 04 06 04
wth money Rec. of the Gift of Customer Peter due at Christide *in the year* 1608 and is 01 00 00
wth money of Mr Barters Gifte the whole beinge £5 yerelie to be pd and is 01 00 00
wth money Rec. by Mr Newby of the profftt of the £20, given by Mr Hayman & is 02 00 00
wth mony made of Fines for absence from Church pd to the hands of Mr Newby and is 00 09 00
for so much d[elivered]d to the hands of wm Micholls made allso of Fines & is 00 04 00
[total] 29 00 10

[page 8]

['*in contrast*' in margin] They Crave to be allowed of money pd weekelie to the poore & to the sicke men in the Mawdlin as by Aldred Staplehill his Account of paiements herewith exlned appeereth and is the some of £14 19s 02d
pd to William Cole wch a poore child bound apprentice to him as p Indentures appeer & is 03 00 00
pd to Diggins in pt of paiemt wch a poore childe by order & is 00 15 00
They Crave allowance of mony wch cannot be receaved by the Rates of such are dead & gone out of Towne & decayed as appereth & is 01 01 06
The said William Niell craveth to be allowed of mony by him pd to Shutland being sicke by Mr Maiors order at 3 severall tymes 3s & to a poore women allso by order 6d in all 00 03 06
Mr Newby Craveth allowance of mony byd him paid to Diggins wth a poore Orphan & is the some of 01 05 00
for money paid by him wth a Child sett to Brocke and is the some of 01 00 00
So there resteth in Stocke upon this Account wch is delivered over to the Overseers for the next yere and is the some of 06 16 08
[total] 29 00 10

[page 9]

13 6
5
[total] [1]8 6 for he S.

1610 We have Rec for Wekly paiments from the 14 Aprill till the 22th of June being 10 weks 01 18 4
for light since the 14th of Aprill 10 weeks till the 22th of June 00 05 00
[total] 02 03 04
Mr Newby Oweth here to this yeres account 00 04 00
& Wm Nuell 00 00 06

74. **Dartmouth** (St Saviour), Poor Rate, 1615

DHC, DD61892

Note: This rate was written on six sheets of paper, of approximately 8 inches in width and 12 inches in length, which have been folded and stitched together to form a booklet of twelve pages.

Overseers Nominated for the yeare 1615
Mr Thomas Holland Mr Robert Martin Zachary Gould Edward Hollister
John Holligrove Churchwarden
Collectors George Couch Charles Parsons
Mr Tho Holland Wm Plomleighe Tho Ball Roger Mathew

[page 2]

Dartmouth A Rate for the poore of the Parish of St Saviors *otherwise* Northtowne Dartmouth received at Easter *in the year* 1615 for one yeare to ende at easter 1616, to be paid quarterly

Mr Thomas Gourney maior	||||	3s 4d	Mr John Smyth	||||	2s 6d
Mr Walter Fraucies	||||	3s	Mr William Niell	||||	2s
Mr John Follett	||||	2s	Mr John Geffery	||||	2s
Mr Thomas Holland	||||	3s	[total]		01 03 10
Mr Robert Martin	||||	3s	Wm plumlyghe	||	0 02 06
Mr Thomas Paydge	||||	3s	Sept. 29		

A

Thomas Axfford	||||	6d	George Axfforde	||||	2d
John Austine Carpenter	||||	6d	John Ameridith	||||	2d
Christopher Adames	||||	2d	[total]		00 01 08
John Austen	||||	2d			

[page 3]

B

Mr Thomas Ball	||||	18d	Peter Boye	||||	2d
Henry Boone	||||	6d	Nicholas Bartter		1d
Christopher Blacker	||||	1d	William Beard	||||	2d
Peter Basterd		2d	gone Nicholas Ball	||||	3d
Edward Brackerd	||||	2d	Walter Birde	|||	3d
Lawrence Brocke	||||	2d	Roger Browne	||||	2d
William Booden	||||	2d	James Browne	||||	2d
Simon Browen	||||	2d	Richard Boodem	||||	2d
William Bradford	||||	2d	[total]		4s 8d
Nicholas Blackler	||||	2d			

C

Mrs Cade Wyddowe	|||	married 7d	Nicholas Coyte	||||	2d
Mr Edward Coake	||||	18d	Jn Coleworthey	||||	2d
Richard Crouste	||||	12d	dead Fraucces Cooke	|	2d
dead William Coxsall	||||	4d	Jn Collynes	||||	3d
William Carey	||||	12d	George Couch	||||	4d
Robert Cade	|||	2d	Bartholomew Clynton	||||	2d
William Cutt	||||	4d	John Collyns fordlane	||	2d
Amy Calles	||||	3d	is to be crosst out		
John Cutt	||||	6d	[total]		6s 6d

D

John Dollyn	||||	2d	William Davey	||||	2d
Nicholas Domyng	||||	2d	[total]		6d

E

John Ellett	||||	12d	Edward Evans	||||	2d
			[total]		1s 2d

F

Lewis Fortescue	||||	2d	Tobias Frencham	||||	6d
Mrs Flute Wyddowe	||||	6d	Edmund Follett	||||	6d
Robert Follett	||||	16d	Edward Follett	||||	6d
John Fursman	||||	6d	Nicholas Foster	||||	1d
Mathew Fisher	||||	6d	Jn Frances	||	6d
Bartholemew Fry	||||	2d	[total]		6 8
John Folett thelder	||||	1d			

G

Zacharias Gould	||||	20d	Richard Goslin [blank]		
James Gudridge	||||	3d	Thomas Gouff	||||	2d
Phillip Godffrey	||||	3d	[total 2 5]		
Joan Gudridge widowe	||||	1d			

[page 4]

H

Mr Henry Haward		6d	Nicholas Hullett	||||	3d
John Holligrove	||||	20d	Richard Hullett	||||	3d
Mary Hawkes widow	||||	4d	Roger Harwode	||||	2d
Edward Hollister	||||	12d	Richard Hillies	||||	2d
Robert Hullett	||||	6d	James Hole	||||	1d
Nicholas Hand	||||	3d	John Hodge Junior	||||	2d
gone Richard Haradon		6d	[total]		5 8

J

Pascoe Jagoe	||||	2s	Thomas Jackman	||||	2d
William Irish	||||	6d	Christopher Jackson	||||	3d
William Jackman	||||	2d	Walter Jackman	||	2d
Robert Geoffrey	||||	1d	[total]		3 5
Thomas Jerome	||||	1d			

K

William Kempe	||||	18d	John Knight	||||	2d
Benjamin Knowles	||||	8d	Thomas Kinge	||||	2d
Stephen Knowlyn	||||	8d	Widdowe Lowdwell		2d
Thomas Knowlyes	||||	12d	[total]		4 8
gone Edward Kingman	||||	4d			
Margery Kelley widdowe	||||	2d			

[page 5]

L

Andrew Langdon	||||	12d	John Lux for the salte miles	||||	20d
Tristram Lane	||||	12d	Tristram Langdon	||||	8d

Richard Lumley						18d	John Lowey						1d
John Leprey						12d	John Lome						12d
Henry Longe						16d	Richard Leprey						2d
William Labie						4d	John Lyson						1d
Phillip Loveringe						18d	dead Charles Lovering			6d
Peter Luscome						6d	[total]		12 0
Phillip Lymbery						6d			

M

Walter Myllerd						2s	Adrian Maccey						2d
Roger Mathewe						18d	Robert Mooddey						3d
Ellies Maye						4d	Henry Mylles						12d
Tobias Marttin						6d	dead Henry Moore			2d
John Morries						2d	Richard Mayne		4d
Richard Millman						1d	[total]		6 10
Henry Mayne						1d	never dwelte heere		
Walter Mancfild						3d			

[page 6]

N

Widdowe Newman						1d	Martin Norman						2d
dead Robert Nicholas			8d	gon Bartholomew Nyller		2d
William Neweland						8d	John Norber		3d
Phillip Nortton						3d	[total]		2s 3d
The widdowe Nancarowe						

O

| John Oliver thelder | |||| | 6d | Henry Oldyn | |||| | 3d |
| John the younger his sonn | |||| | 3d | [total] | | 1s 0 |

P

John Plumleigh theldr						18d	Alexander Pemorey					2d
John Pascowe						8d	John Paddon						1d
Nicholas Plumbell						8d	Thomas Parsons						2d
Vincent Payne						3d	Frances Portman						2d
Thomas Pilletton						3d	The widdowe Penne						2d
William Plumleigh Junior						3d	Charles Parssons						2d
Thomas Penney						2d	Phillip Philmore			2d
Edmund Puckell bated		6d 18d	gone Awaie		
Thomas Porcke						1d	[total]		6s 1d

R

Mr Jn Richards						18d	John Rowe						2d
Arthur Richards						2d	Richard Renolls						1d
Nicholas Redwoode						3d	John Rockett					1d
John Risdon hellier					3d	[total]		2 6

S

Mrs Agnes Smyth						3d	Amy Squyer Widdow						4d
John Streate						3s	Gawen Starkey						4d
Alex: Staplhill						12d	Robert Stabb						2d
William Scouch						12d	dead John Sayer				6d
Lawrence Swanson						2d	Richard Sharpham						3d

William Sherome	||||	2d	Nicholas Sander Carpenter	||||		6d
John Stone	||||	1d	John Staplehill	||||		18d
Nicholas Sander	||||	2d	gone 25 June Humprey Sheere			18d
Richard Speede			Thomas Smyth	|||		3d
Thomas Scouch	||||	1d	[total]			9s 9d

[page 7]

T:

James Tremiles	||||	2d	Nicholas Towse	||||		3d
Richard Tack	||||	4d	gon Thomas Terry	||		3d
Nicholas Townsende	||||	2d	Abraham tynner or Budly	||||		2d
Stephen Tayllor			[total] 1s 7d			
Peter Tyller		1d				

V

Andrew Voyze	[blank]	

W

Mr Walter Wilsman		[blank]	Richard Waye		[blank]
Christopher Welworth	||||	18d	George Williams backer		[blank]
Andrew Weex theldr	||||	2d	gon 25th June John Wilkox	|	4d
Christopher Woode	||||	12d	Robert Wadland	||||	3d
Edward Winchester	||||	12d	Bennett Wattes	||||	2d
Margaret Whittinge Widdow	||||	4d	dead Christopher Woode Junior	|	2d
Robert Woode	||||	3d	David Weecks	||||	2d
William Whitheare	||||	2d	Mr Andrew Wottenn		18d
gone 25th paid 1615 Jeromy Wilkox |		2d	[total]		5 9

This Booke at the first casting over was found to be £21 00s 04d but since being revewed over againe by the Collectors is found but £20 19s 0 so that there is 1s 4d to bee paid for back to the Collectors.

[page 8]

This boock is Chardges wth money For the gift off Costmer peter due at Christmas Last & is 20s
more For money due by the said Costermer at Christmas next & is 20s
more For money geven to the use off the poore by the Last will off E. Harridone deceased & is 40s
more the Collecters are Chardged wth money dlld then in stock & is 20s

This boock rated by the overseers and Church Wardenn Under mencioned
[signed] Tho: holland
[sign of] Robert Martinn
[signed] Zachary Gould
John holygrove ChurchWarden
by me [signed] Edward Hollester

[signed] Tho: Gourney Maior
Joh: Plumleigh

£5 5s 9d

[page 9]

moneys wecklie to be paid to the porre the first paiment to beginn the 15th off June 1615 by the Collectors

To Alice in the kitchinn	..	6[d]	To Mearrie Carpenter	..	4
To Joan macy	..	3	To Joanes downes Child		1 1
To avic Kydney	..	3	To Mother Dymont	..	4
To Thomas Light For the alstron	..	4	*Sum*		3 5
To Joan speed	..	4			

Here Followth the quartely payments

To William Mayne in the mawdlinn house off Tottnes quartrly 17s 4d

To John Drew For part off the rent off the house wherin John Weeks dwells quarterlie 2s 6d

to Mr Wm Neyle For the rent off a house wherein a poore widowe and Walter Phelp quarterlie 3s 6d

Aprill the 26ᵗʰ 1617

I have dd my Cossyn Robert follett for halfe a yeare to the maudlinge £2 7s 8d

p totnis for william mayne which money I rec of Jn Staply

more to by him Clothes

which I payd owt of the pores stocke 0 13 1

More gave William Kynge to help him backe agayne from tyverton beyinge sent here for that he was deseasyd the 4ᵗʰ of May 1617 0 1 0

[page 10]

to paye Henry the blynd boye wecklye 4d the Fyrste payment to begen the 14 of Julye   4d

The 21th of July is the Laste payment of Joan Dotons Chylde

thes 17 of november 1615 paye to walter phylpe wecklye 4d & dyd beffor the daye of payment.

from thes 19 of november ys rd to pay Joan Speed by the wecke the som of   6d

from the 26 november your [illegible] to paye Eleanor grayns For the kyppyn of a pore Chyld of als the bastards wekcly   6d

from the 10 of desember In Docte deryon that Jn Dollens doth mayntyne his mother he is from hense Forth to be discharged of his payment to the pore.

[page 11]

June the 21th 1616

First first payd Jane Awstyn   1s 0d

more the 30ᵗʰ of June to hir   1 0

more payd Will Iryshe by the Consent of the howse for to appear aprynttyse by hym tacken the 3th of July   £1 5s 0d

More to Jane Awstyn for a weekly payment for the keppynge of 2 Children of on Nic Wylles payd hir more the 6ᵗʰ of July   0 1 0

More payd hyr the 13 of July   0 1 0

More payd hir the 19 of July   0 1 0

More payd hir the 26ᵗʰ   0 1 0

More payd hir the 2th of August   0 1 0

More the 10ᵗʰ   0 1 0

More payd to Lawrence brocke for tacken of appreyntces Gyrdell   2 0 0

More dd to Mr Jago by the order of Mr Holland and Mr Mr [sic] ball and my selfe for Hugh Richardes and his Wife and Child beynge sycke the 26ᵗʰ of August   0 10 0

More dd Mr Jago by the former order the fyrst of septtember   £0 10s 00d

more I dd October 7ᵗʰ Will Nichells wyfe for hir husband beynge very sycke   0 0 1 0

More dd hir the 9ᵗʰ   00 01 0

More dd to hir the 13   0 01 0

More dd to goode nicholles the 21th October22th 1616   0 01 0

More dd antonye normen as by the agrement made in the Churche for tackinge of a boye for the keepynge of him on yeare   0 10 0

More dd to William Nicholles wyfe the fyrst of November   0 1 00 more payd for 2 of penes Chilldren before bownde pryntis to the Clarke and to thomas Jackman

2 0 00

more dd to Will nicholles wyfe the 13th of november

0 1 00

[total]

7 09

[page 12]

Apryll the 22th 1616

First first Rc from Mr Robert marttyn overseere of the northtowne

£5 4s 0d

more Rc from the Collecttors

10 6 10

more Rc from harryddons wyddowe the seccond of may as a gyft geven by hir husband 02 0 00

more Rc from Mr Roger mathewes for Costomer petters gyft for the yeare 1614 the some of 00 19 10

[total]

£18 10s 8d

Aprill the 18th 1617

Gave towardes the settynge forof a felloney that hurt Jn Roupe

4s 00d

more to marke Will mayne Clothes

13 01

more gave to Rynge

01 00

for Payments begynnynge the 5th of May 1616

First first payd to Jn staplleehill on of the collectors for the poore

£2 0s 0d

Desember the 20th 1616

I gave to a woman for heallinge of Drewes bastardes head

10s 00d

More to Mr hand for tackynge hir to appryntys

12 00

Januare 25th

More dd to Dyggynshs wyfe for the Releafe of a pore Child beyng almost skourved

01 00

More to Diggynshs wyfe

01 00

February the 7th 1616

More Gave Mr Holland for to marke Cotherd for Rulles boye when he did tacke him to [ap]prentiss

14 00

More to Dyggyns for the Releafe of the poor Child

01 00

March the 11th 1616

More dd Durchard browne in part of payment of £3 for the Caryage of on fostardes Wyfe beynge overcome with the poxe

30s 00d

[page 13]

The Sume of the Receipts of mony dd wth this boke is

£18 10s 8d

paiemts extraordinary as on the other side appereth

£13 17s 1d

[04 13 7

[page 14]

The Some of the Collectors Recepts this yere as by their boke appeereth amounteth to £23 15s 08d

their paiements as by their acc. appeereth amount to

17 09 04

So resteth to ballanc this account from the Collectors

06 06 04

& on the other side

04 13 07

Sum total

£10 19s 11d

More there is pd 4d omitted in the account So the whole acco of money Rc.

£11 0 3d

Wch Some of £10 19s 11d was paid in the 15th day of May 1617 at wch tyme this Account was Audited and the money Delivered to the handes of Mr Thomas Gourney one of the Overseers for the next yere.

[signed] Will Plumleigh maior   Tho: Spurwaie

[page 15]

The 3th of Maie 1616

To Alice in the kichen	6d *for the* week	to Eleanor graine	6d *for the* weeke
to avis kidney	3d	to Mother Dymond	4d
to the blind boy	4d	to Joan Speed	6d

75. **Dartmouth** (St Saviour), Poor Rate, 1618

DHC, DD61943

Note: This rate was written on seven pieces of paper which measure nearly 6 inches in width and about 16 inches in length. These have been stitched together with white thread to form a booklet of fourteen pages. The rate's inside page notes the overseers as being Mr Robert Martin, Mr Jon. Jeffery, Mr Andrew Voysie, Mr Alexander Staplehill and Mr Phillip Lovering as the church-warden. The collecters were John Carpenter and Richard Tack. The pages following the rate noted receiving money and expenditure. The latter includes general payments to 'the old Russell', Alice Kitchin, Thomas Light, Joan Speed, Widow Deymond, Joan Hodge, David Grimes, Michael Adams, Eleanor Graynes for an illegitimate child, Moses' wife for Pennye's child, Joan Straw for Browne's child, Rowland's wife for Slowman's child and Joan Harris for Wiles' boy. It was also noted on 14 March that 'there was brought unto us at the church 3 children of Wlliam Bradfords, he being in the King Majesty's service and his wife being dead the 10th day before, by which occasion the children being a maid of 5 years old & 2 boys, one of 3 years & the youngest of ¾ old was left to the disposing of the Overseers of St Saviours'. The four overseers placed the children with local women until the father returned to claim them.

A rate for the poore of the pishe of St Saviors in the North Towne of Dartmouth recved at Easter 161[torn] to be paid Quarterly.

Mr Thomas Piadge ~~maior~~	||||	3s 3d	Mr John Smith Mayor	||||	2s 6d
Mr John Follett	||||	18d	Mr William Plumleigh | away at michelmes 3s		
Mr Thomas Holland	||	3s	Mr William Niell	||||	2s
Mr Robert Martin	||||	3s 4d	Mr John Jefferye	||||	2s
Mr Thomas Gourney	||||	2s 6d	[total]	,	1 0 8

A

Thomas Axford	||||	6d	George Axford	||||	3d
John Asten Carpenter	||||	12d	John Amerydeth	||||	6d
Christopher Adams	||||	2d	9 8 ye'		

B

[in later hand 'John Budlye']	||||	12d	Peter Boyey	||||	2d
~~Mr Thomas Ball~~			Nicholas Blackler	||||	2d
Nicholas Ball [blank]			['Mychell' in margin] ~~Andrew~~ Barter his land 3d		
Henry Boone	||||	5d	William Beard	||||	3d
Edward Brockett	||||	3d	~~Rodger Brown~~		~~2d~~
Lawrence Brocke	||||	2d	James Browen		3d
dead William Bouden	||	3d	Richard Bowden	||||	~~Bowden~~ 3d
William Bradford	[blank]	d	The widow Band	||||	~~5d~~ 4

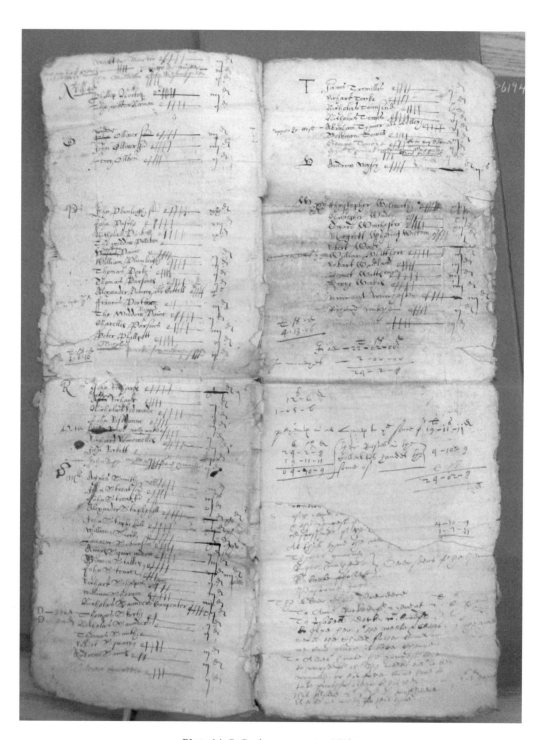

Plate 14. St Saviour poor rate, 1618.

Walter Byrd of Custome howse‖‖ 4d [in later hand 'Robert Blackaller for mydsomer
[in margin 'left']   qrter']   ‖‖‖   3d
John Bromfelld   ‖‖‖‖ 4d [total]   18s 6d
~~John Bodleigh~~ Bodleye

C

Mr Edward Coake   ‖‖‖‖ 17d William Cutt   ‖‖‖‖   4d
[in margin 'not paid'] George Cade‖‖‖‖ 18d Amy Collines widow   ‖‖‖‖   3d
Richard Croaste   ‖‖‖‖ 12d John Cutt   ‖‖‖‖   4d
William Carye   ‖‖‖‖ 15d Nicholas Coyte   ‖‖‖‖   2d
Robert Card   ‖‖‖‖ 2d

[page 2]

John Colseworthey   ‖‖‖‖ 2d   John Collines the Boucher ‖‖‖‖   2d
John Collines senior   ‖‖‖‖ 3d   ~~George Card~~
George Couch   ‖‖‖‖ 6d   [in later hand 'Peter Caseley ‖‖‖‖   2d']
Bartholomew Clynton   ‖‖‖‖ 2d   [total]   £1 13s 4d
John Carpenter   ‖‖‖‖ 6d

D

John Dollin   ‖‖‖‖ ~~3d~~ 2d Cimon Dodony Boboney   ‖   3d
Nicholas Domyney   ‖‖‖‖ 2d   [in margin 'Widow bakers son in law']
John Dottin lawyer   2d   Chrisopher Dicke from mysomer qrter ‖‖‖   2d

E

John Ellett   ‖‖‖‖ 12d Edward Evenes   ‖‖‖‖   2d

F

Mr Lewis Fortescue   ‖‖‖‖ ~~20d~~ 2s Margaret Frencham wyddow ‖   6d
Mrs Flute widow   ‖‖‖‖ 6d   Edward follett   ‖‖‖‖ ~~12d~~ 10d
Robert follett   ‖‖‖‖ 18d Edmund follett   ‖   8d
~~John~~ Widow fursman   ‖‖‖‖ 3d   [in margin 'gone shomaker']
Matthew fisher absent   ~~Nicholas foster agone before mydsomer   2d~~
Nicholas Flute for makler   ‖   12d Thomas Francis   ‖‖   20 2d
Bartholomew frye   ‖‖‖‖ 2d   [in margin 'not payd'] ~~Richard Feris   1d~~

G

Zachary Gould from maklemas quarter ‖ 18d Andrew Glanfill   ‖‖‖‖   3d
[in margin 'will pay butt 6d']   John Gadinge   ‖‖‖‖   2d
James Goodrige   ‖‖‖‖ 13d [in margin 'to the higher end of the towne']
Phillip Godfrye   ‖‖‖‖ 2d   Mark Gosewill   ‖‖‖from mydsomer   2d
Thomas ~~Gough~~ Goaffe   2d

H

Mr John Hollygove senior   ‖‖‖‖ 20d Roger Harwood   ‖‖‖‖   2d
John Hollygrove Junior   ~~8d~~ Richard Hilley   ‖‖‖‖   6d
Mary Hawkes widdow   ‖‖‖‖ 4d   James Holle   ‖‖‖‖   2d
Edward Hollester   ‖‖‖‖ 6d   John Hodge   ‖‖‖‖   2d
Robert Hallett   ‖‖‖‖ ~~7d~~ 6d Andrew Harwood   ‖‖‖‖   2d
[in margin 'will pay butt 6d']   Nicholas Hynde   ‖‖‖‖   3d
Nicholas Hand   ‖‖‖‖ 6d   Stephen Harwood   ‖‖‖‖   3d
Nicholas Hallett   ‖‖‖‖ 6d   Thomas Hart   ‖‖‖‖   8d
Richard Hallett   ‖‖‖‖ 6d

[page 3]

[in margin 'gone before mydsummer qurt']   [total] £1 15s 6d
Richard Harvy   6d

I

Pascoe Jago	||||	20d	Thomas Jherom			3d
William Irish	||||	6d 4d	Christopher Jackson	||||	6d
William Jackman	||||	2d	Walter Jackman	||	2d
Robert Jhefferye aligt		[blank]	Richard Ferris		2d
Thomas Jackman	||||	2d			

K

William Kente	|||	18d	John Knight	||||	2d
Benjamin Knowelles	||||	12d	Thomas Kinge	||||	6d
Stephen Knowlen	||||	9d	Margaret Kelley widow	||||	2d
The widdowe Knowles	||||	6d			

L

Andrew Langdon		[blank]	John Lambe	||||	3d
Tristram Lane	||||	12d	Richard Lepraye	||||	3d
Mingo and others to the salt mielles	||||	20d	Walter Lapp	|||	3d
[in margin 'litle dartmouth muste pay']			William Leach	||||	6d
Tristram Langdon	||||	12d	Henry Lumley	||||	2d
Richard Lumley	||||	18d	Thomas Liston brewer	||||	3d
John Lepraye	||||	16d	John Lomer	||| from	
Henry Longe		3d		mydsomer	6d
Phillip Loveringe	||||	20d	Samuel Lea sayler from Caryes house |		
Peter Luscombe	||||	2d	mydsomer qur		2d
Phillip Limberey	||||	6d 8d	[total]		£3 16s 9d
[in margin 'not pay'] John Loye	||||	2d			

M

Mr Walter Miller	||||[illegible]	20d	Walter Mansell	||||	4d
Mr Roger Matthew	||||	2s	Richard Meane from Michaelmas		6d 8d
Ellis Maye	|	died 26 September 4d	[in margin 'dead'] Adrian Macye	||	2d
Toby Martin	||||	6d	Robert Muddye	||||	6d
Richard Millman	||||	2d	Henry Mylles	||||	15d
Robert Meane	||||	2d	John Martin	||||	[torn]

[page 4]

Walter Martin	||||	3d	John Middleton from mydsomer qrter		2d
wil pay butt 8d p yeere as before Mingo the			[total]		£1 13s 4d
miller		3d			

N

Phillip Norton	||||	4d	The widdow Norman	||||	2d

O

John Widow Olliver sen		4d	Henry Ollden	||||	2d
John Olliver Junior	||||	4d			

P

John Plumleigh senior	||||	20d	Nicholas Pimbell	||||	9d
John Pascho	||||	8d	The widdow Pilliton [blank]		

~~Vincent~~ Vincent Paine |||| 2d

William Plumleigh |||| 3d

Thomas Pocke |||| 2d

Thomas Parsones |||| 2d

Alexander Pumcey *otherwise* Cottell |||| 2d

['pay butt 8d' in margin] Frances Portorn || 3d

The Widdow ['Richard' inserted] Paine ||||2d

Charles Parsons |||| 4d

Peter Phillpott |||| 7d

~~Thomas~~ Nicholas Parcke from medsomer quarter 2d

[total] £1 6s 10d

R

Mr John Richards |||| ~~17s~~ 2s

~~Arter~~ Arthur Richards |||| 3d

Nicholas Redwoode |||| 2d

John Risdonne |||| 3d

Peter ~~John~~ Rowe polly maker |||| 2d

Richard Rennowelles |||| 2d

John Rockett 2d

[in later hand 'John Riche'] workes wth hurde the shoemaker |||| 2d

S

Mrs Agnes Smith widow |||| 3d

John Streat senior |||| 3s

John Streat Junior || 6d

Alexander Staplehill |||| ~~12d~~ 15d

John Staplehill |||| ~~12d~~ 9d

William Scoch ~~16d~~ 15d

Lawrence Swanson |||| 2d

Amy Squire widow |||| 3d

Gawen Stalley |||| ~~6d~~ 4d

John Stonne ||| 2d

Richard Shapon ||| 3d

William Shoram |||| 4d

Nicholas Saunders Carpenter |||| 12d

[in margin D – dead] Thomas Skoch | 2d

[in margin D – dead] Nicholas Saunders 3d

Thomas smith [blank]

Robert Squarye |||| 3d

Andrew Sames || 3d

[in later hand 'Andrew Swaddle'] ||| 2d

[page 5]

T

James Tremilles |||| 2d

Richard Tacke |||| 10d

Nicholas Tounsend |||| 2d

Nicholas Towes |||| 6d

[in margin 'uppon the Fosse'] Abraham Tynner *otherwise* Kelley |||| 6d

Solomon Towes |||| 3d

George Tereye ||| from mydsommer 3d

John Thomas right against pemble from mdsomer 2d

V

Andrew Voysey |||| ~~20d~~ 2s

W

15d Christopher Welworth |||| 16d

Christopher Woode |||| 12d

Edward Winchester |||| 12d

Margaret Whiting Widdow |||| 4d

Robert Woode ~~3d~~

~~he will pay but 10d~~ the yeer William Whitthere |||| 3d

Robert Wadland |||| 3d

Bennet Watts caper 4d

Davy Weekes |||| 4d

Vincent Winchester |||| ~~5~~ 4d

Richard Wakeham |||| 2d

[in later hand 'Warren Wills'] |||| 2d

[total] £4 13s 06d

In all £22 02s 0d8

In monyes 2 00 00

24 2 8

Plate 15. Door of St Saviour's Church, Dartmouth.

76. **Dartmouth** (St Saviour), Poor Rate, 1619

DHC, DD61971

Note: This rate was written on three pieces of paper, which measure 12 inches in width and 16 inches in length, which have been folded and stitched together with brown thread to make up a booklet of six pages.

Mr John Smith Mayor	||	3s 4d	Mr Thomas Gorney	||	2s 6d
Mr Thomas Pasco	||	3s 4d	Mr Willim Neyle	|||	2s
~~Mr John Follett~~			Mr John Jeffery	||	2s
Mr Robert Martin	||	3s 4d	[total]		£0 16s 6d

A.

Thomas Axford	||	6d	George Axford	||	3d
John Awsten Carpenter	||	12d	John Ameredeth	||	6d
Christopher Adams		2d	[total]		0 2 5d

B.

John Budley	||	15d	Andrew Bawtter	||	3d
Nicholas Ball		6d	Richard Bowden	||	4d
Henry Boone	||	6d	The widow Band		4d 4d
Edward Breckett	||	3d	Walter Bearde custome house	||	6d
Lawrence Brocke	||	2d	brunton		
William Bowden dead			John Bromfield		4d
Peter Bowyee		2d	Robert Blackallar	||	3d
Nic: Blackallar		2d	James Bennet	||	2d
Michael Barter	||	2d	Simon Balbine the Currier	||	2d
William Bearde	||	3d	John Bagwell	||	3d
Roger Browne		~~2d~~	[total]		£0 5s 5d
James Browne	||	3d			

C.

Edward Coake	||	18d	Amy Collings widow	||	3d
George Cade	||	18d	John Cutt	||	4d
Richard Crouste	||	12d	Nicholas Coyte	||	2d
William Carye	||	15d	John Coale	||	2d
Robert Carde	||	2d	John Collings senior	||	3d
William Cutt baker		4d	George Couche	||	6d

[page 2]

C

Bartholomew Clinton	||	2d	Edward Coopp	||	6d
John Carpenter		6d	Wm Cutt the yonger	||	2d
John Collings boucher	||	3d	[total]		0 9 0
Peter Caselly		2d			

D

John Dollin	||	2d	Simon Dodeney		3d
Nicholas Donnynge		2d	Christopher Dycke		2d
John Dottin	||	2d	[total]		0 0 11d

E

| John Ellett | ‖ | 12d | [total] | | 0 1 2 |
| Edward Ewnes | | 2d | | | |

F

Mr Lewis Forteskew	‖	2s	not to paye mor then the ½ year pd		
Mrs Flute widow	‖	6d	Edward Follett	‖	12d
Robert Follett	‖	18d	Thomas Francis		2d
Widow Joan Fursman	‖	3d	Richard Feris		[blank]
Nicholas Flute	‖	12d	Mr John Fowntaine	‖	2s
Bartholomew Frye	‖	2d	[total]		0 8 7d

G

Zachary Goulde	‖	18d	Andrew Glanfield			3d
James Goodridge	‖	8d	Joan Goodridge	‖	2d
Phillip Godfrye	‖	2d	Mark Gosewill	‖	3d
Thomas Goffe		2d	[total]		0 3 2

H

Widow Weltin Holigrofe	‖	18d	James Hole	‖	2d
Jn Holligrofe		6d	John Hodge	‖	2d
Mary Hawkes widow	‖	4d	Andrew Harwood	‖	2d
Edward Hollister	‖	6d	Nicholas Hynde	‖	4d
Robert Hallett	‖	6d	Stephen Harwood			2d
Nicholas Hande	‖	6d	Mr Holland widow	‖	18d
Nicholas Hallett	‖	6d	Ric Haradon		2d
Richard Hallett	‖	6d	[total]		0 8s 10d
Roger Harwood		2d			
Richard Hillye	‖	6d			

[page 3]

I

Pascoe Jago	‖	20d	Christopher Jackson	‖	6d
William Irish	‖	4d	Walter Jackman		2d
William Jackman	‖	2d	John Irish hooke seller			3d
Robert Jeffery			[total]		0 3 3d
Thomas Jackman	‖	2d			

K

Benjamin Knowles	‖	12d	Thomas Kinge		6d
Stephen Knowling	‖	9d	Margaret Kellye widow	‖	2d
The widow Knowles	‖	6d	Edward Kingman	‖	6d
John Knighte		2d	[total]		0 3 7d

L

Tristram Lane	‖	12d	Peter Luskome	‖	6d
Tristram Langdon	‖	12d	Phillip Lymbery	‖	8d
Richard Lumley	‖	18d	John Loye		2d
John Lepray	‖	16d	John Lambe	‖	3d
Henry Longe		[blank]	Richard Lepray	‖	4d
Phillip Lovering	‖	20d	Walter Lapp dead		-

William Leach	‖	6d	Samuel Lea ‖	2d
Henry Lumley		3d	Mynge & others to the salte mylls	20d 20d
Thomas Lidstone	‖	4d	[total]	0 11 10d
John Lomer	‖	6d		

M

Mr Walter Myller	‖	20d	Henry Mylles ‖	16d
Mr Roger Mathew	‖	2s	John Martin ‖	6d
Toby Martin	‖	6d	Walter Martin ‖	6d 6d
Richard Mylman		2d	Jn Mydleton ‖	2d
Robert Mayne	‖	4d	Mynge the Myller [illegible crossed through]	
Walter Manfill	‖	6d	3d 20d	
Richard Mayne	‖	8d	John Mead ‖	2d
Adrian Macye dead			[total]	0 9 1
Robert Muddey		6d		

N

Phillip Norton	‖‖	6d	Robert Noresh 2d
The widow Norman	‖‖‖	2d	

[page 4]

O

Widow Olliver	‖	4d	Henry Olden 2d
John Olliver	‖	4d	[total] 0 1 8

P

John Plumleigh	‖	20d	Alexander Pomery	2d
John Pasco	‖	8d	ffraucis Porter	3d
Nicholas Pimbell	‖	9d	The widow Richord Payne ‖	2d
The widow Paine	‖	2d	Charles Parsons ‖	4d
William Plumley	‖	3d	Peter Phillpott ‖‖‖	8d
Thomas Porke		3d 3d	Nicholas Porke	2d
Thomas Parsons	‖	2d	[total]	0 5 8d

R

Mr John Richards	‖	2s	Richard Renells ‖	2d
Arthur Richards		3d	John Rockett	[blank]
Nicholas Reddwood		2d	John Riche ‖	3d
John Risdonne	‖	3d	[total]	0 3 4
Peter Rowe	‖	3d		

S

Mrs Agnes Smith widow		3d	Richard Sharpon ‖	3d
Mr John Street senior	‖	3s	William Shorom ‖	4d
Mr Alexander Staplehill	‖	18d	Nicholas Sanders Carpenter ‖	12d
Mr John Staplehill	‖	16d	Robert Squarey ‖	6d
William Skoche	‖	15d	Andrew Swaddell ‖‖‖	2d
Lawrence Swanson	‖	2d	John Streatt Junior	6d
Amy Squire widow	‖	3d	Andrew Samwes baker	4d
Gawen Stallkey	‖	4d	George Sheeres	2d
John Stone		[blank]	[total]	01 11 4

T

James Tremells	|	2d	Solomon Towes		3d
Richard Tacke		10d	George Tonye		2d
Nicholas Townsend	||	4d	John Thomas	|||	2d
Nicholas Towes	||	6d	George Tapley	||	6d
Abram Tynner *otherwise* Kelly	||	6d	[total]		0 2 11d

[page 5]

V

V Andrew Voysey	||	2s	[total]	0 2 0

W

Christopher Wellworth	||	16d	Vincent Winchister	||	6d
Christopher Wood	||	12d	Richard Wakhame		3d
Edward Winchister	||||	16d	Warren Wills		2d
Margaret Whiting widow	||	6d	~~Richard Wakham~~		~~3d~~
William Whitheire		3d	Henry Wood	||	4d
Robert Wadland	||	4d	Henry Weger		2d
Bennet Wats	|	4d	Robert Wood	||	2d
David Weeks		6d	[total]		0 6 10d

1619 Maye the 9th we Find this Rate to amount to the sum of five pownds eightein shilleings & seven penc the quarter wittnes our hands the daye & year above written.
[signed] John Geffry   John Plumleigh thelder   Andrew Voysey   Alexander Staplehill
Philip Loveringe Churchwarden   John Smyth maior   Thomas Payge

[page 6]

1619

Aprell 23th payd Ric Tack the daye & year written Fourtey shilleings is £2 00s 00d [signed] Richard Tacke

Jn Carpenter and Richard Take £4 8s
[signed] Richard Tacke
more d[elivere]d Richard Tacke of mony of Mickellmas quarter £3
more paid Richard Tacke of mony Recd of mickls quarter £2
More in money of the last 2 quarters 12s
More pad Tacke 10s
More pd Richard Take of money Rced of Christyd quarter £3 10s
More pad Richard Tacke 20s
more pad him £4
more paid him £2
more paid him 20s
Receaved wth this booke of the overseers the some of £2 00 00
more Collected as by the booke appears the some of 23 08 10
[total] 25 08 10d

[page 7]

23th of April 1619.
The Overseers of the poore Receaved wth this Booke as by the last yeres acc. made by the Overseers it appereth   £07 09s 03d
They are to receave of Customers Peters gifte due at Christyde last   01 00 00

They are to receave from Alexander Pomerye for mony disbursed for a Chest & for his Childrens
maintenance & Clothes as appereth & is   02 10 00
for so much bestowed on his wyffe as by Mr Gourneyes account appeereth & is [blank]
They are to receave of Mr John Smith maior for so much by receaved from Hellier the Smith and
is in money   02 00 00
Paid out as *by* the account doth appere the sum of   23 17 9.
more delivered in with this booke   1 11 1.
[total]   25 08 10

77. DARTMOUTH (St Saviour), Poor Rate, 1622

DHC, DD62094

Note: This rate was written on six pieces of paper which measure some 8 inches in width and 12
inches in length, which have been folded and stitched together with white thread to make up a
boolet of twenty-four pages.

The Booke of Rates for the poore of the Northtowne of Dartmouth for this yeare 1622

[page 2]

the names of the poore pepell wch have [been] payed wickelye as Followeth
Joan Whittcott is 0s 9d, Davey grayne 10d, Weddo fenge 4d, Wm Eleatt 6d, Tho: Adames 4d,
Rich: Rowl and for Ciping of a Childe is 1s 13d, Tho: Goffe is 1s, Joan Sttrawe 1s, Widdo Lieght
8d, harrod the Caperes wife 6d, Joan heward is 1s, Mary Egber is 1s, Joan Downe is 6d   7s 9d
[total] 9 8
John Osborne 2d
the gardners daughter 3d

[page 3]

Mr Maior	['and 4s' in later hand]	3s 4d	Mr William Neille		2s 4d
Mr John Plumleigh	|||	2s	Mr Robert Follett	||||	2s 6d
Mr Robert Martin	||||	3s 4d	Mr Walter Myller	||||	2s 6d
Mr John Smyth	||||	2s 6d	Mr Pascoe Jago	||||	2s 6d
Mr John Jefferye	||||	2s	[total]		1 5 6
Mr Roger Mathewe	||||	2s 6d			

A

Thomas Abraham	||||	20d	James Archer	||||	4d
Thomas Axforde	||||	8d	John Amerideth	||||	8d
George Axford	||||	4d	[total]		0 4 10
John Austinge Carpenter	||||	12d	[in later hand 'Walter Austing Mary Archer		
Christopher Addams	||||	2d	Wid']		

B

John Budleigh	||||	18d	Andrew Barter	||	3d
Nicholas Ball	||||	6d	Richard Bowden	||||	4d
Henry Bowen	||||	6d	Walter Beard	||||	8d
Edward Breckard	||||	3d	John Bromfild	||||	4d
Lawrence Brocke	||||	3d	Robert Blackler	||||	4d
Peter Bowey	||||	2d	Simon Baboine	||||	4d
Nicholas Blackler	||||	2d	Daniel Bowne	||||	2d
Michael Barter	||||	2d	John Bownser	||||	8d
William Beard	||||	3d	[total]		0 6 10

[page 4]

C

Edward Coake	‖‖	12d	George Couche	‖‖	3d
George Cade	‖‖	6d	Bartholomew Clynton	‖‖	3d
x Widowe Crowste		12d	John Collings	‖‖	4d
William Carye	‖‖	20d	William Cutt Junier	‖‖	2d
Robert Cade	‖‖	2d	John Carpenter	‖‖	8d
William Cutt	‖‖	6d	James Colle	‖‖	2d
Amy Collings		3d	John Cuttinge	‖‖	2d
Nicholas Coyte		4d	John Colle Junior	‖‖	2d
John Coale senior	‖‖	3d	[total]		7 10

D

John Dottyn	‖‖	4d	Anthony Deymont	‖‖	3d
John Dollyn	‖‖	2d	[total]		11⌈d⌉
X Nicholas Donnyne		2d	Gorge Dier		

E

John Elliott	‖‖	14d	[total]		1 5
Edward Ewines	‖‖	3d			

[page 5]

F

Mr Lewis Fortescue	‖‖	20d	Mr John Fowatayne	‖	2s 4d
Mrs Anne Flute	‖‖	6d	John Frawnces	‖‖	3d
Joan Fursman	‖‖	3d	X John Farrys		2d
X Mr Nicholas Flute		6d	Owen Forde	‖‖	3d
Edward Follett	‖‖	6d	[total]		6 5

G

James Godridge	‖‖	8d	Mark Goswill	‖‖	3d
Philip Godfrey	‖‖	3d	William Gould	‖‖	4d
X Andrew Glanfild		2d	[total]		1 11
Joan Godridge	‖‖	3d			

H

John Hollygrowe	‖‖	20d	Andrew Herwood	‖‖	2d
Walter Harlyn	‖‖	12d	Nicholas Hyne	‖‖	4d
Mary Hawkes	‖‖	4d	Stephen Harwoode	‖‖	3d
Edward Hollyster	‖‖	6d	William Hamett	‖‖	18d
Robert Hollett senior	‖‖	6d	Edward Hollacom		2d
Nicholas Hande	‖‖	6d	William Holland	‖	12d
Nicholas Hollett	‖‖	6d	Richard Hollett	‖‖	8d
Richard Helley	‖‖	4d	Joan Holland	‖	6d
X John Hodge	‖	2d	[total]		10 1

[page 6]

I

William Irishe	‖‖	4d	John Irishe	‖‖	4d
Thomas Jackman	‖‖	2d	[total]		1 4
Margaret Jackson	‖‖	6d			

K

Benjamin Knowles	||||	18d	Edward Kingman	||||	6d
Stephen Knowlinge	||||	12d	Nicholas Knowles	||||	4d
Widow Knighte	||||	2d	Abraham Kelley	||||	3d
X ~~Margaret Kellye~~	||||	2d	[total]		3 11

L

Richard Lumley	||||	20d	Richard Leypraye	||||	4d
Tristram Lane	||||	14d	William Leache	|||	10d
Tristram Langdon	||||	12d	Henry Lumley	||||	6d
['to much' in margin] John Lepraye	||||	14d	Thomas Lydston	|||	6d
Mr Philip Loveringe	||||	20d	['to much' in margin] John Lomver	||||	10d
Peter Luscome	||||	6d	X Samuel Leay		2d
Philip Lymbrye	||||	12d	[total]		12 0
X John Loye		2d	[in later hand 'Simon Leaye		12d']
John Lambe	||||	6d			

M

Toby Martin	||||	12d	Henry Mills	||||	20d
Robert Mayne	||||	8d	John Martin	||||	14d
Walter Manfild	||||	8d	Walter Martin	||||	6d
Robert Moodey	|||	6d	[total]		6 2

[page 7]

John Meade	||||	2d	[total]	0 6
The salte Mylls	||||	2s	[total of those who have paid who have surnames beginning with the letter M]	2 4d
[in margin 'to paye'] Allse mayne widowe ┼┼┼	2d		

N

William Norman	||||	3d	Philip Norton	||||	8d
Widow Norman	||||	3d	[total]		1. 1 5
Robert Norishe	||||	3d			

O

John Ollever	||||	6d	[total]	9
Henry Olding	||||	3d		

P

John Pascoe	||||	12d	Charles Parson	||||	6d
Nicholas Pymble	||||	12d	Peter Philpott	||||	12d
William Plumleigh	||||	6d	Lawrence Peprell	||||	2d
Thomas Pocke	||||	3d	X Thomas Parnell	||||	2d
X Thomas Parsons	||	3d	[total]		5 0
Frances Porter		2d			

R

Mr Nicholas Roope	||||	3s	Richard Renowlls	||||	3d
John Richards	||||	2s 6d	John Riche	||||	4d
Arthur Richards	||||	3d	John Rowlson	||||	4d
Nicholas Redwoode	||||	2d	John Roope	||||	6d
John Risdon	||||	3d	[total]		7 11
Peter Rowe	||||	4d			

[page 8]

S

Mr John Shapleigh		2s 6d	Richard Sharpham	||||	3d
Mrs Smythe widowe	||||	3d	Nicholas Sanders	||||	18d
Mr John Streate senior	||||	3s	X Robert Squarye		4d
John Streate Junior	||||	12d	X Andrew Swadell		2d
Mr Alexander Staplehill	||||	2s	George Sheeres	||||	2d
John Staplhill	||||	20d	Richard Smythe	||||	20d
X Lawrence Swanson	||	2d	William Stocker	|||	2d
Amy Squyre	||||	2d	[total]		15 4
Gawen Stoickey	||||	4d	[in later hand 'Peter Sparke']		

T

Richard Tacke	||||	15d	Gregory Taplye	||||	8d
Nicholas Townsend	||||	6d	Peter Tillye	||||	2d
Nicholas Towse	||||	12d	[total]		3 9
X John Thomas	|||	2d			

V

Mr Andrew Vesey	||||	2s 6d	[total]	2 6

[page 9]

W

Edward Winchester	||||	18d	Henry Wigger	||||	2d
Christopher Woode	||||	10d	Robert Woode	||||	2d
Margaret Whitting	||||	10d	John White	||||	2d
Bennett Watts	||||	4d	William Whitheare	||||	3d
Vincent Winchester	||||	12d	X William Winchester	||	2d
Richard Wakham	||||	6d	Thomas Wardrope	||||	20d 1s
Warren Willes	||||	2d	[illegible sum crossed through] [total]		7 7

the sign RM of Robert Marten
[signed] John Smyth
the signe of Walter WM Miller
[signed] Pascoe Jago Nich: Strawe

[page 10]

by Mr Pascoe Jago   Delevered over unto Richard Smyth and John Martin Collecters for the pore in moneyes the 15th of september 1622 the full some of 26s & paid over by mr Jago unto John Beerkye being sicke 6d. 26s

[page 11]

Collectors Mr Richard Smyth & Mr John Martyne who did begyn to pay the weckely pay the 13th 15th day of September beynge Fryday
To William Mene in the madlen of Tottnes quarterlye to be payed from the overseres of the powre is 17s 4d.
13th October the weekly payments

X John Borage	4d	William Ellyott	6d
John Whitcoate	9d	Thomas Addams	4d
David Grime	8d	Richard Roland for keeping of a Childe	1s 3d
Widowe Leache	4d	Thomas Goffe	12d

Joan Strawe	12d	Joan heawarde	12d
Widowe lighte for her Alstrowe	8d	Mary Egber	6d
Harewode the Coupers wife towards the		Widdo Olliver	[blank]
mayntainse of her Children	6d		

[page 12]

~~The Oversyers for the poore are charged wyth £24 18s 8d and is for so mech Reserved by oure~~
~~boweke of Colecton as me apere is of the 15ᵗʰ of 1622~~   ~~£24 18s 8d~~
The Oversyers for the poore for the yere *in the year* [sic] 1622 are charged wth the Resecpt of £24
8s 8d as by thar Boke of Collection me a pere is   £24 18s 8d
mor theye are charged wth the gefte of Coustomer Petre Des att Chrismas 1622 is   1 . .
more theye ar charfed wth £1 6s 6d Reseved wth book the 15ᵗʰ of September is   1 6 6
mor theye ar charged wth 5s geven by Jerom Wilkexe   . 5[s] .
more theye are charged wth wth [sic] 25s wch was mad of Stephen Lucraftes goods kepe tow
orfants by the deth of father & mother to the Townne is   1 5 .
mor theye are charged wth £1 5s and is for so meche Reseved of Mr mayor of the poors Rent
moneye   1 5 .
[total]   30 00 2
At the Delyveringe up of this booke the 16ᵗʰ daye of June 1623 ther Remayneth an areradge from
Mr Myell of one whole yere   0 09s 4
from John Shaplye for ¾ of a yere at our Ladie Day laste   0 7 6
from Mr John Plumligh thelder for ¼ wch he is to paye our ladie day quarter & is   0 2 0
It is to be understode that all thease arrerags were dew at our ladie daye last past & to be
Remebered by the next Colleckters to be Colleckted.

[page 13]

for against theye Oversyers of the poore Craves to be aloyed £23 3s 5d. And is for some chas will
apere by the booke of the wicklye payment is   £23 3s 5d.
more the[y] crave to be alowed £2 and is for so mech geven to the wedow Trat of kingswar wch
Mary Lucracte of orfant bound an aprentes accordene to the law provided in that bee halfe is
                                                                                               [£]2
more the[y] crave to be alowed £3 10s and is for so meche geven to Richard Reneles wch Ruth
Lorcraft orfant an apprentes accorden to the law provyded in that bee halfe   [£]3 10[s].
more they crave alouance 11s 8s and is for so meche payde the 13ᵗʰ of June for that wick [£]12 8[s]
[total]   29 6 1
pd in by the Colleckters the 16ᵗʰ of June to balance this accompte wch money is d[elivere]d to the
Colleckters for the yere to Come and is   00 14 1
[total]   30 00 2
[signed] Tho: Spurwaie maior   Tho: Gourney
[page 14] Rec. *by* me Nicholas Ball from the Collectors of the last yere the *sum* of 14s 1d.

78. DARTMOUTH (St Saviour), Poor Rate, 1624

DHC, DD62128

Note: This rate was written on four pieces of paper, which measure 12 inches in height and 8
inches in width, which have been folded and stitched with white thread to make up a booklet of
sixteen pages. The cover page has a series of numerical figures.

Mr Roger Mathew Mayor	||||	3s 4d	Mr John Jeffery	||||	2s
Mr Robert Martyne	||||	3s 4d	Mr William Niell		6s is paid 1s 6d
Mr John Smyth	||||	2s 6d	Mr Robert Follett	||||	

Plate 16. Communion table carving, Dartmouth.

Mr Pascoe Jago	||||	2s 6d	Mr Thomas Gorney	||||	2s
Mr Andrew Voysey	||||	2s 6d	23s 2d [total]		4 8 8d

A

Mr Thomas Abraham	||||	2s	Walter Austynn	||||	2d
Thomas Axforde	||||	1s 4d	Mary Archer widow	||||	6d
George Axford	||||	3d	Thomas Adames	||||	
Christopher Adams	||||	2d	Anthony Anthoney sonne	||||	2d
James Archer	||||	6d	6s 5d [total]		1 5 8d
John Amerideth	||||	8d			

B

Mr John Budly	||||	2s	John Bromfeild	||||	4d
Nicholas Ball	||||	8d	Robert Blackler	||||	4d
Henry Bowen	||||	6d	Simon Babonie	||||	4d
Edward Breickard	||||	3d	Daniel Bowen	||||	4d
Lawrence Brock	||||	4d	John Bownser	||||	1s
Peter Bowey	||||	2d	Thomas Burges	||||	8d
Nicholas Blackler	||||	2d	John Bwayes the Toucker	||||	2d
Michael Barter	||||	2d	21s [total]		1 17
William Beerd	||||	4d			

[page 2]

C

Edward Coake	||||	6d	John Collins	||||	6d
George Carde	||||	6d	William Cutt Junior	||||	
William Carye	||||	1s 10d	John Carpenter	||||	8d
Joan Cutt *widow*	||||	3d	James Cole	||||	2d
Anne Collins	||||	3d	John Cuttyngs	||||	2d
Nicholas Coyte	||||	4d	John Cole Junior	||||	2d
John Cole senior	||||	3d	Bartholomew Clentyn	||||	2d
George Couche	||||	3d	6s 3d [total]		1 5 0

D

John Dottin	||||	6d	George Dyer	||||	3d
John Dollyn	||||	2d	Christopher Dicke	||||	2d
Anthony Deymont	||||	3d	16s 4d [total]		0 5 4

E

John Eliott	||||	1s 2d	10s 5d [total]		0 5 8
Edward Evenes	||||	3d			

[page 3]

F

Mr Lewis Fortescue	||||	1s 8d	John Farmes in lew of 2 tennats that he hath	
Mrs Ann Flute	||||	6d	taken in	6s
Edward Follett	||||	6d	3s 6d [total]	0 14 0
John Frances	||||	4d	Ric Flute in lew of a tenant wth wif & chilldren	
William Foxe	||||	3d	that he hath taken in out of another parish 4s	
Thomas Fabies Junior	||||			

G

James Goodridge	||||	8d	William Golile gone of the parish |||		6d
Phillip Godferie	||||	3d	Zachary Goolile	||||	1s 4d
Joan Goodridge	||||	3d	Nicholas Goodredg	||||	3d
Markes Goswill	||||	3d	3s 6d [total] 0 13 6		

H

John Holligrove	||||	1s 8d	Nicholas Hyne	||||	4d
Mrs Harlowyn	||||	1s	Stephen Harrowde	||||	3d
Mary Hawks	||||	4d	William Hamett	||||	1s 6d
Edward Hollester	||||	2d	Edward Hollacombe	||||	2d
Robert Hollet senior	||||	3d	William Holland		1s
Nicholas Hand	||||	8d	Richard Hollett	||||	1s
Nicholas Hollett	||||	6d	~~Joan Holland 2d~~		
Richard Helly	||||	4d	~~Samuel Hingston~~		
Andrew Herwood	||||	3d	10s 1d [total]		1 13 8

J

William Irishe	||||	4d	John Irishe	||||	6d
Thomas Jackman	||||	2d	10s 8d [total] 0 4 0		

[page 4]

K

Benjamin Knowells	||||	1s 6d	Nicholas Knowes	||||	4d
Stephen Knowling	||||	1s	Abraham Kelley	||||	4d
Edward Kingman	||||	6d	3s 8d [total]		0 14 08

L

Richard Lumblye	||||	2s	Henry Lumbly	||||	8d
Tristram Lane	||||	1s 3d	John Lomer	||||	10d
John Lepray	||||	1s 2d	Simon Ley	||||	1s
Mr Phillip Loveraigne	||||	2s	Richard Luke	||||	8d
Peter Luscombe	||||	6d	Thomas Liston	||||	6d
Phillip Lymbery	||||	1s	William Lynes	||||	2d
John Lambe	||||	6d	Henry Longe	||||	3d
Richard Lippraie	||||	4d	13s 10d [total]		2 15 4
William Leach	|||	1s			

M

Toby Martyne	||||	1s	the Salt mylls	||||	2s
Robert Mayne	||||	8d	Alice Mayne *widow*	||||	2d
Walter Manfeild	||||	8d	Mrs Miller *widow*	||||	2s
Robert Moodie	||||	4d	Richard mayne	||||	1s 6d
Mr Henry Myll	||||	2s	William Mathewe	||||	2d
John Martyn	||||	1s 6d	Edward Manneing	||||	2d
Walter Martynn	|||	4d	12s 6d [total]		2 10 4
John Meaden	||||	2d			

[page 5]

N

William Norman	||||	3d	Wydow Norman	||||	3d

Robert Norishe	||||	3d	[on opposite sheet 'Receaved of Phillip Norton
Phillip Norton	||||	1s 2d	3s']
1s 11d [total]		0 7 8	

O

John Olyver	||||	1s	1s 6d [total]		0 6 02
Henry Olding	||||	6d			

P

John Pasche	||||	1s 3d	Peter Philpott	||||	1s
Nicholas Pymble	||||	1s	Lawrence Pepperell	||||	2d
William Plumbligh	||||	8d	Thomas Parnell	||||	2d
Thomas Porke	||||	6d 4d	John Peren	||||	2d
Francis Porter	[blank]		5s 4d [total] 1 00 10		
Charles Parsons	||||	8d			

R.

Mr Nicholas Roope		~~3s~~	Richard Reynolls	||||	3d
Mr John Richards	||||	2s 6d	John Riche	||||	4d
Arthur Richards	||||	3d	John Rowlston	||||	4d
Nicholas Redwoode	||||	2d	John Roope	||||	8d
John Risdon	||||	3d	7s 11d [total]		0 19 0
Peter Rowe		~~2d~~			

[page 6]

S.

Mr Nicholas Strawe	||||	2s	George Sheeres	||||	2d
Mr John Shaplighe	||||	2s 6d	Richard Smyth	||||	1s 8d
Mrs Smythe *widow* [blank]			William Stocker		~~2d~~
Mr John Streate	||||	3s	Peter Sparke	||||	2d
John Streate junior	||||	1s 3d	Jeremy Salter		6d
Mr Alexander Staplehill	||||	2s	William Samoies	||||	4d
Mr John Staplehill	||||	2s	Edward Sporewaye	||||	8d
Amy Squire	||||	2d	Roger Sparke		~~3d~~
Gawen Storekey	||||	4d	~~Robert Spark~~		~~6d~~
Richard Sharpham	||||	3d	[total]	19s 5d	3 12 0
Nicholas Saunders	||||	2s 6d			

T

Richard Tack	||||	1s 4d	Peter Tillye		~~2d~~
Nicholas Townesend	||||	8d	George Tonney		~~3d~~
Nicholas Towse	||||	1s	3s 4d	[total] 0 12 0	

W

Edward Winchester	||||	1s 6d	John White	||||	2d
Christopher Wood	||||	1s 2d	William Whitheare	||||	2d
Margaret Whiteing	||||	10d	Thomas Wardroppe	||||	1s 6d
Bennett Watts	||||	4d	Andrew Waymouth	||||	1s 3d
Vincent Winchester	||||	1s	[on opposite sheet 'came out of the parrish']		
Richard Wakeham	||||	6d	William Widger			2d
Warren Wills	||||	2d	John Walter	||||	3d
Henry Widger	||||	2d	Andrew W	[blank]	
Robert Wood	||||	4d	9s 6d [total]		1 17 6

[page 7]

[signed] John Geffry   Andrew Voysey   Tho: Abraham   John Richards   Alexander Staplehill

[page 8]

Mche 29th 1624

Overseers for this yere following Mr John Jefferie, Mr Andrew Voysie, Mr Thomas Abraham, Mr John Richards

Mr Alexander Staplehill Churchwarden

for Collectors Thomas Waldrope, Thomas Burges

[page 9]

Rc wth this booke the 15th of Aprill 1624 the *sum* of £6 19s 3d ½

by me [signed] Thomas Wardrobe

[signed] Thomas Burgis

The Wekley payments for the poore Aprell 26th 1624:

Davey Graynes 10d, + Widow Knight 12d, + Thomas Adames July 3 4d, William Ellet 6d, – Joan Hayward 6d 6d, Joan Whitcote 9d, Widoe olever 6d, Widoe Light for kepeing in of her daughter 8d, July 11th Ric Rowland | August 8th 1s 3d, Joan Straw 6d, Roger harwods wife 6d, + Joan Downe | 6d, Widowe Leuge 4d, [total] 8s 8d, May 8th Elizabeth Tremills for kepeing her yongest sone wth her 6d, July 11th Ellen Cokwill 6d, August 09 Joan Gerey | 16d, Mch 13th Margaret Pope | 6d, Wilmot Chete for Andrew bear his daughter & for formerly 4s 6d, Joan Browne 4d, Lawrence Pascoe 6d

[page 10]

Overseers for the year Following Mr John Smyth, Mr Pascoe Jago, Mr Nicholas Strawe, Mr John Staplehill Budley

Churchwarden, Mr William Gurney

Collecktors, Edward Spurway, John Knight Walter

£	s	d
4	8	8
1	5	8
1	17	0
1	05	0
	5	4
	5	8
	14	0
	13	6
1	13	8
	4	0
	14	8
2	15	4
2	10	4
	7	8
	6	0
1	00	10
	19	00
3	12	00
	12	00
1	17	06
27	07	10

[page 11]

Receved wth thir Booke & is £6 19 09

mor Receved as by the ptickelers on the other side sum is 27 07 10

Receved by Andrew Voysey of Sir John Mtyne of cockenten being the guift of his Father & is 5 00 00

Mor rc [illegible] of valorpitt Lovering the guift of his Father & is 1 00 00

More found in the pore mans box 0 01 00

May 5ᵗʰ 1625 40 08 01

[signed] Robtt Follett maior Roger Matheaw

[page 12]

pd out in sevrall payments as by the pteckoler apeares 21 06 03¼   payd out to the pore and sike follkes by Andrew Voysey as by his ac. 05 00 04 Rest in money pd in hearby to the oversears for the year Followeing 14 01 7 ¼ May 5ᵗʰ 1625 [total]   40 08 02½

[signed] Robtt Follett maior   Roger Mathew

May 5ᵗʰ 1625 Dellyvrd Jn Walter of the abovenamed sonne   £5 00s 00d

mor he is to Receve of Mr Tokerman for Costemor Petters guift dew at Christmas Last past 1 00 00

the rest of the some abov being nyne pownds one shilleing & seven pence ¼ was payd to Mr Nic Flute the daye & year above written   9 01 07 ¼

[total]   15 01 07 ¼

79. DARTMOUTH (St Saviour), Poor Rate, 1625

DHC, DD62215

Note: This rate was written on four pieces of paper some 9½ inches in width and 13 inches in length which have been folded and stitched with cream-coloured thread to make up a booklet of sixteen pages. DD62216 is a copy in which the crossed names were omitted. Additional details from it have been noted in square brackets. The covering sheet of the rate has details of expenditure. The first of two notes recorded 'Maye the 5ᵗʰ 1625 paid Edward Spurwaie with this booke the some of Five pounds & Twentie shillings to Receave of James Tookerman for Customer petters guift dew at Christid Last past all is £06 00s 00d [signed] Edward Spurwaie' and the second 'more pd me Nicholas Strawe with this booke the daie & yeare above written the some of nyne pounds one shillings seven pence farthing is £09 01 07¼ [signed] Nic: Strawe'. These are followed by 'The weekly payments for the poore' which comprises payments to David Graynes 10d, William Ellett 6d, Joan Haywoode 6d, Joan Whitecoate 9d, Widow Oliver 6d, Widow Light for keeping in her Daughter 8d, Elizabeth Tremills for keeping her youngest sonne 6d, Ellen Cockwell 9d, William [Cheate for keeping in of] Andrew Beares daughter 6d, Joan Browne 4d, John Brakett 15ᵗʰ of Jully 1625 6d, Widow Roberts 13ᵗʰ october 1625 4d, Lucy Pascow 18ᵗʰ november 6d, The 23th december Jn Breckett had *by* your order 12d week, Esbell Fleather the 30ᵗʰ December 1625 2d, The 3th February 1625 I had order to paie Jn Braket 18d a week'. A note was crossed through on page 2 that 'for a warrant for a Rate for the poore pd John Dottin 12d'.

[page 3]

Mr Robert Follett maior	‖	3s 4d	Mr Pascoe Jago	‖‖	2s 6d
Mr Robert Marttinn	‖‖	3s 4d	Mr Andrew Voysey	‖‖	3s 00
Mr John Smyth	‖‖	2s 6d	Mr Thomas Abram	‖‖	2s 6d
Mr John Jeffrie	‖‖	2s 00	[total]		01 02 02
Mr Roger Mathew	‖‖	3s 00			

A

Thomas Axford	‖‖	1s 6d	George Axford	‖‖	3d

Christopher Addams	||||	2d	Mary Archer *widow*		6d
James Archer	||||	3d	Widdow [copy 'Joane'] Addams	||||	6d
John Amerideth	||||	8d	[total]		4 03
Walter Austin	||	2d			

B

Mr John Budley	||||	2s	John Bromefilde		4d
henry Bowen	||||	6d	Robert Blackhall		4d
Edward Breckard		3d	Simon Babovie	||||	4d
Lawrence Brock	||||	4d	Daniel Bowen		3d
~~Peter Bowey~~		~~2d~~	John Bownser	||||	12d
Nicholas Blackhall	||	2d	Thomas Burgis	||||	8d
Michael Barter	||||	2d	~~John Boyes tucker~~		~~2d~~
William Bearde	||||	4d	John Bawden	||||	2d
~~Andrew Barter~~		~~2d~~	John Bagwell 6d		
Richard Bowden	||||	4d	[total]		9s 02d
Walter Beearde	||||	12d			

[page 5]

C

Edward Coake	||	4d	John Collins	||||	6d
George Cade	||||	6d	William Cutt Junior		3d
William Carye	||||	1s 10d	John Carpenter	||||	6d
Joan Cutt *widow*		3d	James Cole		2d
Amy Collins	||||	3d	John Cutting		2d
Nicholas Coyte	|||	4d	John Cole Junior	||||	2d
John Coale senior	||||	3d	Bartholomew Klinton		2d
George Couch	||	2d	[total]		5 10

D

John Dottin	|||	6d	George Dyer	||||	3d
John Dollin		2d	Christopher Dicke		2d
Anthony Dymont	||	3d	[total]		1 4d

E

John Elliott	||||	1s 2d	[total]		1 5
Edward Evines	||||	3d			

[page 7]

F

Mr Lewis Fortescue	||||	1s 8d	Thomas Fabis senior		2d
Mrs Anne Flute	||||	6d	Thomas Fabis Junior	|||||	6d
Edward Follett	||||	6d	John Folliott		6d
John Fraunces	||||	4d	~~Grace Flute~~		~~widow~~
William Foxe	||||	4d			

G

Rcd 3s of Mrs Gurney			Joan Goodridge	||||	3d
Mrs Grace Gurney widow	||||	1s 3d	Mark Gooswell	|	3d
James Goodridge	|||	8d	Zachary Goolds widow		10d
Phillip Godferie	||	3d	Nicholas Goodridge		3d

Mrs Gills widow		12d	John Garland		3d
William Golde			[total]		4 03

H

John Holigrove	||||	1s 10d	Andrew Harwoode	||||	4d
Mrs Harlewin			12d	Nicholas Hyne	||||	4d
Mary Hawkes [copy 'widow']		4d	Stephen Harwoode	||||	3d
Edward Hollester	|||	3d	William Hammett	||||	1s 6d
Robert Hollett senior	|||	3d	Edward Hallacombe		2d
Nicholas Casse *otherwise* hande	||||	8d	Richard Hollett	||||	12d
Nicholas Hollett		4d	Samuel Hingston		2d
Richard Hilley		4d	[total]		8 06

I

William Irishe	||||	4d	Widow Jackman		2d
John Irishe	||||	6d	[total]		1 4d
Richard Jagoe	||||	4d			

[page 13]

K

Benjamin Knowles	||||	1s	Abraham Kelley		4d
Stephen Knowling	||||	12d	William Kent Junior		15d
Edward Kingman	||||	6d	[total]		3s 4d
Nicholas Knowles		4d			

L

Mr Andrew Langdon	|||	2s	Henry Lumblye	||||	8d
Richard Lumblye	||||	2s	John Loamer	|||	8d
Tristram Lane	|||	1s 3d	Simon Leye	||||	12d
John Lepraye	||||	10d	Richarde Luke	||||	8d
Mr Phillip Loveringe	||||	2s	Thomas Lidstoane	||||	8d
Peter Luskombe	|||	6d	William Lynnes			3d
Phillip Liembree	||||	12d	Henry Longe	||||	3d
John Lambe	||||	6d	Mr Andrew Langdon		
Richard Lepreye	||||	4d	[total]		15 07d
William Leache	||||	12d			

M

Toby Marttin	||||	12d	the Salte mylls	||||	2s
Robert Maine	||||	9d	Alice Maine *widow*	||||	2d
Walter Manfeilde	||||	8d	Mrs Miller widow	||||	2s
Robert Modie			4d	Richard Maine	|||	1s
Mr Henry Myll	|||	2s	William Mathewes		2s
John Marttin	|||	1s	Edward Manning	||||	
Walter Marttins wido		2d	[total]		12 5d
John Meade		2d			

[page 9]

N

William Norman	||	3d	Phillip Norton	||||	1s 0d
Widow Norman	|||	3d	Mrs Neild Widow	||||	6d
Robert Norishe		2d			

O

John Olyver	||||	12d	Henry Oldinge	|||	6d

P

M John Plumleighe	|||	12d	Peter Phillpott	||||	12d
John Paschoe	||||	1s 4d	Lawrence Pepperell	|||	2d
Nicholas Pymble	|	12d	Thomas Parnell		2d
William Plumleighe	|||	8d	John Perein		2d
Thomas Porke		3d	Thomas Pheris		2d
Charles Parsons	||||	8d			

R

Mr Nicholas Roope	|	3s	Richard Renneolds	|||	3d
Mr John Richards	||	2s 6d	John Rich	||||	4d
Arthur Richards	||||	4d	John Rowlston	||||	4d
Nicholas Redwoode	||||	4d	John Roope	||	7d
~~John Risden~~		~~3d~~	Gilles Rownsevall		2s

[page 15]

S

Alex: Staplehill	|||	2s	Nicholas Sannders	||||	1s 6d
Mr Nicholas Strawe	||||	2s	~~George Sheers~~		~~2d~~
Mr John Shapleigh	|	2s 6d	Mr Richard Smyth	||||	1s 8d
~~Mrs Smyth widow~~		~~2d~~	Peter Sparke		2d
Mr John Streette	|||	3s	Jeremy Salter		6d
John Streeet Junior	|||	2s 3d	William Samoies	|||	4d
~~Mr Alexander Shapleigh~~		~~2s~~	Edward Spurwaie	||||	8d
Mr John Staplehill	|||	2s	~~William Stocker~~		
+~~Amye Suire~~		~~2d~~	[total]		8 0
Gawyne Storekeyn	||||	3d	~~Mrs Smyth widow~~		~~2d~~
Richard Shapham	|||	4d	Mr Wm Seavey	|	1s 4d

T

Richard Tacke	||||	1s 4d	~~George Tondye~~		
Nicholas Townesend		8d	[total]		3s 4d
Nicholas Towse	||||	12d	['The 3th Marche 1625 I had order to paie the
Peter Tilles widow marian		4d	widow Lang 8d a weeke' on opposite sheet]

W

Edward Winchester		6d	Robert Woode	|||	4d
Christopher Woode	|||	15d	John White		2d
Margaret Whitting	||||	10d	William Whiteheiare		2d
Bennett Watts	||||	4d	Thomas Waldrobbe	||||	1s 5d
Vincent Winchester	||	12d	Andrew Waymouths widow	||||	10d
Richard Wakeham	||||	6d	John Walter		2d
Warren Wills		3d	[total]		8s
Henry Widger	||||	3d			

[final page] overseers for this yeare Following 1625
Mr John Smyth, Mr Pascoe Jagoe, Mr Nicholas Strawe, Mr John Budlye
Mr William Gurney Churchwarden
Collectors Edward Spurwaie John Walter

[signed] John Smith Pascoe Jago Nic Straw Jn Budley
[signed] Robtt Follett Maior Roger Mathew
The 13th of Januarie 1625 I had order to paie 8d a week for Roger Harwoods Childe
Joan Realicke the 17th February 1625 4d
Tamsin Nobodie 6d

Plate 17. Plaster ceiling, Dartmouth.

80. DARTMOUTH (St Saviour) Poor Rate, 1632

DHC, DD62509

Note: This rate was written on five pieces of paper 11½ inches in width and some 13½ inches in length which have been folded and stitched with brown string to provide a booklet of twenty pages. Two mayors were noted this year. Sums were recorded on each sheet tallying the assessments. The outside cover noted it as 'The booke for the Releife of the Poore *in the year* 1632'. The scribe may have used dots to indicate payment but others are unlikely to have had a purpose.

A rate for the releife of the poore of Dartmouth Quarterly to bee payd *in the year of our Lord* 1632.

Mr William Plumleigh Maior	‖	5s	Mr Andrew Voysey	‖‖		5s
Mr Roger Mathew Mayer	‖	5s	Mr Alexander Staplehill	‖‖		3s 4d
Mr Robert Follett	‖‖	4s	Mr John Budleigh	‖‖		3s 4d
Mr John Richards	‖‖	4s	Mr Andrew Langdon	‖‖		3s
Mr Pascoe Jagoe	‖‖		[total]			31s 8d

A.

Thomas Axford	‖‖	1s 8d	Mary Archer *widow*	‖‖		9d
George Axford	‖‖	2s	Joan Adams *widow*	‖‖		6d
William Ashby	‖‖	3d	John Axford	‖‖		1s 2d
Christopher Adams	‖‖	4d	Thomas Adams	‖‖		3d
X John Ameridith	‖‖	1s 6d	[total]			9s 3d
Walter Austin	‖‖	4d				

B.

Thomas Burges	‖‖	1s	William Bawdon	‖‖		1s
Henry Boone	‖‖	1s 6d	William Booth	‖‖		2s
Edward Breckard	‖‖	4d	Richard Bayly *otherwise* Parker	‖‖		6d
Lawrence Brocke	‖‖	6d	John Bagwell			[blank]
Michael Bartram	‖‖	6d	John Bowdon senior	‖‖		3d
William Beard	‖‖	8d	Tristram Bennett	‖‖		3d
Richard Bowdon	‖‖	6d	Christopher Beeare	‖‖		1s
Walter Bird	‖‖	1s 8d	William Branfield	‖‖		3d
Robert Blackaller	‖‖	1s	William Barnes	‖‖		1s
Simond Bobyny	‖‖	8d	William Bennett			3d
Daniel Boone	‖‖	3d	William Bushe one quarter	‖		4d
John Bownser	‖‖	1s 8d	16s 10d 18s 3d [total]			£2 17s 9d
John Bawdon junior	‖‖	4d				

[page 2]

C.

George Cade	‖‖	1s 6d	Edmund Chade	‖‖		1s
William Carey	‖‖	2s	Walter Cole	‖‖		3d
Amy Collins	‖‖	6d	Richard Cutt	‖‖		1s 8d
John Cole senior		4d	Mr John Cawley	‖ one quarter		1s
George Couch	‖‖	4d	John Cole	‖‖		1s 8d
John Collins	‖‖	1s 6d	[also noted on opposite sheet for 6d] John			
William Cutt junior	‖‖	0 9d	Collenes Junior two quarters	‖		0 3d
James Cole smith	‖‖	3d	Edward Coyte	‖‖		3d
John Cole junior	‖‖	6d	Andrew Cole	‖		2d

Arthur Thomas Choledge |||| 8d
James Cole butcher 3d
Edward Cole |||| 3d

Edward Cutt |||| 4d
[total] 14s 2d

D.

John Dottin |||| 1s
Anthony Dymond |||| 4d
George Dyer |||| 6d

[blank] Dicke *widow* |||| 3d
John Dollinge 1s
[total] 2s 1d

E.

John Elliott |||| 2s
Edward Evens |||| 6d

Thomas Evines
[total] 2s 6d

F.

Mr Lewis Fortescue |||| 2s
Mrs Anne Flute |||| 9d
Thomas Fabis 3d
Mr John Follett |||| 2s
Hugh Fawne |||| 6d
Mr Richard Follett |||| 4d

John Foster |||| 3d
Robert Follett junior |||| 1s 3d
Anne Flute widoe |||| 3d
John Franche one quarter | 6d
[total] 7s 8d

G

Mrs Grace Gourney |||| 1s 8d
James Goodridge |||| 6d
Phillip Godfrey |||
Joan Goodridge *widow* |||| 6d
Nicholas Goodridge |||| 1s

[page 3]

Andrew Glanfield |||| 4d
Humphrey Goodridge |||| 4d
Robert Greenswood |||| 4d
[total] £1 11s 6d

H:

Mr John Holligrove |||| 3s
Mrs Mary Hawkes |||| 6d
Nicholas Hand |||| 1s 8d
Andrew Harwood |||| 8d
Nicholas Hine |||| 6d
William Hammett |||| 2s
Richard Hullett |||| 4d
George Hambleton his wife one quarter 6d
Mr Mark Hawkings |||| 3s
John Holman |||| 9d
John Hernaman |||| 3d
Stephen Hepditch |||| 4d
John Hodge |||| debt 3d 9d

Robert Harris |||| 6d
Edmund Horswell |||| 6d
Thomas Hinckston |||| 6d
Robert Hollecke |||| 4d
Arthur Harradon [also noted on opposite sheet]
|||| 2d
John Hand |||| 3d
Julian Holley widowe 2d
Thomas Hawkings [also noted on opposite sheet] |||| 2d
Peter [illegible crossed through]
Mr Peter Hill 1s
[total] 10s 9d

J.

Mr John Jeffery |||| 1s
William Irish |||| 6d
John Irish |||| 1s 6d
J[blank] Ingram 6d

Richard Jago 1s 6d
Richard James [also noted on opposite sheet] 2d
3s 6d [total] 4s 8d

K.

Stephen Knowlinge |||| 1s 6d
Edward Kingman |||| 1s 6d

Nicholas Knowles 6d
Abraham Kelly |||| 8d

Mr William Kent senior	||||	1s	John Kent	|||||	1s
Mr William Kent Junior	||||	1s 2d	Robert Knowles		6d
Benjamin Knowles	||||	1s 6d	[total]		9s 9d
Robert Kingman [also noted in opposite sheet]	||||	4d			

L.

Mr Richard Lumley	||||	3s	Thomas Lidston	||||	1s 4d
Mr Tristram Lane	||||	2s 6d	William Lynes		8d 8d
John Leprey	||||	6d	Mr Henry Long	||||	6d
Mr Philip Loveraigne	||||	2s 6d	John Lynes	||||	4d
Anne Luscombe *widow*	||||	6d	John Lane	||||	8d
Phillip Limbry	||||	2s 6d	Mr Thomas Leigh	||||	1s 6d
John Lamb	||||	9d	Thomas Lynes	||||	3d
Henry Lumley	||||	1s 6d	John Leavericke	||||	6d
John Lomer	||||	1s	[total]		£2 11s 8d

[page 4]

M.

x Toby Martin	||||	1s 8d	William Mathew		3d
Robert Mayne	||||	1s	Edward Manninge	||||	4d
Walter Manfield	||||	1s 3d	Thomas May		3d
Mrs Mary Mills	||||	6d	Thomas Manfield	||||	2d
Mr John Martin	||||	2s	[blank] Mayne *widow*	||||	4d
John Meade	||||	3d	Henry Milcombe		4d
x The Salt Mills	||||	3s	John Moone		4d
Mrs Sebley Miller *widow*	|||	1s 6d	Thomas Moone [sum crossed through]		
Nicholas Michell	||||	4d	[total]		13s 6d

N.

[blank] Norman *widow*	||||	6d	Evan Norman	||||	4d
William Norman	||||	6d	Christopher Newland		8d
Robert Norrish		3d	Joan Norber *widow*	||||	6d
Phillip Norman	||||	2s	[total]		4s 9d

O.

John Olivers ~~widdow~~	||||	1s	[total]		1s 8d
Henry Oldinge	||||	8d			

P.

Mrs [blank] Perrot one quarter 1s 6d ['Mr Parrott' noted on opposite sheet]			William Payne	||||	4d
			Edmund Plumleigh	||||	1s 6d
John Plumleigh	||||	1s 3d	James Peeke	||||	3d
John Pascoe	||||	1s 8d	Vincent Peeke	||	6d
William Plumleigh	||||	4d	John Peryn	||||	3d
James Pelletton	||||	10d	Miles Pyle		1s ~~6d~~
Thomas Pocke	||||	4d	Nicholas Pocke	||||	2d
x Charles Parsons	||||	1s 6d	Edwd Pempe		~~2d~~
Peter Philpott	||||	1s 8d	~~Robt Parker 2d~~ [noted on opposite sheet]		
Lawrence Pepperell	||||	3d	John Plumleigh Junior		1s 6d
Richard Piper	||||	1s 3d	13s 1d [total]		£1 13s 6d

[page 5]

R:

Giles Rounsevall	||||	3s	John Rolestone	||||	8d
Arthur Richards	||||	9d	John Roope	||||	9d
Richard Reynolds	||||	3d	[total]		5s 5d

S:

Mr John Shapleigh one quarter		4s	Nicholas Stitstone	||||	6d
Mr Nicholas Straw	||||	2s	Richard Speed	||||	3d
Mr John Street senior	||||	3s	Phillip Sparke	||||	3d
Mr John Staplehill	||||	2s 6d	Thomas Spurway Junior	||||	1s
Mr John Street Junior	||||	1s 8d	Gilbert Smith	||||	6d
Gawen Stoakey	||||	3d	Thomas Stoker	||||	6d
Mr Richard Smith	||||	2s 6d	Thomas Saunders	||||	4d

[noted on opposite sheet 'Mr Richard Smith for takeing in of an Inmate weekley tenn shillengs to begine the 10th daye of febrearey 1632 & so to Contenew Weekley']

			Abraham Stent	||||	4d
			John Searle	||||	6d
Mrs Elizabeth Smith *widow*	||||	1s 3d	Mrs Shapleighe wido	|one quarter	8d
Peter Sparke	||||	4d	[also noted on opposite sheet]		
Edward Spurway	||||	1s 8d	Nic Spead	|||	4d [also noted on opposite sheet]
Lawrence Swanson	||||	4d	Robert Stonman one quarter	||	6d
Robert Stone	||||	6d	[total] £1 0s 2d		

T:

Richard Tacke	||||	1s 8d	William Trenecke	||||	4d
Nicholas Townsend	||||	10d	Michael Triggs	||||	2d
Nicholas Towse	||||	2s	Robert Turpin	||||	1s 8d
Nicholas Thorne	||||	6d	James Toucker one qter	|	6d
Roger Templeman	||||	6d	[total]		7s 8d

V:

Phillip Voysey	||||	2d	[total]	£1 13s 5d
[total]		2d		

[page 6]

W:

Christopher Wood	||||	1s 4d	Thomas Wilson	||||	6d
Margaret Whiting	||||	2s 6̶d̶	Stephen Whittocke	||||	4d
Bennett Watts	||||	8d	David Weekes	||||	3d
Richard Wakeham	||||	9d	William Wotton	||||	6d
Henry Widger	||||	8d	Peter Wills	||||	9d
x Robert Wood	||||	2s	John Woods	||||	3d
John White	||||	3d	Edward Wreight	||||	2d [name repeated on opposite sheet]
William Whitheare	||||	3d	Peter Woodey one quarter	|	1s [name repeated on opposite sheet]
Mr Thomas Wardrobe	||||	2s 6d			£1 0s 2d
Mary Weamouth	||||	1s			19s 6d
John Walter	||||	1s 6d			
Lawrence Wheeler	||||	2s			
James Wall		3d			

Z

William Zeavey |||| 2s 3d   ~~recd towards the next qtr 9d~~

total £11 07s 06d *for the* quarter [these sums are copied on the oppposite sheet][signed] Roger Mathew maior Robtt Follett

[page 7]

pd nichole Roberts from the 2th of August but 6d *for the* weeke.

the 30th of 9ber 1632 is alld unto Lucy Pasco 6d *for the* week more.

the 31th of March there is allowed unto the widdowe Parker 6d per weeke more 6d. The same to Joan Stone weekly 6d. the same day allowed Tamsen the gunner 6d. the same day to Tho gammon in his sicknes 6d. pd Jn Rowbutt for 8 Weekes 8s. pd Joan Sheram for 8 weeks 8s.

[page 8]

A rate for the reliefe of the poore of St Saviors weekly to bee paid as followeth *in the year of our lord* 1632.

Nichole Robarts	8d	Margaret Light	9d
David Graynes	1s	Thomas Gammon	1s
X Elizabeth Fletcher	1s ~~8d~~	Anne Parker widdowe for 4 poore Chelldren	
Joan Heywood	6d		1s 6d
X Lucy Pascoe	1s 6d	Phillip Shutland	[blank]
Joan Frye widdow	1s	Robert Williams for his wife	1s 6d
Thomasine Gunner	10d	[blank] Beere widdowe	1s
Thomas Hodge	1s	John Rowe	[blank]
Prothesa Rowland	8d	[blank] Lane Widow	8d
Joan Nicholls widdow	1s	John Thomas his wyffe for 2 of her Childer	
Dorothy Crase	4d	in her husbands absenc begon the 3th of	
Eleanor Roads widdow	8d	november	12d

25th February pd to Moses Gillfords wiffe weekly in tyme of her sicknes 12d

more from the last of march more 6d

The second Day of Aprill 1632: chosen to bee Overseers for the Poore of the Parrishe of St Saviors Mr Andrew Voysey, Mr John Richards, Mr Nicholas Straw, Mr John Martin,   Overseers

Mr Thomas Wardrobe   Churchwarden

Walter Bird, Richard Cutt   Collectors

Edmund Horswill, Edmund Chade   Way Wardens

81. DARTMOUTH (St Saviour), Poor Rate, 1638

DHC, DD62678

Note: This rate was written on six pieces of paper, which measure 11½ inches in width and 16 inches in length, which have been folded and stitched with white thread to make up a booklet of twenty-four pages. The inside cover has a series of sums. The scribe used three different marks possibly to indicate whether payments were made.

A rate for the relieife of the poore of the parrishe St Saveries in Darthmouth quarterly to be paide *in the year of our Lord* 1638.

Mr John Budley	||||	5s	Mr Alexander Staplehill	||||	4s
Mr Robert Folltt	||||	4s	Mr John Richards	||||	4s
Mr Andrew Voysey	||||	5s	X Mr Andrew Langdon	||||	4s
Mr Pascoe Jagoe	||||	4s			

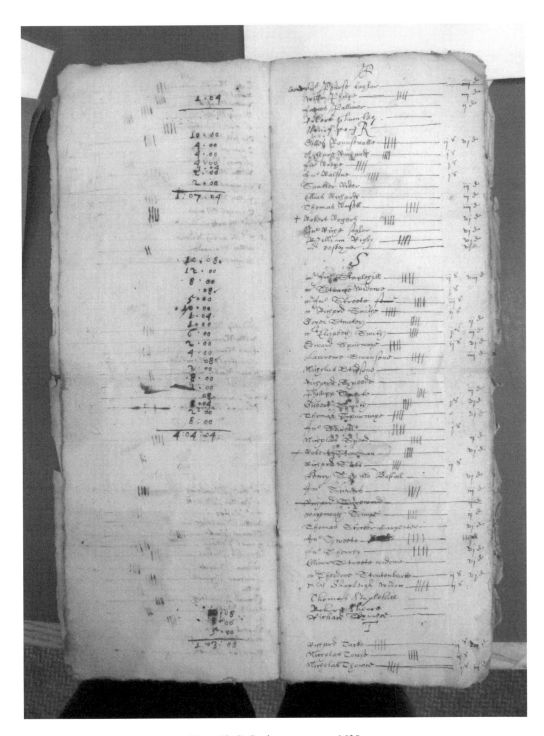

Plate 18. St Saviour poor rate, 1638.

A

Name	Marks	Amount	Name	Marks	Amount
Thomas Axford	IIII	0 10d x	Walter Austine	III	0 4d
George Axford	IIII	2s	Joan Adams	IIII	1s 6d
William Ashbay	IIII	0 6d	Thomas Adams	IIII	4d
Christopher Adams	II	4d	Marie Archer	IIII	0 8d
John Amerideth	IIII	3s			

B

Name	Marks	Amount	Name	Marks	Amount
Thomas Burges	IIII	1s 00	John Bounsey	IIII	1s 6d x
Henry Boones widow	IIII	0 8d	Daniel Boone		4d
Edward Brecard	IIII	0 8d	John Bauden Junior	IIII	1s 6d x
Lawrence Brock	IIII	0 10d	William Booth	II	1s 00
+Michael Barter		0 4d	William Barnes	IIII	3s 00
Walter Bierd	IIII	2s	x William Branfeild		~~4d~~
Rebecca Beard	IIII	1s	Robert Bockland	IIII	6d x
Richard Bowden	IIII	8d	Richard Dayley *otherwise* Parker	III	8d
Tristram Bennett		3d	Henry Beard x		6d x
+Robert Blackler	IIII	1s 6d	John Bowdon Tayler	IIII	3d
William Bauden	IIII	1s	Christopher Beare	IIII	1s 6d
Richard Bauden X		~~3d~~	x Paul Breen		~~x 1s 00~~
Simon Bobeney	III	8d			

[page 2]

B

Name	Marks	Amount	Name	Marks	Amount
William Baddiford	IIII	1s 8d	John Baker bookebinder	IIII	6d
John Barter	IIIII	2d	John Barnes	IIII	1s 6d
William Bickford	IIII	6d	Thomas Boone	III	10d
Alexander Barret	IIII	2d	Leonard Baylie Cuttler		[blank]
Richard Browne	IIII	4d			

C

Name	Marks	Amount	Name	Marks	Amount
George Cade	IIII	1s 6d	Andrew Cole smith	IIII	4d
William Carie	IIII	2s	Thomas Coldich	IIII	1s 8d
Amy Collings		4d	Joseph Cubite	IIII	2s ~~6d~~
Widowe Couch	II	x 4d	x James Cole		[blank]
John Collings	IIII	1s 8d	x Edward Cutt	IIII	x 0 6d
James Cole Smith	IIII	3d	William Clarke Baker	IIII	
Edmond Chade	IIII	1s 4d	Robert Chappell	IIII	4d
Walter Cole smith	IIII	4d	Edward Cocksall	IIII	8d
x Richard Cutte	IIII	1s	Andrew Cornishe house carpenter	IIII	4d
John Calley	IIII	2s	Samuel Chapeltin Sopemaker	III	1s
Mr John Cole	IIII	2s			

D

Name	Marks	Amount	Name	Marks	Amount
John Dottin		1s	Thomas Dier *otherwise* Picher	IIII	6d
Anthony Dinent	IIII	6d	William Dunning	IIII	6d
John Dunning Capp'	IIII	6d	Thomas Drake		[blank]
John Drake	II	6d	~~Jn~~ Richd Deaver	IIII	6d
Elias Drew	IIIII	3d	George Diggins	I	6d
William Drew	IIII	2d			

E

Jn Elliote	||||	2s	James Elliote		[blank]
Edward Elliote	||||	1s	Edward Evens	||||	6d
Ephraim Escote	||||	6d			

[page 3]

E

Henry Ellicote		6d	x Jn Emersone x		~~9d~~
Thomas Elkings	||||	2s	Nicholas Ellitt Shooemaker		

F

Mr Lewis Forteskewe	||||	1s 6d	John Frances	||||	6d
x John Frinde dead		~~2s~~	Joan Forteskew	||||	9d
Mr John Follett	||||	2s 6d	Richard Follett Junior	||||	9d
Hugh Fauns	||||	1s	absent Christopher Flowers cupp		~~4d~~
Mr Richard Follett	||||	4d	John Frye the painter	|||	4d
John Fosterd	||||	4d	Richard Forward Bookebinder	||||	6d
Robert Follett Junior	||||	1s 6d	William Franklin	||	1s
Grace Flute	||||	4d			

G

Mrs Grace Gourney	||||	1s 8d	Robert Greenswoode	||||	1s 00
James Godredge	||||	1s	x James Goodridge Junior x		2d
Catherine Goodredge widowe	||||	3d	x ~~Henry Godfrye~~		~~2d~~
Andrew Glanfeild	||||	4d			

H

Mr John Holligrove	||||	3s 6d	John Hodge	||||	9d
Nicholas Hand	||||	2s	Robert Harris	||	1s
Nicholas Hine	||||	8d	Edmund Horswell	||||	1s
x ~~Andrew Harwoode~~		~~3d~~	Thomas Hingston	||||	6d
Richard Hullit		3d	x ~~Arthur Harradon x~~		~~2d~~
Mr Mark Hawkings	||||	4s	John Hand	||||	6d
John Holman		1s	Thomas Hawkings	||||	3d
John Hernaman	||||	2d	Thomas Huchings Joyner	||||	3d
Stephine Heedeth	||||	9d			

[page 4]

H

George Hockey		0 3d	Elizabeth Hawkes	||||	6d
Ralph Harrie	||||	3d	[blank] huette		
Turkey ~~William husband~~		~~2d~~			

J

½ + William Irishe	||||	6d	Nicholas James		3d
John Irishe	||||	2s 4d	John Jacksone	||||	3d
Richard Jagoe	||	1s	[illegible crossed through]		
Walter Jagoe	||||	2s	Thomas Jagoe	||	6d

K

Edward Kingman	||||	1s 6d	~~William Kents Junior~~		~~1s 6d~~
Abraham Kellye	||||	8d	Benjamin Knowles		1s

Robert Kingeman	|||	8d	Widowe Knowlinge		6d
John Kent	||||	2s	George Kenicote	||||	1s
Robert Knowles		6d	Edward Kingman Junior		3d
~~Hugh Knowles~~		~~3d~~	Margery Kentt widdow	||||	1s 6d
Joseph Knowles	||||	1s 6d			

L

~~Mr Richard~~ Sarah Lumleys widow	||||	2s			
Mr Tristram Lane	||||	3s 6d	John Lane	||||	1s 6d
Phillip Limbery	||||	2s ~~6d~~	~~Hen~~ widowe Longe	||||	0 3d +
Margeret Lepreye		4d	Mr Thomas Leighe	||||	2s 6d
John Lambe	||||	1s	+ Thomas Lines	||||	3d
Henry Lumley	||||	1s 8d +	+ Jn Lapthorne	||||	2d
John Lomer	||||	1s 8d	Mrs Loveringe widow	||||	2s 6d
Thomas Lidstone	||||	1s 8d +	John Laye	||||	3d
William Lewes	||||	9d +	~~Richard Layght~~		~~2d~~

[page 5]

M

Toby Martin	||||	1s 8d	William More	||||	4d
Robert Maine	||||	1s	x ~~George Miller~~		~~3d~~
Walter Manfeild	||||	1s 6d	William Maber	||||	3d
Mary Mills	||||	6d	Thomas Moane	||||	2d
Mr John Martin	||||	1s 6d	x John Marks dead		
The salt Mills	||||	4s	x Mrs Martin Widowe		
~~Thomas Maye~~		~~4d~~	William Marroode	||	4d
Henry Milcome	||||	4d	Michael Martin		6d

N

Phillip Norton	||||	2s 6d	Joan Norber widow	||	6d
William Norman		~~6d~~	Charles Narracott		2d
Ewen Norman	||||	9d	x John Laramore		
Christopher Newland		3d	Thomas Newcomen			2s

O

Henry Oldinge	||||	6d	

P

+Mr John Plumleigh	||||	1s 3d	Lawrence Peperell	||||	4d
Mr William Pettett			1s 6d	William Paynd	||||	4d
John Pascoe	||||	1s 6d	Edmund Plumleigh	|||||	1s 6d
Willliam Plumleigh		2d	James Picke	|||	4d
Thomas Pocke	||||	1s	John Perren	||||	4d
x James Pelliton	||||	6d	x Vincent Pecke		
Charles Persons	||||	1s	Miles Pile	|||||	2s
Widowe Philpote	||||	4d	Nicholas Porcke x		4d

[page 6]

R

ded John Pearse taylor		~~4d~~	Robert Plumley	
William Philpe	||||	4d	Henry Penny	
James Pallimer		2d		

R

Gilles Rounsevalle	||||	2s 6d	Thomas Rusell	||||	4d
Arthur Richards	||||	1s	+ Robert Rogers	||||	6d
John Roope	||||	1s	John Riche saylor		6d
John Ralsone	||||	1s	William Rigby	||||	6d
Sankler Rider		3d	Mrs Reskeymer		6d
Ellias Richards		3d			

S

Mr John Staplehill	||||	2s 8d	x Robert Stoneman	||||	6d
Mrs Strawe Widowe		1s	Richard Saks	|||	2s
Mr John Streete ~~senior~~	||||	3s	Henry Sop *otherwise* Bascell		6d
Mr Richard Smithe	||||	2s	John Simmes	||||	3d
Gawen Stawkey	||||	2d	~~Richard Sayeward~~		~~2d~~
Mrs Elizabeth Smith	||||	1s 3d	Wayemouth Simmes	||||	2d
Edward Spurwaye	||||	2s 6d	Thomas Stocker Carpenter		6d
Lawrence Swansone	||||	4d	John Sweete [illegible crossed through]	||||	4d
Nicholas Stidsone			John Sherrey	||||	6d
Richard Speede			Eleanor Streete widowe		6d
Phillip Sparke	||||	3d	Mr Theodore Stoutenbacke		2s 6d
Gilbert Smith	||||	1s 6d	Mrs Shapeligh widow	||||	2s
Thomas Spurwaye	||||	0 6d	Thomas Staplehill		
John Sarell	||||	1s	Richard Sheare		
Nicholas Speed	||	2d	Richard Skynnere		

T

Richard Tacke	||||	2s 8d	Nicholas Thorne	||||	1s 3d
Nicholas Towse	||||	2s			

[page 7]

T

Robert Turpin	||||	2s 8d	turkey ~~Robert Thomas~~		~~3d~~
William Trenicke	||||	4d	~~George Tayler Cupp~~		~~3d~~
Michael Trigs	||||	3d	William Tapper Tayler	||||	8d
Robert Templman	||	3d	Walter Trenicke tayler	||||	4d
+ James Toucker	||||	6d	Anne Tapley widow	||||	1s

V

Phillip Voyzey	||||	2d	William Vensen	||||	4d
+ Richard Voyzey	||||	6d			

W

Christopher Woode	||||	1s 4d	Peter Wills	||||	8d
Benedict Watts	||||	1s	Edward Wright	||||	4d
Richard Wakehame	||||	6d	Peter Woodye	||||	3d
Robert Woode	||||	2s 6d	Christopher Wheeler	||||	1s 3d
Mary Wayemouth	||||	6d	x Peter Welber		2d
John Walter	||||	2s	Benedict Whiterowe	||||	2s
Lawrence Wheeler	||||	2s 8d	x Richard Wadland lives not in this towne		4d
Thomas Wilson dead			John Woode	||||	3d
William Wotton	||||	1s 6d	David Weeks	||||	3d

[signed] Jn Bodley Maior   Tho: Spurwaie

[page 8]

We are to Receive of Mr Tockerman of Corneworthye twentye shillings at Christide next, given to the poore by Jn Peter Esq.

Rec. in wth his booke the 7th day of June 1638 som of £03 18s 02d

Whereof paid the Widdow cockwell in her sicknes 00 01 00

Resteth 3 17 02

9ber the 10th 1638 rec of Mr Jn Budleigh moneyes that was Resting in his hands for the pooer is 0 07 06

Overseers 1638 Mr Robert Follett Mr Andrew Langdon Mr Jn Holligrove Mr Richard Tacke Mr Edward Spurway Church Warden

Collectors   Mr Richard Sickes Mr Walter Jago

Waywardens   Edward Elliott Edmund Huswill

[page 9]

~~A nott of the Re~~

1638 A weekly Allowance for the Releafe of the Poore of St Saviours whose names are here subscribed

Nicholas Roberts Widdow	1s 00d	Widdow Mingoe	0 8d
Joan Hayward widdow	8d	Joan Pretter	0 6d
Persie Rowland	0 8d	Basses wiffe for on of Collivers Children 1s 6d	1s 6d
Dorothy Crase	0 6d		
Joan Nicholls widdow	0 6d	Burgesses wiffe for on of Collivers Children	
~~Ellinor Roads widdow~~	0 6d		1s 5d
Ann Parker widdow	1s	Jn Whittins wiffe	0 6d
Widdow Beare	1s	Ebbett hannaper	0 4d
Widdow Lane	0 8d	Christian Colsworthe widdow for her three	
Tamsin Tremills		Children	1s
Widdow Duke	1s	Jaen David	0 6d
Jullii 4th Widdow Mark	1 8d	Alice wilkins	0 4d

the 27th 10ber on of these Children was taken away & is to have but 15d *each* week

John Rowe for keeping two of John Collins his Children	2s	Ann hatch for her three Children	1s
		Edward Clement Sailor	0 4d
Elizabeth Row widdow	0 6d	Joan Gearie widdow	0 4d
Ann Camp for her Child	0 8d	Elizabeth Webber	0 6d
Elizabeth Tremills	0 6d		

Elizabeth Coming of Tottnes for keeping on of Abraham streets Children at 1s 3d *by the* week paid monethly 1s 3d

[page 10]

A noat of the names of the overseers Churchwarden Collecteers and waie wardens chosen the 19th of Aprill 1639, According to the statute etc

Mr Pascoe Jagoe, John Follett, Mr Wm Cadreye, Mr Wm Barnes,   Overseers

Mr Lawrence Wheller, Churche warden

Mr Benedict Whiterewe, Thomas Listonce Collectors

Nicholas Hande, Jn Collines way wardenes

[page 14]

Rec of the Maistratts £05 14s 00d

A   01 17 00

B   04 13 08

C	03 19 04
D	00 17 02
E	01 04 00
F	02 04 00
G	00 17 00
H	03 02 08
I	01 03 04
K	01 14 08
L	04 06 08
M	02 04 04
N	00 16 00
O	00 02 00
P	01 16 02
R	01 07 04
S	04 04 04
T	02 07 05
V	00 03 04
W	03 08 00
[total]	48 02 05

82. **Dartmouth** (St Saviour), Poor Rate, 1649

DHC, DD62747

Note: Seven pieces of paper, mostly 6 inches in width and 15 inches in length, were stitched together with white thread to make up a book.

A Rate for the releife of the poore of the Parish of St Saviours, and is to be paide quarterly from the 25th of March to the 24th of June 1649

Mr	John Staplehill Maior	||||	5s	Mr	Lawrence Wheeler	||||	6s
Mr	William Barnes	||||	6s	Mr	John Holygrove	||||	5s 6d
Mr	Andrew Voysey	||||	5s 6d	Mr	Tristram Lane	||||	4s
Mr	Alexander Staplehill	||||	5s 6d	Mr	Walter Jagoe	||||	5s
Mr	John Budley	||||	5s	[total] £2 7s 6d			

A

James Allward	||||	3s 6d	John Austine	||||	4d
William Ashby	||||	2d	John Adames Taylor	||||	8d
Widdow Addames		[blank]	John Adames Barber	||||	8d
John Amerideth	||||	2s 8d	Thomas Axford	||||	4d
George Axford	||||	nott able 8d	[total]		8[s] 6[d]

B

Mrs Grace Beare widow	||||	1s 3d	James Brockadon	||||	3d
not able Thomas Burgis	||||	not able to	Thomas Blackaller	||||	8d
pay to much		8d	Mr John Barnes |||| left the last yeare to pay		
Lawrence Brocke	||||	not able 3d	10s Reced.		3s
Walter Byrd	||||	2s 3d	John Bowdon	||||	4d
William Bawden	||||	10d	John Baker	||||	6d
Mary Bounser *widow*	||||	1s	John Boone	||||	1s
Henry Byrd	||||	1s 4d	Robert Bake	||||	1s
Matthew Bonefeild gone	||	6d	Richard Browne	||||	4d

	Thomas Browne not able ‖‖		2d	[total] [torn]		16 7
Mr	Thomas Bulley	‖‖‖	1s			£3 12s 7d
	William Bickeford	‖‖‖	3d			

[page 2]

C

Mr	George Cade	‖‖‖	8d	James Cole	‖‖‖		4d
	Widdow Coale	‖‖‖	3d	Tristram Couch	‖‖‖		3d
	John Cawley	‖‖‖	4s	William Carey	‖‖‖		2s
	Andrew Cole	‖‖‖	3d	John Cape	‖‖‖		4d
Mr	Joseph Cubitt	‖‖‖	4s	Andrew Cornish	‖‖‖		3d
	Widdow Clarke	‖‖‖	1s	Keeps an ould tenement Milcombe			
	Edward Coxall	‖‖‖	1s 4d	Not able John Collings			6d
	Nicholas Coulton	‖‖‖	6d	Widdow Carpenter			[blank]
	Edmund Courtis	‖‖‖	6d	~~Thomas~~ Robert Carey	‖‖‖		6d
Mr	Henry Crue	‖‖‖	2s 6d	John Cole	‖‖‖		4d
	John Cutt	‖‖‖	6d	[total]			1 1 9
	John Coombe	‖‖‖	1s 8d	[added] John Cole Junior [blank]			

D

Anthony Dymond		[blank]	George Diggons	‖‖‖	2s 9d
John Dottyn junior	‖‖‖	1s	Thomas Dyers	ded	4d
William Dunninge	‖‖‖	10d	[total]		5 8
John Dottyn Senior	‖‖‖	9d			

E

Abel Ekines	‖‖‖	2s	Walter Ellyott	gone	6d
John Elliott		9d	John Elmes ~~Carpenter~~	‖‖‖	4d
Edward Evens	‖‖‖	4d			7 0
Nicholas Ellyott	‖‖‖	1s 3d			1 14 5
James Ellyott		[blank]	[added] Richard English	[blank]	
William Evens		2d			3 12 7
Edward Elliott	‖‖‖	1s 8d			5 7 0

[page 3]

F

Mr	John Follett	‖‖‖	5s	Katherine Fursman		[blank]
Mr	Richard Follett Widdow	‖‖‖	4d	Richard Forward	‖‖‖	1s 6d
	John Fosterd	‖‖‖	4d	Widdow Franklyn	‖‖‖	4d
Mrs	Grace Flute	‖‖‖	4d	[total]		10 8
	Joan Foscoe widow	‖‖‖	6d	~~Mrs Fontaine~~		~~1s 6d~~
	Edward Follett	‖‖‖	2s 4d			

G

Robert Greenswood	recd 5d	1s 6d	James Golsworthy	dead ‖‖	6d
Katherin Goodridge	‖‖‖	3d	John Gould	‖	4d
Edward Gribble	‖‖‖	6d	[total]		5 4
Mrs Grace Gourney widow	‖‖‖	1s 3d			

H

Mr	Mark Hawkings		2s	Stephen Hepditch	‖‖‖	6d
	Nicholas Hande		9d	Edmund Horswell	‖‖‖	1s 4d

Thomas Hyngstone Senior ||||	6d	not able John Hodge mr		[blank]
John Hande ||||	4d	Widdow Holeman		3d
John Hatch lives in torr |||	3d	John Hayman	||||	3d
John Hoyle ||||	2s	Thomas Huckmore	||||	6d
Thomas Harney ||||	4d	[total]		9 6

J

Richard Jagoe	1s	Richard Johnsonne	||||	3d
Thomas Jagoe ||||	1s 8d	[total]		2 11

K

Mr George Kynnecott ||||	3s	Walter Knight	||||	4d
Stephen Knowlinge ||||	2s	[total]		6 5
Thomas Knight ||||	3d			1 14 10
Robert Knowles ||||	3d			7 0
Jacob Kerswell ||||	3d			£7 1s 10d
Robert Kingdonn ||||	4d			

[page 3 dorse]

Distrained
from Richard Lumley one kittle
from Robert Greenswood a quarter of mutton
from Widdow Philpott one beam for scales

[page 4]

L

Mr Thomas Leigh	2s 6d	William Lynes		4s
William Lee ||||	2s	Andrew Lee	||||	6d
Mrs Lambe *widow* ||||	2s 4d	William Lambe		[blank]
Henry Lumley ||||	6d	+ ~~Thomas Lee~~		[blank]
John Lomer ||||	1s 9d	Richard Lecey		3d
Thomas Lydstone ||||	2s 2d	William Lawrence		[blank]
[M]r Richard Lumley	2s 3d	Mrs Lymberry	||||	3d
Mrs Blanch Langdon ||||	1s 10d	[total]		16 1
Mrs Samuel Lomer	4d			

M

Robert Mathew ||||	9d	The Salt Mills	||||	6s
William Malborough || dead	6d	[M]r John Malborough	||||	1s 6d
Tobias Martyn ||||	3d	Edward Manninge	||||	8d
Robert Mayne ||||	1s 8d	[illegible crossed through]		[blank]
~~Tobias Martyn~~	[blank]	[M]r Ambrose Mudd	||||	1s 9d
Walter Manfeild ||||	10d	Edward Masters	||||	1s 6d
Mary Mills widow ||||	4d	[total]		15 10
Mrs Martyn widow ||||	6d	[added] Thomas Mayd		[blank]

N

Katherine Norton ||||	2s	[M]r John Norman	1s
Mr Thomas Newcomen ||||	4s 6d	[total]	8 4d
Even Norman ||||	4d	[added] John Newte weaver	[blank]
Thomas Nicholes	6d		

O

Henry Oldinge	||||	9d	[total]			9

P

Oliver Peirce	||||	3d	Widdow Phillpott	||||	2d
~~John Pasmore~~		[blank]	Miles Pyles	||||	1s 8d
Thomas Porke	||||	6d	Widdow Philpe	|	4d
Charles Parsons	||||	6d	[total]		5 5
Edmund Plumleigh	||||	2s			6 10

[page 5]

P

Widdow Pelliton	not able	2d	Henry Poolyn	||||	3d
Anthony Plumleigh	||||	1s 6d	Widdow Pattenden		[blank]
William Payne	||||	3d	Thomas Porke Junior	||||	3d
Robert Plumleigh	||||	1s	Joseph Porke	||||	3d
John Perriton	||||	3d	+ Henry Poyle		[blank]
+ Matthew Penny		[blank]	Thomas Pitcher	||||	10d
William Prout	||||	2d	Henry Punchion	||||	6d
Phillip Pearce	||||	2d	[total]		5 7

R

Nicholas Roope Esq.		1s 8d	Robert Rogers		2d
John Rounsevall	||||	2s 6d	Walter Roads		3d
Widdow Roulestonne	||||	3d	John Reeve	|	9d
William Rigby	||||	4d	[total]		6 1
Robert Rodes	||||	1d	[added] John Randall		[blank]

S

	Joyce Sanders	||||	4d		Mrs Straw widow	||||	6d
	William Streete for his houses	||||	1s 6d	Mr	John Staplehill junior		1s
Mrs	Eliz. Smyth widow	dead	1s 3d	Mr	Richard Salte	||||	3s 6d
Mr	Edward Spurwaie	||||	4s		Jeromy Stone	||||	2s 4d
	John Skinner	||||	6d		Samuel Shaldon	||	6d
	Phillip Sparke	||||	2d		+ Edmund Searle	||||	[blank]
	Elizabeth Smyth widow	|||	6d		Thomas Sharpeham	||||	2d
	Robert Stoneman	||||	6d		Michael Sanders	||||	3d
	Andrew Sanders	||||	3d		Servanton Shinner	||||	6d
	Thomasine Siks widow	||||	2s		[total]		1 1 9
	Walter Siks	||||	2s				

T

	Elizabeth Tacke	||||	6d	Mr	William Taylor apothecary	||||	1s 6d
	+ Widdow Thorne		[blank]	Groat	Joseph Tooker	||||	4d
	Ann Tapley *widow*	||||	1s 6d		Nicholas Taylor	||||	3d
	~~William Trenycke~~		[blank]		[total]		10 0
Mr	John Terry	||||	3s 6d				2 03 3
Mrs	Tracy widow	||||	8d				9 08 8
	~~Nicholas Treworthy~~	||	1s 9d				£11 11s 11d

[page 6]

W

	Benedict Watts	||||	6d		Obadiah Widger	||||	9d
	Nicholas Watts	||||	6d	Mr	Christopher Wheeler	||||	2s
Mr	Robert Wood	||||	3s 6d		William Wotton		4d
	Mary Waymouth	||||	2d		William Woodmasone		[blank]
Mr	John Walter	||||	2s				[total] 10 11
	Henry Wills	||||	8d				11 11 11
	Phillip Wallys	||||	2d				£12 2s 10d
	Corram Williams	||||	4d				

[signed] Law: Wheeler John Terrye Walter Manfield [overseers]
Stephen Knowlinge, Church warden
Jo: Staplehill Mayor   Will: Barnes

[page 7]

You are to receave of Mr Hugh Hody of Cornworthy Twenty shillings at Christide next being formerly paid by Mrs Joan Tookerman, and now his wife; being given to the poore of St Saviours by John Peters Esquire and is 20s.
February 3d 1649 [1650] Recevde of Mr Huddy 20 shillings
you are to receive of Nicholas Pimble Fowre pound p *year* the first halfe yeare wilbe due the 29th of September 1649
Overseers for the poore this year following chosen the 26th day of March 1649
Mr Lawrence Wheeler, Mr Richard Salte, Mr John Terrie, Walter Manfilde overseers
Mr Stephen Knowling Churchwarden
Walter Sicke, Robert Bake Collectors
John Combe, Walter Ellett Waywardens

Recede of William Trinick for Elizabeth White the summe of five shillings which was due the 24th of June 1649
Recede of William Malborough For Elizabeth White the summe of Five shillings which was due the 24th of June 1649
Recede of Mr Edward Spurway January the 9th [1650] 10 shillings & 4d which was due to the poore upon account from him

[page 8]

What the Poore of St Saviours are to have weekely

Elizabeth Collens	£00 00s 06d	Elizabeth Kingman	00 00 08
Joan Clements for a childe	00 01 06	Tobias Weaver	00 00 06
Marian Yeo	00 00 10	Tomsin Barrett	00 00 08
Widow Duke	00 01 00	Anne Narowcot	00 00 04
Elizabeth White	00 01 00	dead Joan Browne	00 00 04
Anne Duninge	00 00 06	out Jane Beare	00 00 04
Margaret Luscombe	00 00 08	Eliz. Ingram	00 00 06
Katherine Goffe	00 00 08	Widow Chade	00 00 08
Katherine Follett	00 00 08	Widow Reason	00 00 06
Margaret Lapthorne	00 00 10	Richard Lock	00 00 06
Jullian Jackman		Walter Leach	00 00 04
Anne Parker	00 00 06	Joan Wakely for Haritons Children	00 00 06
Christian Cole	00 00 04	Daniel Boone	00 00 02
Chest. Hine	00 00 09	dead Widow Dever	00 00 08

Widow Boaden for the keeping her sisters
child, the mother drowned   00 01 00
~~Widow Jullian Barrens & Children~~   ~~00 00 06~~
~~Widow Eliz. Kingdons Children~~
Julian Jackman   00 00 06

~~William Mathew~~   ~~00 00 06~~
~~William Shorland's children~~
[illegible crossed through]
~~Joan Gall for her keeping a boy~~   ~~00 00 10~~

[page 12]

The twelfe day of aprill 1649 we the Collectors Walter Sikes and Robert Bake land resieved wth this booke for the behafe and use of the poore of the parish of St Saviours in Dartmouth the sum of fower pounds seven shillings and three pence Walter Sicke esquire. Robert Bake

83. DARTMOUTH (St Saviour), Poor Rate, 1649

DHC, DD62750

Note: This rate was written on one piece of paper, measuring 13½ inches in width by 16½ inches in length, which has been folded to provide four pages. An enclosure noted expenditure. The rate shows that a considerable sum was raised nearly every Sunday from the parishioners. This was additional to the quarterly rate paid by the wealthiest of the parish.

An account of what monyes hath been collected in the Church of St Saviours by the Churchwarden & overseers of the poore of the said parrish this year 1649

Aprill	29th	This Day was Collected	£00 12s 0d
May	6th	This Dayes Collection was	00 10 10
	13th	This Dayes Collection was	00 12 1
	19th	Rece. of Xtopher Wheller with the booke	00 11 10 ½

Rece. of Mr John Staplehill then Mayor of Dartmouth & afterward pd by his order unto John Rastall   13[s] 7[d]

	20th	This Daye was Collected	00 09 2
	27th	This Dayes Collection was	00 03 2
June	3th	This Daye was Collected	00 08 6 ½
	10th	This Dayes Collection was	00 08 11 ½
	17th	This Daye was Collected	00 09 9
	24th	This Dayes Collection was	00 10 10
July	8th	This Daye was Collected	00 12 7
	15th	This Daye was Collected	00 10 0
	22th	This Dayes Collection was	00 10 0 ½
	29th	This Daye was Collected	00 07 7
August	5th	This Dayes Collection was	00 09 6
	12th	This Daye was no Collection for our poore	
	19th	This Daye was Collected	00 09 8
	26th	This Dayes Collection	00 09 3
7ber	2th	This Dayes Collection	00 08 3
	9th	This Dayes Collection	00 11 6
	16th	This Daye was Collected	00 08 6
	23th	This Dayes Collection was	00 11 0
	30th	This Daye was Collected	00 09 6
8ber [October]			
7th		This Daye was no Collection for our poore	
	14th	This Dayes Collection was	00 08 9
	21th	This Daye was Collected	00 08 0

	28th	This Dayes Collection was	00 08 8
9ber [November]			
	4th	This Daye was Collected	00 09 8
	11th	This Dayes Collection was	00 08 10 ½
	18th	This Daye was Collected	00 04 11
	25th	This Dayes Collection was	00 09 9
10ber [December]			
	2th	This Daye was Collected	00 13 7
	9th	This Dayes Collection was	00 11 0
	16th	This Daye was Collected	00 07 0
	23th	This Daye was no Colleciton for our poore	
	30th	This Dayes Collection was	00 10 10
January	6th	This Daye was Collected	00 13 0 ½
	13th	This Dayes Collection was	00 11 7
	20th	This Daye was Collected	00 10 7
	27th	This Dayes Collection was	00 11 10 ½
February	3th	This Dayes was Collected	00 12 0
	10th	This Dayes Collection was	00 09 10 ½
	17th	This Daye was Collected	00 07 4
	24th	This Dayes Collection was	00 08 2
March	3th	This Dayes Collection was	00 11 0
	10th	This Daye was no Collection for our poore	
	17th	This Dayes Collection was	00 09 0
	24th	This Daye was Collected	00 12 0
1650	31th	This Dayes Collection was	00 06 5
	7th	This Daye was Collected	00 06 6
	14th	This Dayes Collection was	00 17 0
	21th	This Daye was Collected	00 07 5
	28th	This Dayes Collection was	00 07 6

January Reced of the Worshipful Mr Walter Jago Mayor the some of £10 being for the use of the
poore I say   10 00 0
[total]   35 06 11
[signed] John Terrye

Disbursments of the monye Collected one the other syde

April	27th	Item gave to Margery Richards	00 00 6
		to Larrence Swanson	00 00 6
May	4th	To Joan Walle for Hoskings boye	00 01 0
		To the Widdow Deever	00 00 6
	11th	for a sut of Clothes a shirt a pare of stockings and a pare of shooes for wykings boy	00 14 0
		pd for making this boyes indentures	00 02 0
	12th	gave to goodman Millman	00 01 0
	16th	To Elizabeth Bawdon	00 01 0
		pd for making a pare of Indentures for John Davis	00 02 0
	19th	pd Mr John Staplehill then mayor the balance of his account which he laid out for the poore being	00 03 2
	30th	gave to Henry Milcombe	00 00 4
June	3th	gave to Thomasin Brunton	00 00 6
	11th	gave to Margery Blundy	00 00 2
	20th	Distributed to the poore	00 01 8

	28th	pd for a Smock for the widdow Deever	00 03 2
July	20th	gave to the widdow Narrocott	00 01 0
August	9th	pd for a lyne a lead & hooks for Marryan Yeos boye	00 01 6
	13th	gave to Jane Beere her daughter being sick	00 00 6
	15th	gave to the Widdow Deever	00 01 0
		gave to the Widdow Skynner	00 01 0
	16th	gave to Jane Beere	00 00 6
	24th	gave to Phillip Voyse	00 00 6
	25th	gave to Jane Beere	00 00 6
	30th	gave to Phillip Voyse	00 00 6

7ber [September]

	7th	pd to John Rastell by order of Mr John Staplehill	00 13 7
	8th	pd to one to tend William Shutlands Wife	00 00 6
		pd for making of her grave	00 00 6
	10th	pd for making a grave for Jane Beeres daughter	00 00 6
	24th	gave to the Widdow harracott	00 00 9
		pd Lapthorne for Crying of Paskowes howse	00 00 4

8 ber [October]

	29th	gave to Kattherne Evall	00 01 6

9ber [November]

	30th	pd for a Shirt for William Matthews	00 03 8

10ber [December]

	10th	gave to Kattherne Penny her Child being sikk	00 01 0
	12th	gave to Margerett Luscombe	00 00 6

Cannuary [sic]

	2th	gave to the Churchwarden of Tounstall	00 06 8
		gave to the Churchwarden of St Patricks	00 10 0
	8th	pd Dorrothie Philp for healling of Leathery daughter – 06 8	
	10th	pd for toling the bell & making the grave for the Widdow Deever	
			00 00 10

February

	10th	gave to the Widdow Godfrye	00 01 0
		gave to Jane Row	00 00 6
		gave to Anne Parker	00 00 6
	14th	gave to Margaret Luskombe	00 00 4
	20th	gave unto Julian Thomas	00 01 0
March	6th	gave to the Widdow Godfrye	00 01 0
	12th	gave to William Plumleigh	00 00 4
	19th	gave to Joan Browne	00 01 0
	29th	gave to Elizabeth Rowe	00 01 0
Aprill	22th	sent to Lapthornes Daughter	00 01 0
		pd for 28 yds ⅛ of woolen Cloth at 2s 10d p yd	01 19 8
		pd for 12 yard of karsy stockings	01 00 0
		pd for 12 yard of karsy stockings	00 14 0
		for a Smocke for the Widdow Duke	00 03 4
		for a pare of Shooes for William Matthewes	00 03 0

1649

April 30th		pd to Elizabeth Hinckson 53 weeks at 12d p week	02 13 0
		pd to Julian Barnes 53 weeks at 6d p week	01 06 6
		pd to Larrence Swanson 53 weeks at 6d p week	01 06 6
		pd to Margery Richards 39 weeks at 6d p week	00 19 6

	pd to Margery Richards 14 weeks at 12d p week	00 14 0
May 7th	pd to William Matthes 52 weeks at 6d p week	01 06 0
	pd to William Shutland 17 weeks at 6d p week	00 08 6
	pd to William Shutland 35 weeks at 12d p week	01 15 0
	pd to Thomasin Branton 4 weeks at 6d p week	00 02 0
	pd to Thomasin Branton 20 weeks at 12d p week	01 00 0
	pd to Thomasine Branton 28 weeks at 8d p week	00 18 8
	pd to Joan Walle for hoskings boy 7 weeks at 10d	00 05 10
June 4th	pd to Henry Milcombe 48 weeks at 4d p week	00 16 0
	pd to Joan Harper being sikk	00 01 0
	pd to Mr Tristram Lane for Clothing for the poore	
April 29th	as by his Receit appeeres being	05 03 10
1650		
	pd John Ricle for shooes for the poore pnot apeer	02 04 6
	pd Mr Christopher Wheeler for ½ peece of Doulas	02 15 0
	pd for making of Joan Brownes grave	00 00 6

Remaines to balance this account which I do here deliver with this account the somm of

00 14 7

[total]   35 06 7

[signed] John Terry 24 07 6

[attached sheet] December 31th 1649. The Distribution of the Clothing mentioned one the other syde being distributed by the overseers of the Parrish of St Saviour beeing
Item

20 shirts & smocks	5 dubletts
7 Coates for wemen	4 pare of breeches
2 long coates for men	2 do[zen] of Stockings
7 wash coates for wemen	16 pare of Shooes

Distributed
Item

Daniel Boone a long coate	Katherine follett a Coate & Shooes
Lawrence Swanson a Shirte	William Mans Wife a wastCoate
Abraham Kells a Shirte	William Lapthorne a Shirte
Widdow Gefry a Smock	Anne Stone a Smocke
Goodwife Way a Smock	Widdow Goule a Smocke
Mary Speed a Smocke	Thomasine Branton a Coate
Margery Richards a Coate	Soapers boy a Shirte
Widdow Collings a pare of Shooes	Widdow Skynner a Smocke
Joan Row a Smocke	William Lascomb pare of Shooes
Thomas Collever a Shirte	Walter Leach a pare of breeches
William Shutland a pare breeches	Elizabeth Ingrame a Shirte
Widdow Charde a Smocke	Goodwife Devery a little Smocke
Julian Barnes 3 pare of Shooes for her	Widdow Coale awastCoate
children	Joan Browne awastCoat
Widdow Risdon a Smocke	Elizabeth Phillips awastCoat
Julian Jackman a Coate	Margaret Lapthorne wastCoat & Shooes
Toby Wever a dublett	Widdow Band a wastCoate
Richard Locke dublett breeches & stockings	Anne Parker a pare of Stockings
Henry Milcombe a dublett & stockings	Susan Cooke a pare of Shooes
Joan Beere a Smocke	Margaret Beate a pare of Shooes

Cheston Hayne a Coate
John Burges a pare of breeches
Dorothy Lane a pare of Stockings
Joan Millmans boy a pare of Shooes
Margery Reynolds a pare of Stockings
Widdow Jackman a Coate
Elizabeth Hinckson a Coate
[illegible crossed through]
Thomasine Barrett a Smocke
Marian Yeo a Shirte
Lucy Peters a pare of Stockings
Widdow Willson a wastCoate

Elizabeth Streatt a pare of Stockings
Barbara Ingramme a pare of Stockings
Christian Coale a pare of Stockings
Michael Babbidge a Dublett
Grace Bennett a pare of Shooes
Anne Commin a pare of Shooes
Curretton Stavenge a pare of breeches
Richard Nations Wife a pare of Stockings
George SquinterCombe pr of Stockings
Goodow Baddaford a pare of stockings
Anne Stancombe a pare of stockings

84. DARTMOUTH (Townstal), Military Rate, c.1592

DHC, 3799M/3/O/4/50, no page numbers

Note: This rate is recorded in a volume with pages approximately 7¾ inches in width and 12 inches in length.

Townstall

John Roope	2 muskett ps 2 Corslet ps	Richard Shapley	a musket ps
Nicholas Roope	a musket ps 2 Corslet ps	Thomas Plumligh	2 Corslt ps 3 musket ps
Andrew Wotoon	a musket ps a Corslt ps	The parish armour	Corslt ps 2
Nicholas Ball	a musket ps		

85. Dartmouth (Townstal), Poor Rate, 1610

DHC, DD61790

Note. This rate was written on two sheets of paper folded to make pages of 5¾ inches in width by 15½ inches in length. The cover recorded 'Evan Whiller his Writing'.

Tunstall   A Rate for the poore of that pishe made by the Churchwardens and Overseers there according to the forme of a Statute in that behalf for one yeares payment that is from the 25th daye of March last *in the year of our Lord* 1610 Quarterly to levyed and gathered.

+ Sir Thomas Rudgewaye knight for his Tenemt in Townstall ~~6s 8d~~

Mr John Roowpe	||||	12s	Mr Nicholas Ball	||||	4s
Mr Andrew Wootton	||||	20s	Mrs Joan Sayer widowe	||||	4s
Mr Nicholas Roowpe	||||	12s	Mr John Smythe for the furse pareke and Coate		
Mr Richard Shaplye	||||	8s		||||	8d
Mr Humphrey Reynell	||||	4s	Richard Peeke for barons pke and the Rudge		
Mr Robert Holland	||||	8s		||||	3s
Phillip Coake and Thomas Baddyforthe for the grounde they Joynetly holde there	||||	1s 4d	John Ellett for Heaforde and other grounde	||||	2s
Edward Coake for grounde he holdeth there	||||	2s	Henry Bownde for grounde he holdeth	||||1s 4d	
Thomas Wakeham	||||	8d	~~James Searle~~ Mr John Smythe for his pte of		
William Neill for grounde hee holdeth	||||	6d	Milton	||	2s
Mr Gilbert Staplehill for a close of grounde hee holdeth	||||	6d	Humphrey Pryce for his howse and parsons meadowe	||||	8d

Mr Bennett Flute for his meadowe ||||	6d
Mr William Putt for his Tenement ||||	1s 4d
Mr Edward Coake for grounde he holdeth ||||	10d
Humphrey Pryce for his meadowes ||||	16d
Thomas Wakeham ||||	12d
John Hollygrove for Wallfleete mylls ||||	12d
and for his horse Mills	6d
Mrs Agnes Smyth for twoo Cloases ||||	4d
[in margin 'William Shillaber'] Nicholas	
Rytche for [blank] ||||	12d
John Horwell his his house he dwelleth in ||||	[blank]
John Stoyle for Mrs Haymans grounde ||||	1s 8d
Mrs John Plumleigh for the woode ||||	12d
Mr Arthur Wootton for the woode ||||	12d
William Ellett of Tounstall ||||	16d
Maurice Jeffery	6d

John Harrys ||||	16d
John Layton ||||	2s
John Bowser ||||	12d
John Luxe ||||	12d
Augustine Dennys ||||	8d
Ralph Cooke ||||	8d
[in margin 'Edward kerswell'] Thomas Adruscowe ||||	16d
John Hyll the yonger ||||	8d
Richard Lovett ||||	6d
William Bobbeney ||||	6d
John Whittocke ||||	~~6d~~ 8d
John Wheeler ||||	16d
John Walshe ||||	12d
Thomas Jarvys ||||	7d
Phillip Boyes ||||	16d
Nicholas Smythe ||||	12d
William Jackman ||||	12d

[page 2]

George Kelly ||||	8d
Thomas Webber ||||	8d
William Terry |||	16d
Richard Tole ||||	4d
Emanuel Cardye ||||	12d
Clement Pawlmer ||||	8d
John Baggwell ||||	8d
John Lashe the yonger ||||	Reseved 4d 6d
John Creeping ||||	6d
John Chope ||||	16d
Richard Cowsen the yonger ||||	4d
John Omeale ||||	6d
William Symons ~~thelder~~ the yonger ||||	12d
Thomas Peryn ||||	6d
Richard Courtyce ||||	8d
William Wynchester ||||	8d
Christopher Collyper	12d
William Waye ||||	12d
Richard Harvy ||||	6d
William Younge ||||	12d
Thomas Ford plaisterer ||||	4d
William Ellett ||||	12d
Thomas Dicke ||||	8d
John Smythe ||||	4d
James Marche ||||	4d
Roger Mathew ||||	8d
Edward Burgeis ||||	4d
Thomas Woodeforde ||||	7d
Edward Wright ||||	4d
Humphrey Heathman ||||	4d
Richard Davye ||||	4d

['Jo. carter' in margin] Samuel Wylls ||||	4d
Peter Kynge ||||	4d
Walter Androwes ||||	4d
Vincent Davies ||||	6d
Nicholas Norton ||||	8d
Thomas Browne ||||	4d
Gilbert Wrayford ||||	8d
William Wreath ||||	6d
Roger Yeoman ||||	4d
Christopher Bond ||||	4d
Nicholas Skynner ||||	8d
John Cornesh ||||	4d
Walter Tooker ||||	4d
George Cole ||||	8d
Robert Coleman ||||	4d
John Cooke ||||	4d
Henry Mellcombe	6d
Thomas Vyncent ||||	4d
William Vyncent |||	4d
John Baylye	4d
Henry Churchwarde ||||	4d
Andrew Bickley ||||	12d
Jerome Nicholls ||||	6d
John Neale ||||	4d
Hext Eggbeere ||||	4d
The Guyfte of Customer Peter ||||	20s
Alice Horwell widowe ||||	4d
[page 3] Peter Terry ||||	16d
John Bremblecombe ||||	6d
Davy Cowle ||||	4d
Jane Jeffery widowe ||||	8d

[in margin] George Spark

Joan Walshe widow	||||	8d
Agnes Walshe widowe	||||	6d

[in margin 'fleete'] ~~John hollygrove for his~~
~~horsemill~~

Gilbert Rowpe	16d

Overseers Andrew Wotton Nicholas ball
the signe of Clement Pawlmer
Churchwardens
[signed by] Thomas Adrisboll
the signe of William Ellett
Tho: Paydge

George Davys	||||	8d
Andrew gribble	||||	8d
John Gabrick	||||	4d
William Rowe by the Olde Myll	||||	4d
Sum total		£9 1s 6d

86. DARTMOUTH (Townstal), Poor Rate, 1611

DHC, DD61791

Note: This rate is included within the overseers of the poor account. It was written on two pieces of paper, which have been stitched to make up four pages which measure 6 inches by 16 inches. The account includes two pages of expenditure including to Jane Betts, John Galsworthy, 'Irish Katherine', 'the blind boy', Widow Veale, John Deever, Elizabeth Cosen, 'old Mother Maye' and 'old Mother Veale' for a cape, shoes, stockings and cloth.

Tounstall A rate for the Poore of that Parrishe made by the ChurchWardens and Overseers there according to the forme of a Statute in that behalf for one yeares payment That is from the 25th daye of Marche last *in the year of our Lord* 1611 quarterly to be levyed and gathered by Nicholas Skynner and Ralphe Cooke Collectors

Sir Thomas Rudgwaye knight for his tenement in Tounstall 6s 8d

Mr John Roowpe	||||	12s	Humphrey Pryce for his howse and parsons		
Mr Andrew Wootton	||||	20s	meadowe	||||	8d
Mr Nicholas Roowpe	||||	12s	Mr Bennett Flute for his meadowe	||||	6d
Mr Richard Shapleye	||||	8s	Mr William Putt for his tenement	||||	1s 4d
Mr Humphrey Reynell	|	4s	Mr Edward Coake for grounde he holdeth	||||	10d
Mr Robert Hollande	||||	8s	Humphrey Pryce for his meadowes	||||	16d
Phillip Coake and Thomas Baddyforthe for the			Thomas Wakeham	|||| win	1s 12d
grounde they Joinetly holde there	||||	1s 4d	John Hollygrove for Wallfleete mylls and for		
Thomas Wakeham	||||	8d	his horse myls	||||	18d
William Nyell for grounde he holdeth	||||	6d	Mrs Agnes Smythe for twoo Closes	||||	4d
Mr Gilbert Staplehill for a Cloase of grounde			Nicholas Ritche for [blank]	||||	12d
hee holdeth	||||	6d	William Shillaber	||||	8d
Mr Nicholas Ball	||||	4s	John Horwell for [blank]	||||	4d
Mr John Plumley merchant in place of Mrs			John Stoyle for Mrs Haymans grounde	||||	1s 8d
Joan Sayer decessed	||||	4s	Mrs John Plumleigh for Purseforth woode	||||	12d
Mr John Smythe for the fourseparcke and			Mr Andrew Wootton for Purseforth woode		
Coate	||||	8d		||||	12d
Richard Peeke for the barons pke and the			William Ellett of Tounstall	||||	16d
Rudge	||||	3s	John Harrys	||||	16d
John Ellett for Heaford and other grounde	||||	2s	John Layton	||||	2s
Henry Bownde for grounde he holdeth	||||1s	4d	John Bowser	||||	16d
Mr John Smythe for his part of Milton	||	2s	John Luxe	||||	12d

Richard Scover	IIII	8d	Humphrey Heathman	IIII	4d
Ralph Cooke	IIII	8d	Richard Davye	IIII	4d
Thomas Adruscoll	IIII	16d	Samuel Wylls	IIII	4d
John Hill the yonger	IIII	8d	John Carter	IIII	4d
Richard Lovett	IIII	8d	+ Peter Kynge	IIII	4d
William Bobbeney	IIII	6d	Walter Androwes	IIII	4d
John Whittocke	IIII	8d	William Johns	IIII	4d
John Whealer	IIII	12d	Vincent Davyes	IIII	6d
John Walshe	IIII	12d	Nicholas Norton	IIII	8d
Thomas Jarvers	IIII	12d	Thomas Browne	IIII	4d
Phillip Boyes	IIII	16d	Gilbert Wrayford	IIII	8d
Nicholas Smythe	IIII	6d	William Wreathe	IIII	6d
William Jackman	IIII	4d	Roger Yoman	IIII	4d
George Sparke	IIII	12d	Christopher Bonde	IIII	4d
Edward Kerswell shippwright	IIII	6d	Nicholas Skynner	IIII	8d
George Kellye	IIII	8d	John Corney	IIII	4d
Thomas Webber	IIII	8d	Walter Tooker	IIII	4d
William Terry	III	12d	Robert Coleman	IIII	4d
Richard Tole	IIII	4d	John Cooke	IIII	4d
Emanuell Cardye	IIII	8d	Thomas Vyncent	IIII	4d
Clement Pawmer	III	8d	William Vyncent	IIII	4d
[page 2] John Bagwell	IIII	8d	Robert Every	IIII	4d
John Creeping	IIII	4d	Henry Churchward	IIII	4d
John Chope	IIII	16d	Andrew Bickley	IIII	12d
Richard Cosen the yonger	IIII	4d	Jerom Nicholls	IIII	6d
John Omeale	IIII	6d	John Neale	IIII	4d
William Symons the yonger	IIII	12d	Hext Eggbeere	IIII	4d
Thomas Peryn	III	6d	The Guyfte of Customer Peter	IIII	20s
X Richard Courteis	IIII	8d	Peter Terry	IIII	16d
William Wynchester	IIII	8d	John Bremblecombe	IIII	6d
Thomas Beere shippwright	IIII	8d	Davy Cowle	IIII	4d
William Waye	IIII	12d	Jane Jeffery widowe	IIII	8d
Richard Harvye	IIII	6d	~~Joan Walshe wydowe~~		~~6d~~
Edward Johns Shippwright		8d	Agnes Walshe widowe	IIII	6d
James Lowde *otherwise* Farr	IIII	4d	Gilbert Rowpe		16d
William Ellett	IIII	12d	George Davyes	IIII	8d
Thomas Dicke	IIII	8d	Andrew Gribble	IIII	8d
Charles Goode	IIII	4d	John Gabricke	IIII	4d
James Marche	IIII	4d	William Rowe by the Old Myll	IIII	4d
Roger Mathew	IIII	8d	Michael Babidge		4d
Edward Burgeis	IIII	4d	~~Henry Robyns for his tucking mill at Wallfleete 8d~~		
Thomas Woodeforde	IIII	6d	*Sum total* of the receiptes is		£8 18s 2d
Edward Wright	IIII	4d			

[back cover] Overseers for the poore
[signed] Richard Shapley the signe of John Wheler the signe of Phill Boyes

Churchwardens
~~the signe of Phillip Edward Burgeis~~
[signed] Jn Smyth Maior

Receved the sixt daye of Janneare being 1611 of John Welley for monne Due to the pore upon this a Count the somme of 30 shillines and tow Pence

87. Dartmouth (Townstal), Poor Rate, 1617

DHC, DD61942

Note: This rate was written on three pieces of paper which measure 12 inches in width and 16 inches in length which have been folded and stiched with brown thread in order to make up a booklet of twelve pages.

[cover] M[emorandu]m. the Churchwardens now chosen William Ellett John Bagwell
Overseers Christopher Collaper John Hellier
Collectors William Reve John Whittock

[page 1]

Townstall 1617   A Rate for the poore of the parish of Townstall Renewed at Easter 1617 made by William Bogan gent and Clement Pallmer, Churchwardens, and by Humphrey Price and John Saunders overseers of the pore for one yere next insueinge as followeth

First the Lord Ridgewaie for his Tenement	6s 8d	+ Robert Martin for Cowpks Aller meadow Crossepks furspks & Allgars Coate in all	8s
John Roope gent	20s	John Smyth	10s
Andrew Wotton gent	26s 8d	Phillip Coake & Thomas Baddaford for the great Meadow & other grounds thereunto adjoyneinge wth Putts frounds	9s
Nicholas Roope gent	20s		
John Plumleigh Lewis Fortescue and William Nyell Fermers of the Rectory	10s	John Mayne for a moitie of the Cowpk	18d
Richard Shaplye gent	14s	Andrew Voysey	6s
Mr Walter Wilshman vicar ~~there~~	2s	John Holligrove for Mr Haymans ground	3s 4d
William Bogan gent	18s 4d	Johnn Holligrove for Wallfleet mills	18d
George Gale gent for the Barne hoppyard and garden	2s	Humphrey Price for Butt pk & Cowhowse meadow	2s
George Roope gent	4s	Nicholas Hane for the willpke	4d
Nicholas Roope the yonger	4s	James Tremills for Churchpk	6d
Walter Wotton gent	6s 8d	Julian Whyt for ground she holdeth	2s
Peter Cliffe & Roger Oldreeve for parte of great Norton	3s	William Ellett of Townstall	2s
		Roger Narramore	4d
John Neyle for a moitie of the Cowpkes	18d	Toby Martin for a meadow	6d
Edward Coke for vowells meadow Townepk & Riches ground	4s	Elizabeth Lovett widow	12d
		John Hellier the Smith	12d
John Plumleigh gent for Puddefford wood	20d	Thomas Wakeham	16d
William Niell for his meadow	6d	Nicholas Riche	~~16d~~ 12d
Mrs Joan Ball widow	6s 8d	William Shillaber	18d
John Plumleigh senior for Weeke	6s 8d	John Beare	12d
		£10 12s 2d	~~£10 16s 2d~~

[page 2]

John Bowncer	2s	Alice Luxe widow	12d
Joan Waye widoe	8d	John Tabb *otherwise* Dryller	6d
William Johns	4d	William Kennycott	6d
Andrew Beere	4d	Joan Courtis	12d
Simon Pettigue	8d	John Webber	6d

Thomas Browne	2s	William Symons thelder	8d
Richard Scover	12d	Edward Wright	4d
['John Hovet' inserted]	[blank]	Thomas Peryn	6d
Welthian Cooke ~~widow~~	8d	Alexander Withicombe	6d
John Harris	3s	John Wheeler	20d
Peter Terrye	2s	Christopher Collaper	12d
Benjamin Luxe	6d	John Cooke	4d
John Bremblecombe	4d	William Ellett	2s
Robert Yoman	4d	Joseph Bowden	6d
Richard Tole	6d	John Omeale	8d
Vincent Davye	8d	Elizabeth Sperke widow	4d
William Vincent	6d	James Prowte	4d
Humphrey Heathman	6d	Pascoe Mathew	8d
Robert Lydden	4d	John Carter	4d
Peter Bastard	12d	Joan Jarons widow	8d
Daniel Tucker	4d	Owen Ford	4d
John Gibbons	12d	Richard Cosen	6d
John Whittocke	12d	Thomas Woodford	6d
Richard Harvye	8d	[total]	35s 8d

[page 3]

Walter Tocker	4d	Joan Jles widow by the millpark	4s
John Chope	18d	John Neale for the Lord Ridgwaies ground he	
Thomas Dick	12d	holdeth	2s
Thomas Beere	16d	William Terry	12d
Thomas Webber	12d	John Churchward	4d
John Francis	2s	John Osborne	4d
Jane Jeffry widow	8d	Robert Bagwell	4d
Phillip Boyes	16d	William Rowe	4d
William Roberts thelder	4d	Edward Burges	4d
William Roberts yonger	4d	George Davis	2s
Thomas Blackaller	4d	John Saunders Smith	2s
Michael Babidge	4d	Richard Robins the miller	12d
Christopher Band	4d	Anstice Tocker widow	4d
Christopher Dicke	4d	Thomas Tocker her sonne	4d
John Hill thelder	8d	Henry Boone for the hilles	12d
Edward Johnson	4d	The holders of whiteings ground	8d
Charles Good	4d	Daniel Walter	4d
Samuel Wills	4d	John Salter	4d
John Bagwell	18d	Alice Luxe widow togeather wth William	
Gilbert Wreightford	12d	Scorch Thomas Axford & William Mingo for	
Clement Pallmer	2s	the salt mills	3s
The widow Horwell	4d	[total]	33s 10d

[page 4]

Richard Luther	6d	The gifte of John Luscombe of	
William Labere	6d	Stokeffleminge	
John Wolcombe	4d		10s
Stephen Cockrell	4d	~~Sum~~ total	31s 8d
The gifte of Customer Peter	20s		

10 12 02   *Sum* totall truelie exaied & cast £15 13s 4d

1 15 08
1 13 10
1 11 08
15 13 4

[page 5 has notes which were crossed through and rewritten as a fair copy on pages 6–7]

[page 6]

Townstall The Accompt of the Churchwardens & overseers of the pore of Townstall ended the 8ᵗʰ of May 1616

First   They are chardged wth money in stocke of the last yere dd them wth their Booke & is £04 06s 08d

A   wth money due by the Rates of the same yere and is 15 13 04

Sum total £20 00 00

Memorandum That the sd Overseers deld by this Acc. make good 5s 4d in arreages viz.

for Nicholas Roope the yonger 4s

for Thomas Webber 12d

for John Horwell 4d

Sum 5s 4d

[page 7]

p Contr. They Crave allowance of money Distributed by Humphrey Price as by his note pticuleerlie appereth and is £00 09 04

A   of money paid to sundrie poore people in their sicknes and for shrowdes & placeing out poore Children as by the pticulars there of appeereth and is 09 14 08

A   of money not to be recovered of such as are become poore & dead & gone & abated by Consent and is 00 10 04

A   of money Rec for the use of Luscombes gifte wch was distributed by the pishners and is 00 10 00

[total]   11 04 04

So resteth in the handes of the sd Overssers to balance this Acc. 08 15 08

[signed] Tho Paidge maior Will Plumleighe

The stock remaineing is d[elivere]d to the overseers for the next yere in the Guildhalle.

88. DARTMOUTH (Townstal), Poor Rate, 1620

DHC, DD61975

Note: This rate was written on three pieces of paper, which measure 12 inches in width and 16 inches in length, which have been folded and stitched together with green thread to make up a booklet of twelve pages.

Townstall 1620

Churchwardens Nicholas Roope senior John Sannders

Overseers wth the said Churchwardens John Rowe John Whitticke

[page 2]

Townstall ~~1619~~ 1619

A Rate for the Reliefe of the poore of the parish of Townstall renwed at Easter 1619 made & Rated by Nicholas Roope and John Saunders Churchwardens & John Rose and John Whitticke being nominated & appeared Overseers of the poore of the same parishe for the yere to come as followeth

First Lord Rudgeway for Tuckers Bargaine with the howse and appurtenances £00 08s 00d

John Roope gentleman	01 00 00
Andrew Wotton gent	01 00 00
Nicholas Roope senior gent	02 00 00
Mr Lewis Hele Esquier	00 10 00
Mr Anthony Roope Esquier	00 04 00
Mr Walter Welshman Vicar	00 02 00
Mr John Plumleigh Lewis Fortescue and Mr William Niell gentleman for the Rectory	00 10 00

Mr William Bogan gentleman for his howse he now dwelleth in and grownds thereto, wth the Barne, hoppeyards garden and the hills 00 10 00

Mr Richard Shapleigh	00 14 00
George Roope gentleman	00 04 00
Nicholas Roope Junior Gentleman	00 04 00
Walter Wotton gentleman	00 03 06
Peter Cliffe & ~~Walter~~ Roger Olderive for parcell of great Norton	00 03 00
John Neile for pcell of the Cow pke	00 01 06
Edward Coake for west Townstall & Towne pke	00 01 04
Jn Plumleigh gentleman for Puddiforth woode	00 04 02
William Neill gentleman for his Meadowe	00 00 04
Mrs Joan Ball widdow	00 06 08
John Plumleigh Marcht for Weeke	00 06 08
Mr Robert Martin for Crosse pke Allen meadowe wth the lower & the higher Bacons pkes	00 08 00
Mr John Smith for Cowhowse meadowe	00 00 04

Phillip Coake and Thomas Baddaver for the great meadowe and other grownds thereunto adioyninge wth Puttes grownde 00 09 00

Jn Mayne for a moytie of Cow pkes	00 01 06
James Tremills for the Butt pke Church pke & Whiteings meadowe	00 02 00
Nicholas Hand for the Weld pkes and for one other meadow	00 00 06
William Neile gentleman for pcell of West Norton	00 04 00
John Wakeham & Thomas Luscombe for Midledowne pcell of the Bargaine of Norton	00 03 00
John Hellier for Walshes grownde Devonshieres meadowe Whitings meadowe and Ex pke	00 02 10
Wm Eliot for his Coate and grownd	00 02 00
Nicholas Pinwell for Shapleighes meadowe and Mr Wilshman meadowe	00 00 10
John Collins for silver meadowe Custome meadowe and a meadowe at Croterhill	00 00 04
Richard Lather	00 00 08
[total]	09 05 02

[page 3]

William Row	00 00 06	Wm Roberts Junior	00 00 04
John Bagwill	00 01 00	Phillip Boyes	00 01 04
Nicholas Chilston	00 00 04	Jane Jeffery *widow*	00 00 08
Gilbert Wrayforde	00 01 00	Christopher Dicke	00 00 06
William Labbey	00 00 08	Edward Johnsonne	00 00 04
Clement Palmer	00 02 00	John Lashe ~~senior~~ Junior	00 00 04
Richard Palmer	00 00 08	John Fraunces	00 02 00
Alice Horwill *widow*	00 00 04	Richard Cozens	00 00 06
John Hill senior	00 00 08	Thomas Dicke	00 01 00
Thomas Giles	00 00 06	Thomas Beere	00 01 04
Christopher Bande	00 00 04	John Salter	00 00 06
Robert Hollacombe	00 00 04	Charles Woode	00 00 04
William Roberts senior	00 00 00 [sic]	John Choape	00 01 04

James Farr	00 00 04	John Coake	00 00 04
Walter Tucker	00 00 04	Alexander Wythicomb	00 00 06
Samuel Wills	00 00 04	Thomas Perin	00 00 06
Thomas Woddyforde	00 00 06	Christopher Colliver	00 01 00
Owen Forde	00 00 06	John Wheeler	00 01 00
Richard Hill	00 00 06	William Foster	00 00 04
James Proute	00 00 04	Walter Lambe	00 00 04
Edward Wright	00 00 04	William Vincent	00 00 08
~~Edward~~ Margaret Shillaber widow	00 00 06	Richard Harvye	00 00 08
Roger Yeoman	00 00 04	John Whitticke	00 01 00
John Trickey	00 01 00	John Osburne	00 00 04
Elizabeth Sparke *widow*	00 00 04	John Gibbens	00 01 00
Thomas Blackaller	00 00 04	Humphry Heathman	00 00 04
John Omrealle	00 00 08	Robert Lidden	00 00 04
Richard Tole	00 00 06	Peter Pasterd	00 01 00
Thomas Browne	00 01 00	*Sum*	[blank]
Pascoe Mathew	00 00 08		
William Eliot	00 02 00		

[page 4]

Daniel Tucker	00 00 04	John Tabb	00 00 06
John Beere	00 01 00	William Widger	00 00 08
Robert Younge	00 00 04	Joan Courtes *widow*	00 01 00
Robert Everye	00 00 04	John Webber	00 00 06
John Horwill	00 00 04	Richard Scover	00 01 00
John Row	00 02 00	John Hewett	00 00 06
Thomas Wakeham	00 01 04	Stephen Cockwill	00 00 04
Elizabeth Lovett *widow*	00 01 00	John Brimblecomb	00 00 04
Joan Olles *widow*	00 00 04	William Dennis	00 00 04
John Churchyarde	00 00 04	John Harris	00 03 00
James Crippyn	00 00 04	Peter Terrye	00 02 00
Henry Millcombe	00 00 06	Vincent Davies	00 01 00
John Wollcombe	00 00 04	John Saunders	00 02 00
Peter Trevisard	00 00 04	George Davyes	00 02 00
Benjamin Lux	00 00 06	Richard Robins	00 01 00
Nicholas Riche	00 00 06	John Snellinge	00 00 06
John Bownser	00 02 00	Mrs Holligrove for Waflett mills	00 01 06
William Terry	00 01 00	Edward Burgeis	00 00 04
Joan Waye *widow*	00 00 00 [sic]	Richard Reckley	00 00 04
John Waye	00 01 00	William Scotch Thomas Axforde & William	
William Johns	00 00 06	Minge for the salt mills	00 03 00
William Kennicott	00 00 06		

89. DARTMOUTH (Townstal), Poor Rate, 1649

DHC, DD62746

Note: This rate was written in a booklet of five pieces of paper, which measure 6 inches in width and 14½ inches in length, which have been stitched together with brown thread. The binding has obscured some numerals.

A rate made by the Churchwardens and Overseers of the Parish of Tonstall for the releife of the poore of the said parish.

A

| George Aggener | £00 1s 6d | [total] | 1s 6d |

B

-Thomas Boone Esquire	||||	0 10 0	-Francis Barnard		0 2 0
Mr -William Baddeford	||||	0 3 1	-John Bowden	||||	0 0 2
Mr William Baddeford	||||	0 16 6	-Thomas Boone		0 0 9
Mr -John Budley	||||	0 3 3	John Ballimore		0 0 3
-Josephe Bowden	||	0 0 6	Benjamin Ball		0 0 3
-William Bunkard |||| paid [illegible] 0 0 8			Richard Bartter		0 0 6
-John Burgis	||||	0 0 6	-Richard Bourrier	||	0 0 6
-John Bounsers house	||||	0 0 6	[total]		£4 0s 2d
-William Burgan paid a shilling	0 1 3				

C

-Hingstons Coote	||||	0 1 3	-Nicholas Cruse	||||	0 0 9
-Robert Cawley	paid 6d	0 0 7	-Edward Cooke	||	0 0 6
-Richard Cossens	||||	0 1 0	Ambrose Couch	||||	0 0 6
-John Cutt	||||	0 2 0	John Coting	||||	0 0 3
Jane Cooke		[blank]	-Jarvis Chike	||||	0 0 3
-William Cruse	||	0 0 8	William Campin		0 0 3
John Crossman	||||	0 0 [torn]	-Edward Coole	||||	0 0 6
Richard Cumminge		0 0 [torn]	James Colle for his house 0 0 6		
-William Courtis	||	0 0 6	[total]		18s 8d

D

Roger Deereinge	||||	0 1 0	John Dicke	0 0 2
6	Thomas Dicke	0 0 6	[total]	2s

E

-Edward Elliott for his meddow |||| 0 0 4			-Robert Emmett	||||	0 2 6
-Mr Ekines Mills	||||	0 1 6	-Oades Edwardes	||	0 [torn]
Roger Ellyott	||||	0 0 9			

[page 2]

F

Mr -Fortescues ground	||||	0 1 [0]	Mr -Edward Follett for his house||||		0 1 [0]
Mr -Robert Follett for his house	||||	0 1 [0]	-Owen foorde	||||	0 0 [0]

G

-John Gillard	|	0 1 [torn]	-Richard Graye	||||	0 0 9
-Roger Gray [illegible] on shilling	0 1 6		-Robert Grendell	||||	0 0 4
-Edmund Goodridge	||||	0 0 6	[total]		18s 8d
-Andrew Goodyeare	||||	0 0 4			

H

- ~~The holders of Sir John Hawkins his means at~~			Mr -Crispin Hooper	||||	[blank]
~~Weeke~~	||||	0 3 [0]	Mr -Holygroves Mills	||||	0 2 0
[illegible crossed through]		[blank]	-Richard Hellyer	||||	0 1 0

-Edmund Horswell	||||	0 0 6	Jane Quicke	||||	0 0 6
Henry Haries		0 0 3	[total]		£18 2d

-Jane Sparke [illegible crossed through]
            \|\|\|\| 0 0 6

J

-Nicholas Jacksonne	||||	0 0 3	[total]	1s 10
-John Jefferri	||||	0 0 8		

K

-Edward Knowles		0 0 [obscured]	[total]	2s 3d
-John Kinge	||||	0 0 [obscured]		

L

-Richard Lee	||||	0 0 [obscured]	Mrs -Laskey for her house or tennetes	
-Thomas Little	||	0 0 [obscured]		0 2 [obscured]

Mr -Ambrose Lane for his house or tennete
     \|\|\|\| 0 1 [obscured]   Robert Luoo \|\|\|\| 0 0 [obscured]

                                          -Osselay Lux \|\| 0 0 [obscured]

                                          [total]   11s 4d

[page 3]

M

Mrs	-Joan Mathew *widow*	||||	0 10 0	-John Moone	||||	0 1 3
	-The holders of Milton		0 10 0	-Henry Mills	||||	0 0 6
	-Robert Maine	||||	0 2 0	-Edward Masters or his holders		0 1 6
	Nicholas Marwood	||||	0 1 3	-Walter Manfeild		0 0 10
Mr	-John Martyne or his holder	||||	0 8 0	-Phillip Mayne	||||	0 0 6
	-The salt mills	||	0 2 0	-James March paid 6 penies	||||	0 0 9
Mr	-John Martyn of Cockington or holders			-John Martten		0 0 6
		||||	0 1 6	William Maien		0 0 0
	-Whiteings Meddow	||||	0 0 6	[total]		£4 2s 8d
	-Thomas Manfeild	||||	0 0 6			

N

-John Neile	||||	0 6 0	Daniel Naramore	||	0 0 4
-Nicholas Neile	||||	0 2 6	[total]		17s 8d

P

-The heires of Mr John Plumleigh	||||	0 2 0	-Thomas Parnell	||	0 0 6
-John Paige	||||	0 2 6	-Nicholas Pymble	||||	0 1 6
-Mr John Plumleigh	||||	0 3 4	-John Pomeroy	||	0 0 3
-Clement Palmer	||||	0 2 6	-Customer Petteres		1 0 [obscured]
-Richard Perriton	||||	0 0 6	[total]		£3 0s 2d

R

-Nicholas Roope Esqr.	||||	0 11 0	-The Rectory	||||	0 13 4
-John Roope Esqr.	||||	0 16 0	-Thomas Russell	||||	0 1 0
-Henry Robins recevd of Mr Robines 2s			Ralph Raddon	||	0 1 0
more 5s		0 8 6	-John Roodes paid 4 penes	||	0 0 3
Lord Ridgways ground		0 0 6	[total]		£4 9s 9d

[page 4]

S

-Mrs Mary Shapleigh	||||	0 0 9	-James Symmons	||||	0 0 9
-The heires of Mr Shapleigh of Tonstall		0 9 0	-John Sanders	||	0 0 9
Mr Streete for his house		0 1 0	-John Skinner		0 0 3
-Mr John Staplehill for his house	||	0 0 4	Thomas snelling		0 0 6
Roger Sparke	pd	[illegible]	-John salter	||	0 0 6
shilllinges		0 2 6	[total]		£1 8s 2d

T

Mr John Terry for his house		0 0 6	-Peter Terry	||||	0 0 6
-Matthew Tooker	||||	0 0 6	Peter Tocker		0 0 4
-Richard Towle	||||	0 0 8	[total]		3s 10d

V

Mr Andrew Voysey for his house ~~Voysie~~ 0 1 0

W

-Emanuell Wolley	||||	0 1 [obscured]	-Thomas Willsonne	||||	[blank]
-George Woodvine	||||	0 1 [obscured]	-Jellbord Wreford	||||	0 0 6
-John Whittocke	||||	0 0 [obscured]	~~Thomas Willson~~		0 0 [obscured]
-John Whittocke yonger	||	0 0 0	[total]		11s 04d
-William Widger	||||	0 0 [obscured]			
-Thomas Weekes	||||	0 0 9	[total]		10s 2d

marke of Nicholas Pimbwell
[blank]   Churchwardens
[signed] Richard Kellherd, [initialled] Frances Barnard   overseers
Jo: Staplehill Maior
Will: Barnes

90. DARTMOUTH (Townstal), Poor Rate, 1649

DHC, DD62745

Note: This rate was written on four pieces of paper, some 12 inches in width and 16½ in length, which have been folded and stitched to make up twelve pages. The pages have some damage.

dated 23 of 9ber 1649 A rate made by the Churchwardens & overseers of the parrish of Tounstall for the releife of the poore of the said parish weekly to be payde to be continued untell Ester mondaye next Ensuing 1650.

A

George Aggenner	|	£00 00 09	[total]	1s 6d

B

Mr -Thomas Boone Esquire or his holders			·John Burgis		00 00 06
	|	00 10 00	·John Bounsers house		00 00 06
Mr -William Baddeford	|	00 16 06	-William Burgan	|	00 01 08
Mr -William Baddeford	|	00 03 11	-Francis Barnard	|	00 02 00
Mr -John Budley		00 03 09	-John Bowden	|	00 00 02
-Joseph Bowden		00 00 06	-Thomas Boone		00 00 09
-William Bunkard	|	00 00 08	John Ballimore		00 00 03

Benjamin Ball	00 00 08	-Richard Bourier	00 00 08
Richard Barter	00 00 06	[total]	£1 18s 8d

C

-Hingstons Coote	00 01 03	-Nichollas Cruse	00 00 09
·Robert Cauley	00 00 06	Edward Cooke	00 00 06
-Richard Cossens	00 01 00	-Ambrose Couch	00 00 06
-John Cutt	00 02 00	John Cottinge	00 00 03
Jane Cooke	00 00 08	-Jarvis Chicke	00 00 03
-William Cruse	00 00 08	William Campine	00 00 03
-John Crossman	00 00 08	Edward Coole	00 00 06
Richard Cumminge	00 00 06	James Cole for his house	00 00 06
William Courtis	00 00 06	[total]	8s 4d

D

-Roger Deereinge	00 01 00	John Dicke	00 00 2
Thomas Dicke	00 00 06	[total]	1s

E

-Edward Elliott for his meddow	00 00 04	-Robert Emett	00 02 08
-Mr Ekines Milles	00 01 06	-Oads Edwards	00 00 06
-Roger Elliott	00 00 09	[total]	5s 1d

[page 2]

F

Mr -ffortescues ground	00 01 06	·Owen Foorde	00 00 06
Mr -Robert Follett for his house	00 01 00	[total] 4s	
Mr ·Edward Follett for his house	00 01 00		

G

John Gillard	00 00 06	Richard Graye	00 00 09
Roger Gray	00 01 06	Robert Grendell	00 00 04
-Edmund Goodridge	00 00 06	[total]	3s 7d
-Andrew Goodyer	00 00 06		

H

Mr -John haukings or his holders	- 03 09	henry harris	00 00 03
Mr -Crispin hooper	00 00 10	-Jane sparke	00 00 06
Mr -holligroves Milles or his holders	00 02 00	Jane Quicke	00 00 06
Richard hilliard	00 01 00	[total]	£2 1d
Edmund horswell	00 00 06		

J

Nicholas Jacksonne	00 00 03	[total]	11d
John Jeffery	00 00 08		

K

Edward Knowlles	00 00 06	[total]	6d
John Kinge	00 00 06		

L

Richard Lee	00 00 00	Mrs -Laskey for her house or tennants	00 02 00
Thomas Little	00 00 00	Robert Lues	00 00 08
Mr Ambrose Lane for his house	00 01 00	Ussillagh Lux	00 00 06

[total]   5s 2d

[page 3]

M

-Joan Mathewes *widow*	|	00 10 00	-John Moone	|	00 10 03
-The holders of Milton		00 10 00	-Henry Milles	|	00 00 06
-Robert Maine	|	00 02 00	-Edward Masters or his holders	00 01 06
-Nicholas Marrwood	|	00 01 03	Walter Manfield	|	00 00 10
-John Martyne or his holder	|	00 08 00	-Phillip Maine	|	00 00 06
-The salt Mills	|	00 02 00	-James March	|	00 00 09
-John Martyn of Cockington or holders		00 01 06	John Marten	|	00 00 06
			William Maine		00 00 06
-Whiteings Meddow	|	00 00 06	[total]		£2 1s 1d
-Thomas Manfield	|	00 00 06			

N

-John Neile	|	00 06 00	Samuel Narrimoore	|	00 00 04
-Nicholas Neile	|	00 02 06	[total]		8s 10d

P

-The heirs of Mr John Plumlegh	|00 09 00	Thomas Parnell		00 00 06
-John Paige	|	00 02 06	-Nicholas Pimble	|	00 01 06
Mr -John Plumleigh or his holders	|	00 03 04	-John Pommroy		00 00 03
-Clement Palmer	|	00 02 06	-Christopher Peeters		[blank]
-Richard Perriton	|	00 00 06	[total]		19s 10d

R

-Nicholas Roope Esqr. or his holders	| 00 11 00	-Thomas Russell	|	00 01 00
-John Roope Esqr. or his holders	|00 16 00	Ralph Raddon		00 01 00
-Henry Robbins	|	00 08 06	John Roodes		00 00 03
Lord Rigways ground		00 00 06	[total] £2 8s 10d		
-The Rectory	|	00 13 04			

[page 4]

S

-Mrs Mary Shapleigh	|	00 00 09	-James Simmons	|	00 00 09
-the heirs of Mr Shapleigh of Tounstall or holders		00 09 00	-John Sanders		00 00 03
			John Skinner		00 00 03
Mr Streete for his house		00 01 00	Thomas snellinge		00 00 06
Mr -Jn. Staplehill for his house	|	00 00 04	-John salter		00 00 06
-Roger Sparke	|	00 02 06	[total]		13s

T

Mr John Terry for his house or holders	00 00 06	Peter Terry		00 00 06
Matthew Toker		00 00 06	Peter Tocker		00 00 04
Richard Towle		00 00 08			

V

Mr Andrew Voysey for his house or his holders   0 1 0

W

-Emanuell Willey	|	00 01 03	-John Whittocke	|	00 00 08
-George Woodvine	|	00 01 03	John Whittocke yonger		00 00 06

William Widger	00 00 06	Jilbert Wreford	00 00 06
Thomas Weekes	00 00 09	[total]	3s 8d
Thomas Willsonne	00 00 06		

~~Nicholas Pimbley and William Bauncker churchwardens' William Hellier Francis Bernard Overseers~~

[final page]

this ratte hereon mentioned was made by the churwardens & overseers of the pish of Townstall as here under apyeereth
[signed] Nicholas Penell William Banke Churchwardens
[signed] Richard Hellierd [sign of] Frances Barnard over seeers
[signed] Wal. Jago Maior Jo: Staplehill Senior

91. DARTMOUTH, Militia Rate, 1601

DHC, DD61642

Note: More properly termed a muster book, this account was written on seven pieces of paper which measured 12 inches in width and 13 inches in length and which have been folded and stitched with brown string to make up a booklet of twenty-eight pages. There has been considerable damage by the chewing of at least one rodent. There are a considerable number of other ward lists including a partial muster book for 1618 and lists of the borough's free tenants who owed suit to the manorial court between 1600 and 1632.[8] A total of 494 men were listed while in 1642 there were 776 Dartmouth men who signed the Protestation Return. The difference between these figures may relate to a population increase or to the number of men unfit for military service being included in 1642. The number of tenants recorded also varied between some 500 and nearly 1,000.

Sundaies Warde
The muster booke Mr Haward maiore *in the year* 1601

John Terrie a Muskett performed	George Jewell a holbert
John Harris a Muskett performed	John Hill senior a bill
John Jackman a bill	Thomas Hill
Peter Arnolde a Musket performed	Humphrey Heathman a bill
Thomas Drescoll a bill	Edward Clement a halbert
William [blank]	Thomas Docton a bill
Thomas Toser	John Whittocke a bill
William Honnywell a holbert performed	William Strange
John Smith a bill	Alexander Narracott a bill
Richard Davye	John Wheeler a Calliver performed
John Bownser a Calliber performed	Robert [blank]
Richard Tolle	Richard Curtes a bill
Humphrey price a Muskett performed	William Waie
John Lux	Stephen Voizie A Calliber performed
John [blank]	Robert maie a holbert
John Nightingall	John Lashe a bill
Thomas Hollacombe a bill	William Cosens a bill
Anthony Beare a borespeare	[torn] Comings a bill
William Putt a Muskett performed	

---

[8]   The Dartmouth corporation archive includes DD61941 for Sunday Ward and five men from Monday Ward in 1618, DD61631 (1600), DD62127 (1624), DD62217 (1625), DD62250 & DD62254 (1626), DD62329 (1628), DD62419 (1629), DD62467 (1630), DD62498 (1631), DD62522 (1632).

[page 2]

Peter Luskom a bill
Henry Tucker
Michael Trefacye
Philip Boyes a holbert
Robert hollocombe a bill
William Roberts a bill
James Searle

Absent
Peter Terrie
Raphe Cooke a Muskett performed
Thomas Vitterie a Muskett performed
John Hill a bill
John Chope
William Linge a Muskett performede
William Counter
[blank] Jerman
William Nyell a holbert
Thomas West
William Symons
William Symons [?sic]
Richard Wilson
James Marche a Calliver performed
Alexander [blank]
William Bobbonye a Calliver

Robert Chapin a bill
Thomas Turpin a bill
Richard Smith
John Bagwell a Musket performed
george Axall
Richard Palmer
Clement Palmer

Michael Woodye
Richard Harvye
Thomas Efford
Euon Necke
Thomas perring a bill
Richard Cosen
John Lashe
John Teagg a Calliver #
John Mudge a Calliver performed
Alexander Clarke a Muskett #
Peter Welshe a Muskett performed
John Welshe
Thomas Welshe
William Welshe
M[uskets] 15
C[alivers]   0

[page 3]

Mondaies Warde
Anthony Norman a bill
Thomas paine a bill
John Arrenden
William Maine a muskett performed
William willmead a bill
William weeger a muskett performed
Edward Brecker a muskett performed
Robert Bonclarke
Thomas pennie a bill
John Quoyne
Moses gilforde a bill
John Jant harp a bill
William Charde a bill
Phillip godfrey senior
Phillip godfrey Junior a bill performed
Ellis Maie a muskett performed
John Coleserie a bill performed
William Jackman Junior
Walter husbandes a bill
Roger Foster
Matthew Sheare a bill performed

William Bowden a holbert
Richard Manfielde a bill
Walter Symons a bill
Robert hullett a Calliver performed
Nicholas Narracott a Muskett performed
John Smithe two Musketts performed
Jullian Smith a Musketts performed
William yonnge a Muskett performed
John Lay a Muskett performed
Edward Coke a Muskett performed & a holbert
James Soryer
Robert Stabb a holbert performed
Richard Luke a bill
Richard Kidney
John Plomleighe a Muskett performed
Walter Phillpp a holbert performed
John Collins a bill
Nicholas Goodyere
Martin Norman a holbert performed
John kidlye a Muskett performed
William Irishe a Muskett performed
Robert [torn]

[page 4]

Thomas deparke *otherwise* Martin a Calliver performed
John Yab a bill
Antony Randall two Musketts & a Calliver
Humphrey Randall
William Randall
Arthur Wootton two Musketts performed
John Wootton
Andrew Weeks a Calliver performed Muskett performed
Lancelot Teapp a Muskett performed
phillip baker
John Clarke
John Norris a bill performed
Richard Speede a bill
John pasco a Muskett performed
Andrew pasco
Henry Maine a Muskett performed
John Collin Senior a bill
James warren
James Tremill a bill
Roger Drewe a Muskett performed

Henry Robins a Bill performed
John White a Muskett performed
John Ellett
John Cooke a bill
William Coleserye a bill
Walter Francis two Musketts & a Calliver
John Robertes
George Tapper
William woodeforde
Thomas Ruswell a [blank]
Robert Hodge
Robert pasco a Calliver performed
Edmund Fuersham a bill performed
William Ellett a holbert performed
William hooper
Thomas Collyer
David graine
John Tucker a bill
William White a bill
Thomas Adams a bill Calliver performed
Matthew Stevens a bill
Alexander Brabon a bill

[page 5]

John Fursman Junior
John Walter a musket performed
Bartholomew picher a Muskett performed
Ellis Harradon a bill
Peter goodridge a Calliver performed
Josias fellow a holbert
John Barber a bill
Robert pyke a bill
John furseman senior Muskett performed
William Tomson a Muskett performed
Richard Wallis a bill
William Coxall a Calliver performed
William Cutt a bill performed
Gawen Starkye a holbert performed
Thomas Smith a Muskett performed
Walter Pecke a Calliver performed

Christopher Phillip a Calliver performed
William Kempt a Muskett performed
Walter Dosens a bill
William Channon
Alexander Frie a bill
Elizabeth perrin widowe a halberd
William Richards a bill performed
Lewis Triplyn a bill performed
Margaret whitinge widowe a holbert performed
Jane Blackaller widowe a bill
Rie William Manninge a bill
Henry Deacon a bill
Andrew Churchward a bill
M[uskets] 35
C[alivers] [illegible]

[page 6]

Tewsdaies warde
William Allen a Calliver performed
John Jeffrie a Muskett performed
Robert Carie a Muskett
Lawrence Swainson a Muskett performed
John Sheare a Muskett performed
Richard Reynolls a bill
William Robartes a bill

John Lomer a bill
Thomas Wall a bill
Mrs walter a holbert
Richard Grappole a Calliver performed
Mr Henry Haywoode three Musketts performed
Henry Moore
Thomas Hole

Hugh Edwards a Calliver & holbert performed
Alexander Barter
Walter Wright a bill
Richard Cruste a Muskett & Calliver performed
Zachary gold two Musketts performed
pascoe Jago a Muskett performed
Richard Whitinge a holbert
George Duringe a Muskett performed
John Kellye a Muskett performed
Roger Warren
Thomas Luke a Calliver performed
William ~~Richard~~ Rodes a bill
Bartholomew frie a Muskett performed
Thomas hodge a Muskett performed
Henry Bowne a Muskett performed

[page 7]

Alexander Hellier a bill
Thomas Narracott a holbert
John Olliver senior a Calliver performed
Robert Hoper a Calliver performed
Christopher Woode a Muskett performed
Stephen Coombe
Roger Mathew
Thomas Fabes
William Hawkes
Mr Robert Martin two Musketts one Calliver performed
Richard Kenawaie a Calliver performed

[page 8]

Wednesdaies warde
John Newman the elder 2 Musketts performed
John Bennett
Richard Drewe
William Herringe
Michael barter
Jerome Wilcox a halberd performed
Thomas Fortescue esquire 3 Musketts performed
Lewis Fortescue
Mr Nicholas Hayman 3 Musketts 4 Callivers performed
Robert Hayman
Peter Mograge
Alice Nancarro Widow a Calliver performed
Robert Cole
John paige a Muskett performed & holbert
William Bayle a Calliver performed
Andrew Langdon a Muskett performed
John lowdwell a holberd performed

Nicholas Squire a Muskett performed
Richard Kingdom a bill
John Baker a bill
Benjamin Haywoode
Phillip Joslin
John Rowe a bill
John Diggins
Richard James a halberd
Thomas Skoche a halberd
Richard Meade a bill
John Breckere
Nicholas Carpenter a halberd
John Risedon a bill
Giles Warde
[torn] a Calliver performed

William Cole a bill
John Sherewell
John Aprey a Calliver performed
Richard player a bill
Julian hullett a Calliver performed
Robert Nicholls
John Teagg
Robert Teagg
Mrs Agnes Smith two Musketss two Callivers two pikes
M[uskets] 24
C[alivers] 17

William Lowdwell
William Cade a Muskett & a Calliver performed
Thomas paige a Muskett & a Calliver performed
Nicholas Skynner
John Kinge a Muskett performed
John Winchester a Muskett
John Follett senior a Calliver performed
Osmonde Follett
Edward Follett
Richard Follett
John Beare a holberde
James Clarke
Lawrick Blackford
Tristram Lane a Calliver performed
John Bunker
John Keymer a Calliver performed
John prattin a Muskett performed
Gabriel follett

Mr Thomas Holland
Arthur Richardes
William Courte
Digory Jacob
John Lesiberye

[page 9]

William Wattes
Roger Harwoode a Calliver performed
Robert Knighte
Mr Bennett Flute a Muskett & 2 Calliver
performed
Andrew Flute
John Stone
Peter [blank]
Nicholas Flute the elder a Calliver performed
Christopher pope a bill
Lawrence Brocke a bill
John Drayton a Calliver
Richard Leane a holbert
John Newbye a Muskett & a Calliver
performed
John Knight a holbert
David Banister
Walter Miller a Muskett performed
Phillip Collins
Raphe blackaller
John Hixte a holberte
Thomas Crockwell a Muskett

[page 10]

Thursdaies Warde
Mr William Norris 2 Musketts 2 Callivers
performed
Henry Ashlye a holbert
John Cornishe
John Knowles
Richard Reeve a Calliver
Richard Harris
Phillip Bourne a Calliver performed
Christopher Wilson a Muskett
John Lynes
Matthew Masye
John Blackaller a Muskett performed
Robert Downe a Muskett performed
Alexander Cosen
John Homes
Thomas Mors
Richard Hewett
Richard Cornye

John [blank]
Hugh Richards a bill performed
Richard [blank]
Mr William Flute 3 Musektts & 2 Callivers
[torn]

Phillip [blank]
Andrew Bicklye a Calliveer performed
Thomas Sparke
Thomas Gournye a Muskett & Calliver
performed
Mr John Follett a Muskett & 2 Calliver
performed
Edward Stevens a Calliver performed
William Sherum
Robert Stevens
William Coker
Henrick Clauson a Muskett
John Thomas
Thomas Abraham a Muskett performed
Benjamin Knowles
Thomas Axforde
John Starte a Muskett performed
Christopher Wellworthe a Muskett
Richard Archer
William Newland a Calliver performed
John Skynner
Christopher Wallis a Muskett

Edmund Averie a Muskett & a Calliver
performed
William Waymouth
John Waymouth
Mr John Plomlye 2 Musketts performed
Mr Gilbert Staplehill 3 Musketts performed
Alred Staplehill
Robert homes
Thomas Spurwaie a Muskett performed
John Rockett a holbert
Thomas Watson a Muskett
John Lewes a Calliver
Hugh Bowdon
John Bowden
Robert Bicklye a Muskett
Nicholas Deane
Roger Lewes a Muskett & a Calliver
performed
Thomas Lewes
James Searle a Muskett performed

John Salter
Robert Peerce
James Haywoode a Calliver performed

[page 11]

Phillip boyes a bill
Thomas Viney
Robert Williams
Robert Woode
John Russell a Muskett Calliver & Corsletts
performed
John phillipps a Muskett performed
Thomas Wardroppe a Calliver performed
William Crosse

[page 12]

Fridaies warde
Mr Richard Wakeham a Muskett & a Calliver
performed
Phillip Shutland
Robert Furseman a Calliver performed
William plomleighe a Muskett
Arthur Goodridge a Muskett performed
Richard Trosse a Muskett performed
William Morris *otherwise* Toser 2 Musketts 2
Callivers performed
John Strange
William Roper a Calliver performed
John Furnes a Calliver performed
George Hamleton a Muskett performed
Thomas Hingstone a Muskett performed
Thomas Downinge a Muskett performed
Robert Gyles a Muskett & a Calliver
performed
John Weekes
Richard Spragges a Calliver performed
Robert Rule a holbert
John Ashlye a Muskett performed
Henry Blake a Calliver performed
William [blank]
Maurice Cosen a Muskett performed
Matthew Woodye a Muskett performed

[page 13]

Mrs Lay Widowe 2 Musketts 2 Callivers
performed
Richard pearde
Geoffrey Leagr a bill
Nicholas Beaple a Calliver performed
Nicholas Bennett
John Martin
Richard Norber

John Markes
John prince a Calliver performed
[torn] Weekes a Calliver performed

John Bill a Calliver
William pennybreeche a Calliver performed
Richard Ellis
Phillip Egar
Henry Sparke
Nicholas Hande
John Bartlett a bill
John Antonie a Muskett

Richard Androwes a holbert performed
John Archer a Calliver performed
Anthony White
John Rownsyvall a holbert
Robert Crosse a holbert
William Clayton a Calliver performed
Walter Gunne a Calliver performed bowe &
arrows
John Lucombe a Calliver performed
James Saverie a holbert performed
Thomas Kellye a Muskett performed
William Toollocke a Muskett performed
Nicholas Waterton a Musketts & two Callivers
performed
Arthur Goodridge
William Prowse a halbert performed a
Calliver performed
Thomas Pettyvin
Thomas Creswell
William Wakeham a holbert
Andrew Wakeham
Adrian Starre a Calliver performed
John Cowle a bill
Thomas Cane a bill
[torn] White
[torn]

William Norwoode
William Colline a holbert performed
Phillip Taplye a Calliver performed
Robert Phillpott a Muskett & a Calliver
performed
John Cripiere
Lewis Sayer a Calliver performed
Robert Parker a bill performed

Robert Fletcher a bill performed
~~John Archer~~
Ambrose Constable
John Ham a bill
William Homes
Richard Hollidaie a bill
Richard Crossinge
John Newton
John Goborne
Robert Sparke senior a Calliver performed
John Sparke
John Beaple
Gregory Isacke a Muskett performed
Thomas Carter a Calliver performed
James Foster a Muskett performed

[page 14]

George Davies ~~a Calliver performed~~ muskett
performed
John Tope
John Flinte
Nicholas Roope 2 Musketts 1 Calliver
performed

Thomas Cooche a Muskett performed
Richard Dominicke
~~William~~ John Hawkins a Muskett Calliver
holbert performed
David Collyton
Nicholas Jeffrey a bill
Harry Milton
John Boucher
James Prowte
George Sparke a Muskett performed
Nicholas Ascott a Calliver performed
Richard ~~Gressett~~ Grace a Calliver performed
Lambert Bastwell
[torn] Searle a Muskett performed

Reuben Skynner
William West
John Clymett
Thomas Perrett
John Barnes a Muskett performed
Andrew Phillpott a Calliver performed

M[uskets] 31
C[alivers] 33

[page 15]

		[torn. Muskets]	Calivers
New	Sunday	15	09
	Mondaie	35	13
	Tewsdaie	24	17
	Wednesdaie	34	26
	Thursdaie	22	16
	Fridaie	31	33
	[total]	161	114
			114
			161
	[total]		275

		Musketts	Callivers
Old	Sundaie	12	19
	Mondaie	28	36
	Tewsdaie	12	26
	Wednesdaie	16	46
	Thursdaie	23	25
	Fridaie	22	33
	[total]	113	185
			185
			113
	[total]		298

DEAN PRIOR

A high number of rates survive for this parish which is located on the main road between Plymouth and Exeter. The two main volumes are in fragile states which do not allow, at this time, a proper examination of their contents. The first manuscript, in which much of the ink has faded, is a parish book in that it comprises business relating to the poor, the church and highways from 1567 to 1599. Items relating to the militia include a note that the parish armour was loaned on 20 August 1595 to Robert Bonevin who had been pressed by Sir Francis Drake and Sir John Hawkins. Eight years earlier the parish gave six pence for the tinners to 'the man' of Sir Walter Raleigh, Warden of the Stannaries. Other incidental expenses were for the making of new seats church in 1597. The second manuscript includes poor accounts and rates from the early 1600s to 1657 but many have sustained considerable damage. A selection of the rates have been edited for this volume but the accompanying accounts have not been read or analysed in full.[1]

A scribe recorded the names of those parishioners who were appointed on an annual basis to serve as the four sidemen (often referred to simply as the 'Four Men') from 1565 to 1622 (with the exception of 1584 to 1587 when there were eight men), two wardens (otherwise churchwardens but sometimes known as the 'head wardens' or 'head wardens of the church') from 1554 to 1628, two, three or four 'collectors' (otherwise referred to as the 'overseers' of the poor)[2] from 1569 to 1626 and two 'supervisors of the ways' (otherwise known as waywardens) from 1569 to 1628 who were responsible for the maintenance of public thoroughfares. Their accounts appear to have normally been independent of one another but were sometimes referred to in common. The sidemen appear to have acted for the parish in an overall manner. One rate, that of 1599 jointly from the churchwardens and overseers of the poor, distinguished contributions from forty inhabitants from those of seventeen non-parishioners who held land in Dean Prior.

In other parts of Devon parish roles were decided by a rota of householders of larger properties. It may be that those Dean Prior women who were appointed to serve as churchwardens, such as Agnes Knowlinge in 1626 and Elizabeth Hore in 1628, were widows whose duties were carried out by men nominated on their behalf. This was the case in 1625 for John Collinges who served as an overseer of the poor in the place of his mother and in 1599 John Phillip acted as the deputy for the two churchwardens Peter Leate and Margaret Phillip, widow.[3] The above-named Agnes Knowlinge, a widow, was brought to the church court three years before her term of being a churchwarden. She was accused of living immorally with Nicholas Lavers, but the minister, two churchwardens, four sidemen and another fourteen principal men of the parish disputed this and testified that 'she hath behaved herself honestly and very sufficiently ever since she came to the said parish about 18 years since'.[4]

The first volume shows church ales took place from the 1570s into the 1590s: there were five separate 'brewings' by Joan Kinge, Thomas Gule, William Hede, John Durnruge and John Tolcharde recorded in 1571 and in subsequent years rentals of 'the church vessel' and 'church kettle' were also noted. In 1570 £3 8s 2d was raised from the church ale that year, a shilling more the following year and £6 2d in 1572.[5] When in 1589 thirteen of the principal men of the parish made an agreement regarding a legacy only five of them could sign their own names.

---

[1]   DHC, 4567A-99/PW1 & PO1.
[2]   The number who served as overseers changed: there were two from 1568 to 1598, four from 1599 to 1604, three from 1605 to 1615 and two from 1616 to 1626.
[3]   DHC, 4567A-99/PW1.
[4]   DHC, CC5.
[5]   DHC, 4567A-99/PW1.

Two nationally known men were parish clergymen when some of these rates were written. Barnaby Potter, later the bishop of Carlisle, was presented in 1615 to the rectory of Diptford. By then Potter had been living outside Totnes at Bowden, the home of Sir Edward Giles, the town's Member of Parliament for 1597, 1621, 1624 and 1628. In 1615 Giles moved to Dean Prior and James I presented Potter to the vicarage. Fourteen years later Potter was consecrated at Carlisle. His Calvinist beliefs led to Potter becoming known as the 'penetential preacher' and later as the 'puritanical bishop'. Potter was succeeded at Dean Prior by Robert Herrick, the poet, who celebrated two of Potter's daughters in his *Hesperides*. Herrick, a Royalist, was deprived in 1646 but returned fourteen years later when the king was restored.[6] A later hand added in the margin of one page of the first parish volume 'If that it chance the warrior for to fight, more than to wit trust not to thy sight, for wit without strength much more doth prevail than strength without wit to continue in battle'. The lines are not likely to have been written by Herrick.[7]

92. DEAN PRIOR, Sidemen Rate, 1580

DHC, 4567A-99/PW1

Note: The document is headed 'the accounpt of the 4 men of the prysh John Hele, John Phelyp, Richard P[ar]nell & George Bartor for one hole yeare last past made the 12th day of June in the yeare of our Lord 1580'. The first half of the document recorded other church income including the rental of brewing equipment and the sale of 'the old bible'. Two payments were exacted for this rate although some men were recorded for only one. The account of the Four Men on 11 June 1579 recorded rates were paid by William Gyles, William Stedelston, Walter Tolcharde, John Hele, John Mudge, Richard Hedle, Hugh Hele, William Ascote, John Cudleforde, Henry Perye, Thomas Tolcharde, Roger Cokerman, John Phill[ip], John Cropper, John Fox, Richard P[ar]nyll, Thomas Phill[ip], Christopher Boyse, Robert Perye and William Stidston Junior.

The first-ranked parishioner in Item 90, John Giles, died in 1606 and left his estate to his wife Agnes and son Edward.[8] The second parishioner, Robert Furse, died in 1593. He was the only one to have written a memoir for the benefit of his descendants. Amongst his advice was to:
'have no delight to keep company with liars, cozeners, whisperers, flatterers, tale-tellers, rowlers, scolders or malicious and vicious persons but keep company with the best, wise and honest company for the proverb is *The like will to the like*'.[9]
Receats by the Ratement of the pyshe

Item of Mr John Giles	first 6s 8d & second 6s 8d	Item Thomas Dodd	2s 8d
Item of Mr Robert Furse	6s 8d & 6s 8d	Item Henry Perye	2s 8d & 2s 8d
Item of Mr William Giles	3s 4d	Item Robert Tolchard	12d
Item of John Mudge	13s 4d & 13s 4d	Item of Christopher Boysye	3s 4d & 3s 4d
Item of Hugh Hele	6s 8d & 6s 8d	Item of Edward Jule	3s 4d
Item of John Hele	6s 8d & 6s 8d	Item of John Edwards	12d
Item of William Stydsan	6s 8d	Item of John Ascote	2s 8d
Item of William Hedd	6s & 6s	Item of William Lavers	16d & 16d
Item of John Phelyp	3s 8d & 3s 8d	Item of Robert Spry the [illegible]	8d & 8d
Item of John Cudleforde	3s 4d & 3s 4d	Item of Matthew Tolchard	
Item of Richard Foxe	3s 4d & 3s 4d		

6   A. J. Hegarty, 'Barnaby Potter' and Tom Cain, 'Robert Herrick', https://www.oxforddnb.com/view/10.1093/ref:odnb/9780198614128.001.0001/odnb-9780198614128-e-22605, accessed 12 Feb. 2022.
7   DHC, 4567A-99/PW1. This was added to a page of the overseers of the poor account. I am grateful to Prof. Tom Caine for sharing his expertise of Herrick's writing.
8   TNA, PROB 11/109/407.
9   Travers, *Furse*, p. 14.

Plate 18. Monument to Giles family, Dean Prior.

[new page]

Ratement first second

Item of William Arscot 3s 8d & 3s 8d
Item of Richard Pnell 16d & 16d
Item of John Collyng 12d & 12d
Item of Christopher Croppyn 3s 4d & 3s 4d
Item of John Tockerman 2s & 2s
Item of John Foxe 2s 6d & 2s 6d
Item of Walter Shere 8d & 8d
Item of Andrew Foxe 6d

Item of Andrew Goodrudge 8d & 8d
Item of George Bartor 12d & 12d
Item of Thomas Phelyps 12d & 12d
Item of John Heathyard 6d & 6d
Item of Elizabeth Flacher 8d & 8d
Item of Richard Rudge 8d & 8d
Item of Andrew Hannaford 6d
Item of John Foxe labourer 6d & 6d
Item of William Ryder 6d & 6d

Sum total Recets by the Ratement £9 19s 10d

93. **DEAN PRIOR**, Highway Rate, 1586

DHC, 4567A-99/PW1

Note: A church rate taken four years earlier (on 14 June 1582) reflected the inconsistent nature of spelling and of the number of individuals in taxation lists: the parishioners included John Giles, Esquire, Mr Robert Furse, John Hele, Hugh Hele, William Hedde, William Arscot, John Fox, John Philip, Christopher Croppinge, Richard Fox, John Dunridge, Henry Perrye, Paul Luscombe, John Tocaman, Mother Rudge, William Lavers, Christopher Dodd, Robert Sing, Matthew Turner, Thomas Philip, George Barter, Richard P[ar]nell, Andrew Goodridge, John Pnell, Robert Mudge, John Badford, Matthew Lenard, Andrew Hanniford, Ambrose Hanniford, Richard Ayshelye, William Fox, Walter Addam, Richard Addam, John Edwards helier, Edward Dyver, William Rider, Richard Wearing, Joyce Pereman, John Arscot, Thomas Churchwaye, William Tirner, Christopher Arscot, John Miller, John Tolchard, William Tolchard, the widow Tolchard, Geoffrey Harden, Edward Willyams, John Voyse, Richard Donne, Edward Pnell, Edward Jule, John Heathyeard, Thomas Badford, Robert Tolchard, Edward Badford, John Mudge, Robert Row, John Bard and Walter Sheere.

There are differences between the seventy-four individuals assessed for this rate of 5 April 1586 with those seventy men and one woman rated by the head wardens three months later on 3 July 1586. A year later, on 25 June 1587 only thirty-seven men and women were assessed for the 'rate for the service of the queen'. They were Robert Furse, Hugh Hele, John Hele, William Hedd, John Foxe, John Edwards, John Phillippe, William Arscote, Richard Foxe, John Dunridge, Joan Mudge, Christopher Mudge, Simon Mudge, Walter Sheare, Henry Perry, John Toukerman, Christopher Croppny, Andrew Goodridge, George Barter, Thomas Phillippe, Elizabeth Flacher, Richard Parnell, John Bearde, Mathewe Turnare, Christopher Dod, Phillip Steephen, William Lane, John Arscote, Robert Singe, Robert Mudge, Andrew Hannaford, Robert Tolcherd, George Maddicke, Edward Windyeate, John Pnell, Peter Leate and William Horswill. On the same day, 25 June 1587, forty-three men and women were rated for the maintenance of the poor.

Dean Pryer This is the accounte of Thomas Phyllyppe & Walter Shere, Supervisors of the parish for this yearlaste paste made the 5ᵗʰ Daye of Apryll in the 28 yere of our Soverente Lady Quene Ellezebethe in manner & forme folloynge

First Received of Mr John Gyles	18d	Hugh Hele	18d
more of Robert Furse	18d	John Foxse clothier	12d
John Mudege	2s 6d	John Phillip	12d
John Hele	18d	John Edwards of Semston [Zempson]	12d
William Hedde	18d	Edward Jule	9d

Walter Shere	8d	John Myllyr	1d
Christopher Croppen	6d	Robert Synge	6d
Edward Wyndeyette	3d	Robert Mudege	4d
Christopher Dodle	8d	Robert Rowe	1d
John Tockerman	6d	Walter Adom	3d
Richard Foxse	6d	Richard Adom	3d
William Laveres	6d	Edward Badforde	3d
John Edwards hellier	3d	William Ryder	1d
Elizabeth Fletcher	4d	John Berde & Thomas [illegible]	6d
John Donnerudege	8d	Ambrose Hannaforde	1d
John Foxse labourer	3d	Andrew Hannaforde	3d
George Barter	4d	William Ascotte	6d
Richard Pnyll	4d	John Pnyll	4d
Andrew Gooderudege	3d	Richard Downe	1d
Thomas Phyllyppe	4d	William Foxse	3d
Geoffrey Haredon	2d	John Dever	1d

[new page]

Anthony Weger	1d	John Torner	1d
Henry Perye	6d	Peter Pere	1d
Matthew Torner	4d	Walter Arscott	1d
John Ascotte	6d	George Maddycke	2d
Christopher Ascott	1d	John Masye	1d
Matthew Lenarde	2d	John Voysye	1d
Bartholomew Baille	1d	Richard Werrynge	2d
Richard Cornyshe	1d	Edward Dever	1d

Sum to pay 26s 10d

Item these persones beyinge likewyse taxsede for the charge of the Reprasyon of the weyes by the 8 men howse nemes do followe have not payed

First Thomas Badforde	3d	William Tynkeham	1d
Richard Aysheleye	2d	John Tolcharde	2d
Robert Tolcharde	4d	Sander Downynge	3d
Thomas Churchewaye	2d	George Peryman	7d
Andrew Foxse	2d	Robert Cole	2d
Stephen Fowle	1d	Robert Foxse	1d
William Tolcharde	2d		
Thomas Webber	2d	*Sum* total	2s 8d
Thomas Tomlyn of Netherdene	4d		

94. DEAN PRIOR, Poor & Church Rate, 1590

DHC, 4567A-99/PW1

Note: This rate records the contributions to the maintenance of the poor and of the parish church. It also notes the weekly amount assessed for each parishioner. The scribe neglected to record all of their first names and some of these have been supplied from other rates including one for the poor dated 30 May 1591 which recorded the contributors as John Gyles, Robert Furse, Henry Hele, John Hele, John Edwards, William Hedle, John Foxse, William Ascott, John Phillyppe, Henry Pery, Philip Stevens, Christopher Dodle, John P[ar]nyll, Richard Pnyll, John Berde, Walter Shere, Walter Cokerman, Robert Synge, Robert Tolchard, Richard Sperke, Margaret

Phe, Matthew Torner, Robert Mudge, Christopher Mudge, John Ascott Senior, Austin Lovering, Edward Wyndett, Andrew Hannaford, Richard Adam, John Voysye, Thomas Miller, John Hele Junior, William Fox and Simon Mudge.

This the juste Accounte of Richard Cornyshe general Warden for the Somes of money by him Collectede for the yere Laste made the 24 Daye of June *in the year* 32 of Elizabeth [15]89 [sic]

	for the poor	for the churche	wiklye
Mr John Gyles	17s 4d	5s 5d	6d
Robert Furse	16s	4s	6d
John Hele	13s	4s	6d
Hugh Hele	13s	4s	6d
William Hedle	13s	4s	6d
John Edwards	14s	4s	6d
John Foxse	13s	3s	6d
William Ascott	6s 8d	2s	3d
Henry Perye	3s 4d	20d	2d
Christopher Croppen	3s 4d	2d	3d
Phillip Stevenes	16d	12d	2d
John Phellip	6s 8d	0	3d
[Christopher] Dodle	4s 4d	16d	2d
Richard P[ar]nyll	12d	8d	2d
John Pnyll	2s 8d	8d	2d
John Berde	2s 2d	8d	2d
Donnerudege	0	6d	1d
[Walter] Shere	4s 4d	2s	2d
[Walter] Cokerman	0	6d	0
Robert Synge	16d	12d	2d
Robert Tolchyde	16d	16d	2d
Richard Sperke	16d	10d	2d
Thomas Phillip	2s	10d	2d
[Mathew] Torner	4s 4d	12d	1d
[William] Norrawaye	0	12d	0
[Edward] Prowse	0	10d	0
Robert Mudge	6d	4d	1d
Christopher Mudge	16d	12d	2d
Simon Mudege	0	4d	0
John Ascot Senior	2s 8d	20d	2d
Austin Lovering	12d	12d	0
John Abrom	0	6d	0
Peter Lete	0	4d	0
[Edward] Wyndeyate	4d	4d	1d
Richard Cornyshe	0	2d	1d
John Edwards	0	2d	1d
Matthew Lennard	0	2d	1d
John Boayes	0	2d	1d
Richard Aysheley	0	0	1d
Edward Badforde	4d	2d	1d
Thomas Badford	4d	0	1d
John Foxse lab[ourer]	0	2d	1d
John Miller	0	2d	1d

George Middycke	0	0	1d
William Foxse	4d	~~2d~~	1d
[Alexander] Downynge	0	0	1d
[Thomas] Webber	0	0	1d
Edward Jule	3s 4d	~~20d~~	3d
Stephen Fole	0	2d	1d
Walter Prowse	0	2d	1d
Walter Adam	0	2d	1d
Richard Adam	0	2d	1d
Andrew Foxse	0	2d	1d
Anthony Weger	0	2d	1d
[Andrew] Goodrudege	0	2d	1d
Edward Dever	0	2d	1d
[Bartholomew] Baille	0	2d	0
William Tolcharde	0	2d	1d
[Geoffrey] Haredone	0	0	1d
Robert Scobbe	0	0	1d
Richard Downe	0	2d	1d
Andrew Hannerford	8d	2d	1d
John Voysye	8d	2d	2d
Robert Knolle	4d	0	0
Thomas Hedle	4d	0	0
John Dener	0	2d	1d
John Synge	0	2d	1d
Peter Pere	0	0	1d
Jasper Whithedon	0	2d	1d

95. DEAN PRIOR, Military Rate, c.1592

DHC, 3799M/3/O/4/50, no page numbers

Note: This rate is recorded in a volume which has pages approximately 7¾ inches in width and 12 inches in length. Sixteen men were assessed for their weaponry.

Deanprior

Francis Alley	a corslet ps	John Hele	a musket ps
Thomas Head	a bill 2 Call ps a musket ps	Roger Cole & Nicholas Lavers	a musket ps
Apollo Barry	a musket ps	Walter Tuckerman	a musket ps
Jeffry Wyndeat & Edward Wyndeat	a musket ps	Augustine Lavers	a sword dagger a halbert
Matthew Turner	a bow ps, a Callr ps	William Abraham	a Callr ps
Thomas Knell	a musket ps	Robert Mudge	a musket ps
Thomas Mylls	a bow 12 arrows a bill	John Foxe	a Corslet ps

The parish armour   Corslet ps 1, musket ps 1, Callr ps 1, almaynr 1

96. DEAN PRIOR, Highway Rate, 1598

DHC, 4567A-99/PW1

Note: Amongst the expenses of 10s 4d incurred that year were the transportation of stone to repair roads to Clampitts, 'Bickwill' and John Edwards' garden.

This is the accompt of Richard Adame & Elizabeth Harris, supervisers for one hole yeare last past mad the 18th day of Aprell in the 40th yeare of the raigne of our sovereign Elizabeth that nowe is 1598.

First Mr John Giles Esquire	6d	of Bartholomew Ball	1d
of Mr Arthur Hart gent.	6d	of William Fox	1d
of John Heale	6d	of David Deve	1d
Of John Edwardes	6d	of John Edwards	1d
of William Head	6d	of Thomas Miles	1d
of John Foxe	4d	of John Wyshe	2d
of John Phillip	3d	of Peter Maddocke	1d
of John Pnell	3d	of John Symons	1d
of Walter Shere	3d	of Robert Knowle	1d
of Joan Pnell widow	2d	of Stephen Pnell	1d
of Walter Tockerman	3d	of Robert Arskot	1d
of Pascoe Perrye	2d	of Andrew Hanneford	1d
of John Tolchard	2d	of Matthew Lenarde	1d
of Austin Lavers	2d	of Walter Graye	1d
of John Collinge	2d	of William Tolchard	1d
of John Heale younger	2d	of John Read	1d
of Christopher Mudge	2d	of Thomas Mole	1d
of Phillip Stephen	2d	of Robert Stabb	1d
of Christopher Dod	2d	of Davy Marten	2d
of Robert Saye	2d	of Richard Downe	1d
of Elliz. Harris	2d	of Jasper Weathertone	1d
of Matthew Torrner	2d	of Richard Adame	1d
of Roger Coole	2d	of Thomas Torner	1d
of Edward Windeat	2d	of Robert Heale	1d
of Edward Prowse	2d	of Peter Ellet	1d
of William Abraham	2d	of Robert Fox	1d
of Robert Mudge	4d	of Jasper Phillip	1d
of Edward Badford	1d	of John Ashlye	1d
of Peter Payne	1d	of Edward Arskot	1d
of Anthony Wigger	1d	of Daniel Pnell	1d
of Margaret Phillip	1d	of William Hardon	1d
of Geoffrey Hardone	1d	of Richard Warringe	1d
of John Boyes	1d	Sum total is	10s 4d
of Thomas Badford	1d		

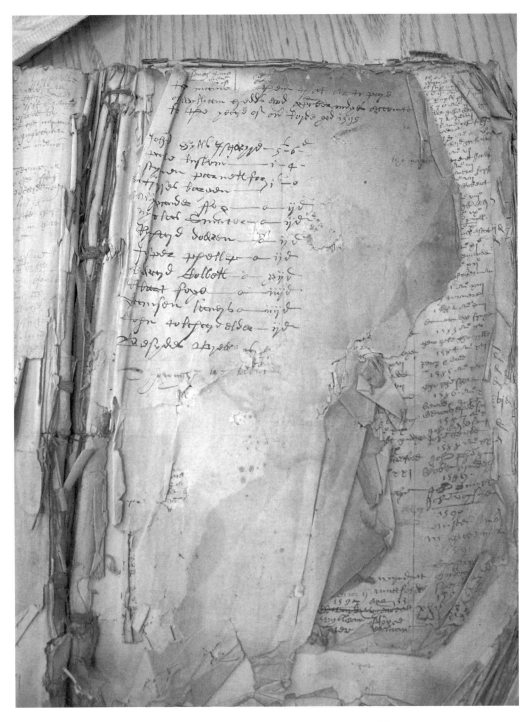

Plate 20. Parish account book, Dean Prior, 1567–99.

97. DEAN PRIOR, Sidemen Rate, 1598

DHC, 4567A-99/PW1

Note: The sidemen received £10 1s in militia expenses including for the maintenance of armour and weapons, the purchase of gunpowder and military training.

This is the accompte of the syde men John Edwards, William Heade, John Phillip & John Collinge for one hole yeare laste past made the 25th daye of June in the yeare of our Majesty 40th 1598 Rescayts
First reseved of the parrishe money that did remayne uppon the accompt of the syde men for the laste yeare 3s 1d
more reseved that did remayne of the accompt of the Churchwardens of the laste yeare 25s 8d
More reseved a booke of Common charge as followeth

First Mr John Gyles esquire	7s	Walter Tockerman	1s 2d
John Healle	6s 4d	John Deard	0 10d
William Head	5s 0d	Thomas Mowle	0 5d
John Edwards	6s 8d	Roger Colle	1s 0d
John Fox	3s 0d	Robert Singe	1s 0d
John Phillip	2s 0d	Phillip Stephen	1s 0d
John Pnell	2s 4d	William Abraham	0 10d
Robert Mudge	3s 0d	Elizabeth Harris	0 10d
John Coone	2s 4d	Edward Windeat	0 8d
John Edwards for Riddeclefe [Redicleave]	1s 8d	John Voyse	0 6d
John Collinge	2s 0d	Richard Adam	0 6d
Walter Sheere	2s 0d	Stephen Pnell	0 4d
John Tolchard	1s 6d	Robert Knowle	0 4d
Edward Prowse	1s 6d	William Fox	0 3d
Christopher Dod	1s 4d	Thomas Milles	0 4d
Pascoe Perrye	0 8d	The some of hole resets is	£10 8s 11d
Matthew Torner	1s 2d		

The names of them that are to paye upon the book of common shares is
Christopher Mudge	2s	Simon Mudge	8d
Pascoe	4d	Thomas Badford	2d
Austin Lavers	1s	[total]	4s 2d

The names of them that are to pay of the book of 40 dayes vitts
Roger Coole	2s	Thomas Badford	8d

Reseved more a booke that was Collected by Christopher Mudge for the provision of the 40 dayes vittling even the 14th daye of November in her maigestyes rayne that was 38
Recets
First Arthur Hart gentleman	8s 0d	Robert Mudge	6s 0d
John Heale	8s 0d	John Collinge	4s 0d
John Edwards	16s 4d	Pascoe Perrye	3s
William Heard	8s 0d	Christopher Dad	2s 8d
John Fox	6s 0d	John Tolchard	2s 8d
John Pnell	6s 0d	Edward Prowse	3s 0d
Walter Shere	4s 0d	John Beard	2s 4d
John Phillip	4s 0d	Walter Tockerman	3s 0d

Matthew Tourner	3s 0d	Robert Fox	0 6d
Davy Marten	1s 4d	John Heale Junior	2s 8d
Robert Singe	2s 0d	Robert Heale	1s 4d
Christopher Mudge	3s 0d	Richard Adam	1s 4d
Phillip Stephen	2s 0d	William Fox	1s 0d
Elizabeth Harris	1s 8d	Stephen Parnell	1s 4d
Margaret Phillip & her sone in lawe	1s 0d	Simon Mudge	1s 4d
Joan Pnell widdowe	1s 4d	Jasper Phillip	0 8d
Austin Lavers	2s 0d	Richard Phillip	0 8d
John Voyse	1s 0d	Peter Madoke	0 8d
William Abraham	1s 0d	Thomas Mills	0 8d
Edward Windeat	1s 4d	Robert Knowle	1s 4d

98. DEAN PRIOR, Highway Rate, 1602

DHC, 4567A-99/PW1

Note: This rate has substantial additions in the individuals who were rated compared to Item 95. The wardens' expenses, which included work at Dean Marshes and Denborne Bridge, amounted to 11s 5d which left them with a surplus of 3d.

This is the Ackompte of Edward Prowse & Robert Knoll Surveyores of the Wayes for one hole yere Laste paste mad the 6th daye of Aprell & in the forteth & forith yere of her Majesty's Raigne that nowe is etc. *year* 1602

Rectes

First of John Geles Esquire	6d	Thomas Coleman	2d
Arthur Harte gentleman	6d	Matthew Turnerd	2d
John Heale	6d	Robert Syng	2d
William Headd	6d	Roger Cole	2d
John Edwards	6d	Simon Mudg	1d
John Foxe	4d	Margaret Phillip	1d
Robert Mudge	4d	Anthony Widger	1d
John Parnell	3d	William Toulcheade	1d
The same John	2d	John Boyse	1d
John Phillip	3d	John Hardon	1d
John Conne	3d	William Hardon	1d
John Colyn	3d	Thomas Wollerdon	1d
Walter Sheare	3d	Jasper Weatherdon	1d
Walter Toukerman	3d	Matthew Leanerd	1d
John Luscomb	3d	Robert Stabbe	[blank]
Christopher Dood	3d	Andrew Hanaford	1d
Austin Lavers	2d	Thomas Turnerd	1d
Edward Wyndyeat	2d	Daniel Parnell	1d
William Abraham	2d	Edward Dev[er]	1d
John Toulcherd	2d	James Stephin	1d
Phillip Stephyn	2d	Peter Payne	1d
Pascoe Perye	2d	William Foxe	1d
Edward Prowse	2d	Richard Downe	1d
Ellis Harrys	2d	Robert Arscote	1d
Christopher Mudg	2d	John Synge	1d

John Ayshlye	1d	Bartholomew Ball	1d
Thomas Badford	1d	John Voysye	1d
Margaret Marten	1d	Richard Adam	1d
Robert Knowle	1d	Robert Foxe	1d
John Hele Junior	1d	Thomas Webber	1d
Stephen Parnell	1d	Sinclair Windyeat	1d
Thomas Wylls	1d	John Penhaye	1d
Robert Hele	1d	Nicholas Luscomb	1d
Waltere Graye	1d	John Dev[er]	1d
Edward Arscote	1d	John Rider	1d
Peter Madicke	1d	Resevyd more that Remend uppon the laste	
John Symons	1d	Ackontt	6d
Peter Ellett	1d	*Sum* of Resetes	11s 8d

99. DEAN PRIOR, Poor Rate, 1616

DHC, 4567A-99/P01

Note: This rate is included in a badly damaged volume that is too fragile to examine closely. The following year an unusual event involved Philip Michelmore, one of those listed in this rate. In the home of Sir Edward Giles, a magistrate, it was claimed that Michelmore had been overcome with alcohol in Buckfastleigh and that a local woman 'did take out the said Michelmore's privy members out of his breeches and put them in again and the said Michelmore did not awake or understand thereof'.[10]

Deane prior

The Ackount of Stephen Parnell & Geoffrey Wyndeat Church wardens: Franncis Alley gentleman: Edward Wyndeat and John Luscombe Overseers for the poore of the saide pishe made the fower & Twenteth daye of Aprill *in the year of our Lord* 1616: before his Majesties Justices of the Peace here under mentioned by force of a Statute in that behalfe made & provided:

Receits:

First of Sir Edward Gyles Knight	£1 14s 4d	the Occupiers of Henry Legassicks Tenement	
the Occupiers of the glebe lande	0 8s 0		0 4s 4d
ffrauncis Alley gentleman	0 12s 6d	Thomas Coleman	0 4s 0
John Hele	0 13s 9d	Walter Tuckerman	0 4s 0
Thomas Hed	0 17s 6d	Robert Dod	0 4s 0
Robert Mudge	0 11s 6d	Edward Prowse	0 4s 0
John Cowne	0 7s 6d	Thomas Knowlinge	0 4s 0
Apollo Barry	0 7s 6d	William Gyll	0 4s 0
Walter Sheare	0 7s 6d	Nicholas Lavers	0 4s 0
John Parnell	0 6s 9d	Matthew Turner	0 2s 4d
Robert Knight	0 6s 9d	Roger Coole	0 2s 8d
Thomas Maddicke	0 8s 0	William Hed	0 3s 0
John Fox	0 5s 0	William Maddicke	0 2s 4d
John Luscombe	0 5s 10d	Edward Wyndeate	0 2s 0
the Occupiers of Reddicleife [Redicleave] 0 5s 10d		John Lavers	0 2s 0
		William Abraham	0 2s 4d
Geoffrey Wyndeate	0 5s 0	Richard Lavers	0 2s 2d
Jasper Tolchard	0 6s 6d	Peter Maddicke	0 2s 6d

[10] Gray, *Strumpets*, p. 57; DHC, Chanter 867/fol. 666.

John Veosey	0 1s 8d	Stephen Parnell	0 2s 4d
Thomas Parnell	0 1s 4d	Ellize Harris	0 1s 4d
John Wyndeat	0 1s 8d	[total]	11 18 05
Margaret Martyn	0 1s 8d		

John Mudge	0 1s 8d	Christopher Dunridge	0 2s [torn]
Thomas Mylles	0 1s	the Occupiers of Blackwills	0 [torn] 4d
Thomas Dod	0 1s	Thomas Nosworthie	0 0 4d
the Occupiers of Anthony Crouts lyving	0 0 4d	Simon Stondich	0 2s 1d
		William Harris	0 1s 3d
Edward Welbrooke	0 1s 8d	Richard Tuckermoor	0 0 8d
Ralph Dench	0 1s 4d	James Stokey	0 0 8d
John Dunridge from him selfe & Mr Troses ground	0 1s 4d	Henry Goodman	0 1s 4d
		Bennett Sheare	0 0 8d
John Hore	0 1s 6d	John Hardon for Mr Troses ground	0 0 2d
Phillip Mychelmoore	0 3s 0	Edmund Jewzell	0 0 4d
Thomas Callard	0 3s 0	Henry Lovers	0 0 4d
Edward Luscombe	0 3s 8d	the Occupiers of John Stidstons ground	0 0 6d
John Greene	0 [torn]	Simon Ball	0 0 4d
John Pomeroy from him selfe & Mr Troses ground	0 3s [torn]	[total]	01 19 03

[new page]

Richard Maddocke	0 12s 6d	Thomas Austyn	0 0 6d
The Occupiers of John Maddicks Tenement	0 3s 2d	Emanuell Caseley	0 0 6d
Richard Harris	0 2s 8d	more we receved for John Devers goods beinge solde	0 8d 9d
Henry Veele	0 2s 8d	more which remayned in his purse when he dyed	0 2s 5d
William Eaton	0 3s 9d		
John Baker	0 1s 0	*Sum* is	01 19 03
Thomas Maddicke	0 0 10d	*Sum total* of receipts is	£15 16s 11d
William Austyn	0 0 6d		

100. DEAN PRIOR, Poor Rate, 1629

DHC, 4567A-99/PO1

Note: See Item 99.

Deane Prior
The accompt of Robt Mudge and William Gill Churchwardens Geoffrey Windiat and Jasper Tollchard Overseers of the poore of the said Parrish for the yere past made the nynteenth day of Aprill *in the year of our Lord* 1629 allowed by his Majesties Justices of the peace by force of A Statute in that case made & pvided &c

Receipts as followeth

First of Sir Edward Giles knight	27s 6d	Thomas Head	14s 10d
Barnaby Potter Doctor of Divinitie	6s 0	John Cowne	10s 0
more for Jasp Tolchards living	4s 8d	Robert Mudge	10s 0
Robert Furse gentleman	10s 0	William Gill for Sempson [Zempson]	
John Heale	9s 6d	Clampitts & Morshead [Moors Head]	10s 0

John Parnell	4s 6d	Mary Standish	1s 8d
Christopher Dundridge	8s 4d	the Occupiers of Richard Massies grownd	1s 0
Marian Knight	5s 0	Hugh Lavers	1s 10d
Walter Sheere	4s 0	Richard Harris for moorepks	1s 0
John Roper	4s 0	Richard Harris for himselfe	2s 2d
Geoffrey Scobble	6s 0	Richard Maddicke	10s 0
Thomas Colman	4s 6d	Henry Veale	2s 2d
Henry Legassicke	3s 6d	Valentine Prowse	3s 0
Gabriel Gest	5s 0	Thomas Maddicke	0 8d
Walter Tuckerman	3s 2d	William Eaton	3s 00
Agnes Knowling	3s 2d	William Baker	1s 00
Robert Dodd	3s 0	Phillip Michelmore	2s 6d
Geoffrey Windiat	2s 8d	Samuel Michelmore	2s 6d
Nicholas Lavers	1s 10d	Mary Luscombe	2s 6d
William Head	2s 6d	Thomas Callard	2s 4d
more for broomepke & the little meade	0 4d	Abraham Harwood	0 10d
John Dundridge	1s 8d	William Rider	0 10d
Richard Maddicke	3s 0	Simon Ball	1s 00
John Cole	1s 6d	Emanuell Casley	1s 00
Edward Windiat	1s 10d	John Faule	0 6d
William Abraham	2s 6d	Daniel Weatherne	00 10d
William Caseley	1s 6d	John Hext	1s 00
Richard Lavers	1s 6d	John Lavers	0 8d
John Parnell	0 10d	James Pomery	1s 00
Thomas Parnell	1s 6d	Edward Cowne	00 6d
John Mudge	1s 4d	Thomas Turner	00 6d
John Windiatt	1s 4d	Adrian Sheere	00 4d
Edward Welbrooke	1s 4d	Anthony Croft	00 4d
Elizabeth Hoare	1s 4d	John Parnell Junior	00 4d
Henry Goodman	1s 6d	Jarvis Colman	00 4d
John Cowne Junior	1s 6d	Edward Collings	00 4d
Mary Prowse	2s 00	Ralph Dench	00 4d
John Collings	0 6d	William Collinge	00 4d
Joan Harris	1s 4d	William Lavers	00 6d

Rec more for Joan Foxes Clothes and houshould implements wch weare sold as followeth

sold to Joan Brocke a pr of gloves & a ptlett	1s 0
sold to Geoffrey Windiat a coat and wastcoat & a smocke for	4s 6d
sold to Robert Arscot her bedding for	0 1d
sold to Robt Mudge her tymber vessell for	2s 10d
sold to William Rider 3 aprons 2 napkins & 2 kercheifs for	3s 6d
wch said 3s 6d the said William Rider refuseth to pay	
receved more of Robert Mudge	20s 0
Sum rec.	£13 8s 4d
Those wch refuse to pay are these	
John Herne	0 6d
more for Denches Marsh	0 6d
Thomas Stitston	1s 0d

101. DEAN PRIOR, Poor Rate, 1631

DHC, 4567A-99/PO1

Note: See Item 99.

Deane Prior

The account of John Cowne Junior Henry Goodman Church Wardens, William Gile and Christopher Dudndridge Overseers of the poore of the said pish for the yere last past made the daie of Aprill in the year of our Lord 1631 Allowed by his Majesties Justices of the peace by force of a Statute in that case made & pvided.

Receipts

First Sir Edward Giles knight	27s 6d	Henry Goodman	1s 6d
The occupiers of the Glebe land	6s 0	John Cowne Junior	1s 6d
Robert Furse gentleman	10s 0	Mary Prowse	2s 00
John Heale	9s 6d	Crispine Lavers	1s 0
Thomas Head	14s 10d	Valentine Prowse	3s 0
John Cowne	10s 0	Joan Harris	1s 4d
Robert Mudge	10s 0	Mary Standish	1s 8d
William Gile	10s 0	The Occupiers of Richard Massies grownd	1s 0
John Parnell	4s 6d	Richard Harris for moore pks	1s 0
Alice Dundridg	8s 4d	Richard Harris for himselfe	2s 2d
Marian Knight	5s 0	Richard Maddicke	10s 0
Gabriel Gist	5s 0	Joan Veale	2s 2d
Walter Sheere	4s 0	Thomas Maddocke	0 8d
Geoffrey Scobble	6s 0	William Eaton	3s 00
Jasper Tolchard	4s 8d	William Baker	1s 00
John Rop	4s 0	Phillip Michelmore	2s 6d
Thomas Colman	4s 6d	Samuel Michelmore	2s 6d
Henry Legassicke	3s 6d	Henry Luscombe	2s 6d
Walter Tuckerman	3s 2d	Thomas Callard	2s 4d
Agnes Knowling	3s 2d	Abram Harwood	0 10d
Robert Dodd	3s 0	William Rider	0 10d
Geoffrey Windiat	2s 8d	Simon Ball	1s 00
more for Sandhills	1s 4d	Emanuell Casley	1s 00
Nicholas Lavers	0s 10d	John Faule	0 6d
William Head	2s 6d	Daniel Weatherdone	00 10d
John Dundridge	2s 8d	John Hext	1s 00
Richard Maddocke	3s 0	John Lavers	0 8d
John Cole	1s 6d	Edward Cowne	00 6d
Edward Windiat	1s 10d	Thomas Turner	00 6d
John Abram	2s 6d	Adrian Sheere	00 4d
William Caseley	1s 6d	Anthony Croft	00 4d
Richard Lavers	1s 6d	John Parnell Junior	00 4d
Thomas Parnell	1s 6d	Jervis Colman	00 4d
John Parnell	0 10d	Edward Collings	00 4d
John Mudge	1s 4d	Ralph Dench	00 4d
John Windiatt	1s 4d	William Collinge	00 4d
Edward Welbrooke	1s 4d	William Lavers	00 6d
Elizabeth Hore	1s 4d		

the occupiers of Thomas Turners tenement in Deanecombe 0 8d

Thomas Stitston 1s 0

Received of the last overseers   £1 3s 3d
~~Some is~~   ~~£13 7s 1d~~ [in Roman substituted for Arabic numerals]

102. DEAN PRIOR, Poor Rate, 1634

DHC, 4567A-99/PO1

Note: See Item 99.

Deane prior

The Accounpte of John Collings and John Abraham Churchwardens, Thomas Head senior and John Cowne senior Overseers of the poore of the said pishe for this yeare last paste made the Seaventhe Day of aprill in *the year* 1634 allowed by his Majesty's Justices of the peace by force of a statute in that case made and provided

Receipts

First Sir Edward Giles knight	27s 6d	John Mudge	1s 4d
the occupiers of the gleebe lande	10s 0	Edward Welbrooke	1s 4d
Robert Furse gent	17s 3d	The occupiers of hores Tenemente	1s 4d
Thomas Head	14s 10d	Henry Goodman	1s 10d
more for moore pks	1s 0	Ferdinando Furse	1s 6d
John Cowne senior	10s 0	Crispin Lavers	1s 00
Robert Mudge	11s 8d	Joan Harris *widow*	1s 4d
William Gill	10s 0	The occupiers of mary Standishes Tenement	
John Cowne Junior	6s 6d		1s 8d
Christopher Parnell	4s 6d	The occupiers of Masies Tenement	1s 00
Alice Dunderidge widow	5s 2d	Richard Maddicke and Thomas Maddicke	10s 00
Mary Dunderidge	1s 4d	Robert Veale	2s 2d
Gabriel Geste	6s 00	more for the Tenement that was Richard	
for Laverses Tenement	0 6d	Harrises	2s 2d
John Collinge	5s 00	Vallentine Prowse	3s 00
Geoffrey Scobble	6s 00	Thomas Maddicke	00 8d
Walter Sheere	4s 00	William Eaton	3s 00
Jasper Tolchard	4s 8d	William Bakers Tenement	1s 00
John Rop	4s 00	Judith Michelmore *widow*	2s 6d
Geoffrey Windeatt	4s 00	Sam. Michelmore	2s 6d
Henry Legasicke	3s 6d	Henry Luscombe and Samuel Luscombe	2s 6d
Walter Tuckerman	2s 8d	Thomas Collard	2s 4d
Agnes Knowlinge	3s 2d	Alexander Fos for Nurson	1s 2d
Robert Dodd	3s 00	William Rider	1s 00
William Head	2s 10d	Simon Ball	1s 00
John Dunderidge	2s 8d	Emanuell Casley	1s 00
Richard Maddicke	3s 00	Hugh Lavers	1s 10d
John Coale	[blank]	Edward Cowne	00 6d
Edward Windeatt	1s 10d	John Foale	00 6d
John Abraham	2s 6d	Daniel Weatherdon	00 10d
William Casley	1s 6d	John Hexte	1s 00
Rich: Lavers	1s 6d	Thomas Turner	00 6d
Thomas Parnell	1s 6d	Anthony Crooke	00 4d
Nicholas Lavers	00 10d	Joan Harwood	01s 00
more for Deancombe	00 10d	John Pnell	00 4d
John Parnell	00 10d	Ralph Denche	00 6d

William Collings	00 4d	Thomas Nosworthe	00 8d
the occupiers of Turners Tenement in		Edward Collinge	00 4d
Deanecombe	00 8d	Thomas Maddicke	00 4d
Thomas Stidston	00 10d	Phillip Knowlinge	00 4d
Thomas Heade Junior	00 4d	John Harwood	00
Richard Arscott	00 6d	*Sum total*	£12 6s 5d

103. DEAN PRIOR, Poor Rate, 1640

DHC, 4567A-99/PO1

Note: See Item 99.

Deane Prior

Receits
A rate & halfe
The accompt of William Gill & Thomas Parnell Church-Wardens and Thomas Maddocks & richard Currier Overseers of the poore of the pish aforesaid for the yere last past made the 6th Day of Aprill *in the year of our Lord* 1640.

First the Ladie Mary Giles	£2 1s 3d	John Laver for Blackwills	0 2 3
the Gleabe land	0 15 0	Nicholas Laves	0 2 6
Robert Furse gentleman	1 4 4	John Hamling	0 2 7
Thomas Head	1 0 9	Thomas Edwards tenement	1s 9d
John Cowne senior	0 15 0	John Parnell Deaneton	1 0
Giles Lowman gentleman	0 2 3	John Mudge senior	2 1
Robert Mudge	0 18 9	Edward Welbrooke	2 0
William Gill	0 14 3	Simon Ball	1 9
John Cowne Junior	0 9 9	Ferdinando Furse gentleman	2 3
Thomas Parnell	0 8 3	Henry Goodman	3 9
Alice Dundridg *widow*	0 7 6	hores tenement	2 0
Geoffrey Scobble	0 9 0	Crispin Lavers	1 6
Mary Dundridge	0 2 3	Joan Harris *widow*	2 0
Gabriel Gest	0 9 3	Mr Masies tenement	1 6
more for Lavers grownd	0 0 9	Richard Maddocke of B:	6 0
John Colling	0 7 6	Thomas Maddocke	9 0
Jasper Tolchard	0 7 0	Robert Veale	6 6
Walter Shere	0 6 0	Valentine Prowse	4 6
Geoffrey Windiat	0 6 0	Thomas Maddock of B	1 0
John Roper	0 4 6	William Eaton	4 6
Henry Legassicke	0 2 7	Marks tenement	1 9
Walter Tuckerman	0 2 6	Judith Michelmore	3 9
Agnes Knowling *widow*	0 3 0	Samuel Michelmore	3 9
Elizabeth Dodd	0 5 0	Henry & Samuel Luscombe	4 3
William Head	0 4 3	Thomas Callard	3 6
John Dundridge	0 4 0	Hugh Lavers	1 6
Robert Veale for Deane	0 5 0	Alexander Foxes tenement	1 6
Richard Currier	0 2 9	William Rider	0 4
Edward Cowne	0 2 6	Richard Maddocke	1 0
William Casleigh	0 2 3	~~Nich~~ Tho: Luscombe	2 0
Joan Lavers widow	0 3 0	John Faule	0 9

Daniel Weatherdon	1 9	Thomas Stitston	1 0
John Hext	1 6	Tho: Nosworthie	0 6
Mr Luce Marten	2 6	Simon Lombshead	0 6
Joan Harwood *widow*	1 0	Henry Putt	0 4
Abrams meaddow	1 3	Robert Dodd	0 4
Thomas Head Junior	0 8	John Harwood	0 6
Thomas Mudge	0 6	Ellis Colling	0 4
Henry Gill	0 6	Peter Cutimor	0 4
Tho: Maddocke of Deantone	0 6	more rec of the last wardens	4s 8
John Parnell Junior	0 6	more for Edward Hannafords goods	7 0
[new page] Phillip Knowlinge	0s 4d	Receits is	£18 17s 2d

104. DEAN PRIOR, Poor Rate, 1644

DHC, 4567A-99/PO1

Note: See Note 99.

Deane Prior
The accompt of Thomas Head & John Harwood Churchwardens and Robert Furse gent and Robert Mudg Overseers of the poore for the yeere last past made the 22th of Aprill *in the year of our Lord* 1644.

Receipts

Imprimis of Mrs Elizabeth Potter	£1 7s 6d	of John Dundridg	0 2 8
of the Occupiers of the Gleabe	0 10 0	of Robt Veale for Deanecombe	0 3 0
of Robert Furse gent	0 16 0	of Robt Veale for his home tenement	0 4 4
of Thomas Head	0 14 10	of Richard Currier	0 1 8
of John Chowne senior	0 10 0	of Edward Cowne	0 1 8
of Giles Lowman gent	0 1 6	of William Casley	0 1 6
of William Gill	0 10 0	of Joan Lavers	0 2 6
more for Eatons	0 2 4	of John Lavers for Blackwills	0 1 0
of Robert Mudge	0 11 7	of Nicholas Lavers	0 1 2
of John Cowne Junior	0 6 6	more for Deanecombe	0 0 10
of Thomas Parnell	0 5 6	of the Occupiers of Edwards tenement	0 1 2
of Alice Dundridge	0 5 0	of John Parnell of Deantowne	0 0 8
of Mary Dundridge	0 1 4	of John Mudge	0 1 6
of Geoffrey Scobble	0 6 0	of Edward Welbrooke	1s 4d
of Gabriel Gest	0 6 0	of Ferdinando Furse gentleman	1 6
more for Lavers ground	0 0 6	of Simon Ball	1 0
of John Colling	0 5 0	of Henry Goodman	2 6
of Jasper Tolchard	0 4 8	The Occupiers of hores tenement	1 4
of Walter Sheere	0 4 0	of Crispen Lavers	1 0
of Geoffrey Wintiat	0 4 0	of Joan Harris	1 4
of John Roper	0 3 0	of Mr Masies tenement	1 0
of John Hamling	0 3 4	of Richard Maddocke	4 0
of the Occupiers of Mr Skinners tenement	0 2 8	of Thomas Maddocke of Whitixton [Whiteaxton]	4 0
of Agnes Knowling	0 2 0	of Bridget Prowse	3 0
of Elizabeth Dodde	0 3 4	of Thomas Maddocke of Brent	0 8
of William Head	0 2 10	The occupiers of Eatons Meade	0 3

of William Marks	1 2	of John Parnell	0 6
of Judith Michelmore	2 2	of Thomas Stitson	0 8
of Edward Robins	2 6	of Richard Casleigh	0 4
of Henry & Samuel Luscombe	2 8	of John Lavers to Crosse	0 4
of Thomas Callard	2 4	of John Hext	1 0
of Alexander Fox	1 0	of Thomas Parnell	0 6
of Duletta Luscombe	1 0	of Thomas Nosworthie	0 4
of John Faule	[blank]	of Simon Lamshead	0 4
of Daniel Weatherdon	1 0	of Thomas Knowling	0 4
of Mr Richard Merten	1 8	of John Harwood	0 6
of Joan Harwood	0 8	of Ellis Colling	0 4
of Abrams Meadowe	0 6	of Peter Cutmore	0 4
of Thomas Head Junior	0 8	of Robert Mudge	0 4
of Thomas Mudge	0 8	of William Marks for arrerages	1 9
of Henry Gill	0 6	Geoffrey Scobble for arrerages	2 0

[new page]

of Henry & Samuel Luscombe for arrerags 4s 0d	Alexander Fox for arrerages	1 6

Received of the old Overseers   £2 11s 3d
Receipts ~~Sum total £14 18s 10d~~
Receipts £15 1s 2d
Expences £16 8s 1d
So wee have expended more then wee have received £1 6s 11d

Witnes to the passing of this account
[signed] John Cowne senior   Richard Cowne   John Collinge
[the signatures of two churchwardens have been crossed through]

105. DEAN PRIOR, Poor Rate, 1649

DHC, 4567A-99/PO1

Note: See Item 99.

Deane Prior
The accompt of Giles Lowman gent and Thomas Maddocke Churchwardens Thomas Head Senior and John Hext Overseers of the poore for the yeere last past made the 28th Day of March *in the year of our Lord* 1649.

Receits

First Mrs Elizabeth Potter	£1 7s 6d	Geoffrey Scobble	0 5 0
Robert Furse gentleman	0 16 0	Alice Dundridge	0 5 0
Mr John Symes Vicar	0 7 0	Elizabeth Gest	0 3 8
Thomas Head senior	0 14 10	Joan Lavers of Deane tone	0 0 4
Richard Cowne	0 9 0	Mrs Bridget Lowman	0 2 4
Giles Lowman gentleman	0 1 6	more for Abrams Meado	0 0 10
William Gill	0 10 0	The occupiers of Sheers tenement	0 4 0
more for Eatons tenement	0 2 4	Jasper Tolchard	0 4 6
Thomas Mudge	0 11 7	Geoffrey Windiat	0 2 8
John Cowne Junior	0 6 6	John James	0 3 0
Thomas Parnell senior	0 5 6	John Hamling	0 2 10

Francis Jackson	0 2 0	Thomas Maddocke	6 0
Elizabeth Dodd	0 3 3	Bridget Prowse	3 0
more for Whitixton	0 0 6	William Luscombe	0 8
Judith Head	0 2 10	The occupiers of Eatons Meadowe	0 3
John Dundridg	0 2 2	William Marks	1 2
Ames Freind	0 0 4	Hugh Hanks	2 2
Robert Veale for Deancombe	0 3 0	Edward Robins	2 8
mor for his home seate	0 4 4	Henry & Sam: Luscomb	2 8
Richard Currier	0 1 6	Thomas Callard	2 4
Edward Cowne	0 1 2	Alexander Fox	1 2
Ellis Pomery	0 1 6	Dulett Luscombe	1 0
John Lavers for Blackwills	0 1 6	John Hext	1 4
Joan Laver of Overdeane	0 2 0	more for Stocks Tenement	0 8
Elizabeth Lavers	0 0 6	Agnes Weatherdon	0 10
William Lavers	0 1 6	Richard Matyn gentleman	1 8
The Occupiers of Edwards grownd	0 1 2	Joan Harwood	0 6
John Parnell of Deane towne	0 0 8	John Harwood	1 4
John Colling	0 3 4	Thomas Head Junior	0 8
John Mudge	1s 6d	Henry Gill	0 6
The occupiers of Skinners Tenement	2 4	John Parnell Junior	0 6
Robert Dodd for Berrell	0 10	Thomas Stitston	0 8
Ferdinando Furse	1 4	Thomas Parnell Junior	0 8
Simon Ball	1 0	Thomas Nosworthie	0 8
William Goodman	2 0	Robert Mudge	0 6
more for John Collings grownd	1 8	Ellis Colling	0 4
William Hore	1 4	Thomas Dodd	0 6
Crispen Lavers	1 0	Richard Andrew	0 4
Samuel Hore	0 8	John Hearne	0 6
John Michell	1 0	Rec of the former Overseers	13 [obscured]
Richard Maddocke	4 0	*Sum total*	£12 [obscured]

DIPTFORD

One rate survives for this village located fifteen miles east of Plymouth. No poor rates survive but the glebe terrier of 1613 noted that the 'rate for the maintenance of our poor is yearly £10 or thereabout'.[1]

106. DIPTFORD, Military Rate, c.1592

DHC, 3799M/3/O/4/50, no page numbers

Note: This rate is recorded in a volume with pages approximately 7¾ inches in width and 12 inches in length.

Stanborough Hundred **Dipford**

William Fowell gent.	a Corslett ps, 2 musketts ps
William Newton gent	2 Corsletts ps, musketts ps
John Lavers	a musket ps, a Callr ps a Corslet ps
John Hele gent.	2 Corsletts ps a musket ps
Peter Harby	a musket ps a Callr ps
~~Robert~~ John Distayn	a musket ps
William Symon	a Callr ps, a Corslet ps
~~John~~ William Lavers of Lapland	a Corslett ps
Henry Downinge	a musket ps, a Callr ps
Nicholas Forde	a musket ps, a Callr ps
~~William~~ William Toser	a bowe sheafe arr[ows] a Callr, a halbert
~~Henry~~ Henry Lavers of Combshed [Combeshead]	a musket ps
John Hingston	a musket ps
Thomas Oldreve	a Callr ps
Thomas Mychell	a musket & bandalere
Thomas Downinge	a sword, Dagger & hedpeece
~~Henry~~ Henry Bynmore	a musket ps
~~Richard~~ John Dorres & John Sheere	a musket ps
Thomas Parnell	a musket ps
John Downinge	a Callr ps
John Kinge	a musket & bandalere
William Comminge	a hedpeece sword & dagger
Richard Crossinge	a musket ps
Phillip Woodye	a muskett & bandalere
Hugh Woodye	a hedpece sword & dagger
Richard Tom	a Corslet ps
Thomas Lavers & Thomas Disteyn	a musket ps
Peter Collyn	a musket ps
~~Thomas Cole~~	a musket & bandalere
Hortas Cole, Dennis Cole & Thomas Rider	a hadpece sword & dagger
William Mychell	a halbert

1 DHC, Diocese of Exeter, Principal Registry, Glebe Terriers, Diptford, 1613.

John Egbear	a halbert
John Damerell	a halbert
Henry Crossinge	a halbert
Robert Basse	a halbert
Jobe Campe	a halbert
Robert Lavers gent.	a Corslet ps
Richard Jackson	a musket ps
Alice Lancastre	a musket & bandalere
Walter Lancaster senior	hadpece sword & dagger

The parish armour	Corsletts ps 5
	Muskets ps 2
	Pikes 6

DITTISHAM

Only one rate survives for this parish on the River Dart located five miles from Dartmouth.

107. DITTISHAM, Military Rate, c.1592

DHC, 3799M/3/O/4/50, no page numbers

Note: This rate is recorded in a volume with pages approximately 7¾ inches in width and 12 inches in length.

Dittisham

Ambrose Billett esquire	2 Corsletts ps
John Badaford	a musket ps a Callr ps a Corslet ps
William Leach	a musket ps, a Callr ps a bill ps a Corslet ps
George Pyne	2 Corslet ps
Gregory Sharpham	a Corslet ps a musket ps
William Yoldon	a musket ps, a Corslet ps
Nicholas Browse	a Callr ps, a musket ps a Corslet ps
William Downinge	a musket ps, a Corslet ps
William Baddaford	a musket ps, a Callr ps a halbert a bill
John Harradon	a musket ps a Callr ps
John Ostion	a Callr ps, a musket ps
Henry Austin	a musket ps
Richard Collaford	a musket ps
Richard Ellyott	a musket ps
Adam Lymer	a musket ps
Nicholas Flute	a musket ps
Richard Lane	a musket ps
Nicholas Hoyle	a Callr ps
The parish armour	Corslet ps 2, alminier ps 2, Calbr ps 2, musket ps 1, pikes 14

DODBROOKE

Only one rate survives for this parish which was divided by a stream from Kingsbridge. It makes up one half of Kingsbridge in a manner similar to Newton Bushel regarding Newton Abbot. Of Dodbrooke it was later noted by Polwhele that 'the custom of this place [has been] to pay a tithe to the clergyman in white ale'. Another writer observed it was 'a liquor peculiar to this part of Devonshire' and that the tithe was paid by the landlords of every public house.[1] Dodbrooke, which historically comprised one street, had become a borough by 1319 and was later incorporated into Kingsbridge.[2] It was at the time of this rate that a poor man of the parish was excommunicated after the church bell was cracked during his ringing.[3] A few years after this rate John Markell, who was listed in 1613 as paying sixteen pence for the rate, allegedly called the rector a knave, arrant knave, dissembling knave and a 'shit breech knave'.[4] About 11 per cent of the parishioners contributed to the rate.

108. Dodbrooke, Poor Rate, 1613

DHC, Diocese of Exeter, Principal Registry, Dodbrooke Church Rates, 1613

Note: This rate was written on a single sheet of folded paper which measures 12 inches by 16 inches.

Dodbrooke (114)
The Ratemente there made for the releife of the poore the 6th daie of Aprill *in the year of our Lord* 1613.

Inhabitants					
	James Weymouth	13s 4d	William Angior	16d
	John Angior	4s	John Luscombe	16d
	Phillippe Brockedon	4s	Tristram Cole	16d
	Robert Preste	4s	Anthony Michell	16d
	Leonarde Kente	3s 4d	Nicholas Tracye	12d
	Joan Peyrs widow	3s	Lawrence Emmotte	12d
	Thomas Downman	3s	Walter Graye	12d
	John Michell senior	2s 8d	William Dollinge	12d
	Anne Tracye widow	2s	John Tracye	12d
	Katherine Marshe widow	2s	Pascoe Harradon	12d
	Hercules Ball	2s	Grace Lane widowe	12d
	Robert Poolinge	2s	Robert Browne	12d
	John Downman	20d	William Giles	12d
	John Hyll	20d	Henry Addames	12d
	Pascoe Luckrafte	20d	Robert Angior	8d
	William Pynhaie	20d	Andrew Peyrs	8d
	Phillippe Downman	16d	John Downman carpenter	8d
	John Markell	16d	George Bastarde	8d

[1] Richard Polwhele, *The History of Devonshire* (Exeter, 1806), II, 477; Lysons, *Magna*, p. 165.
[2] W. G. Hoskins, *Devon* (Newton Abbot, 1954), pp. 419–20.
[3] DHC, CC4/50.
[4] DHC, CC19B/219.

John Angior weaver	8d	Hercules Giles	4d
John Hearde	8d	Phillippe Luckrafte	4d
George Stanton	8d	John Hooper	4d
John Michell Junior	8d	Richarde Howse	4d
Thomas Trebell	8d	John Michelmore	6d
Richarde Lane	8d	Sum	[blank]

[page 2]

Outholders

Richarde Baker gent.	6d	John Scobbell	2d
Thomas Clarke	20d	William Browne	1d
John Winchelsie	18d	Mr John Rumbelow clearke	4d
William Cleife	8d	Alexander Wolcote	12d
George Brockedon	2d	John Clarke for salt milles	3s
Richarde Hillarie	2d	William Hele	16d
John Farwell	4d	William Horwill	2d
John Howse	4d	Widow Ellys	2d
Walter Lappe	2d	Walter Rogers for high house	16d
William Neale	3d	*Sum*	14s 16d

Subscribed by us
Robert Poolinge James Marthen churchwardens
Leonard Kente Sideman

DODDISCOMBSLEIGH

One rate survives for this parish which is located seven miles south-west of Exeter. About 11 per cent of the parishioners contributed to the rate.

109. Doddiscombsleigh, Church Rate, 1612

DHC, Diocese of Exeter, Principal Registry, Doddiscombsleigh Church Rates, 1612

Note: This rate was written on a sheet of paper which measures 8 inches by 12 inches. In 1628 there was a dispute with Malachi Dewdney over non-payment of his third church rate that year. His land holdings comprised closes named Howcombe Meadow, the Willparke, Oakhay Meadow, Broad Meadow, Pound Meadow, Marshe Meadow, Vogsleigh, White Downe, Taddaven Meadow, Bubwills and Rodes. They comprised 50½ acres.[1] A separate list noted he held 35 closes which had combined acreage of 151 acres. These were Dux Meadow, Houndicombe Meadow, Wilparke, Okehay, Broad Meadow, Newparke, Pound Meadow, Piscombe, Challowill, Grasshay, White Downe, Hare Hill, Greaterhay, Miscliffs, Miscliff Wood, Bubwills, Roades, Caddavin Meadow, Caddavin, The Woods, Marsh Meadow, Vogsleigh, Broome Marsh, Little Marsh and West Marsh.[2]

Doddiscombsleigh   The Rate   90

Mrs Judith Duedny	13s 4d	John Monger	18d
Mr William Babb	13s 4d	William Burnell	12d
Mr William Bayly	3s 4d	Sibbilla Pethabridge	12d
Walter Eastabrocke	3s 2d	Bartholomew Norrowmoore	14d
William Allerhead	2s 10d	Michael Cole	12d
Thomas Luckis	2s 8d	John Pethabridge	12d
Michael Dollinge	2s 8d	Jane Tremayne	9d
John Luckis	2s 8d	Thomas Pethabridge	10d
William Cheynye	2s 8d	John Berry	12d
Alice Babb	2s	Richard Langaller	8d
Mris Simons Bargaine	2s	William Sampford	8d
Markes Moore	2s	William monger	12d
Richard Wills	22d	Robert Potter	8d
Bennott Voyce	2s	Streat head	4d
Richard Preeston for Wilhaye [Wilhays]	18d	John Connett	8d
Vincent Collinges	16d	Robert Jerston	6d
John Wills for his Bargaine & Poundcombe	2s	Richard Godsland for his Cawte	4d

A True Copie of the Rate which Walter Eastabroke beinge warden gathered in the year of our Lord God one Thousand Six hunderd & Twelve
the signe of Richard Godsland warden
the signe of John Luckis side man
the signe of Michael Cole side man

---

[1] DHC, CC166.
[2] DHC, CC22.

DOLTON

Three rates survive for this parish located fifteen miles north of Okehampton but the poor condition of that of 1613, held at the Devon Heritage Centre,[1] does not allow examination.

110. DOLTON, Church Rate, 1613

DHC, Diocese of Exeter, Principal Registry, Dolton Church Rates, 1613

Note: This rate was written on paper, some 6 inches in width and 12 inches in length, which has suffered considerable damage.

[torn] of the Aunchent Church rate of Corne Within the parrish of [torn] used and accustomed to be paid towards the mayntynance of the same Church, Until this present Yeere of our Lord God One thousand and six Hundred and Thirteene, as here Showeth

Richard Stafford Esquier for the Barton of Stafford   one Bushell of wheat & three bushels of Oatts
[torn] Stafford for the Tenement called Newcomb   halfe a bushel of wheat & two bushels of oats
[torn] Stafford for the Tenement of Aller   halfe a bushel of wheat & a bushel & halfe of Oatts
[torn]t & Robert Avery for the Tenement of Hettacott   halfe a bushel of wheat & a bushel and [torn]
[torn] for one Tenement in Hame   halfe a bushel of wheat and a bushel of Oatts
[torn]b for his Tenement in Ham   halfe a bushel of wheat and a bushel of Oatts
[torn]oore one Tenement in Woodtowne   one pecke of wheat and a bushel of Oatts
[torn]on his Tenement in Woodtowne   one pecke of wheat and a bushel of Oatts
[torn]aton his Tenement in Kellaway   one pecke of wheat
[torn] his Tenement in Westlake   one pecke of wheat & a bushel of Oatts
[torn] for his Tenement in Langham   one pecke of wheat & a bushell of Oatts
[torn]per for his Tenement in Langham   one pecke of wheat & a bushell of Oatts
[torn] for his Tenement in Langham   one pecke of wheat & halfe a bushell of Oatts
[torn]ll for his Tenement in Langham   one pecke of wheate & halfe a bushell of Oatts
[torn]alkey for his tenement in Langham   one pecke of Wheat & a halfe a bushel of Oatts
[torn] for his Tenement in Lower Chaple   halfe a bushel of wheat & a bushel & half of Oats
[torn] for her Tenement in Chaple   halfe a bushel of wheat & a bushel & halfe of Oatts
[torn] Tockleigh   one pecke of wheat & one bush [torn]
[torn] in Tockleigh   one pecke of wheat & one bushell [torn]
[torn] his Tenement in Tockleigh   one pecke of wheat & one bushe[torn]
[torn] Handcocke for his Tenement in Brightleigh   halfe a bushel of wheat & a bushel [torn]
[torn] for his Tenement in Brightleigh   halfe a bushel of wheat & a bushell [torn]
[torn]nnybear for the Tenement of Wolridge   A pecke of wheat and a bushell of O[torn]
[torn] John Burgen for the Tenement of Halsdon   halfe a bushel of wheat & a bushell & half of Oatts.
Item John Avery for his Tenement in Yeddlecott [Iddlecott]   halfe a bushel of wheat and two bushells of Oatts.
Item Alice Hooper for her Tenement in yeddlecotte   halfe a bushel of wheat & a bushel & halfe of Oatts.
Item Thomas Hooper for the Tenement of Venton   a pecke of wheat and a bushel of Oatts.

[1]   DHC, Diocese of Exeter, Principal Registry, Devon church rates.

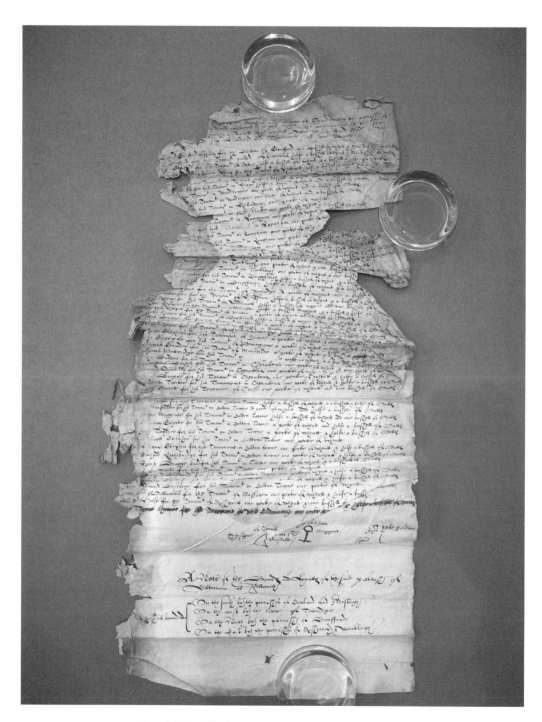

Plate 21. Heavily damaged church rate for Dolton, 1613.

Item Thomas Hooper for his Tenement of Buckland   halfe a bushell wheat & two Bushells of Oatts.

[torn] Robert Bragge senior for his Tenement in fursse   a pecke of wheat & halfe a bushel of Oatts.

[torn] Margery Leviton for her Tenement in fursse   a pecke of wheat & halfe a Bushell of Oatts.

[torn] Stephen Pawe for his Tenement of East Cudworthie [Cudworthy]   halfe a bushel of wheat & two bushels of Oats.

[torn] William Stephens for his Tenement of Downe [Down]   a pecke of wheat & one bushel of Oatts.

[torn]n Screagan for his Tenement of Pennygrewe   a pecke of wheat & one bushel of Oatts.

[torn] Thomas Saunder for his Tenement of Merefilde [Meravin]   a pecke of wheat & a halfe bushel of Oatts.

[torn] Thomas Putteridge for his Tenement in [blank]   a pecke of wheat & a bushel & halfe of Oatts.

[torn] John Burdon for his Tenement of Woodtowne   halfe a bushell of wheat & a bushel & halfe of Oatts.

[torn] William Bright for his Tenement in Cherubear   one pecke of wheat & one bushell of Oatts.

[torn] Richard Chamberly for his Tenement in Cherubear   one pecke of wheat & halfe a bushell of Oatts.

[torn] John Bragge for his Tenement in Cherubear   one pecke of wheatt & halfe a bushell of Oatts.

[torn] Walter Toocker for his Tenement in Cherubear   one pecke of wheatt & halfe a bushell of Oatts.

[torn] John Sweett for his Tenement of Crosse   one pecke of wheatt and one bushell of Oatts.

[Dolton Town]

[torn] John Heaman for his Tenement in Dolton Towne,   halfe a bushel of wheat & a bushell & halfe of Oatts.

Item John Murfeilde for his Tenement in Dolton Towne   A pecke of wheat and halfe a bushell of Oatts.

Item Peter Maggente for Tenement in Dolton Towne   halfe a bushel of wheat and one bushell of Oatts.

Item Humphrey Shorte for his Tenement in Dolton Towne   a pecke of wheat and halfe a bushell of Oatts.

[torn] John Taylder for this Tenement in Dolton Towne   a pecke of wheat & halfe a bushell of Oatts.

Item Wilmot Stephen for her Tenement in Dolton Towne   one pecke of wheat.

Item Henry Stephen for his Tenment in Dolton towne   one pecke of wheat & halfe a bushell of Oatts.

[torn] Richard Lethebridge for his Tenement in Dolton towne   one pecke of wheat & halfe a bushell of Oatts.

[torn] Robert Bragge Junior for his Tenement in Cleive   one pecke of wheat & a bushell of Oatts.

[torn] Seale for his Tenement in Cleive   one pecke of wheatt.

[torn] Richard Haiwood for his Tenement in Dolton Towne   one pecke of wheat & halfe a bushell of Oatts.

[torn] William Hill for his Tenement in Dolton Towne for   one pecke of wheat & halfe a bushell of Oatts.

Item Edward Baseleigh for his Tenement in Dolton Towne   one pecke of wheat.

Item. Mrs Wollacomb for the Tenement of Mussaven   one pecke of wheat & halfe a bushel of Oatts.

Item Mr Halse for the Tenement of Aishwill [Ashwell]   one pecke of wheat & one bushel of Oatts.

[line crossed through]

The sign of Thomas Hooper, constable

The sign of Peter Maggent

The sign of John Zeale, guardian

111. DOLTON, Churchyard Rate, 1623

NDRO, 834A/PR1

Note: This rate was recorded in the bound parish register which has vellum pages which measure aproximately 6 inches in width and 12 inches in length. A preceding memorandum, dated 15 January 1764, recorded 'Whereas the church yards and hedges in the parish of Dolton in the county of Dolton [sic] have hereto for been Repaired by the Occupiers of the Several Estates in the Said Parish (that is to Say) some two yards, some one yards and some a halfe a yard – in proportion to the Value of the Estate and there is a list in this Booke Bearin date the 21th of march 1622 [sic] But that this list being of so Long gone and only the names of the Ocupiers & not the names of all the Estates mentioned, we are at a loss how to measure out those yards So, as it may be properly repaired, we Robt Shute and Wm Shute Churchardens of the Parish aforesd finding the church yards in a Ruinous Condition and having no proper Rule to Enforce the Repair thereof have Summoned a Vestry'. Four men were listed in favour, six were against.

Dolton pish March 21ᵗʰ 1622

A list taken and agreed upon by Mr William Knaplocke Rect. Thomas Hoop: Churchwarden. Stephen Partrig and william Shorte Constabels. Mr Henry Bellew Rowland Hoop William White William Leavaten Edward Bragg William Drake Tho: Wonnacott Sampson Northam Jerimy Webber, with Divers others of every yard aboute the Church chard *that is to say*:
The church gate is to be repared by the pish.

John Graddon
John eale
Widdo Attkin for Towne
Mr Stoffor for Stofford [Stafford] and Aller two yards
Hettacott
Lower Ham
Higher ham
Elizabeth Godfry and Pett: Arscott for Dolton Mill one yarde
Halfe yard by each side the stile for John Moore
Joan Attkin
Lower Chappell
Higher Chapple
Margery Jenkin
Wm Leciton for Kelway halfe yarde
Rowland Hoop Junior for Tockly to yards
Wm Rudge
Wm White
William Drake
Tho: Wonnacott
Phillip Bragg
Susan Clarke
Wm Leveton for Langham
Mr Voysey
Tho: Naylder
W. Crudge
Borden to yards

Newcomb to yards
Harton to yards
Buckland two yards
Robert Bragg for ~~to yards~~ west furse
Phillip Liboton for east Furse
Phillip Hoop for West Cudworthy
John fleaman for east Cudworthy
Robert Stringgon
Monsaven
Phillip Liveton ['Alling' smudged]
Downe
Tho: Tayder for towne
West Iddelcoott [Iddlecott]
East Iddelcott
a yard and halfe by the pish
Timothy Tayder
Mrs Goodwin
Nich: Webber: Jerimy Webber
Rickiard more and John Bragg one yarde
Edward Bragg the Stares and halfe a yarde
Pett: Arscott and Joan Friggon one yarde
Sampson Northam
Robert Bragg for cline
Henry Hearde two yards
Stephen Partridge
Agnes Bright
John Bright
Edmund fleaman and Wm: White the stocke house doore

DUNKESWELL

One rate survies for this parish located five miles north of Honiton. Its Cistercian abbey was dissolved in 1539. Tristram Risdon wrote 'its ruins now lie low in the dust' but more can be seen today than he had suggested nearly four hundred year ago.

112. **Dunkeswell**, Church Rate, 1610

DHC, Diocese of Exeter, Principal Registry, Dolton Church Rates, 1610

Note: This rate was written on single sheet of folded paper which measures 12 inches by 16 inches.

Dunkeswell   *In the year of our Lord* 1610   **9**

A rate made by the Churchwarden, sydemen & others of the parishe of Dunkeswell in the countye of Devon for the repayring of theire church, to be gathered yerely & as often as neede shall require every yere by the Churchwarden made the 13th daye of June in the yere of our Lord God ~~160~~ 1610, made by those whose names are hereunder written Anthony Philip, Rafe Deman, John Rawe, Richard Maunsell, Andrew Whitehorne, Robert Gally, Thomas Burrowe, Ellis Phillip, Alexander Richardes, William Asheforde, William Bruford, Richard Phillip, Thomas Horwoode, & Ambrose Pringe, as followeth.

Ambrose Serle for deepe grange	4s 4d	Pitland	9d
Ambrose Serle for great Oulforchurch		John Blackemore	8d
[Wolford Church] 2s		Robert Rudge	5d
Ambrose Serle for pit place	20d	John Dewdny for Huckedrise[Hookedrise]	5d
Anthony Philpe	3s 4d	Rugg Crafte	3d
John Troude	16d	Alexander Richardes	4d
John flea	9d	John Bennet	3d
Richard Maunsell	6d	Ellis Bucher	2d
Andrew Whitehorne	8d	George Potter	2d
Ellis Philpe	5d	John Thomas for Shildon grange	20d
Ellis Philpe for Whorewoodes lande	5d	William Praft	5d
Thomas Burrowe	8d	John Gally	3d
Parker Northeaver	8d	John Philpe	6d
Robert Gally	5d	fearne hill	1d
William Daniel	9d		*turn page*
Edmund Burrowe	6d		

[page 2]

Bower hayes [Bowerhayes] farme		The southe parte of middle wood & the	
Joan Vicary	22d	childrens chraftes 5d	
Robert Leman	5d	Peter Marke	3d
Ambrose Pringe	14d	John Rawe	16d
Andrew Butson	9d	Matthew Butson	6d
Richard Philpe	5d	Bartholomew Batson	6d
William Bruforde	5d	Nicholas Marke	9d
John More	3d	Robert Hurly	4d

Trots downe [Trott's Down Moors] & shepherdes vally	8d	William Serle of Honiton for his grownde	12d
The little downe close	2d	John Coxe	2d
Humphrey, Dowdny & Nicholas	5d	John Bowdon	2d
Nicholas Lacke	5d	John Trowd for the Parke [Park]	5d
John Vitter	3d	Thomas Burrowe for the Parke	5d
Henry Smith	5d	John Blackemore for Southe stente woode [Stentwood]	
Thomas Pulman	3d		6d

Plate 22. Medieval font in the Church of St Nicholas, Dunkeswell.

APPENDICES

Appendix 1. Letter regarding financing church repairs at Colyton, 1 June 1606

DHC, 1585F/14/4/d

Note: In 1606 the financing of necessary repairs to the parish church did not involve local taxation but a plea from the feoffees and churchwardens for loans from wealthier parishioners. The document has the signs or signatures of John Yonge, William Boucknoll, Robert Tucker, I. Buckland, John Ham, Francis Bagwyll, Stephen Byrde, Robert Boucknoll, William Michell, Michael Bara[illegible], Edward Holwill, Hugh Newton, Walter Teape, Joseph Carswell, John Butter, John Carswell, Peter Blackaller, John Walkelyn, George Macye, Edward Clarke, Gregory Sampson, Robert Carsswell and John Markell.

The fifth daie of June *in the year of our Lord* 1606 *in the year of the reign of James the first of England and thirty-ninth year of Scotland*

Colyton in Devon

Whereas the parrishe Churche of this parrishe of Colyton being nowe in verie great reparation and decaye not onelie in the tymber worke of the Roofe of the bodie of the said Churche, but also all the Leaddes over the north side thereof are so much decayed, that if the same be not presentlie repaired, it will in verie shorte tyme growe to a farre greater charge unto the parrishe. Wherefore uppon good Consideration had thereof, it is thought fit aswell by the feoffees of the parrishe lande of the said parrishe, as also by the Twentie men and others the chiefest of the Inhabitants, That the said [obscured] shalbee presentlie sett fourth and so goe on with [obscured] expedition. And forasmuch as there is [obscured] sufficient at this presente, in the parrishe Stock to defraye the Charge thereof, neither canne the said worke presentlie be sett forwarde except some monyes be disbursed before hande by some well disposed persons by waye of Lone towards the same, but in such tympe as the same maye been repaied againe out of the Revenues and profits wch shallbee received upon the parrishe lands. Wee therefore the feoffees and Twentie men aforesaid and other the Chiefest Inhabitants of the said parrishe whose names are hereunder subscribed Doe by these presente firmelie promise to repaye and satisfie all and every such some and somes of money as shall by any personne or personnes whatsoever by waye of Lone delivered unto the Churchewardens of the said parrishe, (they giving Notes under their handes for the Receite thereof) out of the parishe moneys that shalbee by any waye or meanes receaved of the revenues and profitts of the parrishe lande aforesaid (Excepting onelie some twentie nobles or tenne pounds yeerelie towards the most necessarie payments of such moneys as the parrishe Bayliffes of the said parrishe for the tyme being, nowe and hereafter shalbee appointed by my Note subscribed wth the hands of the said feoffees and Twentie men or the more parte of them to pay for & in the behalf of the parrishe aforesaid). In witness whereof wee the Feoffees and twentie men aforesaid and other the Inhabitants of the said parrishe have hereunto subscribed our names and sett to our Signs on the daie and yeere above written.

Appendix 2. Letter to the churchwardens and overseers of the poor of St Saviour, Dartmouth, 6 March 1610

DHC, DD61784

Note: In 1610 the mayor was compelled to instruct the churchwardens and overseers of the poor to seize the goods of ninety-eight parishioners who refused to pay the poor rate.

Clifton, Dartmoth Hardnes Townstall

Thomas Holland Maior of the Boroughe aforesaid and Thomas Paige the laste or next predent Maior of the same, Twoo of his Majesty's Justices of the Peace aswell within the said Boroughe as also in the said pishe ot Townstall whereof one is of the Quorom, to the Churchwardens of the pishe and Church of Saviours in Dartmoth and unto John Newbye, William Neale & John Jefferye and others beinge inhabitants wthin the said pishe nominated overseers of the poore of the said pishe according to the statue in such case made and pvided in the three and fortieth yeere of the Raigne of Elizabeth late queene of England of famous memorye for a tyme not yet expired and to every of them greeting whereas you have according to the statute wth the consent of two Justices of the peace of the said Boroughe and pishe whereof one of them is of the Quorum, taxed sundrye psones inhabiting wthin the said pishe and divers not dwelline wthin yet occupiers of lande wthin the said pishe to paye certaine somes of money towards the relieffe of the lame, impotent, olde, blinde and other good Charitable deeds in the same acte expressed wch psones being taxed have refused and yet doe refuse to contribute according as they are taxed or assessed, wee the Justices by force of the said statute doe hereby give you the said Churchwardens and oversers and every of your warrant to levye by severall distresses of the goodes of every psone in this schedule hereunto annexed specified and expressed, and by you as aforesaid is taxed for the said purposes and hath refused and doth refuse to paye the same, such somes of money as by you on that psone whose goodes you shall distraine shall fortune to be unpaid rendering to the ptye the overplus, In witness whereof we have hereunto see our hands and seales, yeoven the sixth daye of Marche in the Seaventh yeere of the Raigne of our soveraigne Lord James by the grace of god of England, Fraunce and Ireland Kinge defender of the faith And of Scotland the three and fortieth, 1609 [signed] Thomas Holland mayor   Thomas Payge

The names of those that will not pay to the poore
Thomas Adames *otherwise* Paynter 3d, Edward Breckett 6d, Andrew Bickley 3d, Geoffrey Band 4d, John Cutt 6d, Henry Churchward 2d, John Collesworthie 4d, William Cole 3d, William Daniell 3d, Osmond Follett 3d, Mr Lewis Fourtescue for ½ his howse 18d, Peter Goodriche 1d, Richard Goslinge 3d, Mr Henry Haywoode 18d, Walter Jackman 4d, Timothy Jette 3d, Widow Kelley 10d, Widow Kenaway 3d, Joseph Knolles 3d, Phillip Lovering gent. 3d, John Lowdwell 8d, William Leerfant 6d, Peter Luscombe 14d, William Richards 7d, Nicholas Squire 13d, John Strete 4d, Richard Speede 4d, Matthew Shere 2d, John Scobell 10d, Peter Terrie 3d, Mr Wellesman 18d, Richard Wallis 3d, [illegible] 3d, Giles Wall 6d, John Austine 1d, Peter Bastard 2d, John Brownston 1d, Lawrence Brock 3d, Alexander Barter 2d, Simon Browne 2d, Philip Boyes 2d, Thomas Bodman 1d, Roger Bodome 1d, William Bradford 1d, John Bawden 3d, William Cutt 6d, Christopher Dove 4d, John Davie 2d, Bartholomew Frye 2d, John Follet senior 3d, John of Garnesey [Guernsey] 12d, James Goodriche 3d, Moses Guilford 6d, Robert Grindall 2s 8d, William Grose 1d, Thomas Goss 2d, Widow Hawks 8d, Widow Hollett 1d, Thomas Hodge 15d, William Hoop 1d, Robert Hullett, Robert Hollett 6d, Ellis Harowden 2d, John Harward 1d, Thomas Hawk 4d, Nicholas Hard 2d, Thomas Jackman 2d, Robert Jeffrey 2d, Gilbert Kidley 2d, Richard Kingdome 1d, John Lowey 2d, Lodwick Blackmore a taylor 2d, John Lomer 2d, Thomas Martin 2d, William Mayne 6d, John Maye 3d, Leonard Maye 2d, William Man 1d, Mark Norman 3d, Widow Newcarrowe 1d, Thomas Nevill 3, Thomas Oxford 6d, Alexander Pomeroy 3d, Henry Olden 4d, Nicholas Pambell 2d, John Paddon 2d, Arthur Richards 3d, John Rising 4d, Walter

Ronciball 2d, Robert Rule 2d, John Rowe 2d, John Sayer 4d, Nicholas Townesand 4d, Arthur Wotten 6d, Richard Waye 1d, William Whithear 2d, Christopher Wallis his widowe 2d, Jerome Wilcocks 2d

Appendix 3. Dartmouth electors, 1626

DHC, 3889M/box 7

Note: In 1626 the parliamentary election was contested between three men who received forty-nine, forty and twenty-seven votes from an electorate of sixty men.

The Names of such Men as were on the Election for Burgesses and also the Names of the Electors which Election was made in the Guildhall of Dartmouth the 19th of January 1625 [1626]

Mr John Upton Esquire had Voices
Alexander Staplehill, Nicholas Strawe, John Staplehill, Richard Smithe, William Spurwaie, John Budlie, Philip Lovering, John Plumleigh, John Richardes, John Holligrove, Christopher Searell, John Martin, Edward Spurwaie, Richard Lumleye, William Davie, Thomas Wardropp, George Cadd, Alexander Coozens, Richard Tarke, Charles Parsons, Thomas Alford, Giles Rounsevall, Philip Limbrie, John Ameredithe, Thomas Wakeham, Nicholas Lynne, John Riche, Richard Randall, Lawrence Swanson, Benedict Watts, John Watson, Walter Manfield, Christopher Adames, Lewis Fortescue, Nicholas Knowlles, Richard Jago, John Furnere, Robert Follett, Robert Martin, Thomas Spurwaie, John Smith, John Jefferie, Roger Mathews, Pascoe Jago, Andrew Voysey, Thomas Abraham, William Kent Senior, Henry Lumleye, Jonas Pinsent, John Crewkerne

Mr Roger Matthew had Voices
Alexander Staplehill, Nicholas Straw, John Staplehill, Andrew Langdon, Richard Smith, William Spurwaie, John Holligrove, Christopher Sarrell, John Martyn, Edward Spurwaie, Gilbert Staplehill, Thomas Waldropp, George Cadd, Alexander Coozens, John Streete Junior, William Kent Junior, Giles Rounswall, Richard Mayne, Phillip Norton, Phillip Limbrye, John Ameredith, Thomas Wakeham, Nicholas Skinner, Edward Follett, William Trise, Benedict Watts, Christopher Adames, Nicholas Knowles, Richard Hullett, Robert Follett, Robert Martin, Thomas Spurwaie, John Smythe, John Jefferie, Pascoe Jago, Andrew Voysey, Thomas Abraham, William Kent Senior, Jonas Pinsent, John Crewkerne

Mr Nicholas Roope had Voices
John Budlie, Phillip Lovring, John Plumleigh, John Richardes, Gilbert Staplehill, Richard Lumleye, William Davie, Richard Tacke, Charles Parsonnes, Thomas Axford, John Strete Junior, William Kent Junior, Richard Maine, Philip Norton, Nicholas Skinner, Edward Follett, Nicholas Lyne, John Rich, Richard Randall, William Triss, Lawrence Swanson, John Watson, Walter Mansfield, Lewis Fortescue, Richard Hullett, Richard Jago, John Furnise, Henry Lumlie

Appendix 4. Account of the head wardens of Dean Prior, 1580

DHC, 4567A-99/PW1

Note: The church rented out its equipment for the brewing of ale including its 'vessel' and its 'kettle' and the 'Ayshes'. The second half of this account lists expenditure including sums spent on the bells and other maintenance work included employing a hellier (known today as a slater or tiler) and the purchase of 'shindle', otherwise shingles, the thin pieces of wood or stone used as house-tiles, and 'lasts' (lathes). The account made the following year recorded twenty-three instances of the rental by fifteen men for the vessel, four men for the kettle and four men for the church house and the vessel.

Deane Prior This is the acont of the hedde wardens John Mudge & William Norrawaie writyn the 23rd daie of June in the yeere of our lorde god 1580 for one whole yeere last paste in manner and forme foloinge

Recetes

First receved of the	4 men 23s
Item of John Phillippe for brouinge in the churche house	12d
Item of Joan Jule for brouing in the churche house	12d
Item of Robert Tolchard for brouing in the churche house	12d
Item of Thomas Webber for brouing in the churche house	12d
Item of Christopher Arscot for the vessel	6d
Item of William Tincombe for brouing wth the vessel	6d
Item of John Arscot for the vessel	6d
Item of John Heathyeard for brouing wth the vessel	6d
Item John Fox for the vessel	6d
Item of Anthony Weeger for the vessel	6d
Item of Sander Donninge for the vessel	6d
Item of John Fox for the vessel	6d
Item of Thomas Phillipe for the vessel	6d
Item of John Edwardes for the vessel	6d
Item of Henry Perre for the vessel	6d
Item of John Toncerman for the vessel	6d
Item of Robert Fox for the vessel	6d
Item of Christopher Arscot for the chetill	4d
Item of Anthony Weger for the chettill	4d
Item of William Arscot for the ayshes	20d
made of our ale	£3 5s 9d
Sum of our recetes is	£6 20d

Expencis

Item payd for mendinge of the churche yeard hadge	1d
Item payd to Robert Tolcharde for mending of the churche yeate	7d
Item payd to Nicholas Cunde for the bringing of a bayne for Coliton [Colyton] haven	4d
Item payd at the byshops visitation at totnas [Totnes]	4s 1d
Item payd for mending of the churche vessel	12d
Item payd for a newe bible	31s
Item chargis at exon [Exeter] curte	5s 9d
Item paid for eyght yeardes of lasts for the bible	8d
Item payd for bred and wine	10d
Item payd for the newe belroopes	3s 4d
Item payd for the mending of a bolte	1d
Item payd for nayles	1d
Item paid for greace for the belles	1d
Item paid for a yeard of creascloth	10d
Item paid for bred and wine	12d
Item payd for the lying of the stones in the churche	6d
Item payd to Nicholas Cund. for a brind for bath church	4d

Item payd for 5 boysheles of lyme	20d
Item payd for halfe a thousand of laths	2s
Item payde for halfe a boyshell of helyapines	6d
Item payd for bred and wine agenst easter	3s 6d
Item paid Walter Addam for mending of the churche wall	4d
Itempaid to John Sparke for shindell stones	4s 4d
Item paid to the towne of charde [Chard]	6d
Item payd for lath nayles	2d
Item paid to John Edwards for healyinge of the churche howse	1s 6d
Item payde at the acsdecons vicitacion at totnas	4s 2d
Item payd for wine	10d
Item payd for a newe belle coller	20d
Item payd at the aresdecons vicitation at Totnas	12d
Item payd for wyne	1d
Item payd to Robert Tolchard for keeping of the belles	20d
Item payd for a new booke	8d
Item payd for soope	2d
Item payd for the making of this accont	4d
Sum of exp[enses]	£4 5s 6d
So that ther did remayne	16s 1d

INDEX

DEVON AND CORNWALL
RECORD SOCIETY PUBLICATIONS

Previous volumes are available from Boydell & Brewer Ltd.

A Shelf List of the Society's Collections, ed. S. Stride, revised 1986

New Series